Supply Chain Management

Supply Chain Management:

Strategy, Planning, and Operation

Sunil Chopra

Kellogg Graduate School of Management
Northwestern University

Peter Meindl

i2 Technologies

Upper Saddle River, New Jersey

Chopra, Sunil.
Supply chain management : strategy, planning, and operation / Sunil Chopra, Peter Meindl.
p. cm.
Includes bibliographical references and index.
ISBN 0-13-026465-2
1. Marketing channels—Management. 2. Delivery of goods—Management. 3. Physical distribution of goods—Management. 4. Customer services—Management. 5. Industrial procurement. 6. Materials management. I. Meindl, Peter. II. Title.

HF5415.13.C533 2001
658.7—dc21 00-062419

Vice President/Editorial Director: James Boyd
Executive Editor: Tom R. Tucker
Assistant Editor: Jennifer Surich
Media Project Manager: Cindy Harford
Senior Marketing Manager: Debbie Clare
Production/Manufacturing Manager: Gail Steier de Acevedo
Production Coordinator: Maureen Wilson
Senior Prepress/Manufacturing Manager: Vincent Scelta
Manufacturing Buyer: Natacha St. Hill Moore
Cover Design: Kiwi Design
Cover Art/Photo: PhotoDisc
Composition: UG / GGS Information Services, Inc.

10 9 8 7 6 5 4 3 2

ISBN 0-13-026465-2

I would like to thank my colleagues at Kellogg for all that I have learned from them about logistics and supply chain management. I am grateful for the love and encouragement my parents, Krishan and Pushpa, and sisters, Sudha and Swati, have always provided during every endeavor in my life. I thank my children Ravi and Rajiv for the joy they have brought me. Finally, none of this would have been possible without the constant love, caring, and support of my wife Maria Cristina.

Sunil Chopra

I would like to thank three mentors: Sunil Chopra my co-author, Hau Lee my advisor at Stanford University and beyond, and Gerry Lieberman, also of Stanford University, all of whom have taught me a great deal and inspired me even more. I would like to thank my parents, Freddy and Jim, and sister, Candace, for their constant love and support. And, most importantly, I would like to thank my wife, Sarah, who makes my life wonderful and whom I love with all of my heart.

Pete Meindl

Contents in Brief

Contents

Preface

This book has grown from a course on supply chain management taught to second-year MBA students at the Kellogg Graduate School of Management. The goal of this class is to cover not only high-level supply chain strategy and concepts, but also to give students a solid understanding of the analytical tools necessary to solve supply chain problems. With this class goal in mind, our objective was to create a book that would develop an understanding of the following three key areas and their interrelationships:

- The strategic role of the supply chain
- Key drivers of supply chain performance
- Analytical tools and techniques for supply chain analysis

Our first objective in this book is for the reader to learn the strategic importance of good supply chain design, planning, and operation for every firm. The reader will be able to understand and visualize how good supply chain management can be a competitive advantage for a firm. Similarly, a reader should understand how weaknesses in supply chain design, planning, and operation can hurt the performance of a firm. We use several examples to illustrate this idea and develop a strategic framework for supply chain management.

Within the strategic framework we identify inventory, transportation, information, and facilities as the key drivers of supply chain performance. Our second goal in the book is to convey how these drivers may be used on a conceptual level during supply chain design, planning, and operation to improve performance. For each driver of supply chain performance, our goal is to provide readers with practical managerial levers and concepts that may be used to improve supply chain performance.

Utilizing these managerial levers optimally during the design, planning, and operational phases requires knowledge of logistics and supply chain methodologies. Our third goal is to give the reader knowledge of these methodologies. Every methodological discussion is illustrated with its application in Excel. When discussing methodologies and techniques, we stress the managerial context in which they are used and the managerial levers for improvement that they support.

The strategic framework and concepts discussed in the book are tied together through a variety of examples that show how a combination of concepts is needed to achieve significant increases in performance. There is a particular focus on the analysis of e-business and how it can help firms in different industries improve their supply chain performance.

The book is targeted toward an academic as well as a practitioner audience. On the academic side, it should be appropriate for MBA, engineering management, or senior undergraduate courses in logistics and supply chain management. It should also serve as a suitable reference for both concepts as well as methodology for practitioners in consulting as well as industry.

There are many people we would like to thank who helped us throughout this process. We thank the reviewers whose suggestions significantly improved the book: James Noble, University of Missouri-Columbia; Sime Curkovic, Western Michigan University; Effie Stavrulaki, Penn State University; and James K. Higginson, University of Waterloo (Ontario). We are grateful to the students at the Kellogg Graduate School of Management who suffered through typo-ridden drafts of earlier versions of the book. Specially, we thank Christoph Roettelle and Vikas Vats for carefully reviewing several chapters and solving problems at the end of chapters. Our developmental editor, Libby Rubenstein, who read all our writing with a critical eye and raised all the right issues, was instrumental in improving the book. The book is much better because of her involvement. We would also like to thank our editor Tom Tucker and the staff at Prentice-Hall for their effort with the book. Finally, we'd like to thank you, our readers, for reading and using this book. We hope it contributes to all your efforts to improve the performance of companies and supply chains throughout the world.

Sunil Chopra
Kellogg Graduate School of Management
Northwestern University

Peter Meindl
i2 Technologies

PART ONE

Building a Strategic Framework to Analyze Supply Chains

The goal of the three chapters in this module is to provide a strategic framework to analyze design, planning, and operational decisions within supply chains. Such a framework helps clarify supply chain goals and identify managerial actions that improve supply chain performance in terms of the desired goals.

Chapter 1 defines a supply chain and establishes the impact that supply chain decisions have on a firm's performance. A variety of examples are used to illustrate supply chain decisions, their influence on performance, and their role in a firm's competitive strategy. Chapter 2 describes supply chain strategy in the context of a firm's value chain. The relationship between supply chain strategy and the competitive strategy of a firm is established and used to emphasize the importance of ensuring that strategic fit exists between the two strategies. The rest of the chapter discusses how expanding the scope of strategic fit across all functions and stages within the supply chain improves performance. Chapter 3 describes the four supply chain performance drivers: inventory, transportation, facilities, and information. Key decisions related to each driver are identified and linked to a company's ability to support its competitive strategy.

CHAPTER 1

Understanding the Supply Chain

Learning Objectives
After reading this chapter, you will be able to

1. describe the cycle and push/pull views of a supply chain;
2. identify the three key supply chain decision phases and explain the significance of each one; and
3. discuss the goal of a supply chain and explain the impact of supply chain decisions on the success of a firm.

In this chapter, we provide a conceptual understanding of what a supply chain is and explore the various issues that need to be considered when designing, planning, or operating a supply chain. We discuss the significance of supply chain issues to the success of a firm. We also provide several supply chain examples from different industries to emphasize the variety of supply chain issues that companies need to consider at the strategic, planning, and operational levels.

1.1 WHAT IS A SUPPLY CHAIN?

A **supply chain** consists of all stages involved, directly or indirectly, in fulfilling a customer request. The supply chain not only includes the manufacturer and suppliers, but also transporters, warehouses, retailers, and customers themselves. Within each organization, such as a manufacturer, the supply chain includes all functions involved in filling a customer request. These functions include, but are not limited to, new product development, marketing, operations, distribution, finance, and customer service.

Consider a customer walking into a Wal-Mart store to purchase detergent. The supply chain begins with the customer and his or her need for detergent. The next stage of this supply chain is the Wal-Mart retail store that the customer visits. Wal-Mart stocks its shelves using inventory that may have been supplied from a finished-goods warehouse that Wal-Mart manages or from a distributor using trucks supplied by a third party. The distributor in turn is stocked by the manufacturer (say, Procter & Gamble [P&G] in this case). The P&G manufacturing plant receives raw material from a variety of suppliers, who may themselves have been supplied by lower-tier suppliers. For example, packaging material may come from Tenneco, and Tenneco might receive raw material to manufacture the packaging from other suppliers. This supply chain is illustrated in Figure 1.1.

A supply chain is dynamic and involves the constant flow of information, product, and funds between different stages. Each stage of the supply chain performs different processes and interacts with other stages of the supply chain. Wal-Mart provides the product, as well as pricing and availability information, to the customer. The customer transfers funds to Wal-Mart. Wal-Mart conveys point-of-sale data as well as replenishment orders to the distribution center (DC), which transfers the replenishment order via trucks back to the store. Wal-Mart transfers funds to the distributor after the replenishment. The distributor also provides pricing information and sends delivery schedules to Wal-Mart. Similar information, material, and fund flows take place across the entire supply chain.

In another example, when a customer purchases on-line from Dell Computer, the supply chain includes, among others, the customer, the Web page that takes the customer's order, the Dell assembly plant, and all of Dell's suppliers and their suppliers. The Web page provides the customer with information regarding pricing, product variety, and product availability. Having made a product choice, the customer enters the order information and pays for the product. The customer may later return to the Web page to check the status of the order. Stages further up the supply chain use customer order information to fill the order. That process involves an additional flow of information, product, and funds between various stages of the supply chain.

These examples illustrate that the customer is an integral part of the supply chain. The primary purpose for the existence of any supply chain is to satisfy customer needs, in the process generating profits for itself. Supply chain activities begin with a

FIGURE 1.1 Stages of a Detergent Supply Chain

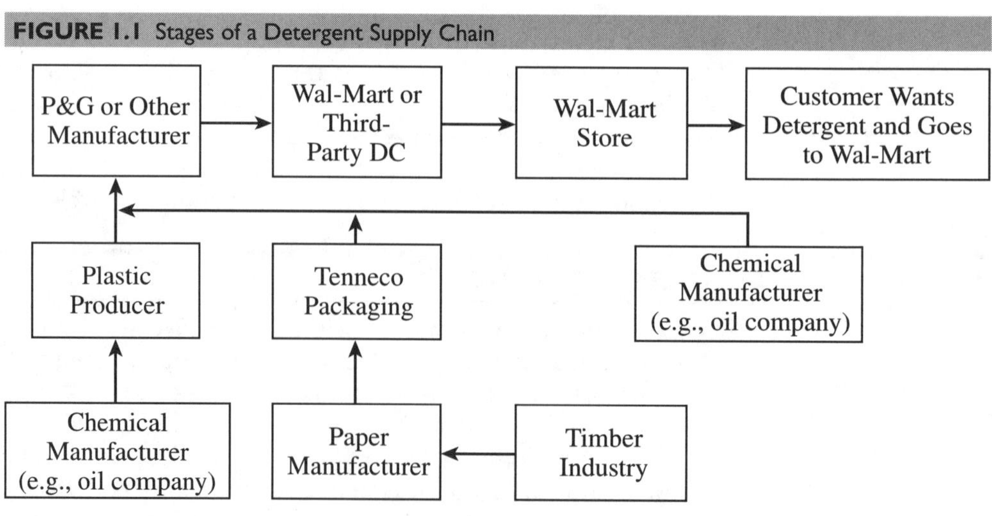

customer order and end when a satisfied customer has paid for his or her purchase. The term *supply chain* conjures up images of product, or supply, moving from suppliers to manufacturers to distributors to retailers to customers along a chain. It is important to visualize information, funds, and product flows along both directions of this chain. The term may also imply that only one player is involved at each stage. In reality, a manufacturer may receive material from several suppliers and then supply several distributors. Therefore, most supply chains are actually networks. It may be more accurate to use the terms *supply network* or *supply web* to describe the structure of most supply chains.

A typical supply chain may involve a variety of stages. These supply chain stages are shown in Figure 1.2 and include the following:

- Customers
- Retailers
- Wholesalers/distributors
- Manufacturers
- Component/raw material suppliers

Each stage in Figure 1.2 need not be present in a supply chain. The appropriate design of the supply chain will depend on both the customer's needs and the roles of the stages involved in filling those needs. In some cases, such as Dell, a manufacturer may fill customer orders directly. Dell **builds to order**, that is, a customer order initiates manufacturing at Dell. Dell does not have a retailer, wholesaler, or distributor in its supply chain. In other cases, such as the mail order company L.L. Bean, manufacturers do not respond to customer orders directly. L.L. Bean maintains an inventory of products from which it fills customer orders. Compared with the Dell supply chain, the L.L. Bean supply chain contains an extra stage (the retailer, L.L. Bean itself) between the customer and the manufacturer. In the case of a small retail store, the supply chain may also contain a wholesaler or distributor between the store and the manufacturer.

The Objective of a Supply Chain

The objective of every supply chain is to maximize the overall value generated. The **value** a supply chain generates is the difference between what the final product is worth to the customer and the effort the supply chain expends in filling the customer's request. For most commercial supply chains, value will be strongly correlated with *supply chain profitability*, the difference between the revenue generated from the customer and the overall cost across the supply chain. For example, a customer purchasing a computer from Dell pays $2,000, which represents the revenue the supply chain receives. Dell and other stages of the supply chain incur costs to convey information, produce components, store them, transport them, transfer funds, and so on. The dif-

FIGURE 1.2 Supply Chain Stages

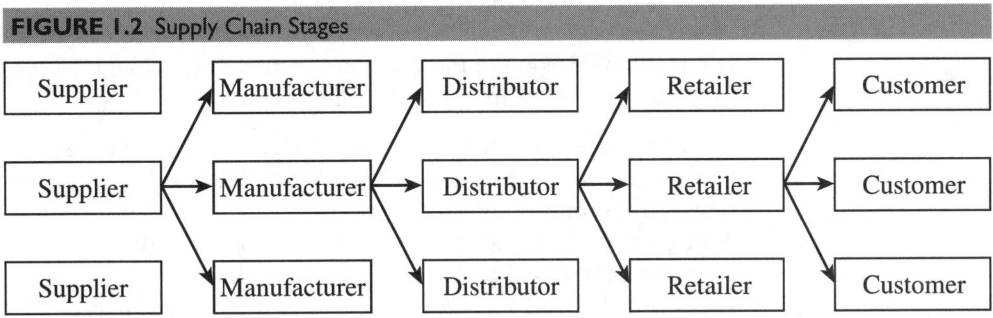

ference between the $2,000 that the customer paid and the sum of all costs incurred by the supply chain to produce and distribute the computer represents the supply chain profitability. **Supply chain profitability** is the total profit to be shared across all supply chain stages. The higher the supply chain profitability, the more successful the supply chain. Supply chain success should be measured in terms of supply chain profitability and not in terms of the profits at an individual stage. (We demonstrate in subsequent chapters that a focus on profitability at individual stages may lead to a reduction in overall supply chain profits.)

We define the success of a supply chain in terms of supply chain profitability. The next logical step is to look for sources of revenue and cost. For any supply chain, there is only one source of revenue: the customer. The customer is the only real point of positive cash flow in a supply chain. In the Wal-Mart example, the customer purchasing detergent is the only one providing positive cash flow for the supply chain. All other cash flows are simply fund exchanges that occur within the supply chain, given that different stages have different owners. When Wal-Mart pays its supplier, it is taking a portion of the funds the customer provides and passing that money on to the supplier. This cash transfer adds to the supply chain's costs. All flows of information, product, or funds generate costs within the supply chain. Therefore, the appropriate management of these flows is a key to supply chain success. **Supply chain management** involves the management of flows between and among stages in a supply chain to maximize total profitability.

In the next section, we categorize supply chain decision phases based on their duration.

1.2 DECISION PHASES IN A SUPPLY CHAIN

Successful supply chain management requires several decisions relating to the flow of information, product, and funds. These decisions fall into three categories or phases, depending on the frequency of each decision and the time frame over which a decision phase has an impact:

1. **Supply chain strategy or design**. During this phase, a company decides how to structure the supply chain. It decides what the chain's configuration will be and what processes each stage will perform. Decisions made during this phase are also referred to as strategic supply chain decisions. Strategic decisions made by companies include the location and capacities of production and warehousing facilities, products to be manufactured or stored at various locations, modes of transportation to be made available along different shipping legs, and type of information system to be utilized. A firm must ensure that the supply chain configuration supports its strategic objectives during this phase. Dell's decisions regarding the location and capacity of its manufacturing facilities, warehouses, and supply sources are all supply chain design or strategic decisions. Supply chain design decisions are typically made for the long term (a matter of years) and are very expensive to alter on short notice. Consequently, when companies make these decisions, they must take into account uncertainty in anticipated market conditions over the next few years.

2. **Supply chain planning**. As a result of the planning phase, companies define a set of operating policies that govern short-term operations. For decisions made during this phase, the supply chain's configuration determined in the strategic phase is fixed. This configuration establishes constraints within which planning must be done. Companies start the planning phase with a forecast for the coming year (or a comparable time frame) of demand in different markets. Planning includes decisions regarding which

markets will be supplied from which locations, the planned buildup of inventories, the subcontracting of manufacturing, the replenishment and inventory policies to be followed, the policies that will be enacted regarding backup locations in case of a stockout, and the timing and size of marketing promotions. Dell's decisions regarding the markets a given production facility will supply and target production quantities at different locations are classified as planning decisions. Planning establishes parameters within which a supply chain will function over a specified period of time. In the planning phase, companies must include uncertainty in demand, exchange rates, and competition over this time horizon in their decisions. Given a shorter time horizon and better forecasts than the design phase, companies in the planning phase try to incorporate whatever flexibility may have been built into the supply chain in the design phase and exploit it to optimize performance in the shorter term.

3. **Supply chain operation**. The time horizon here is weekly or daily, and during this phase companies make decisions regarding individual customer orders. At the operational level, supply chain configuration is considered fixed and planning policies already defined. The goal of supply chain operations is to implement the operating policies in the best possible manner. During this phase, firms allocate individual orders to inventory or production, set a date that an order is to be filled, generate pick lists at a warehouse, allocate an order to a particular shipping mode and shipment, set delivery schedules of trucks, and place replenishment orders. Because operational decisions are being made in the short term (minutes, hours, or days), there is often less uncertainty about demand information. The goal during the operation phase is to exploit the reduction of uncertainty and optimize performance within the constraints established by the configuration and planning policies.

The design, planning, and operation of a supply chain have a strong impact on overall profitability and success. Consider Dell Computer. In 1993, Dell performed poorly, and its stock price dropped sharply. This led Dell management to focus on improving the design, planning, and operation of the supply chain, resulting in significantly improved performance. Both profitability and the stock price subsequently have soared due to this increase in performance.

In later chapters, we develop concepts and present methodologies that can be used at each of the three decision phases described previously. Most of our discussion addresses the supply chain design and planning phases.

> ***Key Point*** Supply chain decision phases may be categorized as design, planning, or operational, depending on the time frame over which the decisions made apply.

1.3 PROCESS VIEW OF A SUPPLY CHAIN

A supply chain is a sequence of processes and flows that take place within and between different supply chain stages and combine to fill a customer need for a product. There are two different ways to view the processes performed in a supply chain:

1. **Cycle view**. The processes in a supply chain are divided into a series of cycles, each performed at the interface between two successive stages of a supply chain.

2. **Push/pull view**. The processes in a supply chain are divided into two categories depending on whether they are executed in response to a customer order or in anticipation of customer orders. **Pull** processes are initiated by a customer order, and **push** processes are initiated and performed in anticipation of customer orders.

Cycle View of Supply Chain Processes

Given the five stages of a supply chain shown in Figure 1.2, all supply chain processes can be broken down into the following four process cycles, as shown in Figure 1.3:

- Customer order cycle
- Replenishment cycle
- Manufacturing cycle
- Procurement cycle

Each cycle occurs at the interface between two successive stages of the supply chain. The five supply chain stages thus result in four supply chain process cycles. Not every supply chain will have all four cycles clearly separated. For example, a grocery supply chain in which a retailer stocks finished-goods inventories and places replenishment orders either with the manufacturer or the distributor is likely to have all four cycles separated. Dell, in contrast, sells directly to customers, thus bypassing the retailer and distributor.

A cycle view of the supply chain is very useful when considering operational decisions, because it clearly specifies the roles and responsibilities of each member of the supply chain. The cycle view provides clarity, for example, when setting up information systems to support supply chain operations, as process ownership and objectives are clearly defined. In the following sections, we describe the various supply chain cycles in greater detail.

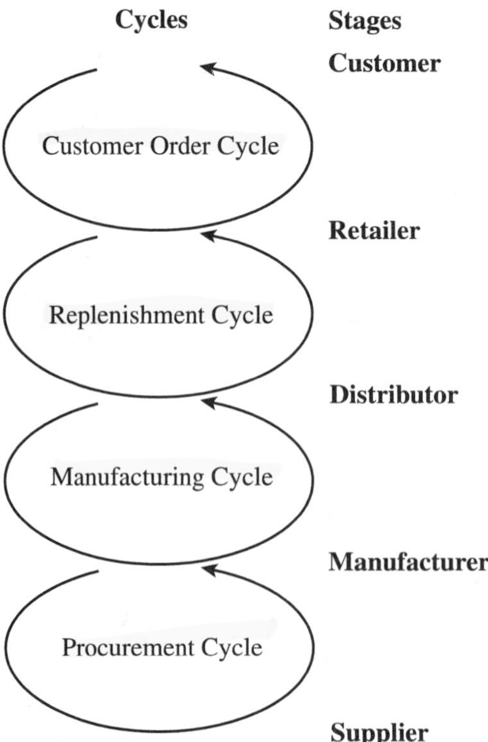

FIGURE 1.3 Supply Chain Process Cycles

Customer Order Cycle

The **customer order cycle** occurs at the customer/retailer interface and includes all processes directly involved in receiving and filling the customer's order. Typically, the customer initiates this cycle at a retailer site, and the cycle primarily involves filling customer demand. The retailer's interaction with the customer starts when the customer arrives or contact is initiated and ends when the customer receives the order. The processes involved in the customer order cycle are shown in Figure 1.4 and include the following:

- Customer arrival
- Customer order entry
- Customer order fulfillment
- Customer order receiving

Customer Arrival The term customer arrival refers to the customer's arrival at the location where he or she has access to his or her choices and makes a decision regarding a purchase. The starting point for any supply chain is the arrival of a customer. Customer arrival can occur when

- the customer walks into a supermarket to make a purchase,
- the customer calls a mail order telemarketing center, or
- the customer uses the Web or an electronic link to a mail order firm.

From the supply chain perspective, a key goal is to facilitate the contact between the customer and the appropriate product so that the customer's arrival turns into a customer order. At a supermarket, facilitating a customer order may involve managing customer flows and product displays. At a telemarketing center, it may mean ensuring that customers do not have to wait on hold for too long. It may also mean having systems in place so that sales representatives can answer customer queries in a way that turns calls into orders. At a Web site, a key system may be search capabilities with tools such as personalization that allow customers to quickly locate and view products that may interest them. The objective of the customer arrival process is to maximize the conversion of customer arrivals to customer orders.

Customer Order Entry The term customer order entry refers to customers telling the retailer what products they want to purchase and the retailer allocating products to customers. At a supermarket, order entry may take the form of customers loading all items that they intend to purchase onto their carts. At a mail order firm's telemarketing center or Web site, order entry will involve customers informing the retailer of

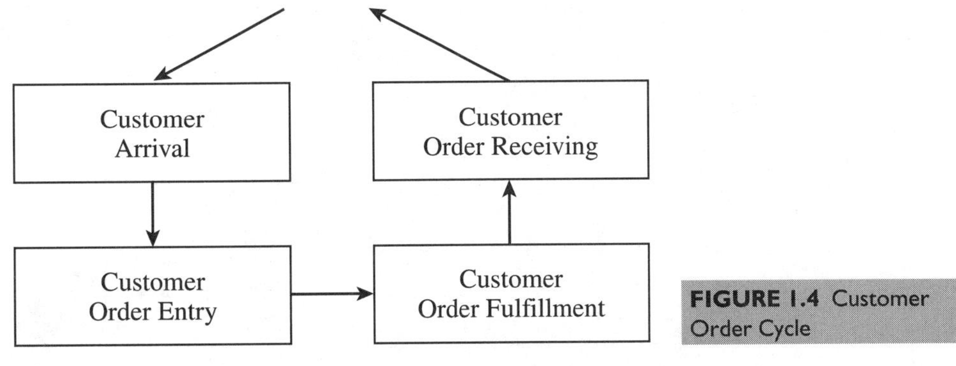

FIGURE 1.4 Customer Order Cycle

the items and quantities they selected. The retailer then allocates the product to the customer order and may also provide a delivery date to the customer. The objective of the customer order entry process is to ensure that the order entry is quick and accurate and is communicated to all other supply chain processes that are affected by it.

Customer Order Fulfillment During the customer order fulfillment process, the customer's order is filled and sent to the customer. At a supermarket, the customer performs this process. At a mail order firm this process generally includes picking the order from inventory, packaging it, and shipping it to the customer. All inventories will need to be updated, which may result in the initiation of the replenishment cycle. In general, customer order fulfillment takes place from retailer inventory. In a build-to-order scenario, in contrast, order fulfillment takes place directly from the manufacturer's production line. The objective of the customer order fulfillment process is to get the correct and complete orders to customers by the promised due dates and at the lowest possible cost.

Customer Order Receiving During the customer order receiving process, the customer receives the order and takes ownership. Records of this receipt may be updated and cash payment initiated. At a supermarket, receiving occurs at the checkout counter. For a mail order firm, receiving occurs when the product is delivered to the customer.

Replenishment Cycle

The **replenishment cycle** occurs at the retailer/distributor interface and includes all processes involved in replenishing retailer inventory. It is initiated when a retailer places an order to replenish inventories to meet future demand. A replenishment cycle may be triggered at a supermarket that is running out of stock of detergent or at a mail order firm that is low on stock of a particular shirt. In some cases replenishment takes place from a distributor that is holding finished-goods inventory. In other cases replenishment may occur directly from a manufacturer's production line.

The replenishment cycle is similar to the customer order cycle except that the retailer is now the customer. The objective of the replenishment cycle is to replenish inventories at the retailer at minimum cost while providing the necessary product availability to the customer. The processes involved in the replenishment cycle are shown in Figure 1.5 and include the following:

- Retail order trigger
- Retail order entry
- Retail order fulfillment
- Retail order receiving

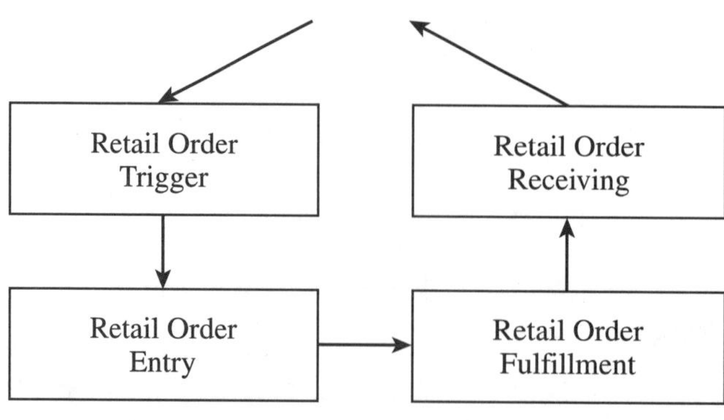

FIGURE 1.5 Replenishment Cycle

Retail Order Trigger As the retailer fills customer demand, inventory is depleted and must be replenished to meet future demand. A key activity the retailer performs during the replenishment cycle is to devise a replenishment or ordering policy that triggers an order from the previous stage (possibly the distributor or the manufacturer). The objective when setting replenishment order triggers is to maximize profitability by balancing product availability and cost. The outcome of the retail order trigger process is that a replenishment order is generated.

Retail Order Entry The retail order entry process is similar to customer order entry at the retailer. The only difference is that the retailer is now the customer placing the order with the distributor or manufacturer. The objective of the retail order entry process is that an order be entered accurately and conveyed quickly to all supply chain processes affected by the order.

Retail Order Fulfillment The retail order fulfillment process is very similar to customer order fulfillment except that it takes place either at the distributor or manufacturer. A key difference is the size of each order. Customer orders tend to be much smaller than replenishment orders. The objective of the retail order fulfillment is to get the replenishment order to the retailer on time while minimizing costs.

Retail Order Receiving Once the replenishment order arrives at a retailer, the retailer must receive it physically, update all inventory records, and settle all payable accounts. This process involves product flow from the distributor to the retailer as well as information and financial flows. The objective of the retail order receiving process is to update inventories and displays quickly and accurately at the lowest possible cost.

Manufacturing Cycle

The **manufacturing cycle** typically occurs at the distributor/manufacturer (or retailer/manufacturer) interface and includes all processes involved in replenishing distributor (or retailer) inventory. The manufacturing cycle is triggered by customer orders (as is the case with Dell), replenishment orders from a retailer or distributor (e.g., Wal-Mart ordering from P&G), or by the forecast of customer demand and current product availability in the manufacturer's finished-product warehouse.

In general, a manufacturer produces several products and fills demand from several sources. One extreme in a manufacturing cycle is an integrated steel mill that collects orders that are similar enough to enable the manufacturer to produce in large quantities. In this case, the manufacturing cycle is reacting to customer demand (referred to as a pull process earlier in the chapter). Another extreme involves certain types of consumer products firms that must produce in anticipation of demand. In this case, the manufacturing cycle is anticipating customer demand (referred to as a push process earlier in the chapter). The processes involved in the manufacturing cycle are shown in Figure 1.6 and include the following:

- Order arrival from the distributor, retailer, or customer
- Production scheduling
- Manufacturing and shipping
- Receiving at the distributor, retailer, or customer

Order Arrival During the order arrival process, a distributor sets a replenishment order trigger based on the forecast of future demand and current product inventories. The resulting order is then conveyed to the manufacturer. In some cases, the customer or retailer may be ordering directly from the manufacturer. In other cases, a manufacturer may be producing to stock a finished-products warehouse. In the latter situation,

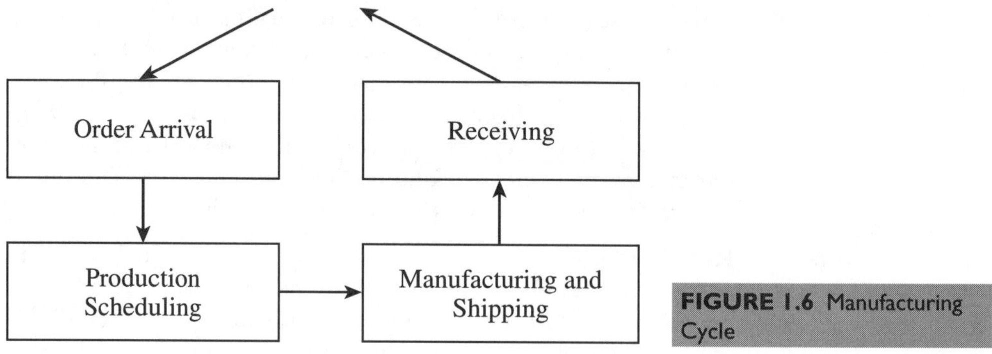

FIGURE 1.6 Manufacturing Cycle

the order is triggered based on product availability and a forecast of future demand. This process is similar to the retail order trigger process in the replenishment cycle.

Production Scheduling The production scheduling process is similar to the order entry process in the replenishment cycle where inventory is allocated to an order. During the production scheduling process, orders are allocated to a production plan or schedule. Given the desired production quantities, the manufacturer must decide on the precise production sequence. If there are multiple lines, the manufacturer must also decide which products to allocate to each line. The objective of the production scheduling process is to maximize the proportion of orders filled on time while keeping costs down.

Manufacturing and Shipping The manufacturing and shipping process is equivalent to the order fulfillment process described in the replenishment cycle. During the manufacturing phase of the process, the manufacturer produces to the production schedule while meeting quality requirements. During the shipping phase of this process, the product is shipped to the customer, retailer, distributor, or finished-product warehouse. The objective of the manufacturing and shipping process is to ship the product by the promised due date while meeting quality requirements and keeping costs down.

Receiving In the receiving process, the product is received at the distributor, finished-goods warehouse, retailer, or customer, and inventory records are updated. Other processes related to storage and fund transfers also take place.

Procurement Cycle 

The **procurement cycle** occurs at the manufacturer/supplier interface and includes all processes necessary to ensure that materials are available for manufacturing to occur according to schedule. During the procurement cycle, the manufacturer orders components from suppliers that replenish the component inventories. The relationship is quite similar to that between a distributor and manufacturer, with one significant difference: Whereas retailer/distributor orders are triggered by uncertain customer demand, component orders can be determined precisely once the manufacturer has decided what the production schedule will be. Component orders are dependent on the production schedule. Thus, it is important that suppliers be linked to the manufacturer's production schedule. Of course, if a supplier's lead times are long, the supplier has to produce to forecast because the manufacturer's production schedule may not be fixed that far in advance.

In practice, there may be several tiers of suppliers, each producing a component for the next tier. A similar cycle would then flow back from one stage to the next. The processes in the procurement cycle are shown in Figure 1.7.

We do not detail each process here because this cycle has processes similar to those discussed in the context of other cycles.

> ***Key Point*** A cycle view of the supply chain clearly defines the processes involved and the owners of each process. This view is very useful when considering operational decisions, because it specifies the roles and responsibilities of each member of the supply chain and the desired outcome for each process.

Push/Pull View of Supply Chain Processes

All processes in a supply chain fall into one of two categories, depending on the timing of their execution relative to customer demand. In pull processes, execution is initiated in response to a customer order. Push processes are those that are executed in anticipation of customer orders. At the time of execution of a pull process, demand is known with certainty. At the time of execution of a push process, demand is not known and must be forecast. Pull processes may also be referred to as reactive processes because they react to customer demand. Push processes may also be referred to as speculative processes because they respond to speculated (or forecast) rather than actual demand. The **push/pull boundary** in a supply chain separates push processes from pull processes. At Dell, for example, the beginning of personal computers (PC) assembly represents the push/pull boundary. All processes before PC assembly are push processes, and all processes after and including assembly are initiated in response to a customer order and are thus pull processes.

A push/pull view of the supply chain is very useful when considering strategic decisions relating to supply chain design. This view forces a more global consideration of supply chain processes as they relate to a customer order. Such a view may, for instance, result in responsibility for certain processes being passed on to a different stage of the supply chain if making this transfer allows a push process to become a pull process.

FIGURE 1.7 Procurement Cycle

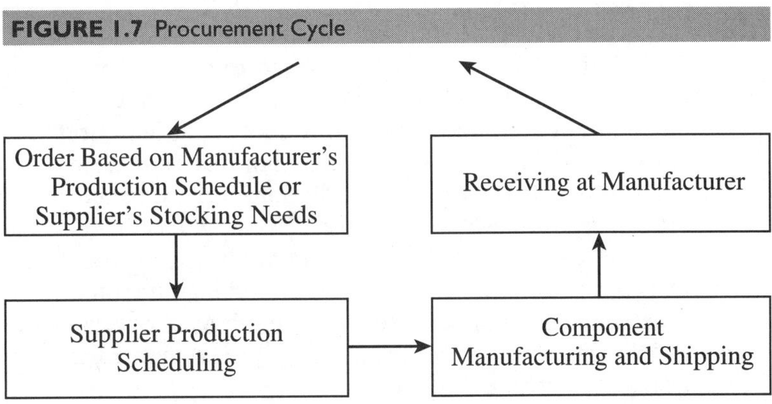

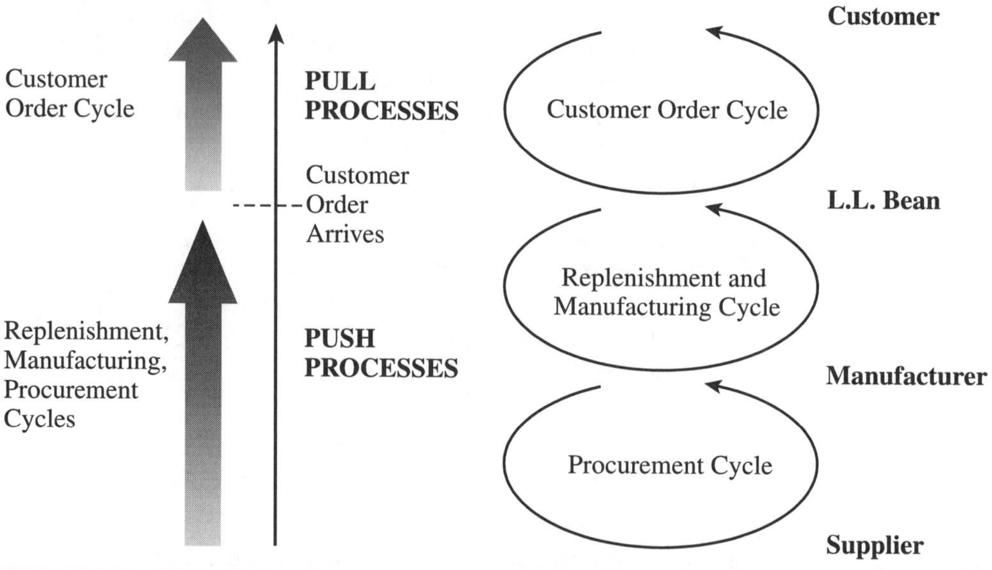

FIGURE 1.8 Push/Pull Processes for the L.L. Bean Supply Chain

Let us consider two distinct supply chains that we have discussed and relate them to the push/pull and the cycle views. One supply chain is a mail order company like L.L. Bean that receives customer orders through its telemarketing center or Web site. The other is a build-to-order computer manufacturer like Dell.

L.L. Bean executes all processes in the customer order cycle *after* the customer arrives. All processes that are part of the customer order cycle are thus pull processes. Order fulfillment takes place from product inventory that is built up in anticipation of customer orders. The goal of the replenishment cycle is to ensure product availability when a customer order arrives. All processes in the replenishment cycle are performed in anticipation of demand and are thus push processes. The same holds true for processes in the manufacturing and procurement cycle. In fact, raw material like fabric is often purchased six to nine months before customer demand is expected. Manufacturing itself begins three to six months before the point of sale. All processes in the manufacturing and procurement cycle are thus push processes. The processes in the L.L. Bean supply chain break up into pull and push processes, as shown in Figure 1.8.

The situation is different for a build-to-order computer manufacturer like Dell. Dell does not sell through a reseller or distributor but rather directly to the consumer. Demand is not filled from finished-product inventory but from production. The arrival of a customer order triggers production in final assembly. The manufacturing cycle is thus part of the customer order fulfillment process in the customer order cycle. There are effectively only two cycles in the Dell supply chain: (1) a customer order and manufacturing cycle and (2) a procurement cycle, as shown in Figure 1.9.

All processes in the customer order and manufacturing cycle at Dell are thus classified as pull processes because they are initiated by customer arrival. Dell, however, does not place component orders in response to a customer order. Inventory is replenished in anticipation of customer demand. All processes in the procurement cycle

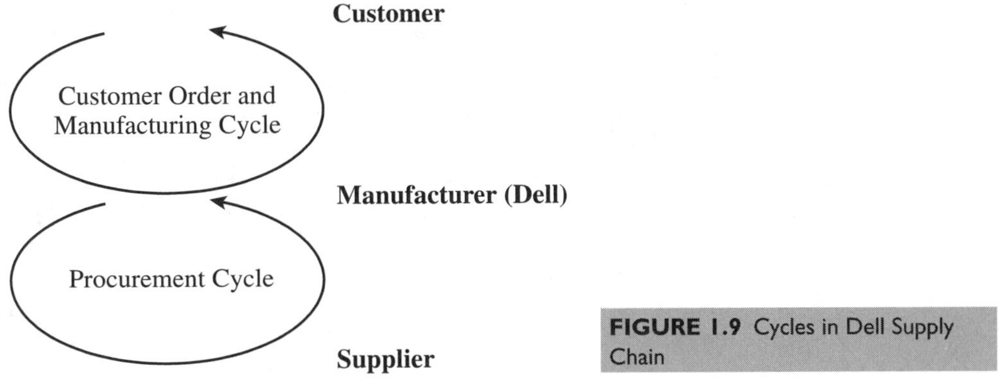

FIGURE 1.9 Cycles in Dell Supply Chain

for Dell are thus classified as push processes because they are a response to a forecast. The processes in the Dell supply chain break up into pull and push processes, as shown in Figure 1.10.

One clear distinction between the two supply chains discussed previously is that the Dell supply chain has fewer stages and more pull processes than the L.L. Bean supply chain. As we indicate in the following chapters, this fact has a significant impact on supply chain performance.

> ***Key Point*** A push/pull view of the supply chain categorizes processes based on whether they are initiated in response to a customer order (pull) or in anticipation of a customer order (push). This view is very useful when considering strategic decisions relating to supply chain design.

FIGURE 1.10 Push/Pull Processes for Dell Supply Chain

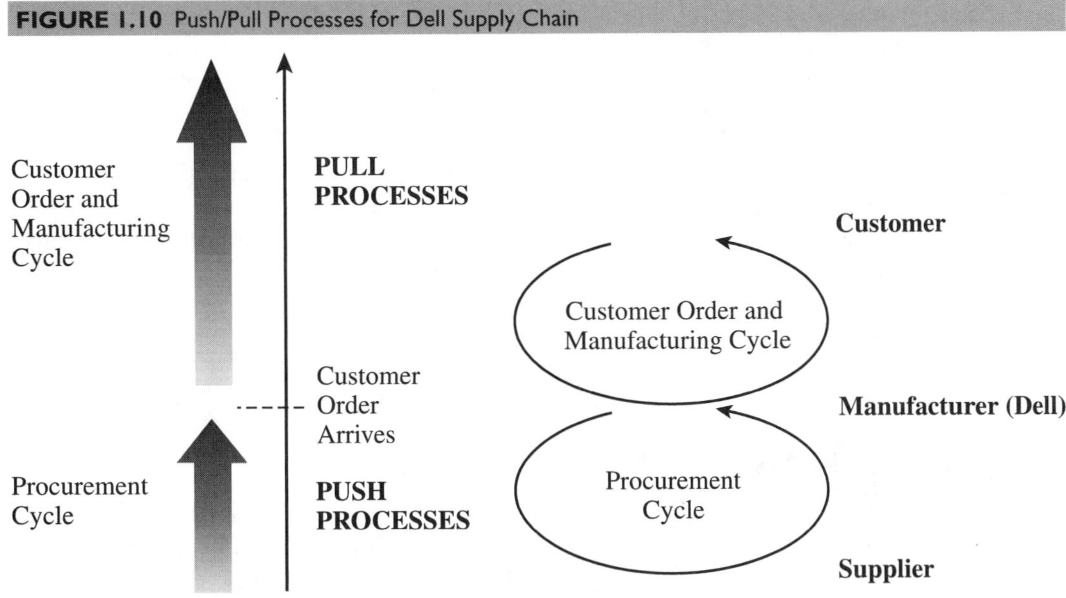

1.4 THE IMPORTANCE OF SUPPLY CHAIN FLOWS

There is a close connection between the design and management of supply chain flows (product, information, and cash) and the success of a supply chain. Dell Computer is an example of a firm that has successfully used good supply chain practices to support its competitive strategy. In contrast, Quaker Oats is an example in which the inability to design and manage flows appropriately in the supply chain led to the failure of its acquisition of Snapple.

Dell was established in 1984. By 1998, it had grown into a $12 billion company. Since 1993, Dell has experienced earnings growth of more than 65 percent per year. Its earnings growth is anticipated to be more than 30 percent per year over the next five years. Dell's stock price has also grown significantly since 1993. Dell has attributed a significant part of its success to the way it manages flows—product, information, and cash—within its supply chain.

Dell's basic supply chain model is direct sales to customers. As distributors and retailers are bypassed, the Dell supply chain has only three stages—customers, manufacturer, and suppliers, as shown in Figure 1.11.

Because Dell is in direct contact with its customers, it has been able to finely segment them and analyze the needs and profitability of each segment. Close contact with its customers and an understanding of customers' needs also allows Dell to develop better forecasts. To further improve the match between supply and demand, Dell makes an active effort to steer customers in real time, on the phone or via the Internet, toward PC configurations that can be built given the components available.

On the operational side, inventory turns is a key performance measure that Dell watches very closely. Each computer chip carries a date code to indicate how old a part is. Dell carries only about 10 days' worth of inventory; in contrast, the competition, selling through retailers, has been carrying in the vicinity of 80 to 100 days. If Intel introduces a new chip, the low level of inventory allows Dell to go to market with a PC containing the chip faster than the competition. If prices suddenly drop, as they did in the early part of 1998, Dell has less inventory that loses value relative to its competitors. For some products, such as monitors manufactured by Sony, Dell maintains no inventory. The transportation company simply picks up the appropriate number of computers from Dell's Austin plant and monitors from Sony's factory in Mexico, matches them by customer order, and delivers them to the customers. This procedure allows Dell to save time and money associated with the extra handling of monitors.

The success of the Dell supply chain is facilitated by sophisticated information exchange. Dell provides real-time data to suppliers on the current state of demand. Suppliers are able to access their components' inventory levels at the factories along with

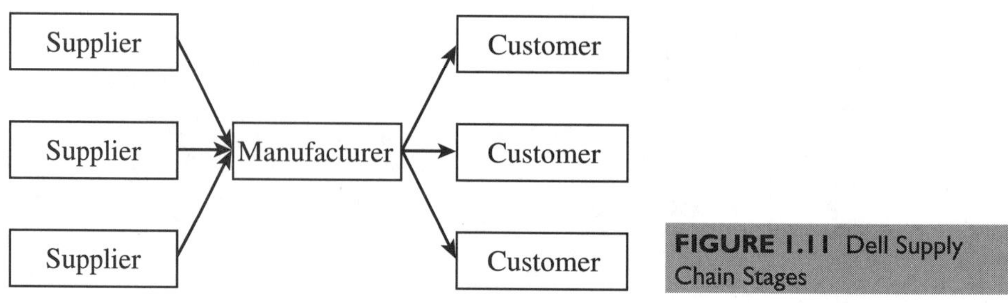

FIGURE 1.11 Dell Supply Chain Stages

daily production requirements. Dell has created customized Web pages so that its major suppliers can view demand forecasts and other customer-sensitive information, thus helping suppliers to get a better idea of customer demand and better match their production schedules to that of Dell. The company has production concentrated in five manufacturing centers: Austin, Texas; Brazil; China; Ireland; and Malaysia. Because demand at each location is relatively large and stable, suppliers are able to replenish component inventories regularly, allowing Dell to maintain low levels of component inventories. In some cases, Dell carries only hours of component inventory at its factory.

Dell's low levels of inventory also help ensure that defects are not introduced into a large quantity of product. When a new product is launched, supplier engineers are stationed right in the plant. If a customer calls in with a problem, production is stopped and design flaws are fixed in real time. As there is no finished product in inventory, the amount of defective merchandise produced is minimized.

Dell also outsources service and support to third-party providers. To ensure a high quality of service, Dell coordinates the delivery of the parts the customer requires with the arrival of the service person. Once again, a coordinated flow of information and material minimizes the cost necessary to provide a high level of service.

Dell also manages its cash flows very effectively. By tracking and managing receivables and payables very closely, it is able to collect cash from its customers, on average, five days before it has to pay its suppliers.

Clearly, Dell's supply chain design and appropriate management of product, information, and cash flows play a key role in the company's success. This approach has positioned Dell very well within the PC industry. Given that good product performance is common in the PC industry, the competitive battlefield is now focused on service delivery and supply chain efficiency.

Quaker Oats, with its acquisition of Snapple, provides an example in which failure to design and manage supply chain flows led to financial failure. Quaker owns Gatorade, the top-selling brand in the sports drink segment. In December 1994, Quaker purchased Snapple at a cost of $1.7 billion. Snapple sold all-natural drinks. At that time, Gatorade was very strong in the south and the southwest of the United States, while Snapple was strong in the northeast and on the west coast.

Quaker announced that it hoped to exploit synergies between the two distribution systems to gain efficiencies, but the company was unable to remedy several problems that prevented it from achieving these synergies. Gatorade was manufactured in plants owned by Quaker, while Snapple was produced under contract by outside plants. Gatorade sold significant amounts through supermarkets and grocery stores, while Snapple sold primarily through restaurants and independent retailers. Over the two years following its acquisition of Snapple, Quaker was unable to gain much synergy between the two distribution systems. In trying to merge two disparate distribution systems, Quaker helped neither and may have hurt both. Just 28 months later, Quaker sold Snapple to Triarc Companies for about $300 million, about 20 percent of the purchase price. The inability to achieve synergies between the two supply chains was a significant reason for the failure of Snapple at Quaker.

Key Point Supply chain decisions play a significant role in the success or failure of a firm.

1.5 EXAMPLES OF SUPPLY CHAINS

In this section, we consider several supply chains and raise questions that would have to be answered during the design, planning, and operations phases of these supply chains. In later chapters, we discuss concepts and present methodologies that can be used to answer these questions.

Example 1.1 Micron Electronics Inc.: A Direct Sales Manufacturer

Micron Electronics Inc. is a manufacturer of PCs that sells directly to customers who place orders either through the telephone or the Internet. Micron has one assembly facility, located in Idaho. It also has a subcontractor that is able to assemble the most popular models. A typical customer order comes in via the Internet or a toll-free number. Depending on the type of order (individual or corporate; high-volume or low-volume item), it is allocated either to the Idaho facility or the subcontractor. Large corporate orders, for example, are handled out of Idaho. Micron carries almost no finished-goods inventory and assembles PCs in response to customer orders.

A typical order may include a monitor and a printer in addition to the PC. Micron does not manufacture peripherals such as monitors and printers. They are stored in Memphis at a depot that Federal Express (FedEx) operates for Micron with some peripherals also held at the Idaho facility. Thus, the order taker must allocate product to the peripheral order from items in the depot. For an individual order, FedEx transports the assembled PC (either from Idaho or the subcontractor) to Memphis, where it is merged with the peripherals from the depot. Another possibility is for FedEx to do the merge at a station close to the customer site. For example, an order from Chicago can be merged in Chicago itself. The merged order is then delivered to the customer. To facilitate this in-transit merge, Micron shares detailed electronic information with the FedEx warehouse as PCs ship out of Idaho. Customers can track the status of their orders after they have placed them.

For large corporate orders within the United States, Micron does not use FedEx. It uses less-than-truckload (LTL) companies to move the product. Currently, these orders are filled using peripherals that are stocked in Idaho.

Micron outsources both PC components and peripherals throughout the world. The company uses airfreight as well as ocean transport to move product to the United States, and then a combination of truck and rail to move it into warehouses.

The following supply chain design, planning, and operational decisions have a bearing on the performance of the Micron supply chain:

1. Why has assembly of certain PCs been outsourced? What characterizes PCs or orders that have been outsourced?
2. Why does Micron have only one manufacturing site?
3. Why are individual orders shipped using FedEx and large corporate orders shipped using LTL?
4. Why are individual orders merged in transit rather than at the assembly site itself?
5. How much inventory of components and finished products is maintained? What inventory policies are used to manage replenishment?
6. Why are some components brought by airfreight and others by ocean? On what basis is the transportation mode selected for a shipment?

Answers to these questions determine the appropriateness of the design, planning, and operation of the supply chain. Manufacturers that sell both direct and through resellers, like Hewlett Packard and Compaq, will need a different supply chain design to best support their strategy. How should they design and manage their supply chains?

Example 1.2 7-Eleven: A Convenience Store

With more than 17,000 stores in more than 20 countries, 7-Eleven is one of the largest convenience store chains in the world. It has more than 7,000 stores in Japan and almost 5,000 in the United States. Its growth in Japan has been phenomenal, given that the first 7-Eleven store opened in Japan in 1974. 7-Eleven Japan is one of the most profitable companies listed on the Tokyo stock exchange. It has seen tremendous growth in sales and profitability while simultaneously decreasing its inventory relative to sales. 7-Eleven Japan's success is attributed primarily to its supply chain design and management ability.

A key reason for its success is 7-Eleven's efforts to obtain a strategic fit between its competitive strategy and its location, transportation, inventory, and information strategy in the supply chain.

7-Eleven aims to provide customers with what they want, when they want it. From a strategic perspective, one of the company's key objectives is to micro-match supply and demand by location, season, and time of day. 7-Eleven designs and manages location, inventory, transportation, and information to support this objective.

7-Eleven follows a dominant location strategy and opens new stores in target areas to establish or enhance a strong presence. In Japan, for example, 7-Eleven stores are present in less than half of the prefectures (roughly equivalent to a county in the United States). However, 7-Eleven has a strong presence, with several stores, in each prefecture where they are located. In the United States, 7-Eleven stores were not as concentrated prior to 1994. Between 1994 and 1997, 7-Eleven closed several of its stores in isolated locations. Today, the company targets new stores in areas that already have a strong 7-Eleven presence. This strategy is consistent with the location strategy in Japan. This dominant location strategy allows the company the benefits of consolidation in both warehousing and transportation.

In Japan, fresh food constitutes a significant percentage of 7-Eleven's sales. Most of the fresh food is cooked off site and delivered to the stores. In Japan, a store placing an order by 10 A.M. has it delivered by dinnertime the same day. There are at least three fresh food deliveries a day per store so that the stock can change for breakfast, lunch, and dinner. All stores are electronically connected to the head office, distribution centers (DCs), and suppliers. All store orders are passed on to the suppliers who package store-specific orders and deliver them to the DC. At the DC, all orders of like products (categorized by temperature at which they are maintained) from different suppliers are combined and delivered to the stores. Each delivery truck delivers to more than one store and tries to visit stores during the off-peak hours. 7-Eleven Japan has made an effort to have no direct store delivery from vendors to the stores. Rather, all deliveries pass through and are aggregated at a 7-Eleven DC from which they are shipped to the stores. Note that the location strategy helps facilitate this supply strategy.

In the United States, 7-Eleven is taking a similar approach to the one used in Japan. Fresh foods are being introduced into the stores. 7-Eleven has once again decided to avoid on-site cooking by having suppliers that cook the fresh foods for them. These foods are then delivered to the stores on a daily basis. In the United States, 7-Eleven has tried to replicate the Japanese model with combined DCs where product is received from suppliers and then shipped to the stores. The success of this strategy is reflected by the improved performance of 7-Eleven in the United States.

In both Japan and the United States, 7-Eleven has invested a lot of money and effort on a retail information system. Scan data are collected and analyzed. The resulting information is then made available to the stores for use in ordering, product assortment, and merchandising. 7-Eleven uses this information system to identify slow-moving items and to analyze the performance of new products. Information systems play a key role in 7-Eleven's ability to micro-match supply and demand.

7-Eleven has made clear choices in the design of its supply chain. Other convenience store chains have not always made the same choices. We can ask a variety of questions, listed next, regarding 7-Eleven's supply chain choices and its key success factors.

1. What factors influence the decision regarding the opening and closing of stores? Why does 7-Eleven choose to have a preponderance of its stores in a particular location?
2. Why has 7-Eleven chosen off-site preparation of fresh foods and subsequent delivery to stores?
3. Why does 7-Eleven discourage direct store delivery from vendors and make an effort to move all products through combined distribution centers?
4. Where are distribution centers located and how many stores does each center serve? How are stores assigned to distribution centers?
5. Why does 7-Eleven combine fresh food shipments by temperature?
6. What point-of-sale data does 7-Eleven gather and what information is made available to store managers to assist them in their ordering and merchandising decisions? How should the information system be structured?

Example 1.3 W.W. Grainger and McMaster-Carr: Maintenance, Repair, and Operations Suppliers

W.W. Grainger and McMaster-Carr sell maintenance, repair, and operations (MRO) products. Both companies have catalogs, as well as Web pages through which orders can be placed. Grainger also has several hundred stores throughout the United States. Customers can walk into a store, call in an order, or place it via the Web. Grainger orders are either shipped to the customer or picked up by the customer at one of the stores. McMaster-Carr, in contrast, ships all orders. Grainger has several DCs that both replenish stores and fill customer orders. McMaster has DCs from which all orders are filled. Neither McMaster nor Grainger manufacture any product. They serve the role of a distributor or retailer. Their success is thus largely linked to their supply chain management ability.

Both firms offer several hundred thousand products to their customers. Each firm stocks about 200,000 products; the rest are obtained from the supplier as needed. Both firms face the following strategic and operational issues:

1. How many DCs should there be, and where should they be located?
2. How should product stocking be managed at the DCs? Should all DCs carry all products?
3. What products should be carried in inventory and what products should be left with the supplier?
4. What products should Grainger carry at a store?
5. How should markets be allocated to DCs in terms of order fulfillment? What should be done if an order cannot be completely filled from a DC? Should there be specified backup locations? How should they be selected?
6. How should replenishment of inventory be managed at the various stocking locations?

7. How should Web orders be handled relative to the existing business? Is it better to integrate the Web business with the existing business or to set up separate distribution?
8. What transportation modes should be used for order fulfillment and stock replenishment?

Example 1.4 Toyota: A Global Auto Manufacturer

Toyota Motor Corporation is Japan's number-one auto manufacturer and has experienced significant growth in global sales over the last two decades of the 20th century. A key issue facing Toyota is the design of its global production and distribution network. Part of Toyota's global strategy is to open factories in every major market it serves. Toyota must decide what the production capability of each of the factories will be, as this has a significant impact on the desired distribution system. At one extreme, each plant is equipped only for local production. At the other extreme, each plant is capable of supplying every market. Prior to 1996, Toyota used specialized local factories for each market. After the Asian financial crisis in 1996/1997, Toyota focused on redesigning its plants so that they could be shifted quickly to exporting to markets that remain strong. Toyota calls this strategy "global complementation."

Whether to be global or local is also an issue for Toyota's parts plants: Should they be designed for local consumption, or should there be few parts plants globally that supply multiple assembly plants?

For any global manufacturer like Toyota, several questions arise regarding the configuration and capability of the supply chain:

1. Where should the plants be located, and what degree of flexibility should be built into each? What capacity should each plant have?
2. Should plants be able to produce for all markets or only specific contingency markets?
3. How should markets be allocated to plants, and how frequently should this allocation be revised?
4. What kind of flexibility should be built into the distribution system?
5. How should this flexible investment be valued?
6. What actions may be taken during product design to facilitate this flexibility?

Example 1.5 Amazon.com: An E-Business

Amazon.com sells books, music, and other items over the Internet. It is one of the largest e-commerce firms, with a market capitalization of more than $20 billion. This figure is particularly impressive, considering that the firm was incorporated in 1994. The firm had annual sales of $1.6 billion in 1999, but it has yet to turn a profit.

Amazon.com is based in Seattle and started by filling all orders using books purchased from a distributor in response to customer orders. This practice differs from that of a traditional bookstore that purchases directly from publishers and stocks books in anticipation of customer orders. Today, Amazon.com has seven warehouses where it holds inventory. Amazon.com stocks best-selling books, though it still gets other titles from distributors. It uses the U.S. Postal Service and other package carriers like United Parcel Service (UPS) and FedEx to send books to customers. Given that Amazon.com has not yet turned a profit, there are several questions to be answered about the use of the e-commerce channel for retailing in general and selling books in particular.

Traditional booksellers like Borders and Barnes and Noble have also started selling using the Internet channel. Barnes and Noble has set up BarnesandNoble.com as a separate company. The two supply chains, however, share common warehousing and transportation to some extent, a change from Barnes and Noble's original supply chain strategy when BarnesandNoble.com was not visible in any Barnes and Noble bookstore.

Several questions arise regarding how Amazon.com is structured and how traditional booksellers have responded:

1. Why is Amazon.com building more warehouses as it grows? How many warehouses should it have, and where should they be located?
2. What advantages does selling books via the Internet provide over a traditional bookstore? Are there any disadvantages to selling via the Internet?
3. Why does Amazon.com stock best-sellers while buying other titles from distributors?
4. Does the Internet channel provide greater value to a bookseller like Borders with retail outlets or to an e-business like Amazon.com?
5. Should traditional booksellers like Barnes and Noble integrate e-commerce into their current supply chain or manage it as a separate supply chain?
6. For what products does the e-commerce channel offer the greatest advantage? What characterizes these products?

1.6 SUMMARY OF LEARNING OBJECTIVES

1. Describe the cycle and push/pull views of a supply chain.

   A cycle view of a supply chain divides processes into cycles, each performed at the interface between two successive stages of a supply chain. Each cycle starts with an order placed by one stage of the supply chain and ends when the order is received from the supplier stage. A push/pull view of a supply chain characterizes processes based on their timing relative to that of a customer order. Pull processes are performed in response to a customer order, and push processes are performed in anticipation of customer orders.
2. Identify the three key supply chain decision phases and explain the significance of each one.

   Supply chain decisions may be characterized as strategic (design), planning, or operational depending on the duration over which they apply. Strategic decisions relate to supply chain configuration. These decisions have a long-term impact lasting several years. Planning decisions cover a period of three months to a year and include decisions such as production plans, subcontracting, and promotions over that period. Operational decisions span a few days and include sequencing production and filling specific orders. Strategic decisions define the constraints for planning decisions, and planning decisions define the constraints for operational decisions.
3. Discuss the goal of a supply chain and explain the impact of supply chain decisions on the success of a firm.

   The goal of a supply chain should be to maximize overall supply chain profitability. Supply chain profitability is the difference between the revenue generated from the customer and the total cost incurred across all stages of the supply chain. Supply chain decisions have a large impact on the success or failure of each firm because they significantly influence both the revenue generated and the cost incurred. Successful supply chains manage flows of product, information, and funds to provide a high level of product availability to the customer while keeping costs low.

Discussion Questions

1. Consider the purchase of a can of soda at a convenience store. Describe the various stages in the supply chain and the different flows involved.
2. Why should a firm like Dell take into account total supply chain profitability when making decisions?
3. What are some strategic, planning, and operational decisions that must be made by an apparel retailer like The Gap?
4. Consider the supply chain involved when a customer purchases a book at a bookstore. Identify the cycles in this supply chain and the location of the push/pull boundary.
5. Consider the supply chain involved when a customer orders a book from Borders.com. Identify the push/pull boundary and two processes each in both the push and the pull phases.
6. In what way do supply chain flows affect the success or failure of a firm like Amazon.com? List two supply chain decisions that have a significant impact on supply chain profitability.

Bibliography

Chopra, S. *Seven Eleven Japan* Case, Kellogg Graduate School of Management, 1995.

Fisher, Marshall L. "What Is the Right Supply Chain for Your Product?" *Harvard Business Review* (March–April 1997), 83–93.

Fuller, J. B., J. O'Conner, and R. Rawlinson. "Tailored Logistics: The Next Advantage." *Harvard Business Review* (May–June 1993), 87–98.

Magretta, Joan. "The Power of Virtual Integration: An Interview with Dell Computer's Michael Dell." *Harvard Business Review* (March–April 1998), 72–84.

Quinn, Francis J. "Reengineering the Supply Chain: An Interview with Michael Hammer." *Supply Chain Management Review* (Spring 1999), 20–26.

Robeson, James F., and William C. Copacino (eds.). *The Logistics Handbook.* New York: The Free Press, 1994.

Shapiro, Roy D. "Get Leverage from Logistics." *Harvard Business Review* (May–June 1984), 119–127.

CHAPTER 2

Supply Chain Performance: Achieving Strategic Fit and Scope

Learning Objectives
After reading this chapter, you will be able to

1. explain why achieving strategic fit is critical to a company's overall success;
2. describe how a company achieves strategic fit between its supply chain strategy and its competitive strategy; and
3. discuss the importance of expanding the scope of strategic fit across the supply chain.

In Chapter 1, we discuss what a supply chain is and the importance of supply chain design, planning, and operation to a firm's success. In this chapter, we define supply chain strategy and explain how creating a strategic fit between a company's competitive strategy and its supply chain strategy affects performance. We also discuss the importance of expanding the scope of strategic fit from one operation within a company to all stages of the supply chain.

2.1 COMPETITIVE AND SUPPLY CHAIN STRATEGIES

A company's **competitive strategy** defines the set of customer needs that it seeks to satisfy through its products and services. For example, Wal-Mart aims to provide high availability of a variety of reasonable quality products at low prices. Most products sold at Wal-Mart are commonplace (everything from home appliances to clothing) and can be purchased elsewhere. What Wal-Mart provides is a low price and product availability. McMaster-Carr sells maintenance, repair, and operations (MRO) products. It offers more than 200,000 different products through both a catalog and a Web site. Its competitive strategy is built around providing the customer convenience. McMaster-Carr does not compete based on low price. However, it guarantees product availability and delivery within a day. Customers do not come to McMaster-Carr looking for the lowest-price product; rather, they come because of the wide variety of products available and the promise of next-day delivery. Clearly, the competitive strategy at Wal-Mart is different from that at McMaster-Carr.

We can also contrast Dell, with its build-to-order model, with a firm like Compaq, selling personal computers (PCs) through retailers. Dell has stressed customization and variety at a reasonable cost, with customers having to wait about a week to get their product. In contrast, a customer can walk into a computer retailer, be helped by a salesperson, and leave the same day with a Compaq computer. However, the amount of variety and customization available at the retailer is limited. In each case, the competitive strategy is based on how the customer prioritizes product cost, product delivery or response time, product variety, and product quality. A McMaster-Carr customer places greater emphasis on product variety and response time than on cost. A Wal-Mart customer, conversely, places greater emphasis on cost. A Dell customer, purchasing on-line, places great emphasis on product variety and customization. A customer purchasing a PC at a retailer is most concerned with the help in product selection and faster response time. Thus, a firm's competitive strategy will be defined based on the customer's priorities. Competitive strategy targets one or more customer segments and aims to provide products and services that will satisfy these customers' needs.

To see the relationship between competitive strategy and supply chain strategy, we start with the value chain for any organization, as shown in Figure 2.1.

The value chain begins with new product development, which creates specifications for the product. Marketing and sales generates demand by publicizing the customer priorities that the product and services will satisfy. Marketing also brings customer input back to new product development. Using new product specifications, operations transforms inputs to outputs to create the product. Distribution either takes the product to the customer or brings the customer to the product. Service responds to customer requests during or after the sale. These are core functions that must be performed for a successful sale. Finance, accounting, information technology, and human resources support and facilitate the functioning of the value chain.

To execute a company's competitive strategy, all these functions play a role, and each must develop its own strategy. *Strategy* here refers to what each function will try to do particularly well.

A **product development strategy** specifies the portfolio of new products that a company will try to develop. It also dictates whether the development effort will be made internally or outsourced. A **marketing and sales strategy** specifies how the mar-

FIGURE 2.1 The Value Chain in a Company

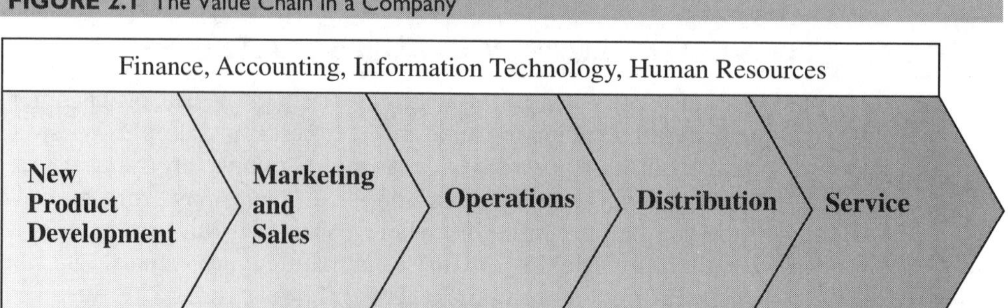

ket will be segmented and the product positioned, priced, and promoted. A **supply chain strategy** determines the nature of procurement of raw materials, transportation of materials to and from the company, manufacture of the product or operation to provide the service, and distribution of the product to the customer, along with any follow-up service. From a value chain perspective, supply chain strategy specifies what operations, distribution, and service will try to do particularly well. Additionally, in each company, strategies will be devised for finance, accounting, information technology, and human resources.

As our focus here is on supply chain strategy, we define it in a little more detail. Supply chain strategy includes what many traditionally call supplier strategy, operations strategy, and logistics strategy. Decisions regarding inventory, transportation, operating facilities, and information flows in the supply chain are all part of supply chain strategy.

The value chain emphasizes the close relationship between all the functional strategies within a company. Each function is crucial if a company is to profitably satisfy customer needs. Therefore, the various functional strategies cannot be formulated in isolation. They are closely intertwined and must fit and support each other if a company is to succeed. We are particularly concerned here with the link between a company's competitive and supply chain strategies. We will seek to answer this question: Given its competitive strategy, what should a company's supply chain try to do particularly well?

2.2 ACHIEVING STRATEGIC FIT

This chapter is built on the idea that for any company to be successful, its supply chain strategy and competitive strategy must fit together. **Strategic fit** means that both the competitive and supply chain strategies have the same goal. It refers to consistency between the customer priorities that the competitive strategy is designed to satisfy and the supply chain capabilities that the supply chain strategy aims to build. The issue of achieving strategic fit is a key consideration during the supply chain strategy or design phase discussed in Chapter 1.

All functions that are part of a company's value chain contribute to its success or failure. These functions do not operate in isolation; no one function can ensure the chain's success. However, failure at any one function may lead to failure of the overall chain. This failure can occur in coordinating strategies and achieving strategic fit, or it can occur when the strategies are being executed. A company's success or failure is thus closely linked to the following keys:

1. The competitive strategy and all functional strategies must fit together to form a coordinated overall strategy. Each functional strategy must support other functional strategies and help a firm reach its competitive strategy goal.
2. The different functions in a company must appropriately structure their processes and resources to be able to execute these strategies successfully.

A company may fail either because of a lack of strategic fit or because its processes and resources do not provide the capabilities to support the desired strategic fit. In thinking of the major tasks of a chief executive officer, there are few greater than the job of aligning all of the core functional strategies with the overall competitive strategy to achieve strategic fit. If this alignment is not achieved at the strategic level, conflicts between different functional goals arise. Such conflicts result in different functions targeting different customer priorities. Because processes and resources are structured to support functional goals, a conflict in functional goals leads to conflicts during execution. Consider, for example, a situation in which marketing is publicizing the company's ability to provide a large variety of products very quickly, and simultaneously, distribution is targeting the lowest-cost means of transportation. In this situation, it is very likely that distribution will delay orders so it can get better transportation economies by grouping several orders together. This action conflicts with marketing's stated goal of providing variety quickly.

To elaborate on strategic fit, let us return to the example of Dell Computer from Chapter 1. Dell's competitive strategy is to provide a large variety of customizable products at a reasonable price; customers can select from among thousands of possible PC configurations. In terms of supply chain strategy, a PC manufacturer has a range of options. At one extreme, a company can have an efficient supply chain with a focus on the ability to produce low-cost PCs by limiting variety and exploiting economies of scale. At the other extreme, a company can have a highly flexible and responsive supply chain that is very good at producing a large variety of products. In this case, costs will be higher than in an efficient supply chain. Both supply chain strategies are viable by themselves. However, both do not fit with Dell's competitive strategy. A supply chain strategy that emphasizes flexibility and responsiveness has a better strategic fit with Dell's competitive strategy of providing a large variety of customizable products.

This notion of fit also extends to Dell's other functional strategies. Its new product development strategy should emphasize designing products that are easily customizable, which may include designing common platforms across several products and using common components. Dell products use many common components; they are designed so that the components that Dell allows to be customized can be easily and quickly assembled. This feature allows Dell to assemble customized PCs quickly in response to a customer order. The design of new products at Dell supports the supply chain's ability to assemble customized PCs in response to customer orders. This capability, in turn, supports Dell's strategic goal of offering customization to its customers. Dell clearly has achieved strong strategic fit between its different functional strategies and its competitive strategy.

How Is Strategic Fit Achieved?

What does a company need to do to achieve that all-important strategic fit between the supply chain and competitive strategies? A competitive strategy will specify, either explicitly or implicitly, one or more customer segments that a company hopes to satisfy. To achieve strategic fit, a company must ensure that its supply chain capabilities support its ability to satisfy the targeted customer segments.

There are three basic steps to achieving this strategic fit:

1. **Understanding the customer**. First, a company must understand the customer needs for each targeted segment. These needs help the company define the desired cost and service requirements.

2. **Understanding the supply chain**. There are many types of supply chains, each of which is designed to perform different tasks well. A company must understand what its supply chain is designed to do well.

3. **Achieving strategic fit**. If any mismatch exists between what the supply chain does particularly well and the desired customer needs, the company will either need to restructure the supply chain to support the competitive strategy or alter its strategy.

Step 1: Understanding the Customer

To understand the customer, a company must identify the needs of the customer segment being served. Let us compare 7-Eleven Japan and a discounter such as Sam's Club (a part of Wal-Mart). When customers go to 7-Eleven to purchase detergent, they go there for the convenience and are not necessarily looking for the lowest price. They prefer that the store be nearby and have a sufficient variety of products to enable them to get what they need. In contrast, a low price is very important to a customer going to Sam's Club to purchase detergent. This customer may be willing to tolerate less variety and even purchase very large package sizes as long as the price is low. Even though customers may purchase detergent at both places, the demand varies along certain attributes. In the case of 7-Eleven, customers are in a hurry and want convenience. In the case of Sam's Club, they want a low price and are willing to spend time getting it. In general, customer demand from different segments may vary along several attributes:

- **The quantity of the product needed in each lot**. For example, an emergency order for material needed to repair a production line is likely to be small; an order for material to build a new production line is likely to be large.
- **The response time that customers are willing to tolerate**. The tolerable response time for the emergency order is likely to be short, whereas the allowable response time for the construction order is apt to be long.
- **The variety of products needed**. A customer may place a high premium on all parts of the emergency repair order being available from a single supplier. This may not be the case for the construction order.
- **The service level required**. A customer placing an emergency order expects a high level of product availability. This customer may go elsewhere if all parts of the order are not immediately available and he or she has to wait. This is not apt to happen in the case of the construction order, where a long lead time is likely.
- **The price of the product**. The customer placing the emergency order is apt to be much less sensitive to price than the customer placing the construction order.
- **The desired rate of innovation in the product**. Customers at a high-end department store expect a lot of innovation and new designs in the store's apparel. Customers at a Wal-Mart may be less sensitive to new product innovation.

Each customer in a particular segment will tend to have similar needs, whereas customers in different segments can have very different needs.

Although we have described the many attributes along which customer demand varies, our goal is to identify one key measure that captures variation for all these attributes. This single measure then helps define what the supply chain should be able to do particularly well.

Implied Demand Uncertainty At first glance, it may appear that each of the customer need categories should be viewed differently, but in a very fundamental sense, each customer need can be translated into the metric of implied demand uncertainty. **Implied demand uncertainty** is the uncertainty that exists due to the portion of demand that the supply chain is required to meet.

We make a distinction between demand uncertainty and implied demand uncertainty. **Demand uncertainty** reflects the uncertainty of customer demand for a prod-

TABLE 2.1 Impact of Customer Needs on Implied Demand Uncertainty

Customer Need	*Causes implied demand uncertainty to . . .*
Range of quantity required increases	increase because a wider range of the quantity required implies greater variance in demand
Lead time decreases	increase because there is less time in which to react to orders
Variety of products required increases	increase because demand per product becomes more disaggregate
Number of channels through which product may be acquired increases	increase because the total customer demand is now disaggregated over more channels
Rate of innovation increases	increase because new products tend to have more uncertain demand
Required service level increases	increase because the firm now has to handle unusual surges in demand

uct. Implied demand uncertainty, in contrast, is the resulting uncertainty for the supply chain given the portion of the demand that the supply chain must handle and the attributes the customer desires. For example, a firm supplying only emergency orders for a product will face a higher implied demand uncertainty than a firm that supplies the same product with a long lead time.

Implied demand uncertainty is also affected by the attributes the customer desires. For example, demand for steel exhibits a certain level of uncertainty in terms of the type and quantity of steel needed. Steel service centers are willing to supply a wide variety of steel with less than a one week lead time. Mini-mills supply less variety and require a larger lead time. Integrated steel mills require a lead time of months. In each of the three cases, the physical product is the same. However, the supply chain faces a different level of implied demand uncertainty. The short lead time and high variety results in steel service centers having the highest implied demand uncertainty; customers come with small orders that they need urgently. Integrated mills, conversely, have a much lower implied demand uncertainty; customers come with steel requirements that can be planned far in advance.

Another illustration of the need for this distinction is the impact of service level. As a supply chain raises its level of service, it must be able to meet a higher and higher percentage of actual demand, forcing it to prepare for rare surges in demand. Thus, raising the service level increases the implied demand uncertainty even though the product's underlying demand uncertainty does not change.

Both the product demand uncertainty and various customer needs that the supply chain tries to fill affect implied demand uncertainty. Table 2.1 illustrates how various customer needs affect implied demand uncertainty.

As each individual customer need contributes significantly to the implied demand uncertainty, we can use implied demand uncertainty as a common metric with which to distinguish different types of demand. We can then think of the different types of demand along a spectrum of implied uncertainty. Figure 2.2 is a spectrum that has examples of products with the level of implied demand uncertainty that each product's customers generate. We call it the implied uncertainty spectrum.

Fisher has pointed out that implied demand uncertainty is often correlated with other characteristics of the demand, as shown in Table 2.2. An explanation follows:

1. Products with uncertain demand are often less mature and have less direct competition. As a result, margins tend to be high.
2. Forecasting is more accurate when demand is more certain.

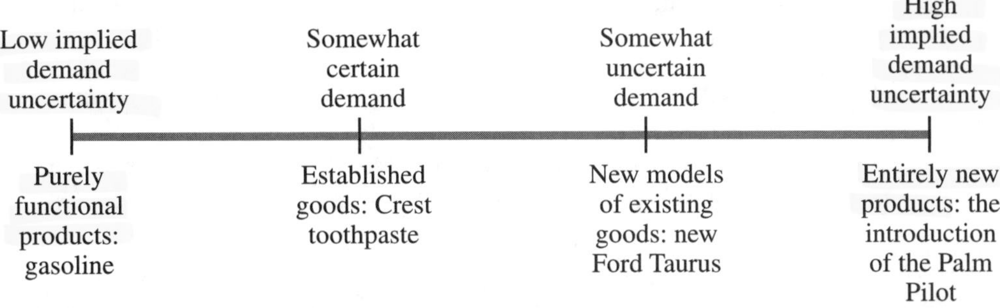

FIGURE 2.2 The Implied Uncertainty Spectrum

3. Increased implied demand uncertainty leads to increased difficulty matching supply with demand. For a given product, this dynamic can lead to either a stockout or an oversupply situation. Increased implied demand uncertainty thus leads to both higher oversupply and a higher stockout rate.
4. Markdowns are high for products with high implied demand uncertainty because oversupply often results.

First, let us take an example of a product with low implied demand uncertainty from Figure 2.2: gasoline. Gasoline has a very low contribution margin, accurate demand forecasts, low stockout rates, and virtually no markdowns. These characteristics match well with Fisher's chart of characteristics for products with highly certain demand.

On the other end of the spectrum, a new "palmtop" computer will likely have a high margin, very inaccurate demand forecasts, high stockout rates (if it is successful), and large markdowns (if it is a failure). This too matches well with Table 2.2.

Another example is a circuit board supplier whose customers include two different types of PC manufacturers. One of its customers is a build-to-order PC manufacturer such as Dell that requires same-day lead times. In this case, the supplier might need to build up inventory or have very flexible manufacturing to be prepared for whatever demand Dell had that day. Forecast error would be high, and stockouts could be high; because of these factors, margins would likely be higher. The supplier's other customer builds a small variety of PCs and specifies in advance the number and type of PCs to be built. This information gives the supplier a much longer lead time and reduces the forecasting errors and stockout rates. Thus, the supplier would likely get smaller margins from this PC manufacturer. These examples demonstrate that even with the same product, different customer segments can have different implied demand uncertainty given different service requirements.

TABLE 2.2 Correlation Between Implied Demand Uncertainty and Other Attributes

Attribute	*Low Implied Uncertainty*	*High Implied Uncertainty*
1. Product margin	Low	High
2. Average forecast error	10%	40% to 100%
3. Average stockout rate	1% to 2%	10% to 40%
4. Average forced season-end markdown	0%	10% to 25%

Adapted from "What Is the Right Supply Chain for Your Product?" Marshall L. Fisher, *Harvard Business Review* (March–April 1997), 83–93.

Clearly, these descriptions are generalizations along the implied uncertainty spectrum. Many types of demand may include a mixture of the characteristics discussed previously and fall somewhere between the two extremes. This spectrum, however, gives a good feel for many of the characteristics of products that tend to have either certain or uncertain demand.

Having completed step 1, we now understand the customer needs and have mapped their demand on the implied uncertainty spectrum.

> ***Key Point*** The first step in achieving strategic fit between competitive and supply chain strategies is to understand customers by mapping where their demand is located on the implied uncertainty spectrum.

Step 2: Understanding the Supply Chain

After understanding the characteristics of the demand that the company faces, the next question is this: How does the firm best meet that demand? Creating strategic fit is all about creating a supply chain strategy that best meets the particular type of demand that a company has targeted.

We now consider characteristics of supply chains and categorize them. Similar to the way we placed demand on a one-dimensional spectrum (the implied uncertainty spectrum), we can also place each supply chain on such a spectrum. Like customer needs, supply chains have many different characteristics. However, if we search for a single idea to which all characteristics of the supply chain contribute, it is the idea of the trade-off between responsiveness and efficiency.

First we provide some definitions. **Supply chain responsiveness** includes a supply chain's ability to do the following:

- Respond to wide ranges of quantities demanded
- Meet short lead times
- Handle a large variety of products
- Build highly innovative products
- Meet a very high service level

These abilities are similar to many of the characteristics of demand that led to high implied uncertainty. The more of these abilities that a supply chain has, the more responsive it is.

Responsiveness, however, comes at a cost. For instance, to respond to a wider range of quantities demanded, capacity must be increased, which increases costs. This increase in cost leads to the second definition: **Supply chain efficiency** is the cost of making and delivering a product to the customer. Increases in cost lower efficiency. For every strategic choice to increase responsiveness, there are additional costs that lower efficiency.

The **cost-responsiveness efficient frontier** is the curve in Figure 2.3 showing the lowest possible cost for a given level of responsiveness. *Lowest* is defined based on existing technology. Not every firm is able to perform on the efficient frontier. The efficient frontier represents the cost-responsiveness performance of the best supply chains. A firm that is not on the efficient frontier can improve both its responsiveness and its cost performance by moving toward the efficient frontier. In contrast, a firm on the efficient frontier can improve its responsiveness only by increasing cost and be-

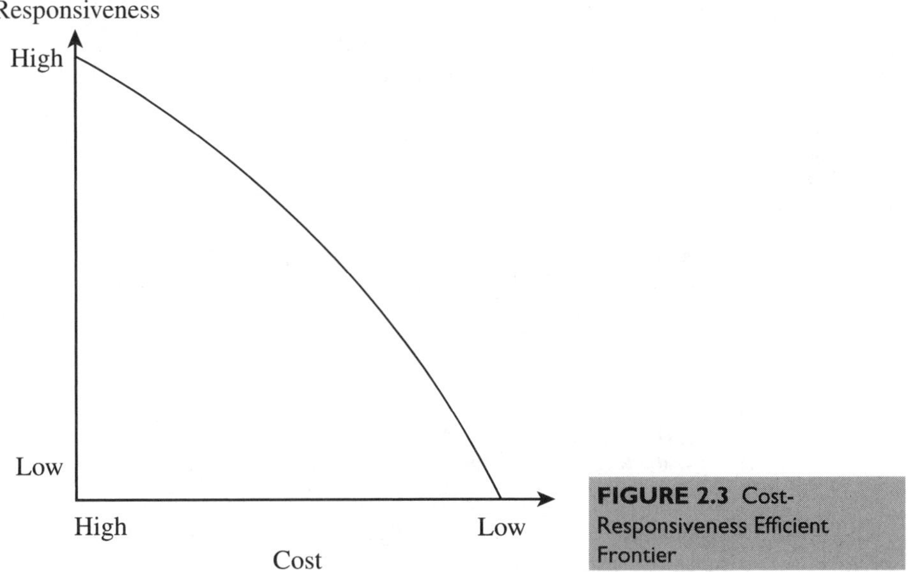
Responsiveness
High
Low
High
Low
Cost

FIGURE 2.3 Cost-Responsiveness Efficient Frontier

coming less efficient. Such a firm must then make a trade-off between efficiency and responsiveness. Of course, firms on the efficient frontier are also continuously improving their processes and changing technology to shift the efficient frontier itself. Given the trade-off between cost and responsiveness, a key strategic choice for any supply chain is the level of responsiveness it seeks to provide.

Supply chains range from those that focus on being responsive to those that focus on efficiency with a goal of producing and supplying at the lowest possible cost. Figure 2.4 shows the responsiveness spectrum and where some different supply chains fall on this spectrum.

The more capabilities constituting responsiveness that a supply chain has, the more responsive it is. 7-Eleven Japan replenishes its stores with breakfast items in the morning, lunch items in the afternoon, and dinner items at night. As a result, the available product variety changes by time of day. 7-Eleven responds very quickly to orders, with store managers placing replenishment orders less than 12 hours before they are supplied. This practice makes the 7-Eleven supply chain very responsive. The Dell supply chain allows a customer to customize any of several thousand PC configurations. Dell then delivers the appropriate PC to the customer within days. The Dell

FIGURE 2.4 The Responsiveness Spectrum

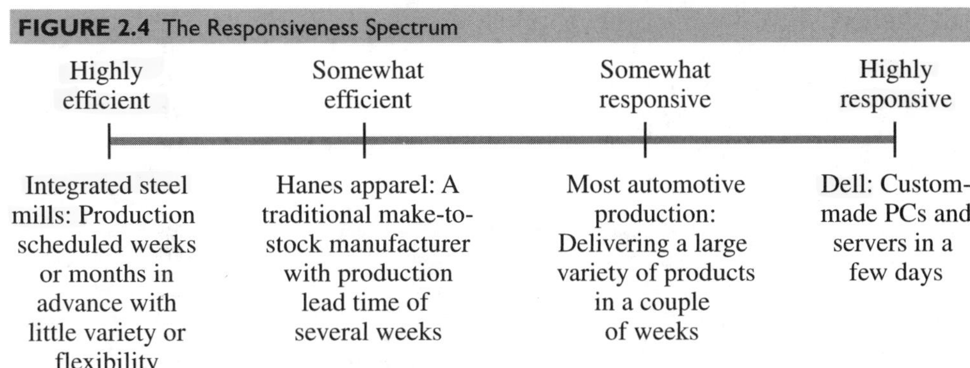
Highly efficient
Somewhat efficient
Somewhat responsive
Highly responsive
Integrated steel mills: Production scheduled weeks or months in advance with little variety or flexibility
Hanes apparel: A traditional make-to-stock manufacturer with production lead time of several weeks
Most automotive production: Delivering a large variety of products in a couple of weeks
Dell: Custom-made PCs and servers in a few days

supply chain would also be considered very responsive. An efficient supply chain, in contrast, lowers cost by eliminating some of its responsive capabilities. For example, Sam's Club sells a limited variety of products in large package sizes. The supply chain is very good at keeping costs down and the focus of this supply chain is clearly on efficiency.

Key Point The second step in achieving strategic fit between competitive and supply chain strategies is to understand the supply chain and map it on the responsiveness spectrum.

Step 3: Achieving Strategic Fit

We have now looked at demand and mapped it to gauge its level of implied uncertainty. We have examined a supply chain to understand where it lies on the responsiveness spectrum. The third and final step in achieving strategic fit is to ensure that what the supply chain does particularly well is consistent with the targeted customer's needs. The degree of supply chain responsiveness should be consistent with the implied demand uncertainty.

A useful exercise is to think of the spectrums that we have discussed as two axes on a graph, as shown in Figure 2.5, with implied uncertainty increasing as we move along the horizontal axis (the implied uncertainty spectrum) and responsiveness increasing along the vertical axis (the responsiveness spectrum). This graph is referred to as the uncertainty/responsiveness map. A point in this graph represents a combination of implied demand uncertainty and supply chain responsiveness. The implied demand uncertainty represents customer needs or the firm's strategic position. The supply chain's responsiveness represents the supply chain strategy. We can now ask the following question: Which combinations of implied demand uncertainty and supply chain responsiveness result in strategic fit?

Consider again the example of Dell Computers. For Dell, the competitive strategy targets customers who value having the latest PC models customized to their

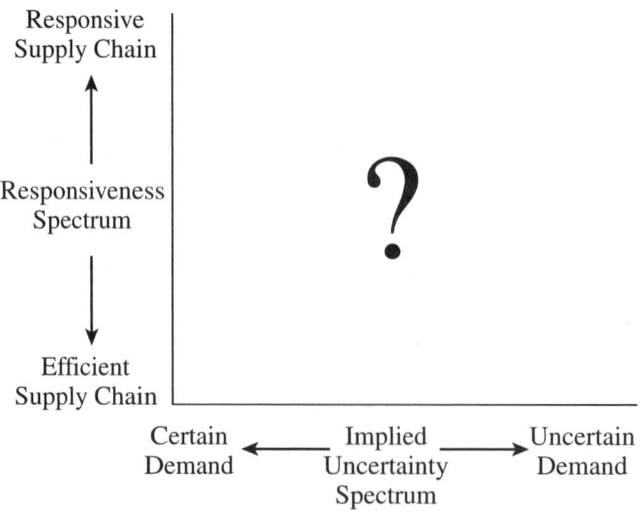

FIGURE 2.5 Uncertainty/Responsiveness Map

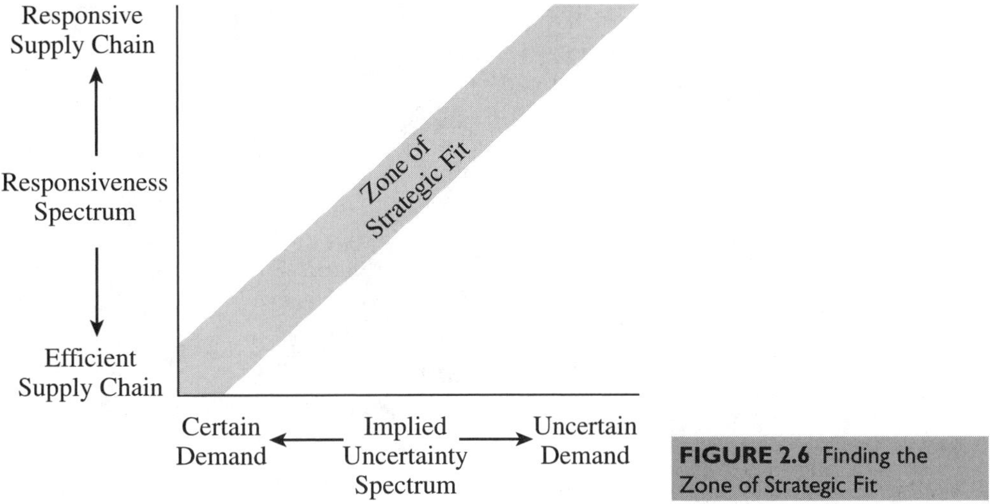

FIGURE 2.6 Finding the Zone of Strategic Fit

needs. Further, these customers want the PCs delivered within days. Given the vast variety of PCs, the high level of innovation, and rapid delivery, demand from Dell customers can be characterized as having high demand uncertainty. Dell has the option of designing an efficient or responsive supply chain. An efficient supply chain may use slow, inexpensive modes of transportation and economies of scale in production. If Dell made both of these choices, it would have difficulty supporting the customer's desire for rapid delivery and a wide variety of customizable products. Building a responsive supply chain, however, will allow Dell to meet its customers' needs. Therefore, a responsive supply chain strategy is best suited to meet the needs of Dell's targeted customers.

Now, consider a pasta manufacturer like Barilla. Pasta is a commodity product with relatively stable customer demand. Demand for pasta has lower implied demand uncertainty than is the case for Dell. Barilla could design a highly responsive supply chain, in which pasta is custom-made in very small batches in response to customer orders and shipped via a rapid transport mode such as Federal Express. This choice would make the pasta prohibitively expensive, resulting in a loss of customers. Barilla, therefore, is in a much better position if it designs a more efficient supply chain with a focus on cost reduction.

From the preceding discussion, it follows that in order to achieve strategic fit, the greater the implied demand uncertainty, and the more responsive the supply chain should be. Increasing implied demand uncertainty from customers is best served with increasing responsiveness from the supply chain. This relationship is represented by the "zone of strategic fit" illustrated in Figure 2.6. For a high level of performance, companies should gear their competitive strategy (and resulting implied demand uncertainty) and supply chain strategy (and resulting responsiveness) toward the zone of strategic fit.

To achieve complete strategic fit, a firm must consider all functional strategies within the value chain; it must ensure that all functions in the value chain have consistent strategies that support the competitive strategy, as shown in Figure 2.7. All functional strategies must support the goals of the competitive strategy, and all substrategies within the supply chain—such as manufacturing, inventory, and purchasing—must also be consistent with the supply chain's level of responsiveness.

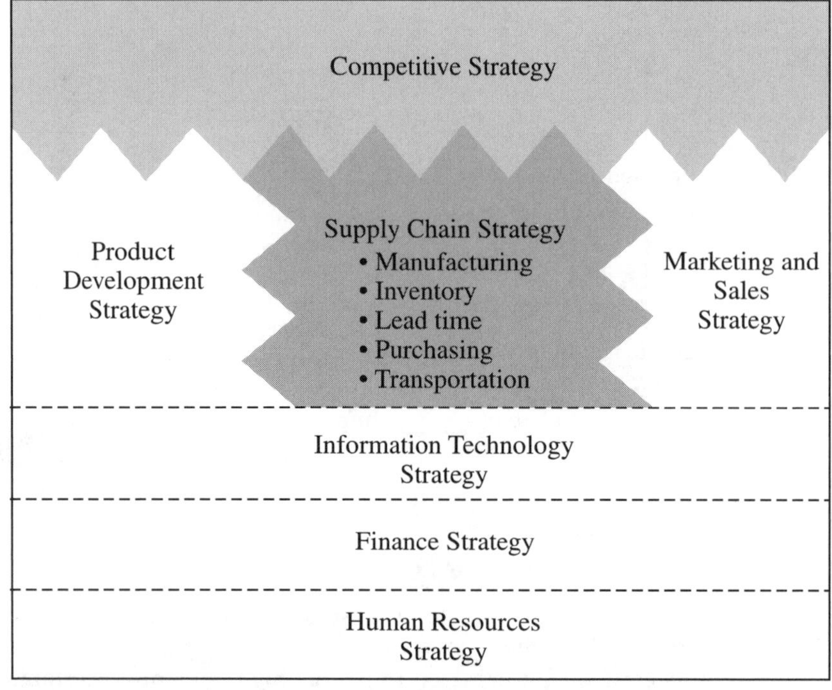

FIGURE 2.7 Fit Between Competitive and Functional Strategies

Thus, firms with different locations along the responsiveness spectrum must have different functional strategies that support their responsiveness. A highly responsive supply chain must devote all its functional strategies to responsiveness, whereas an efficient supply chain must focus all its functional strategies on efficiency. Table 2.3 lists some of the major differences in functional strategy between supply chains that are efficient and those that are responsive.

TABLE 2.3 Comparison of Efficient and Responsive Supply Chains

	Efficient Supply Chain	***Responsive Supply Chains***
Primary goal	Supply demand at the lowest cost	Respond quickly to demand
Product design strategy	Maximize performance at a minimum product cost	Create *modularity* to allow postponement of product differentiation
Pricing strategy	Lower margins because price is a prime customer driver	Higher margins, as price is not a prime customer driver
Manufacturing strategy	Lower costs through high utilization	Maintain capacity flexibility to meet unexpected demand
Inventory strategy	Minimize inventory to lower cost	Maintain *buffer inventory* to meet unexpected demand
Lead time strategy	Reduce but not at the expense of costs	Aggressively reduce even if the costs are significant
Supplier strategy	Select based on cost and quality	Select based on speed, flexibility, and quality
Transportation strategy	Greater reliance on low cost modes	Greater reliance on responsive modes

Adapted from Marshall L. Fisher, "What Is the Right Supply Chain for Your Product?" *Harvard Business Review* (March–April 1997), 83–93.

Key Point The final step in achieving strategic fit is to match supply chain responsiveness with the implied demand uncertainty in the zone of strategic fit. All functional strategies within the value chain must also support the supply chain's level of responsiveness.

Changing the strategies to achieve strategic fit may sound easy enough to do, but in reality it can be quite difficult. In later chapters, we discuss many of the obstacles to achieving this fit. Right now, the important points to remember from this discussion are the following:

1. There is *no* right supply chain strategy independent of the competitive strategy.
2. There *is* a right supply chain strategy for a given competitive strategy.

The drive for strategic fit should come from the highest levels of the organization. In many companies, different groups devise competitive and functional strategies. Without proper communication between the groups and coordination by high-level management such as the chief executive officer, these strategies are not likely to achieve strategic fit. For most firms, the failure to achieve strategic fit is a key reason for their inability to succeed.

Other Issues Affecting Strategic Fit

Our previous discussion focuses on achieving strategic fit when a firm serves a single market segment and the result is a well-defined strategic position. We now consider how multiple products or multiple customer segments and product life cycle affect strategic fit.

Multiple Products and Customer Segments

Most companies produce and sell multiple products and serve multiple customer segments, each with different characteristics. A department store may sell seasonal products with high implied demand uncertainty, such as ski jackets, along with products with low implied demand uncertainty, such as T-shirts. The demand in each case maps to different parts of the uncertainty spectrum. W.W. Grainger sells MRO products to both large firms, like Ford and Boeing, and small manufacturers and contractors. The customer needs in the two cases are very different. A large firm is much more likely to be concerned with price given the large volumes they generate for Grainger, whereas a smaller company is apt to go to Grainger because it is responsive. The two segments served map to different positions along the implied uncertainty spectrum. Another example is that of Levi Strauss, which sells both customized and standard-sized jeans. Demand for standard-sized jeans has a much lower implied demand uncertainty than demand for customized jeans.

In each of the preceding examples, the firm sells multiple products and serves customer segments with very different needs. As a result, the different products and segments have different implied demand uncertainty. When devising supply chain strategy in these cases, the key issue for a company is to create a supply chain that balances efficiency and responsiveness given its portfolio of products and customer segments.

There are several possible routes a company can take. One is to set up independent supply chains for each different product or customer segment. This strategy is feasible if each segment is large enough to support a dedicated supply chain. It fails, however, to take advantage of any economies of scope that often exist between a company's different products. Therefore, a preferable strategy is to tailor the supply chain to best meet the needs of each product's demand.

Tailoring the supply chain requires sharing some links in the supply chain with other products while having separate operations for other links. The links are shared to achieve maximum possible efficiency while providing the appropriate level of responsiveness to each segment. For instance, all products may be made on the same line in a plant, but products requiring a high level of responsiveness may be shipped using FedEx. Other products coming off the line that do not have high responsiveness needs may be shipped by slower and less expensive means such as truck, rail, or even ship. In other instances, products requiring high responsiveness may be manufactured using a very flexible process in response to customer orders, whereas products that require less responsiveness may be manufactured using a less responsive but more efficient process. The mode of transportation used in both cases may be the same. Levi's has set up a very flexible manufacturing process for customized jeans and a more efficient manufacturing process for standard-sized jeans. In other cases, some products may be held at regional warehouses close to the customer, whereas others may be held in a centralized warehouse far from the customer. W.W. Grainger holds fast-moving items in its decentralized locations close to the customer. It holds slow-moving items with higher implied demand uncertainty in a centralized warehouse. Appropriate tailoring of the supply chain helps a firm achieve varying levels of responsiveness for a low overall cost. The level of responsiveness is tailored to each product or customer segment. We provide various examples of tailored supply chains in subsequent chapters.

Product Life Cycle

As products go through their life cycles, the demand characteristics and the needs of the customer segments being served change. High-tech products are particularly prone to these life cycle swings over a very compressed time span. A product goes through life cycle phases from the introductory phase, when only the leading edge of customers is interested in it, all the way to the point at which the product becomes a commodity and the market is completely saturated. Thus, if a company is to maintain strategic fit, its supply chain strategy must evolve as its products enter different phases.

Let us consider changes in demand characteristics over the life cycle of a product. Toward the beginning stages of a product's life cycle, the following are common:

1. Demand is very uncertain.
2. Margins are often high, and time is crucial to gaining sales.
3. Product availability is crucial to capturing the market.
4. Cost is often of secondary consideration.

Consider a pharmaceutical firm introducing a new drug. Initial demand for the drug is highly uncertain, margins are typically very high, and product availability is the key to capturing market share. The introductory phase of a product's life cycle corresponds to high implied demand uncertainty. In such a situation, the goal of the supply chain is responsiveness and high product availability.

In the case of the pharmaceutical firm, the supply chain's initial goal is to ensure that the drug is available to support any level of demand. At this stage, the pharmaceutical firm needs a responsive supply chain.

As the product becomes a commodity product later in its life cycle, the demand characteristics change. At this stage, the following are typically the case:

1. Demand has become more certain.
2. Margins are lower due to an increase in competitors and more competitive pressure.
3. Price becomes a significant factor in customer choice.

In the case of the pharmaceutical company, these changes occur when the drug goes out of patent and generic drugs are introduced. At this stage, demand for the drug stabilizes and margins shrink. Customers make their selections from the various choices based on price. This stage corresponds to a low level of implied demand uncertainty. As a result, the supply chain needs to change. In such a situation, the goal of the supply chain is minimum cost at an acceptable service level. This makes efficiency the most important characteristic of the supply chain.

In the case of the pharmaceutical industry, only firms with efficient supply chains can compete in the generic drug market. Because firms without efficient supply chains are unable to compete on price, they exit the market.

This discussion illustrates that as products mature, the corresponding supply chain strategy should, in general, move from being responsive to being efficient, as illustrated in Figure 2.8.

To illustrate the ideas discussed previously, consider the example of Intel Corporation. Each time Intel introduces a new processor, there is great uncertainty with respect to demand for this new product. Demand for the new processor depends on the sales of new high-end PCs. Typically there is high uncertainty regarding how the market will receive these PCs and what the demand will be. At this stage, the Intel supply chain must be very responsive so it can react if demand is very high.

As the Intel processor is accepted by the market, demand begins to stabilize. At this point demand typically displays lower implied demand uncertainty and price becomes a greater determinant of sales. Now it is important that Intel has an efficient supply chain in place for producing processors.

All PC manufacturers are subject to the cycle just described. When a new model is introduced, margins are high, but demand is highly uncertain. In such a situation, a

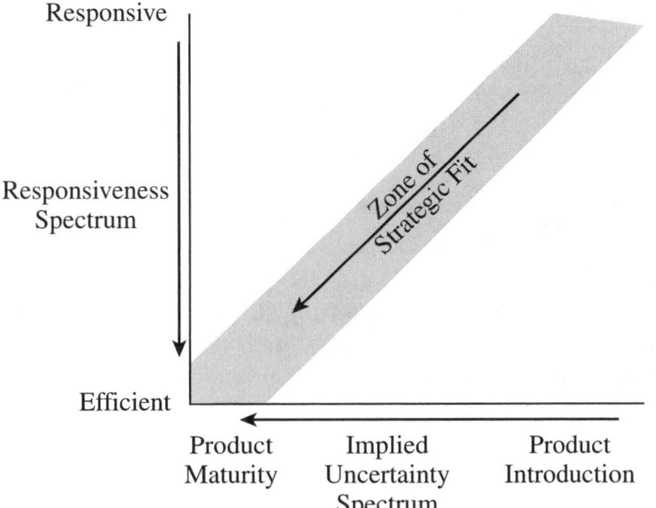

FIGURE 2.8 Changes in Supply Chain Strategy over a Product's Life Cycle

responsive supply chain best serves the PC manufacturer. As the model matures, demand stabilizes and margins shrink. At this stage it is important that the manufacturer have an efficient supply chain. Apple Computer is an example of a firm that had difficulty during product introduction—specifically when it introduced the G4 in 1999. Demand for the machine far exceeded the available supply of processors, resulting in significant lost sales. The supply chain in this case did not display sufficient responsiveness during the product's introductory phase.

The key point here is that demand characteristics change over a product's life cycle. Because demand characteristics change, the supply chain strategy must change over the product's life cycle as well if a company is to continue achieving strategic fit. The change in supply chain strategy and the change in demand characteristics must mesh.

Competitive Changes Over Time

A final dimension to consider when matching supply chain and competitive strategy is changes in competitor behavior. Like product life cycles, competitors can change the landscape, thereby requiring changes in a firm's competitive strategy. An example is the growth of mass customization in various industries over the last decade of the 20th century. As competitors flood the marketplace with product variety, customers are becoming accustomed to having their individual needs satisfied. Thus, the competitive focus today is on producing sufficient variety at a reasonable price. In this regard the Internet plays a significant role because the Web makes it easy to offer high levels of product variety. Competition from firms on the Internet forces supply chains to develop the ability to supply this variety. As the competitive landscape changes, a firm is forced to alter its competitive strategy. With the change in competitive strategy, a firm must also change its supply chain strategy to maintain strategic fit.

Key Point To achieve strategic fit, a firm must tailor its supply chain to best meet the needs of different customer segments. To retain strategic fit, supply chain strategy must be adjusted over the life cycle of a product and as the competitive landscape changes.

In the next section, we describe how the scope within the supply chain over which strategic fit has been achieved has expanded. We also discuss why expanding the scope of strategic fit is critical to supply chain success.

2.3 EXPANDING STRATEGIC SCOPE

A key issue related to strategic fit is the scope, in terms of supply chain stages, across which the strategic fit applies. **Scope of strategic fit** refers to the functions and stages within a supply chain that devise an integrated strategy with a shared objective. At one extreme, every operation within each functional area devises its own independent strategy with the objective of optimizing its own performance. In this case, the scope of strategic fit is restricted to an operation in a functional area within a stage of the supply chain. At the opposite extreme, all functional areas within all stages of the supply chain devise strategy jointly with a common objective of maximizing supply chain profit. In this case, the scope of strategic fit extends across the entire supply chain.

In this section, we discuss how expanding the scope of strategic fit improves supply chain performance. We represent the scope of strategic fit on a two-dimensional grid. Horizontally, the scope of strategic fit is considered across different supply chain stages, starting from suppliers and moving all the way along the chain to the customer. Vertically, the scope is applied to the fit achieved across different functional strategies—competitive, product development, marketing, and supply chain.

Intracompany Intraoperation Scope: The Minimize Local Cost View

The most limited scope over which strategic fit has been considered is one operation within a functional area in a company. This is referred to as **intracompany intraoperation scope**. Here each operation within each stage of the supply chain devises strategy independently. For example, consider a particular warehouse at a distributor in a supply chain. The warehouse's objective is to minimize its own cost. This strategic objective is local to the warehouse and is not necessarily consistent with the distributor's strategy or the strategy of other stages in the supply chain. In such a setting, minimizing warehousing costs results in actions that may increase transportation costs and will not necessarily maximize supply chain profit. In fact, it will not even minimize the distributor's supply chain costs. The intracompany intraoperation scope often results in different operations and functions having conflicting objectives.

Limited scope was the dominant view during the 1950s and 1960s when every operation within each stage of the supply chain attempted to minimize its own costs. The performance evaluation methods in place at the time, when many operations were judged based on local cost performance, were a prime reason for this view.

Consider a transportation operation within a distribution company. The transportation operation is evaluated based on average shipping cost per unit. Shipping the product individually costs $5/item and shipping by truckload costs only $1/item. To minimize cost, the transportation group ships product in full trucks, as this practice results in the lowest shipping cost per unit. This decision, while minimizing transportation cost per unit, increases response time and may undermine a competitive strategy based on responsiveness. The key point here is that the transportation decision was made independent of the rest of the supply chain within and outside of the company. In this case, the scope of strategic fit is restricted to a portion (transportation) of the distributor stage within the supply chain. The shaded area in Figure 2.9 represents the scope of strategic fit at the distributor in this instance.

Intracompany Intrafunctional Scope: The Minimize Functional Cost View

Given that many operations together form each function within a firm, over time managers recognized the weakness of the intracompany intraoperation scope. Supply chain operations include manufacturing, warehousing, and transportation, among others. With the **intracompany intrafunctional scope**, the strategic fit is expanded to include all operations within a function. In this case, a warehousing manager no longer minimizes warehousing costs while the transportation manager independently minimizes transportation costs. By working together and developing a joint strategy, the two minimize the total functional cost.

Applying the intracompany intrafunctional scope and continuing with the distribution example, managers now look at not just transportation costs, but also warehousing and other supply chain–related costs. Although truckload transportation saves the company $4/item, it costs an additional $8/item due to increased inventory

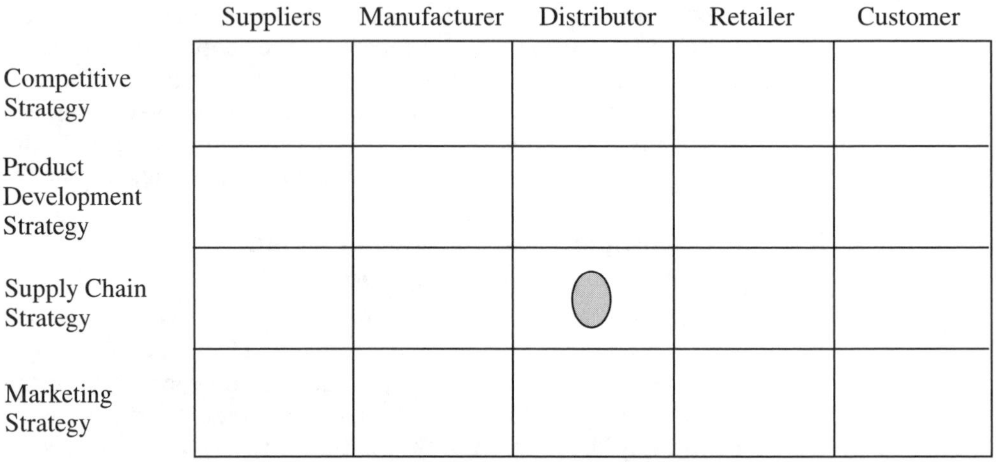

	Suppliers	Manufacturer	Distributor	Retailer	Customer
Competitive Strategy					
Product Development Strategy					
Supply Chain Strategy					
Marketing Strategy					

FIGURE 2.9 The Intracompany Intraoperation Scope of Supply Chain Strategy

and warehousing costs. Therefore, it costs less for the company to ship each item individually because the extra \$4 transportation charge saves the company \$8 in inventory-related costs.

In this case the scope of strategic fit expands to an entire function within a stage of the supply chain. Figure 2.10 shows the intracompany intrafunctional scope as it applies to the supply chain strategy at the distributor.

Intracompany Interfunctional Scope: The Maximize Company Profit View

The key weakness of the intracompany intrafunctional view is that different functions may have conflicting objectives. Over time, companies became aware of this weakness as they saw, for example, marketing and sales focusing on revenue generation and manufacturing and distribution focusing on cost reduction. Actions the two functions took were often in conflict and hurt the firm's overall performance. Compa-

FIGURE 2.10 The Intracompany Intrafunctional Scope of Supply Chain Strategy

	Suppliers	Manufacturer	Distributor	Retailer	Customer
Competitive Strategy					
Product Development Strategy					
Supply Chain Strategy					
Marketing Strategy					

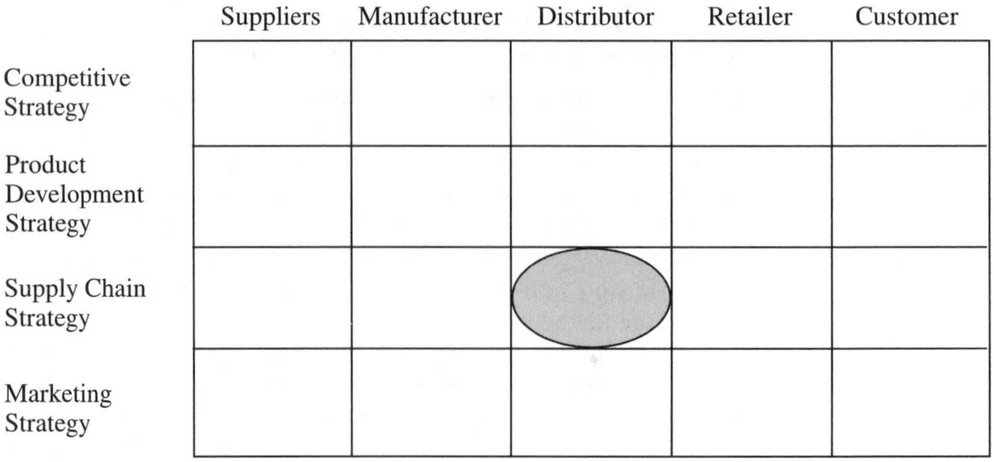

nies realized the importance of expanding the scope of strategic fit across all functions within the firm. With the **intracompany interfunctional scope**, the goal is to maximize company profit. To achieve this goal, all functional strategies are developed to support each other and the competitive strategy.

How does this change manifest itself? To return to the distribution company example, instead of looking only at the warehousing and transportation costs, the company will now look at revenue as well. Although the company had already decided to ship individual units to bring down inventory costs, management realized that by increasing its inventory, the company could increase sales because its service level would improve. The company would gain sales if it were able to build a reputation for having items in stock. If the revenues gained from holding more inventory outweighed the additional inventory costs, the company reasoned that it should go ahead and increase inventory. A company like McMaster-Carr follows this model and is thus able to charge premium prices due to the high level of service and availability it can provide. The basic point is that both operational and marketing decisions have a revenue and a cost impact. They must thus be coordinated and fit together. The intracompany interfunctional scope of strategic fit as it applies to the distributor is shown in Figure 2.11.

Intercompany Interfunctional Scope: The Maximize Supply Chain Surplus View

The intracompany interfunctional scope of strategic fit has two major weaknesses. The first derives from the fact that the only positive cash flow for the supply chain occurs when the customer pays for the product. All other cash flows are simply a resettling of accounts within the supply chain and add to supply chain cost. The difference between what the customer pays and the total cost generated across the supply chain represents the supply chain surplus. The supply chain surplus represents the total profit to be shared across all companies in the supply chain. Increasing supply chain surplus increases the amount to be shared among all members of the supply chain. The intracompany interfunctional scope leads to each stage of the supply chain trying to maximize its own profits, which does not necessarily result in the maximization of supply chain surplus. Supply chain surplus is maximized only when all supply chain

FIGURE 2.11 The Intracompany Interfunctional Scope Strategic Fit

	Suppliers	Manufacturer	Distributor	Retailer	Customer
Competitive Strategy					
Product Development Strategy					
Supply Chain Strategy					
Marketing Strategy					

stages coordinate strategy together. This occurs with the **intercompany interfunctional scope**, in which all stages of the supply chain coordinate strategy across all functions to ensure that together they best meet the customer's needs and maximize supply chain surplus.

The second major weakness of the intracompany scope was noted in the 1990s, when speed became a key driver of supply chain success. Today more and more companies are succeeding not because they have the lowest-priced product and not because they have the highest-quality or best-performing product, but because they are able to respond quickly to market needs and get the right product to the right customer at the right time. Companies like Dell have used speed as their primary competitive advantage to succeed in the marketplace.

This shift toward speed has forced companies to ask what creates the level of speed that customers are demanding. When this question is examined, the answer for most companies lies to a degree within their own boundaries. The most significant delays, however, are created at the interface between the boundaries of different stages of a supply chain. Therefore, managing these interfaces becomes a key to providing speed to customers. The intracompany scope restricts strategic attention within each stage of the supply chain, leading to the interfaces being neglected. The intercompany scope forces every stage of the supply chain to look across the entire supply chain and evaluate the impact of its actions on other stages as well as on the interfaces.

The intercompany interfunctional scope of strategic fit is shown in Figure 2.12.

> ***Key Point*** The intercompany scope of strategic fit is essential today because the competitive playing field has shifted from company versus company to supply chain versus supply chain. A company's partners in the supply chain may well determine the company's success, as the company is intimately tied to its supply chain.

FIGURE 2.12 The Intercompany Interfunctional Scope of Strategic Fit

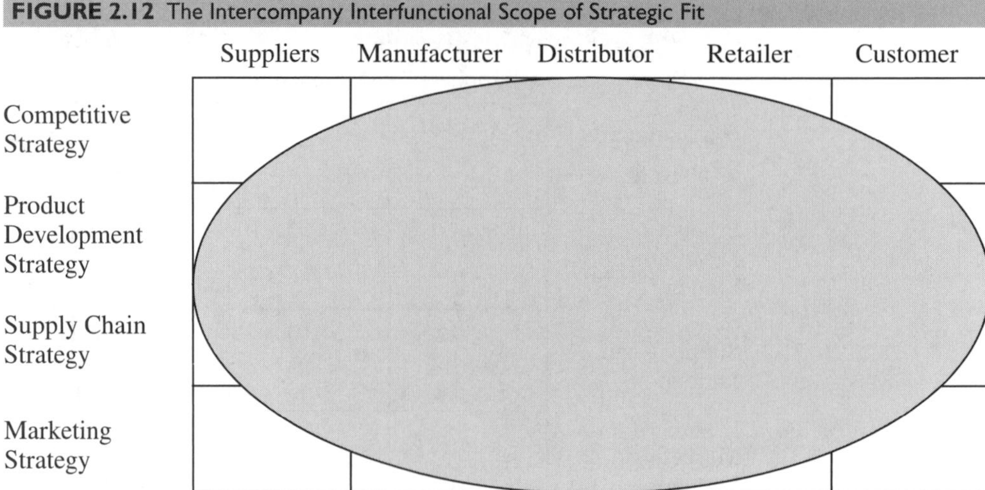

Taking this view requires that each company evaluate its actions in the context of the entire supply chain. This means treating stages in the supply chain that a company does not own as if they belonged to the company. For example, a major supply chain theme that has received a great deal of press in recent years is the reduction of inventory. Many companies strive to reduce their own inventories because they assume that the less inventory they have, the better. This assumption leads to a rash of changes in ownership of inventory from stage to stage in the supply chain without necessarily achieving any real reduction in overall inventory. Manufacturers feel that if they force their suppliers to own the parts inventory, they will not have to finance this inventory, and therefore, their costs will go down. But in many cases, the suppliers simply take ownership of the parts inventory without making any changes in the way this inventory is managed. Because holding this inventory increases the suppliers' costs, they are forced to raise their prices to the manufacturer or lower their margins. In the end, there is no real reduction in cost to the members of that chain because the supply chain merely shifts costs back and forth between its links.

The intercompany interfunctional scope proposes a different approach. Instead of just forcing the inventory on the supplier, who then increases price, the manufacturer and the supplier need to work together to actually reduce the amount of inventory that is required to meet the manufacturer's needs. Any inventory carried should be positioned in the supply chain at a point that maximizes supply chain surplus. The decision about where in the supply chain to hold inventory should not be made based on a single stage. Any actions the manufacturer and the supplier take will result in improvements only if they reduce overall supply chain inventory, not just inventory at a single stage. For example, by sharing demand information with the supplier, the manufacturer can lower the amount of inventory needed in the chain, thus reducing overall cost in the supply chain and making the firms in that supply chain better able to compete.

The intercompany scope will result in a supply chain with greater surplus than the intracompany scope. This result will allow the supply chain to either increase profits by sharing the extra surplus or reduce price by passing along some of the surplus to the customer. This makes the supply chain more competitive.

> ***Key Point*** The intercompany scope of strategic fit requires firms to evaluate every action in the context of the entire supply chain. This broad scope increases the size of the surplus to be shared among all stages of the supply chain.

Flexible Intercompany Interfunctional Scope

Up to this point, we have discussed strategic fit in a static context; that is, the players in the supply chain and customer needs do not change over time. The situation in reality is much more dynamic, as product life cycles get shorter and companies try to satisfy the changing needs of individual customers. In such a situation, a company may have to partner with many different firms, depending on the product being made and the customer being served. In such a situation, it is crucial that strategic fit have a flexible intercompany scope.

Flexibility refers to a firm's ability to achieve strategic fit when partnering with stages that change over time in the supply chain. Firms must think in terms of supply chains consisting of many players at each stage. For example, a manufacturer may interface with different suppliers and distributors, depending on the product being made and the customer being served. The strategy and operations at firms must be flexible enough to maintain strategic fit in a changing environment. Further, as customer needs vary over time, firms must have the ability to become part of new supply chains while ensuring strategic fit. Customer needs may change because of changes in technology or because of actions taken by competitors. The flexible intercompany scope allows strategic fit to apply to a moving target. Flexibility becomes more important as the competitive environment becomes more dynamic.

2.4 SUMMARY OF LEARNING OBJECTIVES

1. Explain why achieving strategic fit is critical to a company's overall success.

A lack of strategic fit between the competitive and supply chain strategy can result in the supply chain taking actions that are not consistent with customer needs, leading to a reduction in supply chain surplus and decreasing supply chain profitability. Strategic fit forces all functions and stages in the supply chain to target the same goal, one that is consistent with customer needs.

2. Describe how a company achieves strategic fit between its supply chain strategy and its competitive strategy.

To achieve strategic fit, a company must first understand the needs of the customers being served and identify the implied demand uncertainty. The second step is to understand the supply chain's capabilities in terms of efficiency and responsiveness. The key to strategic fit is then ensuring that supply chain responsiveness is consistent with customer needs and implied demand uncertainty.

3. Discuss the importance of expanding the scope of strategic fit across the supply chain.

The scope of strategic fit refers to the functions and stages within a supply chain that coordinate strategy and target a common goal. When the scope is narrow, individual functions focus on optimizing their performance based on their own goals. This practice often results in conflicting actions taken across the supply chain and reduces supply chain surplus. As the scope of strategic fit is enlarged to include the entire supply chain, actions are evaluated based on their impact on overall supply chain performance, which helps maximize supply chain surplus.

Discussion Questions

1. How would you characterize the competitive strategy of a high-end department store chain such as Nordstrom? What are the key customer needs that Nordstrom aims to fill?
2. Where would you place the demand faced by Nordstrom on the implied demand uncertainty spectrum? Why?
3. What level of responsiveness would be most appropriate for Nordstrom's supply chain? What should the supply chain be able to do particularly well?
4. How can Nordstrom expand the scope of strategic fit across its supply chain?
5. Reconsider the preceding four questions for other companies such as Amazon.com, a supermarket chain, an auto manufacturer, and a discount retailer such as Wal-Mart.
6. Give arguments to support the statement that Wal-Mart has achieved very good strategic fit between its competitive and supply chain strategies.

Bibliography

Blackwell, Roger D., and Kristina Blackwell. "The Century of the Consumer: Converting Supply Chains Into Demand Chains." *Supply Chain Management Review* (Fall 1999), 22–32.

Bovet, David M., and David G. Frentzel. "The Value Net: Connecting for Profitable Growth." *Supply Chain Management Review* (Fall 1999), 96–104.

Fine, Charles H. *Clock Speed, Winning Industry Control in the Age of Temporary Advantage*. Reading, Mass.: Perseus Books, 1999.

Fisher, Marshall L. "What Is the Right Supply Chain for Your Product?" *Harvard Business Review* (March–April 1997), 83–93.

Fuller, J. B., J. O'Conner, and R. Rawlinson. "Tailored Logistics: The Next Advantage." *Harvard Business Review* (May–June 1993), 87–98.

Gilmore, James H., and B. Joseph Pine II. *Markets of One: Creating Customer Unique Value Through Mass Customization.* Boston: Harvard Business School Press, 2000.

Magretta, Joan. "The Power of Virtual Integration: An Interview With Dell Computer's Michael Dell." *Harvard Business Review* (March–April 1998), 72–84.

Pine, B. Joseph, II. *Mass Customization.* Boston: Harvard Business School Press, 1999.

Shapiro, Roy D. "Get Leverage From Logistics." *Harvard Business Review* (May-June 1984), 119–127.

———, and James L. Heskett. *Logistics Strategy: Cases and Concepts.* St. Paul, Minn.: West Publishing Company, 1985.

Stalk, George, Jr., and Thomas M. Hout. *Competing Against Time.* New York: The Free Press, 1990.

CHAPTER 3

Supply Chain Drivers and Obstacles

Learning Objectives
After reading this chapter, you will be able to

1. identify the major drivers of supply chain performance;
2. discuss the role each driver plays in creating strategic fit between the supply chain strategy and the competitive strategy; and
3. describe the major obstacles that must be overcome to manage a supply chain successfully.

In this chapter, we introduce the four major drivers—inventory, transportation, facilities, and information—that determine the performance of any supply chain. We discuss how these drivers are used in the design, planning, and operation of the supply chain. We also introduce many of the obstacles managers face in designing, planning, and operating their supply chains.

3.1 DRIVERS OF SUPPLY CHAIN PERFORMANCE

The strategic fit discussed in Chapter 2 requires that a company achieve the balance between responsiveness and efficiency in its supply chain that best meets the needs of the company's competitive strategy. To understand how a company can improve supply chain performance in terms of responsiveness and efficiency, we must examine the four drivers of supply chain performance: inventory, transportation, facilities, and information. These drivers not only determine the supply chain's performance in terms of responsiveness and efficiency, they also determine whether strategic fit is achieved across the supply chain.

First we define each driver and discuss its impact on the performance of the supply chain:

1. **Inventory** is all raw materials, work in process, and finished goods within a supply chain. Inventory is an important supply chain driver because changing inventory policies can dramatically alter the supply chain's efficiency and responsiveness. For example, a clothing retailer can make itself more responsive by stocking large amounts of inventory. With a large inventory, the likelihood is high that the retailer can immediately satisfy customer demand with clothes from its floor. A large inventory, however, will increase the retailer's cost, thereby making it less efficient. Reducing inventory will make the retailer more efficient but will hurt its responsiveness.

2. **Transportation** entails moving inventory from point to point in the supply chain. Transportation can take the form of many combinations of modes and routes, each with its own performance characteristics. Transportation choices have a large impact on supply chain responsiveness and efficiency. For example, a mail order catalog company can use Federal Express (FedEx) to ship products, thus making its supply chain more responsive but also less efficient given the high costs associated with FedEx. Or the company can use ground transportation to ship product, making the supply chain efficient but limiting its responsiveness.

3. **Facilities** are the places in the supply chain network where inventory is stored, assembled, or fabricated. The two major types of facilities are production sites and storage sites. Whatever the function of the facility, decisions regarding location, capacity, and flexibility of facilities have a significant impact on the supply chain's performance. For instance, an auto parts distributor striving for responsiveness could have many warehousing facilities located close to customers even though this practice reduces efficiency. Alternatively, a high-efficiency distributor would have fewer warehouses to increase efficiency despite the fact that this practice will reduce responsiveness.

4. **Information** consists of data and analysis regarding inventory, transportation, facilities, and customers throughout the supply chain. Information is potentially the biggest driver of performance in the supply chain as it directly affects each of the other drivers. Information presents management with the opportunity to make supply chains more responsive and efficient. For example, with information on customer demand patterns, a pharmaceutical company can produce and stock drugs in anticipation of customer demand, which makes the supply chain very responsive because customers will find the drugs they need when they need them. This demand information can also make the supply chain more efficient because the pharmaceutical firm is better able to forecast demand and produce only the required amount. Information can also make this supply chain more efficient by providing managers with shipping options, for instance, that allow them to choose the lowest-cost alternative while still meeting the necessary service requirements.

Before we discuss each of the four drivers in detail, we put these drivers into a framework that helps to clarify the role of each driver in improving supply chain performance.

3.2 A FRAMEWORK FOR STRUCTURING DRIVERS

Recall from Chapter 2 that the goal of a supply chain strategy is to strike the balance between responsiveness and efficiency that results in strategic fit with the competitive strategy. To reach this goal, a company uses the four supply chain drivers discussed previously. For each of the individual drivers, supply chain managers must make a trade-off between efficiency and responsiveness. The combined impact of these four drivers then determines the responsiveness and efficiency of the entire supply chain.

We provide a visual framework for supply chain decision making in Figure 3.1. Most companies begin with a competitive strategy and then decide what their supply chain strategy ought to be. The supply chain strategy determines how the supply chain should perform with respect to efficiency and responsiveness. The supply chain must then use the supply chain drivers to reach the performance level the supply chain strategy dictates. Although this framework is generally viewed from the top down, in many instances, a study of the four drivers may indicate the need to change both the supply chain and potentially even the competitive strategy.

Consider this framework with Wal-Mart as an example. Wal-Mart's competitive strategy is to be the reliable, low-cost retailer for a very wide variety of mass consumption goods. This strategy dictates that the ideal supply chain will emphasize efficiency but also will be quite responsive. Wal-Mart uses the four drivers to achieve this type of supply chain performance. With the inventory driver, Wal-Mart maintains an efficient supply chain by keeping relatively low levels of inventory. For instance, Wal-Mart's distribution centers pioneered "crossdocking," a system in which inventory is not stocked in a warehouse but rather is shipped to stores from the manufacturer. These shipments make only brief stops at distribution centers, where they are transferred to trucks making deliveries to stores. This significantly lowers inventory since inventory is stocked only at stores, not at both stores and warehouses. With respect to inventory, Wal-Mart favors efficiency over responsiveness. On the transportation front, Wal-Mart runs its own fleet to keep responsiveness high. This increases cost and investment, but the benefits in terms of responsiveness justify this cost in Wal-Mart's

FIGURE 3.1 Supply Chain Decision-Making Framework

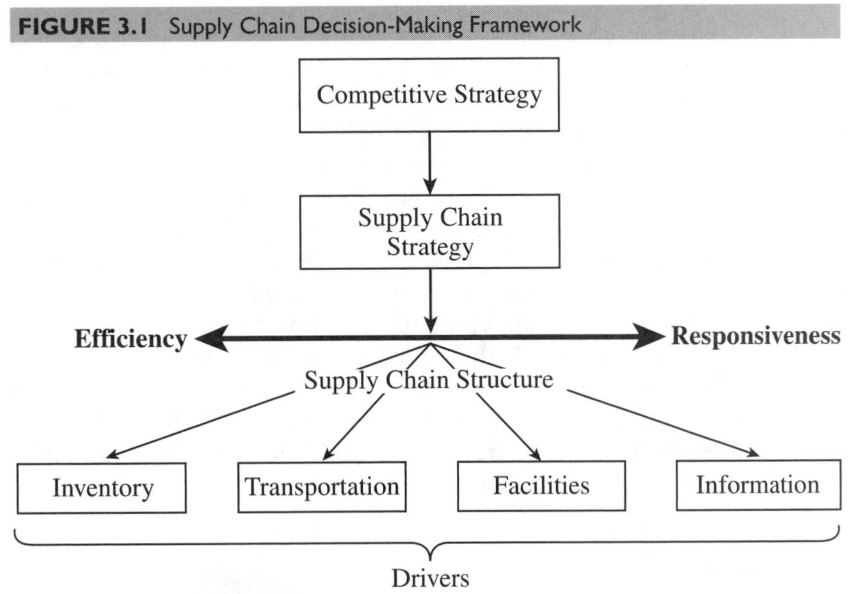

case. In the case of facilities, Wal-Mart uses central distribution centers within its network of stores to keep the number of facilities low and efficiency high. Wal-Mart builds facilities only where the demand is sufficient to justify having them, thereby increasing efficiency. To utilize information in the supply chain, Wal-Mart has invested significantly more than its competitors to take advantage of the benefits information can offer. This has led Wal-Mart to be a leader in its use of the information driver to improve responsiveness. Wal-Mart feeds demand information all the way back up the supply chain to suppliers, which manufacture only what is being demanded. The supply chain's ability to share demand information has required large investments, but the result is an improved supply chain in terms of both responsiveness and efficiency. Wal-Mart uses each supply chain driver to achieve the right balance between responsiveness and efficiency so that its competitive strategy and supply chain strategy are in harmony.

We devote the next four sections to a detailed discussion of each of the four drivers and its role in the supply chain.

3.3 INVENTORY

In this section we discuss the role inventory plays in the supply chain and how managers use inventory to drive supply chain performance.

Role in the Supply Chain

Inventory exists in the supply chain because of a mismatch between supply and demand. This mismatch is intentional at a steel manufacturer, where it is economical to manufacture in large lots that are then stored for future sales. The mismatch is also intentional at a retail store, where inventory is held in anticipation of future demand. An important role that inventory plays in the supply chain is to increase the amount of demand that can be satisfied by having the product ready and available when the customer wants it. Another significant role inventory plays is to reduce cost by exploiting any economies of scale that may exist during both production and distribution.

Inventory is spread throughout the supply chain from raw materials to work in process to finished goods that suppliers, manufacturers, distributors, and retailers hold. Inventory is a major source of cost in a supply chain, and it has a huge impact on responsiveness. If we think of the responsiveness spectrum discussed in Chapter 2, the location and quantity of inventory can move the supply chain from one end of the spectrum to the other. For example, a clothing supply chain with high inventory levels has a high level of responsiveness, since a consumer can walk into a store and walk out with the shirt he or she was looking for. In contrast, a clothing supply chain with little inventory would be very unresponsive. A customer wanting a shirt would have to order it and wait several weeks or even months for it to be manufactured, depending on how little inventory existed in the supply chain.

Inventory also has a significant impact on the material flow time in a supply chain. **Material flow time** is the time that elapses between the point at which material enters the supply chain to the point at which it exits. Another important area where inventory has a significant impact is **throughput**, the rate at which sales to the end consumer occur. If inventory is represented by I, flow time by T, and throughput by R, the three can be related using Little's law as follows:

$$I = RT \quad \textbf{(3.1)}$$

For example, if the flow time of an auto assembly process is 10 hours and the throughput is 60 units an hour, Little's law tells us that the inventory is $60 \times 10 = 600$ units. If we were able to reduce inventory to 300 units while holding throughput constant, we would reduce our flow time to five hours (300/60). Note that in this relationship, inventory and throughput must be in the same units.

The logical conclusion here is that inventory and flow time are synonymous in a supply chain. Because reduced flow time can be a significant advantage in a supply chain, managers should use actions that lower the amount of inventory needed without increasing cost or reducing responsiveness.

Role in the Competitive Strategy

Inventory plays a significant role in a supply chain's ability to support a firm's competitive strategy. If a firm's competitive strategy requires a very high level of responsiveness, a company can use inventory to achieve this responsiveness by locating large amounts of inventory close to the customer. Conversely, a company can also use inventory to make itself more efficient by reducing inventory through centralized stocking. The latter strategy would support a competitive strategy of being a low-cost producer. The trade-off implicit in the inventory driver is between the responsiveness that results from more inventory and the efficiency that results from less inventory.

Example 3.1: Nordstrom

Nordstrom's competitive strategy targets upper-end customers with high responsiveness requirements. These customers are willing to pay a premium to have the products they want when they want them. To support this competitive strategy, Nordstrom uses inventory; the company stocks a large variety and quantity of products to ensure a high level of availability. In fact, Nordstrom stocks a significantly larger amount of inventory than other department stores. Nordstrom incurs higher costs because of its large inventory, but it gains extra margin from its customers, who are willing to pay for the level of service that Nordstrom's inventory makes possible.

Components of Inventory Decisions

We now identify major inventory-related decisions that supply chain managers must make to create more responsive and more efficient supply chains effectively.

Cycle Inventory

Cycle inventory is the average amount of inventory used to satisfy demand between receipt of supplier shipments. The size of the cycle inventory is a result of the production or purchase of material in large lots. Companies produce or purchase in large lots to exploit economies of scale in the production, transportation, or purchasing process. With the increase in lot size, however, also comes an increase in carrying costs. As an example of a cycle inventory decision, consider an on-line book retailer. This retailer's sales average around 10 truckloads of books a month. The cycle inventory decisions the retailer must make involve how much to order for replenishment and how often to place these orders. The e-retailer could order 10 trucks once each month or it could order one truck every three days. The basic trade-off supply chain managers face is the cost of holding larger lots of inventory (when cycle inventory is high) versus the cost of ordering product frequently (when cycle inventory is low).

Safety Inventory

Safety inventory is inventory held just in case demand exceeds expectation; it is held to counter uncertainty. If the world were perfectly predictable, only cycle inventory would be needed. However, because demand is uncertain and may exceed expectations, companies hold safety inventory to satisfy an unexpectedly high demand.

Managers face a key decision when determining how much safety inventory to hold. For example, a toy retailer such as Toys 'R' Us must calculate its safety inventory for the holiday buying season. If it has too much safety inventory, toys go unsold and may have to be discounted after the holidays. However, if the company has ordered too little safety inventory, then Toys 'R' Us will lose sales and the margin those sales would have brought. Therefore, choosing safety inventory involves making a trade-off between the costs of having too much inventory and the costs of losing sales due to not having enough inventory.

Seasonal Inventory

Seasonal inventory is inventory that is built up to counter predictable variability in demand. Companies using seasonal inventory will build up inventory in periods of low demand and store it for periods of high demand when they will not have the capacity to produce all that is demanded. Managers face key decisions in determining whether to build seasonal inventory and, if they do build it, in deciding how much to build. If a company can rapidly change the rate of its production system at very low cost, then it may not need seasonal inventory because the production system can adjust to a period of high demand without incurring large costs. However, if changing the rate of production is expensive (e.g., when workers must be hired or fired), then a company would be wise to have a smooth production rate and build up its inventory during periods of low demand. Therefore, the basic trade-off supply chain managers face in determining how much seasonal inventory to build is the cost of carrying the additional seasonal inventory versus the cost of having a more flexible production rate.

Overall Trade-off: Responsiveness Versus Efficiency

The fundamental trade-off managers face when making inventory decisions is between responsiveness and efficiency. Increasing inventory will generally make the supply chain more responsive to the customer. However, this choice comes at a cost, as the added inventory decreases efficiency. Therefore, a supply chain manager can use inventory as one of the drivers for reaching the level of responsiveness and efficiency that the competitive strategy targets.

3.4 TRANSPORTATION

In this section, we discuss the role transportation plays in the supply chain as well as key transportation-related decisions that supply chain managers need to make.

Role in the Supply Chain

Transportation moves the product between different stages in a supply chain. Like the other supply chain drivers, transportation has a large impact on both responsiveness and efficiency. Faster transportation, whether in the form of different modes of transportation or different amounts being transported, allows a supply chain to be more responsive but reduces its efficiency. The type of transportation a company uses also affects the inventory and facility locations in the supply chain. Dell, for example, flies components from Asia because doing so allows the company to lower the level of inventory it holds. Clearly, such a practice increases responsiveness but decreases transportation efficiency because it is more costly than transporting parts by ship.

Role in the Competitive Strategy

The role of transportation in a company's competitive strategy figures prominently when the company is considering the target customer's needs. If a firm's competitive strategy targets a customer that demands a very high level of responsiveness and that customer is willing to pay for this responsiveness, then a firm can use transportation as one driver for making the supply chain more responsive. The opposite is true as well. If a company's competitive strategy targets customers whose main decision criterion is price, then the company can use transportation to lower the cost of the product at the expense of responsiveness. As a company may use both inventory and transportation to increase responsiveness or efficiency, the optimal decision for the company often means finding the right balance between the two.

Example 3.2: Laura Ashley

Laura Ashley sells clothing and other household items through a mail order catalog and uses transportation as part of its competitive strategy. Laura Ashley's customers are willing to pay a premium price for a high level of responsiveness. To meet this level of responsiveness, Laura Ashley has located its main warehouse near the FedEx hub in Memphis to better utilize the responsive transportation that FedEx offers. When an order is placed, the goods can easily and quickly be sent from the Laura Ashley warehouse to the FedEx hub where they are sent overnight to the customer. This transportation policy enables Laura Ashley's customers to order their goods later than they can at other companies and still receive them next day.

Components of Transportation Decisions

We now identify key components of transportation that companies must analyze when designing and operating a supply chain.

Mode of Transportation

The mode of transportation is the manner in which a product is moved from one location in the supply chain network to another. Companies have six basic modes from which to choose:

- **Air**: the most expensive mode but also very fast
- **Truck**: a relatively quick and inexpensive mode with high levels of flexibility
- **Rail**: an inexpensive mode used for large quantities
- **Ship**: the slowest mode but often the only economical choice for large overseas shipments
- **Pipeline**: used primarily to transport oil and gas
- **Electronic transportation**: the newest mode that "transports" goods such as music, previously sent solely by physical modes, electronically via the Internet

Each mode has different characteristics with respect to the speed, size of shipments (individual parcels to pallets to full trucks to entire ships), cost of shipping, and flexibility that lead companies to choose one particular mode over the others.

Route and Network Selection

Another major decision managers must make is the route and network along which products are shipped. A **route** is the path along which a product is shipped, and a **network** is the collection of locations and routes along which a product can be shipped. For example, a company needs to decide whether to ship products directly to customers or to use a series of distribution layers. Companies make some routing decisions at the supply chain's design stage, and they make others daily or on a short-term basis.

In House or Outsource

Traditionally, much of the transportation function has been performed in house. Today, however, much of transportation (and even entire logistics systems) is outsourced. Having to choose between bringing parts of transportation in house or outsourcing leads to another dimension of complexity when companies are designing their transportation systems.

Overall Trade-off: Responsiveness Versus Efficiency

The fundamental trade-off for transportation is between the cost of transporting a given product (efficiency) and the speed with which that product is transported (responsiveness).

3.5 FACILITIES

In this section, we discuss the role facilities play in the supply chain as well as critical facility-related decisions that supply chain managers need to make.

Role in the Supply Chain

If we think of inventory as *what* is being passed along the supply chain and transportation as *how* it is passed along, then facilities are the *where* of the supply chain. They are the locations to or from which the inventory is transported. Within a facility, inventory is either transformed into another state (manufacturing) or stored before being shipped to the next stage (warehousing).

Role in the Competitive Strategy

Facilities and their corresponding capacities to perform their functions are a key driver of supply chain performance in terms of responsiveness and efficiency. For example, companies can gain economies of scale when a product is manufactured or stored in only one location; this centralization increases efficiency. However, the cost reduction comes at the expense of responsiveness, as many of a company's customers may be located far from the production facility. The opposite is also true. Locating facilities close to customers increases the number of facilities needed and consequently reduces efficiency. However, if the customer demands and is willing to pay for the responsiveness that having numerous facilities adds, then this facilities decision helps meet the company's competitive strategy goals.

Example 3.3: Toyota and Honda

Both Toyota and Honda make facilities decisions to be more responsive to their customers. These companies have an end goal of opening manufacturing facilities in every major market that they enter. Although there are other benefits to opening local facilities, such as protection from currency fluctuation and trade barriers, the increase in responsiveness plays a large role in Toyota's and Honda's decisions to locate in their local markets.

Components of Facilities Decisions

Decisions regarding facilities are a crucial part of supply chain design. We now identify components of facilities decisions that companies must analyze.

Location

Deciding where a company will locate its facilities constitutes a large part of the design of a supply chain. A basic trade-off here is whether to centralize to gain economies of scale or decentralize to become more responsive by being closer to the customer. Companies must also consider a host of issues related to the various characteristics of the local area in which the facility may be situated. These include macroeconomic factors, strategic factors, quality of workers, cost of workers, cost of facility, availability of infrastructure, proximity to customers and the rest of the network, and tax effects.

Capacity (Flexibility Versus Efficiency)

Companies must also decide what a facility's capacity to perform its intended function or functions will be. A large amount of excess capacity allows the facility to be very flexible and to respond to wide swings in the demands placed on it. Excess capacity, however, costs money and therefore can decrease efficiency. A facility with little excess capacity will likely be more efficient per unit of product it produces than one with a lot of unused capacity. The high utilization facility will, however, have difficulty responding to demand fluctuations. Therefore, a company must make a trade-off to determine the right amount of capacity to have at each of its facilities.

Manufacturing Methodology

Companies must make a major decision regarding the manufacturing methodology that a facility will use. They must decide whether to design a facility with a product focus or a functional focus. A product-focused factory performs many different functions (such as fabrication and assembly) in producing a single type of product. A functional focused factory performs few functions (such as only fabrication or only assembly) on many types of products. A product focus tends to result in more expertise about a particular type of product at the expense of the functional expertise that comes from a functional manufacturing methodology. Firms must decide which type of expertise will best enable them to meet customer needs. Firms must also make a decision regarding the relative level of flexible versus dedicated capacity in their portfolios. Flexible capacity can be used for many types of products but is often less efficient, whereas dedicated capacity can be used for only a limited number of products but it is more efficient. The trade-off, as in previous instances, is between efficiency and responsiveness.

Warehousing Methodology

As with manufacturing, there are a variety of methodologies from which companies can choose when designing a warehouse facility, including the following:

- **Stock-keeping unit (SKU) storage**: a traditional warehouse that stores all of one type of product together. This is a fairly efficient way to store products.
- **Job lot storage**: a methodology in which all the different types of products needed to perform a particular job or satisfy a particular type of customer are stored together. This generally requires more storage space but can create a more efficient picking and packing environment.
- **Crossdocking**: a methodology (pioneered by Wal-Mart) in which goods are not actually warehoused in a facility. Instead, trucks from suppliers, each carrying a different type of product, deliver goods to a facility. There, the inventory is broken into smaller lots and quickly loaded onto store-bound trucks that carry a variety of products, some from each of the supplier trucks.

Overall Trade-off: Responsiveness Versus Efficiency

The fundamental trade-off managers face when making facilities decisions is between the cost of the number, location, and type of facilities (efficiency) and the level of responsiveness that these facilities provide the company's customers.

3.6 INFORMATION

In this section, we discuss the role information plays in the supply chain as well as key information-related decisions that supply chain managers must make.

Role in the Supply Chain

Information could be overlooked as a major supply chain driver because it does not have a physical presence. Information, however, deeply affects every part of the supply chain in many ways. Consider the following:

1. Information serves as the connection between the supply chain's various stages, allowing them to coordinate their actions and bring about many of the benefits of maximizing total supply chain profitability.
2. Information is also crucial to the daily operations of each stage in a supply chain. For instance, a production scheduling system uses information on demand to create a schedule that allows a factory to produce the right products in an efficient manner. A warehouse management system uses information to give the warehouse's inventory visibility. The company can then use this information to determine whether new orders can be filled.

Role in the Competitive Strategy

Information is a driver whose importance has grown as companies have used it to become both more efficient and more responsive. The tremendous growth of the importance of information technology is a testimony to the impact information can have on improving a company. Like all the other drivers, however, even with information, companies reach a point where they must make the trade-off between efficiency and responsiveness.

Another key decision involves what information is most valuable in reducing cost and improving responsiveness within a supply chain. This decision will vary depending on the supply chain structure and the market segments served. Some companies, for example, target customers who require certain customized products that carry a premium price tag. These companies might find that investments in information allow them to respond more quickly to their customers. The following examples illustrate this kind of investment.

Example 3.4: Andersen Windows

Andersen Windows, a major manufacturer of residential wood windows located in Bayport, Minnesota, has invested in an information system that enables it to get customized products to the market rapidly. This system, called "Window of Knowledge," allows distributors and customers to actually design windows to custom-fit their needs. Users can select from a library of more than 50,000 components that can be combined in any number of ways. The system immediately gives the customer price quotes and automatically sends the order to the factory if the customer decides to buy. This information investment not only gives the customer a much wider variety of products, but it allows Andersen to be much more responsive to the customer as it gets the customer's order to its factory as soon as the order is placed.

Example 3.5: Dell

Dell operates differently from most personal computer (PC) manufacturers in that it has invested in building up its own channel—a direct channel to the consumer. Most PC manufacturers sell their product to a distributor, who then either sells it to a dealer or a corporate customer. Dell takes orders directly from consumers over the phone and via the Internet. This direct channel required an investment to build, given the added functions Dell must perform. A large part of that cost can be attributed to information. However, with the direct channel model, Dell is able to view the actual consumer demand much sooner than most PC manufacturers, and therefore, the company can respond more quickly to changes in consumer needs. Dell can then modify its product offering to meet these new needs. Dell is not the low-cost provider. The company is, however, the most responsive provider, and a large part of its responsiveness is due to the information flow between Dell and its customers and Dell and its suppliers that is made possible by its investment in information.

Components of Information Decisions

We now consider key components of information within a supply chain that a company must analyze to increase efficiency and improve responsiveness within its supply chain.

Push Versus Pull

When designing processes in the supply chain, managers must determine whether these processes are part of the push or pull phase in the chain. We discussed this distinction in Chapter 1, but we mention it again here because different types of systems require different types of information. Push systems generally require information in the form of elaborate material requirements planning (MRP) systems to take the master production schedule and roll it back, creating schedules for suppliers with part types, quantities, and delivery dates. Pull systems require information on actual demand to be transmitted extremely quickly throughout the entire chain so that production and distribution of parts and products can accurately reflect the real demand.

Coordination and Information Sharing

Supply chain coordination occurs when all the different stages of a supply chain work toward the objective of maximizing total supply chain profitability rather than each stage devoting itself to its own profitability. Lack of coordination can result in a significant loss of supply chain profit. Managers must decide how to create this coordination in the supply chain and what information must be shared in order to accomplish this goal. Coordination between different stages in a supply chain requires each stage to share appropriate information with other stages. For example, if a supplier is to produce the right parts in a timely manner for a manufacturer in a pull system, the manufacturer must share demand and production information with the supplier. Information sharing is thus crucial to the success of a supply chain.

Forecasting and Aggregate Planning

Forecasting is the art and science of making projections about what future needs and conditions will be. Obtaining forecasting information frequently means using sophisticated techniques to estimate future demand or market conditions. Managers must decide how they will make forecasts and to what extent they will rely on them to make decisions. Companies often use forecasts both on a tactical level to schedule production and on a strategic level to determine whether to build new plants or even whether to enter a new market.

Once a company creates a forecast, the company needs a plan to act on this forecast. **Aggregate planning** transforms forecasts into plans of activity to satisfy the projected demand. A key decision managers face is how to use aggregate planning both at the manager's stage in the supply chain and throughout the entire supply chain. The aggregate plan becomes a critical piece of information to be shared within the supply chain. A company's aggregate plan significantly affects the demand on both its suppliers and its supply to its customers.

Enabling Technologies

Many technologies exist that share and analyze information in the supply chain. Managers must decide which technologies to use and how to integrate these technologies into their companies and their partners. The consequences of these decisions are becoming more and more important as the capabilities of these technologies grow. Some of these technologies include:

1. **Electronic data interchange** (EDI) allows companies to place instantaneous, paperless purchase orders with suppliers. EDI is not only efficient, but it also decreases the time needed to get products to customers, as transactions can occur more quickly and accurately than when they are paper-based.

2. **The Internet** has critical advantages over EDI with respect to information sharing. The Internet can be accessed by all and conveys much more information and therefore offers much more visibility than EDI. Better visibility enables stages in the supply chain to make better decisions. Internet communication between stages in the supply chain is also easier because a standard infrastructure (the World Wide Web) already exists. Thanks to the Internet, e-commerce has become a major force in the supply chain.

3. **Enterprise resource planning** (ERP) systems provide the transactional tracking and global visibility of information from any part of a company and its supply chain that allows intelligent decisions to be made. This real-time information helps a supply chain to improve the quality of its operational decisions. ERP systems keep track of the information, whereas the Internet provides one method with which to view this information. SAP, Peoplesoft, Oracle, JD Edwards, and Baan are some major ERP software vendors that experienced tremendous growth due to the power of this system.

4. **Supply chain management** (SCM) software adds a higher layer to ERP systems. This software provides analytical decision support in addition to the visibility of information. ERP systems show a company what is going on, whereas SCM systems help a company decide what it should do. The leader in this area is i2 Technologies.

Overall Trade-off: Responsiveness Versus Efficiency

As with the entire supply chain, the fundamental trade-off with the information driver is between responsiveness and efficiency. Many information systems increase both responsiveness and efficiency. However, managers will soon need to make the trade-off between the cost of information (a reduction in efficiency) and the responsiveness that information creates in the supply chain.

3.7 OBSTACLES TO ACHIEVING STRATEGIC FIT

A company's ability to find a balance between responsiveness and efficiency along the responsiveness spectrum that best matches the type of demand it is targeting is the key to achieving strategic fit. In deciding where this balance should be located on the responsiveness spectrum, companies face many obstacles.

In this section we discuss some of the obstacles and provide a feel for how the supply chain environment has changed over the years. On one hand, these obstacles have made it much more difficult for companies to create the ideal balance. On the other hand, they have afforded companies increased opportunities for improving supply chain management. Managers need a solid understanding of the impact of these obstacles because they are critical to a company's ability to reap the maximum profitability from its supply chain.

Increasing Variety of Products

Product proliferation is rampant today. With customers demanding ever more customized products, manufacturers have responded with mass customization and even segment-of-one (in which companies view each customer as an independent market segment) views of the market. Products that were formerly quite generic are now custom-made for a specific consumer. For example, PCs used to come from the manufacturer in a standard set of configurations. Now, one can order a custom PC, built from a variety of configurations that numbers in the millions. Market segments have become increasingly fragmented as customers demand that products be custom-made to their needs. The increase in product variety complicates the supply chain by making forecasting and meeting demand much more difficult. The rise of e-commerce, which makes it easy to offer variety to the customer, reinforces the customization trend. For example, reflect.com sells personalized beauty care products that are customized to individual tastes. Increased variety tends to raise uncertainty, and uncertainty frequently results in increased cost and decreased responsiveness within the supply chain.

Decreasing Product Life Cycles

In addition to the increasing variety of product types, the life cycle of products has been shrinking. Today, there are products whose life cycles can be measured in months, compared with the old standard of years. These are not just niche products, either. PCs now have a life cycle of several months, and even some automobile manufacturers have lowered their product life cycles from five-plus years to three years. This decrease in product life cycles makes the job of achieving strategic fit more difficult, as the supply chain must constantly adapt to manufacture and deliver new products in addition to coping with these products' demand uncertainty. Shorter life cycles increase uncertainty while reducing the window of opportunity within which the supply chain can achieve fit. Increased uncertainty combined with a smaller window of opportunity has put additional pressure on supply chains to coordinate and create a good match between supply and demand.

Increasingly Demanding Customers

Companies can clearly see how customer demands have increased when considering delivery lead times, cost, and product performance. Many companies used to have periodic, standard price increases—not due to a rise in demand or any other factor, but simply because raising prices was the way business was done. Now, one hears repeatedly about companies that cannot force through *any* price increases without losing market share. Today's customers are demanding faster fulfillment, better quality, and better performing products for the same price they paid years ago. This tremendous growth in customer *demands* (not necessarily *demand*) means that the supply chain must provide more just to maintain its business.

Fragmentation of Supply Chain Ownership

Over the past several decades, most firms have become less vertically integrated. As companies have shed noncore functions, they have been able to take advantage of supplier and customer competencies that they themselves did not have. However, this new ownership structure has also made managing the supply chain more difficult. With the chain broken into many owners, each with its own policies and interests, the chain is more difficult to coordinate. Potentially, this problem could cause each stage of a supply chain to work only toward its own objectives rather than the whole chain's, resulting in the reduction of overall supply chain profitability.

Globalization

Over the past few decades, governments around the world have loosened trade restrictions, which has resulted in a dramatic increase in global trade. This increase in globalization has had two main impacts on the supply chain. The first is that supply chains are now more likely than ever to be global. Having a global supply chain creates many benefits, such as the ability to source from a global base of suppliers who may offer better or cheaper goods than were available in a company's home nation. However, globalization also adds stress to the chain because facilities within the chain are farther apart, making coordination much more difficult.

The second impact of globalization is an increase in competition, as once protected national players must now compete with companies from around the world. In the past, if there were not many companies offering to satisfy customers' needs, then individual companies could take more time responding to these needs. However, in most industries, there are now many more firms aggressively pursuing their competitors' business. This competitive situation makes supply chain performance a key to maintaining and growing sales while also putting more strain on supply chains and thus forcing them to make their trade-offs even more precisely.

Difficulty Executing New Strategies

Creating a successful supply chain strategy is not easy. However, once a good strategy is formulated, actually executing the strategy can be even more difficult. For instance, Toyota's production system, which is a supply chain strategy, was and is widely known and understood. Yet this strategy has been a sustained competitive advantage for Toyota for more than two decades. Does Toyota have a brilliant strategy that no one else can figure out? Their strategy *is* brilliant, but many others have figured it out. The difficulty other firms have had is in executing that strategy. Many highly talented employees at all levels of the organization are necessary to make a supply chain strategy successful. Although we deal mostly with the formulation of strategy in this book, one should keep in mind that skillful execution of a strategy can be as important as the strategy itself.

All of the obstacles discussed here are making it more difficult for companies to create the proper balance between responsiveness and efficiency in the supply chain and therefore to achieve strategic fit. These obstacles also represent a tremendous opportunity in terms of untapped improvement within the supply chain. The increasing impact of these obstacles has led to supply chain management's becoming a major factor in the success or failure of firms.

Key Point Many obstacles, such as growing product variety and shorter life cycles, have made it increasingly difficult for supply chains to achieve strategic fit. Overcoming these obstacles offers a tremendous opportunity for firms to use supply chain management to gain competitive advantage.

3.8 SUMMARY OF LEARNING OBJECTIVES

1. Identify the major drivers of supply chain performance.

The major drivers of supply chain performance are inventory, transportation, facilities, and information.

2. Discuss the role of each driver in creating strategic fit between the supply chain strategy and the competitive strategy.

A company achieving strategic fit has found the right balance between responsiveness and efficiency. Each driver affects this balance. Holding higher levels of inventory increases the responsiveness of a supply chain, whereas keeping inventory low increases the chain's efficiency. Using faster modes of transportation increases a chain's responsiveness, whereas using slower modes generally increases efficiency. Having more facilities generally makes a chain more responsive, whereas having few, central facilities creates higher efficiency. Investing in information can vastly improve the supply chain performance on both dimensions. However, at some point supply chain managers need to decide whether the increased cost of information is worth the responsiveness it brings to the supply chain.

3. Describe the major obstacles that must be overcome to manage a supply chain successfully.

Increasing product variety, decreasing product life cycles, demanding customers, and global competition all make creating supply chain strategies more difficult as these factors can hamper supply chain performance. The increase in globalization of the supply chain and fragmentation of supply chain ownership have also made it more difficult to execute supply chain strategies.

Discussion Questions

1. How could a grocery retailer use inventory to increase the responsiveness of the company's supply chain?
2. How could an auto manufacturer use transportation to increase the efficiency of its supply chain?
3. How could a bicycle manufacturer increase responsiveness through its facilities?
4. How could an industrial supplies distributor use information to increase its responsiveness?
5. How has globalization made strategic fit even more important to a company's success?
6. What are some industries in which products have proliferated and life cycles have shortened? How have the supply chains in these industries adapted?
7. How can the full set of four drivers be used to create strategic fit for a PC manufacturer targeting time-sensitive customers?

Bibliography

Marien, Edward J. "The Four Supply Chain Enablers." *Supply Chain Management Review*, (March/April 2000), 60–68.

PART TWO

Planning Demand and Supply in a Supply Chain

The goal of the three chapters in this module is to explain the significance of planning in a supply chain, identify decisions that are part of the planning process, and discuss tools that supply chain managers can use for planning. Planning allows a supply chain manager to be proactive and manage demand and supply to ensure that profits are maximized.

All supply chain decisions are based on an estimate of future demand. Chapter 4 describes methodologies that can be used to forecast future demand based on historical demand data. Given a demand forecast, Chapter 5 describes the aggregate planning methodology that a supply chain manager can use to plan production, distribution, and allocation of resources for the near future (typically a quarter to a year) by making appropriate trade-offs among capacity, inventory, and backlogged orders. Chapter 6 then discusses how a supply chain manager can plan pricing and promotions to manage customer demand, along with production and distribution planning to manage supply from production facilities, to maximize supply chain profits.

CHAPTER 4

Demand Forecasting in a Supply Chain

Learning Objectives

After reading this chapter, you will be able to

1. understand the role of forecasting in a supply chain;
2. identify the components of a demand forecast;
3. forecast demand in a supply chain given historical demand data using time series methodologies; and
4. analyze demand forecasts to estimate forecast error.

Forecasts of future demand are essential to a supply chain manager's decision-making and planning processes. In this chapter, we explain how historical demand information can be used to forecast future demand. We describe several methods to forecast demand and estimate a forecast's accuracy. We also discuss how these methods can be implemented using Microsoft Excel.

4.1 THE ROLE OF FORECASTING IN A SUPPLY CHAIN

The forecast of future demand forms the basis for all strategic and planning decisions in a supply chain. Consider the push/pull view of the supply chain discussed in Chapter 1. All push processes are performed in anticipation of customer demand, and all pull processes are performed in response to customer demand. For push processes, a manager must plan the level of production. For pull processes, a manager must plan the level of capacity to make available. In both instances, the first step a supply chain manager must take is to forecast what customer demand will be in the future.

Consider, for example, Dell Computer. Dell builds personal computers (PCs) to customer order. Dell orders components in anticipation of customer orders, and it performs assembly in response to a customer order. The production manager must ensure that Dell orders the appropriate number of components in anticipation of customer demand. The production manager must also ensure that the required capacity is available in the assembly plant to meet the demand for assembly. For both decisions, the manager requires a forecast of future demand.

Supply chain managers plan all the supply chain's activities based on an estimation of when the final sale to the customer will occur. In the case of Dell, a supplier such as Intel provides processors for Dell PCs. Intel takes several weeks to manufacture processors, but Dell cannot wait that long after a customer order to have a processor order filled. Customers demand their PCs in days after an order, not weeks. Therefore, Intel must produce processors in advance of a customer order, which requires that Dell and Intel forecast future demand for processors and plan production accordingly. Production at Intel drives demand for Intel's suppliers; they too must forecast future demand and produce so that Intel can meet its production plan.

In addition to production and distribution decisions, firms also use forecasts of future demand as the basis for many other decisions made in the push phase of a supply chain. We list some important decisions by functional area that are based on demand forecasts as follows:

- **Production**. Scheduling, inventory control, aggregate planning
- **Marketing**. Sales-force allocation, promotions, new product introduction
- **Finance**. Plant/equipment investment, budgetary planning
- **Personnel**. Workforce planning, hiring, layoffs

Ideally, in a supply chain, these decisions should not be segregated by functional area, as they influence each other and are best made jointly (see Chapters 5 and 6). For example, Coca-Cola considers the demand forecast over the coming quarter and decides on the timing of various promotions. The promotion information is then used to update the demand forecast. Based on this forecast, Coca-Cola will decide on a production plan for the quarter. This plan may require additional investment, hiring, or perhaps subcontracting of production. Coke will make these decisions based on the production plan and existing capacity, and it must make them all in advance of actual production. Thus, the decisions are based on a forecast. We can see from this example that all these decisions are interrelated. Mature products with stable demand are usually easiest to forecast. Staple products at a supermarket, such as milk or paper towels, fit this description. Forecasting and the accompanying managerial decisions are extremely difficult when either the supply of raw materials or the demand for the finished product is highly variable. One example of a product with variable seasonal demand is chocolate; the majority of chocolate sales take place close to the holiday season. Other examples include skiing equipment, parkas, gardening equipment, bathing suits, and snow clearing equipment. Good forecasting is very important in these cases, because the time window for sales is narrow and if a firm has either over- or underproduced, it has little chance to recover and ensure that supply matches demand. For a product with stable demand, in contrast, the impact of a forecasting error is less significant. We identify a forecasting method appropriate for products with seasonal demand later in the chapter.

Before we begin an in-depth discussion of the components of forecasts and forecasting methods, we briefly list characteristics of forecasts that companies must understand to design and manage their supply chains effectively.

4.2 CHARACTERISTICS OF FORECASTS

Companies and supply chain managers should be aware of the following characteristics of forecasts:

1. Forecasts are always wrong and should thus include both the expected value and a measure of forecast error. To understand the importance of forecast error, consider two car dealers. One of them expects sales to range between 100 and 1,900, whereas the other expects sales to range between 900 and 1,100. Even though both dealers anticipate average sales of 1,000, the sourcing policies for each dealer should be very different given the difference in forecast accuracy. Thus, the forecast error (or demand uncertainty) must be a key input into most supply chain decisions.

2. Long-term forecasts are usually less accurate than short-term forecasts; that is, long-term forecasts have a larger standard deviation of error relative to the mean than short-term forecasts. 7-Eleven Japan has exploited this key property to improve its performance. The company has instituted a replenishment process that enables it to respond to an order within hours. For example, if a store manager places an order by 10 A.M., the order is delivered by 7 P.M. the same day. The store manager thus has to forecast what will sell that night less than 12 hours before the actual sale. The forecast in this case is likely to be much more accurate than if the store manager had to forecast demand a week in advance.

3. Aggregate forecasts are usually more accurate than disaggregate forecasts. Aggregate forecasts tend to have a smaller standard deviation of error relative to the mean. For example, it is easy to forecast the gross domestic product (GDP) of the United States for a given year with less than a 2 percent error. However, it is much more difficult to forecast yearly earnings for a company with less than a 2 percent error, and it is even harder to forecast demand for a given product with the same degree of accuracy. The key difference between the three forecasts is the degree of aggregation. The GDP is an aggregation across many companies, and the earnings of a company are an aggregation across several product lines. The greater the degree of aggregation, the more accurate the forecast.

In the next section, we discuss the basic components of a forecast and explain the four classifications into which forecasting methods fall. We also introduce the notion of forecast error.

4.3 COMPONENTS OF A FORECAST AND FORECASTING METHODS

Yogi Berra, the former New York Yankees catcher who was famous for his malapropisms, has been quoted as saying, "Predictions are usually difficult, especially about the future." One may be tempted to treat demand forecasting as magic or art and leave everything to chance. A company can create useful forecasts, however, if it interprets the past correctly. What a firm knows about its customers' past behavior sheds light on their future behavior as well as the responses they are apt to have to actions the firm may take. Demand does not arise in a vacuum. Rather, customer demand is influenced by a variety of factors and can be predicted if a company can determine the relationship between the current value of these factors and future demand. In good demand forecasting, companies will first identify the factors that influence future demand and then ascertain the relationship between these factors and future demand.

Companies must balance objective and subjective factors when forecasting demand. Although we focus on quantitative forecasting methods in this chapter, companies must include human input when they make their final forecast. 7-Eleven Japan illustrates this point.

7-Eleven Japan provides its store managers with a state-of-the-art decision support system to forecast demand. The decision support system makes a forecast and provides a recommended order. The store manager, however, is responsible for making the final forecast and placing the order because he or she may have access to information about market conditions that is not available in historical demand data. This knowledge of market conditions is likely to improve the forecast. We use the demand for ice cream as an example of the importance of the human factor. If the store manager knows that the weather is likely to be rainy and cold the next day, he or she can use this information to reduce the size of the ice cream order even if demand was high during the previous few days when the weather was hot. In this instance, a change in market conditions (the weather) could not have been predicted using historical demand data. A company can experience substantial payoffs from improving its demand forecasting through qualitative human inputs. Thus, proper human intervention is crucial for good forecasting within a supply chain.

Before a company selects a forecasting method, it must clearly understand what the supply chain's response time is because this information will determine when the forecast needs to be made. For example, if a mail order company is going to use its forecast to determine the number of units of a particular product to order, the company should know how long it takes the supply chain to respond to such an order. If the supply chain takes six months, the mail order company must make a forecast six months before it needs the product.

A company must also be knowledgeable about numerous factors that may be related to the demand forecast, including the following:

- Past demand
- Planned advertising or marketing efforts
- Display position in a catalog
- State of the economy
- Planned price discounts
- Actions competitors have taken

A company must understand such factors before it can select an appropriate forecasting methodology. For example, historically a firm may have experienced low demand for chicken noodle soup in October and high demand in December and January. If the firm decides to discount the product in October, the situation is likely to change, with some of the future demand shifting to the month of October. The firm should make its forecast taking this factor into consideration.

Forecasting methods are classified according to the following four types:

1. **Qualitative**: **Qualitative forecasting methods** are primarily subjective; they rely on human judgment and opinion to make a forecast. They are most appropriate when there are little historical data available or when experts have market intelligence that is critical in making the forecast. Such methods may be necessary to forecast demand several years into the future in a new industry. Initially, forecasts of demand on the Internet were often made using qualitative methods, as the Internet had little historical data on which to base a forecast.

2. **Time series**: **Time series forecasting methods** use historical demand to make a forecast. They are based on the assumption that past demand history is a good indicator of future demand. These methods are most appropriate when the environmental situation is stable and the basic demand pattern does not vary significantly from one year to the next. These are the simplest methods to implement and can serve as a good starting point for a demand forecast.

3. **Causal**: **Causal forecasting methods** involve assuming that the demand forecast is highly correlated with certain factors in the environment (e.g., the state of the economy, interest rates). Causal forecasting methods find this correlation between demand and environmental factors and use estimates of what environmental factors will be to forecast future demand. For example, product pricing is strongly correlated with demand. Companies can thus use causal methods to determine the impact of price promotions on demand.

4. **Simulation**: **Simulation forecasting methods** imitate the consumer choices that give rise to demand to arrive at a forecast. Using simulation, a firm can combine time series and causal methods to answer such questions as these: What will the impact of a price promotion be? What will the impact be of a competitor opening a store nearby? Airlines simulate customer buying behavior to forecast demand for higher-fare seats when there are no seats available at the lower fares.

A company may find it difficult to decide which method is most appropriate for forecasting. In fact, several studies have indicated that using multiple forecasting methods and then using the combination of their forecasts as the actual forecast is more effective than any individual method.

In this chapter we deal primarily with time series methods. Time series methods are most appropriate when future demand is expected to follow historical patterns. When a company attempts to forecast demand based on historical information, clearly, the current demand, any historical growth patterns, and any historical seasonal patterns will influence that company's future demand. Moreover, with this forecasting method, there is always a random element that cannot be explained by current demand, historical patterns, or seasonality. Therefore, any observed demand can be broken down into a systematic and a random component:

$$\text{Observed demand } (O) = \text{Systematic component } (S) + \text{Random component } (R)$$

The **systematic component** measures the expected value of demand and consists of **level**, the current deseasonalized demand; **trend**, the rate of growth or decline in demand for the next period; and **seasonality**, the predictable seasonal fluctuations in demand.

A company may forecast demand's level, trend, and seasonality by using historical data to obtain the forecast's systematic component. The **random component** is that part of the forecast that deviates from the systematic part. A company cannot (and should not) forecast the random component. All a company can forecast is its estimated size and variability, which provides a measure of forecast error. Randomness also means that a company cannot forecast this component's direction. On average, a good forecasting method will have an error whose size is comparable to the random component of demand. A manager should be skeptical of a forecasting method that claims to have no forecasting error on historical demand. In this case, the method has merged the historical random component with the systematic component. As a result, the forecasting method will perform poorly. The objective of forecasting is to filter out the random component (noise) and estimate the systematic component. The **forecast error** measures the difference between the forecast and actual demand. The forecast is based on a measure of the systematic component, and the random component is estimated based on the forecast error.

One of the most common and effective forecasting techniques is time series forecasting. Time series forecasting methods fall into two basic categories: static and adaptive. We explain each category as follows:

1. **Static**: In **static forecasting methods**, companies estimate various parts (e.g., level, trend, seasonality) of the systematic component of demand once and then do not update these estimates even as they observe new demands. Static methods treat all future forecast error as part of the random component of demand. As a result, they do not update the systematic component based on new demand observations.

2. **Adaptive**: In **adaptive forecasting methods**, companies update their estimates of the various parts (e.g., level, trend, seasonality) of the systematic component of demand after they make each demand observation. Adaptive methods assume that a portion of the error is attributed to incorrect estimation of the systematic component, with the rest attributed to the random component. These methods thus update the systematic component after each demand observation.

Static forecasting methods include finding the average values (or obtaining regression estimates) of trend and seasonality. Adaptive methods include moving averages, simple exponential smoothing, and exponential smoothing with corrections for trend and seasonality. We discuss these forecasting methods in the following sections.

In the next section, we describe a six-step approach to demand forecasting.

4.4 BASIC APPROACH TO DEMAND FORECASTING

The choice of a forecasting methodology is only one component of a comprehensive approach to demand forecasting. All parties in the supply chain should reach consensus regarding forecast assumptions, techniques, and final forecast numbers. With consensus, all plans within the supply chain are consistent and are able to support each other. The following basic, six-step approach to forecasting helps an organization perform effective forecasting:

1. Understand the objective of forecasting
2. Integrate demand planning and forecasting
3. Identify the major factors that influence the demand forecast
4. Understand and identify customer segments
5. Determine the appropriate forecasting technique
6. Establish performance and error measures for the forecast

Each organization must use all six steps to forecast effectively.

Understand the Objective of Forecasting

The first step a company must take is to clarify the objective of the forecast to be created. The objective of every forecast is to support decisions that are based on the forecast, so the company must clearly identify these decisions. All parties affected by a supply chain decision should be aware of the link between the decision and the forecast. For example, if Wal-Mart plans a promotion in which it will discount detergent during the month of July, this information must be shared with the manufacturer, the transporter, and others involved in filling demand. All parties must then come up with a common forecast for the promotion and a shared plan of action based on the forecast. Failure to make these decisions jointly may result in either too much or too little product in various stages of the supply chain. It may also result in a last-minute scramble for trucks or warehouse space because those two stages were not informed of the planned promotion and its impact on demand during the planning phase. At this stage, the company should specify whether it wants a forecast based on geography, product, customer segment, or aggregate plan.

The **forecast horizon** is the time lag between the point at which the forecast is made and the event being forecasted. A firm should also specify the desired forecast horizon. For example, if the forecast is to be used to determine the resource capacity a firm will allocate to a particular process and the lead time for changing capacity is two months, the forecast must be ready two months before the firm makes any change in capacity.

Integrate Demand Planning and Forecasting

A company should link its forecast to all planning activities within the supply chain that will use the forecast or influence demand. These include capacity planning, production planning, promotion planning, and purchasing, among others. This link should exist at both the information system and the human resource management level. As a variety of functions are affected by the outcomes of the planning process, it is important that all of them are integrated into the forecasting process. In one unfortunately common scenario, sales and marketing develop forecasts to drive marketing activities, while manufacturing develops a different forecast for production planning. Marketing may plan a large promotion for a specific time of the coming year. Simultaneously, manufacturing makes its forecast based on historical data that do not include any promotions. As a result, the company may not build the impact of the promotion into its aggregate plan, leading ultimately to poor customer service.

In general, it is a good idea for a firm to have a cross-functional team, with members from each affected function responsible for forecasting demand. A firm should also involve the people responsible for executing a plan in the forecasting and planning process, as doing so ensures that all operational issues are taken into consideration during the forecasting and planning phase.

Identify Major Factors That Influence the Demand Forecast

Next, a firm must identify major factors that influence the demand forecast. A proper analysis of these factors is central to developing an appropriate forecasting technique. The main factors influencing forecasts are demand, supply, and product-related phenomena.

On the demand side, a company must ascertain whether demand is growing, declining, or has a seasonal pattern. These estimates must be based on demand—not sales data. For example, a supermarket may have promoted a certain brand of cereal in July 2000. As a result, the demand for this cereal may have been high while the demand for other, comparable cereal brands was low in July. The supermarket should not use the sales data from 2000 to estimate that demand for this brand will be high in July 2001, because this will only be the case if the same brand is promoted again in July 2001 and other brands respond as they did the previous year. When making the demand forecast, the supermarket must understand what the demand would have been in the absence of promotion activity and how demand is affected by promotions. A combination of these two pieces of information will allow the supermarket to forecast demand for July 2001, given the promotion activity planned for that year.

A company should also determine whether there is any relationship (complementary or substitution) between its different products. If promoting one product is likely to steal demand from another product, the company must account for this fact in the forecast. Finally, the firm should be aware of any planned change in lead times and service policies and their influence on demand.

On the supply side, a company must consider the available supply sources to decide on the accuracy of the forecast desired. If alternative supply sources with short lead times are available, a highly accurate forecast may not be especially important. However, if only a single supplier with a long lead time is available, an accurate forecast will have great value.

On the product side, a firm must know the number of variants of a product being sold and whether these variants substitute for or complement each other. If demand for a product influences or is influenced by demand for another product, the two forecasts are best made jointly. For example, when a firm introduces an improved version of an existing product, it is likely that the demand for the existing product will decline because new customers will buy the improved version. Although the decline in demand for the original product would not be indicated by historical data, the historical demand is still useful in that it allows the firm to estimate the combined total demand for the two versions. Clearly, demand for the two products should be forecast jointly.

Understand and Identify Customer Segments

To understand and identify customer segments, customers may be grouped by similarities in service requirements, demand volumes, order frequency, demand volatility, and seasonality. In general, companies may use different forecasting methods for different segments. A clear understanding of the customer segments facilitates an accurate and simplified approach to forecasting.

Determine the Appropriate Forecasting Technique

In selecting an appropriate forecasting technique, a company should first understand the dimensions that will be relevant to the forecast. These dimensions include geographical area, product groups, and customer groups. The company should understand the differences in demand along each dimension. A firm would be wise to have different forecasts and techniques for each dimension. At this stage, a firm selects an appropriate forecasting method from the four methods discussed previously—qualitative, time series, causal, or simulation. As mentioned earlier, using a combination of these methods is often the most effective approach.

Establish Performance and Error Measures for Forecast

Companies should establish clear performance measures to evaluate the accuracy and timeliness of the forecast. These measures should correlate with the objectives of the business decisions based on these forecasts. For example, consider a mail order company that uses a forecast to place orders with its suppliers. Suppliers send in the orders with a two-month lead time, and the products are then sold. The objective of the order is to provide the company with a quantity that minimizes the amount of extra product left over at the end of the sales season and eliminates any lost sales that would result if the product were not available. The mail order company must ensure that the forecast is created at least two months before the start of the sales season because suppliers take two months to send the ordered quantities. At the end of the sales season, the company must compare actual demand with forecasted demand to estimate the accuracy of the forecast. The observed accuracy should be compared with the desired accuracy, and the resulting gap should be used to identify corrective actions that the mail order company needs to take. The desired accuracy may be unattainable given the current ordering and fulfillment process. In this case, the company may find that sending an early version of its catalog to a select set of customers will provide sufficient advance information to improve forecast accuracy.

In the next section, we begin by discussing basic techniques for static and adaptive forecasting. We then present a variety of forecasting methods for complex demand patterns, including demand patterns with both growing and declining trends, and demand patterns with seasonal variation. These time series methods are most useful when future demand is strongly correlated with historical demand.

4.5 TIME SERIES FORECASTING METHODS

The goal of any forecasting method is to predict the systematic component of demand and estimate the random component. The systematic component of demand data, in its most general form, contains a level, a trend, and a seasonal factor. The systematic component may take a variety of forms, as shown in the following equations:

- Multiplicative: Systematic component = level × trend × seasonal factor
- Additive: Systematic component = level + trend + seasonal factor
- Mixed: Systematic component = (level + trend) × seasonal factor

The specific form of the systematic component applicable to a given forecast will depend on the nature of demand. Companies may develop both static and adaptive forecasting methods for each form.

Static Methods

A static method assumes that the estimates of level, trend, and seasonality within the systematic component do not vary as new demand is observed. In this case, we estimate each of these parameters based on historical data and then use the same values for all future forecasts. In this section, we discuss a static forecasting method for use when demand has a trend as well as a seasonal component. We assume that the systematic component of demand is mixed, that is,

$$\text{Systematic component} = (\text{level} + \text{trend}) \times \text{seasonal factor}$$

A similar approach can be applied for other forms as well. We begin with a few basic definitions:

L = Estimate of level for period 0 (the deseasonalized demand estimate for period 0)
T = Estimate of trend (increase or decrease in demand per period)
S_t = Estimate of seasonal factor for period t
D_t = Actual demand observed in period t
F_t = Forecast of demand for period t

In a static forecasting method, the forecast in period t for demand in period $t + l$ is as follows:

$$F_{t+l} = [L + (t + l)T]S_{t+l} \quad \textbf{(4.1)}$$

We now describe one method for estimating the three parameters. As an example, we consider the demand for natural gas from the new on-line utility, NaturalGas.com. NaturalGas uses the pipelines of existing utilities and fills emergency orders that arrive on line from various distributors. NaturalGas has been in existence since the second quarter of 1998, and it has seen demand grow. The planning year at NaturalGas starts in the second quarter of a given year and extends into the first quarter of the following year. The company is planning its capacity requirements and gas purchases from the second quarter of 2001 to the first quarter of 2002 and wants to forecast quarterly demand for the coming year. It estimates that the demand pattern and growth for the coming year are captured in the pattern and growth observed over the past three years. Quarterly demand for the past three years is shown in Table 4.1 and charted in Figure 4.1.

From Figure 4.1 observe that demand for gas is seasonal, with demand increasing from the second quarter of a given year to the first quarter of the following year. The second quarter of each year has the lowest demand of all quarters in the year. Each cycle lasts four quarters, and the demand pattern repeats itself every year. There is also a growth trend in the demand, with sales at NaturalGas growing over the past three years. The company estimates that growth will continue in the coming year. We now describe how each of the three parameters—level, trend, and seasonal factors—may be estimated. The following two steps are necessary to making this estimation:

1. Deseasonalize demand and run linear regression to estimate level and trend
2. Estimate seasonal factors

TABLE 4.1 Quarterly Demand for NaturalGas.com

Year	*Quarter*	*Period t*	*Demand D_t*
1998	2	1	8,000
1998	3	2	13,000
1998	4	3	23,000
1999	1	4	34,000
1999	2	5	10,000
1999	3	6	18,000
1999	4	7	23,000
2000	1	8	38,000
2000	2	9	12,000
2000	3	10	13,000
2000	4	11	32,000
2001	1	12	41,000

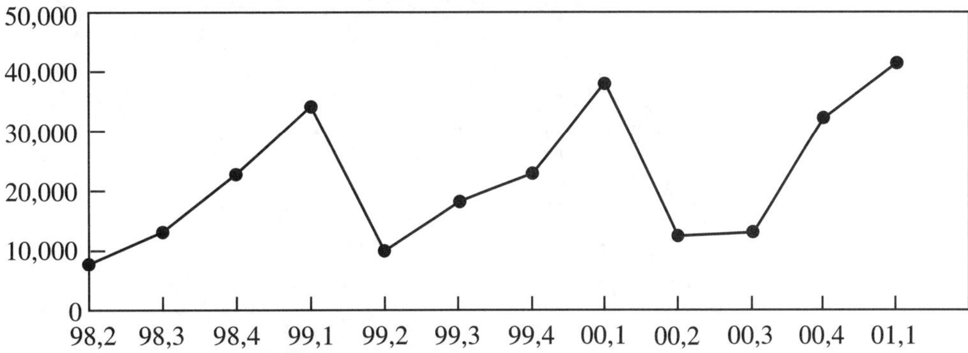

FIGURE 4.1 Quarterly Demand at NaturalGas.com

Estimating Level and Trend

Before estimating level and trend, we must deseasonalize the demand data. **Deseasonalized demand** represents the demand that would have been observed in the absence of seasonal fluctuations. The **periodicity** p is the number of periods after which the seasonal cycle repeats itself. For the demand at NaturalGas, the pattern repeats every year. Given that we are measuring demand on a quarterly basis, the periodicity for the demand in Table 4.1 is $p = 4$.

In order to ensure that each season is given equal weight when deseasonalizing demand, we take the average of p consecutive periods of demand. The average of demand from period $l + 1$ to $l + p$ provides deseasonalized demand for period $l + (p + 1)/2$. If p is odd, this method provides deseasonalized demand for an existing period. If p is even, this method provides deseasonalized demand at a point between period $l + (p/2)$ and $l + 1 + (p/2)$. By taking the average of deaseasonalized demand provided by periods $l + 1$ to $l + p$ and $l + 2$ to $l + p + 1$, we obtain the deseasonalized demand for period $l + 1 + (p/2)$. This procedure for obtaining the deseasonalized demand, $\overline{D_t}$, for period t is formulated as follows:

$$\overline{D_t} = \begin{cases} \left[D_{t-(p/2)} + D_{t+(p/2)} + \sum_{i=t+1-(p/2)}^{t-1+(p/2)} 2\,D_i \right] / 2p \ \ for\ p\ even \\ \sum_{i=t-\lfloor p/2 \rfloor}^{t+\lfloor p/2 \rfloor} D_i / p \ \ for\ p\ odd \end{cases} \tag{4.2}$$

In our example, $p = 4$ is even. For $t = 3$, we obtain the deseasonalized demand using Equation 4.2. That demand is as follows:

$$\overline{D_3} = \left\{ D_{t-(p/2)} + D_{t+(p/2)} + \sum_{i=t+1-(p/2)}^{t-1+(p/2)} 2\,D_i \right\} / 2p = \left\{ D_1 + D_5 + \sum_{i=2}^{4} 2\,D_i \right\} / 8$$

With this procedure we can obtain deseasonalized demand between periods 3 and 10 as shown in Figures 4.2 and 4.3.

Microsoft Excel - chapter4-forecasting-example4.1.xls

	A	B	C	D	E	F	G
1	*Period t*	*Demand D_t*	*Deseasonalized Demand*				
2	1	8,000					
3	2	13,000					
4	3	23,000	19,750				
5	4	34,000	20,625				
6	5	10,000	21,250				
7	6	18,000	21,750				
8	7	23,000	22,500				
9	8	38,000	22,125				
10	9	12,000	22,625				
11	10	13,000	24,125				
12	11	32,000					
13	12	41,000					
14							
15							
16							

FIGURE 4.2 *Excel* Workbook with Deseasonalized Demand for NaturalGas

The cell formulas in column C of Table 4.2 are based on Equation (4.2). In particular, cell C4 contains the Excel formula "= (B2 + B6 + 2*SUM(B3:B5))/8." This formula corresponds to the deseasonalized demand for period 3 and is expressed as $\left\{D_1 + D_5 + \sum_{i=2}^{4} 2\,D_i\right\}/8$.

Once demand has been deseasonalized, it is either growing or declining at a steady rate. Thus, there is a linear relationship between the deseasonalized demand, $\overline{D_t}$, and time t. This relationship is defined as follows:

$$\overline{D_t} = L + tT \tag{4.3}$$

Note that in Equation 4.3, we use $\overline{D_t}$ to represent deseasonalized demand in period t and not the demand in period t, L represents the *level* or deseasonalized demand at period 0, and T represents the rate of growth of deseasonalized demand or *trend*.

FIGURE 4.3 Deseasonalized Demand for NaturalGas

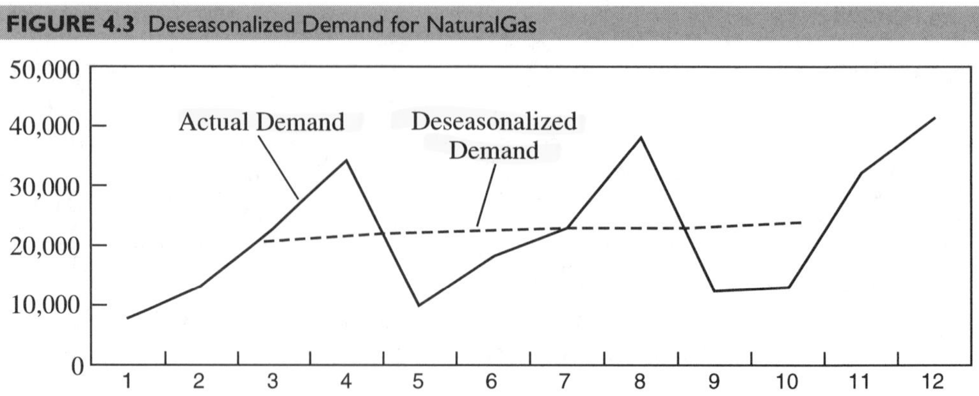

We need to estimate the values of L and T for the deseasonalized demand given in Figure 4.2. We can estimate these two quantities using linear regression with deseasonalized demand in Figure 4.2 as the dependent variable and time as the independent variable. Such a regression can be run using Excel (Tools | Data Analysis | Regression). This sequence of commands opens the Regression dialog box in Excel. For the NaturalGas workbook in Figure 4.2, in the resulting dialogue box we enter the following:

Input *Y* Range: C4:C11
Input *X* Range: A4:A11

and click the OK button. A new sheet containing the results of the regression opens up. This new sheet contains estimates for both the initial *level* L and the *trend* T. The initial level, L, is obtained as the *intercept coefficient* and the trend, T, is obtained as the *X variable coefficient* (or the slope) from the sheet containing the regression results. For the NaturalGas example, we obtain $L = 18{,}439$ and $T = 524$. For this example, deseasonalized demand $\overline{D}_t$ for any period t is thus as follows:

$$\overline{D}_t = 18{,}439 + 524t \tag{4.4}$$

Note that it is not appropriate to run a linear regression between the original demand data and time to estimate level and trend because the original demand data are not linear, and the resulting linear regression will not be accurate. The demand must be deseasonalized before we run the linear regression.

Estimating Seasonal Factors

We can now obtain deseasonalized demand for each period using Equation 4.4. The seasonal factor $\overline{S}_t$ for period t is the ratio of actual demand D_t to deseasonalized demand $\overline{D}_t$ and is as follows:

$$\overline{S}_t = D_t/\overline{D}_t \tag{4.5}$$

For the NaturalGas example, the deseasonalized demand estimated using Equation 4.4 and the seasonal factors estimated using Equation 4.5 are shown in Figure 4.4. The cell formulas in columns C and D for row 2 are shown in Table 4.2.

Given the periodicity, p, we can obtain the seasonal factor for a given period by averaging seasonal factors that correspond to similar periods. For example, if we have a periodicity of $p = 4$, periods 1, 5, and 9 will have similar seasonal factors. The seasonal factor for these periods is obtained as the average of the three seasonal factors. Given r seasonal cycles in the data, for all periods of the form $pt + i, 1 \leq i < p$ we obtain the following seasonal factor:

$$S_i = \left(\sum_{j=0}^{r-1} \overline{S}_{jp+i}\right)/r \tag{4.6}$$

	A	B	C	D	E	F	G	H
1	*Period t*	*Demand D_t*	*Deseasonalized Demand*	*Seasonal Factor*				
2	1	8,000	18963	0.42				
3	2	13,000	19487	0.67				
4	3	23,000	20011	1.15				
5	4	34,000	20535	1.66				
6	5	10,000	21059	0.47				
7	6	18,000	21583	0.83				
8	7	23,000	22107	1.04				
9	8	38,000	22631	1.68				
10	9	12,000	23155	0.52				
11	10	13,000	23679	0.55				
12	11	32,000	24203	1.32				
13	12	41,000	24727	1.66				
14								
15								
16								

FIGURE 4.4 Deseasonalized Demand and Seasonal Factors for NaturalGas

For the NaturalGas example, a total of 12 periods and a periodicity of $p = 4$ implies that there are $r = 3$ seasonal cycles in the data. We obtain seasonal factors using Equation 4.6 as follows:

$$S_1 = (\overline{S}_1 + \overline{S}_5 + \overline{S}_9)/3 = (0.42 + 0.47 + 0.52)/3 = 0.47$$
$$S_2 = (\overline{S}_2 + \overline{S}_6 + \overline{S}_{10})/3 = (0.67 + 0.83 + 0.55)/3 = 0.68$$
$$S_3 = (\overline{S}_3 + \overline{S}_7 + \overline{S}_{11})/3 = (1.15 + 1.04 + 1.32) = 1.17$$
$$S_4 = (\overline{S}_4 + \overline{S}_8 + \overline{S}_{12})/3 = (1.66 + 1.68 + 1.66)/3 = 1.67$$

At this stage, we have estimated the level, trend, and all seasonal factors. We can now obtain the forecast for the next four quarters using Equation 4.1. In the example, the forecast for the next four periods using the static forecasting method is as follows:

$$F_{13} = (L + 13T)S_{13} = (18{,}439 + 13 \times 524)0.47 = 11{,}868$$
$$F_{14} = (L + 14T)S_{14} = (18{,}439 + 14 \times 524)0.68 = 17{,}527$$
$$F_{15} = (L + 15T)S_{15} = (18{,}439 + 15 \times 524)1.17 = 30{,}770$$
$$F_{16} = (L + 16T)S_{16} = (18{,}439 + 16 \times 524)1.67 = 44{,}794$$

Adaptive Forecasting

In adaptive forecasting, the estimates of level, trend, and seasonality are updated after each demand observation. We now discuss a basic framework and several methods that can be used for adaptive forecasting. The framework is provided in the most general setting when the systematic component of demand data contains a level, trend, and seasonal factor. The framework we present is for the case in which the systematic

TABLE 4.2 Cell Formulas for Figure 4.4

Cell	*C2*	*D2*
Spreadsheet formula	= 18439 + A2*524	= B2/C2
Actual formula	18,439 + 1 × 524	$D_1/\overline{D}_1$

component has the mixed form. It can, however, easily be modified for the other two cases. The framework can also be specialized for the case in which the systematic component contains no seasonality or trend. We assume that we are given a set of historical data for n periods. The demand is seasonal with periodicity, p, that is, every p periods the seasonal pattern repeats itself. Given quarterly data, where the pattern repeats itself every year, we would have a periodicity of $p = 4$.

We begin by defining a few terms:

L_t = Estimate of level at the end of period t
T_t = Estimate of trend at the end of period t
S_t = Estimate of seasonal factor for period t
F_t = Forecast of demand for period t (made in period $t - 1$ or earlier)
D_t = Actual demand observed in period t
E_t = Forecast error in period t
A_t = Absolute deviation for period $t = |E_t|$
MAD = Mean absolute deviation = average value of A_t

In adaptive methods, the forecast for period $t + l$ in period t is as follows:

$$F_{t+l} = (L_t + lT_t)S_{t+l} \qquad \textbf{(4.7)}$$

The four steps in the adaptive forecasting framework are as follows:

1. **Initialize**. Compute initial estimates of the level (L_0), trend (T_0), and seasonal factors ($S_1, \ldots, S_p$) from the given data. This is done exactly as in the static forecasting method discussed earlier in the chapter.

2. **Forecast**. Given the estimates in period t, forecast demand for period $t + 1$ using Equation 4.7. The first forecast is for period 1 and is made with the estimates of level, trend, and seasonal factor at period 0.

3. **Estimate error**. Record the actual demand D_{t+1} for period $t + 1$ and compute the error E_{t+1} in the forecast for period $t + 1$ as the difference between the forecast and the actual demand. The error for period $t + 1$ is stated as follows:

$$E_{t+1} = F_{t+1} - D_{t+1} \qquad \textbf{(4.8)}$$

4. **Modify estimates**. Modify the estimates of level (L_{t+1}), trend (T_{t+1}), and seasonal factor (S_{t+p+1}), given the error E_{t+1} in the forecast. It is desirable that the modification be such that if the demand is lower than forecast, the estimates are revised downward, whereas if the demand is higher than forecast, the estimates are revised upward. The revision is thus proportional to the actual error size.

The revised estimates in period $t + 1$ are then used to make a forecast for period $t + 2$, and steps 2, 3, and 4 are repeated until all historical data up to period n have been covered. The estimates at period n are then used to forecast future demand.

We now discuss various adaptive forecasting methods. The method that is most appropriate depends on the characteristic of demand and the composition of the systematic component of demand. In each case we assume the period under consideration to be t.

Moving Average

We use the moving average method when demand has no observable trend or seasonality. In this case, the following equation applies:

$$\text{Systematic component of demand} = \text{level}$$

In this method, we estimate the level in period t as the average demand over the most recent N periods. This represents an N-period moving average. Thus, we have the following:

$$L_t = (D_t + D_{t-1} + \cdots + D_{t-N+1})/N \qquad \textbf{(4.9)}$$

The current forecast for all future periods is the same and is based on the current estimate of level. The forecast is stated as follows:

$$F_{t+1} = L_t, \qquad \text{and} \qquad F_{t+n} = L_t \qquad \textbf{(4.10)}$$

After observing the demand for period $t + 1$, we revise the estimates as follows:

$$L_{t+1} = (D_{t+1} + D_t + \cdots + D_{t-N+2})/N,\ F_{t+2} = L_{t+1}$$

That is, to compute the new moving average, we simply add the latest observation and drop the oldest one. The revised moving average serves as the next forecast. The moving average corresponds to giving the last N periods of data equal weight when forecasting and ignoring all data older than this new moving average. As we increase N, the moving average becomes less responsive to the most recently observed demand. We illustrate the use of the moving average in Example 4.1.

Example 4.1: Consider the demand data for NaturalGas.com in Table 4.1. Forecast demand for period 5 using a four-period moving average.

Analysis: We make the forecast for period 5 in period 4. Therefore, assume the current period to be $t = 4$. Our first objective is to estimate the level in period 4. Using Equation 4.9, with $N = 4$, we obtain the following:

$$L_4 = (D_4 + D_3 + D_2 + D_1)/4 = (34{,}000 + 23{,}000 + 13{,}000 + 8{,}000)/4 = 19{,}500$$

The forecast of demand for period 5 (using Equation 4.10) is expressed as follows:

$$F_5 = L_4 = 19{,}500$$

As demand in period 5, D_5 is 10,000, we have a forecast error for period 5 of

$$E_5 = F_5 - D_5 = 19{,}500 - 10{,}000 = 9{,}500$$

After observing demand in period 5, the revised estimate of level for period 5 is given as follows:

$$L_5 = (D_5 + D_4 + D_3 + D_2)/4 = (10{,}000 + 34{,}000 + 23{,}000 + 13{,}000)/4 = 20{,}000$$

Simple Exponential Smoothing

The simple exponential smoothing method is appropriate when demand has no observable trend or seasonality. In this case, the following equation applies:

$$\text{Systematic component of demand} = \text{level}$$

The initial estimate of level, L_0, is taken to be the average of all historical data because demand has been assumed to have no observable trend or seasonality. Given demand data for periods 1 though n, we have the following:

$$L_0 = \frac{1}{n}\sum_{i=1}^{n} D_i \qquad \textbf{(4.11)}$$

The current forecast for all future periods is equal to the current estimate of level and is given as follows:

$$F_{t+1} = L_t, \quad \text{and} \quad F_{t+n} = L_t \qquad \textbf{(4.12)}$$

After observing the demand, D_{t+1}, for period $t + 1$, we revise the estimate of the level as follows:

$$L_{t+1} = \alpha D_{t+1} + (1 - \alpha)L_t \qquad \textbf{(4.13)}$$

where α is a smoothing constant for the level, $0 < \alpha < 1$. The revised value of the level is a weighted average of the observed value of the level (D_{t+1}) in period $t + 1$ and the old estimate of the level (L_t) in period t. Using Equation 4.13, we can express the level in a given period as a function of the current demand and the level in the previous period. We can thus rewrite Equation 4.13 as follows:

$$L_{t+1} = \sum_{n=0}^{t+1} \alpha(1 - \alpha)^n D_{t+1-n}$$

The current estimate of the level is a weighted average of all of the past observations of demand, with recent observations weighted higher than older observations. A higher value of α corresponds to a forecast that is more responsive to recent observations, whereas a lower value of α represents a more stable forecast that is less responsive to recent observations. We illustrate the use of exponential smoothing in Example 4.2.

Example 4.2: Consider the NaturalGas demand data in Table 4.1. Forecast demand for period 1 using simple exponential smoothing.

Analysis: In this case we have demand data for $n = 12$ periods. Using Equation 4.11, the initial estimate of level is expressed as follows:

$$L_0 = \frac{1}{12}\sum_{i=1}^{12} D_i = 22{,}083$$

The forecast for period 1 (using Equation 4.12) is thus as follows:

$$F_1 = L_0 = 22{,}083$$

The observed demand for period 1 is $D_1 = 8{,}000$. The forecast error for period 1 is as follows:

$$E_1 = F_1 - D_1 = 22{,}083 - 8{,}000 = 14{,}083$$

Assuming a smoothing constant $\alpha = 0.1$, the revised estimate of level for period 1 using simple exponential smoothing Equation 4.13 is as follows:

$$L_1 = \alpha D_1 + (1 - \alpha)L_0 = 0.1 \times 8{,}000 + 0.9 \times 22{,}083 = 20{,}675$$

Observe that the estimate of level for period 1 is lower than for period 0 because the demand in period 1 is lower than the forecast for period 1.

Trend-Corrected Exponential Smoothing (Holt's Model)

This method is appropriate when demand is assumed to have a level and a trend in the systematic component but no seasonality. In this case, we have the following:

$$\text{Systematic component of demand} = \text{level} + \text{trend}$$

We obtain an initial estimate of level and trend by running a linear regression between demand D_t and time period t of the following form:

$$D_t = at + b$$

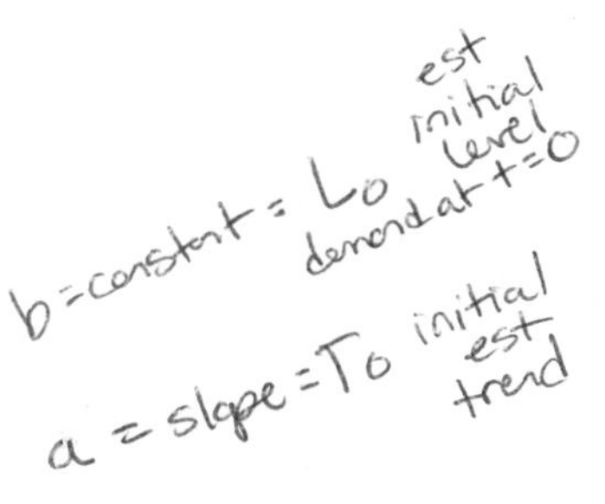

In this case, running a linear regression between demand and time periods is appropriate because we have assumed that demand has a trend but no seasonality. The underlying relationship between demand and time is thus linear. The constant b measures the estimate of demand at period $t = 0$ and is an estimate of the initial level L_0. The slope a measures the rate of change in demand per period and is the initial estimate of the trend T_0.

In period t, given estimates of level L_t and trend T_t, the forecast for future periods is expressed as follows:

$$F_{t+1} = L_t + T_t, \qquad \text{and} \qquad F_{t+n} = L_t + nT_t \tag{4.14}$$

After observing demand for period t, we revise the estimates for level and trend as follows:

$$L_{t+1} = \alpha D_{t+1} + (1 - \alpha)(L_t + T_t) \tag{4.15}$$

$$T_{t+1} = \beta(L_{t+1} - L_t) + (1 - \beta)T_t \tag{4.16}$$

where α is a smoothing constant for the level, $0 < \alpha < 1$, and β is a smoothing constant for the trend, $0 < \beta < 1$. Observe that in each of the two updates, the revised estimate (of level or trend) is a weighted average of the observed value and the old estimate. We illustrate the use of Holt's model in Example 4.3.

Example 4.3: Consider the NaturalGas demand data in Table 4.1. Forecast demand for period 1 using trend corrected exponential smoothing.

Analysis: The first step is to obtain initial estimates of level and trend using linear regression. We first run a linear regression (using the Excel tool Regression Tools|Data Analysis|Regression) between demand and time periods. For the NaturalGas workbook in Figure 4.2, in the Regression dialog box, we enter the following:

Input *Y* Range: B2:B11
Input *X* Range: A2:A11

and click the OK button. A new sheet containing the results of the regression opens up. The estimate of initial level L_0 is obtained as the intercept coefficient and the trend T_0 is obtained as the X variable coefficient (or the slope). For the NaturalGas example, we obtain the following:

$$L_0 = 12{,}015 \quad \text{and} \quad T_0 = 1{,}549$$

The forecast for period 1(using Equation 4.14) is thus given by the following:

$$F_1 = L_0 + T_0 = 12{,}015 + 1{,}549 = 13{,}564$$

The observed demand for period 1 is $D_1 = 8{,}000$. The error for period 1 is thus given by the following

$$E_1 = F_1 - D_1 = 13{,}564 - 8{,}000 = 5{,}564$$

Assuming smoothing constants $\alpha = 0.1$, $\beta = 0.2$, the revised estimate of level and trend for period 1 using trend corrected exponential smoothing (Equations 4.15 and 4.16) is given by the following:

$$L_1 = \alpha D_1 + (1 - \alpha)(L_0 + T_0) = 0.1 \times 8{,}000 + 0.9 \times 13{,}564 = 13{,}008$$
$$T_1 = \beta(L_1 - L_0) + (1 - \beta)T_0 = 0.2 \times (13{,}008 - 12{,}015) + 0.8 \times 1{,}549 = 1{,}438$$

Observe that the initial estimates have overforecast demand for period 1. As a result, our updates have decreased the estimate of level for period 1 from 13,564 to 13,008 and the estimate of trend from 1,549 to 1,438. Using Equation 4.14, we thus obtain the following forecast for period 2:

$$F_2 = L_1 + T_1 = 13{,}008 + 1{,}438 = 14{,}446$$

Trend- and Seasonality-Corrected Exponential Smoothing (Winter's Model)

This method is appropriate when the systematic component of demand is assumed to have a level, trend, and seasonal factor. In this case we have the following:

$$\text{Systematic component of demand} = (\text{level} + \text{trend}) \times \text{seasonal factor}$$

Assume periodicity of demand to be p. To begin we need initial estimates of level (L_0), trend (T_0), and seasonal factors ($S_1, \ldots, S_p$). We obtain these estimates using the procedure for static forecasting described earlier in the chapter.

In period t, given estimates of level, L_t, trend, T_t, and seasonal factors, $S_t, \ldots, S_{t-p+1}$, the forecast for future periods is given by the following:

$$F_{t+1} = (L_t + T_t)S_{t+1} \quad \text{and} \quad F_{t+n} = (L_t + nT_t)S_{t+n} \qquad \textbf{(4.17)}$$

On observing demand for period $t + 1$ we revise the estimates for level, trend, and seasonal factors as follows:

$$L_{t+1} = \alpha(D_{t+1}/S_{t+1}) + (1 - \alpha)(L_t + T_t) \qquad \textbf{(4.18)}$$
$$T_{t+1} = \beta(L_{t+1} - L_t) + (1 - \beta)T_t \qquad \textbf{(4.19)}$$
$$S_{t+p+1} = \gamma(D_{t+1}/L_{t+1}) + (1 - \gamma)S_{t+1} \qquad \textbf{(4.20)}$$

where α is a smoothing constant for the level, $0 < \alpha < 1$, and β is a smoothing constant for the trend, $0 < \beta < 1$, and γ is a smoothing constant for the seasonal factor, $0 < \gamma < 1$. Observe that in each of the updates (level, trend, or seasonal factor), the revised estimate is a weighted average of the observed value and the old estimate. We illustrate the use of Winter's model in Example 4.4.

Example 4.4: Consider the NaturalGas demand data in Table 4.1. Forecast demand for period 1 using trend and seasonality corrected exponential smoothing.

Analysis: We obtain the initial estimates of level, trend, and seasonal factors exactly as in the static case. They are expressed as follows:

$$L_0 = 18{,}439,\ T_0 = 524,\ S_1 = 0.47,\ S_2 = 0.68,\ S_3 = 1.17,\ S_4 = 1.67$$

The forecast for period 1 (using Equation 4.17) is thus given by

$$F_1 = (L_0 + T_0)S_1 = (18{,}439 + 524)0.47 = 8{,}913$$

The observed demand for period 1 is $D_1 = 8{,}000$. The forecast error for period 1 is thus given by the following

$$E_1 = F_1 - D_1 = 8{,}913 - 8{,}000 = 913$$

Assuming smoothing constants $\alpha = 0.1, \beta = 0.2, \gamma = 0.1$, the revised estimate of level and trend for period 1, and seasonal factor for period 5, using trend and seasonality corrected exponential smoothing (using Equations 4.18, 4.19, and 4.20) is given by the following

$$L_1 = \alpha(D_1/S_1) + (1 - \alpha)(L_0 + T_0) = 0.1 \times (8{,}000/0.47) + 0.9 \times (18{,}439 + 524) = 18{,}769$$
$$T_1 = \beta(L_1 - L_0) + (1 - \beta)T_0 = 0.2 \times (18{,}769 - 18{,}439) + 0.8 \times 524 = 485$$
$$S_5 = \gamma(D_1/L_1) + (1 - \gamma)S_1 = 0.1(8{,}000/18{,}769) + 0.9 \times 0.47 = 0.47$$

The forecast of demand for period 2 (using Equation 4.17) is thus given by the following:

$$F_2 = (L_1 + T_1)S_2 = (18{,}769 + 485)0.68 = 13{,}093$$

The forecasting methods discussed previously and the situations in which they are generally applicable are summarized as follows:

Forecasting Method	*Applicability*
Moving average	Demand displays no trend or seasonality
Simple exponential smoothing	Demand displays no trend or seasonality
Holt's model	Demand displays trend but no seasonality
Winter's model	Demand displays trend and seasonality

A measure of forecast error is important because it estimates the random component of demand and also helps identify instances in which the forecasting method being used is inappropriate. In the next section, we describe the way in which a manager can estimate and use forecast error.

4.6 MEASURES OF FORECAST ERROR

As mentioned earlier, every demand has a random component. A good forecasting method should capture the systematic component of demand but not the random component. The random component manifests itself in the form of a forecast error. Forecast errors contain valuable information and must be analyzed carefully. Managers perform a thorough error analysis on a forecast for the following two key reasons:

1. Managers can use error analysis to determine whether the current forecasting method is accurately predicting the systematic component of demand. For example, if a forecasting method consistently results in a positive error, the manager can assume that the forecasting method is overpredicting the systematic component and take appropriate corrective action.

2. Managers estimate forecast error because any contingency plan must account for such an error. For example, consider a mail order company that has a supplier in Asia with whom orders are placed two months in advance and another local supplier who

supplies with a week's notice. The local supplier is more expensive, whereas the Asian supplier costs less. The mail order company wants to contract a certain amount of contingency capacity with the local supplier to be used if the demand exceeds the quantity the Asian supplier provides. The decision regarding the quantity of local capacity to contract is closely linked to the size of the forecast error.

As long as observed errors are within historical error estimates, firms can generally continue to use their current forecasting method. If a firm observes an error that is well beyond historical estimates, this finding may indicate that the forecasting method it is using is no longer appropriate. If all of a firm's forecasts tend to consistently over- or underestimate demand, this may be another signal that the firm should change its forecasting method.

As defined earlier, forecast error for period t is given by E_t, where the following holds:

$$E_t = F_t - D_t$$

That is, the error in period t is the difference between the forecast for period t and the actual demand in period t. It is important that a manager estimate the error of a forecast made at least as far in advance as the lead time required for the manager to take whatever action the forecast is to be used for. For example, if a forecast will be used to determine an order size, and the supplier's lead time is six months, a manager should estimate the error for a forecast made six months before demand arises. In a situation with a six-month lead time, there is no point in estimating errors for a forecast made one month in advance.

One measure of forecast error is the **mean squared error** (MSE), where the following holds:

$$MSE_n = \frac{1}{n} \sum_{t=1}^{n} E_t^2 \qquad \textbf{(4.20)}$$

The MSE estimates the variance of the forecast error.

Define the **absolute deviation** in period t, A_t, to be the absolute value of the error in period t, that is, the following:

$$A_t = |E_t|$$

Define the **mean absolute deviation** (MAD) to be the average of the absolute deviation over all periods, expressed as follows:

$$MAD_n = \frac{1}{n} \sum_{t=1}^{n} A_t \qquad \textbf{(4.21)}$$

The MAD can be used to estimate the standard deviation of the random component, assuming that the random component is normally distributed. In this case, the standard deviation of the random component is as follows:

$$\sigma = 1.25\ MAD \qquad \textbf{(4.22)}$$

We then estimate that the mean of the random component is 0 and the standard deviation of the random component of demand is σ.

The **mean absolute percentage error (MAPE)** is the average absolute error as a percentage of demand and is as follows:

$$MAPE_n = \frac{\sum_{t=1}^{n} \left| \frac{E_t}{D_t} \right| 100}{n} \tag{4.23}$$

To determine whether a forecast method consistently over- or underestimates demand, we can use the sum of forecast errors to evaluate the **bias**, where the following holds:

$$bias_n = \sum_{t=1}^{n} E_t \tag{4.24}$$

The bias will fluctuate around 0 if the error is truly random and not biased one way or the other. Ideally, if we plot all the errors, the slope of the best straight line passing through should be 0.

The **tracking signal** (TS) is the ratio of the bias and the MAD and is given by the following:

$$TS_t = \frac{bias_t}{MAD_t} \tag{4.25}$$

If the TS at any period is outside the range ± 6, this is a signal that the forecast is biased and is either under- (tracking signal below -6) or overforecasting (tracking signal above $+6$). In this case, a firm may decide to choose a new forecasting method. One instance in which a large negative tracking signal will result is when demand has a growth trend and the manager is using a forecasting method such as moving average. Because trend is not included, the average of historical demand will always be lower than future demand. The negative tracking signal will detect that the forecasting method consistently underestimates demand and alert the manager.

4.7 FORECASTING DEMAND AT NATURALGAS.COM

Recall that NaturalGas.com supplies gas in response to emergency orders. The company began operating in the second quarter of 1998 and has seen a rapid growth in demand as shown in Table 4.1 and Figure 4.1. The demand data are also shown in column B of Figure 4.5. NaturalGas is currently negotiating contracts for pipeline capacity for the four quarters between the second quarter of 2001 and the first quarter of 2002. An important input into this negotiation is the forecast of demand over that period. NaturalGas puts together a team consisting of the vice president of sales and

Microsoft Excel - chapter4-forecasting-example4.1.xls

	A	B	C	D	E	F	G	H	I	J	K
1	Period t	Demand D_t	Level L_t	Forecast F_t	Error E_t	Absolute Error A_t	Mean Squared Error MSE_t	MAD_t	% Error	$MAPE_t$	TS_t
2	1	8,000									
3	2	13,000									
4	3	23,000									
5	4	34,000	19,500								
6	5	10,000	20,000	19,500	9,500	9,500	90,250,000	9,500	95	95	1.00
7	6	18,000	21,250	20,000	2,000	2,000	47,125,000	5,750	11	53	2.00
8	7	23,000	21,250	21,250	-1,750	1,750	32,437,500	4,417	8	38	2.21
9	8	38,000	22,250	21,250	-16,750	16,750	94,468,750	7,500	44	39	-0.93
10	9	12,000	22,750	22,250	10,250	10,250	96,587,500	8,050	85	49	0.40
11	10	13,000	21,500	22,750	9,750	9,750	96,333,333	8,333	75	53	1.56
12	11	32,000	23,750	21,500	-10,500	10,500	98,321,429	8,643	33	50	0.29
13	12	41,000	24,500	23,750	-17,250	17,250	123,226,563	9,719	42	49	-1.52

FIGURE 4.5 NaturalGas Forecasts Using Four-Period Moving Average

the vice president of operations to come up with this forecast. The forecasting team decides to apply each of the adaptive forecasting methods discussed in this chapter to the given historical data. Their goal is to select the most appropriate forecasting method and then use it to forecast demand for the next four quarters. The team decides to select the forecasting method based on the errors that result when each method is used on the 12 quarters of historical demand data.

Demand in this case clearly has both a trend and seasonality in the systematic component. Therefore, the team initially expects Winter's model to produce the best forecast. They decide to test this hypothesis by using each of the methods to make the forecast.

Moving Average

The forecasting team initially decides to test a four-period moving average for the forecasting. All calculations are shown in Figure 4.5 and are as discussed in the moving average method section earlier in this chapter. The team uses Equation 4.9 to estimate level and Equation 4.10 to forecast demand.

The cell formulas for row 6 (period 5) are shown in Table 4.3. All other cell formulas are obtained similarly in Excel.

As indicated by column K in Figure 4.5, the tracking signal is well within the ± 6 range, which indicates that the forecast using the four-period moving average does not contain any significant bias. It does, however, have a fairly large MAD of 9,719 and MAPE of 49 percent in period 12. From Figure 4.5, observe the following:

$$L_{12} = 24{,}500$$

Thus, using a four-period moving average, the forecast for periods 13 through 16 (using Equation 4.10) is as follows:

$$F_{13} = F_{14} = F_{15} = F_{16} = L_{12} = 24{,}500$$

Given that the MAD is 9,719, the estimate of standard deviation of forecast error, using a four-period moving average, is $1.25 \times 9{,}719 = 12{,}148$. In this case, the standard deviation of forecast error is fairly large relative to the size of the forecast.

TABLE 4.3 Cell Formulas for Figure 4.5 Using Moving Average

Cell	*Quantity*	*Spreadsheet Formula*	*Actual Formula*
C6	Level	Average(B3:B6)	$(D_2 + D_3 + D_4 + D_5)/4$
D6	Forecast	C5	L_4
E6	Error	D6 − B6	$F_5 - D_5$
F6	Absolute error	Abs(E6)	$\lvert E_5 \rvert$
G6	MSE	Sumsq($E$6:E6)/(A6-4)	$\frac{1}{1}\sum_{t=5}^{5} E_t^2$
H6	MAD	Sum($F$6:F6)/(A6-4)	$\frac{1}{1}\sum_{t=5}^{5} A_t$
I6	Percent error	100*(F6/B6)	$100 \times \lvert E_5 \rvert / D_5$
J6	MAPE	Average($I$6:I6)	$\frac{1}{1}\sum_{t=5}^{5} \frac{\lvert E_t \rvert}{D_t} 100$
K6	TS	Sum($E$6:E6)/H6	$\frac{\sum_{t=5}^{5} E_t}{MAD_5}$

Simple Exponential Smoothing

The forecasting team next uses a simple exponential smoothing approach with $\alpha = 0.1$ to forecast demand. This method is also tested on the 12 quarters of historical data. Using Equation 4.11, the team estimates the initial level for period 0 to be the average demand for periods 1 through 12. The initial level is the average of the demand entries in cells B3 to B14 in Figure 4.6 and results in the following:

$$L_0 = 22{,}083$$

The team then uses Equation 4.12 to forecast demand for the succeeding period. The estimate of level is updated each period using Equation 4.13. The results are shown in Figure 4.6.

FIGURE 4.6 NaturalGas Forecasts Using Simple Exponential Smoothing

Microsoft Excel - chapter4-forecasting-example4.1.xls

	A	B	C	D	E	F	G	H	I	J	K
1	Period t	Demand D	Level L_t	Forecast F_t	Error E_t	Absolute Error A_t	Mean Squared Error MSE_t	MAD_t	% Error	$MAPE_t$	TS_t
2	0		22,083								
3	1	8,000	20,675	22,083	14,083	14,083	198,340,278	14,083	176	176	1.00
4	2	13,000	19,908	20,675	7,675	7,675	128,622,951	10,879	59	118	2.00
5	3	23,000	20,217	19,908	-3,093	3,093	88,936,486	8,284	13	83	2.25
6	4	34,000	21,595	20,217	-13,783	13,783	114,196,860	9,659	41	72	0.51
7	5	10,000	20,436	21,595	11,595	11,595	118,246,641	10,046	116	81	1.64
8	6	18,000	20,192	20,436	2,436	2,436	99,527,532	8,777	14	70	2.15
9	7	23,000	20,473	20,192	-2,808	2,808	86,435,714	7,925	12	62	2.03
10	8	38,000	22,226	20,473	-17,527	17,527	114,031,550	9,125	46	60	-0.16
11	9	12,000	21,203	22,226	10,226	10,226	112,979,315	9,247	85	62	0.95
12	10	13,000	20,383	21,203	8,203	8,203	108,410,265	9,143	63	63	1.86
13	11	32,000	21,544	20,383	-11,617	11,617	110,824,074	9,368	36	60	0.58
14	12	41,000	23,490	21,544	-19,456	19,456	133,132,065	10,208	47	59	-1.38
15											
16	alpha	0.1									
17											
18											
19											

TABLE 4.4 Cell Formulas for Figure 4.6 Using Simple Exponential Smoothing

Cell	*Quantity*	*Spreadsheet Formula*	*Actual Formula*
C3	Level	0.1*B3 + (1 − 0.1)*C2	$\alpha D_1 + (1 - \alpha) L_0$
D3	Forecast	C2	L_0
E3	Error	D3 − B3	$F_1 - D_1$
F3	Absolute error	Abs(E3)	$\lvert E_1 \rvert$
G3	MSE	Sumsq($E$3:E3)/A3	$\frac{1}{1}\sum_{t=1}^{1} E_t^2$
H3	MAD	Sum($F$3:F3)/A3	$\frac{1}{1}\sum_{t=1}^{1} A_t$
I3	Percent error	100*(F3/B3)	$100 \times \lvert E_1 \rvert / D_1$
J3	MAPE	Average($I$3:I3)	$\frac{1}{1}\sum_{t=1}^{1} \frac{\lvert E_t \rvert}{D_t} 100$
K3	TS	Sum($E$3:E3)/H3	$\frac{\sum_{t=1}^{1} E_t}{MAD_1}$

The cell formulas for row 3 (period 1) are shown in Table 4.4. All other cell formulas are obtained similarly in Excel.

As indicated by the tracking signal that ranges from −1.38 to 2.25, the forecast using simple exponential smoothing with $\alpha = 0.1$ does not indicate any significant bias. However, it has a fairly large MAD of 10,208 and MAPE of 59 percent. From Figure 4.6, observe the following:

$$L_{12} = 23{,}490$$

Thus, the forecast for the next four quarters (using Equation 4.12) is as follows:

$$F_{13} = F_{14} = F_{15} = F_{16} = L_{12} = 23{,}490$$

In this case, MAD_{12} is 10,208 and $MAPE_{12}$ is 59 percent. Thus, the estimate of standard deviation of forecast error using simple exponential smoothing is 1.25 × 10,208 = 12,760. In this case, the standard deviation of forecast error is fairly large relative to the size of the forecast.

Trend-Corrected Exponential Smoothing (Holt's Model)

The team next investigates the use of the Holt's model. In this case the systematic component of demand is as follows:

$$\text{Systematic component of demand} = \text{level} + \text{trend}$$

The team applies the methodology discussed earlier. As a first step, they estimate the level at period 0 and the initial trend. As described earlier in Example 4.3, this estimate is obtained by running a linear regression between demand D_t and time period t. From the regression of the available data, the team obtains the following:

$$L_0 = 12{,}015 \quad \text{and} \quad T_0 = 1{,}549.$$

The team now applies Holt's model with $\alpha = 0.1$ and $\beta = 0.2$ to obtain the forecasts for each of the 12 quarters for which demand data are available. They make the

Microsoft Excel - chapter4-forecasting-example4.1.xls

	A	B	C	D	E	F	G	H	I	J	K	L
1	Period t	Demand D	Level L_t	Trend T_t	Forecast F_t	Error E_t	Absolute Error A_t	Mean Squared Error MSE_t	MAD_t	% Error	$MAPE_t$	TS_t
2			12,015	1,549								
3	1	8,000	13,008	1,438	13,564	5,564	5,564	30,958,096	5,564	70	70	1.00
4	2	13,000	14,301	1,409	14,445	1,445	1,445	16,523,523	3,505	11	40	2.00
5	3	23,000	16,439	1,555	15,710	-7,290	7,290	28,732,318	4,767	32	37	-0.06
6	4	34,000	19,594	1,875	17,993	-16,007	16,007	85,603,146	7,577	47	40	-2.15
7	5	10,000	20,322	1,645	21,469	11,469	11,469	94,788,701	8,355	115	55	-0.58
8	6	18,000	21,570	1,566	21,967	3,967	3,967	81,613,705	7,624	22	49	-0.11
9	7	23,000	23,123	1,563	23,137	137	137	69,957,267	6,554	1	42	-0.11
10	8	38,000	26,018	1,830	24,686	-13,314	13,314	83,369,836	7,399	35	41	-1.90
11	9	12,000	26,262	1,513	27,847	15,847	15,847	102,010,079	8,338	132	52	0.22
12	10	13,000	26,298	1,217	27,775	14,775	14,775	113,639,348	8,981	114	58	1.85
13	11	32,000	27,963	1,307	27,515	-4,485	4,485	105,137,395	8,573	14	54	1.41
14	12	41,000	30,443	1,541	29,270	-11,730	11,730	107,841,864	8,836	29	52	0.04
15												
16												
17		Alpha	0.1									
18		Beta	0.2									
19												

FIGURE 4.7 Trend-Corrected Exponential Smoothing

forecast using Equation 4.14; they update level using Equation 4.15; and they update trend using Equation 4.16. The results are shown in Figure 4.7.

The cell formulas for row 3 (period 1) are shown in Table 4.5. All other cell formulas are obtained similarly in Excel.

As indicated by a tracking signal that ranges from −1.90 to 2.00, trend-corrected exponential smoothing with $\alpha = 0.1$ and $\beta = 0.2$ does not seem to significantly over- or underforecast. However, the forecast has a fairly large MAD of 8,836 and MAPE of 52 percent. From Figure 4.7 observe the following

$$L_{12} = 30{,}443,\ T_{12} = 1{,}541$$

TABLE 4.5 Cell Formulas for Figure 4.7 Using Holt's Model

Cell	*Quantity*	*Spreadsheet Formula*	*Actual Formula*
C3	Level	0.1*B3 + (1 − 0.1)*(C2 + D2)	$\alpha D_1 + (1-\alpha)(L_0 + T_0)$
D3	Trend	0.2*(C3 − C2) + (1 − 0.2)*D2	$\beta(L_1 - L_0) + (1-\beta)T_0$
E3	Forecast	C2 + D2	$L_0 + T_0$
F3	Error	E3 − B3	$F_1 - D_1$
G3	Absolute error	Abs(F3)	$\lvert E_1 \rvert$
H3	MSE	Sumsq($F$3:F3)/A3	$\frac{1}{1}\sum_{t=1}^{1} E_t^2$
I3	MAD	Sum($G$3:G3)/A3	$\frac{1}{1}\sum_{t=1}^{1} A_t$
J3	Percent error	100*(G3/B3)	$100 \times \lvert E_1 \rvert / D_1$
K3	MAPE	Average($J$3:J3)	$\frac{1}{1}\sum_{t=1}^{1} \frac{\lvert E_t \rvert}{D_t} 100$
L3	TS	Sum($F$3:F3)/I3	$\frac{\sum_{t=1}^{1} E_t}{MAD_1}$

Thus, using Holt's method (Equation 4.14), the forecast for the next four periods is as follows[1]:

$$F_{13} = L_{12} + T_{12} = 30{,}443 + 1{,}541 = 31{,}984$$
$$F_{14} = L_{13} + 2T_{13} = 30{,}443 + 2 \times 1{,}541 = 33{,}525$$
$$F_{15} = L_{13} + 3T_{13} = 30{,}443 + 3 \times 1{,}541 = 35{,}066$$
$$F_{16} = L_{13} + 4T_{13} = 30{,}443 + 4 \times 1{,}541 = 36{,}607$$

In this case, MAD = 8,836. Thus the estimate of standard deviation of forecast error using Holt's model with $\alpha = 0.1$ and $\beta = 0.2$ is $1.25 \times 8{,}836 = 11{,}045$. In this case, the standard deviation of forecast error relative to the size of the forecast is smaller than it was with the previous two methods. However, it is still fairly large.

Trend- and Seasonality-Corrected Exponential Smoothing (Winter's Model)

The team next investigates the use of Winter's model to make the forecast. Winter's model assumes that the systematic component of demand is as follows

Systematic component of demand = (level + trend) seasonal factor

The team applies the methodology as we discussed earlier. As a first step, they need to estimate the level and trend for period 0, and seasonal factors for periods 1 through $p = 4$. This estimation is done by first deseasonalizing the demand and then estimating initial level and trend by running regression between deseasonalized demand and time. This information is then used to estimate the seasonal factors. For the demand data in Figure 4.2, as discussed in Example 4.4, the team obtains the following:

$$L_0 = 18{,}439,\ T_0 = 524,\ S_1 = 0.47,\ S_2 = 0.68,\ S_3 = 1.17,\ S_4 = 1.67$$

They then apply Winter's model with $\alpha = 0.05$, $\beta = 0.1$, $\gamma = 0.1$ to obtain the forecasts. All calculations are shown in Figure 4.8. The team makes forecasts using Equation 4.17; they update level using Equation 4.18; they update trend using Equation 4.19; and they update seasonal factors using Equation 4.20.

FIGURE 4.8 Trend- and Seasonality-Corrected Exponential Smoothing

Microsoft Excel - chapter4-forecasting-example4.1.xls

	A	B	C	D	E	F	G	H	I	J	K	L	M
1	Period t	Demand D_t	Level L_t	Trend T_t	Seasonal Factor S_t	Forecast F_t	Error E_t	Absolute Error A_t	Mean Squared Error MSE_t	MAD_t	% Error	$MAPE_t$	TS_t
2			18,439	524									
3	1	8,000	18,866	514	0.47	8,913	913	913	832,857	913	11	11	1.00
4	2	13,000	19,367	513	0.68	13,179	179	179	432,367	546	1	6	2.00
5	3	23,000	19,869	512	1.17	23,260	260	260	310,720	450	1	5	3.00
6	4	34,000	20,380	512	1.67	34,036	36	36	233,364	347	0	4	4.00
7	5	10,000	20,921	515	0.47	9,723	-277	277	202,036	333	3	3	3.34
8	6	18,000	21,689	540	0.68	14,558	-3,442	3,442	2,143,255	851	19	6	-2.74
9	7	23,000	22,102	527	1.17	25,981	2,981	2,981	3,106,508	1,155	13	7	0.56
10	8	38,000	22,636	528	1.67	37,787	-213	213	2,723,856	1,037	1	6	0.42
11	9	12,000	23,291	541	0.47	10,810	-1,190	1,190	2,578,653	1,054	10	7	-0.72
12	10	13,000	23,577	515	0.69	16,544	3,544	3,544	3,576,894	1,303	27	9	2.14
13	11	32,000	24,271	533	1.16	27,849	-4,151	4,151	4,818,258	1,562	13	9	-0.87
14	12	41,000	24,791	532	1.67	41,442	442	442	4,432,987	1,469	1	8	-0.63
15	13				0.47	11,940							
16	14				0.68	17,579							
17	15				1.17	30,930							
18	16				1.67	44,928							
19													
20	alpha	0.05											
21	Beta	0.1											
22	Gamma	0.1											

[1]Due to rounding, calculations done with only significant digits shown in the text may yield a different result. This is the case throughout the book.

TABLE 4.6 Cell Formulas for Figure 4.8 Using Winter's Model

Cell	*Quantity*	*Spreadsheet Formula*	*Actual Formula*
C3	Level	0.05*(B3/E3) + (1 – 0.05)*(C2 + D2)	$\alpha(D_1/S_1) + (1-\alpha)(L_0 + T_0)$
D3	Trend	0.1*(C3 – C2) + (1 – 0.1)*D2	$\beta(L_1 - L_0) + (1-\beta)T_0$
E7	Seasonal factor	0.1*(B3/C3) + (1 – 0.1)*E3	$\gamma(D_1/L_1) + (1-\gamma)S_1$
F3	Forecast	(C2 + D2)*E3	$(L_0 + T_0)S_1$
G3	Error	F3 – B3	$F_1 - D_1$
H3	Absolute error	Abs(G3)	$\|E_1\|$
I3	MSE	Sumsq($G$3:G3)/A3	$\frac{1}{1}\sum_{t=1}^{1} E_t^2$
J3	MAD	Sum($H$3:H3)/A3	$\frac{1}{1}\sum_{t=1}^{1} A_t$
K3	Percent error	100*(H3/B3)	$100 \times \|E_1\|/D_1$
L3	MAPE	Average($K$3:K3)	$\frac{1}{1}\sum_{t=1}^{1} \frac{\|E_t\|}{D_t} 100$
M3	TS	Sum($G$3:G3)/J3	$\frac{\sum_{t=1}^{1} E_t}{MAD_1}$

The cell formulas for row 3 (period 1) are shown in Table 4.6. The seasonal factor update is in period 5 or row 7. All other cell formulas are obtained similarly in Excel.

In this case the MAD of 1,469 and MAPE of 8 percent are significantly lower than with any of the other methods. From Figure 4.8 observe the following:

$$L_{12} = 24{,}791,\ T_{12} = 532,\ S_{13} = 0.47,\ S_{14} = 0.68,\ S_{15} = 1.17,\ S_{16} = 1.67$$

Using Winter's model, (Equation 4.17), the forecast for the next four periods is as follows:

$$F_{13} = (L_{12} + T_{12})S_{13} = (24{,}791 + 532) \times 0.47 = 11{,}902$$
$$F_{14} = (L_{12} + 2T_{12})S_{14} = (24{,}791 + 2 \times 532) \times 0.68 = 17{,}581$$
$$F_{15} = (L_{13} + 3T_{13})S_{15} = (24{,}791 + 3 \times 532) \times 1.17 = 30{,}873$$
$$F_{16} = (L_{13} + 4T_{13})S_{16} = (24{,}791 + 4 \times 532) \times 1.67 = 44{,}954$$

In this case, MAD = 1,469. Thus the estimate of standard deviation of forecast error using Winter's model with $\alpha = 0.05$, $\beta = 0.1$, and $\gamma = 0.1$ is $1.25 \times 1{,}469 = 1{,}836$. In this case, the standard deviation of forecast error relative to the demand forecast is much smaller than in the other methods.

The team compiles the error estimates for the four forecasting methods as shown in Table 4.7.

TABLE 4.7 Error Estimates for NaturalGas Forecasting

Forecasting Method	*MAD*	*MAPE (%)*	*TS Range*
Four-period moving average	9,719	49	−1.52 to 2.21
Simple exponential smoothing	10,208	59	−1.38 to 2.25
Holt's model	8,836	52	−1.90 to 2.00
Winter's model	1,469	8	−2.74 to 4.00

Based on the error information in Table 4.7, the forecasting team decides to use Winter's model. It is not surprising that Winter's model results in the most accurate forecast because the demand data have both a growth trend and seasonality. Using Winter's model, the team forecasts the following demand for the coming four quarters:

Second Quarter, 2001: 11,902
Third Quarter, 2001: 17,581
Fourth Quarter, 2001: 30,873
First Quarter, 2002: 44,954

The standard deviation of forecast error is 1,836.

4.8 SUMMARY OF LEARNING OBJECTIVES

1. Understand the role of forecasting in a supply chain.
   All supply chain design and planning decisions are based on a forecast of customer demand. These decisions include investment in plant and equipment, production scheduling, sales force allocation, and workforce hiring. Thus, good demand forecasts have a significant impact on supply chain performance.
2. Identify the components of a demand forecast.
   Demand consists of a systematic and a random component. The systematic component measures the expected value of demand. The random component measures fluctuations in demand from the expected value. The systematic component consists of level, trend, and seasonality. Level measures the current deseasonalized demand. Trend measures the current rate of growth or decline in demand. Seasonality indicates predictable seasonal fluctuations in demand.
3. Forecast demand in a supply chain given historical data using time series methodologies.
   Time series methods for forecasting are categorized as static or adaptive. In static methods the estimates of parameters and demand patterns are not updated as new demand is observed. Static methods include regression. In adaptive methods the estimates are updated each time a new demand is observed. Adaptive methods include moving averages, simple exponential smoothing, Holt's model, and Winter's model. Moving averages and simple exponential smoothing are best used when demand displays no trend or seasonality. Holt's model is best when demand displays a trend but no seasonality. Winter's model is appropriate when demand displays both trend and seasonality.
4. Analyze demand forecasts to estimate forecast error.
   Forecast error measures the random component of demand. This measure is important because it reveals how inaccurate a forecast is likely to be and what contingencies a firm may have to plan for. The mean absolute deviation (MAD) and the mean absolute percentage error (MAPE) are used to estimate the size of the forecast error. The bias and tracking signal are used to estimate if the forecast consistently over- or underforecasts.

Discussion Questions

1. What role does forecasting play in the supply chain of a build-to-order manufacturer such as Dell?
2. What role does forecasting play in the supply chain of a mail order firm such as L.L. Bean?
3. What systematic and random components would you expect in demand for chocolates?
4. Why should a manager be suspicious if a forecaster claims to forecast historical demand without any forecast error?
5. Give examples of products that display seasonality of demand.
6. What is the problem if a manager uses the previous year's sales data instead of the previous year's demand to forecast demand for the coming year?
7. How do static and adaptive forecasting methods differ?
8. What information does the MAD and MAPE provide to a manager? How can the manager use this information?
9. What information does the bias and tracking signal provide to a manager? How can the manager use this information?

Exercises

1. Consider monthly demand for the ABC Corporation as shown in Table 4.8. Forecast the monthly demand for 2001 using the static method for forecasting. Evaluate the bias, TS, MAD, MAPE, and MSE. Evaluate the quality of the forecast.
2. Weekly sales of pizzas at Hot Pizza are as follows:

Week	*Demand*	*Week*	*Demand*	*Week*	*Demand*
1	108	5	96	9	112
2	116	6	119	10	102
3	118	7	96	11	92
4	124	8	102	12	91

Estimate demand for the next four weeks using a four-week moving average as well as simple exponential smoothing with $\alpha = 0.1$. Evaluate the MAD, MAPE, MSE, bias, and TS in each case. Which of the two methods would you prefer? Why?

TABLE 4.8 Monthly Demand for ABC Corporation

Sales	*1997*	*1998*	*1999*	*2000*	*2001*
JAN	2,000	3,000	2,000	5,000	5,000
FEB	3,000	4,000	5,000	4,000	2,000
MAR	3,000	3,000	5,000	4,000	3,000
APR	3,000	5,000	3,000	2,000	2,000
MAY	4,000	5,000	4,000	5,000	7,000
JUN	6,000	8,000	6,000	7,000	6,000
JUL	7,000	3,000	7,000	10,000	8,000
AUG	6,000	8,000	10,000	14,000	10,000
SEP	1,000	12,000	15,000	16,000	20,000
OCT	12,000	12,000	15,000	16,000	20,000
NOV	14,000	16,000	18,000	20,000	22,000
DEC	8,000	10,000	8,000	12,000	8,000
Total	78,000	89,000	98,000	115,000	113,000

3. Quarterly sales of flowers at a wholesaler are as follows:

Year	*Quarter*	*Sales (in thousands)*	*Year*	*Quarter*	*Sales (in thousands)*
1997	I	$ 98	1999	I	$138
	II	106		II	130
	III	109		III	147
	IV	133		IV	141
1998	I	130	2000	I	144
	II	116		II	142
	III	133		III	165
	IV	116		IV	173

Forecast quarterly sales for 2001 using simple exponential smoothing with $\alpha = 0.1$ as well as Holt's models with $\alpha = 0.1$ and $\beta = 0.1$. Which of the two methods would you prefer? Why?

4. Consider monthly demand for the ABC Corporation as shown in Table 4.8. Forecast the monthly demand for 2001 using moving average, simple exponential smoothing, Holt's model, and Winter's model. In each case evaluate the bias, TS, MAD, MAPE, and MSE. Which forecasting method would you prefer? Why?

Bibliography

Bernstein, Peter L., and Theodore H. Silbert. "Are Economic Forecasters Worth Listening To?" *Harvard Business Review* (September–October 1984), 2–8.

Box, G.E.P., and G.M. Jenkins. *Time Series Analysis: Forecasting and Control*. Oakland, Calif.: Holden-Day, 1976.

Bowerman, Bruce L., and Richard T. O'Connell. *Forecasting and Time Series: An Applied Approach*, 3d ed. Belmont, Calif.: Duxbury Press, 1993.

Brown, R.G. *Statistical Forecasting for Inventory Control*. New York: McGraw-Hill, 1959.

Chambers, J.C., K.M. Satinder, and D.D. Smith. "How to Choose the Right Forecasting Technique." *Harvard Business Review* (July–August 1971), 45–74.

"Forecasting with Regression Analysis." *Harvard Business School* Note #9-894-007, Cambridge, Mass.: Harvard Business School.

Georgoff, David M., and Robert G. Murdick. "Manager's Guide to Forecasting." *Harvard Business Review* (January–February 1986), 2–9.

Makridakis, Spyros and Steven C. Wheelwright. *Forecasting Methods for Management*. New York: John Wiley & Sons, 1989.

Yurkiewicz, Jack. "Forecasting 2000." *ORMS Today* (February 2000), 58–65.

CASE STUDY

Specialty Packaging Corporation, Part A

Julie Williams had a lot on her mind when she left the conference room at Specialty Packaging Corporation (SPC). Her divisional manager had informed her that her manufacturing plant would now be responsible for the management of work-in-process material and that all costs associated with the storage of this material would be charged to the plant in the coming year. As facility production planning manager, Julie's responsibility would be to minimize the total cost of production, including storage of in-process material. Until this time, a corporate overhead account had absorbed costs associated with the transportation and storage of all materials. As a planner, Julie's goal had been to optimize production efficiencies within the plant without having to consider storage requirements. The new structure would force Julie to develop a low-cost plan for the management and storage of in-process materials. Julie's immediate goal is to forecast quarterly demand for the final product for each quarter over the next three years. This information will help her to make her material management plans.

SPECIALTY PACKAGING CORPORATION

SPC turns polystyrene resin into recyclable/disposable containers for the food industry. Polystyrene is purchased as a commodity in the form of resin pellets. The resin is unloaded from bulk rail containers or overland trailers into storage silos. Making the food containers is a two-step process. First, resin is conveyed to an extruder, which converts it into polystyrene sheets wound into rolls. The plastic comes in two forms: clear and black. The rolls are either used immediately to make containers or are put into storage. Second, the rolls are loaded onto thermoforming presses, which form the sheet into containers and trim the containers from the sheet. The two manufacturing steps are shown in Figure 4.9.

Over the past five years, the plastic packaging business has grown steadily. Demand for containers made from clear plastic comes from grocery stores, bakeries, and restaurants. Demand for black plastic rays comes from caterers and grocery stores, which use them as packaging and serving trays. Demand for clear plastic containers peaks in the summer months, and demand for black plastic containers peaks in the fall. Capacity on the extruders is not sufficient to cover demand for sheets during the peak seasons. As a result, the plant is forced to build inventory of each type of sheet in anticipation of future demand. Table 4.9 and Figure 4.10 display historical quarterly demand for each of the two types (clear and black) of containers.

FORECASTING

The storage requirement for work-in-process material is dependent upon the production plan as well as demand. The production plan itself will be based on a forecast of demand for the years 2001–2003. As a first step in her decision making, Julie wants to forecast quarterly demand for each of the two types of containers for the years 2001–2003. Based on historical trends, demand is expected to continue to grow until 2003, after which it is expected to plateau. Julie must select the appropriate forecasting method and estimate the likely forecast error. Which method should she choose?

FIGURE 4.9 Manufacturing Process at SPC

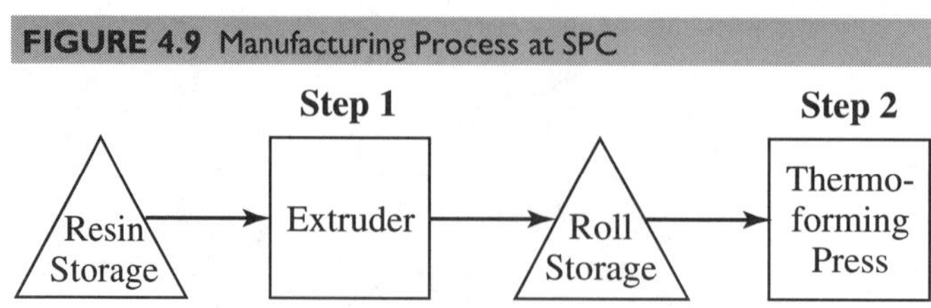

TABLE 4.9 Quarterly Historical Demand for Clear and Black Plastic Containers

Year	*Quarter*	*Black Plastic Demand ('000 lbs.)*	*Clear Plastic Demand ('000 lbs.)*
1996	I	2,250	3,200
	II	1,737	7,658
	III	2,412	4,420
	IV	7,269	2,384
1997	I	3,524	3,654
	II	2,143	8,680
	III	3,459	5,695
	IV	7,056	1,953
1998	I	4,120	4,742
	II	2,766	13,673
	III	2,556	6,640
	IV	8,253	2,737
1999	I	5,491	3,486
	II	4,382	13,186
	III	4,315	5,448
	IV	12,035	3,485
2000	I	5,648	7,728
	II	3,696	16,591
	III	4,843	8,236
	IV	13,097	3,316

FIGURE 4.10 Plot of Quarterly Demand for Clear and Black Plastic Containers

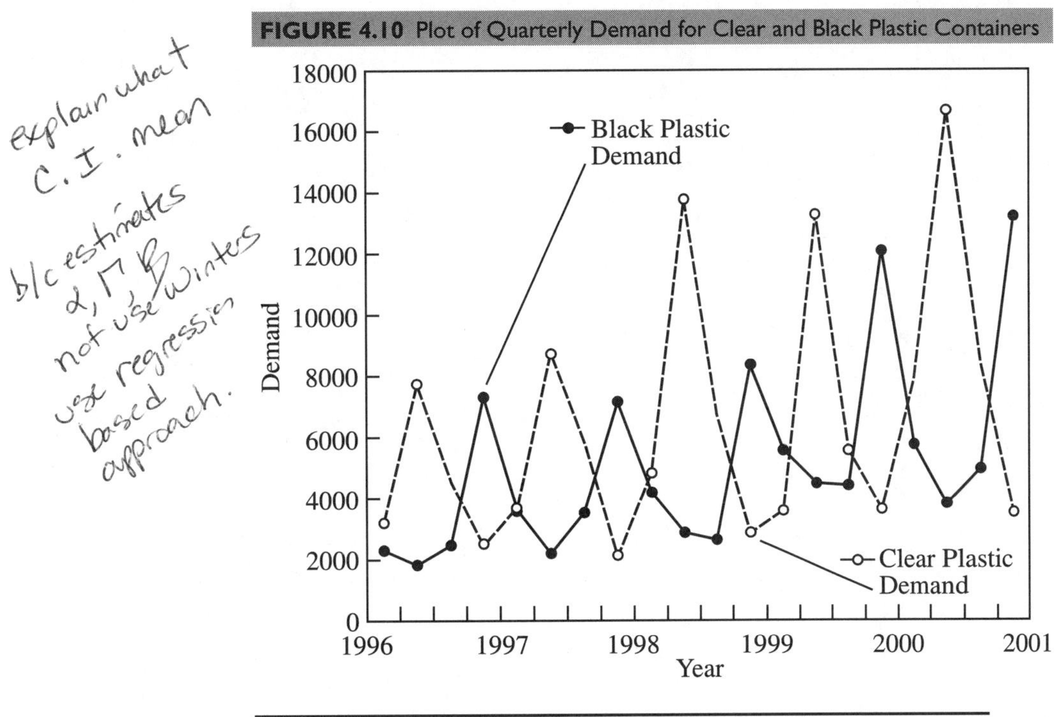

CHAPTER 5

Aggregate Planning in a Supply Chain

Learning Objectives
After reading this chapter, you will be able to

1. identify the types of decisions that are best solved by aggregate planning;
2. describe the kind of information needed to produce an aggregate plan;
3. explain the basic trade-offs a manager makes when producing an aggregate plan; and
4. formulate and solve aggregate planning problems using Microsoft Excel.

In this chapter, we discuss how the aggregate planning methodology is used to make decisions about production, inventory, and backlogs in a supply chain. We identify the information required to produce an aggregate plan and outline the basic trade-offs that must be made to create an optimal aggregate plan. We also describe how the aggregate planning problem can be formulated and solved using Microsoft Excel.

5.1 THE ROLE OF AGGREGATE PLANNING IN A SUPPLY CHAIN

Imagine a world where manufacturing capacity, transportation capacity, storage capacity, and even information capacity are all limitless and without cost. Imagine lead times equal to zero, allowing goods to be produced and delivered instantaneously. In this world, there is no need to plan in anticipation of demand as whenever a customer demands a product, the demand can be instantly satisfied. In this world, aggregate planning plays no role.

In our world, however, capacity has a cost, and lead times are greater than zero. Therefore, companies must make decisions regarding capacity levels, how to use that capacity, and even when to run promotions to spur demand. A company must anticipate demand and determine, in advance of that demand, how it will be met. Should a company invest in a plant with large capacity that is able to produce enough to satisfy demand even in the busiest months? Or should a company build a smaller plant but incur the costs of holding inventory built during slow periods in anticipation of demand in later months? These are the types of questions aggregate planning helps companies answer.

Aggregate planning is a process by which a company determines levels of capacity, production, subcontracting, inventory, stockouts, and even pricing over a specified time horizon. The goal of aggregate planning is to satisfy demand in a way that maximizes profit. Aggregate planning, as the name suggests, solves problems involving aggregate decisions rather than stock-keeping unit (SKU) level decisions. For example, aggregate planning will determine the total production level in a plant for a given month, but it will do so without determining the quantity of each individual SKU that will be produced. This level of detail makes aggregate planning a useful tool for thinking about decisions with an intermediate time frame of between roughly 3 and 18 months. In this time frame, it is too early to determine SKU by SKU production levels, but it is also generally too late to build a new set of facilities. Therefore, aggregate planning answers the question, "How should a firm best utilize the facilities that it currently has?"

For example, paper manufacturers use aggregate planning to determine their production plans. Many types of paper mills face seasonal demand where peaks occur in the spring and fall. However, because mill capacity is very expensive, building a mill to meet capacity in the spring and fall on an as-needed basis would be too costly. To deal with this potential problem, mills use aggregate planning to determine production levels and inventory levels that they should build up in the slower months for sale in the spring and fall when demand is greater than the mill's capacity. Aggregate planning thus allows the mill to maximize profit.

The aggregate planner's main objective is to identify the following operational parameters over the specified time horizon:

- **Production rate**. The number of units completed per unit time (such as per week or per month).
- **Workforce**. The number of workers/units of capacity needed for production.
- **Overtime**. The amount of overtime production planned.
- **Machine capacity level**. The number of units of machine capacity needed for production.
- **Subcontracting**. The subcontracted capacity required over the planning horizon.
- **Backlog**. Demand not satisfied in the period in which it arises but carried over to future periods.
- **Inventory on hand**. The planned inventory carried over the various periods in the planning horizon.

The aggregate plan serves as a broad blueprint for operations and establishes the parameters within which short-term production and distribution decisions are made.

The aggregate plan allows the supply chain to alter capacity allocations and change supply contracts. As we mentioned in Chapter 4, the entire supply chain should coordinate the planning process. If a manufacturer has planned an increase in production over a given time period, the supplier, transporter, and warehouser must be aware of this plan and incorporate the increase into their own plans. Ideally, all stages of the supply chain should work together on an aggregate plan that will optimize supply chain performance. If each stage develops its own aggregate plan, it is extremely unlikely that all the plans will mesh in a coordinated manner. This lack of coordination will result in shortages or oversupply in the supply chain. Therefore, it is important to perform aggregate plans over as wide a scope of the supply chain as is reasonably possible.

In the next section, we formally define the aggregate planning problem. We specify the information required for aggregate planning and discuss the decision outcomes that aggregate planning can provide.

5.2 THE AGGREGATE PLANNING PROBLEM

The objective of the aggregate plan is to satisfy demand in a way that maximizes profit for the firm. We can formally state the aggregate planning problem as follows:

> Given the demand forecast for each period in the planning horizon, determine the production level, inventory level, and the capacity level for each period that maximizes the firm's profit over the planning horizon.

To create an aggregate plan, a company must specify the planning horizon for the plan. A planning horizon is the time period over which the aggregate plan is to produce a solution—usually between 3 and 18 months. A company must also specify the duration of each period within the planning horizon—for example, weeks, months, or quarters. In general, aggregate planning takes place over months or quarters. Next, a company specifies key information required to produce an aggregate plan and the decisions an aggregate plan will develop recommendations for. This information and the recommendations are specified for a generic aggregate planning problem in this section. The model we propose in the next section is flexible enough to accommodate situation-specific requirements.

An aggregate planner requires the following information:

- Demand forecast F_t for each period t in the planning horizon that extends over T periods
- Production costs
  —labor costs, regular time ($/hour) and overtime costs ($/hour)
  —cost of subcontracting production ($/unit or $/hour)
  —cost of changing capacity, specifically, cost of hiring/laying off workforce ($/worker) and cost of adding or reducing machine capacity ($/machine)
- Labor/machine hours required per unit
- Inventory holding cost ($/unit/period)
- Stockout or backlog cost ($/unit/period)
- Constraints
  —limits on overtime
  —limits on layoffs
  —limits on capital available
  —limits on stockouts and backlogs

This information is used to create an aggregate plan, which in turn helps a company make the following determinations:

- **Production quantity from regular time, overtime, and subcontracted time**. Used to determine number of workers and supplier purchase levels.
- **Inventory held**. Used to determine how much warehouse space and working capital is needed.
- **Backlog/stockout quantity**. Used to determine what the customer service levels will be.
- **Workforce hired/laid off**. Used to determine any labor issues that will be encountered.
- **Machine capacity increase/decrease**. Used to determine if new production equipment needs to be purchased.

The quality of an aggregate plan has a significant impact on the profitability of a firm. A poor aggregate plan can result in lost sales and lost profits if the available inventory and capacity are unable to meet demand. A poor aggregate plan may also result in a large amount of excess inventory and capacity, thereby raising costs. Therefore, aggregate planning is a very important tool in helping a company maximize profitability.

5.3 AGGREGATE PLANNING STRATEGIES

The aggregate planner must make a trade-off among capacity, inventory, and backlog costs. An aggregate plan that decreases one of these costs typically results in an increase of the other two. In this sense, the costs represent a trade-off: To lower inventory cost, a planner must increase capacity cost or backlog cost. Thus, the planner has traded inventory cost for capacity or backlog cost. Arriving at the most profitable trade-off is the goal of aggregate planning. Given that demand varies over time, the relative level of the three costs leads to one of them being the key lever the planner uses to maximize profits. If the cost of varying capacity is low, a company may not have to build inventory during off-peak periods or carry backlogs. If the cost of varying capacity is high, a company may compensate by building some inventory and carrying some backlogs from peak demand periods to off-peak demand periods.

In general, the fundamental trade-offs available to a planner are among the following:

- Capacity (regular time, overtime, subcontracted)
- Inventory
- Backlog/lost sales

There are essentially three distinct aggregate planning strategies for achieving balance among these costs. These strategies involve trade-offs among capital investment, workforce size, work hours, inventory, and backlogs/lost sales. Most strategies that a planner actually uses are a combination of these three and are referred to as **mixed strategies**. The three strategies are as follows:

1. **Chase strategy—using capacity as the lever**. With this strategy, the production rate is synchronized with the demand rate by varying machine capacity or hiring and laying off employees as the demand rate varies. In practice, achieving this synchronization can be very problematic because of the difficulty in varying capacity and workforce on short notice. This strategy can be expensive to implement if the cost of varying machine capacity over time is high. It can also have a significant negative impact on the morale of the workforce. The chase strategy results in low levels of inven-

tory in the supply chain and high levels of change in capacity and workforce. It should be used when the cost of carrying inventory is very expensive and costs to change levels of capacity and workforce are low.

2. **Time flexibility from workforce or capacity strategy—using utilization as the lever**. This strategy may be used if there is excess machine capacity—that is, if machines are not used 24 hours a day, seven days a week. In this case, the workforce (capacity) is kept stable, but the number of hours worked is varied over time in an effort to synchronize production with demand. A planner can use variable amounts of overtime or a flexible schedule to achieve this synchronization. Although this strategy does require that the workforce be flexible, it avoids some of the problems associated with the chase strategy, such as changing the size of the workforce. This strategy results in low levels of inventory but lower average utilization than the chase strategy. It should be used when inventory carrying costs are relatively high and capacity is relatively inexpensive.

3. **Level strategy—using inventory as the lever**. With this strategy, a stable machine capacity and workforce are maintained with a constant output rate. Shortages and surpluses result in inventory levels fluctuating over time. Here production is not synchronized with demand. Either inventories are built up in anticipation of future demand or backlogs are carried over from high to low demand periods. Employees benefit from stable working conditions. A drawback associated with this strategy is that large inventories and backlogs may accumulate. This strategy keeps capacity and costs of changing capacity relatively low. It should be used when inventory carrying costs and backlog costs are relatively low.

In the next section, we discuss a methodology that is commonly used for aggregate planning.

5.4 AGGREGATE PLANNING USING LINEAR PROGRAMMING

As discussed earlier, the goal of aggregate planning is to maximize profit while meeting demand. Every company, in its effort to meet customers' demand, faces certain constraints, such as the capacity of its facilities or its workforce. A highly effective tool for a company to use when it tries to maximize profits while being subjected to a series of constraints is **linear programming**. Linear programming finds the solution that will create the highest profit while satisfying the constraints that the company faces.

We illustrate linear programming through a discussion of Red Tomato Tools, a small manufacturer of gardening equipment. Red Tomato's operations consist of the assembly of purchased parts into a multipurpose gardening tool. Due to the limited equipment and space required for their assembly operations, Red Tomato's capacity is determined mainly by the size of its workforce.

For Red Tomato, we use a six-month time period because this is a large enough time horizon to illustrate the points we make without being unwieldy.

Red Tomato Tools

The demand for Red Tomato's gardening tools is highly seasonal, peaking in the spring as people plant their gardens. Red Tomato has decided to use aggregate planning to overcome this obstacle of seasonal demand and maximize profits. The options Red Tomato has for handling the seasonality are adding workers during the peak season, subcontracting out some of the work, building up inventory during the slow months, and building up a backlog of orders that will be delivered late to customers.

TABLE 5.1 Demand Forecast at Red Tomato Tools

Month	*Demand Forecast*
January	1,600
February	3,000
March	3,200
April	3,800
May	2,200
June	2,200

To determine how to best use these options through an aggregate plan, Red Tomato's vice president of supply chain starts with the demand forecast for its tools over the next six months, as shown in Table 5.1.

Red Tomato sells each tool to retailers for $40. The company has a starting inventory in January of 1,000 tools. At the beginning of January the company has a workforce of 80 employees. The plant has a total of 20 working days in each month, and each employee earns $4 per hour regular time. Each employee works eight hours a day on straight time and the rest on overtime. As discussed previously, the capacity of the production operation is determined primarily by the total labor hours worked. Therefore, machine capacity does not limit the capacity of the production operation. Due to labor rules, no employee works more than 10 hours of overtime per month. The various costs are shown in Table 5.2.

Currently, Red Tomato has no limits on subcontracting, inventories, and stockouts/backlog. All stockouts are backlogged and supplied from the following months' production. Inventory costs are incurred on the ending inventory in the month. The supply chain manager's goal is to obtain the optimal aggregate plan that allows Red Tomato to end June with at least 500 units (i.e., no stockouts at the end of June and at least 500 units in inventory).

The optimal aggregate plan is one that results in the highest profit over the six-month planning horizon. Given Red Tomato's desire for a very high level of customer service, assume all demand is to be met. Therefore, the revenues earned over the planning horizon are fixed given the fixed price. In this case, minimizing cost over the planning horizon is the same as maximizing profit. In many instances, a company has the option of not meeting certain demand, or price itself may be a variable that a company will have to determine based on the aggregate plan. In such a scenario, minimiz-

TABLE 5.2 Costs for Red Tomato

Item	*Cost*
Material cost	$10/unit
Inventory holding cost	$2/unit/month
Marginal cost of stockout/backlog	$5/unit/month
Hiring and training costs	$300/worker
Layoff cost	$500/worker
Labor hours required	4/unit
Regular time cost	$4/hour
Overtime cost	$6/hour
Cost of subcontracting	$30/unit

ing cost would not be equivalent to maximizing profits, and therefore, the company's objective would be to maximize profits.

Decision Variables

The first step in constructing an aggregate planning model is to identify the set of decision variables whose values are to be determined as part of the aggregate plan. For Red Tomato, the following decision variables are defined for the aggregate planning model:

W_t = Workforce size for month t, $t = 1, \ldots, 6$,
H_t = Number of employees hired at the beginning of month t, $t = 1, \ldots, 6$,
L_t = Number of employees laid off at the beginning of month t, $t = 1, \ldots, 6$,
P_t = Number of units produced in month t, $t = 1, \ldots, 6$,
I_t = Inventory at the end of month t, $t = 1, \ldots, 6$,
S_t = Number of units stocked out / backlogged at the end of month t, $t = 1, \ldots, 6$,
C_t = Number of units subcontracted for month t, $t = 1, \ldots, 6$,
O_t = Number of overtime hours worked in month t, $t = 1, \ldots, 6$.

The next step in constructing an aggregate planning model is to define the objective function.

Objective Function

Denote the demand in period t by D_t. The values of D_t are as specified by the demand forecast in Table 5.1. The objective function is to minimize the total cost (equivalent to maximizing total profit as all demand is to be satisfied) incurred during the planning horizon. The cost incurred has the following components:

- Regular time labor cost
- Overtime labor cost
- Cost of hiring and layoffs
- Cost of holding inventory
- Cost of stocking out
- Cost of subcontracting
- Material cost

These costs are evaluated as follows:

- **Regular time labor cost.** Recall that workers are paid a regular time wage of \$640 (\$4/hour × 8 hours/day × 20 days/month) per month. Because W_t is the number of workers in period t, the regular time labor cost over the planning horizon is as follows:

$$\text{Regular time labor cost} = \sum_{t=1}^{6} 640\, W_t$$

- **Overtime labor cost.** As overtime labor cost is \$6 per hour (see Table 5.2) and O_t represents the number of overtime hours worked in period t, the overtime cost over the planning horizon is as follows:

$$\text{Overtime labor cost} = \sum_{t=1}^{6} 6\, O_t$$

- **Cost of hiring and layoffs.** The cost of hiring a worker is \$300, and the cost of laying off a worker is \$500 (see Table 5.2). H_t and L_t represent the number hired and the number laid off, respectively, in period t. Thus, the cost of hiring and layoff is as follows:

$$\text{Cost of hiring and layoff} = \sum_{t=1}^{6} 300\, H_t + \sum_{t=1}^{6} 500\, L_t$$

- **Cost of inventory and stockout**. The cost of carrying inventory is \$2 per unit per month, and the cost of stocking out is \$5 per unit per month (see Table 5.2). I_t and S_t represent the units in inventory and the units stocked out, respectively, in period t. Thus, the cost of holding inventory and stocking out is as follows:

$$\text{Cost of holding inventory and stocking out} = \sum_{t=1}^{6} 2\, I_t + \sum_{t=1}^{6} 5\, S_t$$

- **Cost of materials and subcontracting**. The material cost is \$10 per unit, and the subcontracting cost is \$30/unit (see Table 5.2). P_t represents the quantity produced and C_t the quantity subcontracted in period t. Thus, the material and subcontracting cost is as follows:

$$\text{Cost of materials and subcontracting} = \sum_{t=1}^{6} 10\, P_t + \sum_{t=1}^{6} 30\, C_t$$

The total cost incurred during the planning horizon is a sum of all the previously mentioned costs and is given by the following:

$$\sum_{t=1}^{6} 640\, W_t + \sum_{t=1}^{6} 300\, H_t + \sum_{t=1}^{6} 500\, L_t + \sum_{t=1}^{6} 6\, O_t + \sum_{t=1}^{6} 2\, I_t + \sum_{t=1}^{6} 5\, S_t + \sum_{t=1}^{6} 10\, P_t + \sum_{t=1}^{6} 30\, C_t \qquad \textbf{(5.1)}$$

Red Tomato's objective is to find an aggregate plan that minimizes the total cost (see Equation 5.1) incurred during the planning horizon.

The values of the decision variables in the objective function cannot be arbitrarily set. They are subject to a variety of constraints. The next step in setting up the aggregate planning model is to define clearly the constraints linking the decision variables.

Constraints

Red Tomato's vice president now specifies the constraints that the decision variables may not violate. They are as follows:

- **Workforce, hiring, and layoff constraints**. The workforce size W_t in period t is related to the workforce size W_{t-1} in period $t-1$, the number hired H_t in period t, and the number laid off L_t in period t as follows:

$$W_t = W_{t-1} + H_t - L_t \quad \text{for} \quad t = 1, \ldots, 6 \qquad \textbf{(5.2)}$$

The starting workforce size is given by $W_0 = 80$.

- **Capacity constraints.** In each period, the amount produced cannot exceed the available capacity. This set of constraints limits the total production by the total internally available capacity (which is determined based on the available labor hours, regular or overtime). Subcontracted production is not included in this constraint; the constraint is limited to production within the plant. As each worker can produce 40 units per month on regular time (4 hours per unit, as specified in Table 5.2) and one unit for every 4 hours of overtime, we have the following:

$$P_t \leq 40W_t + O_t/4 \quad \text{for} \quad t = 1, \ldots, 6 \qquad \textbf{(5.3)}$$

- **Inventory balance constraints.** The third set of constraints balances inventory at the end of each period. Net demand for period t is obtained as the sum of the current demand D_t and the previous backlog S_{t-1}. This demand is either filled from current production (in-house production P_t or subcontracted production C_t) and previous inventory I_{t-1} (in which case some inventory I_t may be left over) or part of it is backlogged S_t. This relationship is captured by the following equation:

$$I_{t-1} + P_t + C_t = D_t + S_{t-1} + I_t - S_t \quad \text{for} \quad t = 1, \ldots 6 \qquad \textbf{(5.4)}$$

The starting inventory is given by $I_0 = 1{,}000$; the ending inventory must be at least 500 units, that is , $I_6 \geq 500$; and initially there are no backlogs, that is $S_0 = 0$.

- **Overtime limit constraints.** The fourth set of constraints requires that no employee work more than 10 hours of overtime each month. This requirement limits the total amount of overtime hours available as follows:

$$O_t \leq 10W_t \quad \text{for} \quad t = 1, \ldots, 6 \qquad \textbf{(5.5)}$$

In addition, each variable must be non-negative, and there must be no backlog at the end of period 6, that is, $S_6 = 0$.

When implementing the model in Excel, which we discuss later, it is easiest if all the constraints are written so that the right-hand side for each constraint is 0. The overtime limit constraint (Equation 5.5) in this form would be written as follows:

$$O_t - 10W_t \leq 0 \quad \text{for} \quad t = 1, \ldots, 6$$

Observe that one can easily add constraints that limit the amount purchased from subcontractors each month or the maximum number of employees to be hired or laid off. Any other constraints limiting backlogs or inventories can also be accommodated. Ideally, the number of employees should be an integer variable. However, we can obtain a good approximation by allowing the number of employees to take on fractional values. This change significantly speeds up the time taken to solve the problem. Such a linear program can be solved using the tool Solver in Excel.

If we assume the average inventory in period t to be the average of the starting and ending inventories—that is, $(I_{t-1} + I_t)/2$—the average inventory over the planning horizon is given by the following:

$$\text{Average inventory} = \left\{\left[(I_0 + I_T)/2 + \sum_{t=1}^{T-1} I_t\right]/T\right\}$$

The average flow time of the units over the planning horizon is obtained using Little's law (average flow time = average inventory / throughput). The average flow time is as follows:

$$\text{Average flow time} = \left\{\left[(I_0 + I_T)/2 + \sum_{t=1}^{T-1} I_t\right]/T\right\}/\left(\sum_{t-1}^{T} D_t/t\right) \quad \textbf{(5.6)}$$

By optimizing the objective function (minimizing cost in Equation 5.1) subject to the listed constraints (Equations 5.2–5.5), the vice president obtains the aggregate plan shown in Table 5.3. (Later in the chapter we discuss how to perform this optimization using Excel.)

For this aggregate plan we have the following:

Total cost over planning horizon = \$422,275

Red Tomato lays off a total of 15 employees in the beginning of January. After that, the company maintains the workforce and production level. It does not use the subcontractor during the entire planning horizon. The company carries a backlog only from April to May. In all other months, it plans no stockouts. In fact, Red Tomato carries inventory in all other periods. We describe this inventory as seasonal inventory because it is carried in anticipation of a future increase in demand. Given the sale price of \$40 per unit and total sales of 16,000 units, revenue over the planning horizon is as follows:

Revenue over planning horizon = 40 × 16,000 = \$640,000

TABLE 5.3 Aggregate Plan for Red Tomato

Period t	*No. Hired* H_t	*No. Laid Off* L_t	*Workforce Size* W_t	*Overtime* O_t	*Inventory* I_t	*Stockout* S_t	*Subcontract* C_t	*Total Production* P_t
0	0	0	80	0	1,000	0	0	
1	0	15	65	0	1,983	0	0	2,583
2	0	0	65	0	1,567	0	0	2,583
3	0	0	65	0	950	0	0	2,583
4	0	0	65	0	0	267	0	2,583
5	0	0	65	0	117	0	0	2,583
6	0	0	65	0	500	0	0	2,583

TABLE 5.4 Demand Forecast With Higher Seasonal Fluctuation

Month	*Demand Forecast*
January	1,000
February	3,000
March	3,800
April	4,800
May	2,000
June	1,400

The average seasonal inventory during the planning horizon is as follows:

$$\text{Average seasonal inventory} = \left[(I_0 + I_6)/2 + \sum_{t=1}^{5} I_t \right] / T = 5{,}367/6 = 895$$

The average flow time for this aggregate plan over the planning horizon (using Equation 5.6) is as follows:

$$\text{Average flow time} = 895 \,/\, 2{,}667 = 0.34 \text{ months}$$

If the seasonal fluctuation of demand grows, synchronization of supply and demand becomes more difficult, resulting in an increase in either inventory or backlogs as well as an increase in the total cost to the supply chain. This is illustrated in Example 5.1, in which the demand forecast is more variable.

Example 5.1: All the data are exactly the same as in our previous discussion of Red Tomato, except for the demand forecast. Assume that the same overall demand (16,000 units) is distributed over the six months in such a way that the seasonal fluctuation of demand is higher, as shown in Table 5.4.

Obtain the optimal aggregate plan in this case.

Analysis: In this case, the optimal aggregate plan (using the same costs as those used before) is shown in Table 5.5.

Observe that monthly production remains the same, but both inventories and stockouts (backlogs) go up compared with the aggregate plan in Table 5.3 for the demand profile in Table 5.1. The cost of meeting the new demand profile in Table 5.4 is higher at $432,858 (compared with $422,275 for the previous demand profile in Table 5.1).

TABLE 5.5 Optimal Aggregate Plan for Demand in Table 5.4

Period t	*No. Hired* H_t	*No. Laid Off* L_t	*Workforce Size* W_t	*Overtime* O_t	*Inventory* I_t	*Stockout* S_t	*Subcontract* C_t	*Total Production* P_t
0	0	0	80	0	1,000	0	0	
1	0	15	65	0	2,583	0	0	2,583
2	0	0	65	0	2,167	0	0	2,583
3	0	0	65	0	950	0	0	2,583
4	0	0	65	0	0	1,267	0	2,583
5	0	0	65	0	0	683	0	2,583
6	0	0	65	0	500	0	0	2,583

The seasonal inventory during the planning horizon is as follows:

$$\text{Seasonal inventory} = \left\{\left[(I_0 + I_T)/2 + \sum_{t=1}^{T-1} I_t\right]/T\right\} = 6{,}450/6 = 1{,}075$$

The average flow time for this aggregate plan over the planning horizon (using Equation 5.6) is as follows:

$$\text{Average flow time} = 1{,}075 \,/\, 2{,}667 = 0.40 \text{ months}$$

Using the Red Tomato example, we can also see that the optimal trade-off changes as the costs change. This is illustrated in Example 5.2, where we show that as holding costs increase, it is better to carry less inventory and resort to excess capacity, backlogs, or subcontracting.

Example 5.2: Assume that demand at Red Tomato is as shown in Table 5.1 and all other data are the same, except that holding cost per unit is increased from $2 per unit per month to $6 per unit per month. Evaluate the total cost corresponding to the aggregate plan in Table 5.3. Suggest an optimal aggregate plan for the new cost structure.

Analysis: If the holding cost increases from $2 per unit per month to $6 per unit per month, the cost corresponding to the aggregate plan in Table 5.3 would increase from $422,275 to $442,742. Taking this new cost into account and determining a new optimal aggregate plan yields the following plan shown in Table 5.6.

As expected, the inventory carried is reduced (because inventory holding cost has been raised) compared with the aggregate plan in Table 5.3. The aggregate plan has compensated by increasing the amount subcontracted. The total cost of the aggregate plan in Table 5.6 is $441,200 compared with $442,742 (for the aggregate plan in Table 5.3) if the holding cost is $6 per unit per month.

The seasonal inventory during the planning horizon is the following:

$$\text{Seasonal inventory} = \left\{\left[(I_0 + I_T)/2 + \sum_{t=1}^{T-1} I_t\right]/T\right\} = 3{,}350/6 = 558$$

The average flow time for this aggregate plan over the planning horizon (using Equation 5.6) is given by the following

$$\text{Average flow time} = 558 \,/\, 2{,}667 = 0.21 \text{ months}$$

Forecast Error in Aggregate Plans

The aggregate planning methodology we have discussed in this chapter does not take into account any forecast error. However, we know that all forecasts have errors. To improve the quality of these aggregate plans, forecast errors must be taken into account when formulating aggregate plans. Forecasting errors are dealt with using either **safety inventory**, defined as inventory held to satisfy demand that is higher than fore-

TABLE 5.6 Optimal Aggregate Plan for Holding Cost of $6/Unit/Month

Period t	*# Hired* H_t	*# Laid Off* L_t	*Workforce Size* W_t	*Overtime* O_t	*Inventory* I_t	*Stockout* S_t	*Subcontract* C_t	*Total Production* P_t
0	0	0	80	0	1,000	0	0	
1	0	23	57	0	1,667	0	0	2,267
2	0	0	57	0	933	0	0	2,267
3	0	0	57	0	0	0	0	2,267
4	0	0	57	0	0	67	1,467	2,267
5	0	0	57	0	0	0	0	2,267
6	0	0	57	0	500	0	433	2,267

casted, (discussed thoroughly in Chapter 8) or **safety capacity**, defined as capacity used to satisfy demand that is higher than forecasted. A company can create a buffer for forecast error using safety inventory and safety capacity in a variety of ways, such as the following:

- Use overtime as a form of safety capacity
- Carry extra workforce permanently as a form of safety capacity
- Use subcontractors as a form of safety capacity
- Build and carry extra inventories as a form of safety inventory
- Purchase capacity or product from an open or spot market as a form of safety capacity

The actions a company might take depend on the relative cost of the choices. Of course, if in practice a company can vary the capacity on short notice by hiring extra people, this is always an option. The problem with this option relates to the cost (monetary as well as morale) of letting them go later.

In the next section, we explain how to implement the linear programming methodology for aggregate planning using Microsoft Excel.

5.5 AGGREGATE PLANNING IN EXCEL

Aggregate plans can be obtained using linear programming in Microsoft Excel. We now discuss how to generate the aggregate plan for Red Tomato in Table 5.3 using Excel. To access Excel's linear programming capabilities, use Solver (Tools|Solver). To begin, we need to create a table, which we illustrate with Figure 5.1, containing the following decision variables:

W_t = Workforce size for month t, $t = 1, \ldots, 6$
H_t = Number of employees hired at the beginning of month t, $t = 1, \ldots, 6$
L_t = Number of employees laid off at the beginning of month t, $t = 1, \ldots, 6$
P_t = Number of units produced in month t, $t = 1, \ldots, 6$
I_t = Inventory at the end of month t, $t = 1, \ldots, 6$
S_t = Number of units stocked out at the end of month t, $t = 1, \ldots, 6$
C_t = Number of units subcontracted for month t, $t = 1, \ldots, 6$
O_t = Number of overtime hours worked in month t, $t = 1, \ldots, 6$

The first step is to build a table containing each decision variable. Figure 5.1 illustrates what this table should look like. The decision variables are contained in the

FIGURE 5.1 Spreadsheet Area for Decision Variables

Microsoft Excel - aggregateplan-chapter5-april18,00.xls

Aggregate Plan Decision Variables

	Ht	Lt	Wt	Ot	It	St	Ct	Pt	
Period	*# Hired*	*# Laid off*	*# Workforce*	*Overtime*	*Inventory*	*Stockout*	*Subcontract*	*Production*	*Demand*
0	0	0	80	0	1,000	0	0		
1	0	0	0	0	0	0	0	0	1,600
2	0	0	0	0	0	0	0	0	3,000
3	0	0	0	0	0	0	0	0	3,200
4	0	0	0	0	0	0	0	0	3,800
5	0	0	0	0	0	0	0	0	2,200
6	0	0	0	0	0	0	0	0	2,200

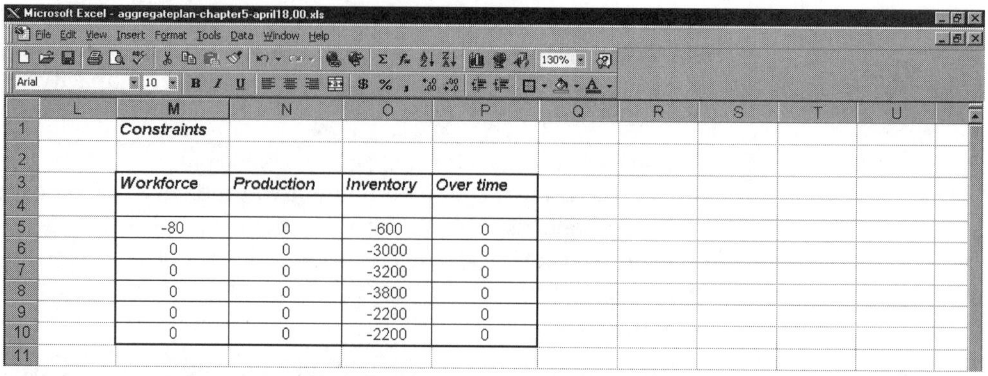

	L	M	N	O	P	Q	R	S	T	U
1		Constraints								
2										
3		Workforce	Production	Inventory	Over time					
4										
5		-80	0	-600	0					
6		0	0	-3000	0					
7		0	0	-3200	0					
8		0	0	-3800	0					
9		0	0	-2200	0					
10		0	0	-2200	0					
11										

FIGURE 5.2 Spreadsheet Area for Constraints

cells B5 to I10, with each cell corresponding to a decision variable. For instance, cell D7 corresponds to the workforce size in period 3. Begin by setting all the decision variables to 0, as shown in Figure 5.1.

Also note that column J contains the actual demand, which is not a decision variable. The demand information is included because it is required to calculate the aggregate plan.

The second step is to construct a table for the constraints in Equations 5.2 to 5.5. The constraint table may be constructed as shown in Figure 5.2. Each cell in this table contains a formula listed in Table 5.7.

The various formulas in Row 5 of the spreadsheet from column M to P correspond to constraints for period 1 and are shown in Table 5.7. Column M contains workforce constraints (Equation 5.2), column N contains capacity constraints (Equation 5.3), column O contains inventory balance constraints (Equation 5.4), and column P contains overtime constraints (Equation 5.5). These constraints are applied to each of the six periods.

Each constraint will eventually be written in Solver as follows:

$$\text{Cell value } \{\leq, =, \text{or} \geq\}\ 0$$

In our case, we will have the following constraints:

$$M5 = 0,\ N5 \geq 0,\ O5 = 0,\ P5 \geq 0$$

The third step is to create a cell containing the objective function, which is how each solution is judged. This cell need not contain the entire formula but can be written as a formula using cells with intermediate cost calculations. For the Red Tomato example, all cost calculations are shown in Figure 5.3. Cell B15, for instance, contains the hiring costs incurred in period 1. The formula in cell B15 is the product of cell B5

TABLE 5.7 Cell Formulas in Constraint Area

Cell	*M5*	*N5*	*O5*	*P5*
Constraint	Workforce (Equation 5.2)	Capacity (Equation 5.3)	Inventory (Equation 5.4)	Overtime (Equation 5.5)
Spreadsheet Formula	D5 − D4 − B5 + C5	40*D5 + E5/4 − I5	F4 − G4 + I5 + H5 − J5 − F5 + G5	− E5 + 10*D5
Actual Formula	$W_1 - W_0 + H_1 - L_1$	$40W_1 + O_1/4 - P_1$	$I_0 - S_0 + P_1 + C_1 - D_1 - I_1 + S_1$	$- O_1 + 10\,W_1$

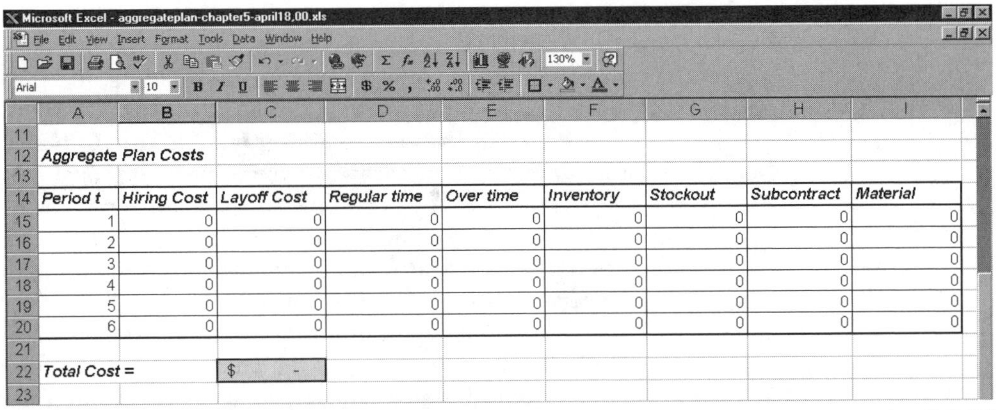

Microsoft Excel - aggregateplan-chapter5-april18,00.xls

Aggregate Plan Costs

Period t	Hiring Cost	Layoff Cost	Regular time	Over time	Inventory	Stockout	Subcontract	Material
1	0	0	0	0	0	0	0	0
2	0	0	0	0	0	0	0	0
3	0	0	0	0	0	0	0	0
4	0	0	0	0	0	0	0	0
5	0	0	0	0	0	0	0	0
6	0	0	0	0	0	0	0	0

Total Cost = $ -

FIGURE 5.3 Spreadsheet Area for Cost Calculations

and the cell containing the hiring cost per worker, which is obtained from Table 5.2 earlier in the chapter. Other cells are similarly filled. Cell C22 contains the sum of cells B15 to I20 and represents the total cost.

The fourth step is to use Tools|Solver to invoke Solver. Within the Solver parameters dialog box, enter the following information to represent the linear programming model:

Set target cell: C22
Equal to: Select *Min*
By changing cells: B5:I10
Subject to the constraints:

B5:I10≥0	{All decision variables are non-negative}
F10≥500	{Inventory at end of period 6 is at least 500}
G10 = 0	{Stockout at end of period 6 equals 0}
M5:M10 = 0	$\{W_t - W_{t-1} - H_t + L_t = 0 \text{ for } t = 1, \ldots, 6\}$
N5:N10≥0	$\{40W_t + O_t/4 - P_t \geq 0 \text{ for } t = 1, \ldots, 6\}$
O5:O10 = 0	$\{I_{t-1} - S_{t-1} + P_t + C_t - D_t - I_t + S_t = 0 \text{ for } t = 1, \ldots, 6\}$
P5:P10≥0	$\{10W_t - O_t \geq 0 \text{ for } t = 1, \ldots, 6\}$

Within the Solver parameters dialog box, click on Options and then select Assume Linear Model. (This will significantly speed up the solution time.) Return to the Solver parameters dialog box and click on Solve. The optimal solution should be returned. In case Solver does not return the optimal solution, solve the problem again after saving the solution that Solver has returned. (In some cases, multiple repetitions of this step may be required because of some flaws in Solver. Add-Ins are available at relatively low cost that do not have any of the problems associated with Solver.) The optimal solution turns out to be the one shown in Table 5.3.

5.6 IMPLEMENTING AGGREGATE PLANNING IN PRACTICE

Consider the following significant issues when implementing aggregate planning in practice:

- **Make plans flexible because forecasts are always wrong.** Aggregate plans are based on forecasts of future demand. Given that these forecasts are always wrong to some degree, the aggregate plan needs to have some flexibility built into it if it is to be useful. By building flexibility into the plan, when future demand changes or other changes occur such as increases in costs, the plan can appropriately adjust to handle the new situation.

How do we create this flexibility? In addition to the suggestions earlier in the chapter, we recommend that a manager perform sensitivity analysis on the inputs into aggregate plan. For example, if the plan recommends expanding expensive capacity while facing uncertain demand, the manager should examine the outcome of a new aggregate plan when demand is higher and when demand is lower than expected. If this examination reveals a small savings from expanding capacity when demand is high but a large increase in cost when demand is lower than expected, deciding to postpone the capacity investment decision is a potentially attractive option. Using sensitivity analysis on the inputs into the aggregate plan will enable the planner to choose the best solution for the range of possibilities that could occur.

- **Rerun the aggregate plan as new data emerges.** As we have mentioned, aggregate plans provide a map for the next 3 to 18 months. This does not mean that a firm should run aggregate plans only once every 3 to 18 months. As inputs into the aggregate plan change, managers should use the latest values of these inputs and rerun the aggregate plan. By using the latest inputs, the plan will avoid suboptimization based on old data and will produce a better solution. For instance, as new demand forecasts become available, aggregate plans should be reevaluated.
- **Use aggregate planning as capacity utilization increases.** Surprisingly, many companies do not create aggregate plans and instead rely solely on orders from their distributors or warehouses to determine their production schedules. These orders are driven either by actual demand or through inventory management algorithms. If a company has no trouble efficiently meeting demand this way, then the lack of aggregate planning may not significantly harm the company. However, when utilization becomes high and capacity is an issue, relying on orders to set the production schedule can lead to capacity problems. When utilization is high, the likelihood of producing for all the orders as they arrive is very low. Therefore, managers should plan to best utilize the capacity to meet the forecasted demand. Therefore, as capacity utilization increases, it becomes more important to perform aggregate planning.

5.7 SUMMARY OF LEARNING OBJECTIVES

1. Identify the types of decisions that are best solved by aggregate planning.

   Aggregate planning is best used to determine capacity, production, and inventory decisions for each period of time over a range of 3 to 18 months. It is most important to perform aggregate planning under conditions in which capacity is limited and lead times are long.
2. Describe the kind of information needed to produce an aggregate plan.

   To create an aggregate plan, a planner needs a demand forecast and cost and production information. The demand forecast consists of an estimate of demand for each period of time in the planning horizon. The production and cost data consist of capacity levels and costs to raise and lower them, costs to produce the product, costs to store the product, costs of stocking out of the product, and any restrictions that limit these factors.

3. Explain the basic trade-offs a manager makes to produce an aggregate plan.
The basic trade-offs involve balancing the cost of capacity, the cost of inventory, and the cost of stockouts in order to maximize profitability. Each of these costs has many components within them. How these costs are balanced to maximize profitability is generally expressed by either the chase, flexibility, or level strategies.

4. Formulate and solve aggregate planning problems using Microsoft Excel.
Aggregate planning problems can be solved in Excel by setting up cells for the objective function and the constraints and using the Solver to produce the solution.

Discussion Questions

1. What are some industries in which aggregate planning would be particularly important?
2. What are the characteristics of these industries that make them good candidates for aggregate planning?
3. What are the main differences among the aggregate planning strategies?
4. What types of industries or situations are best suited to the chase strategy? The flexibility strategy? The level strategy?
5. What are the major cost categories needed as inputs for aggregate planning?
6. How does the availability of subcontracting affect the aggregate planning problem?
7. If a company currently employs the chase strategy and the cost of training increases dramatically, how might this change its aggregate planning strategy?
8. How can aggregate planning be used in an environment of high demand uncertainty?

CASE STUDY

Specialty Packaging Corporation, Part B

Julie Williams, facility production planning manager at Specialty Packaging Corporation (SPC), left the meeting with her planning group with forecasts and error estimates for the next three years. Given that the plant would now be charged for storage and management of all sheet inventories, she had to decide whether to use public or private warehousing. She also had to decide how much warehouse space to lease or build if she chose to use private warehousing.

SPECIALTY PACKAGING CORPORATION

From the discussion of this case in Chapter 4, recall that SPC processes polystyrene resin into recyclable/disposable containers for the food industry. Polystyrene is purchased as a commodity in the form of resin pellets. The resin is unloaded from bulk rail containers or overland trailers into storage silos. Making the food containers is a two-step process. In the first step, resin is conveyed to an extruder, which turns pellets into polystyrene sheet that is wound into rolls. The plastic comes in two forms: clear and black. The rolls are then either used immediately to make containers or are put into storage. In the second step, the rolls are loaded onto thermoforming presses, which form the sheet into container cavities and trim the cavities from the sheet. These manufacturing steps are shown in Figure 4.1 in the previous chapter.

SPC currently operates for 63 working days each quarter. Each workday consists of eight hours of regular time and any overtime that may have been scheduled.

DEMAND FORECAST FOR NEXT THREE YEARS

Julie's planning group has used the historical demand data provided in Table 4.14 to develop a forecast for quarterly demand for both clear and black plastic containers. The demand forecast between 2001 and 2003 is shown in Table 5.8.

EXTRUDERS

The extrusion process is capital-intensive, as is the investment in the facilities required to support it. The plant currently has 14 extruders. Each extruder has a rated processing capacity of 2,400 pounds per hour. A changeover is required whenever the ex-

TABLE 5.8 Demand Forecast for Clear and Black Plastic Containers

Year	*Quarter*	*Black Plastic Forecast ('000 Lbs.)*	*Clear Plastic Forecast ('000 lbs.)*
2001	I	6,650	7,462
	II	4,576	18,250
	III	6,293	8,894
	IV	13,777	4,064
2002	I	7,509	8,349
	II	5,149	20,355
	III	7,056	9,891
	IV	15,399	4,507
2003	I	8,367	9,235
	II	5,721	22,461
	III	7,819	10,889
	IV	17,021	4,950
		MAD = 608	**MAD = 786**

truder switches between clear and black sheet. SPC estimates that there is a 5 percent capacity loss due to changeovers. The effective processing capacity of an extruder is thus 2,280 pounds per hour. Each extruder requires six workers. SPC pays each worker $15 per hour, including benefits. Overtime is paid at 150 percent of regular-time salary. Workers are limited to overtime of 60 hours per quarter.

Extruders are fairly expensive, and the addition of an extruder requires the hiring of six additional people. Each new extruder incurs a fixed cost of $80,000 per quarter. Any new personnel hired need to be trained. Training costs per person are $2,000. As a result, SPC has decided not to purchase any new extruders for the short term. During any quarter, extruders may be idled if they are not to be used. The only savings here is the salary of associated workers. Laying off each worker, however, costs $1,500. If idled extruders are brought on line, SPC incurs a training cost of $2,000 per worker.

THERMOFORMING PRESSES

The plant currently has 25 thermoforming presses. Each thermoforming press requires one operator and can produce containers at the rate of 2,000 pounds per hour. SPC pays each operator $15 per hour including benefits. Overtime is paid at 150 percent of regular time salary. Workers are limited to overtime of 60 hours per quarter. Presses may be idled for the quarter if they are not to be used. Laying off an operator costs $1,500 and training a newly hired operator costs $2,000.

SUBCONTRACTING

SPC has the option of subcontracting the production of plastic sheet; sufficient capacity is always available on the open market. SPC spends $100 per 1,000 pounds of plastic sheet produced by a subcontractor.

MATERIALS MANAGEMENT PRACTICES

Resin is available for $10 per 1,000 pounds. Resin purchased is stored in silos. As there is no shortage of resin in the market, it can easily be purchased at $10 per 1,000 pounds when needed. As a result, SPC's practice has been to purchase resin on a quarterly basis to match the planned production. This practice limits the amount of resin that must be held in inventory.

As the extruders produce rolls of plastic sheet, the amount required at the thermoforming presses is passed forward, with the rest driven via shuttle trailer to one of two public warehouses. Transportation is again required to bring the sheets back from the warehouse when they are needed to feed the thermoforming presses. SPC's total transportation cost is $2 per 1,000 pounds of plastic sheet.

PUBLIC WAREHOUSING

Public warehousing charges customers for both material handling and storage. The SPC plant contracts with local warehouses to store material on a per-1,000-pound basis. Material handling charges are from $4 to $6 per 1,000 pounds unloaded at the warehouse. Storage charges are from $10 to $12 per 1,000 pounds in storage at the end of each quarter. The SPC plant negotiates annually with local warehouses to establish rates for each cost element.

PRIVATE WAREHOUSING

Operating a private warehouse requires capitalized investment either to construct a facility or to lease an existing facility. Lease rates in any location are determined by the economics associated with building costs in that location and the option value of a lease versus a long-term capital commitment. Leases are typically in force for three years, but the time span can be shorter depending on a given company's negotiating strengths. Several viable leasing options exist for the SPC plant, all more favorable than the option of building a new facility. Lease rates average $4 per square foot per year in each location. On average, one square foot is required per 1,000 pounds in storage.

Private warehousing also results in operating costs, both variable and fixed. Private warehousing is available from a third-party logistics provider, who has agreed to charge SPC a variable operating cost of $3 per 1,000 pounds of plastic sheet stored per quarter. To obtain this rate, SPC must sign the lease for a full three years. As a result, SPC will pay for the space each quarter even if it is not used for storage. SPC must take this cost into account when making its decision.

SPC must consider several variables when determining the amount of warehouse space it requires. Usable warehousing space is the fraction of a warehouse that can actually be used to store inventory. Considerations are made for aisle space, shipping and receiving dock space, administrative office space, and ceiling height. Storage density is another consideration. SPC must also take into account velocity and times of materials movement, because the staffing level required and storage configurations are dependent upon both. For example, if materials must be retrieved readily, the warehouse layout must include a greater ratio of aisle and staging space to actual storage space.

THE ACTIONS AND DECISIONS

Julie and her group must take two actions. The first, given a three-year forecast as shown in Table 5.8, is to come up with an aggregate production plan. The second is to choose from the following three options:

1. Continue with the strategy of storing materials off site in public warehousing
2. Lease and run a private warehouse to handle off-site inventory
3. Use a combination of both public and private warehousing

In the case of private warehousing, Julie must make a decision regarding the square footage to be leased. This decision will apply over the period 2001 to 2003. Clearly, this decision must be made in conjunction with the preparation of an aggregate plan over the three-year period. Ideally, the two decisions should be made jointly, as each will affect the other.

What factors do you think influence the actions and decisions? For example, do you think that the price the subcontractor charges has any relationship to the amount of private warehousing space to be leased?

Julie also has to decide how to handle any potential error in the demand forecast. How do you recommend she handle these errors?

CHAPTER 6

Planning Supply and Demand in a Supply Chain: Managing Predictable Variability

Learning Objectives
After reading this chapter, you will be able to

1. manage supply to improve synchronization in the supply chain in the face of predictable variability;
2. manage demand to improve synchronization in the supply chain in the face of predictable variability; and
3. use aggregate planning to maximize profitability when faced with predictable variability.

In Chapter 5 we discuss how companies manage supply by using aggregate planning to make optimal trade-offs in a way that maximizes profits. In this chapter, we build upon the knowledge gained from Chapter 5 and focus on additional ways to manage supply in order to deal with predictable variability of demand. We also discuss how demand may be managed to counter predictable variability through the use of price and promotion. By managing supply and demand, managers can maximize overall profitability.

6.1 RESPONDING TO PREDICTABLE VARIABILITY IN A SUPPLY CHAIN

In Chapter 5 we discuss how companies use aggregate planning to plan supply to maximize profits. For products whose demand is stable with little change in volume from month to month, devising an aggregate plan is very simple. In such cases, a firm arranges for sufficient capacity to match the expected demand and then produces an amount to match that demand. Products are made close to the time when they will be sold. Therefore, the supply chain carries little inventory.

However, demand for many products changes rapidly from period to period, often due to a predictable influence. These influences include seasonal factors that affect products such as lawn mowers and ski jackets, as well as nonseasonal factors such as promotions or product adoption rates that may cause large, predictable increases and declines in sales.

Predictable variability is change in demand that can be forecasted. Products that undergo this type of change in demand cause numerous problems in the supply chain, ranging from high levels of stockouts during peak demand periods to high levels of excess inventory during periods of low demand. These problems increase the cost of products and decrease the responsiveness of the supply chain. Supply and demand management will have the greatest impact when it is applied to predictably variable products.

Faced with predictable variability, a company's goal is to respond in a manner that maximizes profitability. A firm must choose between two broad options to handle predictable variability:

1. Manage supply using capacity, inventory, subcontracting, and backlogs
2. Manage demand using short-term price discounts and trade promotions

To illustrate some of the issues involved, let us consider the garden equipment manufacturer discussed in Chapter 5, Red Tomato Tools. Demand for garden tools is seasonal, with sales concentrated in the spring. Red Tomato needs to plan how it will meet the demand to maximize profit. One way to meet demand requires that Red Tomato carry enough manufacturing capacity to meet demand in any period. The advantage of this approach is that Red Tomato incurs very low inventory costs because no inventory needs to be carried from period to period. However, the disadvantage is that much of the expensive capacity would go unused during most months when demand was lower. Another approach to meeting demand would be to build up inventory during the off season while keeping production stable year round. The advantage of this approach lies in the fact that Red Tomato could get by with a smaller, less expensive factory. However, high inventory carrying costs make this alternative expensive. A third approach would be for Red Tomato to offer a price promotion before the spring months during periods of low demand. This promotion shifts some of the spring demand forward into a slow period, thereby spreading demand more evenly throughout the year and reducing the seasonal surge. As discussed in Chapter 5, such a demand pattern is less expensive to supply. Red Tomato needs to decide which alternative maximizes its profitability.

Often companies divide the task of supply and demand management between different functions: Marketing typically manages demand, and operations typically manages supply. Separating the supply and demand management decisions makes it increasingly difficult to coordinate the supply chain, thereby decreasing profit. Therefore, maximizing profitability depends on these decisions being made in a coordinated fashion. We illustrate how a company can achieve this coordination through our further discussion of Red Tomato.

First, we focus on actions that a supply chain can take to improve profitability by managing supply.

6.2 MANAGING SUPPLY

A firm can vary supply of product by controlling a combination of the following two factors:

- Production capacity
- Inventory

The objective is to maximize profit, which, for our discussion, is the difference between revenue generated from sales and the total cost associated with capacity and inventory. In general, companies use a combination of varying capacity and inventory when managing supply. We list some specific approaches to managing capacity and inventory (the components of supply) with the goal of maximizing profits.

Managing Capacity

When managing capacity to meet predictable variability, firms use a combination of the following approaches:

- **Time flexibility from workforce**. In this approach, a firm uses flexible work hours from the workforce to better match production with demand. In many instances, plants do not operate continually and are left idle during portions of the day and week. Therefore, spare plant capacity exists in the form of hours when the plant is not operational. For example, many plants do not run three shifts, so the existing workforce could work overtime during peak periods to produce more to meet demand. The overtime used is varied to match the variation in demand. This system would allow production from the plant to more closely match the demand from customers. If demand fluctuates by day of the week or week of the month and the workforce is willing to be flexible, a firm may schedule the workforce so that the available capacity better matches demand. In such settings, use of a part-time workforce may further increase the capacity flexibility by enabling the firm to have more people working during peak periods. Telemarketing centers and banks use part-time workers extensively to match supply and demand better.
- **Use of seasonal workforce**. In this approach, a firm uses a temporary workforce during the peak season to increase capacity to match demand. The tourism industry often employs this approach, in which a base of full-time employees exists and the rest are hired only for the peak season. Agriculture also uses seasonal workers for both harvesting and processing. This approach may be hard to sustain if the labor market is tight.
- **Use of subcontracting**. In this approach, a firm subcontracts peak production so that internal production remains level and can be done cheaply. With the subcontractor handling the peaks, the company is able to build a relatively inflexible but low-cost facility where the production rates are kept relatively constant (other than variations that arise from the use of overtime). Peaks are subcontracted out to facilities that are more flexible. A key here is the availability of relatively flexible subcontractor capacity. The subcontractor can often provide flexibility at a lower cost by pooling the fluctuations in demand across different manufacturers. Thus, the flexible subcontractor capacity must have both volume (fluctuating demand from a manufacturer) and variety flexibility (demand from several manufacturers) to be sustain-

able. For example, most power companies do not have the capacity to supply their customers with all the electricity demanded on peak days. They instead rely on being able to purchase that power from suppliers and subcontractors who have excess electricity. This allows the power companies to maintain a level supply and, subsequently, a lower cost.

- **Use of dual facilities—dedicated and flexible**. In this approach, a firm builds both dedicated and flexible facilities. Dedicated facilities produce a relatively stable output of products over time in a very efficient manner. Flexible facilities produce a widely varying volume and variety of products but at a higher unit cost. For instance, a personal computer components manufacturer could have dedicated facilities for different types of circuit boards as well as a flexible facility that could manufacture all types of circuit boards. Each dedicated facility could produce at a relatively steady rate, with fluctuations being absorbed by the flexible facility.
- **Designing product flexibility into the production processes**. In this approach, a firm has flexible production lines whose production rate can easily be varied. Production is then changed to match demand. Hino Trucks in Japan has several production lines for different product families. The production lines are designed such that changing the number of workers on a line can vary the production rate. As long as variation of demand across different product lines is complementary—that is, when one goes up, the other tends to go down—the capacity on each line can be varied by moving the workforce from one line to the other. Of course this requires that the workforce be multiskilled and able to adapt easily to being moved from line to line. Production flexibility can also be achieved if the production machinery being used is flexible and can be changed easily from producing one product to another. This approach can be effective only if the overall demand across all the products is relatively constant. Several firms making products with seasonal demand try to exploit this approach by carrying a portfolio of products that have peak demand seasons distributed over the year. A classic example is lawn mower manufacturers that also make snowblowers. Many strategy consulting firms also offer a balanced portfolio of products, with growth strategies purchased primarily when economic times are good, and cost-cutting projects typically purchased when times are not so good.

Managing Inventory

When managing inventory to meet predictable variability, firms use a combination of the following approaches:

- **Using common components across multiple products**. In this approach, a firm designs common components across multiple products, each with predictably variable demand but with a relatively constant overall demand. Using common components across these products will result in the demand for the components being relatively constant. For example, using a common engine for both lawn mowers and snowblowers allows for engine demand to be relatively stable, even though lawn mower and snowblower demand fluctuates over the year. Therefore, the part of the supply chain producing components can easily synchronize supply with demand, and a relatively low inventory of parts will have to be built up. Similarly, in a consulting firm, many of the same consultants produce growth strategies when they are in demand and cost reduction strategies when they are in demand.

- **Build inventory of high demand or predictable demand products**. When most of the products a firm produces have the same peak demand season, the previous approach is no longer feasible. A firm must then decide which inventory to build during the off season. The answer is to build products with the more predictable demand during the off season because there is less to be learned about their demand by waiting. As more is known about demand closer to the selling season, production of more uncertain items should take place. As an example, imagine a manufacturer of winter jackets that produces jackets both for retail sale and for the New York police and fire departments. Demand for the New York police and fire jackets will be much more predictable, and these jackets can be made in the off season and stocked up until winter. However, the retail jacket's demand will likely be better known closer to the time when it will be sold because fashion trends can change quickly. Therefore, this jacket manufacturer should make the retail jackets close to the peak season when they are being sold to enable them to gain as much knowledge of demand as they can. This strategy helps the supply chain better synchronize supply and demand.

Next we consider actions a supply chain can take to improve profitability by managing demand.

6.3 MANAGING DEMAND

In many instances, supply chains can influence demand in different periods of the year using pricing and other forms of promotion. Typically, marketing and sales make the promotion and pricing decisions, and they make them with the objective of maximizing revenue. But as we know from Chapter 5, changing the demand pattern can change the cost the company incurs to meet that demand. Therefore, pricing decisions based only on revenue considerations often result in a decrease in overall profitability. In this section, our goal is to show how the combination of pricing and aggregate planning (both demand and supply management) may be used to maximize supply chain profitability.

Let us return to Red Tomato Tools, the garden equipment manufacturer. Demand for its garden tools peaks in the spring months of March and April as gardeners prepare to begin planting. Red Tomato is exploring how promotions can increase its profitability. A key decision its managers must make is how to time the promotion. Are they in a better position if they offer the price promotion during the peak period of demand or during a low demand period? The vice president of marketing favors a promotion during the peak period because this will increase revenue by the largest amount. However, the vice president of manufacturing is against such a move because it will increase costs. She favors a promotion during the low demand season because it will level demand and lower production costs.

The optimal timing of a promotion (and the decision of whether to offer it at all) depends on the revenue generated by the promotion at different times and the impact on costs of the change in demand. In the following discussion, we show how different factors influence the promotion decision. Red Tomato must start by considering the forecasted demand and the resulting optimal aggregate plan. (This is the same as discussed in Chapter 5.) Red Tomato's marketing department has forecast demand over the next six months as shown in Table 6.1.

Each tool has a sale price of $40. The company has a starting inventory in January of 1,000 tools. At the beginning of January the company has a workforce of 80 em-

TABLE 6.1 Demand at Red Tomato Tools

Month	*Demand Forecast*
January	1,600
February	3,000
March	3,200
April	3,800
May	2,200
June	2,200

TABLE 6.2 Costs for Red Tomato Tools

Item	*Cost*
Material cost	$10/unit
Inventory holding cost	$2.00/unit/month
Marginal cost of a stockout	$5/unit/month
Hiring and training costs	$300/worker
Layoff cost	$500/worker
Labor hours required	4/unit
Regular time cost	$4/hour
Overtime cost	$6/hour
Cost of subcontracting	$30/unit

ployees. There are a total of 20 working days in each month and Red Tomato workers earn $4 per nonovertime hour. Each employee works 8 hours on normal time and the rest on overtime. Because the Red Tomato operation consists mostly of hand assembly, the capacity of the production operation is determined primarily by the total labor-hours worked; that is, it is not limited by machine capacity. No employee works more than 10 hours of overtime per month. The various costs are shown in Table 6.2.

There are no limits on subcontracting, inventories, and stockouts. All stockouts are backlogged and supplied from the following months' production. Inventory costs are incurred on the ending inventory of each month. Red Tomato's goal is to obtain the optimal aggregate plan that allows the company to end June with at least 500 units (i.e., no stockouts at the end of June and at least 500 units in inventory).

The optimal aggregate plan for Red tomato is shown in Table 6.3.

For this aggregate plan, Red Tomato will obtain the following costs and revenues:

$$\text{Total cost over planning horizon} = \$422{,}275$$

Given the sale price of $40/unit and total sales of 16,000 units, revenue over the planning horizon is given by the following:

$$\text{Revenue over planning horizon} = 40 \times 16{,}000 = \$640{,}000$$
$$\text{Profit over the planning horizon} = \$217{,}725$$

The average seasonal inventory during the planning horizon is given by the following:

$$\text{Average seasonal inventory} = \left[(I_0 + I_6)/2 + \sum_{t=1}^{5} I_t \right] / T = 5{,}367/6 = 895$$

TABLE 6.3 Aggregate Plan for Red Tomato

Period t	*No. Hired* H_t	*No. Laid Off* L_t	*Workforce Size* W_t	*Overtime* O_t	*Inventory* I_t	*Stockout* S_t	*Subcontract* C_t	*Total Production* P_t
0	0	0	80	0	1,000	0	0	
1	0	15	65	0	1,983	0	0	2,583
2	0	0	65	0	1,567	0	0	2,583
3	0	0	65	0	950	0	0	2,583
4	0	0	65	0	0	267	0	2,583
5	0	0	65	0	117	0	0	2,583
6	0	0	65	0	500	0	0	2,583

The average flow time for this aggregate plan over the planning horizon is given by the following:

Average flow time = average inventory / average sales = 895 / 2,667 = 0.34 months

These results all pertain to the situation in which Red Tomato offers no promotion. Now Red Tomato wants to explore if and when to offer a promotion. Four key factors influence the timing of a trade promotion:

- Impact of the promotion on demand
- Product margins
- Cost of holding inventory
- Cost of changing capacity

Managers at Red Tomato would like to identify whether each factor favors offering a promotion during the high or low demand periods. They start by considering the impact of promotion on demand. When a promotion is offered during a period, that period's demand will tend to go up. This increase in demand results from a combination of the following three factors:

1. **Market growth**. An increase in consumption of the product either from new or existing customers. For an example outside the garden tool industry, Red Tomato looks at Toyota. When Toyota offers a price promotion on the Camry, it may attract buyers who were considering the purchase of a lower-end model. Thus, the promotion increases the size of the overall family sedan market as well as increasing Toyota's sales.

2. **Stealing share**. Customers substituting the firm's product for a competitor's product. When Toyota offers a Camry promotion, buyers who might have purchased a Honda Accord may now purchase a Camry. Thus, the promotion increases Toyota's sales while keeping the overall size of the family sedan market the same.

3. **Forward buying**. Customers move up future purchases (as is discussed in Chapter 7) to the present. A promotion may attract buyers who would have purchased a Camry a few months down the road. The promotion does not increase Toyota's sales in the long run and also leaves the family sedan market the same size.

The first two factors increase the overall demand for Toyota, whereas the third simply shifts future demand to the present. It is important to know the relative impact from the three factors as a result of a promotion before making the decision regarding the optimal timing of the promotion. In general, as the fraction of increased demand coming from forward buying grows, offering the promotion during the peak demand period becomes less attractive. Offering a promotion during a peak period that has significant forward buying creates even more variable demand than before the promotion. Product that was once demanded in the slow period is now demanded in the peak period, making this demand pattern even more costly to serve.

The sales department at Red Tomato has estimated that discounting a unit from $40 to $39 (a $1 discount) results in the period demand's increasing by 10 percent because of increased consumption or substitution. Further, 20 percent of each of the two following months demand is moved forward. The management of Red Tomato would like to determine whether it is more effective to offer the discount in January or April.

Red Tomato first considers the impact of offering the discount in January. If the discount is offered in January, the demand forecast is as shown in Table 6.4. The opti-

TABLE 6.4 Demand When Discounting Price in January to $39

Month	*Demand Forecast*
January	3,000
February	2,400
March	2,560
April	3,800
May	2,200
June	2,200

mal aggregate plan is shown in Table 6.5. With a discount in January, Red Tomato obtains the following:

Total cost over planning horizon = $421,915
Revenue over planning horizon = $643,400
Profit over planning horizon = $221,485

Now they consider the impact of offering the discount in April. If Red Tomato offers the discount in April, the demand forecast is as shown in Table 6.6. The optimal aggregate plan is shown in Table 6.7. With a discount in April, we have the following:

Total cost over planning horizon = $438,857
Revenue over planning horizon = $650,140
Profit over planning horizon = $211,283

Observe that the demand fluctuation has increased relative to the profile in Table 6.1 because the discount was offered in the highest demand month. The optimal aggregate plan for this demand pattern is shown in Table 6.7.

Observe that a price promotion in January results in a higher profit than no promotion, whereas a promotion in April results in a lower profit than no promotion. As a result, Red Tomato should offer the discount in the off-peak month of January. Even though revenues are higher when the discount is offered in April, the increase in operating costs makes it a less profitable option. This conclusion supports our earlier statement that it is not appropriate for a firm to leave pricing decisions solely in the domain of marketing and aggregate planning solely in the domain of operations, with each having their own forecasts. It is crucial that forecasts, pricing, and aggregate planning be coordinated in the supply chain.

The conclusion would be different if Red Tomato were in a situation in which most of the demand increase comes from market growth or stealing market share rather than forward buying. Reconsider the Red Tomato situation in which discounting a unit from $40 to $39 results in the period demand's increasing by 100 percent because of increased consumption or substitution. Further, 20 percent of each of the two following months' demand is moved forward. Management would like to determine whether it is preferable to offer the discount in January or April.

Offering the discount in January results in the demand forecast shown in Table 6.8.

TABLE 6.5 Optimal Aggregate Plan for Demand in Table 6.4

Period t	*No. Hired* H_t	*No. Laid Off* L_t	*Workforce Size* W_t	*Overtime* O_t	*Inventory* I_t	*Stockout* S_t	*Subcontract* C_t	*Total Production* P_t
0	0	0	80	0	1,000	0	0	
1	0	15	65	0	610	0	0	2,610
2	0	0	65	0	820	0	0	2,610
3	0	0	65	0	870	0	0	2,610
4	0	0	65	0	0	320	0	2,610
5	0	0	65	0	90	0	0	2,610
6	0	0	65	0	500	0	0	2,610

TABLE 6.6 Demand Profile on Discounting Price in April to $39

Month	*Demand Forecast*
January	1,600
February	3,000
March	3,200
April	5,060
May	1,760
June	1,760

TABLE 6.7 Optimal Aggregate Plan for Demand in Table 6.6

Period t	*No. Hired* H_t	*No. Laid Off* L_t	*Workforce Size* W_t	*Overtime* O_t	*Inventory* I_t	*Stockout* S_t	*Subcontract* C_t	*Total Production* P_t
0	0	0	80		1,000	0	0	
1	0	14	66	0	2,047	0	0	2,647
2	0	0	66	0	1,693	0	0	2,647
3	0	0	66	0	1,140	0	0	2,647
4	0	0	66	0	0	1,273	0	2,647
5	0	0	66	0	0	387	0	2,647
6	0	0	66	0	500	0	0	2,647

TABLE 6.8 Demand Profile from Discounting Price in January to $39 with Large Increase in Demand

Month	*Demand Forecast*
January	4,440
February	2,400
March	2,560
April	3,800
May	2,200
June	2,200

TABLE 6.9 Optimal Aggregate Plan for Demand in Table 6.8

Period t	*No. Hired* H_t	*No. Laid Off* L_t	*Workforce Size* W_t	*Overtime* O_t	*Inventory* I_t	*Stockout* S_t	*Subcontract* C_t	*Total Production* P_t
0	0	0	80		1,000	0	0	
1	0	0	80	0	0	240	0	3,200
2	0	11	69	0	140	0	0	2,780
3	0	0	69	0	360	0	0	2,780
4	0	0	69	0	0	660	0	2,780
5	0	0	69	0	0	80	0	2,780
6	0	0	69	0	500	0	0	2,780

The optimal aggregate plan in this case is shown in Table 6.9.
With a discount in January Red Tomato obtains the following:

Total cost over planning horizon = \$456,750
Revenue over planning horizon = \$699,560
Profit over planning horizon = \$242,810

If the discount is offered in April, the demand forecast is as shown in Table 6.10.

The optimal aggregate plan in this case is shown in Table 6.11.
With a discount in April Red Tomato obtains the following:

Total cost over planning horizon = \$536,200
Revenue over planning horizon = \$783,520
Profit over planning horizon = \$247,320

When forward buying is a small part of the increase in demand from discounting, Red Tomato is better off offering the discount in the peak demand month of April.

Exactly as discussed previously, the optimal aggregate plan and profitability for Red Tomato can also be determined for the case when the unit price is \$31 and the discounted price is \$30. The results of the various instances are summarized in Table 6.12.

TABLE 6.10 Demand Profile on Discounting Price in April to \$39 with Large Increase in Demand

Month	*Demand Forecast*
January	1,600
February	3,000
March	3,200
April	8,480
May	1,760
June	1,760

TABLE 6.11 Optimal Aggregate Plan for Demand in Table 6.10

Period t	*No. Hired* H_t	*No. Laid Off* L_t	*Workforce Size* W_t	*Overtime* O_t	*Inventory* I_t	*Stockout* S_t	*Subcontract* C_t	*Total Production* P_t
0	0	0	80		1,000	0	0	
1	0	0	80	0	2,600	0	0	3,200
2	0	0	80	0	2,800	0	0	3,200
3	0	0	80	0	2,800	0	0	3,200
4	0	0	80	0	0	2,380	100	3,200
5	0	0	80	0	0	940	0	3,200
6	0	0	80	0	500	0	0	3,200

From the results for Red Tomato in Table 6.12, we can draw the following conclusions regarding the impact of promotions:

1. As seen in Table 6.12, average inventory increases if a promotion is run during the peak period and decreases if the promotion is run during the off-peak period.

2. Promoting during a peak demand month may decrease overall profitability if a significant fraction of the demand increase results from a forward buy. In Table 6.12, observe that running a promotion in April decreases profitability for Red Tomato when forward buying is 20 percent and the demand increase from increased consumption and substitution is also 20 percent.

3. As forward buying becomes a smaller fraction of the demand increase from a promotion, it becomes more profitable to promote during the peak period. From Table 6.12, for a sale price of $40, Red Tomato finds it optimal to promote in the off-peak month of January, when forward buying is 20 percent and increased consumption is also 20 percent. However, when forward buying is 20 percent and increased consumption is 100 percent, Red Tomato finds it optimal to promote in the peak month of April.

4. As product margin declines, promoting during the peak demand period becomes less profitable. In Table 6.12, observe that for a unit price of $40 it is optimal for Red Tomato to promote in the peak month of April when forward buying is 20 percent and increased consumption is 100 percent. In contrast, if the unit price is $31, Red Tomato finds it optimal to promote in the off-peak month of January.

TABLE 6.12 Red Tomato Performance Under Different Scenarios

Regular Price	*Promotion Price*	*Promotion Period*	*Percent Increase in Demand*	*Percent Forward Buy*	*Profit*	*Average Inventory*
$40	$40	NA	NA	NA	$217,725	895
$40	$39	January	20%	20%	$221,485	523
$40	$39	April	20%	20%	$211,283	938
$40	$39	January	100%	20%	$242,810	208
$40	$39	April	100%	20%	$247,320	1,492
$31	$31	NA	NA	NA	$73,725	895
$31	$30	January	100%	20%	$84,410	208
$31	$30	April	100%	20%	$69,120	1,492

TABLE 6.13 Summary of Impact on Promotion Timing

Factor	*Impact on Timing of Promotion*
High forward buying	Favors promotion during low demand periods
High ability to steal market share	Favors promotion during peak demand periods
High ability to grow overall market	Favors promotion during peak demand periods
High margin	Favors promotion during peak demand periods
Low margin	Favors promotion during low demand periods
High holding costs	Favors promotion during low demand periods
High costs of changing capacity	Favors promotion during low demand periods

Other factors, such as holding cost and the cost of changing capacity, also affect the optimal timing of promotions. The various factors and their impacts are summarized in Table 6.13.

A key point from the Red Tomato examples we have considered in this chapter is that, faced with seasonal demand, a firm may use a combination of pricing (to manage demand) and production and inventory (to manage supply) to improve profitability. The precise use of each lever varies with the situation. This makes it crucial that marketing and operations coordinate both their forecasting and planning efforts. Only then are profits maximized.

6.4 IMPLEMENTING SOLUTIONS TO PREDICTABLE VARIABILITY IN PRACTICE

Consider the following when implementing solutions to predictable variability:

- **Coordinate marketing and operations**. For a company to manage predictable variability successfully, the entire company must work toward the one goal of maximizing profitability. Everyone in a company will agree with this in principle, but in reality, it is difficult to get an entire organization to agree on how to maximize profitability. Marketing often has incentives based on revenue while operations has incentives based on cost. From the examples considered in this chapter, it is clear that such incentives will result in suboptimal profits because actions that maximize revenues or minimize costs may not maximize profits. Therefore, firms must develop incentives that encourage marketing and operations to coordinate their efforts so that pricing and aggregate planning are always coordinated. Often, it may be necessary to have a single person or group responsible for this coordination. High-level support within the organization, including support from the chief executive officer, will also be needed, because this coordination often requires groups to act counter to their traditional operating procedures.
- **Take predictable variability into account when making strategic decisions**. Predictable variability has a tremendous impact on the operations of a company. A firm must always take this impact into account when making strategic decisions. However, predictable variability is not always taken into account when strategic plans are made, such as what type of products to offer, whether to build new facilities, and what sort of pricing structure a company should have. As indicated in this chapter, the level of profitability is greatly affected by predictable variability, and therefore, the success or failure of strategic decisions can be determined by it.

- **Preempt, do not just react to, predictable variability**. Companies often tend to focus on how they can effectively react to predictable variability. This role often falls on operations, which tries to manage supply to best deal with predictable variability. As discussed in this chapter, the management of supply as well as demand provides the best response to predictable variability. Actions like pricing and promotion that manage demand are preemptive and often in the domain of marketing. It is important for marketing and operations to coordinate their efforts and plan for predictable variability together well before the peak demand is observed. This coordination allows a firm to preempt predictable variability and come up with a response that maximizes profits.

6.5 SUMMARY OF LEARNING OBJECTIVES

1. Manage supply to improve synchronization in the supply chain in the face of predictable variability.

   To manage supply with the goal of maximizing profit, companies must manage their capacity through the use of workforce flexibility, subcontracting, dual facilities, and product flexibility. Companies must also manage supply through the use of inventory by emphasizing common parts and building and holding products with predictable demand ahead of time. These methodologies, combined with aggregate planning, enable a company to manage supply effectively.
2. Manage demand to improve synchronization in the supply chain in the face of predictable variability.

   To manage demand with the goal of maximizing profit, companies must use pricing and promotion decisions. The timing of these tools can often have a tremendous impact on demand. Therefore, using pricing to shape demand can help synchronize the supply chain.
3. Use aggregate planning to maximize profitability when faced with predictable variability.

   To handle predictable variability in a profit-maximizing manner, companies must coordinate the management of both supply and demand. This can be done by selecting aggregate plans that maximize profit.

Discussion Questions

1. What are some obstacles to creating a flexible workforce? What are the benefits?
2. Discuss why subcontractors can often offer products and services to a company more cheaply than if the company produced them itself.
3. In what type of industries would you tend to see dual facility types (some facilities focusing on only one type of product and others able to produce a wide variety)? In what industries would this be relatively rare? Why?
4. What are some product lines that use common parts across many products? What are the advantages of doing this?
5. Discuss how a company can get marketing and operations to work together with the common goal of coordinating supply and demand to maximize profitability.
6. How can a firm use pricing to change demand patterns?
7. When would a firm want to offer pricing promotions in its peak demand periods?
8. When would a firm want to offer pricing promotions during its low demand periods?

CASE STUDY

Mintendo Game Girl

It is late June, and Sandra, head of operations at Mintendo, and Bill, head of marketing for the company, are about to get together to discuss production and marketing plans for the next six months. Mintendo is the manufacturer of the popular Game Girl handheld electronic game. The second half of the year is critical to Game Girl's success, because a majority of Mintendo's sales occur during this period due to the holiday season.

Sandra is worried about the impact that the upcoming holiday surge in demand will have on her production line. Costs to subcontract assembly of the Game Girls are expected to increase, and she has been trying to keep costs down given that her bonus depends on the level of production costs.

Bill is worried about competing products gaining share during the Christmas buying season. He has seen many companies lose their share by failing to keep prices in line with the performance of their products. He would like to maximize the Game Girl market share.

Both Sandra and Bill agree with the marketing department's forecast of demand over the next six months, shown in Table 6.14.

Mintendo sells Game Girls to retailers for $50 a piece. At the end of June, the company has an inventory of 50,000 Game Girls. Capacity of the production facility is set purely by the number of workers assembling the Game Girls. At the end of June, the company has a workforce of 300 employees, each of whom work 8 hours of nonovertime at $15/hour for 20 days each month. Work rules require that no employee work more than 40 hours a week. The various costs are shown in Table 6.15.

TABLE 6.14 Demand for Game Girls

Month	*Demand Forecast*
July	100,000
August	110,000
September	130,000
October	180,000
November	250,000
December	300,000

Sandra, concerned about controlling costs during the periods of surging demand over the holidays, proposes to Bill that the price be lowered by $5 for the month of September. This would likely increase September's demand by 50 percent due to new customers attracted to Game Girl. In addition, 30 percent of each of the following two months of demand would occur in September as forward buys. She strongly believes that this leveling of demand will help the company.

Bill counters with the idea of offering the same promotion in November, during the heart of the buying season. In this case, the promotion increases November's demand by 50 percent due to new customers attracted to Game Girl. In addition, 30 percent of December's demand would occur in November as forward buying. Bill wants to increase revenue and sees no better way to do this than to offer a promotion during the peak season.

QUESTIONS

1. Which option delivers the maximum profit for Mintendo: Sandra's plan, Bill's plan, or no promotion plan at all?
2. How does the answer change if a discount of $10 must be given to reach the same level of impact that the $5 discount received?
3. Suppose Sandra's fears about increasing outsourcing costs come to fruition and the cost rises to $22/unit for subcontracting. Does this change the decision when the discount is $5?

TABLE 6.15 Costs for Mintendo

Item	*Cost*
Material cost	$12/unit
Inventory holding cost	$4.00/unit/month
Marginal cost of a stockout	$10/unit/month
Hiring and training costs	$000/worker
Layoff cost	$5000/worker
Labor-hours required	0.25/unit
Regular time cost	$15/hour
Overtime cost	$22.50/hour
Cost of subcontracting	$18/unit

PART THREE

Planning and Managing Inventories in a Supply Chain

CHAPTER 7

Managing Economies of Scale in a Supply Chain: Cycle Inventory

CHAPTER 8

Managing Uncertainty in a Supply Chain: Safety Inventory

CHAPTER 9

Determining Optimal Level of Product Availability

The goal of the three chapters in this module is to describe the role that inventory plays in a supply chain and discuss actions that managers can take to decrease inventories without increasing cost or hurting the level of product availability. The module also describes how supply chain managers can manage sourcing for their products to improve supply chain profits.

Chapter 7 discusses factors that lead to the increase of cycle inventory within a supply chain. Several managerial actions that allow a supply chain manager to decrease the level of cycle inventory without increasing costs are described. Chapter 8 focuses on the buildup of safety inventory to counter supply or demand uncertainty. Factors influencing the level of safety inventory are discussed. Based on these factors, a variety of managerial levers are explained that can be used to reduce the amount of safety inventory required without hurting the level of product availability within a supply chain. Chapter 9 discusses factors that influence the appropriate level of product availability within a supply chain. Several managerial levers that can be used to increase overall profitability in the supply chain such as quick response and postponement, are described. The use of sourcing strategies and supply chain contracts to increase total profits is also discussed.

CHAPTER 7

Managing Economies of Scale in a Supply Chain: Cycle Inventory

Learning Objectives

After reading this chapter, you will be able to

1. balance the appropriate costs in order to choose the optimal amount of cycle inventory in a supply chain;
2. understand the impact of quantity discounts on lot size and cycle inventory;
3. devise appropriate discounting schemes for a supply chain;
4. understand the impact of trade promotions on lot size and cycle inventory; and
5. identify managerial levers that reduce lot size and cycle inventory in a supply chain without increasing cost.

Cycle inventory exists because producing or purchasing in large lots allows a stage of the supply chain to exploit economies of scale and lower cost. The presence of fixed costs associated with ordering and transportation, quantity discounts in product pricing, and short-term discounts or trade promotions encourages different stages of a supply chain to exploit economies of scale and order in large lots. In this chapter, we study how each of these factors affects the lot size and cycle inventories within the supply chain. We also identify managerial levers that reduce cycle inventory in the supply chain without raising cost.

7.1 THE ROLE OF CYCLE INVENTORY IN A SUPPLY CHAIN

A **lot** or **batch size** is the quantity that a stage of the supply chain either produces or purchases at a given time. Consider, for example, a computer store that sells printers. The store sells an average of four printers a day. The store manager, however, orders 80 printers from the manufacturer each time he places an order. The lot or batch size in this case is 80 printers. All 80 printers do not sell as soon as they arrive. Given daily sales of four printers, it takes on average 20 days before the store sells the entire lot and purchases a replenishment lot. The computer store holds an inventory of printers because the manager purchased a lot size larger than the store's daily sales. **Cycle inventory** is the average inventory that builds up in the supply chain because a stage of the supply chain either produces or purchases in lots that are larger than those demanded by the customer.

In the rest of the chapter we use the following notation:

Q: lot or batch size of an order
R: Demand per unit time

We ignore the impact of demand variability because it has a marginal impact on lot size and cycle inventory. We assume demand to be stable for the rest of this chapter. (Demand variability and its impact on safety inventory is discussed in detail in Chapter 8.)

Consider the sale of jeans at Jean-Mart, a department store. Demand for jeans is relatively stable at $R = 100$ pairs of jeans per day. First, consider the case in which the store manager at Jean-Mart purchases in lots of $Q = 1{,}000$ pairs. We can draw the **inventory profile** of jeans at Jean-Mart, which is a plot depicting the level of inventory over time, as shown in Figure 7.1.

Because purchases are in lots of $Q = 1{,}000$ units, but demand is only $R = 100$ units per day, it takes 10 days for a lot to be sold. The inventory of jeans at Jean-Mart declines steadily from 1,000 (when the lot arrives) to 0 (when the last pair of jeans is sold) over 10 days. This sequence of a lot arriving and demand depleting inventory until another lot arrives repeats itself in a cyclical manner every 10 days, as shown in the inventory profile in Figure 7.1.

FIGURE 7.1 Inventory Profile of Jeans at Jean-Mart

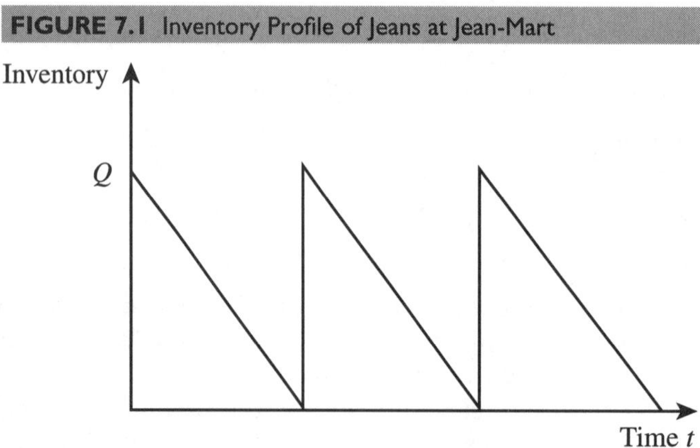

When demand is steady, cycle inventory and lot size are related as follows:

$$\text{Cycle inventory} = \text{lot size}/2 = Q/2 \qquad \textbf{(7.1)}$$

Given a lot size of 1,000 units, Jean-Mart carries a cycle inventory of $Q/2 = 500$ pairs of jeans. From this relationship (Equation 7.1), we see that cycle inventory is proportional to the lot size. A supply chain in which stages produce or purchase in larger lots will have more cycle inventory than a supply chain in which stages purchase in smaller lots. For example, if a competing department store purchases in lot sizes of 200 pairs of jeans, it will carry a cycle inventory of only 100 pairs.

Lot sizes and cycle inventory also influence the flow time of material within the supply chain. Recall Little's law (Equation 3.1) from Chapter 3:

$$\text{Average flow time} = \text{average inventory}/\text{average flow rate}$$

For any supply chain, average flow rate equals the demand. We thus have the following:

$$\begin{aligned}&\text{Average flow time resulting from cycle inventory}\\ &= \text{cycle inventory}/\text{demand} = Q/2R\end{aligned}$$

For Jean-Mart, which purchases lot sizes of 1,000 pairs of jeans and whose daily demand is 100 pairs of jeans, we obtain the following:

$$\text{Average flow time resulting from cycle inventory} = Q/2R = 1{,}000/200 = 5 \text{ days}$$

Cycle inventory at the Jean-Mart store thus adds five days to the amount of time that jeans spend in the supply chain. The larger the cycle inventory, the longer the lag time between when a product is produced and when it is sold. Because large time lags leave a firm vulnerable to changes in the marketplace, a lower level of cycle inventory is always desirable. A lower cycle inventory is also desirable because it decreases the working capital requirement for a firm. Toyota, for example, keeps a cycle inventory of only a few hours of production between the factory and most suppliers. As a result, Toyota is never left with parts that it does not need. It also allocates very little space in the factory to inventory.

Before we can suggest actions that a manager can take to reduce cycle inventory, it is important to understand why stages of a supply chain produce or purchase in large lots and how lot size reduction affects supply chain performance.

Cycle inventory is primarily held to take advantage of economies of scale and reduce cost within the supply chain. Increasing the lot size or cycle inventory often decreases the cost incurred by different stages of a supply chain. To understand how the supply chain achieves these economies of scale, we must first identify supply chain costs that are influenced by the lot size.

The average price paid per unit purchased is a key cost in the lot sizing decision. A buyer may increase the lot size if this action results in a reduction in the price paid per unit purchased. For example, if the jean manufacturer charges \$20 per pair of jeans for orders under 500 pairs and \$18 per pair of jeans for larger orders, the store manager at Jean-Mart may order in lots of at least 500 pairs to get the lower price. The price paid per unit is referred to as the **material cost** and is denoted by C. It is measured in \$/unit. In many practical situations, material cost displays economies of scale and increasing the lot size decreases the material cost.

The **fixed ordering cost** includes all costs that do not vary with the size of the order but are incurred each time an order is placed. For example, a fixed administrative cost may be incurred to place an order, a trucking cost may be incurred to transport the order, and a labor cost incurred to receive the order. Jean-Mart, for example, incurs a cost of $400 for the truck that brings the shipment of jeans from the manufacturer. Assume that the truck can hold up to 2,000 pairs of jeans. The $400 cost is incurred irrespective of the number of jeans shipped on the truck. A lot size of 100 pairs of jeans results in a transportation cost of $4 per pair, whereas a lot size of 1,000 pairs results in a transportation cost of $0.40 per pair. Given the fixed transportation cost per batch, the store manager is inclined to increase lot size to reduce transportation cost per pair of jeans. The fixed ordering cost per lot or batch is denoted by S and is measured in $/lot. The ordering cost also displays economies of scale, and increasing the lot size decreases the fixed ordering cost per unit purchased.

Holding cost is the cost of carrying one unit in inventory for a specified period of time, usually one year. It is a combination of the cost of capital, the cost of physically storing the inventory, and the cost that results from the product becoming obsolete. The holding cost is denoted by H and is measured in $/unit/year. It may also be obtained as a fraction, h, where h is the cost of holding $1 in inventory for one year. Given a unit cost of C, the holding cost H is given by

$$H = hC \tag{7.2}$$

The total holding cost increases with an increase in lot size and cycle inventory.

To summarize, the costs that must be considered in any lot sizing decision are as follows:

- Average price per unit purchased, $$C$/unit
- Fixed ordering cost incurred per lot, $$S$/lot
- Holding cost incurred per unit per year, $$H$/unit/year $= hC$

Later in the chapter, we discuss how the various costs may be estimated in practice. However, for the purposes of this discussion, we can assume that they are already known.

The primary role of cycle inventory is to allow different stages in the supply chain to purchase product in lot sizes that minimize the sum of the material, ordering, and holding cost. If a manager was considering the holding cost alone, he or she would reduce the lot size and cycle inventory. However, economies of scale in purchasing or ordering motivate a manager to increase the lot size and cycle inventory. A manager must make the trade-off that minimizes the total cost when making the lot sizing decision.

Ideally, cycle inventory decisions should be made considering the total cost across the entire supply chain. However, in practice, each stage makes its cycle inventory decisions independently. As we discuss later in the chapter, this practice increases the level of cycle inventory as well as the total cost in the supply chain.

> ***Key Point*** Cycle inventory exists in a supply chain because different stages exploit economies of scale to lower the total cost. The costs considered include material cost, fixed ordering cost, and holding cost.

Any stage of the supply chain exploits economies of scale in its replenishment decisions in the following three typical situations:

1. A fixed cost is incurred each time an order is placed or produced.
2. The supplier offers price discounts based on the quantity purchased per lot.
3. The supplier offers short-term discounts or holds trade promotions.

Next we discuss how the presence of a fixed cost associated with the manufacture or purchase of each lot influences the lot size and cycle inventory.

7.2 ECONOMIES OF SCALE TO EXPLOIT FIXED COSTS

To understand better the trade-offs discussed in this section, consider a situation that often arises in our daily life: the purchase of groceries and other household products. These may be purchased at a nearby convenience store or at a Sam's Club (a large warehouse club selling consumer goods), which is located much further away. The fixed cost of going shopping is the time it takes to go to either location. This fixed cost is much lower for the convenience store. Prices, however, are higher at the local convenience store. Taking the fixed cost into account, we tend to tailor our lot size decision accordingly. When we need only a small quantity, we go to the nearby convenience store because the fixed costs are low. However, if we are buying a large quantity, we go to Sam's Club, where the lower prices over the larger quantity purchased more than make up for the increase in fixed costs.

In this section we focus on the situation in which the supply chain incurs a fixed cost each time an order is placed. As mentioned earlier, this fixed cost may be associated with placing the order, receiving the order, and transporting the order. We identify the appropriate cost trade-offs that need to be considered when making the lot sizing decision. The objective of a lot sizing decision is to minimize the total cost of satisfying demand. We start by considering the lot sizing decision for a single product.

Lot Sizing for a Single Product (Economic Order Quantity)

Consider a computer reseller, like Best Buy, that sells Compaq computers. As it sells its current inventory, the Best Buy manager has to place a replenishment order for a new lot of computers. Compaq ships the order from its distributor using a truck. Best Buy pays for the truck no matter how many computers are on it. The key decision for the manager is how many computers to order from Compaq in a lot. For this decision, we assume the following inputs:

R = Annual demand of the product
S = Fixed cost incurred per order
C = Cost per unit
h = Holding cost per year as a fraction of product cost

Assume that Compaq does not offer any discounts and each unit costs \$$C$ no matter how large an order is. The holding cost is thus given by $H = hC$ (using Equation 7.2).

If all replenishment orders are made in lots of size Q, given a constant demand, the inventory profile at Best Buy is as shown in Figure 7.1. The Best Buy manager makes the lot sizing decision to minimize the total cost the store incurs. He or she must consider three costs when deciding on the lot size:

- Annual material cost: annual cost of material purchased
- Annual order cost: annual order cost for the lots ordered
- Annual holding cost: annual cost of holding inventory

Because purchase price is independent of lot size, we have the following:

$$\text{Annual material cost} = CR$$

Given a lot size of Q, the number of orders must suffice to meet the annual demand. We thus have the following:

$$\text{Number of orders per year} = R/Q \tag{7.3}$$

Because an order cost of S is incurred for each order placed, we infer the following:

$$\text{Annual order cost} = \left(\frac{R}{Q}\right)S \tag{7.4}$$

Given a lot size of Q, we have an average inventory of $Q/2$. The annual holding cost is thus the cost of holding $Q/2$ units in inventory for a year and is as follows:

$$\text{Annual holding cost} = \left(\frac{Q}{2}\right)H = \left(\frac{Q}{2}\right)hC$$

The total annual cost is the sum of all three costs and is given by the following:

$$\text{Total annual cost, } TC = CR + (R/Q)S + (Q/2)hC$$

Figure 7.2 shows the variation in different costs as the lot size is changed.

Observe that the annual holding cost increases with an increase in lot size. In contrast, the annual order cost declines with an increase in lot size. The material cost is independent of lot size because we have assumed price to be fixed. The total annual cost thus first declines and then increases with an increase in lot size. The fundamental trade-off the manager must make is between the fixed order cost and the holding cost incurred by Best Buy because material cost in this case is independent of the lot size.

FIGURE 7.2 Effect of Lot Size on Costs at Best Buy

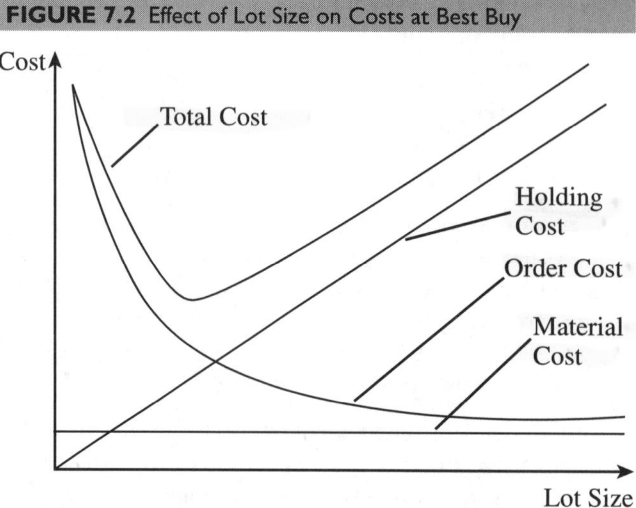

From the perspective of the manager at Best Buy, the optimal lot size is one that minimizes the total cost to Best Buy. It is obtained by taking the first derivative of the total cost with respect to Q and setting it equal to 0 (see Appendix 7A). The optimal lot size is referred to as the **economic order quantity (EOQ)**. It is denoted by Q^* and is given by the following equation:

$$\text{Optimal lot size, } Q^* = \sqrt{\frac{2RS}{hC}} \qquad \textbf{(7.5)}$$

When using the formula, it is important to have the same time units for the holding cost h and the demand R. If the holding cost is per year, the demand should also be per year. With each lot or batch of size Q^*, the cycle inventory in the system is given by $Q^*/2$. The flow time spent by each unit in the system is given by $Q^*/(2R)$. Note that as the optimal lot size increases, so does the cycle inventory and the flow time. The optimal ordering frequency is given by n^* where

$$n^* = \frac{R}{Q^*} = \sqrt{\frac{RhC}{2S}} \qquad \textbf{(7.6)}$$

In Example 7.1 we illustrate the EOQ formula and the procedure to make lot sizing decisions.

Example 7.1 (economic order quantity): Demand for the Deskpro computer at Best Buy is 1,000 units per month. Best Buy incurs a fixed order placement, transportation, and receiving cost of $4,000 each time an order is placed. Each computer costs Best Buy $500, and the retailer has a holding cost of 20 percent. Evaluate the number of computers that the store manager should order in each replenishment lot.

Analysis: In this case, the store manager has the following input:

$$\begin{aligned}\text{Annual demand, } R &= 1{,}000 \times 12 = 12{,}000 \text{ units}\\ \text{Order cost per lot, } S &= \$4{,}000\\ \text{Unit cost per computer, } C &= \$500\\ \text{Holding cost per year as a fraction of inventory value, } h &= 0.2\end{aligned}$$

Using the EOQ formula (Equation 7.5), the optimal lot size is as follows:

$$\text{Optimal order size} = \sqrt{\frac{2 \times 12{,}000 \times 4{,}000}{0.2 \times 500}} = 980$$

To minimize the total cost at Best Buy, the store manager orders a lot size of 980 computers for each replenishment order. For a lot size of $Q^* = 980$, the cycle inventory is the average resulting inventory and (using Equation 7.1) is given by the following:

$$\text{Cycle inventory} = Q^*/2 = 980/2 = 490$$

For a lot size of $Q^* = 980$, the store manager evaluates the situation as follows:

$$\begin{aligned}\text{Number of orders per year} &= R/Q^* = 12{,}000/980 = 12.24\\ \text{Annual ordering and holding cost} &= (R/Q^*)S + (Q^*/2)hC = \$97{,}980\\ \text{Average flow time} &= Q^*/2R = 490/12{,}000 = 0.041 \text{ year} = 0.49 \text{ month}\end{aligned}$$

Each computer thus spends 0.49 month, on average, at Best Buy before it is sold. This flow time in storage is attributed to lot sizes arising from fixed costs.

A few key insights can be gained from the simple scenario used in Example 7.1. First, observe that using a lot size of 1,100 (instead of 980) increases annual costs to \$98,636 (from \$97,980). Even though the order size is more than 10 percent larger than Q^*, total cost increases by only 0.6 percent. This issue can be relevant in practice. For example, Best Buy may find that the EOQ for computer diskettes is 6.5 cases. The manufacturer may be reluctant to ship half a case and may want to charge extra for this service. Our discussion illustrates that Best Buy is perhaps better off with lot sizes of six or seven cases, because this change has a very small impact on its inventory-related costs but can save on any fee that the manufacturer may charge for shipping half a case.

Key Point Total ordering and holding costs are relatively stable around the EOQ. A firm is often better served by ordering a convenient lot size close to the EOQ rather than the precise EOQ.

If demand at Best Buy increases to 4,000 computers a month (demand has increased by a factor of 4 compared with 1,000 per month), we can use the EOQ formula to determine that the optimal lot size doubles and the number of orders placed per year also doubles. However, average flow time decreases by a factor of 2. In other words, as demand increases, cycle inventory measured in terms of days (or months) of demand should reduce if the lot sizing decision is made optimally. This observation can be stated as follows:

Key Point If demand increases by a factor of k, the optimal lot size increases by a factor of $\sqrt{k}$. The number of orders placed per year should also increase by a factor of $\sqrt{k}$. Flow time attributed to cycle inventory should decrease by a factor of $\sqrt{k}$.

Let us return to the instance in which monthly demand for the Deskpro model is 1,000 computers. Now assume that the manager would like to reduce the lot size to $Q = 200$ units to reduce flow time. If this lot size is decreased without any other change, we have the following:

$$\text{Annual inventory-related costs} = (R/Q)S + (Q/2)hC = \$250{,}000$$

This is significantly higher than the total cost of \$97,980 that Best Buy incurred when ordering in lots of 980 units as in Example 7.1. Therefore, there are clear financial reasons why the store manager would be unwilling to reduce the lot size to 200. To make it feasible to reduce the lot size, the Best Buy manager should work to reduce the fixed order cost. For example, if the fixed cost associated with each lot is reduced to \$1,000 (from the current value of \$4,000), the optimal lot size reduces to 490 (from the current value of 980). We illustrate the relationship between desired lot size and order cost in Example 7.2.

Example 7.2 (relationship between desired lot size and order cost): The store manager at Best Buy would like to reduce the optimal lot size from 980 to 200. For this lot size reduction to be optimal, the store manager wants to evaluate how much the order cost per lot should be reduced.

Analysis: In this case we have the following:

Desired lot size, $Q^* = 200$
Annual demand, $R = 1{,}000 \times 12 = 12{,}000$ units
Unit cost per computer, $C = \$500$
Holding cost per year as a fraction of inventory value, $h = 0.2$

Using the EOQ formula (Equation 7.5), the desired order cost is as follows:

$$S = \frac{hC(Q^*)^2}{2R} = \frac{0.2 \times 500 \times 200^2}{2 \times 12{,}000} = \$166.7$$

Thus, the store manager at Best Buy would have to reduce the order cost per lot from \$4,000 to \$166.7 for a lot size of 200 to be optimal.

The observation in Example 7.2 may be stated as follows:

Key Point In order to reduce the optimal lot size by a factor of k, the fixed order cost S must be reduced by a factor of k^2.

Aggregating Multiple Products in a Single Order

To reduce the lot size effectively, the store manager needs to understand the source of the fixed cost. As we pointed out earlier, one major source of fixed costs is transportation. In several companies, the array of products sold is divided into families or groups, with each group managed independently by a separate product manager. For example, Best Buy also purchases the Litepro, the Medpro, and the Heavypro models from the same manufacturer as the Deskpro. Currently, a separate product manager is responsible for the inventory and sales of each model. As a result, the ordering and delivery for each model is independent. The fixed transportation cost of \$4,000 is thus incurred separately for each model. This leads to each product manager ordering a large lot size for his or her product.

Consider the data from Example 7.1. Assume that the demand for each of the four models is 1,000 units per month. In this case, if each product manager orders separately, he or she would order a lot size of 980 units. Across the four models, the total cycle inventory would thus be 1,960 units.

Now consider the case in which the store manager at Best Buy realizes that all four shipments originate from the same source. He or she asks all the product managers to coordinate their purchasing to ensure that all four products arrive on the same truck. In this case, the optimal combined lot size across all four models turns out to be 1,960 units. This is equivalent to 490 units for each model. As a result of spreading the fixed transportation cost across multiple products originating from the same supplier, it becomes financially optimal for the store manager at Best Buy to reduce the lot size for each individual product. This action significantly reduces the cycle inventory as well as cost to Best Buy.

Another way to achieve this result is to have a single delivery coming from multiple suppliers (allows fixed transportation cost to be spread across multiple suppliers) or have a single truck delivering to multiple retailers (allows fixed transportation cost to be spread across multiple retailers). This observation can be stated as follows:

Key Point Aggregating across products, retailers, or suppliers in a single order allows for a reduction in lot size for individual products because fixed ordering and transportation costs are now spread across multiple products, retailers, or suppliers.

When considering fixed costs, one cannot ignore the receiving or loading costs. As more products are included in a single order, the product variety on a truck increases. The receiving warehouse now has to update inventory records for more items per truck. In addition, the task of putting inventory into storage now becomes more expensive because each distinct item must be stocked in a separate location. Therefore, when attempting to reduce lot sizes, it is important to focus on reducing these costs. An **advanced shipping notice** (ASN) is an electronic file sent by the supplier to the customer via electronic data interchange (EDI) that contains precise records of the contents of the truck. These electronic notices facilitate updating of inventory records as well as the decision regarding storage locations, helping to reduce the fixed cost of receiving. The reduced fixed cost of receiving makes it optimal to reduce the lot size ordered, thus reducing cycle inventory.

In the preceding discussion, we focus on the case in which the fixed cost of the order does not change as we include more products in the order. In reality, the fixed cost of the order changes as we increase the product variety in the order. We next analyze how optimal lot sizes may be determined in such a setting.

Lot Sizing with Multiple Products or Customers

Let us return to the example of Best Buy ordering multiple models to be delivered in the same truck. In our earlier discussion, we assume that the fixed ordering cost is associated with a lot and is not dependent on the variety included in the lot. In practice, this will not often be the case. In general, a portion of the fixed cost can be related to transportation. (This is independent of product variety on the truck.) A portion of the fixed cost is related to loading and receiving. (This cost increases with variety on the truck.) We now discuss how optimal lot sizes may be determined in such a setting.

Our objective is to arrive at lot sizes and an ordering policy that minimize the total cost. We assume the following input:

R_i: Annual demand for product i
S: Order cost incurred each time an order is placed independent of the variety of products included in the order
s_i: Additional order cost incurred if product i is included in the order

In the case of Best Buy with multiple models, the store manager may consider three approaches to the lot sizing decision:

1. Each product manager orders his or her model independently.
2. The product managers jointly order every product in each lot.
3. Product managers order jointly, but not every order contains every product; that is, each lot contains a selected subset of the products.

The first approach does not use any aggregation and will result in the highest cost. The second approach aggregates all products in each order. This aggregation should result in a lower cost than the first approach. The weakness with the second approach is that low-volume products are aggregated with high-volume products in every order, which causes a product-specific order cost for the low-volume product to be incurred with each order. In such a situation, it may be better to order the low-volume products less frequently than the high-volume products. This practice will result in a reduction of the product-specific order cost associated with the low-volume product. As a result, the third approach is likely to yield the lowest cost.

Let us use the example of Best Buy purchasing computers to illustrate the effect of each of the three approaches on supply chain costs. We start by considering the case in which each product is ordered and delivered independently.

Lots Are Ordered and Delivered Independently for Each Product

Example 7.3 illustrates how the lot sizing decision is made in the case where lots are ordered and delivered independently. This scenario is simple and equivalent to the single product approach using the EOQ formula applied to each product.

Example 7.3 (multiple products with lots ordered and delivered independently): Best Buy sells three models of computers; the Litepro, Medpro, and Heavypro. Annual demands for the three products are $R_L = 12{,}000$ for the Litepro, $R_M = 1{,}200$ units for the Medpro, and $R_H = 120$ units for the Heavypro. Assume that each model costs Best Buy \$500. A fixed transportation cost of \$4,000 is incurred each time an order is delivered. For each model ordered and delivered on the same truck, an additional fixed cost of \$1,000 is incurred for receiving and storage. Best Buy incurs a holding cost of 20 percent. Evaluate the lot sizes that the Best Buy manager should order if lots for each product are ordered and delivered independently. Also evaluate the annual cost of such a policy.

Analysis: In this example, we have the following information:

$$\begin{aligned}
\text{Demand, } R_L &= 12{,}000\text{/year, } R_M = 1{,}200\text{/year, } R_H = 120\text{/year} \\
\text{Common order cost, } S &= \$4{,}000 \\
\text{Product specific order cost, } s_L &= \$1{,}000,\ s_M = \$1{,}000,\ s_H = \$1{,}000 \\
\text{Holding cost, } h &= 0.2 \\
\text{Unit cost, } C_L &= \$500,\ C_M = \$500,\ C_H = \$500
\end{aligned}$$

Because each model is ordered and delivered independently, a separate truck delivers each model. Therefore, a fixed ordering cost of \$5,000 (\$4,000 + \$1,000) is incurred for each product delivery. The optimal ordering policies and resulting costs for the three products (when the three products are ordered independently) are evaluated using the EOQ formula (Equation 7.5) and are shown in Table 7.1.

The Litepro model is ordered 11 times a year, the Medpro model is ordered 3.5 times a year, and the Heavypro model is ordered 1.1 times each year. The annual ordering and holding cost Best Buy incurs if the three models are ordered independently turns out to be \$155,140.

As mentioned earlier, independent ordering ignores the opportunity of aggregating orders. If the product managers at Best Buy combined orders of the different models in a single truck, the trucking cost of \$4,000 would not be incurred separately in each case. We next consider the scenario in which all three products are ordered and delivered each time an order is placed.

Lots Are Ordered and Delivered Jointly for All Three Models

When all three models are included each time an order is placed, the combined fixed order cost per order is given by the following:

$$S^* = S + s_L + s_M + s_H$$

TABLE 7.1 Lot Sizes and Costs for Independent Ordering

	Litepro	*Medpro*	*Heavypro*
Demand per year	12,000	1,200	120
Fixed cost/order	\$5,000	\$5,000	\$5,000
Optimal order size	1,095	346	110
Cycle inventory	548	173	55
Annual holding cost	\$54,772	\$17,321	\$5,477
Order frequency	11.0/year	3.5/year	1.1/year
Annual ordering cost	\$54,772	\$17,322	\$5,477
Average flow time	2.4 weeks	7.5 weeks	23.7 weeks
Annual cost	\$109,544	\$34,642	\$10,954

Note: While these figures are correct, some may differ from calculations due to rounding.

The next step is to identify the optimal ordering frequency. Let n be the number of orders placed per year. We then have the following:

$$\text{Annual order cost} = S^* n$$

$$\text{Annual holding cost} = (R_L\, h\, C_L/2n) + (R_M h\, C_M/2n) + (R_H\, h\, C_H/2n)$$

The total annual cost is thus as follows:

$$\text{Total annual cost} = (R_L\, h\, C_L/2n) + (R_M\, h\, C_M/2n) + (R_H\, h\, C_H/2n) + S^* n$$

The optimal order frequency minimizes the total annual cost and is obtained by taking the first derivative of the total cost with respect to n and setting it equal to 0. This results in the optimal order frequency n^*, where

$$n^* = \sqrt{\frac{R_L\, h\, C_L + R_M\, h\, C_M + R_H\, h\, C_H}{2S^*}} \quad \textbf{(7.7)}$$

In Example 7.4, we consider the case in which the product managers at Best Buy order all three models each time they place an order.

Example 7.4 (products ordered and delivered jointly): Consider the Best Buy data in Example 7.3. The three product managers have decided to aggregate and order all three models each time they place an order. Evaluate the optimal lot size for each model.

Analysis: Because all three models are included in each order, the combined order cost is as follows:

$$S^* = S + s_A + s_B + s_C = \$7{,}000 \text{ per order}$$

The optimal order frequency is obtained using Equation 7.7 and is given by the following:

$$n^* = \sqrt{\frac{12{,}000 \times 100 + 1{,}200 \times 100 + 120 \times 100}{2 \times 7{,}000}} = 9.75$$

Therefore, if each model is to be included in every order and delivery, the product managers at Best Buy should place 9.75 orders each year. In this case, the ordering policies and costs are as shown in Table 7.2.

Because 9.75 orders are placed each year and each order costs a total of \$7,000, we have the following arrival order cost:

$$\text{Annual order cost} = 9.75 \times \$7{,}000 = \$68{,}250$$

The annual ordering and holding cost, across the three sizes, of this policy is as follows:

$$\text{Annual ordering and holding cost} = \$61{,}512 + \$6{,}151 + \$615 + \$68{,}250 = \$136{,}528$$

Observe that the product managers at Best Buy lower the annual cost from \$155,140 to \$136,528 by ordering all products jointly. This represents a decrease of about 13 percent.

TABLE 7.2 Lot Sizes and Costs for Joint Ordering at Best Buy

	Litepro	*Medpro*	*Heavypro*
Demand per year	12,000	1,200	120
Order frequency	9.75/year	9.75/year	9.75/year
Optimal order size	1,230	123	12.3
Cycle inventory	615	61.5	6.15
Annual holding cost	\$61,512	\$6,151	\$615
Average flow time	2.67 weeks	2.67 weeks	2.67 weeks

Note: While these figures are correct, some may differ from calculations due to rounding.

The main advantage of this approach is that it is easy to administer and implement. The disadvantage is that it is not selective enough in combining the particular models that should be ordered together. Product-specific order costs of $1,000 are incurred for all three models with each order. Total costs can be reduced if low-volume models are ordered less frequently. Next we consider a policy in which the product managers do not necessarily order all models each time an order is placed.

Lots Are Ordered and Delivered Jointly for a Selected Subset of the Products

We now discuss a procedure that is more selective in combining products to be ordered jointly and arriving at an ordering schedule. The procedure we discuss here does not necessarily provide the optimal solution. However, it yields an ordering policy whose cost is close to optimal.

Of the three models, we first identify the one that is to be ordered most frequently. Once this decision has been made, for each successive product we need to identify those orders in which it is to be included. In general, it is not necessarily optimal for a particular model to be included at regular intervals (i.e., it should be included every second or third order). However, in our procedure, we make the assumption that each model is included in the order at regular intervals. Once we have identified the most frequently ordered model, for each successive model i we need to identify the frequency m_i, where model i is ordered every m_i deliveries.

We first describe the procedure in general and then apply it to the specific example. Assume that the products are indexed by i, where i varies from 1 to n (assuming a total of n products). Each product i has an annual demand R_i, a unit cost C_i, and a product specific order cost s_i. The common order cost is S.

Step 1 As a first step we identify the most frequently ordered product, assuming each product is ordered independently. In this case, a fixed cost of $S + s_i$ would be allocated to each product. For each product i, (using Equation 7.6) we evaluate the optimal ordering frequency as follows:

$$\overline{n}_i = \sqrt{\frac{h\, C_i\, R_i}{2(S + s_i)}}$$

This is the frequency at which product i would be ordered if it were the only product being ordered (in which case a fixed cost of $S + s_i$ would be incurred per order). Let $\overline{n}$ be the frequency of the most frequently ordered product; that is, $\overline{n}$ is the maximum among all $\overline{n}_i$. The most frequently ordered product is included each time an order is placed.

Step 2 The next step is to identify the frequency with which other products are included with the most frequently ordered product, that is, calculate the order frequency for each product as a multiple of the order frequency of the most frequently ordered product. We assume that the most frequently ordered product will be ordered each time. All of the fixed cost S is thus allocated to this product. For each of the other products i, we thus only have the product-specific fixed cost component s_i. The order frequency for all other products is thus calculated using only the product-specific fixed cost in Equation 7.6. For each product i (other than the most frequently ordered product), evaluate the ordering frequency as follows:

$$\overline{\overline{n}}_i = \sqrt{\frac{h\, C_i\, R_i}{2\, s_i}}$$

Evaluate the frequency of product i relative to the most frequently ordered product to be $\overline{m_i}$, where

$$\overline{m_i} = \overline{n}/\overline{\overline{n_i}}$$

In general, $\overline{m_i}$ will contain a fractional component. For each product i (other than the most frequently ordered product), define the frequency m_i with which it is included with the most frequently ordered product, where

$$m_i = \lceil \overline{m_i} \rceil$$

In this case, $\lceil \, \rceil$ is the operation that rounds a fraction up to the closest integer.

Step 3 Having decided the ordering frequency of each product, recalculate the ordering frequency of the most frequently ordered product to be n, where

$$n = \sqrt{\frac{\sum h\, C_i\, R_i}{2(S + \sum s_i/m_i)}} \qquad \textbf{(7.8)}$$

The reason for this step is that in the initial calculation of $\overline{n_i}$, the fixed cost allocated to each order is $S + s_i$, where i is the most frequently ordered product. In reality, the most frequently ordered product is ordered each time, whereas others are ordered once every m_i orders. Thus, each product i contributes s_i/m_i to the fixed cost of an order. The effective fixed cost per order thus becomes the following:

$$S + \sum \frac{s_i}{m_i}$$

Using Equation 7.7, we thus obtain the optimal order frequency given in Equation 7.8.

Step 4 Next, for each product, evaluate an order frequency of $n = n/m_i$. We can then evaluate the total cost of such an ordering policy.

The procedure just described results in **tailored aggregation**, with higher-volume products ordered more frequently and lower-volume products ordered less frequently when the products are aggregated appropriately. In Example 7.5, we consider tailored aggregation for the Best Buy ordering decision in Example 7.3.

Example 7.5 (lot sizes ordered and delivered jointly for a selected subset that varies by order): Consider the Best Buy data in Example 7.3. Product managers have decided to order jointly but to be selective about which models they include in each order. Evaluate the ordering policy and costs using the procedure previously discussed.

Analysis: Recall that S = \$4,000, s_L = \$1,000, s_M = \$1,000, s_H = \$1,000. Applying Step 1, we obtain the following:

$$\overline{n_L} = \sqrt{\frac{h\, C_L\, R_L}{2(S + s_L)}} = 11.0, \overline{n_M} = 3.5 \qquad \text{and} \qquad \overline{n_H} = 1.1$$

Clearly, Litepro is the most frequently ordered model. Therefore, we set $\overline{n}$ = 11.0. We now apply Step 2 to evaluate the frequency with which Medpro and Heavypro are included with Litepro in the order. We first obtain the following:

$$\overline{\overline{n_M}} = \sqrt{\frac{h\, C_M\, R_M}{2\, s_M}} = 7.7 \qquad \text{and} \qquad \overline{\overline{n_H}} = 2.4$$

Next, we evaluate the following:

$$\overline{m_M} = \bar{n}/\overline{n_M} = 11.0/7.7 = 1.4 \quad \text{and} \quad \overline{m_H} = 4.5$$

Next, we evaluate the following:

$$m_M = \lceil 1.4 \rceil = 2 \quad \text{and} \quad m_L = \lceil 4.5 \rceil = 5$$

Thus, Medpro is included in every other order, and Heavypro is included in every fifth order. (Litepro, the most frequently ordered model, is included in every order.)

Now that we have decided on the ordering frequency of each model, apply Step 3 (Equation 7.8) to recalculate the ordering frequency of the most frequently ordered model as follows:

$$n = 10.8$$

Thus, the Litepro is ordered 10.8 times per year. Next, we apply Step 4 to obtain an ordering frequency of

$$n_L = 10.8/\text{year}, n_M = 5.4/\text{year}, \text{and } n_H = 10.8/5 = 2.16/\text{year}$$

The ordering policies and resulting costs for the three products (using our heuristic) are shown in Table 7.3.

The annual holding cost of this policy is $69,444. The annual order cost is given by

$$nS + n_A S_A + n_B S_B + n_C S_C = \$61{,}560$$

The total annual cost is thus equal to $131,004. Tailored aggregation results in a cost reduction of $5,524 (more than 4 percent) compared with the case when all models are included in each order. The cost reduction results because each model-specific fixed cost of $1,000 is not incurred with every order.

From the Best Buy examples, it follows that aggregation can provide significant cost savings and reduction in cycle inventory in the supply chain. Simple aggregation of all products into each order will generally do better than the case in which each product is ordered independently. Tailored aggregation, however, will provide an even lower cost because it exploits the difference between low- and high-volume products and adjusts their ordering frequency accordingly. The effectiveness of tailored aggregation increases as the product-specific fixed cost is a larger fraction of the fixed cost S.

Tailored aggregation should also be used when a single truck makes deliveries to multiple customers, some large and some small. Managers must decide on the frequency of deliveries for each customer. There is a major fixed cost of sending the truck and then a minor fixed cost of each customer delivery. It will be less expensive if tailored aggregation is used: Larger customers should receive more frequent deliveries and smaller customers should be visited less often, with the deliveries being aggregated appropriately.

We have looked at fixed ordering costs and their impact on the inventory and costs in the supply chain. What is most significant from this discussion is that the key

TABLE 7.3 Lot Sizes and Costs for Ordering Policy Using Heuristic

	Litepro	*Medpro*	*Heavypro*
Demand per year	12,000	1,200	120
Order frequency	10.8/year	5.4/year	2.16/year
Order size	1,111	222	56
Cycle inventory	555.5	111	28
Annual holding cost	$55,556	$11,111	$2,778
Average flow time	2.41 weeks	4.81 weeks	12.04 weeks

Note: While these figures are correct, some may differ from calculations due to rounding.

to reducing lot sizes is to focus on the reduction of fixed costs associated with each lot ordered. These costs and the processes causing them must be well understood so that appropriate action may be taken.

> ***Key Point*** A key to reducing cycle inventory is the reduction of lot size. A key to reducing lot size without increasing costs is to reduce the fixed cost associated with each lot. This may be achieved by reducing the fixed cost itself or by aggregating lots across multiple products, customers, or suppliers. When aggregating across multiple products, customers, or suppliers, tailored aggregation provides the best solution.

Next we consider lot sizes in the situation that material cost also displays economies of scale.

7.3 ECONOMIES OF SCALE TO EXPLOIT QUANTITY DISCOUNTS

In the previous discussion, we assume that the material cost remains constant regardless of the quantity purchased. However, there are many instances in which the pricing schedule yields economies of scale, with prices decreasing as lot size is increased. This form of pricing is very common in business-to-business transactions. A discount is **lot size–based** if the pricing schedule offers discounts based on the quantity ordered in a single lot. A discount is **volume-based** if the discount is based on the total quantity purchased over a given period, regardless of the number of lots purchased over that period. Two commonly used lot size–based discount schemes are the following:

- All units quantity discounts
- Marginal unit quantity discount or multiblock tariffs

In this section, we investigate the impact of such quantity discounts on the supply chain. We must answer the following two basic questions in this context:

1. Given a pricing schedule with quantity discounts, what is the optimal purchasing decision for a buyer seeking to maximize profits? How does this decision affect the supply chain in terms of lot sizes, cycle inventories, and flow times?

2. Under what conditions should a supplier offer quantity discounts? What are appropriate pricing schedules that a supplier, seeking to maximize profits, should offer?

We start by studying the optimal response of a retailer (the buyer) when faced with either of the two lot size–based discount schemes offered by a manufacturer. Because material costs vary with lot size, the retailer needs to consider annual material, order, and holding costs when making the lot sizing decision. The retailer's objective is to select lot sizes to minimize the total annual cost. Next we evaluate the optimal lot size in the case of all-unit quantity discounts.

All-Unit Quantity Discounts

In **all-unit quantity discounts**, the pricing schedule contains specified break points q_0, $q_1, \ldots, q_r$ where $q_0 = 0$. If an order is placed that is at least as large as q_i but smaller than q_{i+1}, then each unit is obtained at an average cost of C_i. In general, the unit cost decreases as the quantity ordered increases, that is, $C_0 \geq C_1 \geq \ldots \geq C_r$. In the following discussion we focus on a retailer faced with such a pricing schedule. The retailer's objective is to decide on lot sizes in order to maximize profits or equivalently minimize the sum of material, order, and holding costs.

For all-unit discounts, the average unit cost varies with the quantity ordered, as shown in Figure 7.3. Observe that under this discount scheme, ordering $q_1 + 1$ units may be less expensive (in terms of material cost) than ordering $q_1 - 1$ units.

The solution procedure evaluates the optimal lot size for each price C_i (this forces a lot size between q_i and q_{i+1}) and then settles on the lot size that minimizes the overall cost. For each value of i, $0 \leq i \leq r$, evaluate the following:

$$Q_i = \sqrt{\frac{2RS}{h\,C_i}} \tag{7.9}$$

There are three possible cases for Q_i:

1. $q_i \leq Q_i < q_{i+1}$
2. $Q_i < q_i$
3. $Q_i \geq q_{i+1}$

Case 1

If $q_i \leq Q_i < q_{i+1}$, then a lot size of Q_i units will result in the discounted price of C_i per unit. In this case, the total annual cost of ordering Q_i is given by the following (this includes order cost, holding cost, and material cost):

$$\text{Total annual cost, } TC_i = \left(\frac{R}{Q_i}\right)S + \left(\frac{Q_i}{2}\right)h\,C_i + R\,C_i \tag{7.10}$$

FIGURE 7.3 Average Unit Cost With All-Unit Quantity Discounts

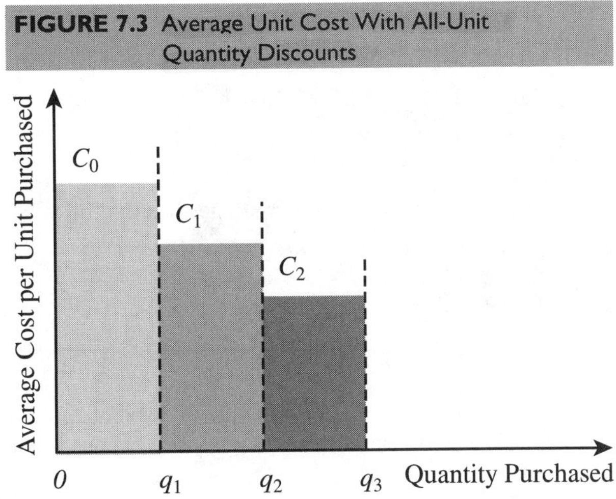

Case 2

If $Q_i < q_i$, then a lot size of Q_i does not result in a discount. Raising the lot size to q_i units will result in the discounted price of C_i per unit. Ordering more than q_i units will raise the order and holding cost without reducing the material cost. In this case, it is thus optimal to order a lot size of units. The annual cost is given by the following:

$$\text{Total annual cost, } TC_i = \left(\frac{R}{q_i}\right)S + \left(\frac{q_i}{2}\right)h\,C_i + R\,C_i \tag{7.11}$$

Case 3

If $Q_i \geq q_{i+1}$, then a lot size of q_{i+1} units will result in the discounted price of C_{i+1} per unit. Ordering more takes us out of the price range. In this case, the total annual cost is based on a lot size of q_{i+1} units and is given by the following:

$$\text{Total annual cost, } TC_i = \left(\frac{R}{q_{i+1}}\right)S + \left(\frac{q_{i+1}}{2}\right)h\,C_{i+1} + R\,C_{i+1} \tag{7.12}$$

For each price C_i, we apply the appropriate case and evaluate the total cost TC_i and the corresponding lot size. The solution is to order the lot size that minimizes the total annual cost across all prices in the schedule.

In Example 7.6, we evaluate the optimal lot size given an all-unit quantity discount.

Example 7.6 (all-unit quantity discount): Drugs Online (DO) is an on-line retailer of prescription drugs and health supplements. Vitamins represent a significant percentage of its sales. Demand for vitamins is 10,000 bottles per month. DO incurs a fixed order placement, transportation, and receiving cost of \$100 each time an order for vitamins is placed with the manufacturer. DO incurs a holding cost of 20 percent. The price charged by the manufacturer varies according to the following all-unit discount pricing schedule. Evaluate the number of bottles that the DO manager should order in each lot.

Order Quantity	*Unit Price*
0–5,000	\$3.00
5,001–10,000	\$2.96
Over 10,000	\$2.92

Analysis: In this case, the manager has the following input:

$q_0 = 0,\ q_1 = 5{,}000,\ q_2 = 10{,}000$
$C_0 = \$3.00,\ C_1 = \$2.96,\ C_2 = \$2.92$
$R = 120{,}000/\text{year},\ S = \$100/\text{lot},\ h = 0.2$

For $i = 0$, evaluate Q_0 (using Equation 7.9) as $Q_0 = \sqrt{\frac{2\,RS}{h\,C_0}} = 6{,}324$.

For $i = 0$, we set the lot size at $q_1 = 5000$ because $6{,}324 > q_1 = 5000$. The total cost incurred in this case is evaluated (using Equation 7.12) as follows:

$$TC_0 = \left(\frac{R}{q_1}\right)S + \left(\frac{q_1}{2}\right)h\,C_1 + RC_1 = \$359{,}080$$

For $i = 1$, using Equation 7.9 we obtain $Q_1 = 6{,}367$ units. Because $5{,}000 < 6{,}367 < 10{,}000$, we set the lot size at $Q_1 = 6{,}367$ units and evaluate the cost of ordering 6,367 units using Equation 7.10 as follows:

$$TC_1 = \left(\frac{R}{Q_1}\right)S + \left(\frac{Q_1}{2}\right)h\,C_1 + RC_1 = \$358{,}969$$

For $i = 2$, using Equation 7.9, we obtain $Q_2 = 6{,}410$ units. Because $6{,}410 < q_2 = 10{,}000$, we set the lot size at $q_2 = 10{,}000$ units and evaluate the cost of ordering 10,000 units using Equation 7.11 as follows:

$$TC_2 = \left(\frac{R}{q_2}\right)S + \left(\frac{q_2}{2}\right)h\,C_2 + RC_2 = \$354{,}520$$

Observe that the lowest total cost is for $i = 2$. Thus, it is optimal for DO to order $q_2 = 10{,}000$ bottles per lot and obtain the discount price of \$2.92 per bottle.

If the manufacturer in Example 7.6 sold all bottles for \$3, it would be optimal for DO to order in lots of 6,324 bottles. The quantity discount is an incentive for DO to order in larger lots of 10,000 bottles, raising both the cycle inventory and the flow time. The impact of the discount is further magnified if DO works hard to reduce its fixed ordering cost to $S = \$4$. The optimal lot size in the absence of a discount would be 1,265 bottles. In the presence of the all-unit quantity discount, the optimal lot size will still be 10,000 bottles. In this case, the presence of quantity discounts leads to an eightfold increase in average inventory as well as flow time at DO.

Pricing schedules with all-unit quantity discounts encourage retailers to increase the size of their lots to take advantage of price discounts, which adds to the average inventory and flow time in a supply chain. This increase in inventory raises a question about the value that all-unit quantity discounts offer in the supply chain. Before we consider this question, we discuss marginal unit quantity discounts.

Marginal Unit Quantity Discount

Marginal unit quantity discounts have also been referred to as **multiblock tariffs**. In this case, the pricing schedule contains specified break points $q_0, q_1, \ldots, q_r$. However it is not the *average cost* of a unit but the *marginal cost* of a unit that decreases at a break point (in contrast with the all-unit discount scheme). If an order of size q is placed, the first $q_1 - q_0$ units are priced at C_0, the next $q_2 - q_1$ are priced at C_1, and so on. The marginal cost per unit varies with the quantity purchased, as shown in Figure 7.4.

FIGURE 7.4 Marginal Unit Cost with Marginal Unit Quantity Discount

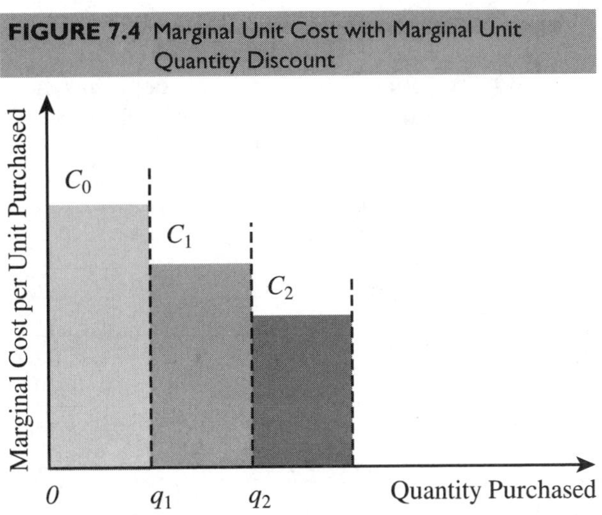

Faced with such a pricing schedule, the retailer's objective is to decide on lot sizes to maximize profits, which in this scenario is equivalent to minimizing cost.

The solution procedure evaluates the optimal lot size for each marginal price C_i (this forces a lot size between q_i and q_{i+1}) and then settles on the lot size that minimizes the overall cost.

For each value of i, $0 \leq i \leq r$, let V_i be the cost of ordering q_i units. Define $V_0 = 0$ and V_i for $0 \leq i \leq r$ as follows:

$$V_i = C_0 (q_1 - q_0) + C_1 (q_2 - q_1) + \ldots + C_{i-1} (q_i - q_{i-1}) \quad \textbf{(7.13)}$$

For each value of i, $0 \leq i \leq r - 1$, consider an order of size Q in the range q_i to q_{i+1} units, that is $q_{i+1} \geq Q \geq q_i$. The material cost of each order of size Q is given by $V_i + (Q - q_i) C_i$. The various costs associated with such an order are as follows:

$$\text{Annual order cost} = \left(\frac{R}{Q}\right)S$$

$$\text{Annual holding cost} = [V_i + (Q - q_i)\, C_i]h/2$$

$$\text{Annual material cost} = \frac{R}{Q}[V_i + (Q - q_i)\, C_i]$$

The total annual cost is the sum of the three costs and is given by the following:

$$\text{Total annual cost} = \left(\frac{R}{Q}\right)S + [V_i + (Q - q_i)C_i]h/2 + \frac{R}{Q}[V_i + (Q - q_i)\, C_i]$$

The optimal lot size for this price range is obtained by taking the first derivative of the total cost with respect to the lot size and setting it equal to 0. This results in an optimal lot size for this price range of the following:

$$\text{Optimal lot size for price } C_i = \sqrt{\frac{2R(S + V_i - q_i\, C_i)}{hC_i}} \quad \textbf{(7.14)}$$

Observe that the optimal lot size is obtained using a formula very much like the EOQ formula (Equation 7.5) except that the presence of the quantity discount has the effect of raising the fixed cost per order by $V_i - q_iC_i$ (from S to $S + V_i - q_iC_i$). There are three possible cases for Q_i:

1. $q_i \leq Q_i \leq q_{i+1}$
2. $Q_i < q_i$
3. $Q_i > q_{i+1}$

Case 1

If $q_i \leq Q_i \leq q_{i+1}$, then a lot size of Q_i will result in the discounted price in this range. In this case, the optimal lot size in this price range is to order Q_i units. The total annual cost of this policy is given by the following:

$$TC_i = \left(\frac{R}{Q_i}\right)S + [V_i + (Q_i - q_i)C_i]h/2 + \frac{R}{Q_i}[V_i + (Q_i - q_i)\, C_i]$$

Cases 2 and 3

If $Q_i < q_i$ or $Q_i > q_{i+1}$, the lot size in this range is either q_i or q_{i+1}, depending on which has the lower total cost. Evaluate the total annual cost:

$$TC_i = \text{Min}\left\{\left(\frac{R}{q_i}\right) S + V_i h/2 + \frac{R}{q_i} V_i, \left(\frac{R}{q_{i+1}}\right)S + V_{i+1}\, h/2 + \frac{R}{q_{i+1}} V_{i+1}\right\}$$

The lot size for this range then corresponds to the break point, giving the minimum total cost. Observe that for each range, the optimal lot size is the quantity defined by Equation 7.14 if it is feasible, or one of the break points if it is not feasible.

For each i we evaluate the optimal lot size and total cost. The solution is to set the lot size to be the one that minimizes the total annual cost across all ranges i. In Example 7.7, we evaluate the optimal lot size given a marginal unit quantity discount.

Example 7.7 (marginal unit quantity discount): Let us return to DO from Example 7.6. Assume that the manufacturer uses the following marginal unit discount pricing schedule:

Order Quantity	*Marginal Unit Price*
0–5,000	\$3.00
5,000–10,000	\$2.96
Over 10,000	\$2.92

This implies that if an order is placed for 7,000 bottles, the first 5,000 are at a unit cost of \$3.00, with the remaining 2,000 at a unit cost of \$2.96. Evaluate the number of bottles that Drugs Online should order in each lot.

Analysis: In this case we have the following:

$q_0 = 0,\ q_1 = 5{,}000,\ q_2 = 10{,}000$
$C_0 = \$3.00,\ C_1 = \$2.96,\ C_2 = \$2.92$
$V_0 = 0;\ V_1 = 3(5{,}000 - 0) = \$15{,}000$
$V_2 = 3(5{,}000 - 0) + 2.96(10{,}000 - 5{,}000) = \$29{,}800$
$R = 120{,}000/\text{year},\ S = \$100/\text{lot},\ h = 0.2$

For $i = 0$, evaluate Q_0 (using Equation 7.14) as follows:

$$Q_0 = \sqrt{\frac{2R(S + V_0 - q_0 C_0)}{hC_0}} = 6{,}324$$

Because $6{,}324 > q_1 = 5{,}000$, we evaluate the cost of ordering lots of $q_1 = 5{,}000$. (We do not consider lots of 0.) The total annual cost of ordering 5,000 bottles per lot is as follows (set $Q = 5{,}000$ and $i = 1$):

$$TC_0 = \left(\frac{R}{Q}\right)S + [V_i + (Q - q_i)\, C_i]h/2 + \frac{R}{Q}[V_i + (Q - q_i)\, C_i] = \$363{,}900$$

For $i = 1$, evaluate Q_1 using Equation 7.14 as follows:

$$Q_1 = \sqrt{\frac{2\, R(S + V_1 - q_1 C_1)}{hC_1}} = 11{,}028$$

Because $11{,}028 > q_2 = 10{,}000$, we evaluate the cost of ordering lots of $q_2 = 10{,}000$. (The cost of ordering lots of 5,000 has already been evaluated.) The total annual cost of ordering 10,000 bottles per lot is as follows (set $Q = 10{,}000$ and $i = 2$):

$$TC_1 = \left(\frac{R}{Q}\right)S + [V_i + (Q - q_i)\, C_i]h/2 + \frac{R}{Q}[V_i + (Q - q_i)\, C_i] = \$361{,}780$$

Because \$361,780 < \$363,900, it is less expensive to order in lots of 10,000 than in lots of 5,000. If the lot size is to be 10,000 units or less, we are better off ordering 10,000 units per lot. Now we investigate the cost of ordering in lots larger than 10,000 units, that is, $i = 2$. For $i = 2$, evaluate Q_2 using Equation 7.14 as follows:

$$Q_2 = \sqrt{\frac{2\, R(S + V_2 - q_2 C_2)}{hC_2}} = 16{,}961$$

The total annual cost of ordering 16,961 bottles per lot is as follows (set $Q = 16{,}961$ and $i = 2$):

$$TC_2 = \left(\frac{R}{Q}\right)S + [V_i + (Q - q_i)\,C_i]h/2 + \frac{R}{Q}[V_i + (Q - q_i)\,C_i] = \$360{,}365$$

DO should order a lot size of 16,961 bottles, because that number has the lowest total cost. This is much larger than the optimal lot size of 6,324 in the case in which the manufacturer does not offer any discount.

If the fixed cost of ordering is \$4, the optimal lot size for DO is 15,755 with the discount compared with a lot size of 1,265 without the discount. Observe that a marginal unit quantity discount results in a larger lot size than an all-unit quantity discount and significantly raises the optimal size of the order, leading to a buildup of cycle inventory at DO and an increase of flow time. This occurs because as the lot size is increased beyond the last break point, the material cost continues to decline for marginal unit quantity discounts but not for all unit quantity discounts.

This discussion demonstrates that there can be significant order sizes and thus cycle inventory in the absence of any formal fixed ordering costs as long as quantity discounts are offered. Thus, quantity discounts lead to a significant buildup of cycle inventory in the supply chain. In many supply chains, quantity discounts contribute more to cycle inventory than fixed ordering costs. This forces us to once again question the value of quantity discounts in a supply chain.

Why Quantity Discounts?

In this section, we develop different arguments supporting the presence of quantity discounts in a supply chain. Quantity discounts can be valuable in a supply chain because they result in the following:

- Improved coordination in the supply chain
- Extraction of surplus through price discrimination

Lot size–based quantity discounts are only justified for commodity products for which the market is competitive and price is fixed by the market. For products for which customer demand increases as price declines, it is better to offer volume-based discounts because supply chain profits increase.

Coordination in the Supply Chain

A supply chain is **coordinated** if the decisions the retailer and supplier make maximize total supply chain profits. This may occur if the supply chain is vertically integrated and the performance at each stage is judged based on total supply chain profits. In reality, each stage has a separate owner and considers its own costs in an effort to maximize its own profits. For example, the retailer makes cycle inventory decisions based on its own profitability considerations. The result of this independent decision making is a lack of coordination in the supply chain because actions that maximize retailer profits may not maximize supply chain profits.

In this section, we discuss how a manufacturer may use appropriate quantity discounts to ensure that coordination results even if the retailer is acting to maximize its own profits given the cost structure.

Quantity Discounts for Commodity Products Economists have argued that for commodity products like milk, a competitive market exists, and prices are driven down to the product's marginal cost. In this case, the market sets the price and the firm's objective is to lower costs. Consider, for example, the on-line drug retailer DO discussed earlier. It can be argued that the vitamins it sells are a commodity product. When placing orders with the manufacturer, DO makes its lot sizing decisions based on its own costs.

Demand for vitamins is 10,000 bottles per month. DO incurs a fixed order placement, transportation, and receiving cost of $100 each time it places an order for vitamins with the manufacturer. DO incurs a holding cost of 20 percent. The manufacturer charges DO $3 for each bottle of vitamins purchased. Using the EOQ formula (Equation 7.5), DO evaluates its optimal lot size to be Q = 6,324 bottles. The annual ordering and holding costs incurred by DO as a result of this policy are $3,795.

Each time DO places an order, the manufacturer has to process, pack, and ship the order. The manufacturer has a line packing bottles at a steady rate. The fixed cost of filling each order is $250 for the manufacturer. Each bottle costs the manufacturer $2, and it incurs a holding cost of 20 percent. Given that DO orders in lot sizes of 6,324 bottles, we evaluate the annual ordering and holding cost for the manufacturer as

Annual order cost at manufacturer = $(120{,}000/6{,}324) \times 250 =$ $4,744
Annual holding cost at manufacturer = $(6{,}324/2) \times 2 \times 0.2 =$ $1,265
Total order and holding cost at manufacturer = $6,009

The manufacturer thus incurs an annual cost of $6,009 as a result of DO ordering in lots of 6,324. The total cost, across the supply chain, as a result of DO ordering in lots of 6,324 is thus $6,009 + $3,795 = $9,804.

If DO can be convinced to order in lots of 9,165 units, the total cost in the supply chain decreases to $9,165. There is thus an opportunity for the supply chain to save $638. Observe that ordering in lots of 9,165 bottles raises the cost for DO by $238 per year to $4,059 (even though it reduces overall supply chain costs). The manufacturer's costs, in contrast, go down by $902 to $5,106 per year. The manufacturer must offer DO a suitable incentive for DO to raise its lot size.

Lot size–based quantity discounts are the appropriate incentive in this case. If the manufacturer were to price vitamins so that each bottle cost $3 for all orders with lot sizes under 9,165 and $2.9978 for all orders in lots of 9,165 or more, DO will have an incentive to order in lots of 9,165 bottles. This is because the quantity discount reduces the material cost for DO by just enough to offset the increase in ordering and holding costs. The manufacturer returns $264 to DO as material cost reduction (in the form of a quantity discount) to make it optimal for DO to order in lots of 9,165 bottles. The manufacturer's and the total supply chain's profits increase by $638 in this case. It can be argued that in practice, the manufacturer may have to share some of the $638 increase with DO. The precise division of the increase in supply chain profits will depend on the relative bargaining power of the different stages in the supply chain.

Observe that offering a lot size–based discount in this case decreases total supply chain cost. It does, however, increase the lot size the retailer purchases and thus increases cycle inventory in the supply chain.

> ***Key Point*** For commodity products for which price is set by the market, manufacturers can use lot size–based quantity discounts to achieve coordination in the supply chain and decrease supply chain cost. Lot size–based discounts, however, increase cycle inventory in the supply chain.

Our discussion on coordination for commodity products highlights the important link between the lot size–based quantity discount offered and the order costs incurred by the manufacturer. As the manufacturer works on lowering its order or setup cost, the discount it offers to retailers should change. This has not always occurred in practice. Often, firms have found that significant efforts to reduce order costs have not reduced cycle inventory in the supply chain because of quantity discounts. In most companies, the marketing and sales divisions design quantity discounts while operations works on reducing the setup or order cost. It is very important that the two functions coordinate these activities.

Quantity Discounts for Products for Which the Firm Has Market Power Now consider the scenario in which the manufacturer has invented a new vitamin pill, vitaherb, that is derived from herbal ingredients and has other properties highly valued in the market. Few competitors have a similar product. In this case, it can be argued that the price at which DO sells vitaherb will influence demand. Assume that the annual demand faced by DO is given by the demand curve 360,000 – 60,000p, where p is the price at which DO sells vitaherb. The manufacturer incurs a production cost of $C_S = \$2$ per bottle of vitaherb sold. In this case, the manufacturer must decide on the price to charge DO, and DO in turn must decide on the price to charge the customer. When the two make their decisions independently, it is optimal for DO to charge a price of $p = \$5$ per bottle and for the manufacturer to charge DO a price of $C_R = \$4$ per bottle. The total market demand in this case is for $360{,}000 - 60{,}000p = 60{,}000$ bottles of vitaherb. The profit at DO as a result of this policy is given by the following:

$$Prof_R = p(360{,}000 - 60{,}000p) - (360{,}000 - 60{,}000p)C_R = \$60{,}000$$

The profit at the manufacturer is given by the following:

$$Prof_M = C_R(360{,}000 - 60{,}000p) - C_S(360{,}000 - 60{,}000p) = \$120{,}000$$

If the two stages coordinate pricing and DO prices at $p = \$4$, market demand would be 120,000 bottles. The total supply chain profit if the two stages coordinate would be $120{,}000 \times (\$4 - \$2) = \$240{,}000$. As a result of each stage setting its price independently, the supply chain thus loses \$60,000 in profit.

Key Point The supply chain profit is lower if each stage of the supply chain independently makes its pricing decisions with the objective of maximizing its own profit. A coordinated solution results in higher profit.

There are two pricing schemes that the manufacturer may use to achieve the coordinated solution and maximize supply chain profits, even though DO acts in a way that maximizes its own profit:

1. **Two-part tariff**. In this case, the manufacturer charges its entire profit as an upfront franchise fee and then sells to the retailer at cost. It is then optimal for the retailer to price as though the two stages are coordinated. In the case of DO, recall that total supply chain profit when the two stages coordinate is \$240,000, with DO charging the customer \$4 per bottle of vitaherb. The profit made by DO when the two stages

do not coordinate is $60,000. One option available to the manufacturer is to construct a two-part tariff, in which DO is charged an up-front fee of $180,000 and material cost of C_R = $2 per bottle. DO maximizes its profit if it prices the vitamins at p = $4 per bottle. It has annual sales of 360,000 − 60,000p = 120,000 and profits of $60,000. The manufacturer, in contrast, makes a profit of $180,000 given its material cost of $2 per bottle.

2. **Volume-based quantity discount**. Observe that the two-part tariff is really a volume-based quantity discount. The average material cost for DO declines as it increases the quantity it purchases per year. This observation can be made explicit by designing a volume-based discount scheme that also achieves coordination. The objective here is to price in a way that the retailer buys the total volume sold when the two stages coordinate pricing. In the case of DO, recall that 120,000 bottles are sold per year when the supply chain is coordinated. The manufacturer must offer DO a volume discount to encourage DO to purchase this quantity. The manufacturer thus offers a price of C_R = $4 per bottle if the quantity DO purchases per year is less than 120,000. If the total volume in the year is 120,000 or higher, DO has to pay only C_R = $3.50. It is then optimal for DO to order 120,000 units and price them at p = $4 per bottle to the customers. The total profit earned by DO is (360,000 − 60,000p) (p − C_R) = $60,000. The total profit earned by the manufacturer is 120,000 (C_R − $2) = $180,000. The total supply chain profit is $240,000.

Key Point For products for which the firm has market power, two-part tariffs or volume-based quantity discounts can be used to achieve coordination in the supply chain and maximize supply chain profits.

At this stage, we can see that even in the absence of inventory-related costs, quantity discounts play a role in supply chain coordination and improved supply chain profits. The discount schemes that are optimal, however, are volume-based and not lot size–based. In our analysis, we do not assume any inventory-related costs, so one may argue that in the presence of inventory costs, lot size–based discounts may be optimal. It can be shown that even in the presence of inventory costs (order and holding), a two-part tariff or volume-based discount, with the manufacturer passing on some of the fixed cost to the retailer, optimally coordinates the supply chain and maximizes profits given the assumption that customer demand decreases when the retailer increases price.

Key Point For products for which a firm has market power, lot size–based discounts are not optimal for the supply chain even in the presence of inventory costs. In such a setting, either a two-part tariff or a volume-based discount, with the supplier passing on some of its fixed cost to the retailer, is needed for the supply chain to be coordinated and maximize profits.

A key distinction between lot size–based and volume-based discounts is that lot size discounts are based on the quantity purchased per lot, not the rate of purchase. Volume discounts, in contrast, are based on the rate of purchase or volume purchased on average per specified time period (say a month, quarter, or year). Lot size–based discounts tend to raise the cycle inventory in the supply chain by encouraging retailers to increase the size of each lot. Volume-based discounts, conversely, focus on increasing supply chain profitability and are compatible with small lots and reduced cycle inventory. A supply chain can have very small lot sizes and be consistent with volume-based discounts.

One can make the point that even with volume-based discounts, retailers will tend to increase the size of the lot toward the end of the evaluation period. For example, the manufacturer offers DO a 2 percent discount if the number of bottles of vitaherb purchased over a quarter exceeds 40,000. This policy will not affect the lot sizes DO orders early during the quarter, and DO will order in small lots to match the quantity ordered with demand. However, consider a situation in which DO has sold only 30,000 bottles with a week left before the end of the quarter. To get the quantity discount, DO may order 10,000 bottles over the last week even though it expects to sell only 3,000. In this case, cycle inventory in the supply chain will go up in spite of the fact that there is no lot size–based quantity discount. The situation in which orders peak toward the end of a financial horizon is referred to as the **hockey stick phenomenon**. It has been observed in many industries. One possible solution to this phenomenon is to base the volume discounts on a rolling horizon. For example, each week the manufacturer may offer DO the volume discount based on sales over the past 12 weeks. Such a rolling horizon dampens the hockey stick phenomenon by making each week the last week in some 12-week horizon.

Thus far, we have only discussed the scenario in which the supply chain has a single retailer. One may ask whether our insights are robust and also apply if the supply chain has multiple retailers, each with different demand curves, all supplied by a single manufacturer. As one would expect, the form of the discount scheme to be offered becomes more complicated in these settings. (Typically, instead of having only one break point at which the volume-based discount is offered, there are multiple break points.) However, the basic form of the optimal pricing scheme does not change. The optimal discount continues to be volume-based with the average price charged to the retailers decreasing as the rate of purchase (volume purchased per unit time) increases.

Price Discrimination to Maximize Supplier Profits

Price discrimination is the practice in which customers are charged different prices based on their individual valuation of the product. An example of price discrimination is the airline industry, in which passengers traveling on the same plane often pay different prices for their seats. We now discuss how price discrimination can increase total supply chain profits.

Let us return to the case in which the manufacturer of vitaherb is selling to DO. In such a situation, the quantity purchased by DO will depend upon the price charged by the manufacturer, with the quantity purchased decreasing as price increases. Assume that the quantity DO purchases is $200{,}000 - 50{,}000C$, where C is the price charged by the manufacturer. The material cost per bottle for the manufacturer is $C_S = \$2$. If the manufacturer is to pick a single price to charge DO, it should charge \$3 per bottle. DO purchases 50,000 bottles at this price, and the manufacturer makes a profit of \$50,000. The demand curve and profits are shown in Figure 7.5.

It is clear that setting a fixed price of \$3 does not maximize profits for the manufacturer. In principle, the manufacturer could obtain the entire area under the demand curve above its marginal cost of \$2 by pricing each unit differently. The manufacturer could price each unit equal to DO's marginal evaluation at each quantity.

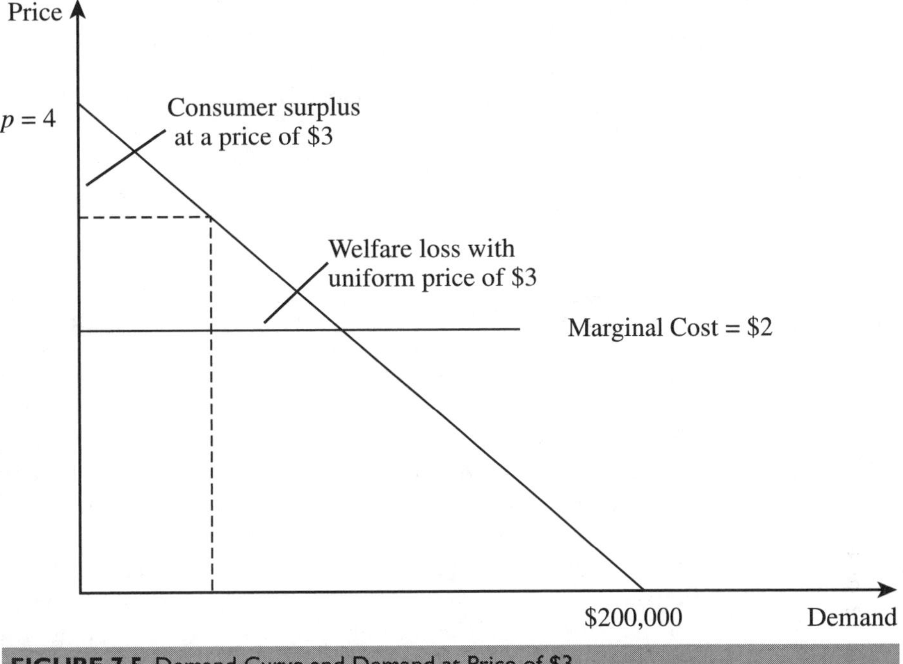

FIGURE 7.5 Demand Curve and Demand at Price of $3

The first unit would be priced so DO purchases exactly one unit at that price, the second unit priced so that DO purchases exactly two units, the third unit priced so that DO purchases exactly three units, and so on. Clearly, the price decreases as the quantity increases. The optimal price charged by the manufacturer is thus a form of a quantity discount.

An equivalent approach would be a two-part tariff in which the manufacturer asks for the entire area under the demand curve (above the marginal cost of $2) as an up-front franchise fee and then prices each bottle at marginal cost ($2 each). In our example, the manufacturer would ask DO for an up-front payment of $100,000 and then offer a price of $2 per bottle. In this case DO orders 100,000 units (because the up-front payment is sunk) and the manufacturer makes a profit of $100,000. In this situation, the pricing scheme with an up-front fee increases the manufacturer's profits compared with the case in which a single fixed price is offered.

Observe that the pricing scheme offered is a quantity discount because the customer pays less per unit as the order increases. However, note that the demand curve represents demand over a specified time period, say a year or a billing period. In other words, the discount offered is a volume discount, not a lot size–based discount. Therefore, the motivation for price discrimination also leads the supplier to offer a volume-based discount, not a lot size–based discount.

Price discrimination has been used effectively by the airline industry, in which business travelers pay a higher rate compared with vacation passengers. The two segments are separated based on various restrictions on length of stay as well as advance time to make a reservation. This form of pricing allows the airline to increase its total profit. Price discrimination can also be used to partially explain the fact that larger retailers get a lower unit price from the manufacturer compared with smaller retailers.

> ***Key Point*** Price discrimination to maximize profits at the manufacturer may also be a reason to offer quantity discounts within a supply chain. Discounts related to price discrimination will also be volume-based and not lot size–based.

Next, we discuss trade promotions and their impact on lot sizes and cycle inventory in the supply chain.

7.4 SHORT-TERM DISCOUNTING: TRADE PROMOTIONS

Manufacturers use **trade promotions** to offer a discounted price and a time period over which the discount is effective. For example, a manufacturer of canned soup may offer a price discount of 10 percent for the shipping period December 15 to January 25. For all purchases within the specified time horizon, retailers get a 10 percent discount. In some cases, the manufacturer may require specific actions from the retailer such as displays, advertising, promotion, and so on to qualify for the trade promotion. Trade promotions are quite common in the consumer packaged goods industry, with manufacturers promoting different products at different times of the year.

The goal of trade promotions is to influence retailers to act in a way that helps the manufacturer achieve its objectives. A few of the key goals (from the manufacturer's perspective) of a trade promotion are as follows:[1]

1. Induce retailers to use price discounts, displays, or advertising to spur sales.
2. Shift inventory from the manufacturer to the retailer and the customer.
3. Defend a brand against competition.

Although these may be the manufacturer's objectives, it is not clear that they are always achieved as the result of a trade promotion. Our goal in this section is to investigate the impact of a trade promotion on the behavior of the retailer and the performance of the entire supply chain. The key to understanding this impact is to focus on how a retailer reacts to a trade promotion a manufacturer offers. In response to a trade promotion, the retailer has the following options:

1. Pass through some or all of the promotion to customers to spur sales.
2. Pass through very little of the promotion to customers but purchase in greater quantity during the promotion period to exploit the temporary reduction in price.

The first action lowers the price of the product for the end customer, leading to increased purchases and thus increased sales for the entire supply chain. The second action does not increase purchases by the customer but increases the amount of inventory held at the retailer. As a result, the cycle inventory and flow time within the supply chain increase.

A **forward buy** is the amount that a retailer purchases in the current period for sales in future periods. A forward buy helps reduce the retailer's future cost of goods for product sold after the promotion ends. Although a forward buy is often the retailer's appropriate response and increases the retailer's own profits, it usually increases demand variability with a resulting increase in inventory and flow times within

[1]See Blattberg and Levin (1990) for more details.

the supply chain. As discussed in Chapters 5 and 6, this can decrease supply chain profitability.

Our objective in this section is to understand a retailer's optimal response when faced with a trade promotion. We identify the factors affecting the forward buy and quantify the size of a forward buy by the retailer. We also identify factors that influence the amount of the trade promotion that a retailer passes on to the customer as well as the optimal amount passed on by a retailer.

We first illustrate the impact of a trade promotion on forward buying behavior of the retailer. Consider a Cub Foods supermarket selling chicken noodle soup manufactured by the Campbell Soup Company. Customer demand for chicken noodle soup is R cans per year. The price Campbell charges is $\$C$ per can. Cub Foods incurs a holding cost of h (per dollar of inventory held for a year). Using the EOQ formula (Equation 7.5), Cub Foods normally orders in the following lot sizes:

$$Q^* = \sqrt{\frac{2\,RS}{hC}}$$

Campbell announces that it is offering a discount of $\$d$ per can for the coming four-week period. Cub Foods must decide how much to order at the discounted price compared with the lot size of Q^* that it normally orders. Let Q^d be the lot size ordered at the discounted price.

When making this decision, the retailer must consider material cost, holding cost, and order cost. Increasing the lot size Q^d will lower the material cost for Cub Foods because it purchases more cans (for sale now and in the future) at the discounted price. Increasing the lot size Q^d will raise the holding cost because inventories increase. Increasing the lot size Q^d will lower the order cost for Cub Foods because some orders that would otherwise have been placed are now not necessary. Cub Food's goal is to make the trade-off that minimizes the total cost.

The inventory pattern when a lot size of Q^d is followed by lot sizes of Q^* is shown in Figure 7.6. The objective is to identify Q^d that maximizes the reduction in total cost

FIGURE 7.6 Inventory Profile for Forward Buying

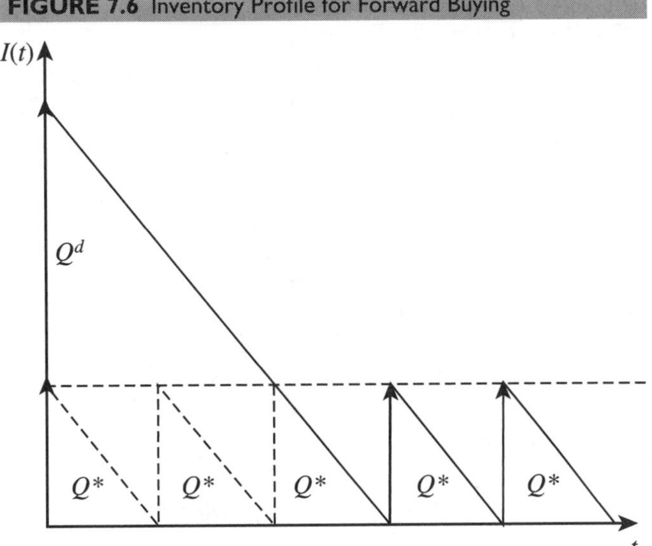

(material cost + ordering cost + holding cost) over the time interval during which the quantity Q^d (ordered during the promotion period) is consumed.

The precise analysis in this case is complex, so we present a result that holds under some restrictions.[2] The first key assumption is that the discount will only be offered once. In all future periods, there will be no discount. The second key assumption is that the order quantity Q^d is a multiple of Q^*. The third key assumption is that the retailer takes no action (such as passing on part of the trade promotion) to influence customer demand. The customer demand thus remains unchanged. With these assumptions, the optimal order quantity at the discounted price is given by the following:

$$Q^d = \frac{dR}{(C-d)h} + \frac{CQ^*}{C-d} \tag{7.15}$$

In practice, retailers are often aware of the timing of the next promotion. If the demand until the next anticipated trade promotion is Q_1, it is optimal for the retailer to order *min* $\{Q^d, Q_1\}$. Observe that the quantity Q^d ordered as a result of the promotion will be larger than the regular order quantity Q^*. The forward buy in this case is given by the following:

$$\text{Forward buy} = Q^d - Q^*$$

Even for relatively small discounts, the order size tends to increase by a large quantity, resulting in a large forward buy. We illustrate the impact of trade promotions on lot sizes using Example 7.8.

Example 7.8 (impact of trade promotions on lot sizes): Recall DO from Example 7.7. DO sells vitaherb, a popular vitamin diet supplement. Demand for vitaherb is 120,000 bottles per year. The manufacturer currently charges \$3 for each bottle, and DO incurs a holding cost of 20 percent. DO currently orders in lots of $Q^* = 6{,}324$ bottles. The manufacturer has offered a discount of \$0.15 for all bottles purchased by retailers over the coming month. Evaluate the number of bottles of vitaherb that DO should order given the promotion.

Analysis: In the absence of any promotion, DO orders in lot sizes of 6,324 bottles. Given a monthly demand of 10,000 bottles, DO normally orders every 0.6324 months. In the absence of the trade promotion, we have the following:

$$\text{Cycle inventory at DO} = Q^*/2 = 6{,}324/2 = 3{,}162 \text{ bottles}$$
$$\text{Average flow time} = Q^*/2R = 6{,}324/(2R) = 0.3162 \text{ months}$$

The optimal lot size during the promotion is obtained using Equation 7.15 and is given by the following:

$$Q^d = \frac{dR}{(C-d)h} + \frac{C\,Q^*}{C-d} = \frac{0.15 \times 120{,}000}{(3.00 - 0.15) \times 0.20} + \frac{3 \times 6{,}324}{3.00 - 0.15} = 38{,}236$$

During the promotion, DO should place an order for a lot size of 38,236. In other words, DO places an order for 3.8236 months' worth of demand. In the presence of the trade promotion, we have the following:

$$\text{Cycle inventory at DO} = Q^d/2 = 38{,}236/2 = 19{,}118 \text{ bottles}$$
$$\text{Average flow time} = Q^*/2R = 38{,}236/(2R) = 1.9118 \text{ months}$$

In the absence of a promotion, DO would have ordered 6,324 bottles. In this case, the forward buy is given by the following:

$$\text{Forward buy} = Q^d - Q^* = 38{,}236 - 6{,}324 = 31{,}912 \text{ bottles}$$

---

[2]See Silver, Pyke, and Petersen (1990) for a more detailed discussion.

As a result of this forward buy, DO will not place any order for the next 3.8236 months. (Without a forward buy, DO would have placed 31,912/6,324 = 5.05 orders for 6,324 bottles each during this period.) Observe that a 5 percent discount causes the lot size to increase by more than 500 percent.

As the example illustrates, forward buying as a result of trade promotions leads to a significant increase in inventory (and thus material flow time) at the retailer. The retailer can justify the forward buying because it decreases the retailer's total cost. However, the manufacturer can justify this action only if it has either inadvertently built up a lot of excess inventory or the forward buy allows the manufacturer to smooth demand by shifting it from peak to low demand periods. In practice, manufacturers often build up inventory in anticipation of planned promotions. During the trade promotion, this inventory shifts to the retailer, primarily as a forward buy. If the forward buy during trade promotions is a significant fraction of total sales, manufacturers end up reducing the revenues they earn from sales because most of the product is sold at a discount. The increase in inventory and the decrease in revenues often leads to a reduction in manufacturer profits as a result of trade promotions.[3] Total supply chain profits also decrease because of an increase in inventory.

Key Point Trade promotions lead to a significant increase in lot size and cycle inventory because of forward buying by the retailer. This generally results in reduced supply chain profits unless the trade promotion reduces demand fluctuations.

Now let us consider the extent to which the retailer may find it optimal to pass through some of the discount to the end customer to spur sales. As we shall see in Example 7.9, in general it is not optimal for the retailer to pass through the entire discount to the customer. In other words, it is optimal for the retailer to capture part of the promotion and only pass through part of it to the customer.

Example 7.9: Assume that DO faces a demand curve for vitaherb of 300,000 − 60,000p. The normal price charged by the manufacturer is C_R = \$3 per bottle. Ignoring all inventory-related costs, evaluate the optimal response of DO to a discount of \$0.15 per unit.

Analysis: The profits for DO are given by the following:

$$Prof_R = (300{,}000 - 60{,}000p)p - (300{,}000 - 60{,}000p)C_R$$

The retailer prices to maximize profits, and the optimal retail price is obtained by setting the first derivative of retailer profits with respect to p to 0. This implies the following:

$$300{,}000 - 120{,}000p + 60{,}000C_R = 0$$

or

$$p = (300{,}000 + 60{,}000C_R)/120{,}000 \qquad \textbf{(7.16)}$$

Substituting C_R = \$3 into Equation 7.16, we obtain a retail price of p = \$4. As a result, the customer demand at the retailer in the absence of the promotion is as follows:

$$R_R = 300{,}000 - 60{,}000p = 60{,}000$$

[3]See Blattberg and Levin (1990) for more details.

During the promotion, the manufacturer offers a discount of \$0.15, resulting in a price to the retailer of C_R = \$2.85. Substituting into Equation 7.16, the optimal price set by DO is as follows:

$$p = (300{,}000 + 60{,}000 \times 2.85)/120{,}000 = \$3.925$$

Observe that the retailer's optimal response is to pass through only \$0.075 of the \$0.15 discount to the customer. The retailer does not pass through the entire discount. At the discounted price, DO experiences the following demand:

$$R_R = 300{,}000 - 60{,}000p = 64{,}500$$

This represents an increase of 7.5 percent in demand. In this case, it is optimal for DO to pass on half the trade promotion discount to the customers. This action results in a 7.5 percent increase in customer demand.

From Examples 7.8 and 7.9, observe that the increase in customer demand resulting from a trade promotion (7.5 percent of demand in Example 7.9) is insignificant relative to the increased purchase by the retailer due to forward buying (500 percent from Example 7.8). The impact of the increase in customer demand may be further dampened by customer behavior. For products like vitamin supplements, it can be argued that customers will increase their consumption if they have purchased more. This is hard to argue for products like detergent and toothpaste, for which most of the increase in customer purchases is a forward buy by the customer; customers are unlikely to start brushing their teeth more frequently simply because they have purchased a lot of toothpaste. For such products, a trade promotion does not truly increase demand.

> ***Key Point*** Faced with a short-term discount, it is optimal for retailers to pass through only a fraction of the discount to the customer, keeping the rest for themselves. Simultaneously, it is optimal for the retailer to increase the purchase lot size and forward buy for future periods. This leads to an increase of cycle inventory in the supply chain as the result of a trade promotion without a significant increase in customer demand.

Both issues have been commonly observed in industry. Manufacturers have always struggled with the fact that retailers pass along only a small fraction of a trade discount to the customer. Almost a quarter of all distributor inventories in the dry-grocery supply chain in 1990 could be attributed to forward buying.[4]

Our previous discussion supports the claim that trade promotions generally increase cycle inventory in the supply chain and hurt performance. This realization has led many firms, including the world's largest retailer, Wal-Mart, and several manufacturers like Procter and Gamble (P&G) to adopt every day low pricing (EDLP). Here the price is fixed over time and no short-term discounts are offered. This eliminates any incentive for forward buying. As a result, all stages of the supply chain purchase in quantities that match demand.

There is one scenario in which trade promotions may make sense: as a competitive response. Consider a situation with competing brands for a product—say, cola. In such a category, some customers may be loyal to their brand while others may switch depending on the brand being offered at the lowest price. Consider a situation in which one of the competitors—say, Pepsi—offers retailers a trade promotion. Re-

[4]See Kurt Salmon Associates, Inc. (1993).

tailers increase their purchases of Pepsi and pass through some of the discount to the customer. Price-sensitive customers increase their purchase of Pepsi. If a competitor like Coca-Cola does not respond, it may lose some market share in the form of price-sensitive customers. A case can be made that a trade promotion may be justified in such a setting. However, observe that with both competitors offering trade promotions, there is no real increase in demand for either. Inventory in the supply chain, however, does increase for both brands. This is then a situation in which trade promotions may be a competitive necessity but they increase supply chain inventory, leading to reduced profits for all competitors.

When trade promotions are offered, they should be designed so that retailers limit their forward buying and pass along more of the discount to end customers. The manufacturer's basic objective is to increase market share and sales without allowing the retailer to forward-buy significant amounts. One approach to achieving this outcome is to discount sales to the retailer based on actual sales to customers rather than the amount purchased by the retailer. The discount price thus applies to items sold to customers (**sell-through**) during the promotion, not the quantity purchased by the retailer (**sell-in**). This eliminates all incentive for forward buying.

Given the information technology in place, many manufacturers today offer scanner-based promotions, in which the retailer receives credit for the promotion discount for every unit sold. It is unlikely, however, that retailers will accept such a scheme for weak brands. Another option is to limit the allocation to a retailer based on past sales. This is also an effort to limit the amount that the retailer can forward buy.

7.5 ESTIMATING CYCLE INVENTORY–RELATED COSTS IN PRACTICE

When setting cycle inventory levels in practice, a common hurdle is estimating the various major costs included in our discussion so far: material cost, order cost, and holding cost. The material cost is typically the easiest to identify in practice. In this section, we focus on the components of order and holding costs and discuss how they may be estimated. A key point here is that it is not terribly important to estimate these costs to a high level of precision. It is better to get a good approximation quickly rather than spend a lot of time trying to estimate costs exactly.

In calculating these costs, remember that what we are really concerned with are incremental costs—that is, costs that change as we change our lot sizing decision. Costs that are unchanged with a change in lot size should not be included in the lot sizing decision. For example, if a factory is running at 50 percent of capacity and all labor is full time and not earning overtime, it can be argued that the incremental setup cost is actually zero. Reducing the lot size in this case will not have any impact on setup cost until either labor is fully utilized (and earning overtime) or machines are fully utilized (with a resulting loss in production capacity).

Inventory Holding Cost

Holding cost is estimated as the sum of the following major components, not all of which are applicable to every type of situation. Holding cost is usually estimated as a percentage of the cost of a product.

- **Cost of capital.** This cost is often the most important component of holding cost. It should always be viewed as the opportunity cost of capital. The appropriate approach is to evaluate the weighted average cost of capital

(WACC).[5] This cost takes into account the return demanded on the firm's equity and the amount the firm must pay on its debt. These are weighted by the amount of debt and equity financing that the firm has. The formula for the WACC is as follows:

$$WACC = \frac{E}{D+E}(R_f + \beta \times MRP) + \frac{D}{D+E} R_b (1 - t)$$

where

E = amount of equity
D = amount of debt
R_f = risk-free rate of return (which is usually in the mid–single digits)
β = the firm's beta
MRP = Market risk premium (which is around the high single digits)
R_b = rate at which the firm can borrow money (related to its debt rating)
t = tax rate

However, we need to keep in mind that the WACC is an after-tax number, whereas inventory level calculations are done pretax. Therefore, we need to adjust the WACC to use in a pretax setting, as follows.

$$Pretax\ WACC = after\text{-}tax\ WACC/(1 - t)$$

The pre-tax WACC is the appropriate cost of capital for a firm that could grow its business using the funds released by reducing inventories. Most of these numbers can be found in a company's annual report or on any equity report on the company. The borrowing rate can come from tables listing the rates charged for bonds from firms with the same credit ratings. The risk-free rate is the return on U.S. treasuries, and the market risk premium is the return of the market above the risk-free rate. If a company is private and access to its financial structure is not available, a good approximation can be made by picking companies in the same industry and of somewhat similar size that are public and then using their numbers.

- **Obsolescence (or spoilage) cost**. The obsolescence cost estimates the rate at which the value of the product being stored drops either because the market value of that product drops or because the product quality deteriorates. This cost can range dramatically from rates of many thousands of percentage points to virtually zero and depends on the type of product we are holding. When setting an inventory level of hamburgers that can sell for only 15 minutes after they are cooked, the obsolescence rate should be high. It is unlikely that we will be able to sell hamburgers cooked half an hour ago. Even nonperishables like microprocessors can have obsolescence rates topping 100 percent. On the other end of the spectrum are products like gasoline that take a long time to become obsolete or spoil. For such products, a very low obsolescence rate may be applied.
- **Handling cost**. Handling cost should only include receiving and storage costs that vary with the volume of product received. Volume-independent handling costs that vary with the number of orders should be included in the order cost. Volume-dependent handling costs are generally small, and often the real cost does not change if volume varies within a range. If the volume

[5]See Brealey and Myers (2000).

is within this range (e.g., the range of inventory a crew of four people can unload per period of time), incremental handling cost added to the holding cost is zero. However, if incremental handling cost is incurred, then handling costs associated with this additional inventory should be included in the holding cost.

- **Occupancy cost**. The occupancy cost should reflect the incremental change in space cost due to changing cycle inventory. If the firm is being charged based on the actual number of units held in storage, we have the direct occupancy cost. Firms often lease or purchase a fixed amount of space. As long as a marginal change in cycle inventory does not change the space requirements, the occupancy cost should be considered zero. Occupancy, or space costs, often take the form of a step function with a sudden increase in cost when capacity is fully utilized and new space must be acquired.
- **Miscellaneous costs**. The final component of holding cost deals with a number of other relatively small costs, including theft, security, damage, tax, and additional insurance charges that may be incurred. Once again, it is important to estimate the incremental change in these costs on changing cycle inventory.

Order Cost

The order cost includes all incremental costs associated with placing or receiving an extra order that are incurred regardless of the size of the order. Components of order cost include the following:

- **Buyer time**. Buyer time is the incremental time of the buyer placing the extra order. This cost should be included only if the buyer is utilized fully. The incremental cost of getting an idle buyer to place an order is zero and does not add to the order cost. Electronic ordering can significantly reduce the buyer time to place an order by making order placement simpler and in some cases automatic.
- **Transportation costs**. A fixed transportation cost is often incurred regardless of the size of the order. For instance, if a truck is sent to deliver every order, it costs the same amount to send a half-empty truck as it does a full truck. Less than truckload pricing also includes a fixed component that is independent of the quantity shipped and a variable component that increases with the quantity shipped. The fixed component should be included in the order cost.
- **Receiving costs**. Some receiving costs are incurred regardless of the size of the order. These include any administration work such as purchase order matching and any effort associated with updating inventory records. Receiving costs that are volume-based should not be included here.
- **Other costs**. Each situation can have costs unique to it that should be considered if they are incurred for each order regardless of the volume of that order.

The order cost is estimated as the sum of all its component costs. As with carrying cost, it is important to determine that all costs included are the incremental change in real cost for an additional order. The order cost is often a step function, in that it is zero when the resource is not fully utilized but takes on a large value when the resource is fully utilized. At that point, the order cost is the cost of the additional resource required.

7.6 SUMMARY OF LEARNING OBJECTIVES

1. Balance the appropriate costs in order to choose the optimal amount of cycle inventory in the supply chain.

   Cycle inventory generally equals half the lot size. Therefore, as the lot size grows, so does the cycle inventory. In deciding on the optimal amount of cycle inventory, the supply chain goal is to minimize the total cost—the order cost, holding cost, and material cost. As cycle inventory increases, so does the holding cost. However, the order cost and, in some instances, the material cost go down with an increase in lot size and cycle inventory. The economic order quantity (EOQ) balances the three costs to obtain the optimal lot size. The higher the order and transportation cost, the higher the lot size and cycle inventory.
2. Understand the impact of quantity discounts on lot size and cycle inventory.

   Lot size–based quantity discounts encourage buyers to purchase in larger quantities to take advantage of the decrease in price. Therefore, lot size–based quantity discounts increase the lot size and cycle inventory within the supply chain.
3. Devise appropriate discounting schemes for a supply chain.

   Quantity discounts are justified to achieve coordination within the supply chain. Volume-based discounts are more effective at coordinating the supply chain without increasing lot size and cycle inventory. They are thus more appropriate than lot size–based discounts.
4. Understand the impact of trade promotions on lot size and cycle inventory.

   Trade promotions increase forward buying within the supply chain. Forward buying shifts future demand to the present and creates a spike in demand. As a result, trade promotions increase inventory and cost in a supply chain.
5. Identify managerial levers that reduce lot size and cycle inventory in a supply chain without increasing cost.

   The key managerial levers for reducing lot size and thus cycle inventory in the supply chain without increasing cost are the following:

- Reduce fixed ordering and transportation costs incurred per order.
- Implement volume-based discounting schemes rather than individual lot size–based discounting schemes.
- Eliminate or reduce trade promotions and encourage EDLP. Base trade promotions on sell-through rather than sell-in to the retailer.

Discussion Questions

1. Consider a supermarket deciding on the size of its replenishment order from P&G. What costs should it take into account when making this decision?
2. Discuss how various costs for the supermarket change as it decreases the lot size ordered from P&G.
3. As demand at the supermarket chain grows, how would you expect the cycle inventory measured in days of inventory to change? Explain.
4. The manager at the supermarket would like to decrease the lot size without increasing the costs he incurs. What actions can he take to achieve this objective?
5. When are quantity discounts justified in a supply chain?
6. What is the difference between lot size–based and volume-based quantity discounts?

7. Why do manufacturers like Kraft and Sara Lee offer trade promotions? What impact do trade promotions have on the supply chain? How should trade promotions be structured to maximize their impact while minimizing the additional cost they impose on the supply chain?
8. Why is it appropriate to include only the incremental cost when estimating the holding and order cost for a firm?

Exercises

1. Harley Davidson has its engine assembly plant in Milwaukee and its motorcycle assembly plant in Pennsylvania. Engines are transported between the two plants using trucks. Each truck trip costs $1,000. The motorcycle plant assembles and sells 300 motorcycles each day. Each engine costs $500, and Harley incurs a holding cost of 20 percent per year. How many engines should Harley load onto each truck? What is the cycle inventory of engines at Harley?
2. Harley has decided to implement just-in-time (JIT) manufacturing at the motorcycle assembly plant. As part of this initiative, it has reduced the number of engines loaded on each truck to 100. If each truck trip still costs $1,000, how does this decision affect annual costs at Harley? What should the cost of each truck be if a load of 100 engines is to be optimal for Harley?
3. Harley purchases components from three suppliers. Components purchased from supplier A are priced at $5 each and used at the rate of 20,000 units per month. Components purchased from supplier B are priced at $4 each and used at the rate of 2,500 units per month. Components purchased from supplier C are priced at $5 each and used at the rate of 900 units per month. Currently, Harley purchases a separate truckload from each supplier. As part of its JIT drive, Harley has decided to aggregate purchases from the three suppliers. The trucking company charges a fixed cost of $400 for the truck with an additional charge of $100 for each stop. Thus, if Harley asks for a pickup from only one supplier, the trucking company charges $500; from two suppliers it charges $600; and from three suppliers it charges $700. Suggest a replenishment strategy for Harley that minimizes annual cost. Compare the cost of your strategy with Harley's current strategy of ordering separately from each supplier. What is the cycle inventory of each component at Harley?
4. Prefab, a furniture manufacturer, uses 20,000 square feet of plywood per month. The trucking company charges Prefab $400 per shipment independent of the quantity purchased. The manufacturer offers an all-unit quantity discount with a price of $1 per square foot for orders under 5,000 square feet, $0.98 per square foot for orders between 5,000 and 10,000 square feet, and $0.96 per square foot for orders larger than 10,000 square feet. Prefab incurs a holding cost of 20 percent. What is the optimal lot size for Prefab? What is the annual cost of such a policy? What is the cycle inventory of plywood at Prefab? How does it compare with the cycle inventory if the manufacturer did not offer a quantity discount but sold all plywood at $0.96 per square foot?
5. Reconsider problem 4 with Prefab. However, the manufacturer now offers a marginal unit quantity discount for the plywood. The first 5,000 square feet of any order are sold at $1 per square foot, the next 5,000 square feet are sold at $0.98 per square foot, and any quantity over 10,000 square feet is sold for $0.96 per square foot. What is the optimal lot size for Prefab given this pricing structure? How much cycle inventory of plywood will Prefab carry given the ordering policy?
6. The Dominick's supermarket chain sells Nut Flakes, a popular cereal manufactured by the Tastee cereal company. Demand for Nut Flakes is 1,000 boxes per week. Dominick's has a holding cost of 25 percent and incurs a fixed trucking cost of $200 for each replenishment order it places with Tastee. Given that Tastee

normally charges \$2 per box of Nut Flakes, how much should Dominick's order in each replenishment lot? Tastee runs a trade promotion lowering the price of Nut Flakes to \$1.80 for a month. How much should Dominick's order given the short-term price reduction?

Bibliography

Blattberg, Robert C., and Scott A. Neslin. *Sales Promotion: Concepts, Methods, and Strategies*. Upper Saddle River, N.J.: Prentice-Hall, 1990.

Brealey, Richard A., and Stewart C. Myers. *Principles of Corporate Finance*. Boston; Irwin McGraw-Hill, 2000.

Buzzell, Robert, John Quelch, and Walter Salmon. "The Costly Bargain of Trade Promotions." *Harvard Business Review* (March–April 1990), 141–149.

Crowther, J. "Rationale for Quantity Discounts." *Harvard Business Review* (March–April 1964), 121–127.

Dolan, Robert J. "Quantity Discounts: Managerial Issues and Research Opportunities." *Marketing Science* (6, 1987), 1–24.

Federgruen, A. and Yu-Sheng Zheng. "Optimal Power-of-Two Replenishment Strategies in Capacitated General Production/Distribution Networks." *Management Science* (39, 1993), 710–727.

Kurt Salmon Associates, Inc. *Efficient Consumer Response*. Washington, D.C.; Food Marketing Institute, 1993.

Lee, Hau L., and Corey Billington. "Managing Supply Chain Inventories: Pitfalls and Opportunities." *Sloan Management Review* (Spring 1992), 65–73.

Maxwell, J. A., and J. A. Muckstadt. "Establishing Consistent and Realistic Reorder Intervals in Production-Distribution Systems." *Operations Research* (33, 1985), 1316–1341.

Roundy, Robin. "98%-Effective Integer-Ratio Lot-Sizing for One-Warehouse Multi-Retailer Systems." *Management Science* (31, 1985), 1416–1429.

Silver, Edward A., David Pyke, and Rein Petersen. *Inventory Management and Production Planning and Scheduling*. New York; John Wiley & Sons, 1998.

CASE STUDY

Delivery Strategy at MoonChem

John Kresge was very concerned as he left the meeting at MoonChem, a manufacturer of specialty chemicals. At the year-end meeting, the company's officers had evaluated financial performance and discussed the fact that the firm was achieving only two inventory turns a year. A more careful look had revealed that more than half the inventory MoonChem owned was consignment inventory with its customers. This was very surprising, given that only 20 percent of its customers carried consignment inventory. John Kresge is vice president of supply chain and thus responsible for inventory as well as transportation. He decided to take a careful look at how consignment inventory was managed and come up with an appropriate plan.

MOONCHEM OPERATIONS

MoonChem is a manufacturer of specialty chemicals used in a variety of industrial applications. MoonChem has eight manufacturing plants and 40 distribution centers (DCs). The plants manufacture the base chemicals, and the DCs mix them to produce hundreds of end products that fit customer specifications. In the specialty chemicals market, MoonChem has decided to differentiate itself in the Midwest region by providing consignment inventory to its customers. MoonChem would like to take this strategy national if it proves effective. MoonChem keeps the chemicals required by each customer in the Midwest region on consignment at the customers' sites. Customers use the chemicals as needed, and MoonChem guarantees replenishment to ensure that the customers do not run out of inventory. In most instances, customers' chemical consumption is very stable. MoonChem is paid for the chemicals as they are used. Thus, all consignment inventories belong to MoonChem.

DISTRIBUTION AT MOONCHEM

MoonChem currently uses Golden trucking, a full truckload carrier, for all its shipments. Each truck has a capacity of 40,000 pounds, and Golden charges a fixed rate given the origin and destination, irrespective of the quantity shipped on the truck. Currently, MoonChem sends full truckloads to each customer to replenish its consignment inventory.

THE ILLINOIS PILOT STUDY

John decided to take a careful look at his distribution operations. He decided to focus on the state of Illinois, which was supplied from the Chicago DC. He broke up the state of Illinois into a collection of contiguous zip codes, as shown in Figure 7.7. He decided to restrict attention within the Peoria region, which was classified as zip code 615. A careful study of the Peoria region revealed 2 large customers, 6 medium-sized customers, and 12 small customers. The annual consumption at each type of customer is as shown in Table 7.4. Golden currently charges \$400 for each shipment from Chicago to Peoria, and MoonChem's policy is to send a full truckload to each customer when replenishment of consignment inventory is needed.

John checked with Golden to find out what it would take to include shipments for multiple customers on a single load. Golden informed him that it would continue to charge \$350 per truck and would then add \$50 for each dropoff that Golden was responsible for. Thus, if Golden carried a truck that had to make one delivery, the total charge would be \$400. However, if a truck had to make four deliveries, the total charge would be \$550.

TABLE 7.4 Customer Profile for MoonChem in Peoria Region

Customer Type	*Number of Customers*	*Consumption (Pounds per Month)*
Small	12	1,000
Medium	6	5,000
Large	2	12,000

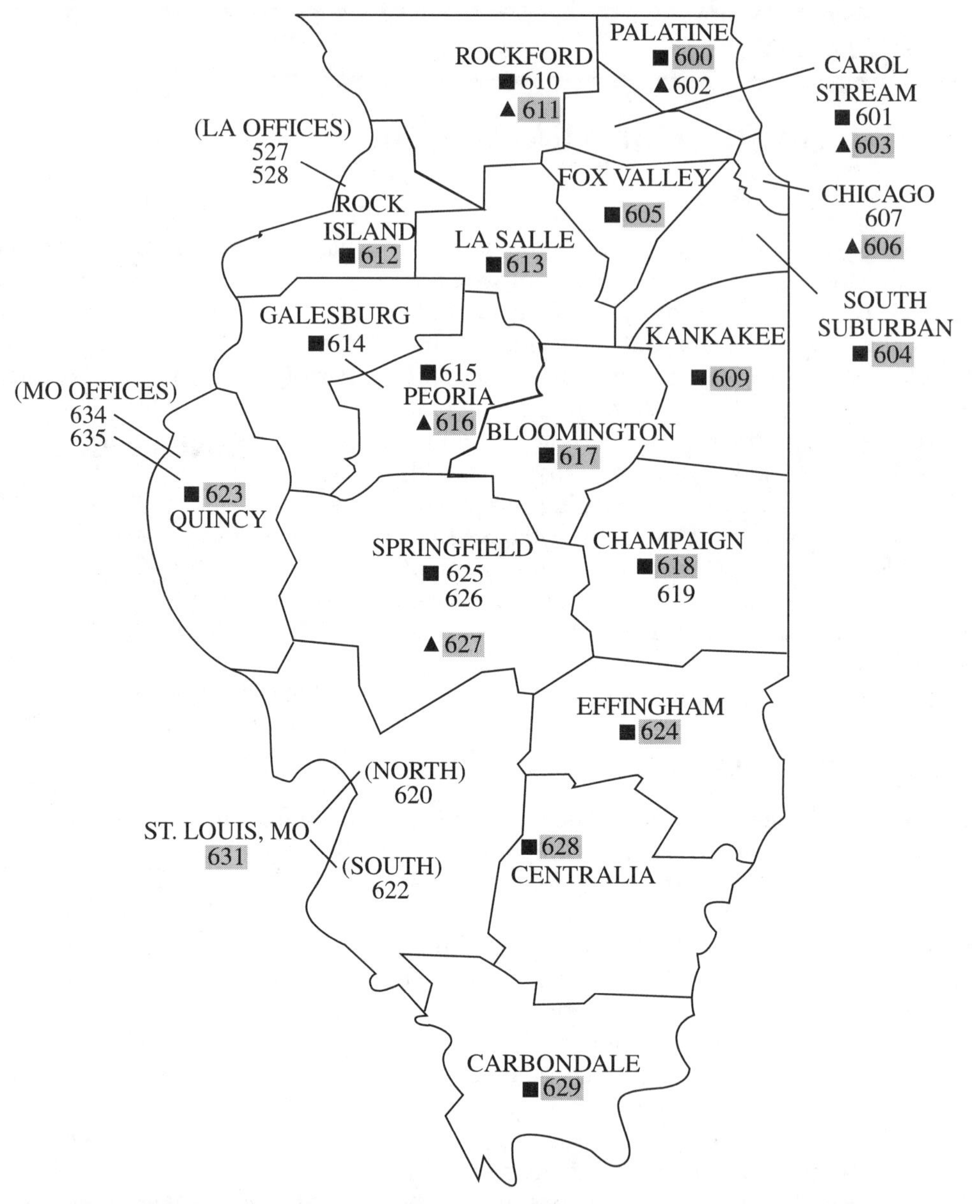

FIGURE 7.7 Illinois Zip Code Map

Each pound of chemical in consignment cost MoonChem $1, and MoonChem had a holding cost of 25 percent. John wanted to analyze different options for distribution available in the Peoria region to decide on the optimal distribution policy. The detailed study of the Peoria region would provide the blueprint for the distribution strategy that MoonChem planned to roll out nationally.

QUESTIONS

1. What is the current annual cost of MoonChem's strategy of sending full truckloads to each customer in the Peoria region to replenish consignment inventory?
2. Consider different delivery options and evaluate the cost of each. What delivery option do you recommend for MoonChem?
3. How does your recommendation affect consignment inventory for MoonChem?

APPENDIX 7A

Economic Order Quantity

Objective: Derive the economic order quantity (EOQ) formula

Analysis: Given an annual demand R, order cost S, unit cost C, and holding cost h, our goal is to estimate the lot size Q that minimizes the total annual cost. For a lot size of Q, the total annual cost is given by the following:

$$\text{Total annual cost, } TC = (R/Q)S + (Q/2)hC + CR$$

To minimize the total cost, we take the first derivative with respect to the lot size Q and set it to zero. Taking the first derivative with respect to Q, we have the following:

$$\frac{d(TC)}{dQ} = -\frac{RS}{Q^2} + \frac{hC}{2}$$

Setting the first derivative to be zero, the EOQ is given by the following:

$$Q^2 = \frac{2\,RS}{hC}, \quad \text{or} \quad Q = \sqrt{\frac{2\,RS}{hC}}$$

CHAPTER 8

Managing Uncertainty in a Supply Chain: Safety Inventory

Learning Objectives
After reading this chapter, you will be able to

1. understand the role of safety inventory in a supply chain;
2. identify factors that influence the required level of safety inventory;
3. describe different measures of product availability; and
4. utilize managerial levers available to lower safety inventory and improve product availability.

In this chapter, we discuss how safety inventory can help a supply chain improve product availability in the presence of supply and demand variability. We discuss various measures of product availability and how managers can set safety inventory levels to provide the desired product availability. We also explore what managers can do to reduce the amount of safety inventory required while maintaining or even improving product availability.

8.1 THE ROLE OF SAFETY INVENTORY IN A SUPPLY CHAIN

Safety inventory is inventory carried for the purpose of satisfying demand that exceeds the amount forecasted for a given period. Safety inventory is carried because demand forecasts are uncertain and a product shortage may result if actual demand exceeds the forecast demand. Consider, for example, Bloomingdales, a high-end department store. Bloomingdales sells purses for women and purchases them from Gucci, an Italian manufacturer. Given the high transportation cost from Italy, the store manager at Bloomingdales orders in lots of 600 purses. Demand for purses at Bloomingdales averages 100 per week. Gucci takes three weeks to respond to a Bloomingdales order and deliver the purses to the store. If there is no demand uncertainty and exactly 100 purses are sold each week, the store manager at Bloomingdales can place an order when the store has exactly 300 purses remaining. In the absence of demand uncertainty, such a policy ensures that the new lot arrives just as the last purse is being sold at the store.

However, as discussed in Chapter 4, demand forecasts are unlikely to be completely accurate. Given forecast errors, actual demand over the three weeks may be higher or lower than the 300 purses forecasted. If the actual demand at Bloomingdales is higher than 300, some customers will be unable to purchase purses, resulting in a loss of potential margin for Bloomingdales. The store manager thus decides to place an order with Gucci when the store still has 400 purses. This policy allows the store manager to improve product availability for the customer, because the store now runs out of purses only if the demand over the three weeks exceeds 400. Given an average weekly demand of 100 purses, the store will have an average of 100 purses remaining when the replenishment lot arrives. Safety inventory is the average inventory remaining when the replenishment lot arrives. Thus, Bloomingdales carries a safety inventory of 100 purses.

Given the lot size of Q = 600 purses, the cycle inventory is $Q/2$ = 300 purses. The inventory profile at Bloomingdales in the presence of safety inventory is shown in Figure 8.1. As Figure 8.1 illustrates, the average inventory at Bloomingdales is the sum of the cycle and safety inventories.

This example illustrates a trade-off that a supply chain manager must consider when planning safety inventory. On the one hand, raising the level of safety inventory increases product availability and thus the margin captured from customer purchases. On the other hand, raising the level of safety inventory increases inventory holding costs in the supply chain. This issue is very significant in high-tech industries, where product life cycles are short and demand is very volatile. Carrying excessive inventory can help counter demand volatility but can really hurt if new products come on the market and demand for the old product in inventory dries up. The inventory on hand then becomes worthless.

In today's business environment, innovations such as the Internet have made it easier for customers to search across stores for product availability. When shopping for books on-line, if Amazon.com is out of a title, a customer can easily check to see if Borders.com has the title available. The increased ease of searching puts pressure on firms to improve product availability. Simultaneously, product variety has grown with increased customization. As a result, markets have become increasingly heterogeneous and demand for individual products is very unstable and difficult to forecast.

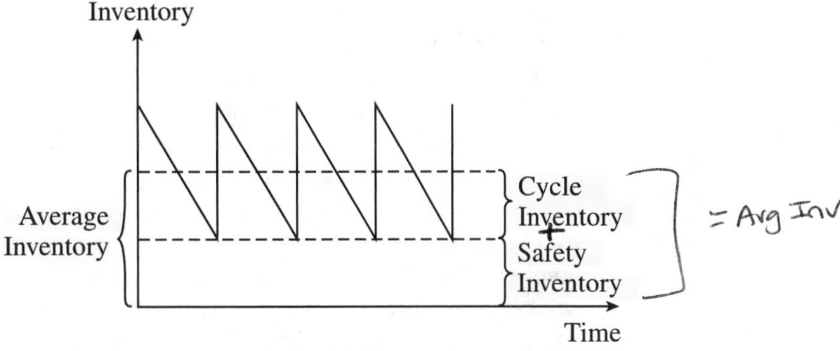

FIGURE 8.1 Inventory Profile with Safety Inventory

Both the increased variety and the increased pressure for availability push firms to increase the level of safety inventory they hold. Given the product variety and high demand uncertainty in most high-tech supply chains, a significant fraction of the inventory carried is safety inventory.

However, as product variety has grown, product life cycles have shrunk. Therefore, it is more likely that a product that is "hot" today will be obsolete tomorrow, which increases the cost to firms of carrying too much inventory. Therefore, a key to the success of any supply chain is to figure out ways to decrease the level of safety inventory carried without hurting the level of product availability.

The importance of reduced safety inventories is emphasized by the experience of Dell and Compaq in the early part of 1998, when prices dropped. Compaq carried 100 days of inventory compared with Dell, which carried only 10. Declining prices hurt Compaq much harder given the extra inventory that it carried. In fact, this situation resulted in Compaq's announcing that it would not make any profits in the first quarter of 1998.

A key to Dell's success has been its ability to provide a high level of product availability to customers while carrying very low levels of safety inventory in its supply chain. This fact has also played a very important role in the success of Wal-Mart and 7-Eleven Japan.

For any supply chain, there are two key questions to consider when planning safety inventory:

1. What is the appropriate level of safety inventory to carry?
2. What actions can be taken to improve product availability while reducing safety inventory?

The remainder of this chapter focuses on answering these questions. Next we consider factors that influence the appropriate level of safety inventory.

8.2 DETERMINING APPROPRIATE LEVEL OF SAFETY INVENTORY

The appropriate level of safety inventory is determined by the following two factors:

- The uncertainty of demand or supply
- The desired level of product availability

As the uncertainty of supply or demand grows, the required level of safety inventories increases. Consider the sale of Palm Pilots at B&M Office Supplies, a distributor of Palm Pilots. When a new Palm Pilot model is introduced, demand is highly uncertain. B&M thus carries a much higher level of safety inventory relative to demand. As the market accepts the model, demand stabilizes and uncertainty reduces. At that point, B&M can carry a lower level of safety inventory relative to demand.

As the desired level of product availability increases, the required level of safety inventory also increases. If B&M targets a higher level of product availability for the new versus the old Palm Pilot model, it must be able to supply a higher level of customer demand for the new model from inventory. Therefore, it must carry a higher level of safety inventory for the new model.

Next we discuss some measures of demand uncertainty.

Measuring Demand Uncertainty

As discussed in Chapter 4, demand has a systematic as well as a random component. The goal of forecasting is to predict the systematic component and estimate the random component. The estimate of the random component is a measure of demand uncertainty. The random component is usually estimated as the standard deviation of demand. We assume the following inputs for demand:

R: Average demand per period
σ_R: Standard deviation of demand per period

For now, we assume that demand is normally distributed. In the case of B&M, weekly demand for the Palm Pilot is normally distributed with a mean of R and a standard deviation of σ_R.

Lead time is the gap between when an order is placed and when it is received. In our discussion, we denote the lead time by L. In the B&M example, L is the time between when B&M orders Palm Pilots and when they are delivered. In this case, B&M is exposed to the uncertainty of demand during the lead time. Whether B&M is able to satisfy all demand from inventory depends on the demand for Palm Pilots experienced during the lead time and the inventory B&M has when a replenishment order is placed. Therefore, B&M must estimate the uncertainty of demand during the lead time, not just a single period. We now evaluate the distribution of demand over k periods, given the distribution of demand during each period.

Assume that demand for each period i, $i = 1, \ldots, k$ is normally distributed with a mean R_i and standard deviation σ_i. Let $cov(i, j)$ be the covariance of demand between periods i and j. In this case, the total demand during k periods is normally distributed with a mean of P and a standard deviation of Ω, where

$$P = \sum_{i=1}^{k} R_i \quad \text{and} \quad \Omega = \sqrt{\sum_{i=1}^{k} \sigma_i^2 + \sum_{i \neq j} \text{cov}(i, j)} \qquad \textbf{(8.1)}$$

The covariance is as follows:

$$cov(i,j) = \rho\sigma_i\sigma_j$$

where ρ is the **correlation coefficient**. Demand in two periods is **perfectly positively correlated** if $\rho = 1$. Demand in two periods is **perfectly negatively correlated** if $\rho = -1$. Demand in two periods is **independent** if $\rho = 0$. Therefore, if demand during each of the k periods is independent and normally distributed with a mean of R and a standard deviation of σ_R, from Equation 8.1 total demand during the k periods is normally distributed with a mean P and a standard deviation of Ω, where

$$P = kR \qquad \text{and} \qquad \Omega = \sqrt{k}\,\sigma_R \tag{8.2}$$

Another important measure of uncertainty is the **coefficient of variation** (cv), which is the ratio of the standard deviation to the mean. Given demand with a mean of μ and a standard deviation of σ, we have the following

$$cv = \sigma/\mu$$

The coefficient of variation measures the size of the uncertainty relative to demand. It captures the fact that a product with a mean demand of 100 and a standard deviation of 100 has greater demand uncertainty than a product with mean demand of 1,000 and a standard deviation of 100. Considering the standard deviation alone cannot capture this difference.

Next we discuss some measures of product availability.

Measuring Product Availability

Product availability reflects a firm's ability to fill a customer order out of available inventory. A **stockout** results if a customer order arrives when product is not available. There are several ways to measure product availability. All availability measures are defined on average over a given time frame, which can range from hours to a year. Some of the important measures follow:

1. **Product fill rate** *(fr)* is the fraction of product demand that is satisfied from product in inventory. It is equivalent to the probability that product demand is supplied from available inventory. Assume that B&M provides Palm Pilots to 90 percent of its customers from inventory, with the remaining 10 percent lost to a neighboring competitor because of a lack of available inventory. In this case, B&M achieves a fill rate of 90 percent.

2. **Order fill rate** is the fraction of orders that are filled from available inventory. In a multiproduct scenario, an order is filled from inventory only if all products in the order can be supplied from the available inventory. In the case of B&M, a customer may order a Palm Pilot along with a calculator. The order is filled from inventory only if both the Palm Pilot and the calculator are available through the store. Order fill rates tend to be lower than product fill rates.

3. **Cycle service level (*CSL*)** is the fraction of **replenishment cycles** that end with all the customer demand being met. A replenishment cycle is the interval between two successive replenishment deliveries. The cycle service level is equal to the probability of not having a stockout in a replenishment cycle. If B&M orders replenishment lots of 600 Palm Pilots, the interval between the arrival of two successive replenishment lots is a replenishment cycle. If the manager at B&M manages inventory such that the store does not run out of inventory in 6 out of 10 replenishment cycles, the store achieves a cycle service level of 60 percent. Observe that a cycle service level of 60 percent will typically result in a much higher fill rate. In the 60 percent of cycles in which B&M does not run out of inventory, all customer demand is satisfied from available inventory. In the 40 percent of cycles in which a stockout does occur, most of

the customer demand is satisfied from inventory. Only the small fraction toward the end of the cycle that arrives after B&M is out of inventory is lost. As a result, the fill rate will be much higher than 60 percent.

The distinction between product fill rate and order fill rate is not very significant in a single product situation. However, when a firm is selling multiple products, this difference may be significant. For example, if most orders include 10 or more different products that are to be shipped, an out-of-stock situation of one product results in the order not being filled from stock. The firm in this case may have a poor order fill rate even though it has good product fill rates. Tracking order fill rates is important when customers place a high value on the entire order being filled simultaneously.

Next we describe two replenishment policies that are often used in practice.

Replenishment Policies

A **replenishment policy** consists of decisions regarding when to reorder and how much to reorder. These decisions determine the cycle and safety inventories along with the product fill rate and the cycle service level. There are several forms that replenishment policies may take. We will restrict attention to two instances:

1. **Continuous review**. Inventory is continuously tracked, and an order for a lot size Q is placed when the inventory declines to the reorder point ROP. As an example, consider the store manager at B&M who continuously tracks the inventory of Palm Pilots. She orders 600 Palm Pilots when the inventory drops below 400. In this case, the size of the order does not change from one order to the next. The time between orders may fluctuate given variable demand.

2. **Periodic review**. Inventory status is checked at regular periodic intervals, and an order is placed to raise the inventory level to a specified threshold. As an example, consider the purchase of film at B&M. The store manager does not continuously track film inventory. Every Saturday, she checks film inventory and orders enough such that the available inventory and the size of the order total 1,000 films. In this case, the time between orders is fixed. The size of each order, however, can fluctuate given variable demand.

These inventory policies are not comprehensive but suffice to illustrate the key managerial issues recording safety inventories.

Evaluating Cycle Service Level and Fill Rate Given a Replenishment Policy

We now discuss procedures for evaluating the cycle service level and fill rate given a replenishment policy. In this section, we restrict attention to the continuous review policy, which is discussed in detail in Section 8.3. The replenishment policy consists of a lot size Q ordered when the inventory on hand declines to the reorder point (ROP). Assume weekly demand to be normally distributed, with mean R and standard deviation σ_R. Assume replenishment lead time of L weeks.

Evaluating Safety Inventory Given a Replenishment Policy

In the case of B&M, safety inventory corresponds to the average number of Palm Pilots on hand when a replenishment order arrives. Given the lead time of L weeks and a mean weekly demand of R, using Equation 8.2, we have the following:

$$\text{Expected demand during lead time} = RL$$

Given that the store manager places a replenishment order when *ROP* Palm Pilots are on hand, we have the following:

$$\text{Safety inventory, } ss = ROP - RL \qquad \textbf{(8.3)}$$

This is because, on average, *RL* Palm Pilots will sell over the period between when the order is placed and when the lot arrives. The average inventory when the replenishment lot arrives will thus be $ROP - RL$.

Example 8.1: Assume that weekly demand for Palm Pilots at B&M Computer World is normally distributed with a mean of 2,500 and a standard deviation of 500. The manufacturer takes two weeks to fill an order placed by the B&M manager. The store manager currently orders 10,000 Palm Pilots when the inventory on hand drops to 6,000. Evaluate the safety inventory carried by B&M and the average inventory carried by B&M. Also evaluate the average time spent by a Palm Pilot at B&M.

Analysis: Under this replenishment policy, we have the following:

$$\text{Average demand per week, } R = 2{,}500$$
$$\text{Standard deviation of weekly demand, } \sigma_R = 500$$
$$\text{Average lead time for replenishment, } L = 2 \text{ weeks}$$
$$\text{Reorder point, } ROP = 6{,}000$$
$$\text{Average lot size, } Q = 10{,}000$$

Using Equation 8.3, we thus have the following:

$$\text{Safety inventory, } ss = ROP - RL = 6{,}000 - 5{,}000 = 1{,}000$$

B&M thus carries a safety inventory of 1,000 Palm Pilots. From Chapter 7, recall the following:

$$\text{Cycle inventory} = Q\,/\,2 = 10{,}000/2 = 5{,}000$$

We thus have the following:

$$\text{Average inventory} = \text{cycle inventory} + \text{safety inventory} = 5{,}000 + 1{,}000 = 6{,}000$$

B&M thus carries an average of 6,000 Palm Pilots in inventory. Using Little's law (Equation 3.1), we have

$$\text{Average flow time} = \text{average inventory / throughput} = 6{,}000\,/\,2{,}500 = 2.4 \text{ weeks}$$

Each Palm Pilot thus spends an average of 2.4 weeks at B&M.

Next, we discuss how to evaluate the cycle service level given a replenishment policy.

Evaluating Cycle Service Level Given a Replenishment Policy

Given a replenishment policy, our goal is to evaluate *CSL*, the probability of not stocking out in a replenishment cycle. We return to B&M's continuous review replenishment policy of ordering *Q* units when the inventory on hand drops to the reorder point *ROP*. The lead time is *L* weeks, and weekly demand is normally distributed with a mean of *R* and a standard deviation of σ_R. Observe that a stockout occurs in a cycle if demand during the lead time is larger than the reorder point *ROP*. Thus, we have the following:

$$CSL = \text{Prob(demand during lead time of } L \text{ weeks} \leq ROP)$$

To evaluate this probability, we need to obtain the distribution of demand during the lead time. From Equation 8.2, we know that demand during lead time is normally distributed with a mean of R_L and a standard deviation of σ_L where

$$R_L = RL \qquad \text{and} \qquad \sigma_L = \sqrt{L}\,\sigma_R$$

Using the notation for the normal distribution from Appendix 8A, the cycle service level is as follows:

$$CSL = F(ROP, R_L, \sigma_L) \tag{8.4}$$

We now illustrate this evaluation in Example 8.2.

Example 8.2: Weekly demand for Palm Pilots at B&M is normally distributed with a mean of 2,500 and a standard deviation of 500. The replenishment lead time is two weeks. Assume that the demand is independent from one week to the next. Evaluate the cycle service level resulting from a policy of ordering 10,000 Palm Pilots when there are 6,000 Palm Pilots in inventory.

Analysis: In this case we have the following:

$Q = 10{,}000$, $ROP = 6{,}000$, $L = 2$ weeks
$R = 2{,}500$/week, $\sigma_R = 500$

Observe that B&M runs the risk of stocking out during the two weeks between when an order is placed and when the replenishment arrives. Thus, whether a stockout occurs depends on the demand during the lead time of two weeks.

The first step is to obtain the distribution of demand during the lead time of two weeks. Because demand across time is independent, we use Equation 8.2 to obtain demand during the lead time to be normally distributed with a mean of R_L and a standard deviation of σ_L where

$$R_L = RL = 2 \times 2{,}500 = 5{,}000 \quad \text{and} \quad \sigma_L = \sqrt{L}\,\sigma_R = \sqrt{2} \times 500 = 707$$

Using Equation 8.4, the cycle service level is evaluated as

$$CSL = \text{probability of not stocking out in a cycle} = F(ROP, R_L, \sigma_L) = F(6{,}000, 5{,}000, 707)$$

Using the relation (Equation 8.19) in Appendix 8B, the cycle service level is evaluated using the Excel function NORMDIST as follows:

$$F(ROP, R_L, \sigma_L) = NORMDIST(ROP, R_L, \sigma_L, 1)$$

We thus obtain a cycle service level for B&M as follows:

$$CSL = F(6{,}000, 5{,}000, 707) = NORMDIST(6{,}000, 5{,}000, 707, 1) = 0.92$$

A cycle service level of 0.92 implies that in 92 percent of the replenishment cycles, B&M is able to supply all demand from available inventory. In the remaining 8 percent of the cycles, stockouts occur, and some demand is not satisfied because of the lack of inventory.

Next we discuss the evaluation of the fill rate given a replenishment policy.

Evaluating Fill Rate Given a Replenishment Policy

Recall that fill rate measures the proportion of customer demand that is satisfied from available inventory. From a retailer's perspective, fill rate is a more relevant measure than cycle service level because it allows the retailer to estimate the fraction of demand that turns to sales. The two measures are very closely related because raising the cycle service level will also raise the fill rate for a firm. Our discussion focuses on evaluating fill rate for a continuous review policy in which Q units are ordered when the quantity on hand drops to the reorder point ROP.

To evaluate the fill rate, it is important to understand the process by which a stockout may occur during a replenishment cycle. A stockout occurs if the demand during the lead time exceeds the reorder point. We thus need to evaluate the average amount of demand in excess of the reorder point in each replenishment cycle.

The **expected shortage per replenishment cycle** (ESC) is the average units of demand that are not satisfied from inventory in stock per replenishment cycle. Given a lot size of Q, the fraction of demand lost is thus ESC/Q. The product fill rate fr is thus given by the following:

$$fr = 1 - ESC/Q = (Q - ESC)/Q \qquad \textbf{(8.5)}$$

A shortage occurs in a replenishment cycle only if the demand during the lead time exceeds the reorder point ROP. Let $f(x)$ be the density function of the demand distribution during the lead time. The expected shortage per replenishment cycle is given by the following:

$$ESC = \int_{x=ROP}^{\infty} (x - ROP)f(x)dx \qquad \textbf{(8.6)}$$

In the case in which demand during the lead time is normally distributed with mean R_L and standard deviation σ_L, given a safety inventory ss, Equation 8.6 can be simplified to the following:

$$ESC = -ss\left[1 - F_s\left(\frac{ss}{\sigma_L}\right)\right] + \sigma_L f_s\left(\frac{ss}{\sigma_L}\right) \qquad \textbf{(8.7)}$$

where F_S is the standard normal cumulative distribution function and f_S is the standard normal density function. A detailed description of the normal distribution is contained in Appendix 8A. Details of the simplification in Equation 8.7 are described in Appendix 8C. Using the Excel functions (Equations 8.22 and 8.23) discussed in Appendix 8B, ESC may be evaluated (using Equation 8.7) as follows:

$$ESC = -ss[1 - \text{NORMDIST}(ss/\sigma_L, 0, 1, 1)] + \sigma_L\,\text{NORMDIST}(ss/\sigma_L, 0, 1, 0). \qquad \textbf{(8.8)}$$

Given the expected shortage per replenishment cycle ESC, we can use Equation 8.5 to evaluate the fill rate fr. Next, we illustrate this evaluation in Example 8.3.

Example 8.3: From Example 8.2, recall that weekly demand for Palm Pilots at B&M is normally distributed with a mean of 2,500 and a standard deviation of 500. The replenishment lead time is two weeks. Assume that the demand is independent from one week to the next. Evaluate the fill rate resulting from the policy of ordering 10,000 Palm Pilots when there are 6,000 Palm Pilots in inventory.

Analysis: From the analysis of Example 8.2, we have the following:

Lot size, $Q = 10{,}000$
Average demand during lead time, $R_L = 5{,}000$
Standard deviation of demand during lead time, $\sigma_L = 707$

Using Equation 8.3, we obtain the following:

Safety inventory, $ss = ROP - RL = 6{,}000 - 5{,}000 = 1{,}000$

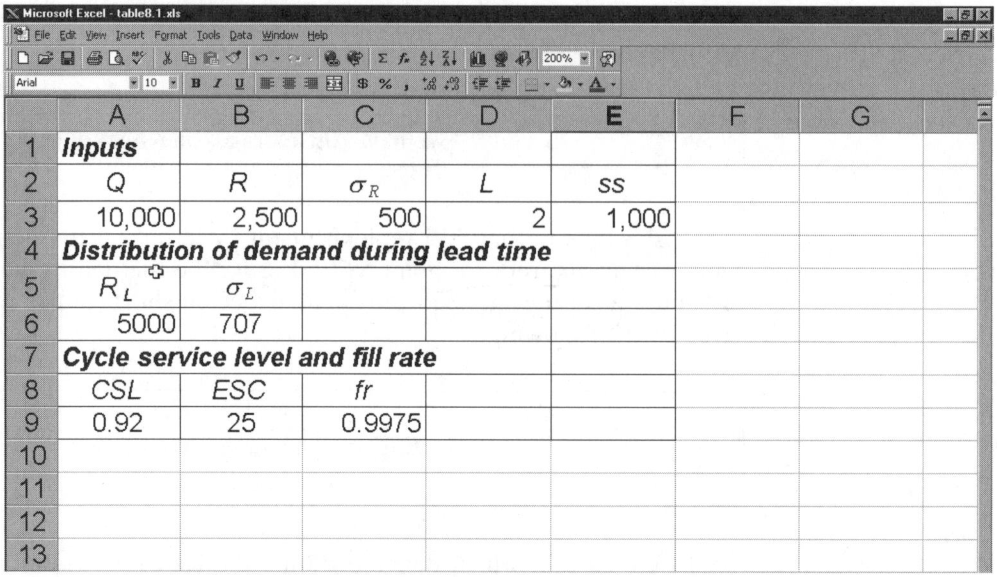

Microsoft Excel - table8.1.xls

	A	B	C	D	E	F	G
1	***Inputs***						
2	*Q*	*R*	σ_R	*L*	*ss*		
3	10,000	2,500	500	2	1,000		
4	***Distribution of demand during lead time***						
5	R_L	σ_L					
6	5000	707					
7	***Cycle service level and fill rate***						
8	*CSL*	*ESC*	*fr*				
9	0.92	25	0.9975				
10							
11							
12							
13							

FIGURE 8.2 Excel Solution of Example 8.3

From Equation 8.8, we thus have the following:

$$ESC = -1{,}000[1 - \text{NORMDIST}(1{,}000/707\,, 0, 1, 1)] + \\ 707\ \text{NORMDIST}(1{,}000/707, 0, 1, 0) = 25.$$

Thus, on average, in each replenishment cycle, 25 Palm Pilots are demanded by customers but not available in inventory. Using Equation 8.5, we thus obtain the following fill rate:

$$fr = (Q - ESC)/Q = (10{,}000 - 25)/10{,}000 = 0.9975$$

In other words, 99.75 percent of the demand is filled from inventory in stock. This is much higher than the cycle service level of 92 percent that resulted in Example 8.2 for the same replenishment policy.

All the calculations for Example 8.3 may be done easily in Excel, as shown in Figure 8.2. The various cell formulas are shown in Table 8.1.

A few key observations should be made. First, observe that the fill rate (0.9975) in Example 8.3 is significantly higher than the cycle service level (0.92) in Example 8.2 for the same replenishment policy. Next, by rerunning the examples with a different lot size, we can observe what the impact of lot size changes is on the service level. Increasing the lot size of Palm Pilots from 10,000 to 20,000 has no impact on the cycle service level (which stays at 0.92). The fill rate, however, now increases to 0.9987. This is because an increase in lot size results in fewer replenishment cycles. In the case of

TABLE 8.1 Cell Formulas for Figure 8.2

Quantity	*Cell*	*Actual Formula*	*Cell Formula*
R_L	A6	*RL*	= B3*D3
σ_L	B6	$\sqrt{L}\,\sigma_R$	= SQRT(D3)*C3
CSL	A9	$CSL = NORMDIST(RL + ss, R_L, \sigma_L, 1)$	= NORMDIST(A6 + E3, A6, B6, 1)
ESC	B9	$-\ ss\,[1 - NORMDIST(ss/\sigma_L, 0, 1, 1)]$ $+\ \sigma_L\ NORMDIST(ss/\sigma_L, 0, 1, 0)$	= −E3*(1 − NORMDIST(E3/B6, 0, 1, 1)) + B6*NORMDIST(E3/B6, 0, 1, 0)
fr	C9	$(Q - ESC)/Q$	= (A3 − B9)/A3

B&M, an increase in lot size from 10,000 to 20,000 results in replenishment occurring once every eight weeks instead of once every four weeks. In other words, the number of replenishment cycles per year decreases from 13 to 6.5. With a 92 percent cycle service level, a lot size of 10,000 results in, on average, one cycle with a stockout per year. With a lot size of 20,000, we have, on average, one stockout every two years. Thus, the fill rate is higher.

> ***Key Point*** Both fill rate and cycle service level increase as the safety inventory is increased. For the same safety inventory, an increase in lot size increases the fill rate but not the cycle service level.

We now discuss how the appropriate level of safety inventory may be obtained given a desired cycle service level or fill rate.

Evaluating Safety Inventory, Given Desired Cycle Service Level or Fill Rate

In many practical settings, firms have a desired level of product availability and want to design replenishment polices that achieve this level. For example, Wal-Mart has a desired level of product availability for each product sold in the store. The store manager must design a replenishment policy with the appropriate level of safety inventory to meet this goal. The desired level of product availability may be determined by trading off the cost of holding inventory with the cost of a stockout. (This trade-off is discussed in detail in Chapter 9.) In other instances, the desired level of product availability (in terms of cycle service level or fill rate) is explicitly stated in contracts, and management must design replenishment policies that achieve the desired target.

Evaluating Required Safety Inventory, Given Desired Cycle Service Level

Our goal is to obtain the appropriate level of safety inventory, given the desired cycle service level. We assume that a continuous review replenishment policy is followed. Consider the store manager at Wal-Mart responsible for designing replenishment policies for all products in the store. He has targeted a cycle service level of CSL for the basic box of Lego building blocks. Given a lead time of L, the store manager wants to identify a suitable reorder point and safety inventory that achieves the desired service level. Assume that demand for Lego at Wal-Mart is normally distributed and independent from one week to the next. We assume the following input:

$$\text{Desired cycle service level} = CSL$$
$$\text{Mean demand during lead time} = R_L$$
$$\text{Standard deviation of demand during lead time} = \sigma_L$$

From Equation 8.3, recall that $ROP = R_L + ss$. The store manager needs to identify safety inventory ss such that

$$\text{Probability(demand during lead time} \leq R_L + ss) = CSL$$

Given that demand is normally distributed, using Equation 8.4, the store manager must identify safety inventory ss such that

$$F(R_L + ss, R_L, \sigma_L) = CSL$$

Given the definition of the inverse normal in Appendix 8A, we obtain the following:

$$R_L + ss = F^{-1}(CSL, R_L, \sigma_L) \qquad \text{or} \qquad ss = F^{-1}(CSL, R_L, \sigma_L) - R_L$$

Using the definition of the standard normal distribution and its inverse from Appendix 8A, it can also be shown that

$$ss = F_S^{-1}(CSL) \times \sigma_L \tag{8.9}$$

In Example 8.4, we illustrate the evaluation of safety inventory given a desired cycle service level.

Example 8.4: Weekly demand for Lego at a Wal-Mart store is normally distributed with a mean of 2,500 boxes and a standard deviation of 500. The replenishment lead time is two weeks. Assuming a continuous review replenishment policy, evaluate the safety inventory that the store should carry to achieve a cycle service level of 90 percent.

Analysis: In this case we have the following:

$$\begin{aligned} Q &= 10{,}000 \\ CSL &= 0.9 \\ L &= 2 \text{ weeks} \\ R &= 2{,}500/\text{week} \\ \sigma_R &= 500 \end{aligned}$$

Because demand across time is independent, we use Equation 8.2 to find demand during the lead time to be normally distributed with a mean of R_L and a standard deviation of σ_L where

$$R_L = RL = 2 \times 2{,}500 = 5{,}000 \qquad \text{and} \qquad \sigma_L = \sqrt{L}\,\sigma_R = \sqrt{2} \times 500 = 707$$

Using Equations 8.9 and 8.24 in Appendix 8B, we obtain the following:

$$ss = F_S^{-1}(CSL) \times \sigma_L = NORMSINV(CSL) \times \sigma_L = NORMSINV(.90) \times 707 = 906$$

Thus, the required safety inventory to achieve a cycle service level of 90 percent is 906 boxes.

Evaluating Required Safety Inventory, Given Desired Fill Rate

We now evaluate the required safety inventory, given a desired fill rate, *fr*, and the fact that a continuous review replenishment policy is followed. Consider the store manager at Wal-Mart targeting a fill rate *fr* for Lego building blocks. The current replenishment lot size is *Q*. The first step is to obtain the expected shortage per replenishment cycle *ESC* using Equation 8.5. The shortage is the following:

$$ESC = (1 - fr)Q$$

The next step is to obtain a safety inventory *ss* that solves Equation 8.7 (and its Excel equivalent, Equation 8.8), given the expected shortage per replenishment cycle, *ESC* evaluated previously. It is not possible to give a formula that provides the answer. The appropriate safety inventory that solves Equation 8.8 can be obtained easily using Excel and trying different values of *ss*. In Excel, the safety inventory may also be obtained directly using the tool GOALSEEK, as illustrated in Example 8.5.

Example 8.5: Weekly demand for Lego at a Wal-Mart store is normally distributed with a mean of 2,500 boxes and a standard deviation of 500. The replenishment lead time is two weeks. The store manager currently orders replenishment lots of 10,000 boxes from Lego. Assuming a continuous review replenishment policy, evaluate the safety inventory the store should carry to achieve a fill rate of 97.5 percent.

Analysis: In this case, we have the following:

Desired fill rate, $fr = 0.975$
Lot size, $Q = 10{,}000$ boxes
Standard deviation of demand during lead time, $\sigma_L = 707$

From Equation 8.5, we thus obtain the following expected shortage per replenishment cycle:

$$ESC = (1 - fr)Q = (1 - 0.975)10{,}000 = 250$$

Now we need to solve Equation 8.7 for the safety inventory ss, where

$$ESC = 250 = -ss\left[1 - F_s\left(\frac{ss}{\sigma_L}\right)\right] + \sigma_L f_s\left(\frac{ss}{\sigma_L}\right) = -ss\left[1 - F_s\left(\frac{ss}{707}\right)\right] + 707 f_s\left(\frac{ss}{707}\right)$$

Using Equation 8.8, this equation may be restated with Excel functions as follows:

$$250 = -ss[1 - NORMSDIST(ss/707)] + 707NORMDIST(ss/707, 0, 1, 0) \quad \textbf{(8.10)}$$

Equation 8.10 may be solved in Excel by trying different values of ss until Equation 8.10 is satisfied. A more elegant approach for solving Equation 8.10 is to use the Excel tool GOALSEEK as follows.

First set up the spreadsheet as shown in Figure 8.3, where cell D3 can have any value for the safety inventory ss and cell A6 has the formula representing Equation 8.10 given by the following equation:

Formula in A6: = −D3*[1 − NORMSDIST(D3/B3)] + B3*NORMDIST(D3/B3, 0, 1, 0)

Invoke GOALSEEK using Tools | Goal Seek. In the GOALSEEK dialog box, enter the following:

Set Cell: A6 {This represents the formula to be evaluated.}
To value: 250 {This represents the desired value of the formula.}
By changing cell: D3 {This represents the variable for which the equation is to be solved.}

Using GOALSEEK, we obtain a safety inventory of $ss = 67$ boxes, as shown in Figure 8.3. Thus, the store manager at Wal-Mart should target a safety inventory of 67 boxes to achieve the desired fill rate of 97.5 percent.

Next we identify the factors that affect the required level of safety inventory.

FIGURE 8.3 Spreadsheet to solve for *ss* using *GOALSEEK*

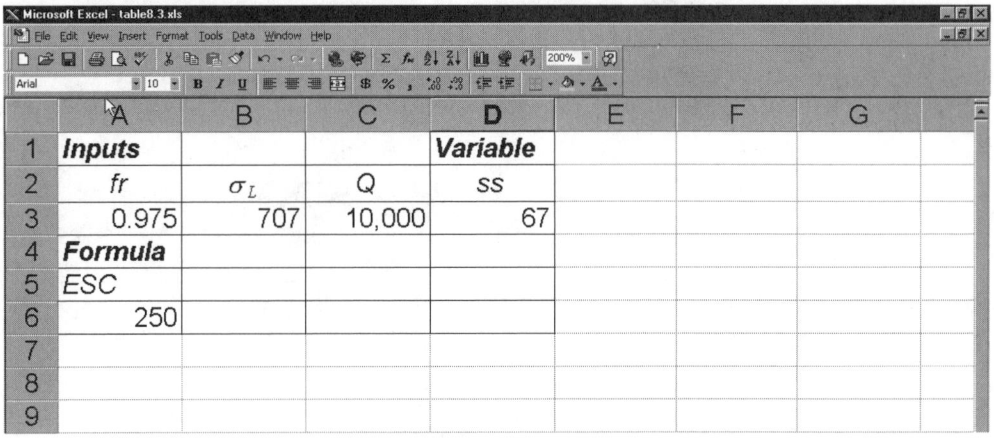

Microsoft Excel - table8.3.xls

	A	B	C	D	E	F	G
1	*Inputs*			*Variable*			
2	*fr*	σ_L	Q	ss			
3	0.975	707	10,000	67			
4	*Formula*						
5	*ESC*						
6	250						
7							
8							
9							

Impact of Required Product Availability and Uncertainty on Safety Inventory

The two key factors that affect the required level of safety inventory are the desired level of product availability and uncertainty. We now discuss the impact that each factor has on the safety inventory.

As the desired product availability goes up, the required safety inventory will also increase, because the supply chain must now be able to accommodate uncommonly high demand or uncommonly low supply. For the Wal-Mart situation in Example 8.5, we evaluate the required safety inventory for varying levels of fill rate, as shown in Table 8.2.

Observe that raising the fill rate from 97.5 percent to 98.0 percent requires an additional 116 units of safety inventory, and raising the fill rate from 99.0 percent to 99.5 percent requires an additional 268 units of safety inventory. Thus, the marginal increase in safety inventory grows as product availability rises. This phenomenon highlights the importance of selecting suitable product availability levels. It is very important for a supply chain manager to be aware of the products that require a high level of availability and only hold high safety inventories in those instances. It is not appropriate to select a very high level of product availability arbitrarily and require it across all products.

> ***Key Point*** The required safety inventory grows rapidly with an increase in the desired product availability.

From Equation 8.9, we see that the required safety inventory *ss* is also influenced by the standard deviation of demand during the lead time, σ_L. The standard deviation of demand during the lead time is influenced by the duration of the lead time L as well as the standard deviation of periodic demand σ_R, as shown in Equation 8.2. The relationship between safety inventory and σ_R is linear in that a 10 percent increase in σ_R results in a 10 percent increase in safety inventory. Safety inventory also increases with an increase in lead time L. The safety inventory, however, is proportional to the square root of the lead time and therefore grows more slowly than the lead time itself.

> ***Key Point*** The required safety inventory increases with an increase in the lead time or the standard deviation of periodic demand.

TABLE 8.2 Required Safety Inventory for Different Values of Fill Rate

Fill Rate	*Safety Inventory*
97.5%	67
98.0%	183
98.5%	321
99.0%	499
99.5%	767

A goal of any supply chain manager is to reduce the level of safety inventory required in a way that does not affect product availability. The preceding discussion highlights two key managerial levers that may be used to achieve this goal:

1. **Reduce the supplier lead time L.** If lead time decreases by a factor of k, the required safety inventory decreases by a factor of $\sqrt{k}$. The only caveat here is that reducing the supplier lead time requires significant effort from the supplier, whereas reduction in safety inventory occurs at the retailer. Therefore, it is important for the retailer to share some of the resulting benefits. Wal-Mart, 7-Eleven Japan, and many other retailers have applied tremendous pressure on their suppliers to reduce the replenishment lead time. Manufacturers like Dell have also required suppliers to reduce their lead times. In each case, the benefit has manifested itself in the form of reduced safety inventory.

2. **Reduce the underlying uncertainty of demand (represented by σ_R).** If σ_R is reduced by a factor of k, the required safety inventory also decreases by a factor of k. A reduction in σ_R may be achieved by better market intelligence and the use of more sophisticated forecasting methods. 7-Eleven Japan provides its store managers with detailed data about prior demand along with weather and other factors that may influence demand. This market intelligence allows the store managers to make better forecasts, reducing uncertainty. However, in most supply chains, the key to reducing the underlying forecast uncertainty is to link all forecasts throughout the supply chain to customer demand data. A lot of the demand uncertainty exists only because each stage of the supply chain plans and forecasts independently. This distorts demand throughout the supply chain, increasing uncertainty. Improved coordination, as discussed in Chapter 13, can often reduce the demand uncertainty significantly. Both Dell and 7-Eleven Japan share demand information with their suppliers, reducing uncertainty and thus safety inventory within the supply chain.

8.3 IMPACT OF SUPPLY UNCERTAINTY ON SAFETY INVENTORY

In our discussion to this point, we focus on situations with demand uncertainty in the form of a forecast error. In many practical situations, supply uncertainty can also play a significant role. Consider the case of the Dell assembly plant in Austin. Dell assembles computers to customer order. However, components are kept in inventory so assembly may start as soon as the order arrives. When planning the level of component inventory, Dell clearly has to take demand uncertainty into account. However, suppliers may not be able to deliver the components required on time because of quality problems. Dell must also account for this supply uncertainty when planning its safety inventories.

In our previous discussion, we consider the replenishment lead time to be fixed. In this section we consider the case in which the lead time is uncertain and identify the impact of lead time uncertainty on safety inventories. We continue with the case of Dell planning its component inventories.

Assume that the customer demand per period for Dell computers and the replenishment lead time from the component supplier are normally distributed. We are provided with the following input:

R: Average demand per period
σ_R: Standard deviation of demand per period
L: Average lead time for replenishment
s_L: Standard deviation of lead time

We consider the safety inventory requirements given that Dell follows a continuous review policy to manage component inventory. Dell experiences a stockout of components if demand during the lead time exceeds the reorder point—that is, the quantity on hand when Dell places a replenishment order. Therefore, we need to identify the distribution of customer demand during the lead time. Given that both lead time and periodic demand are uncertain, demand during the lead time is normally distributed with a mean of R_L and a standard deviation σ_L, where

$$R_L = RL, \sigma_L = \sqrt{L\,\sigma_R^2 + R^2\,s_L^2} \qquad \textbf{(8.11)}$$

Given the distribution of demand during the lead time in Equation 8.11 and a desired cycle service level CSL, Dell can obtain the required safety inventory using Equation 8.9. If product availability is specified as a fill rate, Dell can obtain the required safety inventory using the procedure outlined in Example 8.5. In Example 8.6, we illustrate the impact of lead time uncertainty on the required level of safety inventory at Dell.

Example 8.6: Daily demand for PCs at Dell is normally distributed with a mean of 2,500 and a standard deviation of 500. A key component used in the PC assembly is the hard drive. The hard drive supplier takes an average of $L = 7$ days to replenish inventory at Dell. Dell is targeting a cycle service level of 90 percent (providing a fill rate close to 100 percent) for its hard drive inventory. Evaluate the safety inventory of hard drives that Dell must carry if the standard deviation of the lead time is 7 days. Dell is working with the supplier to reduce the standard deviation to zero. Evaluate the reduction in safety inventory that Dell can expect as a result of this initiative.

Analysis: In this case we have the following:

Average demand per period, $R = 2{,}500$
Standard deviation of demand per period, $\sigma_R = 500$
Average lead time for replenishment, $L = 7$ days
Standard deviation of lead time, $s_L = 7$ days

We first evaluate the distribution of demand during the lead time. Using Equation 8.11, we have the following:

Mean demand during lead time, $R_L = RL = 2{,}500 \times 7 = 17{,}500$
Standard deviation of demand during lead time $\sigma_L = \sqrt{L\,\sigma_R^2 + R^2\,s_L^2} = \sqrt{7 \times 500^2 + 2500^2 \times 7^2} = 17{,}550$

The required safety inventory is obtained using Equations 8.9 and 8.24 as follows:

$$ss = F_s^{-1}(CSL) \times \sigma_L = NORMSINV(CSL) \times \sigma_L = NORMSINV(0.90) \times 17{,}550 = 22{,}491 \text{ hard drives}$$

If the standard deviation of lead time is seven days, Dell must carry a safety inventory of 22,491 drives. Observe that this is equivalent to about nine days of demand for hard drives.

In Table 8.3 we provide the required safety inventory as Dell works with the supplier to reduce standard deviation of lead time down to zero.

From Table 8.3, observe that the reduction in lead time uncertainty allows Dell to reduce its safety inventory of hard drives by a significant amount. As the standard deviation of lead time declines from seven days to zero, the amount of safety inventory declines from about nine days of demand to less than a day of demand.

This example emphasizes the impact of lead time variability on safety inventory requirements (and thus material flow time) and the large potential benefits from reducing lead time variability or improving on-time deliveries. Often, safety inventory calculations in practice do not include any measure of supply uncertainty, resulting in levels that may be lower than required. This hurts product availability.

TABLE 8.3 Required Safety Inventory as a Function of Lead Time Uncertainty

s_L	σ_L	*ss (units)*	*ss (days)*
6	15,058	19,298	7.72
5	12,750	16,109	6.44
4	10,087	12,927	5.17
3	7,616	9,760	3.90
2	5,172	6,628	2.65
1	2,828	3,625	1.45
0	1,323	1,695	0.68

Key Point A reduction in supply uncertainty can help reduce safety inventory required without hurting product availability.

In practice, variability of supply lead time is caused by practices at both the supplier and the party receiving the order. Suppliers often have poor planning tools that do not allow them to schedule production in a way that can be executed. Today, most supply chain planning suites have good production planning tools that allow suppliers to promise lead times that can be met. This should help reduce lead time variability. In other instances, the behavior of the party placing the order often increases lead time variability. In one instance, a distributor placed orders to all suppliers on the same day of the week. As a result, all deliveries arrived on the same day of the week. The surge in deliveries made it impossible for all of them to be received in a day. Often, deliveries did not show up in inventory until several days after they were delivered. This led to a perception that supply lead times were large and variable. By just leveling out the orders over the week, the lead time and the lead time variability were significantly reduced, allowing the distributor to reduce its safety inventory.

Next, we discuss how aggregation can help reduce the amount of safety inventory in the supply chain.

8.4 IMPACT OF AGGREGATION ON SAFETY INVENTORY

In practice, supply chains have varying degrees of inventory aggregation. For example, Compaq and Hewlett Packard sell computers through retail stores like Best Buy with inventory distributed all over the country. Dell, in contrast, has one centralized facility at Austin from which all customer orders are shipped. Borders and Barnes and Noble sell books and music from retail stores with inventory geographically distributed across the country. Amazon.com, in contrast, ships all its books and music from a few facilities. 7-Eleven Japan has small convenience stores densely distributed over areas of Japan where they have a presence. In contrast, supermarkets tend to be much larger with fewer outlets that are not as densely distributed.

A key question to consider is how aggregation in each of these cases affects safety inventories. Our goal is to understand how supply chains can exploit inventory aggregation to reduce the level of safety inventory required without hurting product availability.

As discussed in Chapter 4, we show that geographical aggregation of demand improves forecast accuracy. Consider the case in which weekly demand for computers in each zip code in the Chicago region is normally distributed with the following characteristics:

R_i: Mean weekly demand in zip code i, $i = 1, \ldots, k$
σ_i = Standard deviation of weekly demand in zip code i, $i = 1, \ldots, k$
$cov(i, j)$: Covariance of weekly demand for zip codes i, j, $1 \leq i \neq j \leq k$

Our objective is to find the distribution of aggregate demand across the entire Chicago region. In this case (similar to Equation 8.1), the aggregate demand is normally distributed with a mean of R^C, standard deviation of σ_R^C, and a variance of $var(R^C)$, where

$$R^C = \sum_{j=1}^{k} R_i,\ \text{var}(R^C) = \sum_{i \neq j}^{k} \sigma_1^2 + 2\sum_{i=j} \text{cov}(i, j),\ \sigma_R^C = \sqrt{\text{var}(R^C)} \tag{8.12}$$

Recall that the covariance is given by the following equation:

$$cov(i,j) = \rho_{ij}\,\sigma_i\,\sigma_j$$

where ρ_{ij} is the correlation coefficient. The stronger the positive correlation of demand in two regions, the closer ρ_{ij} is to one. It can be argued that demand for electricity, natural gas for heating, or oil will be strongly positively correlated across all zip codes in the Chicago area because demand is closely linked to temperature. Conversely, demand for milk across the different zip codes is likely to be independent.

When demand across all the zip codes is independent, all correlation coefficients and thus covariances are zero. In this case, variance and standard deviation of aggregate demand are given by the following equation:

$$\text{var}(R^C) = \sum_{i=1}^{k} \sigma_i^2 \text{ and } \sigma_R^C = \sqrt{\text{var}(R^C)} = \sqrt{\sum_{i=1}^{k} \sigma_i^2} \tag{8.13}$$

From Equation 8.13, observe that $\sigma_R^C \leq \sum_{i=1}^{k} \sigma_i$. This implies that when the demands being aggregated are independent, the standard deviation of aggregate demand is less than the sum of the standard deviations of individual demands.

In contrast, if demand across the different zip codes is perfectly positively correlated, we have all correlation coefficients ρ_{ij} equal to one. In this case the variance and standard deviation of aggregate demand are given by

$$\text{var}(R^C) = (\sigma_R^C)^2 = \sum_{i=1}^{k} \sigma_i^2 + 2\sum_{i \neq j} \text{cov}(i, j) = \sum_{i=1}^{k} \sigma_i^2 + 2\sum_{i \neq j} \sigma_i\,\sigma_j = \left(\sum_{i=1}^{k} \sigma_i\right)^2 \tag{8.14}$$

From Equation 8.14, observe that $\sigma_R^C = \sum_{i=1}^{k} \sigma_i$. Thus, if the demands being aggregated are perfectly positively correlated, the standard deviation of aggregate demand is the sum of the standard deviations of individual demands.

From Equations 8.13 and 8.14, it thus follows that aggregation reduces the standard deviation of demand only if demand across the regions being aggregated is not perfectly positively correlated. Because the required safety inventory is proportional to the standard deviation of demand (see Equation 8.9), we can thus argue that aggregating demand that is not perfectly positively correlated will reduce the amount of safety inventory required without hurting product availability.

We illustrate the impact of aggregation on safety inventory in Example 8.7.

Example 8.7: A luxury car dealership has four retail outlets serving the entire Chicago area (disaggregate option). Weekly demand at each outlet is normally distributed with a mean of $R = 25$ cars and a standard deviation of $\sigma_R = 5$. The lead time for replenishment from the manufacturer is $L = 2$ weeks. Each outlet covers a separate geographical area, and the correlation of demand across any pair of areas is ρ. The dealership is considering the possibility of replacing the four outlets by a single large outlet (aggregate option). Assume that the demand in the central outlet would be the sum of the demand across all four areas. The dealership is targeting a cycle service level of 0.90. Compare the level of safety inventory needed in the two options as the correlation coefficient ρ varies between 0 and 1.

Analysis: We provide a detailed analysis for the case when demand in each area is independent, that is, $\rho = 0$. For each retail outlet we have the following:

Standard deviation of weekly demand, $\sigma_R = 5$
Replenishment lead time, $L = 2$ weeks

Using Equation 8.2 we thus have the following:

Standard deviation of demand during lead time, $\sigma_L = 7.07$.

Given the desired cycle service level, $CSL = 0.90$, the required safety inventory at each retail outlet (using Equation 8.9) is given by the following:

$$\text{Required safety inventory, } ss = F_s^{-1}(CSL) \times \sigma_L = F_s^{-1}(0.9) \times 7.07 = 9.06$$

In the disaggregate option, each retail outlet must carry 9.06 cars as safety inventory. Across all four outlets, in the disaggregate option we have the following:

$$\text{Total safety inventory required for } CSL \text{ of } 0.90 = 4 \times 9.06 = 36.24 \text{ cars}$$

Now consider the aggregate option. Because demand in all four areas is independent, using Equation 8.13, we thus have the following:

Mean demand at central outlet, $R^C = 4 \times 25 = 100$
Standard deviation of weekly demand at central outlet, $\sigma_R^C = \sqrt{4} \times 5 = 10$

Given that lead time is two weeks, we have the following:

Standard deviation of demand during lead time at central outlet,
$$\sigma_L^C = \sqrt{L}\,\sigma_R^C = \sqrt{2} \times 10 = 14.14$$

For a cycle service level of 0.90, safety inventory required for the aggregate option (using Equation 8.9) is as follows:

$$ss = F_s^{-1}(\text{CSL}) \times \sigma_L^C = NORMSINV(0.90) \times 14.14 = 18.12$$

Using the same procedure, the required level of safety inventory for the disaggregate as well as the aggregate option can be obtained for different values of ρ. The results are shown in Table 8.4.

Observe that the safety inventory for the disaggregate option is higher than for the aggregate option except in the case in which all demands are perfectly positively correlated. The benefit of aggregation decreases as demand in different areas is more positively correlated.

Example 8.7 and the previous discussion demonstrate that aggregation reduces demand uncertainty and thus the required safety inventory as long as the demand being aggregated is not perfectly positively correlated. Demand for most products does not show perfect positive correlation across different geographical regions. In case demand in different geographical regions is about the same size and independent, aggregation reduces safety inventory by the square root of the number of areas

TABLE 8.4 Safety Inventory in the Disaggregate and Aggregate Options

ρ	*Disaggregate Safety Inventory*	*Aggregate Safety Inventory*
0	36.24	18.12
0.2	36.24	22.92
0.4	36.24	26.88
0.6	36.24	30.32
0.8	36.24	33.41
1.0	36.24	36.24

aggregated. In other words, if the number of independent stocking locations decreases by a factor of n, the average safety inventory is expected to decrease by a factor of $\sqrt{n}$. This principle is referred to as the **square root law**. In general, demand being aggregated is unlikely to be perfectly independent. The square root law is illustrated in Figure 8.4.

There are instances in which companies have physically centralized inventories by having one central warehouse serving the entire United States. In the computer industry, both Dell and Gateway have aggregated their assembly and inventory holding. As for retailers, most e-commerce firms are hoping to exploit the benefits of aggregation in terms of reduced inventories to compete. The best-known example in this regard is Amazon.com, which has aggregated its inventories in a few locations. As a result, it has lower levels of book and music inventories than bookstore chains such as Borders and Barnes and Noble, which must keep inventory in every retail store.

There are, however, situations in which physical aggregation of inventories in one location may not be optimal. There are two major disadvantages of aggregating all inventory in one location:

- Increase in response time to customer order
- Increase in transportation cost to customer

Both disadvantages result because the average distance between the inventory and the customer increases with aggregation. With this situation, either the customer has to travel more to reach the product, or the product has to be shipped over longer distances to reach the customer. For example, a retail chain like The Gap has

FIGURE 8.4 Square Root Law

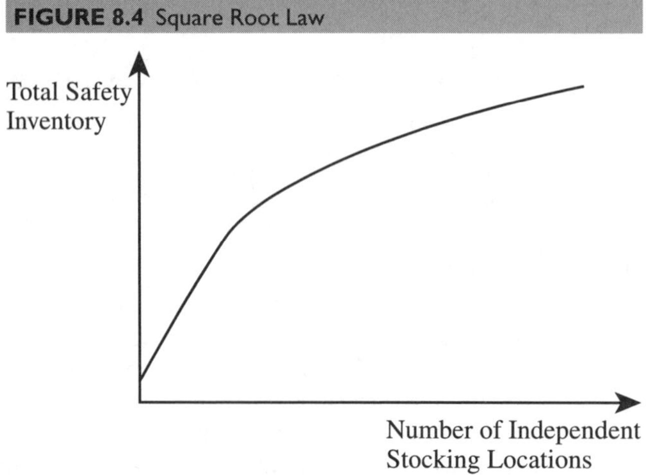

the option of building many small retail outlets or a few large ones. The Gap tends to have many smaller outlets distributed evenly in a region, because this strategy reduces the distance that customers travel to reach a store. If The Gap had one large centralized outlet, the average distance that customers need to travel would increase, and therefore, the response time would increase. Consequently, a desire to decrease customer response time is the impetus for the firm to have multiple outlets. Another example is McMaster-Carr, a distributor of maintenance, repair, and operations (MRO) supplies. McMaster-Carr uses UPS for shipping product to customers. Because shipping charges are based on the origin as well as the destination zone, having one centralized warehouse will increase the average shipping cost as well as the response time to the customer. Therefore, McMaster-Carr has five warehouses that allow it to provide next-day delivery to a large fraction of the United States. Next-day delivery with UPS would not be feasible at a reasonable cost if McMaster had only one warehouse. Another example is that of Amazon.com, which started with one warehouse in Seattle. As it has grown, it has added more warehouses in other parts of the United States in an effort to improve response time and reduce transportation cost to the customer.

These examples highlight instances in which physical aggregation of inventory at one location may not be optimal. However, there are clear benefits to aggregating safety inventory. We now discuss various methods by which a supply chain can extract the benefits of aggregation without having to physically centralize all inventories in one location.

Information Centralization

McMaster-Carr uses **information centralization** to virtually aggregate all its inventories despite having five stocking locations. The company has set up an information system that allows access to current inventory records from each warehouse. Consider, for example, a customer from Chicago ordering a motor and a pump. When the customer order arrives, McMaster-Carr makes an initial check to see if the Chicago warehouse can fill the entire order. If so, the order is shipped from the Chicago warehouse, minimizing the transportation cost.

In case the Chicago warehouse has motors but is out of pumps, McMaster-Carr obtains the pump from the closest warehouse that has the pump in inventory. The pump is shipped from the warehouse to Chicago, where it is merged with the motor into a single shipment and sent to the customer. Thus, inventory at all locations is available to all orders, no matter where they originate. Information centralization allows McMaster-Carr to reduce the level of inventories required while providing a high level of product availability by virtually aggregating inventories.

The benefit of information centralization derives from the fact that most orders are filled from the warehouse closest to the customer, keeping transportation costs low. In case of a stockout, other warehouses fill the order, improving product availability. As a result, McMaster-Carr can reduce its safety inventory without hurting product availability.

Retailers like The Gap have also used information centralization very effectively. If a store does not have the size or color that a customer wants, store employees can use the available information system to inform the customer of the closest store with the product in inventory. The customer can then either go to this store or have the product delivered to his or her house. The Gap thus uses information centralization to virtually aggregate inventory across all retail stores, even though the inventory is physically separated. This allows The Gap to reduce the amount of safety inventory it carries while providing a high level of product availability.

Wal-Mart has an information system in place that allows store managers to search other stores for an excess of items that may be hot sellers at its stores. Wal-Mart provides transportation that allows store managers to exchange products so they arrive at stores where they are in high demand. In this case, Wal-Mart uses information centralization with a responsive transportation system to reduce the amount of safety inventory carried while providing a high level of product availability.

Specialization

Most supply chains provide a variety of products to customers. When inventory is carried at multiple locations, a key decision for a supply chain manager is whether all products should be stocked at every location. Clearly, a product that does not sell in a geographical region should not be carried in inventory by the warehouse or retail store located there. For example, it does not make sense for a Sears retail store in southern Florida to carry snow boots in inventory.

Another important factor that must be considered when making stocking decisions is the reduction in safety inventory that results from aggregation. If aggregation reduces the required safety inventory for a product by a large amount, it is better to carry the product in one central location. If aggregation reduces the required safety inventory for a product by a small amount, it may be best to carry the product in multiple decentralized locations to reduce response time and transportation cost.

The reduction in safety inventory due to aggregation is strongly influenced by the coefficient of variation of demand. For a product with very low coefficient of variation, disaggregate demand can be forecast with accuracy. As a result, the benefit from aggregation is minimal. For a product with a high coefficient of variation of demand, disaggregate demand is very difficult to forecast. In this case, aggregation improves forecast accuracy significantly, providing great benefits. We illustrate this idea in Example 8.8.

Example 8.8: Assume that Grainger, a supplier of MRO products, has 1,600 stores distributed throughout the United States. Consider two products: large electric motors and industrial cleaners. Each motor costs \$500, and each can of cleaner costs \$30. Weekly demand for motors at each store is normally distributed with a mean of 20 and a standard deviation of 40. Weekly demand for cleaner at each store is normally distributed with a mean of 1,000 and a standard deviation of 100. Demand experienced by each store is independent, and supply lead time for both motors and cleaner is four weeks. Grainger has a holding cost of 25 percent. For each of the two products, evaluate the reduction in safety inventories that will result if they are removed from retail stores and only carried in a centralized distribution center (DC). Assume a desired cycle service level of $CSL = 0.95$.

Analysis: The evaluation of safety inventories and the value of aggregation for each of the two products is shown in Table 8.5. All calculations use the approach discussed earlier and illustrated in Example 8.5.

As Table 8.5 shows, the benefit from centralizing motors is much larger than the benefit from centralizing cleaner. Grainger would be advised to stock cleaner at the stores and motors in the DC. Given that cleaner is a high-demand item, customers will be able to pick it up on the same day at the stores. Given that motors are a low-demand item, customers may be willing to wait the extra day that shipping from the DC will entail.

Key Point The higher the coefficient of variation of an item, the greater the reduction in safety inventories as a result of centralization.

TABLE 8.5 Value of Aggregation at Grainger

	Motors	*Cleaner*
Inventory Is Stocked in Each Store		
Mean weekly demand per store	20	1,000
Standard deviation	40	100
Coefficient of variation	2.0	0.1
Safety inventory per store	132	329
Total safety inventory	211,200	526,400
Value of safety inventory	$105,600,000	$15,792,000
Inventory Is Aggregared at the DC		
Mean weekly aggregate demand	32,000	1,600,000
Standard deviation of aggregate demand	1,600	4,000
Coefficient of variation	0.05	0.0025
Aggregate safety inventory	5,264	13,159
Value of safety inventory	$2,632,000	$394,770
Savings		
Total inventory savings on aggregation	$102,968,000	$15,397,230
Total holding cost savings on aggregation	$25,742,000	$3,849,308
Holding cost savings per unit sold	$7.74	$0.046
Savings as a percent of product cost	1.55%	0.15%

Items with a very low demand are referred to as **slow-moving items** and typically have a high coefficient of variation, and items with high demand are referred to as **fast-moving items** and typically have a low coefficient of variation. For many supply chains, specializing the distribution network with fast-moving items stocked at decentralized locations close to the customer and slow-moving items stocked at a centralized location can significantly reduce the safety inventory carried without hurting customer response time or adding to transportation cost. The centralized location then specializes in handling slow-moving items.

Of course, there are other factors that need to be considered when deciding on the allocation of products to stocking locations. For example, an item that is considered an emergency item because the customer urgently needs it may be stocked at the stores even if it has a high coefficient of variation. One also needs to consider the cost of the item. High-value items will provide a greater benefit from centralization than low-value items.

It is important for firms with brick-and-mortar stores to take the idea of specialization into account when they design their e-commerce strategy. Consider, for example, a bookstore chain like Borders. It is able to carry fewer than 100,000 titles at each retail store. The titles carried can be divided into two broad categories: best-sellers with high demand and other books with much lower demand. Borders can design an e-commerce strategy in which the retail stores primarily carry best-sellers in inventory. They would also carry one or at most two copies of each of the other titles to allow customers to browse. Customers could access all titles not in the store via electronic kiosks in the store that provide access to Borders.com inventory. This strategy would allow customers to access an increased variety of books from Borders stores. Customers could place orders for the low-volume titles with Borders.com while purchasing high-volume titles at the store itself. This strategy of specialization would allow Borders to aggregate all slow-moving items to be sold by the on-line channel. All best-sellers would be decentralized and carried close to the customer. The supply chain would thus reduce inventory costs for the slow-moving items at the expense of somewhat higher transportation costs. For the fast-moving items, the supply chain would provide a lower transportation cost and better response time by carrying the items at retail stores close to the customer.

The Gap has followed a similar strategy and integrated its on-line channel with its retail stores. Terminals are available at the retail stores for placing orders on-line. The retail stores carry fast-moving items, and the customer is able to order slow-moving colors or sizes on-line. The Gap is thus able to increase the variety of products available to customers while keeping supply chain inventories down.

Product Substitution

Substitution refers to the use of one product to satisfy demand for a different product. There are two instances in which substitution may occur:

- **Manufacturer-driven substitution**. In this case, the manufacturer or supplier makes the decision to substitute. Typically, the manufacturer will substitute a higher-value product for a lower-value product not in inventory. For example, Dell may install a six-gigabyte hard drive into a customer order requiring a four-gigabyte hard drive, if the smaller drive is out of stock.
- **Customer-driven substitution**. In this case, customers make the decision to substitute. For example, a customer walking into a Wal-Mart store to buy a gallon of detergent may buy the half-gallon size if the gallon size is unavailable. In this case, the customer has substituted the half-gallon size for the gallon size.

In both cases, exploiting substitution allows the supply chain to satisfy demand using aggregate inventories, which permits the supply chain to reduce safety inventories without hurting product availability. In general, given two products or components, substitution may be **one-way**—that is, only one of the products (components) substitutes for the other—or **two-way**—that is, either product (component) substitutes for the other. We briefly discuss one-way substitution in the context of manufacturer-driven substitution and two-way substitution in the context of customer-driven substitution.

Manufacturer-Driven One-Way Substitution

Consider Gateway, a personal computer (PC) manufacturer selling direct to customers. Gateway offers its customers drives that vary in size from 5 to 20 gigabytes. Customers are charged according to the size of drive that they select, with larger sizes being priced higher. If a customer orders a 6-gigabyte drive and Gateway is out of drives of this size, there are two possible choices: (1) delay or deny the customer order or (2) substitute a larger drive that is in stock (say a 8-gigabyte drive) and fill the customer order on time. In the first case, there is potentially a lost sale or loss of future sales because the customer experiences a delayed delivery. In the second case, the manufacturer installs a higher-cost component, reducing the company's profit margin. These factors, along with the fact that only larger drives can substitute for smaller drives, must be considered when Gateway makes inventory decisions for individual drive sizes.

Substitution allows Gateway to aggregate demand across the components, reducing safety inventories required. The value of substitution increases as demand uncertainty increases. Thus, Gateway should consider substitution for components displaying very high demand uncertainty.

The desired degree of substitution is influenced by the cost differential between the higher-value and lower-value components. If the cost differential is very small, Gateway should aggregate most of the demand and carry most of its inventory in the form of the higher-value component. As the cost differential increases, the benefit of substitution decreases. In this case, Gateway will find it more profitable to carry inventory of each of the two components and decrease the amount of substitution.

The desired level of substitution is also influenced by the correlation of demand between the products. If demand between two components is strongly positively correlated, there is little value in substitution. As demand for the two components becomes less positively correlated, the benefit of substitution increases.

Key Point Manufacturer-driven substitution increases overall profitability for the manufacturer by allowing some aggregation of demand, which reduces the inventory requirements for the same level of availability.

Customer-Driven Two-Way Substitution

Consider Grainger selling two brands of motors, GE and SE, which have very similar performance characteristics. Customers are willing to purchase either brand, depending on product availability. If Grainger managers do not recognize customer substitution, they will not encourage it. For a given level of product availability, Grainger will thus have to carry high levels of safety inventory of each brand. If its managers recognize and encourage customer substitution, they can aggregate the safety inventory across the two brands, thereby improving product availability.

Grainger does a very good job of recognizing customer substitution. When a customer calls or goes on-line to place an order and the product he or she requests is not available, he or she is immediately told the availability of all equivalent products that may be substituted. Most customers ultimately buy a substitute product in this case. Grainger exploits this substitution by managing safety inventory of all substitutable products jointly. Recognition and exploitation of customer substitution allows Grainger to provide a high level of product inventory with lower levels of safety inventory.

A good understanding of customer-driven substitution is very important in the retail industry. It must be exploited when merchandising to ensure that substitute products are placed near each other, allowing a customer to buy one if the other is out of stock. In the on-line channel, substitution requires a retailer to present the availability of substitute products if the one the customer requests is out of stock. The supply chain is thus able to reduce the required level of safety inventory while providing a high level of product availability.

Key Point Recognition of customer-driven substitution and joint management of inventories across substitutable products allows a supply chain to reduce the required safety inventory while ensuring a high level of product availability.

The demand uncertainties as well as the correlation of demand between the substitutable products influence the benefit to a retailer from exploiting substitution. The greater the demand uncertainty, the greater the benefit. The less the positive correlation of demand between substitutable products, the greater the benefit from exploiting substitution.

Component Commonality

In any supply chain, a significant amount of inventory is held in the form of components. A single product like a PC often contains hundreds of components. When a supply chain is producing a large variety of products, component inventories can easily become very large. The use of common components in a variety of products has become a very effective supply chain strategy to exploit aggregation and reduce component inventories.

The Dell Corporation sells thousands of different PC configurations to customers. An extreme option for Dell is to design distinct components that are suited to the performance of a particular configuration. In this case, Dell would use different memory, hard drive, modem, and other components for each distinct finished product. The other option is to design common components such that different combinations of the finished products result in different finished products.

Without common components, the uncertainty of demand for any component is the same as the uncertainty of demand for the finished product in which it is used. Given the large number of components in each finished product, demand uncertainty will be very high, resulting in high levels of safety inventory. When common components are designed, each component is used in multiple finished products. The demand for each component is then an aggregation of the demand for all the finished products of which the component is a part. Component demand is thus more predictable than the demand for any one finished product. This fact reduces the component inventories carried in the supply chain. This idea has been a key factor for success in the PC industry and has also started to play a big role in the auto industry. With increasing product variety, component commonality is a key to reducing supply chain inventories without hurting product availability. We illustrate the basic idea behind component commonality in Example 8.9.

Example 8.9: Assume that Dell is to manufacture 27 different PCs with three distinct components: processor, memory, and hard drive. In the disaggregate option, Dell designs specific components for each PC, resulting in $3 \times 27 = 81$ distinct components. In the common component option, Dell designs three distinct processors, three distinct memory units, and three distinct hard drives that can be combined to create 27 different PCs. Each component is thus used in nine different PCs. Monthly demand for each of the 27 different PCs is independent and normally distributed with a mean of 5,000 and a standard deviation of 3,000. The replenishment lead time for each component is one month. Dell is targeting a cycle service level of 95 percent for component inventory. Evaluate the safety inventory requirements with and without the use of component commonality. Also evaluate the change in safety inventory requirements as the number of finished products of which a component is a part varies from one to nine.

Analysis: We first evaluate the disaggregate option, in which components are specific to a PC. For each component we have the following:

$$\text{Standard deviation of monthly demand} = 3{,}000$$

Given a lead time of one month, using Equation 8.9, required safety inventory per component is given by the following:

$$\text{Safety inventory per component} = NORMSINV(0.95) \times 3{,}000 = 4{,}935 \text{ units}$$

Given a total of 81 components across 27 different PCs, we thus have the following:

$$\text{Total safety inventory required} = 81 \times 4{,}935 = 399{,}699 \text{ units}$$

In the case of component commonality, each component ends up in nine different finished products. Therefore, the demand at the component level is the sum of demand across nine different products. Aggregating across the nine products, we get monthly component demand to be normally distributed with the following:

$$\text{Mean demand of common component across 9 products} = 9 \times 5{,}000 = 45{,}000$$
$$\text{Standard deviation of demand of common component across 9 products} = \sqrt{9} \times 3{,}000 = 9{,}000$$

Using Equation 8.9, the safety inventory required for each component is thus as follows:

$$\text{Safety inventory per common component} = NORMSINV(0.95) \times 9{,}000 = 14{,}804 \text{ units}$$

With component commonality there are a total of nine distinct components. The total safety inventory across all nine components is thus as follows:

$$\text{Total safety inventory required} = 9 \times 14{,}804 = 133{,}236$$

Thus, using component commonality, having each component in nine different products results in a reduction in safety inventory for Dell from 399,735 to 133,236.

In Table 8.6, we evaluate the marginal benefit in terms of reduction in safety inventory as a result of increasing component commonality. Starting with the required safety inventory when each component is used in only one finished product, we evaluate the safety inventory as the number of finished products in which a component is used increases to nine.

Observe that component commonality decreases the required safety inventory for Dell. However, the marginal benefit of commonality declines as a component is used in more and more finished products.

As a component is used in more finished products, it needs to be more flexible. As a result, the cost of producing the component typically increases with increasing commonality. Given that the marginal benefit of component commonality decreases as we increase commonality, we need to trade off the increase in component cost and the decrease in safety inventory when deciding on the appropriate level of component commonality.

Key Point Component commonality decreases the safety inventory required. The marginal benefit, however, decreases with increasing commonality.

Postponement

Postponement is the ability of a supply chain to delay product differentiation or customization until closer to the time the product is sold. The goal is to have common components in the supply chain for most of the push phase and move product differentiation as close to the pull phase of the supply chain as possible. For example, Dell

TABLE 8.6 Marginal Benefit of Component Commonality

Number of Finished Products per Component	*Safety Inventory*	*Marginal Reduction in Safety Inventory*	*Total Reduction in Safety Inventory*
1	399,699		
2	282,630	117,069	117,069
3	230,766	51,864	168,933
4	199,849	30,917	199,850
5	178,751	21,098	220,948
6	163,176	15,575	236,523
7	151,072	12,104	248,627
8	141,315	9,757	258,384
9	133,233	8,082	266,466

holds all inventory in the form of components that are common across many PC configurations. A PC is assembled in the pull phase of the supply chain after the customer order arrives. Thus, Dell introduces product variety only when demand is known with certainty. Postponement coupled with component commonality allows Dell to carry significantly lower safety inventories than a manufacturer that sells through retailers, like Compaq. Given that Compaq must stock finished inventory at the retailer, it assembles to stock. Therefore, Compaq must forecast demand for each individual configuration when assembling. The assemble-to-order direct sales model of Dell relies on aggregate inventories in the form of components, whereas the assemble-to-stock sale through retailers model relies on disaggregate inventories for each PC configuration. Compaq has tried to postpone assembly by having distributors located close to retailers that build to reseller order.

Another classic example of postponement is the production process at Benetton to make colored knit garments. The original process called for the thread to be dyed, then knitted, and assembled into garments. The entire process required up to six months. Because the color of the final garment was fixed the moment the thread was dyed, demand for individual colors had to be forecast far in advance (up to six months). Benetton developed a manufacturing technology that allowed it to dye knitted garments to the appropriate color. Now *greige* thread (the term used for thread that has not yet been dyed) can be purchased, knitted, and assembled into greige garments. The dyeing of the garments is done much closer to the selling season. In fact, part of the dyeing is done after the start of the selling season, when demand is known with great accuracy. In this case, Benetton has postponed the color customization of the knit garments. When thread is purchased, only the aggregate demand across all colors needs to be forecast. Given that this decision is made far in advance when forecasts are least likely to be accurate, there is great advantage to this aggregation. However, as Benetton moves closer to the selling season, the forecast uncertainty reduces. At the time Benetton dyes the knit garments, demand is known with a high degree of accuracy. Thus, postponement allows Benetton to exploit aggregation and significantly reduce the level of safety inventory carried. Supply chain flows with and without postponement are illustrated in Figure 8.5.

Without component commonality and postponement, product differentiation occurs early on in the supply chain, and most of the supply chain inventories are disaggregate. Postponement allows the supply chain to delay product differentiation. As a result, most of the inventories in the supply chain are aggregate. Postponement thus

FIGURE 8.5 Supply Chain Flows with and without Postponement

Supply Chain Flows without Postponement

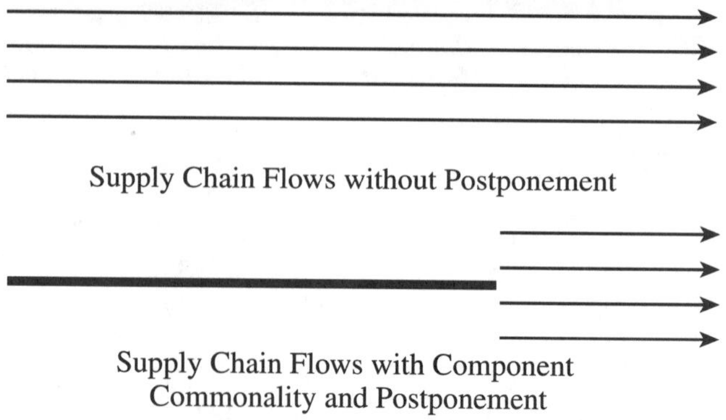

Supply Chain Flows with Component Commonality and Postponement

allows a supply chain to exploit aggregation to reduce safety inventories without hurting product availability.

Postponement can be a powerful concept for the e-commerce channel. When ordering over the Internet, customers are implicitly willing to wait a little for the order to arrive. This delay offers the supply chain an opportunity to reduce inventories by postponing product differentiation until after the customer order arrives. It is important that the manufacturing process be designed in a way that enables assembly to be completed quickly. All PC manufacturers are already postponing assembly for their on-line orders. Several on-line furniture manufacturers have also postponed some of the assembly process for their on-line orders.

8.5 IMPACT OF REPLENISHMENT POLICIES ON SAFETY INVENTORY

In this section, we describe the evaluation of safety inventories for both continuous and periodic review replenishment policies. We will highlight the fact that periodic review policies require more safety inventory than continuous review policies for the same level of product availability. To simplify the discussion, we will focus on the cycle service level as the measure of product availability. The managerial implications are the same if we use fill rate; however, the analysis is somewhat more cumbersome.

Continuous Review Policies

Given that continuous review policies are discussed in detail in Section 8.2, we only reiterate the main points here. When using a continuous review policy, a manager orders Q units when the inventory drops to the reorder point ROP. Clearly, a continuous review policy requires technology that monitors the level of available inventory. This is the case for many firms where inventories are continuously monitored, like Wal-Mart and Dell.

Given a desired cycle service level CSL, our goal is to identify the required safety inventory ss and the reorder point ROP. We assume that demand is normally distributed with the following input:

R: Average demand per period
σ_R: Standard deviation of demand per period
L: Average lead time for replenishment

The reorder point represents the available inventory to meet demand during the lead time L. A stockout occurs if the demand during the lead time is larger than the reorder point ROP. If demand across periods is independent, demand during the lead time is normally distributed with the following:

$$\text{Mean demand during lead time, } R_L = RL$$
$$\text{Standard deviation of demand during lead time, } \sigma_L = \sqrt{L}\,\sigma_R$$

Given the desired cycle service level CSL, the safety inventory ss required is given by Equation 8.9 and the reorder point by Equation 8.3:

$$ss = F_s^{-1}(CSL) \times \sigma_L = NORMSINV(CSL) \times \sigma_L \qquad ROP = R_L + ss$$

When using a continuous review policy, a manager has to account only for the uncertainty of demand during the lead time. This is because the continuous monitoring of inventory allows a manager to adjust the timing of the replenishment order, depending on the demand experienced. If demand is very high, the inventory will reach the reorder point quickly, leading to a quick replenishment order. If demand is very low, inventory will drop to the reorder point slowly, leading to a delayed replenishment order. The manager, however, has no recourse during the lead time once a replenishment order has been placed. The available safety inventory thus must cover for the uncertainty of demand over this period.

Typically, in continuous review policies, the lot size ordered is kept fixed between replenishment cycles. The optimal lot size may be evaluated using the EOQ formula discussed in Chapter 7.

Periodic Review Policies

In periodic review policies, the inventory levels are reviewed after a fixed period of time T and an order placed such that the level of current inventory plus the replenishment lot size equals a prespecified level called the **order up to level**. The **review interval** is the time T between successive orders. Observe that the size of each order may vary, depending on the demand experienced between successive orders and the resulting inventory at the time of ordering. Periodic review policies are simpler to implement for retailers because they do not require that the retailer have the capability of continuously monitoring inventory. Suppliers may also prefer them because they result in replenishment orders placed at regular intervals.

Let us consider the store manager at Wal-Mart responsible for designing a replenishment policy for Lego building blocks. He wants to analyze the impact on safety inventory if he decides to use a periodic review policy. Demand for Lego is normally distributed and independent from one week to the next. We assume the following input:

R: Average demand per period
σ_R: Standard deviation of demand per period
L: Average lead time for replenishment
T: Review interval
CSL: Desired cycle service level

To understand the safety inventory requirement, we track the sequence of events over time as the store manager places orders. The store manager places the first order at time 0 such that the lot size ordered and the inventory on hand sum to the order up to level (OUL). Once an order is placed, the replenishment lot arrives after the lead time L. The next review period is time T when the store manager places the next order, which then arrives at time $T + L$. The order up to level OUL represents the inventory available to meet all demand that arises between periods 0 and $T + L$. The Wal-Mart store will experience a stockout if demand during the time interval between 0 and $T + L$ exceeds the order up to level. Therefore, the store manager must identify an order up to level such that the following is true:

$$\text{Probability(demand during } L + T \leq OUL) = CSL$$

The next step is to evaluate the distribution of demand during the time interval $T + L$. Using Equation 8.2, demand during the time interval $T + L$ is normally distributed with the following:

$$\text{Mean demand during } T + L \text{ periods } (R_{T+L}) = (T + L)R$$
$$\text{Standard deviation of demand during } T + L \text{ periods } (\sigma_{T+L}) = \sqrt{T + L}\,\sigma_R$$

The safety inventory in this case is the quantity in excess of R_{T+L} carried by Wal-Mart over the time interval $T + L$. The order up to level OUL and the safety inventory ss are related as follows:

$$OUL = R_{T+L} + ss \tag{8.15}$$

Given the desired cycle service level CSL, the safety inventory ss required is given by the following:

$$ss = F_s^{-1}(CSL) \times \sigma_{T+L} = NORMSINV(CSL) \times \sigma_{T+L} \tag{8.16}$$

The average lot size equals the average demand during the review period T and is given by the following:

$$\text{Average lot size, } Q = R_T = RT \tag{8.17}$$

We illustrate the periodic review policy for Wal-Mart in Example 8.10.

Example 8.10: Weekly demand for Lego at a Wal-Mart store is normally distributed with a mean of 2,500 boxes and a standard deviation of 500. The replenishment lead time is two weeks, and the store manager has decided to review inventory every four weeks. Assuming a periodic review replenishment policy, evaluate the safety inventory that the store should carry to provide a cycle service level of 90 percent. Evaluate the order up to level for such a policy.

Analysis: In this case, we have the following:

Average demand per period, $R = 2{,}500$
Standard deviation of demand per period, $\sigma_R = 500$
Average lead time for replenishment, $L = 2$ weeks
Review interval, $T = 4$ weeks

We first obtain the distribution of demand during the time interval $T + L$. Using Equation 8.2, demand during the time interval $T + L$ is normally distributed as follows:

Mean demand during $T + L$ periods, $R_{T+L} = (T + L)R = (4 + 2)2{,}500 = 15{,}000$
Standard deviation of demand during $T + L$ periods, $\sigma_{T+L}\ \sqrt{T + L}\ \sigma_R = (\sqrt{4 + 2})\ 500 = 1{,}225$

From Equation 8.16 (evaluated using Equation 8.24 in Appendix 8B), the required safety inventory for a cycle service level of $CSL = 0.90$ is given by the following:

$$ss = F_s^{-1}(CSL) \times \sigma_{T+L} = NORMSINV(CSL) \times \sigma_{T+L} = NORMSINV(0.90) \times 1{,}225 = 1{,}570 \text{ boxes}$$

Using Equation (8.15), the order up to level is given by

$$OUL = R_{T+L} + ss = 15{,}000 + 1{,}570 = 16{,}570$$

The store manager therefore orders the difference between 16,570 and current inventory every four weeks.

We can now compare the safety inventory required when using continuous and periodic review policies. With a continuous review policy, the safety inventory is used to cover for demand uncertainty over the lead time L. With a periodic review policy, the safety inventory is used to cover for demand uncertainty over the lead time and the review interval $L + T$. Given that higher uncertainty must be accounted for, periodic review policies will require a higher level of safety inventory. This argument can be confirmed by comparing the results in Examples 8.4 and 8.11. For a 90 percent cycle service level, the store manager requires a safety inventory of 906 boxes when using a continuous review and a safety inventory of 1,570 boxes when using a periodic review.

> ***Key Point*** Periodic review replenishment policies require more safety inventory than continuous review policies for the same lead time and level of product availability.

Of course, periodic review policies are somewhat simpler to implement because they do not require continuous tracking of inventory. Given the broad use of bar codes and point-of-sales systems, continuous tracking of all inventories is much more commonplace today than it was in the 1980s. In some instances, companies partition their products based on their value. High-value products are managed using continuous review policies, and low-value products managed using periodic review policies. This makes sense if the cost of perpetual tracking of inventory is more than the savings in safety inventory that result from switching all products to a continuous review policy.

8.6 ESTIMATING AND MANAGING SAFETY INVENTORY IN PRACTICE

In this section, we raise some issues that must be considered when putting into practice the ideas discussed in this chapter:

- **Account for the fact that supply chain demand is lumpy**. In practice, a manufacturer or distributor does not order one unit at a time but instead often orders in a large lot. Thus, demand observed by different stages of the supply chain tends to be lumpy. Lumpiness adds to the variability of demand. Lumpiness of demand is not a significant issue when using periodic review policies. However, when using a continuous review policy, it may lead to inventory dropping far below the reorder point before a replenishment order is placed. On average, inventory will drop below the reorder point by about half the average size of an order. The lumpiness can be accounted for in practice by raising the safety inventory suggested by the models discussed earlier by half the average size of an order.
- **Adjust inventory policies if demand is seasonal**. In practice, demand is often seasonal, with the mean and the standard deviation of demand varying by the time of year. Thus, a given reorder point or order up to level may correspond to 10 days of demand during the low-demand season and only 2 days of demand during the peak demand season. If the lead time is a week, stockouts are certain to occur during the peak season. In the presence of seasonality, it is not appropriate to select an average demand and standard deviation over the year to evaluate fixed reorder points and order up to levels. Both the mean and the standard deviation of demand must be adjusted by the time of year to reflect changing demand. Corresponding adjustments in the reorder points, order up to levels, and safety inventories must be made over the year. Adjustments for changes in the mean demand over the year are generally more significant than adjustments for changes in variability.

- **Use simulation to test inventory policies**. Given that demand may not be perfectly normal and may be seasonal, it is a good idea to test and adjust inventory policies using a computer simulation before they are implemented. The simulation should use a demand pattern that truly reflects actual demand, including any lumpiness as well as seasonality. The inventory policies obtained using the models discussed in this chapter can then be tested and adjusted if needed to obtain the desired service levels. Very powerful simulations can be built using Excel or other simulation packages, as we discuss in Chapter 9. Identifying problems in a simulation can save a lot of time and money compared with facing these problems once the inventory policy is in place.
- **Start with a pilot**. Even a simulation cannot identify all problems that may arise when using an inventory policy. Once an inventory policy has been selected and tested using simulation, it is often a good idea to start implementation with a pilot program of products representative of the entire set of products in inventory. By starting with a pilot, many of the problems (both in the inventory policies themselves and in the process of applying the policies) can be solved. Getting these problems solved before the policy is rolled out to all the products can save a lot of time and money.
- **Monitor service levels**. Once an inventory policy has been implemented, it is important that its performance be tracked and monitored. Monitoring is crucial because it allows a supply chain to identify when a policy is not working well and make adjustments before supply chain performance is significantly affected. Monitoring requires not just tracking the inventory levels but also tracking any stockouts that may result. Historically, firms have not tracked stockouts very well, partly because they are difficult to track, and partly because there is the perception that they affect the customer and not the firm itself. Stockouts can be difficult to measure in a situation like a supermarket, where the customer simply does not buy the product when it is not on the shelf. However, there are simple ways to estimate stockouts. At a supermarket, the fraction of time that a shelf does not contain a product may be used to estimate the fill rate. Stockouts are in fact easier to estimate on-line, where the number of clicks on an out-of-stock product can be measured. Given the fraction of clicks that turn into orders and the average size of an order, demand during a stockout can be estimated.
- **Focus on reducing safety inventories**. Given that safety inventory is often a large fraction of the total inventory in a supply chain, the ability to reduce safety inventory without hurting product availability can significantly increase supply chain profitability. This is particularly important in the high-tech industry, where product life cycles are short. In this chapter, we discuss a variety of managerial levers that can help reduce safety inventories without hurting availability. Supply chain managers must focus continuously on using these levers to reduce safety inventories.

8.7 SUMMARY OF LEARNING OBJECTIVES

1. Understand the role of safety inventory in a supply chain.

Safety inventory helps a supply chain provide customers a high level of product availability in spite of supply and demand variability. It is carried just in case demand exceeds the amount forecasted or supply arrives later than expected.

2. Identify factors that influence the required level of safety inventory.

Safety inventory is influenced by demand uncertainty, replenishment lead times, lead time variability, and desired product availability. As any one of them increases, the required safety inventory also increases. The required safety inventory is also influenced by the inventory policy implemented. Continuous review policies require less safety inventory than periodic review policies.

3. Describe different measures of product availability.

The three basic measures of product availability are product fill rate, order fill rate, and cycle service level. Product fill rate is the fraction of demand for a product that is successfully filled. Order fill rate is the fraction of orders that are completely filled. Cycle service level is the fraction of replenishment cycles in which no stockouts occur.

4. Utilize managerial levers available to lower safety inventory and improve product availability.

The required level of safety inventory may be reduced and product availability improved if a supply chain can reduce demand variability, replenishment lead times, and variability of lead times. A switch from periodic monitoring to continuous monitoring can also help reduce inventories. Another key managerial lever to reduce the required safety inventories is to exploit aggregation. This may be achieved by physically aggregating inventories, virtually aggregating inventories using information centralization, specializing inventories based on demand volume, exploiting substitution, using component commonality, and postponing product differentiation.

Discussion Questions

1. What is the role of safety inventory in the supply chain?
2. Explain how a reduction in lead time can help a supply chain reduce safety inventory without hurting product availability.
3. What are the pros and cons of the various measures of product availability?
4. Describe the two types of ordering policies and the impact that each of them has on safety inventory.
5. What is the impact of supply uncertainty on safety inventory?
6. Why can a hardware store chain like Home Depot, with a few large stores, provide a higher level of product availability with lower inventories than a hardware store chain like Tru-Value, with several small stores?
7. Why is Amazon.com able to provide a large variety of books and music with less safety inventory than a bookstore chain selling through retail stores?
8. In the 1980s, paint was sold by color and size in paint stores. Today, paint is mixed at the paint store as per the color required. Discuss what, if any, impact this change has on safety inventories in the supply chain.
9. A new technology allows books to be printed in 10 minutes. Borders has decided to purchase these machines for each store. They must decide which books to carry in stock and which books to print on demand using this technology. Do you recommend it for best-sellers or other books? Why?

Exercises

1. Weekly demand for Motorola cellular phones at a Best Buy store is normally distributed with a mean of 300 and a standard deviation of 200. Motorola takes two weeks to supply a Best Buy order. Best Buy is targeting a cycle service level of 95

percent and monitors its inventory continuously. What level of safety inventory of cellular phones should Best Buy carry? What should its reorder point be?

2. Reconsider the Best Buy store in problem 1. The store manager has decided to follow a periodic review policy to manage inventory of cellular phones. She plans to order every three weeks. Given a desired cycle service level of 95 percent, how much safety inventory should the store carry? What should its order up to level be?
3. Assume that the Best Buy store has a continous review policy of ordering cellular phones from Motorola in lots of 500. Weekly demand for Motorola cellular phones at the store is normally distributed with a mean of 300 and a standard deviation of 200. Motorola takes two weeks to supply an order. If the store manager is targeting a fill rate of 99 percent, what safety inventory should Best Buy carry? What should its reorder point be?
4. Weekly demand for Hewlett Packard (HP) printers at a Sam's Club store is normally distributed with a mean of 250 and a standard deviation of 150. The store manager continuously monitors inventory and currently orders 1,000 printers each time the inventory drops to 600 printers. HP currently takes two weeks to fill an order. How much safety inventory does the store carry? What cycle service level does Sam's Club achieve as a result of this policy? What fill rate does the store achieve?
5. Return to the Sam's Club store in problem 4. Assume that the supply lead time from HP is normally distributed with a mean of 2 weeks and a standard deviation of 1.5 weeks. How much safety inventory should Sam's Club carry if it wants to provide a cycle service level of 95 percent? How does the required safety inventory change as the standard deviation of lead time is reduced from 1.5 weeks to 0 in intervals of 0.5 weeks?
6. The Gap has started selling through its on-line channel along with its retail stores. Management has to decide which products to carry at the retail stores and which products to carry at a central warehouse to be sold only via the on-line channel. The Gap currently has 900 retail stores in the United States. Weekly demand for large khaki pants at each store is normally distributed with a mean of 800 and a standard deviation of 100. Each pair of pants costs \$30. Weekly demand for purple cashmere sweaters at each store is normally distributed with a mean of 50 and a standard deviation of 50. Each sweater costs \$100. The Gap has a holding cost of 25 percent. The Gap manages all inventories using a continuous review policy, and the supply lead time for both products is four weeks. The targeted cycle service level is 95 percent. How much reduction in holding cost per unit sold can The Gap expect on moving each of the two products from the stores to the on-line channel? Which of the two products should The Gap carry at the stores, and which at the central warehouse for the on-line channel? Why? Assume demand from one week to the next to be independent.
7. Epson produces printers for sale in Europe in its Taiwan factory. Printers sold in different countries differ in terms of the power outlet as well as the language manuals. Currently Epson assembles and packs printers for sale in individual countries. The distribution of weekly demand in different countries is normally distributed with mean and standard deviation as shown in Table 8.7.

TABLE 8.7 Weekly Demand for Epson Printers in Europe

Country	*Mean Demand*	*Standard Deviation*	*Country*	*Mean Demand*	*Standard Deviation*
France	3,000	2,000	Italy	2,500	1,600
Germany	4,000	2,200	Portugal	1,000	800
Spain	2,000	1,400	UK	4,000	2,400

Assume demand in different countries to be independent. Given that the lead time from the Taiwan factory is eight weeks, how much safety inventory does Epson require in Europe if it targets a cycle service level of 95 percent?

Epson decides to build a central DC in Europe. It will ship base printers (without power supply) to the DC. When an order is received, the DC will assemble power supplies, add manuals, and ship the printers to the appropriate country. The base printers are still to be manufactured in Taiwan with a lead time of eight weeks. How much saving of safety inventory can Epson expect as a result?

8. Return to the Epson data in problem 7. Each printer costs Epson $200, and they have a holding cost of 25 percent. What saving in holding cost can Epson expect as a result of building the European DC? If final assembly in the European DC adds $5 to the production cost of each printer, would you recommend the move? Suppose that Epson is able to cut the production and delivery lead time from its Taiwan factory to four weeks using good information systems. How much saving in holding cost can Epson expect without the European DC? How much saving in holding cost can they expect with the European DC?
9. Return to the Epson data in problem 7. Assume that demand in different countries is not independent. Demand in any pair of countries is correlated with a correlation coefficient of ρ. Evaluate the holding cost savings that Epson gains as a result of building a European DC as ρ increases from 0 (independent demand) to 1 (perfectly positively correlated demand) in intervals of 0.2.

Bibliography

Feitzinger, Edward, and Hau L. Lee. "Mass Customization at Hewlett Packard." *Harvard Business Review* (January–February 1997), 116–121.

Kopczak, Laura, and Hau L. Lee. "Hewlett-Packard: Deskjet Printer Supply Chain." Stanford University Case 1993.

Lee, Hau L. "Design for Supply Chain Management: Concepts and Examples." In R. Sarin, Ed. *Perspectives in Operations Management.* Norwell, Mass.: Kluwer Academic Publishers, 1993, 45–65.

Lee, Hau L., and Corey Billington. "Managing Supply Chain Inventory." *Sloan Management Review* (Spring 1992), 65–73.

Lee, Hau L., Corey Billington, and B. Carter. "Hewlett-Packard Gains Control of Inventory and Service through Design for Localization." *Interfaces* (July–August 1993), 1–11.

Nahmias, Steven. *Production and Operations Analysis.* Burr Ridge, Ill.: Richard P. Irwin, 1997.

Signorelli, Sergio, and James L. Heskett. "Benetton (A)." Harvard Business School Case 9-685-014, 1984.

Silver, Edward A., David Pyke, and Rein Petersen. *Inventory Management and Production Planning and Scheduling.* New York: John Wiley & Sons, 1998.

Tayur, Sridhar, Ram Ganeshan, and Michael Magazine, Eds. *Quantitative Models for Supply Chain Management.* Boston: Kluwer Academic Publishers, 1999.

CASE STUDY

Managing Inventories at ALKO Inc.

ALKO started in 1943 in a garage workshop set up by John Williams at his Cleveland home. John had always enjoyed tinkering, and in February 1948, he obtained a patent for one of his designs for lighting fixtures. He decided to produce it in his workshop and tried marketing it in the Cleveland area. The product sold well, and by 1957, ALKO had grown to a $3 million company. Its lighting fixtures were well known for their outstanding quality. By then, it sold a total of five products.

In 1963, John took the company public. Since then, ALKO had been very successful, and the company started distributing its products nationwide. As competition intensified in the 1980s, ALKO started introducing many new lighting fixture designs. However, the company's profitability started to worsen despite the fact that ALKO had taken great care to ensure that product quality did not suffer. The problem was that margins started to shrink as competition in the market intensified. At this point, the board decided that a complete reorganization was needed, starting at the top. Gary Fisher was then hired to reorganize and restructure the company.

When Fisher arrived in 1999, he found a company teetering on its laurels. He spent the first few months understanding the company business and the way it was structured. Fisher realized that the key was in the operating performance. Although the company had always been outstanding at developing and producing new products, it had historically ignored its distribution system. The feeling within the company was that once you made a good product, the rest took care of itself. Fisher set up a task force to review the company's current distribution system and come up with recommendations.

THE CURRENT DISTRIBUTION SYSTEM

The task force noted that ALKO had 100 products in its 1999 line. All production took place at three facilities located in the Cleveland area. For sales purposes, the continental United States was divided into five regions, as shown in Figure 8.6. An independent distribution center (DC) owned by ALKO operated in each of these regions. Customers placed orders with the DCs, which tried to supply them from product in inventory. As the inventory for any product diminished, the DC in turn ordered from the plants. The plants scheduled production based on DC orders. Orders were transported from plants

FIGURE 8.6 Sales Regions for ALKO

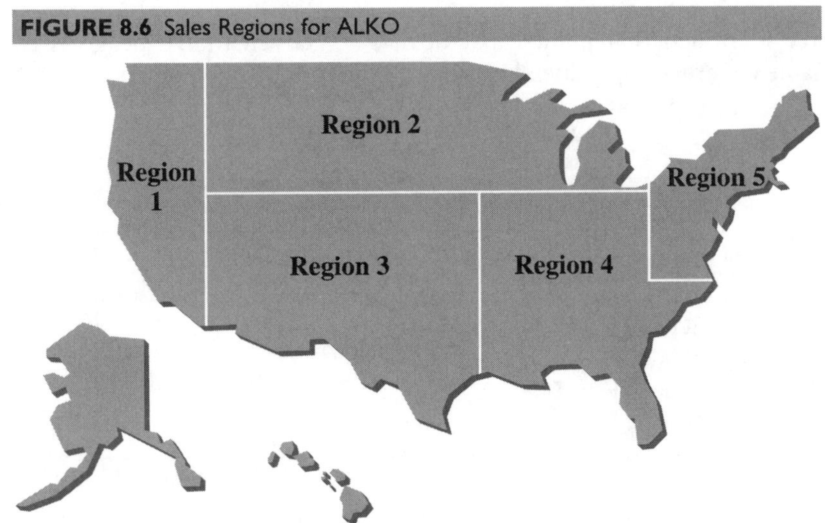

TABLE 8.8 Distribution of Daily Demand at ALKO

	Region 1	*Region 2*	*Region 3*	*Region 4*	*Region 5*
Part 1 Mean	35.48	22.61	17.66	11.81	3.36
Part 1 SD	6.98	6.48	5.26	3.48	4.49
Part 3 Mean	2.48	4.15	6.15	6.16	7.49
Part 3 SD	3.16	6.20	6.39	6.76	3.56
Part 7 Mean	0.48	0.73	0.80	1.94	2.54
Part 7 SD	1.98	1.42	2.39	3.76	3.98

to the distribution centers in truckload (TL) quantities, because order sizes tended to be large. However, shipment from the DC to the customer was less than truckload (LTL). ALKO used a third-party trucking company for both transportation legs. In 1996, TL costs from the plants to DCs averaged $0.09 per unit, and LTL shipping costs from a DC to a customer averaged $0.10 per unit. On average, 14 days were necessary between the time a DC placed an order with a plant and the time the order was delivered from the plant.

The policy at the time was to stock each item in every DC. A detailed study of the product line had shown that there were three basic categories of products in terms of the volume of sales: High, Medium, and Low. Demand data for a representative product in each category are shown in Table 8.8. Products 1, 3, and 7 are representative of High, Medium, and Low products, respectively. Of the 100 products that ALKO sells, 10 are of type High, 20 of type Medium, and 70 of type Low. Each of their demands is identical to those of the representative products 1, 3, and 7, respectively.

The task force identified that plant capacities allow any reasonable order to be produced in 1 day. Thus, a plant ships out an order 1 day after receiving it. After another 4 days in transit, the order reaches the DC. The DCs order using a periodic review policy with a reorder interval of 6 days. The holding cost incurred is $0.15 per unit per day whether the unit is in transit or in storage. All DCs carry safety inventories to ensure a cycle service level of 95 percent.

ALTERNATIVE DISTRIBUTION SYSTEMS

The task force recommended that ALKO build a national distribution center (NDC) outside Chicago. The task force recommended that ALKO close its five DCs and move all inventory to the NDC. Warehouse capacity is measured in terms of the number of units handled per year. The cost of constructing a warehouse is shown in Figure 8.7. However, ALKO is expected to recover $50,000 for each warehouse that it closes. The cycle service level out of the NDC would continue to be 95 percent.

Given that Chicago is close to Cleveland, the inbound transportation cost from the plants to the

FIGURE 8.7 Construction Costs for NDC

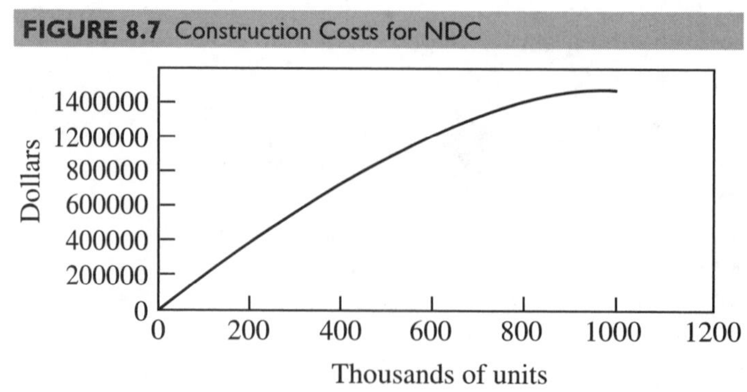

NDC would reduce to $0.05 per unit. However, given the increased average distance, the outbound transportation cost to customers from the NDC would increase to $0.24 per unit.

Other possibilities the task force considered include building an NDC while keeping the regional DCs open. In this case, some products would be stocked at the regional DCs, whereas others would be stocked at the NDC.

FISHER'S DECISION

Gary Fisher pondered the task force report. Task force members had not detailed any of the numbers supporting their decision. He decided to evaluate the numbers before making his decision.

QUESTIONS

1. What is the annual inventory and distribution cost of the current distribution system?
2. What are the savings that would result from following the task force recommendation and setting up an NDC? Evaluate the savings as the correlation coefficient of demand in any pair of regions varies from 0 to 0.5 to 1.0. Do you recommend setting up a NDC?
3. Suggest other options that Fisher should consider. Evaluate each option and recommend a distribution system for ALKO that would be most profitable. How dependent is your recommendation on the correlation coefficient of demand across different regions?

APPENDIX 8A

The Normal Distribution

A continuous random variable X has a **normal distribution** with mean μ and standard deviation $\sigma > 0$, if the probability density function $f(x, \mu, \sigma)$ of the random variable is given by the following:

$$f(x, \mu, \sigma) = \frac{1}{\sigma\sqrt{2\pi}} exp\left[-\frac{(x-\mu)^2}{2\sigma^2}\right] \quad \textbf{(8.18)}$$

The normal density function is as shown in Figure 8A.1. The **cumulative normal distribution function** is denoted by $F(x, \mu, \sigma)$ and is the probability that a normally distributed random variable with mean μ and standard deviation σ takes on a value less than or equal to x. The cumulative normal distribution function and the density function are related as follows:

$$F(x, \mu, \sigma) = \int_{X=-\infty}^{x} f(X, \mu, \sigma)dX$$

A normal distribution with a mean $\mu = 0$ and standard deviation $\sigma = 1$ is referred to as the **standard normal distribution**. The standard normal density function is denoted by $f_S(x)$, and the cumulative standard normal distribution function is denoted by $F_S(x)$. Thus,

$$f_S(x) = f(x, 0, 1) \text{ and } F_S(x) = F(x, 0, 1)$$

Given a probability p, the inverse normal $F^{-1}(p, \mu, \sigma)$ is the value x such that p is the probability that the normal random variable takes on a value x or less. Thus, if $F(x, \mu, \sigma) = p$, then $x = F^{-1}(p, \mu, \sigma)$. The inverse of the standard normal distribution is denoted by $F_S^{-1}(p)$. Thus,

$$F_S^{-1}(p) = F^{-1}(p, 0, 1)$$

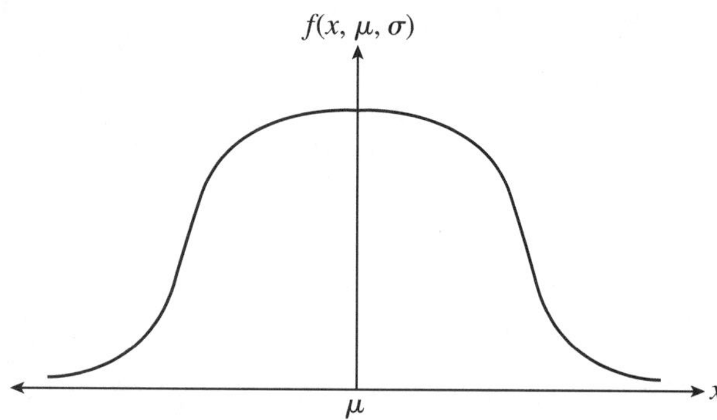

FIGURE 8A.1 Normal Density Function

APPENDIX 8B

The Normal Distribution in Excel

The following Excel functions can be used to evaluate various normal distribution functions:

$$F(x, \mu, \sigma) = NORMDIST(x, \mu, \sigma, 1) \quad \textbf{(8.19)}$$

$$f(x, \mu, \sigma) = NORMDIST(x, \mu, \sigma, 0) \quad \textbf{(8.20)}$$

$$F^{-1}(p, \mu, \sigma) = NORMINV(p, \mu, \sigma) \quad \textbf{(8.21)}$$

The Excel functions to evaluate various standard normal distribution functions are as follows:

$$F_S(x) = NORMDIST(x, 0, 1, 1) \text{ or } NORMSDIST(x) \quad \textbf{(8.22)}$$

$$f_S(x) = NORMDIST(x, 0, 1, 0) \quad \textbf{(8.23)}$$

$$F_S^{-1}(p) = NORMSINV(p) \quad \textbf{(8.24)}$$

APPENDIX 8C

Expected Shortage Cost per Cycle

Objective: Establish alternate formula for expected shortage per replenishment cycle (ESC) to be evaluated using Excel.

Analysis: Given a reorder point of $ROP = R_L + ss$, the expected shortage per replenishment cycle is given by the following:

$$ESC = \int_{x=ROP}^{\infty} (x - ROP)f(x)dx$$

$$= \int_{x=R_L+ss}^{\infty} (x - R_L - ss)f(x)dx$$

Given that the demand during lead time is normally distributed with a mean R_L and a standard deviation σ_L, we have the following (using Equation 8.18):

$$ESC = \int_{x=R_L+ss}^{\infty} (x - R_L - ss)\frac{1}{\sqrt{2\pi}\,\sigma_L} e^{\frac{-(x-R_L)^2}{2\sigma_L^2}} dx$$

Substitute the following:

$$z = (x - R_L)/\sigma_L$$

This implies the following:

$$dx = \sigma_L\, dz$$

Thus, we have the following:

$$ESC = \int_{x=ss/\sigma_L}^{\infty} (z\,\sigma_L - ss)\frac{1}{\sqrt{2\pi}} e^{-z^2/2}\, dz$$

$$= -ss \int_{z=ss/\sigma_L}^{\infty} \frac{1}{\sqrt{2\pi}} e^{-z^2/2}\, dz + \sigma_L \int_{z=ss/\sigma_L}^{\infty} z\frac{1}{\sqrt{2\pi}} e^{-z^2/2}\, dz$$

Recall that $F_S(\cdot)$ is the cumulative distribution function and $f_S(\cdot)$ is the probability density function for the standard normal distribution with mean 0 and standard deviation 1. Using Equation 8.18 and the definition of the standard normal distribution, we thus have the following:

$$1 - F_S(y) = \int_{z=y}^{\infty} f_S(z)dz = \int_{z=y}^{\infty} \frac{1}{\sqrt{2\pi}} e^{-\frac{z^2}{2}} dz$$

Substitute $w = z^2/2$ into the expression for ESC. This implies the following:

$$ESC = -ss[1 - F_S(ss/\sigma_L)] + \sigma_L \int_{w=ss^2/2\sigma_L^2}^{\infty} \frac{1}{\sqrt{2\pi}} e^{-w}\, dw$$

or

$$ESC = -ss[1 - F_S(ss/\sigma_L)] + \sigma_L\, f_S(ss/\sigma_L)$$

Using Equations 8.22 and 8.23, ESC may be evaluated using Excel as follows:

$$ESC = -ss[1 - NORMDIST(ss/\sigma_L, 0, 1, 1)] + NORMDIST(ss/\sigma_L, 0, 1, 1)$$

CHAPTER 9

Determining Optimal Level of Product Availability

Learning Objectives
After reading this chapter, you will be able to

1. identify the factors affecting the optimal level of product availability and evaluate the optimal cycle service level;
2. use managerial levers that improve supply chain profitability through optimal service levels; and
3. construct contracts that increase supply chain profitability.

In this chapter, we explore the process of determining the optimal level of availability to be offered to customers. The chapter examines the components that go into the calculation of the optimal service level and the various ways that this calculation can be performed. We discuss and demonstrate how different managerial levers can be used to improve supply chain profitability by increasing the level of product availability while reducing inventories. We also discuss how product availability and supply chain profits are affected by contracts between different stages of the supply chain. We highlight contracts that can be used to increase supply chain profitability.

9.1 THE IMPORTANCE OF THE LEVEL OF PRODUCT AVAILABILITY

The level of product availability is measured using the cycle service level or the fill rate. The level of product availability measures the fraction of customer demand that is satisfied from available inventory. The level of product availability is also referred to as the **customer service level**. The level of product availability is an important component of any supply chain's responsiveness. A supply chain can use a high level of product availability to improve its responsiveness and attract customers. This increases revenues for the supply chain by increasing sales and ensuring product availability when customers come to make a purchase. However, a high level of product availability requires large inventories, and large inventories tend to raise costs for the supply chain. Therefore, a supply chain needs to achieve a balance between the level of availability and the cost of inventory. The optimal level of product availability is one that maximizes supply chain profitability.

Whether the optimal level of availability is high or low depends on where a particular company believes it can maximize profits. For example, Nordstrom has focused on providing a high level of product availability and has used its reputation for responsiveness to become a very successful department store chain. However, prices at Nordstrom are higher than at a discount store, where the level of product availability tends to be lower. Power plants ensure that they (almost) never run out of fuel because a shutdown is extremely expensive and can result in several days of lost production. Some power plants try to maintain several months of fuel supply to avoid any probability of running out. In contrast, most supermarkets may carry only a few days' supply of product, and out-of-stock situations do occur with some frequency.

In the e-commerce channel, the nature of searching on the Web allows a customer to shop easily at an alternative store if one is out of stock. This competitive environment puts pressure on Web retailers to increase their level of availability. At the same time, significant price competition has lowered prices on the Web. Web retailers with excess inventory find it difficult to be profitable. Providing the optimal level of product availability is thus a key to success on the Web.

In these examples, firms provide different levels of product availability. Every supply chain manager must be aware of the factors that influence the optimal level of product availability. This knowledge can be used to target the optimal level of product availability and identify managerial levers that increase supply chain surplus. Next, we identify factors that affect the optimal level of product availability.

9.2 FACTORS AFFECTING OPTIMAL LEVEL OF PRODUCT AVAILABILITY

To understand the factors that influence the optimal level of product availability, consider L.L. Bean, a large mail order company selling apparel. One of the products L. L. Bean sells is ski jackets. The selling season for ski jackets is from November to February. The buyer at L.L. Bean currently purchases the entire season's supply of ski jackets from the manufacturer before the start of the selling season. Providing a high level of product availability requires the buyers to purchase large numbers of jackets. Although a high level of product availability is likely to satisfy all demand that arises, it is also likely to result in a large number of unsold jackets at the end of the season, with L.L. Bean losing money on unsold jackets. In the opposite scenario, a low level of product availability is likely to result in few unsold jackets. However, it is quite likely that L.L. Bean will have to turn away customers willing to buy jackets because it is sold out. In this scenario, L.L. Bean loses potential profit by losing customers. The buyer at L.L. Bean must balance the loss from having too many unsold jackets (in case the number of jackets ordered is more than demand) and the lost profit from turning away customers (in case the number of jackets ordered is less than demand) when deciding the level of product availability.

The **cost of overstocking** is denoted by C_o and is the loss incurred by a firm for each unsold unit at the end of the selling season. The **cost of understocking** is denoted by C_u and is the margin lost by a firm for each lost sale because there is no inventory on hand. The cost of understocking should include the margin lost from current as well as future sales if the customer does not return. In summary, the two key factors that influence the optimal level of product availability are

- Cost of overstocking the product
- Cost of understocking the product

We illustrate and develop this relationship in the context of a buying decision at L.L. Bean. The first point to observe is that deciding on an optimal level of product availability only makes sense in the context of demand uncertainty. Traditionally, many firms have forecast a consensus estimate of demand without any measure of uncertainty. In this setting, firms do not make a decision regarding the level of availability; they simply order the consensus forecast.

Over the last decade of the 20th century, firms have developed a better appreciation for uncertainty and have started developing forecasts that include a measure of uncertainty. Incorporating uncertainty and deciding on the optimal level of product availability can increase profits relative to using a consensus forecast.

L.L. Bean has a buying committee that decides on the quantity of each product to be ordered. Based on demand over the past few years, the buyers have estimated the demand distribution for the red women's ski parka to be as shown in Table 9.1. This is a deviation from their traditional practice of using the average historical demand as the consensus forecast. To simplify the discussion, we assume that all demand is in hundreds of parkas. The manufacturer also requires that L.L. Bean place orders in multiples of 100. In Table 9.1, p_i is the probability that demand equals D_i, and P_i is the probability that demand is less than or equal to D_i.

From Table 9.1, we can evaluate the expected demand of parkas as follows:

$$\text{Expected demand} = \Sigma D_i p_i = 1{,}026$$

Under the old policy of ordering the expected value, the buyers would have ordered 1,000 parkas. However, demand is uncertain, and Table 9.1 shows that there is a 51 percent probability that demand will be 1,000 or less. Therefore, a policy of ordering 1,000 parkas will result in a cycle service level of 51 percent at L.L. Bean. The buying committee must decide on an order size and cycle service level that maximizes the profits from the sale of parkas at L.L. Bean.

The loss that Bean incurs from an unsold parka as well as the profit that Bean makes on each parka it sells influence the buying decision. Each parka costs Bean c = \$45 and is priced in the catalog at p = \$100. Any unsold parkas at the end of the season are sold at the outlet store for \$50. Holding the parka in inventory and trans-

TABLE 9.1 Demand Distribution for Parkas at L.L. Bean

Demand D_i *('00s)*	*Probability* p_i	*Cumulative Probability of Demand Being* D_i *or Less* (P_i)	*Probability of Demand Being Greater than* D_i
4	0.01	0.01	0.99
5	0.02	0.03	0.97
6	0.04	0.07	0.93
7	0.08	0.15	0.85
8	0.09	0.24	0.76
9	0.11	0.35	0.65
10	0.16	0.51	0.49
11	0.20	0.71	0.29
12	0.11	0.82	0.18
13	0.10	0.92	0.08
14	0.04	0.96	0.04
15	0.02	0.98	0.02
16	0.01	0.99	0.01
17	0.01	1.00	0.00

porting it to the outlet store costs Bean $10. Thus, Bean recovers a salvage value of $s = \$40$ for each parka that is unsold at the end of the season. Bean makes a profit of $p - c = \$55$ on each parka it sells and incurs a loss of $c - s = \$5$ on each unsold parka that is sent to the outlet store.

The expected profit from ordering a thousand parkas is given by the following:

$$\text{Expected profit} = \sum_{i=4}^{10} [D_i(p - c) - (1{,}000 - D_i)(c - s)]\, p_i + (1 - P_i)1{,}000(p - c) = \$49{,}900$$

To decide whether to order 1,100 parkas, the buying committee needs to determine the potential outcome of buying the extra 100 units. If 1,100 parkas are ordered, the extra 100 are sold (for a profit of $5,500) if demand is 1,100 or higher. Otherwise, the extra hundred units are sent to the outlet store at a loss of $500. From Table 9.1, we see that there is a probability of .49 that demand is 1,100 or higher, and a .51 probability that demand is 1,000 or less. Thus, we deduce the following:

$$\text{Expected profit from the extra 100 parkas} = 5{,}500 \times \text{probability[demand} \geq 1{,}100] - 500 \times \text{probability[demand} < 1{,}100] = \$5{,}500 \times .49 - \$500 \times .51 = \$2{,}440$$

The total expected profit from ordering 1,100 parkas is thus $52,340, which is almost 5 percent higher than the expected profit from ordering 1,000 parkas. Using the same approach, we can evaluate the marginal contribution of each additional 100 parkas as in Table 9.2.

Note that the expected marginal contribution is positive up to 1,300 parkas, and it is negative from that point on. Therefore, the optimal order size is 1,300 parkas. From Table 9.2, we have the following:

$$\text{Expected profit from ordering 1,300 parkas} = \$49{,}900 + \$2{,}440 + \$1{,}240 + \$580 = \$54{,}160$$

This is more than an 8 percent increase in profitability relative to the policy of ordering the expected value of 1,000 parkas.

TABLE 9.2 Expected Marginal Contribution of Each Additional 100 Parkas

Additional 100s	*Expected Marginal Benefit*	*Expected Marginal Cost*	*Expected Marginal Contribution*
11th	$5{,}500 \times 0.49 = 2{,}695$	$500 \times 0.51 = 255$	$2{,}695 - 255 = 2{,}440$
12th	$5{,}500 \times 0.29 = 1{,}595$	$500 \times 0.71 = 355$	$1{,}595 - 355 = 1{,}240$
13th	$5{,}500 \times 0.18 = 990$	$500 \times 0.82 = 410$	$990 - 410 = 580$
14th	$5{,}500 \times 0.08 = 440$	$500 \times 0.92 = 460$	$4409 - 460 = -20$
15th	$5{,}500 \times 0.04 = 220$	$500 \times 0.96 = 480$	$220 - 480 = -260$
16th	$5{,}500 \times 0.02 = 110$	$500 \times 0.98 = 490$	$110 - 490 = -380$
17th	$5{,}500 \times 0.01 = 55$	$500 \times 0.99 = 495$	$55 - 495 = -440$

A plot of total expected profits versus the order quantity is shown in Figure 9.1. The optimal order quantity maximizes the expected profit.

For L.L. Bean, the optimal order quantity is 1,300 parkas, which provides a cycle service level of 92 percent. Observe that with a cycle service level of 0.92, Bean has a fill rate that is much higher. If demand is 1,300 or less, Bean achieves a fill rate of 100 percent, because all demand is satisfied. If demand is more than 1,300 (say D), part of the demand ($D - 1{,}300$) is not satisfied. In this case a fill rate of $1{,}300/D$ is achieved. Overall, the fill rate achieved at L.L. Bean if 1,300 parkas are ordered is given by

$$fr = 1 \times \text{probability}(\text{demand} \leq 1{,}300) + \sum_{D_i \geq 1{,}400} (1{,}300/D_i)p_i = 0.99$$

Thus, L.L. Bean, with a policy of ordering 1,300 parkas, satisfies on average 99 percent of its demand from parkas in inventory.

In the L.L. Bean example, we have a cost of overstocking of $C_o = c - s = \$5$ and a cost of understocking of $C_u = p - c = \$55$. As these costs change, the optimal level of product availability also changes. In the next section we develop the relationship between the desired cycle service level and the cost of overstocking and understocking for seasonal items.

Optimal Cycle Service Level for Seasonal Items with a Single Order in a Season

In this section we focus attention on seasonal products such as ski jackets where all leftover items must be disposed at the end of the season. The assumption is that the

FIGURE 9.1 Expected Profit as a Function of Order Quantity at L.L. Bean

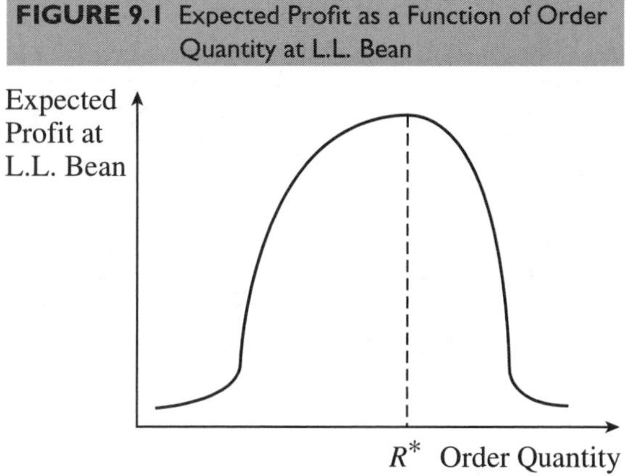

leftover items from the previous season are not used to satisfy demand for the current season. Assume a retail price per unit of p, a purchase price of c, and a salvage value of s. We consider the following input

C_o: cost of overstocking by one unit, $C_o = c - s$
C_u: cost of understocking by one unit, $C_u = p - c$
CSL^*: optimal cycle service level
O^*: corresponding optimal order size

The cycle service level CSL^* is the probability that demand during the season will be at or below O^*. At the optimal cycle service level CSL^*, the marginal contribution of purchasing an additional unit is zero. If the order quantity is raised from O^* to $O^* + 1$, the additional unit sells if demand is larger than O^*. This occurs with probability $1 - CSL^*$ and results in a contribution of $p - c$. We thus have the following:

$$\text{Expected benefit of purchasing extra unit} = (1 - CSL^*)(p - c)$$

The additional unit remains unsold if demand is at or below O^*. This occurs with probability CSL^* and results in a cost of $c - s$. We thus have the following:

$$\text{Expected cost of purchasing extra unit} = CSL^*(c - s)$$

Thus, the expected marginal contribution of raising the order size from O^* to $O^* + 1$ is as follows:

$$(1 - CSL^*)(p - c) - CSL^*(c - s)$$

Because the expected marginal contribution must be zero at the optimal cycle service level, we have the following

$$CSL^* = \text{probability}(\text{demand} \leq O^*) = \frac{p - c}{p - s} = \frac{C_u}{C_u + C_o} = \frac{1}{1 + (C_o/C_u)} \quad \textbf{(9.1)}$$

A more rigorous derivation of this formula is provided in Appendix 9A. The optimal cycle service level CSL^* has also been referred to as the **critical fractile**. The resulting optimal order quantity maximizes the firm's profit. If demand during the season is normally distributed with a mean of μ and a standard deviation of σ, the optimal order quantity is given by the following:

$$O^* = F^{-1}(CSL^*, \mu, \sigma) = NORMINV(CSL^*, \mu, \sigma) \quad \textbf{(9.2)}$$

When demand is normally distributed with a mean of μ and a standard deviation of σ, the expected profit from ordering O units is as follows:

$$\text{Expected profit} = (p - s)\mu F_S\left(\frac{O - \mu}{\sigma}\right) - (p - s)\sigma f_S\left(\frac{O - \mu}{\sigma}\right)$$
$$- O(c - s)F(O, \mu, \sigma) + O(p - c)[1 - F(O, \mu, \sigma)]$$

The derivation of this formula is provided in Appendixes 9B and 9C. Here, F_S is the standard normal cumulative distribution function and f_S is the standard normal density function discussed in Appendix 8A. The expected profit from ordering O units is evaluated in Excel using Equations 8.19, 8.22, and 8.23 as follows:

$$\text{Expected profits} = (p - s)\mu NORMSDIST((O - \mu)/\sigma, 0, 1, 1) - (p - s)\sigma NORMDIST((O - \mu)/\sigma, 0, 1, 0) - O(c - s)NORMDIST(O, \mu, \sigma, 1) + O(p - c)[1 - NORMDIST(O, \mu, \sigma, 1)] \quad \textbf{(9.3)}$$

Example 9.1 illustrates the use of Equations 9.1 and 9.2 to obtain the optimal cycle service level and order quantity.

Example 9.1: The manager at Sportmart, a sports equipment store, has to decide on the number of skis to purchase for the winter season. Considering past demand data and weather forecasts for the year, management has forecast demand to be normally distributed with a mean of $\mu = 350$ and a standard deviation of $\sigma = 100$. Each pair of skis costs $c = \$100$ and retails for $p = \$250$. Any unsold skis at the end of the season are disposed of for \$85. Assume that it costs \$5 to hold a pair of skis in inventory for the season. Evaluate the number of skis that the manager should order to maximize expected profits.

Analysis: In this case, we have the following:

$$\text{Salvage value } s = \$85 - \$5 = \$80$$
$$\text{Cost of understocking} = C_u = p - c = \$250 - \$100 = \$150$$
$$\text{Cost of overstocking} = C_o = c - s = \$100 - \$80 = \$20$$

Using Equation 9.1, we deduce that the optimal cycle service level is as follows:

$$CSL^* = \text{probability}(\text{demand} \le R^*) = \frac{C_u}{C_u + C_o} = \frac{150}{150 + 20} = 0.88$$

Using Equation 9.2, the optimal order size is as follows:

$$O^* = NORMINV(CSL^*, \mu, \sigma) = NORMINV(0.88, 350, 100) = 468$$

Thus, it is optimal for the manager at Sportmart to order 468 skis even though the expected number of sales is 350. In this case, because the cost of understocking is much higher than the cost of overstocking, management is better off ordering more than the expected value to cover for the uncertainty of demand.

Using Equation 9.3, the expected profits from ordering O^* units are as follows:

$$\text{Expected profits} = (p - s)\mu NORMDIST((O^* - \mu)/\sigma, 0, 1, 0) - (p - s)\sigma NORMDIST((O^* - \mu)/\sigma, 0, 1, 0) - O^*(c - s)NORMDIST(O^*, \mu, \sigma, 1) + O^*(p - c)[1 - NORMDIST(O^*, \mu, \sigma, 1)] = 59{,}500 \text{ NORMDIST}(1.18, 0, 1, 1) - 17{,}000 \text{ NORMDIST}(1.18, 0, 1, 0) - 9{,}360 \text{ NORMDIST}(468, 350, 100, 1) + 70{,}200[1 - \text{NORMDIST}(468, 350, 100, 1)] = \$49{,}146.$$

The expected profit from ordering 350 skis can be evaluated at \$45,718. Thus, ordering 468 skis results in a profit that is almost 8 percent higher than the profit obtained from ordering the expected value of 350 skis.

When O units are ordered, a firm is left with either too much or too little inventory, depending on demand. When demand is normally distributed with expected value μ and standard deviation σ, the expected quantity overstocked at the end of the season is given by the following:

$$\text{Expected overstock} = (O - \mu)F_S\left(\frac{O - \mu}{\sigma}\right) + \sigma f_S\left(\frac{O - \mu}{\sigma}\right)$$

The derivation of this formula is provided in Appendix 9D. The formula can be evaluated using Excel as follows:

$$\text{Expected overstock} = (O - \mu)NORMDIST((O - \mu)/\sigma, 0, 1, 1) + \sigma NORMDIST((O - \mu)/\sigma, 0, 1, 0) \qquad \textbf{(9.4)}$$

The expected quantity understocked at the end of the season is given by the following:

$$\text{Expected understock} = (\mu - O)\left[1 - F_S\left(\frac{O - \mu}{\sigma}\right)\right] + \sigma f_S\left(\frac{O - \mu}{\sigma}\right)$$

The derivation of this formula is provided in Appendix 9E. The formula can be evaluated using Excel as follows:

$$\text{Expected understock} = (\mu - O)[1 - NORMDIST((O - \mu)/\sigma, 0, 1, 1)] + \sigma NORMDIST((O - \mu)/\sigma, 0, 1, 0) \qquad \textbf{(9.5)}$$

Example 9.2 illustrates the use of Equations 9.4 and 9.5 to evaluate the quantity expected to be overstocked and understocked as a result of an ordering policy.

Example 9.2: Demand for skis at Sportmart is normally distributed with a mean of $\mu = 350$ and a standard deviation of $\sigma = 100$. The manager has decided to order 450 pairs of skis for the upcoming season. Evaluate the expected overstock and understock as a result of this policy.

Analysis: In this case, we have an order size $O = 450$. An overstock results if demand during the season is below 450. The expected overstock can be obtained using Equation 9.4 as follows:

$$\begin{aligned}\text{Expected overstock} &= (O - \mu)NORMDIST((O - \mu)/\sigma, 0, 1, 1) \\ &\quad + \sigma NORMDIST((O - \mu)/\sigma, 0, 1, 0) \\ &= (450 - 350)NORMDIST((450 - 350)/100, 0, 1, 1) \\ &\quad + 100NORMDIST((450 - 350)/100, 0, 1, 0) \\ &= 108\end{aligned}$$

Thus, the policy of ordering 450 pairs of skis results in an expected overstock of 108 pairs.

An understock occurs if demand during the season is higher than 450 pairs. The expected understock can be evaluated using Equation 9.5 as follows:

$$\begin{aligned}\text{Expected understock} &= (\mu - O)[1 - NORMDIST((O - \mu)/\sigma, 0, 1, 1)] \\ &\quad + \sigma NORMDIST((O - \mu)/\sigma, 0, 1, 0) \\ &= (350 - 450)[1 - NORMDIST((450 - 350)/100, 0, 1, 1)] \\ &\quad + 100NORMDIST((450 - 350)/100, 0, 1, 0) \\ &= 8\end{aligned}$$

Therefore, the policy of ordering 450 pairs results in an expected understock of 8 pairs.

Desired Cycle Service Level for Continuously Stocked Items

In this section, we restrict attention to products that are ordered repeatedly by a retail store like Wal-Mart, such as detergent. In such a situation, Wal-Mart uses safety inventory to increase the level of availability and decrease the probability of stocking out between successive deliveries. If detergent is left over in a replenishment cycle, it can be sold in the next cycle. It does not have to be disposed of at a lower cost. However, a holding cost is incurred as the product is carried from one cycle to the next. The manager at Wal-Mart is faced with the issue of deciding the cycle service level to aim for.

Two extreme scenarios should be considered:

1. All demand that arises when the product is out of stock is backlogged and filled later when inventories are replenished.
2. All demand arising when the product is out of stock is lost.

Reality in most instances is somewhere in between, with some of the demand lost and other customers returning when the product is in stock. Here, we consider both extreme cases.

We assume that demand per unit time is normally distributed along with the following inputs:

Q: Replenishment lot size
S: Fixed cost associated with each order
ROP: Reorder point
R: Average demand per unit time
σ_R: Standard deviation of demand per unit time
ss: Safety inventory. Recall that $ss = ROP - R_L$
CSL: Cycle service level
C: Unit cost
h: Holding cost as a fraction of product cost per unit time
H: Cost of holding one unit for one unit of time. $H = hC$

Demand During Stockout Is Backlogged

We first consider the case in which all demand arising when the product is out of stock is backlogged. Because no demand is lost, minimizing costs becomes equivalent to maximizing profits. As an example, consider a Wal-Mart store selling detergent. The store manager offers a discount of C_u to each customer wanting to buy detergent when it is out of stock. This ensures that all these customers return when inventory is replenished.

If the store manager increases the level of safety inventory, more orders are satisfied from stock, resulting in lower backlogs. This decreases the backlogging cost. However, the cost of holding inventory increases. The store manager must pick a level of safety inventory that minimizes the backlogging and holding costs. In this case, the optimal cycle service level is given by the following:

$$CSL^* = 1 - \frac{HQ}{RC_u} \tag{9.6}$$

Given the optimal cycle service level, the required safety inventory can be evaluated using Equation 8.9 if demand is normally distributed.

From Equation 9.6, observe that increasing the lot size Q allows the store manager at Wal-Mart to reduce the cycle service level and thus the safety inventory carried. This is because increasing the lot size increases the fill rate and thus reduces the quantity backlogged. One should be careful, however, because an increase in lot size raises the cycle inventory. In general, increasing the lot size is not an effective way for a firm to improve product availability.

If the cost of stocking out is known, one can use Equation 9.6 to obtain the appropriate cycle service level (and thus the appropriate level of safety inventory). In many practical settings, it is hard to estimate the cost of stocking out. In such a situation, a manager may want to evaluate the current inventory policy and identify the implied cost of a stockout. Often, when a precise cost of stockout cannot be found, this implied stockout cost will at least give an idea of whether inventory should be increased, decreased, or kept about the same. In Example 9.3 we show how Equation 9.6 can be used to estimate a cost of stocking out implied by a given inventory policy.

Example 9.3: Weekly demand for detergent at Wal-Mart is normally distributed with a mean of $R = 100$ gallons and a standard deviation of $\sigma_R = 20$. The replenishment lead time is $L = 2$ weeks. The store manager at Wal-Mart orders 400 gallons when the available inventory drops to 300 gallons. Each gallon of detergent costs \$3. The holding cost Wal-Mart incurs is 20 percent. If all unfilled demand is backlogged and carried over to the next cycle, evaluate the cost of stocking out implied by the current replenishment policy.

Analysis: In this case, we have the following:

Lot size $Q = 400$ gallons
Reorder point $ROP = 300$ gallons
Average demand per week $R = 100$ gallons
Average demand per year $R_{\text{year}} = 100 \times 52 = 5{,}200$
Standard deviation of demand per week $\sigma_R = 20$
Unit cost $C = \$3$
Holding cost as a fraction of product cost per year $h = 0.2$
Cost of holding one unit for one year $H = hC = \$0.6$
Lead time $L = 2$ weeks

We thus have the following:

$$\text{Mean demand over lead time, } R_L = RL = 200 \text{ gallons}$$
$$\text{Standard deviation of demand over lead-time, } \sigma_L = \sigma_R\sqrt{L} = 20\sqrt{2} = 28.3$$

Because demand is normally distributed, we can use Equation 8.4 to evaluate the cycle service level under the current inventory policy at CSL where

$$CSL = F(ROP, R_L, \sigma_L) = F(300, 200, 28.3)$$

Using Equation 8.19 from Appendix 8B, we thus obtain the following:

$$CSL = NORMDIST(300, 200, 28.3, 1) = 0.9998$$

We can thus deduce that the implied cost of stocking out (using Equation 9.6) is given by the following:

$$C_u = \frac{HQ}{(1 - CSL)R_{\text{year}}} = \frac{0.6 \times 400}{0.0002 \times 5{,}200} = \$230.8 \text{ per gallon}$$

The implication here is that if each shortage of a gallon of detergent costs Wal-Mart \$230.8, the current cycle service level of 0.9998 is optimal. In this particular example, one can claim that the store manager is carrying too much inventory because the cost of stocking out of detergent is unlikely to be \$230.8 per gallon.

A manager can use the preceding analysis to decide if the implied cost of stocking out, and thus, the inventory policy is reasonable.

Demand During Stockout Is Lost

For the case in which unfilled demand during the stockout period is lost, the optimal cycle service level CSL^* is given as follows:

$$CSL^* = 1 - \frac{HQ}{HQ + RC_u} \tag{9.7}$$

In this case, we have assumed that C_u is the cost of losing one unit of demand during the stockout period. In Example 9.4, we evaluate the optimal cycle service level if demand is lost during the stockout period.

Example 9.4: Consider the situation in Example 9.3, but make the assumption that all demand during a stockout is lost. Assume that the cost of losing one unit of demand is \$2. Evaluate the optimal cycle service level that the store manager at Wal-Mart should target.

Analysis: In this case we have the following:

Lot size $Q = 400$ gallons
Average demand per year $R_{\text{year}} = 100 \times 52 = 5{,}200$
Cost of holding one unit for one year $H = \$0.6$
Cost of understocking, $C_u = \$2$

Using Equation 9.7, the optimal cycle service level is given by the following:

$$CSL^* = 1 - \frac{HQ}{HQ + RC_u} = 1 - \frac{0.6 \times 400}{0.6 \times 400 + 2 \times 5{,}200} = 0.98$$

In this case, the store manager at Wal-Mart should target a cycle service level of 98 percent.

In general, the optimal cycle service level will be higher if sales are lost than if sales are backlogged.

9.3 MANAGERIAL LEVERS TO IMPROVE SUPPLY CHAIN PROFITABILITY

Having identified the factors that influence the optimal level of product availability, we now focus on actions a manager can take to improve supply chain profitability. We show in Section 9.2 that the costs of over- and understocking have a direct impact on both the optimal cycle service level and profitability. Two obvious managerial levers to increase profitability are thus as follows:

1. Increasing the salvage value of each unit to increase profitability (as well as the optimal cycle service level)
2. Decreasing the margin lost from a stockout to increase profitability

Strategies to increase the salvage value include selling to outlet stores so that leftover units are not merely discarded. Some companies like Sport Obermeyer selling winter wear in the United States sell the surplus in South America, where the winter corresponds to the North American summer. The increased salvage value of the surplus allows Sport Obermeyer to provide a higher level of product availability in the United States and increase its profits.

Strategies to decrease the margin lost in a stockout include arranging for backup sourcing (which may be more expensive) so customers are not lost forever. The practice of purchasing product from a competitor on the open market to satisfy customer demand is observed and justified by this reasoning. In the maintenance, repair, and operations (MRO) supply industry, McMaster-Carr and Grainger, two major competitors, are also large customers for each other.

The goal of reducing the margin lost from a stockout is also a major justification for the practice of providing customers with a rain check or discount on future purchases in case of a current stockout.

The optimal cycle service level as a function of the ratio of the cost of overstocking and the cost of understocking is shown in Figure 9.2. Observe that as this ratio gets smaller, the optimal level of product availability increases. This fact explains the difference in the level of product availability between a high-end store like Nordstrom

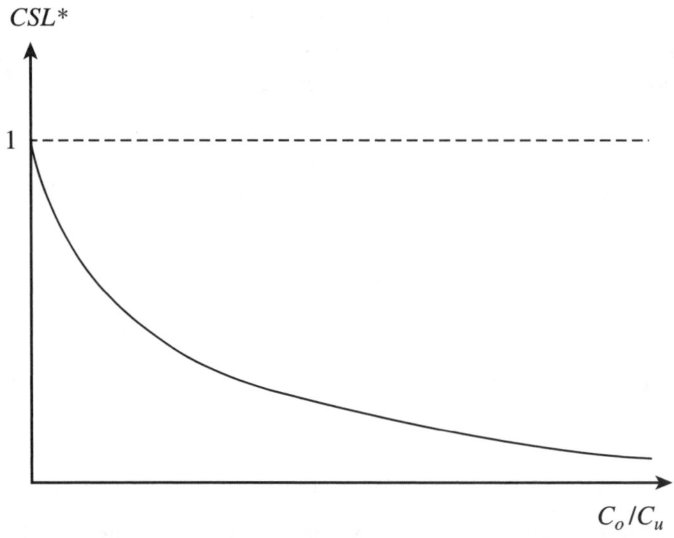

FIGURE 9.2 Impact of Changing C_o/C_u on Optimal Cycle Service Level

and a discount store. Nordstrom has higher margins and thus a higher cost of understocking. It should thus provide a higher level of product availability than a discount store with lower margins and, as a result, a lower cost of stocking out.

Another significant managerial lever to improve supply chain profitability is the reduction of demand uncertainty. With reduced demand uncertainty, a supply chain manager can better match supply and demand by reducing both over- and understocking. A manager can reduce demand uncertainty via the following means:

1. **Improved forecasting**. Use better market intelligence to reduce demand uncertainty.
2. **Quick response**. Reduce replenishment lead time so that multiple orders may be placed in the selling season.
3. **Postponement**. In a multiproduct setting, postpone product differentiation closer to the point of sale.
4. **Tailored sourcing**. Use a low lead time but expensive supplier as a backup for a low-cost but long lead time supplier.

Next we study the impact of each of these on supply chain performance.

Improving Forecasts: Impact on Profits and Inventories

Companies have tried to understand their customers better and coordinate actions within the supply chain to improve forecast accuracy. The use of demand planning information systems has also helped in this regard. We show that improved forecast accuracy can help a firm significantly increase its profitability while decreasing the excess inventory overstocked as well as the sales lost because of understocking. We illustrate the impact of improving forecast accuracy in Example 9.5.

Example 9.5: Consider a buyer at Bloomingdale's responsible for purchasing dinnerware with Christmas patterns. The dinnerware only sells over the Christmas season, and the buyer places an order for delivery in early November. Each dinnerware set costs $c = \$100$ and sells for a retail price of $p = \$250$. Any sets unsold by Christmas are heavily discounted in the post-

TABLE 9.3 Expected Profit and Order Size at Bloomingdale's

Standard Division of Forecast Error σ_R	*Optimal Order Size* O^*	*Expected Overstock*	*Expected Understock*	*Expected Profit*
150	526	186.7	8.6	$47,469
120	491	149.3	6.9	$48,476
90	456	112.0	5.2	$49,482
60	420	74.7	3.5	$50,488
30	385	37.3	1.7	$51,494
0	350	0	0	$52,500

Christmas sales and sold for a salvage value of $s = \$80$. The buyer has estimated that demand is normally distributed with a mean of $R = 350$. Historically, forecast errors have had a standard deviation of $\sigma_R = 150$. The buyer has decided to conduct additional market research to get a better forecast. Evaluate the impact of improved forecast accuracy on profitability and inventories as the buyer reduced σ from 150 to 0 in increments of 30.

Analysis: In this case, we have the following:

Cost of understocking = $C_u = p - c = \$250 - \$100 = \$150$
Cost of overstocking = $C_o = c - s = \$100 - \$80 = \$20$

Using Equation 9.1, we thus have the following

$$CSL^* = \text{probability}(\text{demand} \leq O^*) \geq \frac{150}{150 + 20} = 0.88$$

The optimal order size is obtained using Equation 9.2 and the expected profit using Equation 9.3. The order size and expected profit, as forecast accuracy (measured by standard deviation of forecast error) varies, are shown in Table 9.3.

Example 9.5 illustrates that as a firm improves its forecast accuracy, expected quantity overstocked and understocked decline and expected profit increases. This relationship is shown in Figure 9.3.

FIGURE 9.3 Variation of Profit and Inventories with Forecast Accuracy

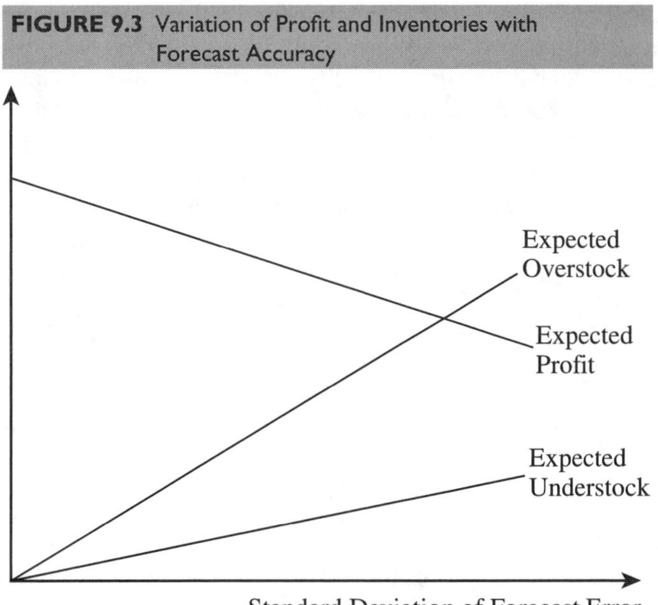

> ***Key Point*** An increase in forecast accuracy decreases both the overstocked and understocked quantity and increases a firm's profits.

Quick Response: Impact on Profits and Inventories

Quick response is the set of actions a supply chain takes that leads to a reduction in the replenishment lead time. Supply chain managers are able to increase their forecast accuracy as lead times decrease, which allows them to match supply with demand better and increase supply chain profitability.

To illustrate the issues, consider the example of Saks Fifth Avenue, a high-end department store, purchasing cashmere shawls from India and Nepal. The selling season for cashmere shawls is about 14 weeks. Historically, replenishment lead time has been on the order of 25–30 weeks. With a 30-week lead time, the buyer at Saks must order all the store expects to sell well before the start of the sales season. It is difficult for a buyer to make an accurate forecast of demand this far in advance. This results in high demand uncertainty, leading the buyer to order either too many or too few shawls each year. If the Asian manufacturers decrease the replenishment lead time to 15 weeks, the buyer at Saks must still place the entire order before the start of the sales season. However, the order can now be placed closer to the sales season, resulting in a more accurate forecast. As discussed earlier in the chapter, this reduction in uncertainty will increase profits at Saks.

Typically, buyers are able to make very accurate forecasts once they have observed demand for the first week or two in the season. Consider the situation in which the manufacturers are able to reduce the replenishment lead time to six weeks. This reduction allows the buyer at Saks to break up the entire season's purchase into two orders. The first order is placed six weeks before the start of the sales season. The buyer orders what the store expects to sell over the first seven weeks of the season. Once sales start, the buyer observes demand for the first week and places a second order after the first week. The second order is to build inventory up to the level that the buyer would like to order for the entire season. The ability to place the second order allows the buyer to match supply and demand much more effectively, resulting in higher profits.

When multiple orders are placed in the season, it is not possible to provide formulas like Equations 9.1–9.5 that specify the optimal order quantity, expected profit, expected overstock, and expected understock. Rather, we must use simulation (see Appendix 9F) to identify the impact of different ordering policies. We illustrate the impact of being able to place multiple orders using the Saks example discussed earlier.

The buyer at Saks must decide on the quantity of cashmere shawls to order from India and Nepal for the upcoming winter season. The unit cost of each shawl is $40, and the shawl retails for $150. A discount store purchases any leftover shawls at the end of the season for $30. Cost of displaying and holding any unsold shawls is $2 per week in inventory. After the sales season of 14 weeks, any leftover shawls are sold to the discount store.

Before the start of the sale season, the buyer forecasts weekly demand to be normally distributed with a mean of 20 and a standard deviation of 15. We compare the impact of the following two ordering policies:

1. A single order must be placed at the beginning of the season to cover the entire season's demand.
2. Two orders are placed in the season, one for the beginning of the season and the other for the beginning of the eighth week.

We consider two instances: one in which the buyer's forecast accuracy does not improve for the second order and one in which it improves and the buyer is able to reduce the standard deviation of the forecast to 3 instead of 15.

The analysis comparing the two policies is done using a simulation. We compare inventory levels as well as profitability for ordering policies in the single- and double-order scenario, which provide the same level of service.

When placing a single order, the ordering policy consists of a quantity to be ordered at the beginning of the season. When placing two orders, the ordering policy consists of an initial order quantity for the first seven weeks followed by an order up to level for the second seven weeks. The idea is that the quantity ordered in the second round should account for sales during the first seven weeks and the inventory remaining. If very little has sold during the first seven weeks, the second order should be small, because a lot of inventory remains from the first order. If a lot has sold during the first seven weeks, the second order should be large. The quantity ordered in the second round is the difference between the order up to level and the inventory remaining after the first seven weeks.

In the simulation we assume that any unfilled demand is lost. In Table 9.4 we report results for the case in which there is no improvement in forecast accuracy for the second order. The results given are an average of 500 different simulations.

From the results in Table 9.4, we observe three important consequences of being able to place a second order in the season:

1. The expected total quantity ordered during the season with two orders is less than that with a single order for the same cycle service level. In other words, it is possible to provide the same level of product availability to the customer with less inventory if a second follow-up order is allowed in the sales season.
2. The average overstock to be disposed of at the end of the sales season is less if two orders are allowed.
3. The profits are higher when a second order is allowed during the sales season.

In other words, as the total quantity for the season is broken up into multiple smaller orders, the buyer is better able to match supply and demand and increase profitability for Saks. These relationships are shown in Figures 9.4 and 9.5.

We now consider the case in which the buyer improves his forecast accuracy for the second order after observing some of the season's demand. As a result, the stan-

TABLE 9.4 Expected Profit and Overstock at Saks with No Improvement in Forecast Accuracy for Second Order

	Single Order for Season			*Two Orders in the Season*				
Cycle Service Level	*Order Size*	*Average Overstock*	*Expected Profit*	*Initial Order*	*Order Up to Level for Second Order*	*Average Total Order*	*Average Overstock*	*Expected Profit*
0.96	378	97	\$23,624	209	209	349	69	\$26,590
0.94	367	86	\$24,034	201	201	342	60	\$27,085
0.91	355	73	\$24,617	193	193	332	52	\$27,154
0.87	343	66	\$24,386	184	184	319	43	\$26,944
0.81	329	55	\$24,609	174	174	313	36	\$27,413
0.75	317	41	\$25,205	166	166	302	32	\$26,915

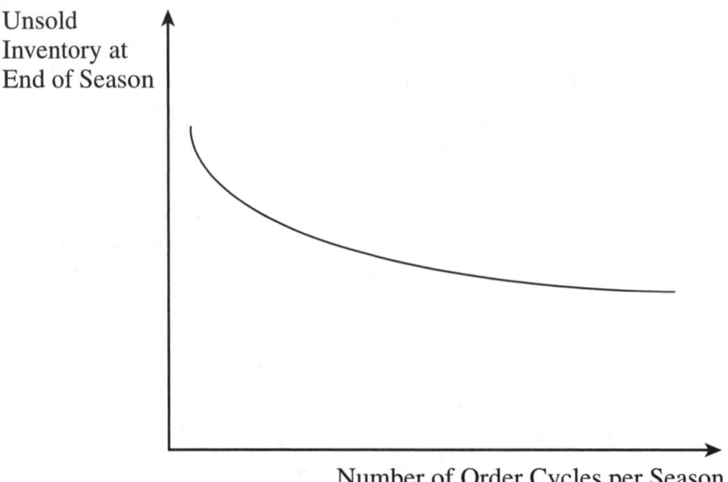

FIGURE 9.4 Leftover Inventory Versus Number of Order Cycles per Season

dard deviation of weekly demand forecast reduces from 15 to 3 for the second seven-week period. To provide the same service level, the second order up to level is adjusted appropriately. The results of the simulations are shown in Table 9.5.

From Table 9.5, observe that the reduction in demand uncertainty that occurs after the first seven weeks further enhances the benefits of quick response and the ability to place a second order. Profits at Saks increase and the expected overstock quantity decreases.

> ***Key Point*** If quick response allows multiple orders in the season, profits increase, and the overstock quantity decreases.

FIGURE 9.5 Expected Profit Versus Number of Order Cycles per Season

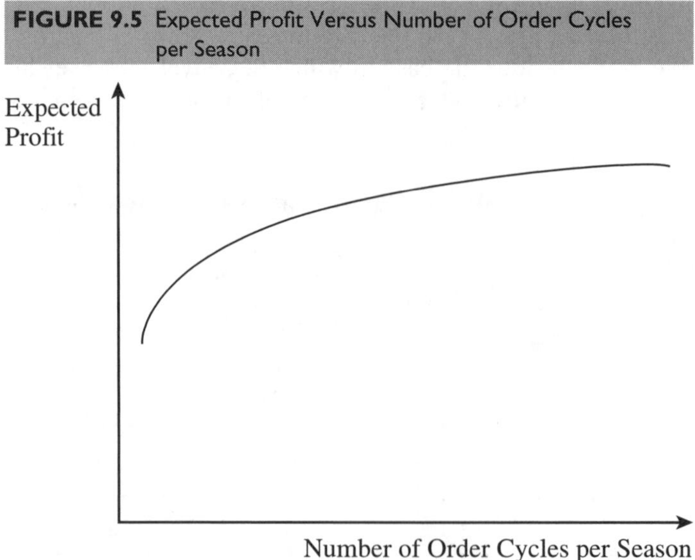

TABLE 9.5 Expected Profit and Overstock at Saks Assuming Forecast Accuracy Improves for Second Order

	Single Order for Season			*Two Orders in the Season*				
Cycle Service Level	*Order Size*	*Average Overstock*	*Expected Profit*	*Initial Order*	*Order Up to Level for Second Order*	*Average Total Order*	*Average Overstock*	*Expected Profit*
0.96	378	96	$23,707	209	153	292	19	$27,007
0.94	367	84	$24,303	201	152	293	18	$27,371
0.91	355	76	$24,154	193	150	288	17	$26,946
0.87	343	63	$24,807	184	148	288	14	$27,583
0.81	329	52	$24,998	174	146	283	14	$27,162
0.75	317	44	$24,887	166	145	282	14	$27,268

From our previous discussion, quick response is clearly advantageous to a retailer in the supply chain—with one caveat: As the manufacturer reduces replenishment lead times allowing for a second order, we have seen that the retailer's order size drops. In effect, the manufacturer sells less to the retailer. Thus, quick response results in the manufacturer's making a lower profit in the short term if all else is unchanged. This is an important point to consider, because decreasing replenishment lead times requires tremendous effort from the manufacturer yet seems to benefit the retailer at the expense of the manufacturer. The benefits resulting from quick response should be shared appropriately across the supply chain.

Postponement: Impact on Profits and Inventories

As discussed in Chapter 8, postponement refers to the delay of product differentiation closer to the time of sale of the product. With postponement, all activities prior to product differentiation require aggregate forecasts that are more accurate than individual product forecasts. Individual product forecasts are required close to the time of sale when demand is known with greater accuracy. As a result, postponement allows a supply chain to better match supply with demand.

Postponement can be a powerful managerial lever to increase profitability. It can be particularly valuable in e-commerce because of the lag that exists between the time customers place an order and when they expect delivery. If the supply chain can postpone product differentiation until after receiving the customer order, a significant increase in profits and reduction in inventories can be achieved.

The major benefit of postponement arises from the improved matching of supply and demand. There is, however, a cost associated with postponement because the production cost using postponement is typically higher than the production cost without it. For example, the production process at Benetton, in which knit garments are dyed, costs about 10 percent more than if dyed thread is knit. Similarly, when Hewlett Packard postpones some assembly steps for its European printers to the European distribution center, manufacturing costs increase because packing, unpacking, and some other steps must be duplicated. Given the increased production cost from postponement, a company should quantify the benefits and ensure that they are larger than the additional costs.

Postponement is valuable for a firm that sells a large variety of products with demand that is independent and comparable in size We illustrate this claim using the Benetton example. A large fraction of Benetton's sales are from knit garments in solid colors. Starting with thread, there are two steps to completing the garment:

dyeing and knitting. Traditionally, thread was dyed and then the garment was knitted (option 1). Benetton developed a procedure in which dyeing is postponed until after the garment is knitted (option 2).

Benetton sells each knit garment at a retail price $p = \$50$. Option 1 results in a manufacturing cost of \$20 per garment, whereas option 2 results in a manufacturing cost of \$22 per garment. Benetton disposes of any unsold garments at the end of the season in a clearance for $s = \$10$ each. The knitting or manufacturing process takes a total of 20 weeks. For the sake of discussion, we assume that Benetton sells garments in four colors. Twenty weeks in advance, Benetton forecasts demand for each color to be normally distributed with a mean of $\mu = 1{,}000$ and a standard deviation of $\sigma = 500$. Demand for each color is independent. Under option 1, Benetton makes the buying decision for each color 20 weeks before the sale period and holds separate inventories for each color. Under option 2, Benetton forecasts only the aggregate uncolored thread to purchase 20 weeks in advance. The inventory held is based on the aggregate demand across all four colors. Benetton decides the quantity for individual colors after demand is known. We now quantify the impact of postponement for Benetton.

Under option 1, Benetton must decide on the quantity of colored thread to purchase for each color. For each color we have the following:

Retail price $p = \$50$
Manufacturing cost $c = \$20$
Salvage value $s = \$10$

Using Equation 9.1, we obtain the optimal cycle service level for each color as follows:

$$CSL^* = \frac{p-c}{p-s} = \frac{30}{40} = 0.75$$

Using Equation 9.2, the optimal purchase quantity of thread in each color is as follows:

$$O^* = NORMINV(CSL^*, \mu, \sigma) = NORMINV(0.75, 100, 500) = 1{,}337$$

Thus, it is optimal for Benetton to produce 1,337 units of each color. Using Equation 9.3, the expected profit from each color is as follows:

Expected profits = \$23,644

Using Equations 9.4 and 9.5, the expected overstock and understock for each color is as follows:

Expected overstock = 412
Expected understock = 75

Using option 1, across all four colors Benetton thus produces 5,348 sweaters. This results in an expected profit of \$94,576, with an average of 1,648 sweaters sold on clearance at the end of the season and 300 customers turned away for lack of sweaters.

Under option 2, Benetton has to decide on the total number of sweaters across all four colors to be produced because they can be dyed to the appropriate color once demand is known. In this case, we have the following:

Retail price $p = \$50$
Manufacturing cost $c = \$22$
Salvage value $s = \$10$

Using Equation 9.1, the optimal cycle service level for each color is this:

$$CSL^* = \frac{p-c}{p-s} = \frac{28}{40} = 0.70$$

Given that demand for each color is independent, aggregate demand across all four colors can be evaluated using Equations 8.12 and 8.13 to be normally distributed with a mean of μ_A and a standard deviation of σ_A, where

$$\mu_A = 4 \times 1{,}000 = 4{,}000 \qquad \sigma_A = \sqrt{4} \times 500 = 1{,}000$$

Using Equation 9.2, the optimal aggregate production for Benetton is given by O_A^* where

$$O_A^* = NORMINV(CSL^*, \mu_A, \sigma_A) = NORMINV(0.7, 4000, 1000) = 4{,}524$$

Under option 2, it is optimal for Benetton to produce 4,524 undyed sweaters to be dyed as demand by color is available. The expected profit is evaluated using Equation 9.3 as follows:

$$\text{Expected profits} = \$98{,}092$$

Using Equation 9.4, the expected overstock is 715 and the expected understock is 190. Thus, postponement increases expected profits for Benetton from $94,576 to $98,092. Expected overstock declines from 1,648 to 715, and the expected understock declines from 300 to 190. Clearly, the use of postponement and production using option 2 is a good choice for Benetton in this case.

Key Point Postponement allows a firm to increase profits and better match supply and demand if the firm produces a large variety of products whose demand is not positively correlated and is of about the same size.

Postponement is not very effective if a large fraction of demand comes from a single product. This is because the benefit from aggregation is small in this case, but the increased production cost applies to all products. We illustrate this idea once again using Benetton as an example.

Assume that demand for red sweaters at Benetton is forecast to be normally distributed with a mean of $\mu_{\text{red}} = 3{,}100$ and a standard deviation of $\sigma_{\text{red}} = 800$. Demand for each of the other three colors is forecast to be normally distributed with a mean of $\mu = 300$ and a standard deviation of $\sigma = 200$. Observe that red sweaters constitute about 80 percent of demand.

Under option 1, the optimal cycle service level is $CSL^* = 0.75$, as evaluated earlier. Using Equation 9.2, the optimal production of red sweaters is given by the following:

$$O^* = NORMINV(CSL^*, \mu_{\text{red}}, \sigma_{\text{red}}) = NORMINV(0.75, 3100, 800) = 3{,}640$$

Using Equation 9.3, the expected profit from red sweaters is $82,831. Using Equation 9.4, the expected overstock of red sweaters is 659, and using Equation 9.5, the expected understock of red sweaters is 119. For each of the other three colors, we can similarly evaluate the optimal production to be 435 sweaters. This results in an expected profit of $6,458, an expected overstock of 165, and an expected understock of 30. Across all four colors, option 1 thus results in the following:

Total production = 4,945
Expected profit = $102,205
Expected overstock = 1,154
Expected understock = 209

Under option 2, Benetton has to decide only the total production across all four colors. Given that demand for each color is independent, total demand across all four colors can be evaluated using Equations 8.12 and 8.13 to be normally distributed with a mean of μ_A and a standard deviation of σ_A, where

$$\mu_A = 3{,}100 + 3 \times 300 = 4{,}000 \qquad \sigma_A = 872$$

Under option 2, we repeat all calculations to obtain the following:

Total production = 4,457
Expected profit = $99,872
Expected overstock = 623
Expected understock = 166

In this case, Benetton sees its profits decline as a result of postponement. This is because a large fraction of demand is from red sweaters, which can already be forecast with reasonably good accuracy. Postponement and the resulting aggregation thus do little to improve the forecasting accuracy of red sweaters. It does, however, improve the forecasting accuracy for the other three colors, but they represent a small fraction of demand. The production costs meanwhile increase for all sweaters. As a result, the increased production costs outweigh the benefits from postponement.

> ***Key Point*** Postponement may reduce overall profits for a firm if a single product contributes the majority of the demand, because the increased manufacturing expense due to postponement outweighs the small benefit that aggregation provides in this case.

In **tailored postponement**, a firm uses production with postponement to satisfy a part of its demand and satisfies the rest without postponement. Tailored postponement produces higher profits than when no postponement is used or all products are manufactured using postponement. Under tailored postponement, a firm produces the amount that is very likely to sell using the lower-cost production method without postponement. The firm produces the portion of demand that is uncertain using postponement. For the portion of the demand that is certain, postponement provides little value in terms of increased forecast accuracy. The firm thus produces it using the lower-cost method to lower manufacturing cost.

For the portion of demand that is uncertain, postponement significantly improves forecast accuracy. The firm is thus willing to incur the increased production cost to achieve the benefit from the improved matching of supply and demand. We illustrate the idea of tailored postponement, returning to the example of Benetton.

Consider the scenario in which Benetton is selling four colors and the forecast demand for each color is normally distributed with a mean of $\mu = 1{,}000$ and a standard deviation of $\sigma = 500$. We observe earlier that the use of postponement increases profits at Benetton. We now consider a situation in which Benetton applies tailored postponement and uses both option 1 (dye thread and then knit garment) and option 2 (dye knit garment) for production. For each color, Benetton identifies a quantity Q_1 to be manufactured using option 1 and an aggregate quantity Q_A to be manufactured using option 2, with colors for the aggregate quantity being assigned when demand is known. We now identify the appropriate tailored postponement policy and its impact on profits and inventories.

TABLE 9.6 Average of 500 Simulations for Tailored Postponement Policies

Quantity Produced Under Each Option				
Q_I	Q_A	*Average Profit*	*Average Overstock*	*Average Understock*
0	4,524	$98,092	715	190
1,337	0	$94,576	1,648	300
700	1,850	$102,730	308	168
800	1,550	$104,603	427	170
900	950	$101,326	607	266
900	1,050	$101,647	664	230
1,000	850	$100,312	815	195
1,000	950	$100,951	803	149
1,100	550	$99,180	1,026	211
1,100	650	$100,510	1,008	185

There is no formula that can be used to evaluate the optimal policy and profits. We thus resort to simulations to study the impact of different policies. The results of various simulations are shown in Table 9.6.

From Table 9.6, we see that Benetton can increase its expected profit to $104,603 by using a tailored postponement policy in which 800 units of each color are produced using option 1 and 1,550 units are produced using option 2. The resulting profit is higher than if all units are produced entirely using option 1 or 2. It is quite likely that demand for each color will be 800 or higher. The tailored postponement policy exploits this fact and produces these units using option 1, which has a low cost. The remaining units are produced using option 2 so that demand uncertainty can be reduced by aggregation.

Key Point Tailored postponement allows a firm to increase its profitability by postponing only the uncertain part of the demand and producing the predictable part at a lower cost without postponement.

Tailored Sourcing: Impact on Profits and Inventories

In **tailored sourcing**, firms use a combination of two supply sources: one focusing on cost but unable to handle uncertainty well and the other focusing on flexibility to handle uncertainty but at a higher cost. For tailored sourcing to be effective, having one supply source serve as a backup to the other is not sufficient. The two sources must focus on different capabilities. The low-cost source must focus on being efficient and should be required to supply only the predictable portion of the demand. The flexible source should focus on being responsive and be required to supply the uncertain portion of the demand. As a result, tailored sourcing allows a firm to increase its profits and match supply and demand better. The value of tailored sourcing depends on the reduction in cost that can be achieved as a result of one source facing no variability. If this benefit is small, tailored sourcing may not be ideal because of the added complexity of implementation. Tailored sourcing may be volume-based or product-based, depending on the source of uncertainty.

In volume-based tailored sourcing, the predictable part of a product's demand is produced at an efficient facility, and the uncertain portion is produced at a flexible facility. Benetton is a good example of volume-based tailored sourcing.

Benetton requires retailers to commit to about 65 percent of their orders about seven months before the start of the sales season. Benetton subcontracts production of this portion without uncertainty to low-cost sources that have long lead times of several months. On the other 35 percent, Benetton allows retailers to place orders much closer to or even after the start of the selling season. All uncertainty is concentrated in this portion of the order. Benetton produces this portion of the order in a plant it owns that is very flexible. Production at the Benetton plant is more expensive than production at the subcontractor's. However, the plant can produce with a lead time of weeks. A combination of the two sources allows Benetton to reduce its inventories while incurring a high cost of production for only a fraction of its demand. This allows it to increase profits.

Volume-based tailored sourcing should be considered by firms that have moved a lot of their production overseas to take advantage of lower costs. The lower costs have also been accompanied by longer lead times. In such a situation, having a flexible local source with short lead times can be very effective even if the local source is more expensive. Long lead times require large safety inventories, and the resulting mismatch of supply and demand hurts profits. The presence of the local source allows the firm to carry low safety inventories and supply any excess demand from the local source. The most effective combination is for the overseas source to focus on replenishing cycle inventories, ignoring uncertainty. The local source is used as a backup any time demand exceeds the inventory available.

In product-based tailored sourcing, low-volume products with uncertain demand are obtained from a flexible source and high-volume products with less demand uncertainty are obtained from an efficient source. An example of product-based tailored sourcing is Levi Strauss. Levi sells standard-sized jeans as well as jeans that can be customized to fit an individual. Standard jeans have relatively stable demand, whereas demand for custom jeans is unpredictable. Custom jeans are produced at a flexible facility, and standard jeans are produced at an efficient facility.

In some instances new products have very uncertain demand, whereas well-established products have more stable demand. Product-based tailored sourcing may be implemented with a flexible facility focusing on new products and efficient facilities focusing on the well-established products.

9.4 SUPPLY CHAIN CONTRACTS AND THEIR IMPACT ON PROFITABILITY

A **contract** specifies the parameters within which a buyer places orders and a supplier fulfills them. A contract may contain specifications regarding quantity, price, time, and quality. At one extreme, a contract may require the buyer to specify the precise quantity required, with a very long lead time. In this case, the buyer bears the risk of over- and understocking, and the supplier has exact order information well in advance of delivery. At the other extreme, buyers may not be required to commit to the precise purchase quantity until they are certain of their demand, with the supply arriving with a short lead time. In this case, the supplier has little advance information, and the buyer can wait until demand is known before ordering. As a result, the supplier must build inventory in advance and bear most of the risk of over- or understocking. As contracts change, the risk different stages of the supply chain bear changes, which affects the retailers' and suppliers' decisions and the supply chain's profitability.

Consider, for example, Tech Fiber (TF), a manufacturer of synthetic fibers used in ski jackets and other winter outerwear. TF has patented a new lightweight fiber that is very inexpensive to manufacture but has the warmth and water-repellent properties of very expensive natural fiber. TF has designed a new jacket using this fiber that it wants to bring to the market. The jacket will be sold exclusively through Ski Adventure (SA), a major retailer of winter apparel and sport equipment. Each jacket costs v = \$10 to produce, and TF plans to charge a wholesale price c = \$100 per jacket from the retailer. The retailer plans to sell the jacket for a price of p = \$200. At this price, the manager at SA estimates the demand for the new jacket to be normally distributed with a mean of $\mu = 1{,}000$ and a standard deviation of $\sigma = 300$. To simplify the discussion, assume that SA is unable to salvage anything for unsold jackets, resulting in a salvage value of s = \$0.

Using Equation 9.1, the manager at SA obtains an optimal cycle service level of $CSL^* = 0.5$. Using Equation 9.2, the manager finds it optimal to order 1,000 jackets. Using Equation 9.3, the manager evaluates expected profit at the end of the season as a result of this policy at \$76,063. In this case, TF sells 1,000 jackets for a total profit of \$90,000. The total expected supply chain profit in this case is \$166,063.

Observe that the supply chain makes \$190 for each jacket sold. The ordering decision, however, is made by the manager at SA, and SA makes a margin of \$100 per jacket, which is lower than the margin for the entire supply chain. Meanwhile, SA loses \$100 for each unsold jacket, whereas the supply chain as a whole loses only \$10. As a result, the manager at SA orders fewer jackets than is optimal from the perspective of the entire supply chain acting as one. From the perspective of the entire supply chain, the cost of understocking is \$190 and the cost of overstocking is \$10. It is thus optimal for the supply chain to provide a cycle service level of 0.95 and produce 1,493 jackets. This results in a total supply chain profit of \$183,812.

The gap in profit exists because of **double marginalization**. Double marginalization refers to the fact that the total supply chain margin of \$190 is divided between \$90 for the manufacturer and \$100 for the retailer. Therefore, each party makes decisions considering only a portion of the total supply chain margin. In this case, a decision by the SA manager (the size of the order) affects profits at TF. The manager at SA, however, does not take TF profits into account when making her decision. As a result, her decision does not maximize supply chain profits.

We next consider how TF can offer buyback contracts to induce the manager at SA to order quantities that increase the total supply chain profit.

Returns Policy: Buyback Contracts

A manufacturer can increase the quantity the retailer purchases by offering to buy back any leftover units at the end of the season at a fraction of the purchase price. This action has the effect of increasing the salvage value per unit for the retailer who, as a result, increases its order size. The manufacturer may benefit by taking on some of the cost of overstocking because the supply chain will, on average, end up selling more products.

In a **buyback contract**, the manufacturer specifies a wholesale price c along with a buyback price b at which the retailer can return any unsold units at the end of the season. We assume that the manufacturer can salvage $\$s_M$ for any units that the retailer returns.

The optimal order quantity O^* for a retailer in response to a buyback contract is evaluated using Equations 9.1 and 9.2, where the salvage value for the retailer is $s = b$. The expected retailer profit is evaluated using Equation 9.3. The expected profit at the manufacturer depends on the overstock at the retailer (evaluated using Equation 9.4) that is returned. We obtain the following:

$$\text{Expected manufacturer profit} = O^*(c - v) - b \times \text{expected overstock at retailer}$$

Table 9.7 provides the outcome for different buyback contracts that TF offers SA. The sale price of jackets at SA is p = \$200, and demand at this price is normally distributed with a mean of $\mu = 1{,}000$ and a standard deviation of $\sigma = 300$. At this stage, we assume that there is no transportation or other cost associated with any returns.

From Table 9.7, observe that a buyback contract allows both the manufacturer, TF, and the retailer, SA, to increase their profits. In Table 9.7, the use of buyback contracts increases total supply chain profits by about 10 percent. In many instances, buyback contracts can be used to increase total supply chain profits. Also observe that the buyback price that maximizes supply chain profits is somewhere between zero and the wholesale price. In general, it is optimal for the manufacturer to offer to buy back at a fraction of the wholesale price.

For a fixed wholesale price, increasing the buyback price always increases retailer profits and may also increase manufacturer profits. Also observe that the manufacturer, TF, makes a higher profit with a wholesale price of \$120 and a buyback price of \$96 than it does with a wholesale price of \$100 and a buyback price of \$60. Thus, manufacturers can increase their profits by increasing the buyback price by a larger amount than they increase the wholesale price.

In 1932, Viking Press was the first book publisher to accept returns. Today, buyback contracts are very common in the book industry, and publishers accept unsold books from retailers. To minimize the cost associated with a return, retailers do not have to return the book but only the cover. This provides publishers with proof that the book did not sell while reducing the cost of the return. Over the years, there has been considerable debate about the impact of publishers' returns policy on profits in the industry. Our discussion provides some justification for the approach taken by the publishers.

From Table 9.7, observe that as the wholesale price increases, it is optimal for the manufacturer to increase the buyback price as well. Also observe that for a fixed wholesale price, as the buyback price increases, the retailer orders more and also returns more. In our analysis in Table 9.7, we have not considered the cost associated with a return. As the cost associated with a return increases, buyback contracts become less attractive because the cost of returns reduces supply chain profits. If return

TABLE 9.7 Order Sizes and Profits at SA and TF Under Different Buyback Contracts

Wholesale Price c	*Buyback Price b*	*Optimal Order Size for SA*	*Expected Profit for SA*	*Expected Returns to TF*	*Expected Profit for TF*	*Expected Supply Chain Profit*
\$100	\$0	1,000	\$76,063	120	\$90,000	\$166,063
\$100	\$30	1,067	\$80,154	156	\$91,338	\$171,492
\$100	\$60	1,170	\$85,724	223	\$91,886	\$177,610
\$100	\$95	1,501	\$96,875	506	\$86,935	\$183,810
\$110	\$78	1,191	\$78,074	239	\$100,480	\$178,555
\$110	\$105	1,486	\$86,938	493	\$96,872	\$183,810
\$120	\$96	1,221	\$70,508	261	\$109,225	\$179,733
\$120	\$116	1,501	\$77,500	506	\$106,310	\$183,810

costs are very high, buyback contracts can reduce the total profits of the supply chain far more than is the case without any buyback.

> ***Key Point*** Manufacturers can use buyback contracts to increase their own profit as well as total supply chain profits.

In some instances, manufacturers use holding cost subsidies to encourage retailers to order more. With **holding cost subsidies**, manufacturers pay retailers a certain amount for every unit held in inventory over a given period. Holding cost subsidies behave very much like buyback contracts in their impact on manufacturer and supply chain profits.

Next we discuss how quantity flexibility contracts allow a supply chain to increase total profits.

Quantity Flexibility Contracts

In **quantity flexibility** contracts, the manufacturer allows the retailer to change the quantity ordered after observing demand. If a retailer orders O units, the manufacturer commits to providing $Q = (1 + \alpha)O$ units, and the retailer is committed to buying at least $q = (1 - \beta)O$ units. Both α and β are between 0 and 1. The retailer can purchase up to Q units, depending on the demand observed. These contracts are similar to buyback contracts in that the manufacturer now bears some of the risk of having excess inventory. Because no returns are required, these contracts can be more effective than buyback contracts when the cost of returns is high. Quantity flexibility contracts increase the average amount the retailer purchases and may increase total supply chain profits.

Assume that the manufacturer incurs a production cost of $\$v$ per unit and charges a wholesale price of $\$c$ from the retailer. The retailer in turn sells to customers for a price of $\$p$. The retailer salvages any leftover units for s_R. The manufacturer salvages any leftover units for s_M. If retailer demand is normally distributed with a mean of μ and a standard deviation of σ, we can evaluate the impact of a quantity flexibility contract. If the retailer orders O units, the manufacturer is committed to supplying Q units. As a result, we assume that the manufacturer produces Q units. The retailer purchases q units if demand R is less than q, R units if demand R is between q and Q, and Q units if demand is higher than Q. We thus obtain the following:

$$\text{Expected quantity purchased by retailer, } Q_R = qF(q) + Q[1 - F(Q)] + \mu\left[F_S\left(\frac{Q-\mu}{\sigma}\right) - F_S\left(\frac{q-\mu}{\sigma}\right)\right] - \sigma\left[f_S\left(\frac{Q-\mu}{\sigma}\right) - f_S\left(\frac{q-\mu}{\sigma}\right)\right]$$

$$\text{Expected quantity sold by retailer } D_R = Q[1 - F(Q)] + \mu F_S\left(\frac{Q-\mu}{\sigma}\right) - \sigma f_S\left(\frac{Q-\mu}{\sigma}\right)$$

Expected overstock at manufacturer $= Q_R - D_R$

Expected retailer profit $= D_R \times p + (Q_R - D_R)s_R - Q_R \times c$

Expected manufacturer profit $= Q_R \times c + (Q - Q_R)s_M - Q \times v$

We return to the example of TF selling jackets to SA at a wholesale price of $c = \$100$. TF incurs a cost of $v = \$10$ to produce each jacket. SA sells jackets to

TABLE 9.8 Profits at TF and SA Under Different Quantity Flexibility Contracts

α	β	*Wholesale Price c*	*Order Size O*	*Expected Purchase by SA*	*Expected Sale by SA*	*Expected Profits for SA*	*Expected Profits for TF*	*Expected Supply Chain Profit*
0.00	0.00	$100	1,000	1,000	880	$76,063	$90,000	$16,063
0.20	0.20	$100	1,050	1,024	968	$91,167	$89,830	$180,997
0.40	0.40	$100	1,070	1,011	994	$97,689	$86,122	$183,811
0.00	0.00	$110	962	962	860	$66,252	$96,200	$162,452
0.15	0.15	$110	1,014	1,009	945	$78,153	$99,282	$177,435
0.42	0.42	$110	1,048	1,007	993	$87,932	$95,879	$183,811
0.00	0.00	$120	924	924	938	$56,819	$101,640	$158,459
0.2	0.2	$120	1,000	1,000	955	$70,933	$108,000	$178,933
0.5	0.5	$120	1,040	1,003	996	$78,874	$104,803	$183,677

consumers at a retail price of $p = \$200$. At this price, demand is normally distributed with a mean of $\mu = 1{,}000$ and a standard deviation of $\sigma = 300$. We assume a salvage value of $0 at both the retailer SA and manufacturer TF. In Table 9.8, we show the impact of different quantity flexibility contracts on supply chain profitability. All contracts considered are such that $\alpha = \beta$.

From Table 9.8, observe that quantity flexibility contracts allow both the manufacturer, TF, and the retailer, SA, to increase their profits. It is often in the manufacturer's best interest to offer a quantity flexibility contract to the retailer. In Table 9.8, observe that for wholesale prices of $110 and $120, the manufacturer, TF, increases its profits by offering a quantity flexibility contract. Total supply chain profits also increase with quantity flexibility. Observe that as the manufacturer increases the wholesale price, it is optimal for it to offer greater quantity flexibility to the retailer.

Quantity flexibility contracts are common for components in the electronic and computer industry. In the preceding discussion, we consider fairly simple quantity flexibility contracts. Benetton has successfully used sophisticated quantity flexibility contracts with its retailers to increase supply chain profits. We describe such a contract in the context of colored knit garments.[1]

Seven months before delivery, Benetton retailers are required to place their orders. Consider a retailer placing an order for 100 sweaters each in red, blue, and yellow. One to three months before delivery, retailers may alter up to 30 percent of the quantity ordered in any color and assign it to another color. The aggregate order, however, cannot be adjusted at this stage. Potentially the retailer may change the order to 70 red, 70 blue, and 160 yellow sweaters. After the start of the sales season, retailers are allowed to order up to 10 percent of their previous order in any color. Potentially the retailer can order another 30 yellow sweaters. In this quantity flexibility contract, Benetton retailers have a flexibility of up to 10 percent on the aggregate order across all colors and about 40 percent for individual colors. Retailers can increase the aggregate quantity ordered by up to 10 percent, and the quantity for any individual color can be adjusted by up to 40 percent. This flexibility is consistent with the fact that aggregate forecasts are more accurate than forecasts for individual colors. As a result, retailers can better match product availability with demand. The quantity flexibility contract Benetton offers allows both the retailers and Benetton to increase their profits.

[1]See Signorelli and Heskett (1984).

> ***Key Point*** Manufacturers can use contracts with quantity flexibility to increase their own profits as well as total supply chain profits.

Vendor-Managed Inventories

With **vendor-managed inventories** (VMI), the manufacturer or supplier is responsible for all decisions regarding product inventories at the retailer. As a result, the control of the replenishment decision moves to the manufacturer instead of the retailer. VMI requires the retailer to share demand information with the manufacturer to allow it to make inventory replenishment decisions. VMI can allow a manufacturer to increase its profits as well as profits for the entire supply chain by mitigating some of the effects of double marginalization. Profits increase only if both retailer and manufacturer margins are considered when making inventory decisions. Several firms, including Campbell Soup and Procter & Gamble (P&G), have had successful VMI relationships with retailers.

VMI also helps by conveying customer demand data to the manufacturer, who can then plan production accordingly. This helps improve manufacturer forecasts and better match manufacturer production with customer demand.

One drawback to VMI arises because retailers often sell products from competing manufacturers that are substitutes in the customer's mind. For example, a customer may substitute detergent manufactured by P&G with detergent manufactured by Lever Brothers. If the retailer has a VMI agreement with both manufacturers, each manufacturer will ignore the impact of substitution when making its inventory decisions. As a result, inventories at the retailer will be higher than optimal. In such a setting, the retailer may be better positioned to decide on the replenishment policy. Demand data can still be shared with the manufacturer responsible for implementing the replenishment policy.

9.5 SETTING OPTIMAL LEVELS OF PRODUCT AVAILABILITY IN PRACTICE

Managers will find the following ideas relevant when considering levels of product availability in practice:

- **Use this analytic framework to increase profits**. Many firms set inventory levels without any supporting analysis. Managers can provide significant value to a firm by introducing the concepts discussed in this chapter. The concepts not only provide an approach for a firm to target the optimal level of product availability, they also help identify key managerial levers that may be used to increase profitability.
- **Beware of preset levels of availability**. Often companies have a preset target of product availability without any justification. In such a situation, managers should probe the rationale for the targeted level of product availability. A manager can provide significant value by adjusting the targeted level of product availability to one that maximizes profits.
- **Use approximate costs because profit-maximizing solutions are quite robust**. Companies should avoid spending an inordinate amount of effort to get exact estimates of various costs used to evaluate optimal levels of product

availability. Levels of product availability close to optimal will often produce a profit that is very close to the optimal profit. Therefore, it is not crucial that all costs be estimated precisely. A reasonable approximation of the costs will generally produce targeted levels of product availability that are close to optimal.

- **Estimate a range for the cost of stocking out**. Firms' efforts to set levels of product availability often get bogged down in debate over the cost of stocking out. The sometimes controversial nature of this cost and its hard-to-quantify components (such as loss of customer goodwill) make it a difficult number for people from different functions to agree upon. However, it is often not necessary to estimate a precise cost of stocking out. Using a range of the cost of stocking out, a manager can identify appropriate levels of availability and the associated profits. Often, profits do not change significantly in the range, thus eliminating the need for a more precise estimation of the cost of stocking out.
- **Ensure that levels of product availability fit with strategy**. A manager should use the level of product availability suggested by the analysis along with the firm's strategic objectives when setting the targeted level of product availability. In some instances, a firm may find it appropriate to provide a high level of product availability for a low-volume item that is not very profitable but is required by important customers. A firm trying to project a reputation for product availability may find it appropriate to provide a high level of availability for all products, irrespective of the margins they provide.

9.6 SUMMARY OF LEARNING OBJECTIVES

1. Identify the factors affecting the optimal level of product availability and evaluate the optimal cycle service level.

   The cost of overstocking by one unit and the lost current and future margin from understocking by one unit are the two major factors that affect the optimal level of product availability. The optimal level of availability is obtained by balancing the costs of over- and understocking. As the cost of overstocking increases, it is optimal to lower the targeted level of product availability. As the lost margin from being out of stock increases, it is optimal to raise the targeted level of product availability.
2. Use managerial levers that improve supply chain profitability through optimal service levels.

   A manager may increase supply chain profitability by (1) increasing the salvage value of each unit overstocked, (2) decreasing the margin lost from a stockout, (3) using improved forecasting to reduce demand uncertainty, (4) using quick response to reduce lead times and allow multiple orders in a season, (5) using postponement to delay product differentiation, and (6) using tailored sourcing with a flexible short lead time supply source serving as a backup for a low-cost long supply source with long lead times.
3. Construct contracts that increase supply chain profitability.

   Using contracts that counteract double marginalization increases supply chain profitability. In many instances, a manager can increase supply chain profitability by structuring contracts that allow (1) return of surplus inventory, (2) subsidies for holding inventory, (3) quantity flexibility when ordering, or (4) vendor-managed inventories.

Discussion Questions

1. Consider two products with the same cost but different margins. Which product should have a higher level of product availability? Why?
2. Consider two products with the same margin carried by a retail store. Any leftover units of one product are worthless. Leftover units of the other product can be sold to outlet stores. Which product should have a higher level of availability? Why?
3. When a firm improves its forecast accuracy using better market intelligence, what impact will this have on supply chain inventories and profitability? Why?
4. How can postponement of product differentiation be used to improve supply chain profitability?
5. Mattel has historically allowed toy retailers to place two orders for the holiday shopping season. Mattel is considering allowing retailers to place only one order. What impact will this have on retailer orders? What impact will this have on supply chain profits?
6. Discuss how an expensive supplier with short lead times that is used as a backup for a low-cost supplier with long lead times can result in higher profits than using only the low-cost supplier.
7. How does a contract with buybacks allow a manufacturer to increase its profits as well as supply chain profits?
8. How does a contract with quantity flexibility allow a manufacturer to increase its profits as well as supply chain profits?

Exercises

1. Green Thumb, a manufacturer of lawn care equipment, has introduced a new product. The anticipated demand is normally distributed with a mean of $\mu = 100$ and a standard deviation of $\sigma = 40$. Each unit costs \$150 to manufacture, and the introductory price is to be \$200 to achieve this level of sales. Any unsold units at the end of the season are unlikely to be very valuable and will be disposed of in a fire sale for \$50 each. It costs \$20 to hold a unit in inventory for the entire season. How many units should Green Thumb manufacture for sale? What is the expected profit from this policy? On average, how many customers does Green Thumb expect to turn away because of stocking out?
2. The general manager at Green Thumb decides to conduct extensive market research for its new product. At the end of the market research the manager estimates demand to be normally distributed with a mean of $\mu = 100$ and a standard deviation of $\sigma = 15$. How should Green Thumb alter its production plans in Problem 1 as a result of the market research? How much increase in profit is it likely to observe? How does the improved forecast affect the demand lost by Green Thumb because of understocking? Use cost and price information from Problem 1.
3. The manager at Goodstone Tires, a distributor of tires in Illinois, uses a continuous review policy to manage its inventory. The manager currently orders 10,000 tires when the inventory of tires drops to 6,000. Weekly demand for tires is normally distributed with a mean of 2,000 and a standard deviation of 500. The replenishment lead time for tires is two weeks. Each tire costs Goodstone \$40, and the company sells each tire for \$80. Goodstone incurs a holding cost of 25 percent. How much safety inventory does Goodstone currently carry? At what cost of understocking is the manager's current inventory policy justified? How much safety inventory should Goodstone carry if the cost of understocking is \$80 per tire in lost current and future margin?
4. Champion manufactures winter fleece jackets for sale in the United States. Demand for jackets during the season is normally distributed with a mean of 20,000 and a standard deviation of 10,000. Each jacket sells for \$60 and costs \$30 to pro-

duce. Any leftover jackets at the end of the season are currently sold for $25 at the year-end clearance sale. Holding jackets until the year-end sale adds another $5 to their cost. A recent recruit has suggested shipping leftover jackets to South America for sale in the winter there rather than running a clearance. Each jacket will fetch a price of $35 in South America, and all jackets sent there are likely to sell. Shipping costs add $5 to the cost of any jacket sold in South America. Would you recommend the South American option? How will this decision affect production decisions at Champion? How will it affect profitability at Champion? On average, how many jackets will Champion ship to South America each season?

5. Snoblo, a manufacturer of snowblowers, currently sells four models. The base model, Reguplo, has demand that is normally distributed with a mean of 10,000 and a standard deviation of 1,000. The three other models have additional features and each has demand that is normally distributed with a mean of 1,000 and a standard deviation of 700. Currently all four models are manufactured on the same line at a cost of $100 for Reguplo and $110 for each of the other three models. Reguplo sells for $200, and each of the other three models sells for $220. Any unsold blowers are sold at the end of the season for $80. Snoblo is considering the use of tailored sourcing by setting up two separate lines, one for Reguplo and one for the other three. Given that no changeovers will be required on the Reguplo line, the production cost of Reguplo is expected to decline to $90. The production cost of the other three products, however, will now increase to $120. Do you recommend tailored sourcing for Snoblo? How will tailored sourcing affect production and profits? Ignore holding costs for snowblowers.

6. AnyLogo supplies firms with apparel containing their logo to be used for promotional purposes. Currently AnyLogo has four major customers: IBM, AT&T, Hewlett Packard (HP), and Cisco. During the holiday season, the logos are adorned with a Christmas motif. Demand from each firm for apparel with the Christmas motif is normally distributed as shown in Table 9.9.

   AnyLogo currently produces all the apparel, including the logo embroidery, in Sri Lanka in advance of the holiday season. Each unit costs $15 and is sold by AnyLogo for $50. Any leftover inventory at the end of the holiday season is essentially worthless and is donated by AnyLogo to charity. Holding the apparel in inventory adds another $3 to the cost per unit donated to inventory. However, the donation allows AnyLogo to recover $6 per unit in tax savings. What production quantities do you recommend for AnyLogo? What is the expected profit from the policy? On average, how much does AnyLogo expect to donate to charity each year?

7. The manager at AnyLogo is considering the purchase of high-speed embroidery machines that will allow the company to embroider on demand. In this case, the apparel will be made in Sri Lanka without any logo; the logo embroidery is postponed and will be done in the United States on demand. This will raise the cost per unit to $18. However, AnyLogo will not have any holiday or company-specific apparel to be disposed at the end of the season. The apparel without logos can be sold for $18 a unit to retailers. The cost of holding inventory and shipping adds $4 to the cost of any apparel left over after the holiday season. With all other information as in Problem 6, do you recommend that the manager at AnyLogo implement postponement? What will the impact of postponement be on profits and inventories?

TABLE 9.9 Demand Distribution for AnyLogo

	IBM	*AT&T*	*HP*	*Cisco*
Mean	5,000	7,000	4,000	4,000
SD	2,000	2,500	2,000	2,200

8. Mattel currently allows toy retailers to place an order in August for delivery in November for the holiday season. The Gigantic Pocket Monster (Gipokmon) is a new toy that Mattel has introduced. It costs Mattel $1.50 to manufacture and ship each Gipokmon. Mattel charges a wholesale price of $10. The Toys 'R' Us manager plans to sell the toy for $20. At this price, demand for the Gipokmon is estimated to be normally distributed with a mean of 10,000 and a standard deviation of 4,000. How many Gipokmons should the manager at Toys 'R' Us order? How much profit does Toys 'R' Us expect to make as a result? How much profit will Mattel make as a result? What is the resulting supply chain profit? What order quantity would maximize supply chain profits? Can you devise a buyback contract that Mattel can offer to induce the manager at Toys 'R' Us to order a quantity that maximizes supply chain profits? Can you devise a quantity flexibility contract that Mattel can offer to induce the manager at Toys 'R' Us to order a quantity that maximizes supply chain profits?

Bibliography

Cachon, G., and M. L. Fisher. "Campbell Soup's Continuous Product Replenishment Program: Evaluation and Enhanced Decision Rules." *Production and Operations Management*, 6 (1997), 266–276.

Clark, T., and J. Hammond. "Reengineering Channel Reordering Processes to Improve Total Supply Chain Performance." *Production and Operations Management*, 6 (1997), 248–265.

Fisher, M. L., J. H. Hammond, W.R. Obermeyer, and A. Raman. "Making Supply Meet Demand in an Uncertain World." *Harvard Business Review* (May–June 1994), 83–93.

Nahmias, Steven. *Production and Operations Analysis*. Burr Ridge, Ill.: Richard P. Irwin, 1997.

Padmanabhan, V., and I. P. L. Png. "Returns Policies: Making Money by Making Good." *Sloan Management Review* (Fall 1995), 65–72.

Paternack, B. A. "Optimal Pricing and Return Policies for Perishable Commodities." *Marketing Science*, 4 (1985), 166–176.

Signorelli, Sergio, and James L. Heskett. "Benetton (A)." Harvard Business School Case 9-685-0141, 1984.

Silver, Edward A., David Pyke, and Rein Petersen. *Inventory Management and Production Planning and Scheduling*. New York: John Wiley & Sons, 1998.

Tayur, Sridhar, Ram Ganeshan, and Michael Magazine, Eds. *Quantitative Models for Supply Chain Management*. Boston: Kluwer Academic Publishers, 1999.

"The Critical-Fractile Method for Inventory Planning." Harvard Business School note 9-191-132, 1991.

APPENDIX 9A

Optimal Level of Product Availability

Objective: Evaluate level of product availability that maximizes profit.
Analysis: In this analysis we assume that the demand is a continuous non-negative random variable with density function $f(x)$ and cumulative distribution function $F(x)$. C_u is the margin per unit and, as a result, the cost of understocking per unit. C_o is the cost of overstocking per unit.

Assume that Q units are purchased and a demand of x units arises. If $Q < x$, all Q units are sold and a profit of QC_u results. However, if $Q \geq x$, only x units are sold, and a profit of $xC_u - (Q - x)C_o$ results. The expected profit $P(Q)$ is thus given by the following:

$$P(Q) = \int_0^Q [xC_u - (Q - x)C_o]f(x)dx + \int_Q^\infty QC_u f(x)dx$$

In order to determine the value of Q that maximizes the expected profit $P(Q)$, we have the following:

$$\frac{dP(Q)}{d(Q)} = -C_o \int_0^Q f(x)dx + C_u \int_Q^\infty f(x)dx = C_u[1 - F(Q)] - C_oF(Q) = 0$$

This implies an optimal order size of Q^* where

$$F(Q^*) = \frac{C_u}{C_u + C_o}$$

It is easy to verify that the second derivative is negative, implying that the total expected profit is maximized at Q^*

APPENDIX 9B

An Intermediate Evaluation

Objective: Given that x is normally distributed with a mean μ and standard deviation σ, show the following:

$$A = \int_{x=-\infty}^{a} xf(x)dx = \mu F_S((a - \mu)/\sigma) - \sigma f_S((a - \mu)/\sigma) \quad \textbf{(9.8)}$$

Here $f(x)$ is the normal density function, $f_S(\,)$ the standard normal density function, and $F_S(\,)$ the standard normal cumulative distribution function.
Analysis: Using Equation 8.18 we have the following:

$$A = \int_{x=-\infty}^{a} xf(x)dx = \int_{-\infty}^{a} x\frac{1}{\sqrt{2\pi}\sigma}e^{\frac{-(x-\mu)^2}{2\sigma^2}}dx$$

Substitute $z = (x - \mu)/\sigma$. This implies $dx = \sigma dz$. Thus, we have the following:

$$A = \int_{x=-\infty}^{(a-\mu)/\sigma} (z\sigma + \mu)\frac{1}{\sqrt{2\pi}} e^{-z^2/2}\, dz$$

$$= \mu \int_{z=-\infty}^{(a-\mu)/\sigma} \frac{1}{\sqrt{2\pi}} e^{-z^2/2}\, dz + \sigma \int_{z=-\infty}^{(a-\mu)/\sigma} z\frac{1}{\sqrt{2\pi}} e^{-z^2/2}\, dz$$

Given the relationship between the cumulative distribution function and the probability density function, we use the definition of the standard normal distribution and Equation 8.18 to obtain the following:

$$F_S(t) = \int_{z=-\infty}^{t} f_S(z)dz = \int_{z=-\infty}^{t} \frac{1}{\sqrt{2\pi}} e^{-z^2/2}\, dz$$

Substitute $w = z^2/2$ into the expression for A. This implies that $dw = zdz$. Thus,

$$A = \mu F_S((a - \mu)/\sigma) + \sigma \int_{w=\infty}^{(a-\mu)^2/2\sigma^2} \frac{1}{\sqrt{2\pi}} e^{-w} dw$$

or

$$A = \mu F_S((a - \mu)/\sigma) - \sigma f_S((a - \mu)/\sigma)$$

APPENDIX 9C

Expected Profit from an Order

Objective: Assume demand to be normally distributed with a mean μ and standard deviation σ. Each unit sells for a price \$$p$ and costs \$$c$. Any unsold units fetch a salvage value of \$$s$. Obtain an expression for the expected profit if O units are ordered.

Analysis: If O units are ordered and demand turns out to be $x < O$, each of the x units sold contribute $p - c$, and each of the $(O - x)$ units unsold result in a loss of $c - s$. If demand is lager than O, each of the O units sold contribute $p - c$. We thus obtain the following:

$$\text{Expected profits} = \int_{x=-\infty}^{O} [(p - c)x - (c - s)(O - x)]f(x)dx + \int_{x=O}^{\infty} O(p - c)f(x)dx$$

$$= \int_{x=-\infty}^{O} [(p - s)x - O(c - s)]f(x)dx + \int_{x=O}^{\infty} O(p - c)f(x)dx$$

Using Equation 9.8 we obtain the following:

$$\int_{x=-\infty}^{O} xf(x)dx = \mu F_S\left(\frac{O - \mu}{\sigma}\right) - \sigma f_S\left(\frac{O - \mu}{\sigma}\right)$$

We can thus evaluate the expected profits as follows:

$$\text{Expected profits} = (p - s)\mu F_S\left(\frac{O - \mu}{\sigma}\right) - (p - s)\sigma f_S\left(\frac{O - \mu}{\sigma}\right)$$
$$- O(c - s)F(O, \mu, \sigma) + O(p - c)[1 - F(O, \mu, \sigma)]$$

APPENDIX 9D

Expected Overstock from an Order

Objective: Assume demand to be normally distributed with a mean μ and standard deviation σ. Obtain an expression for the expected overstock if O units are ordered.
Analysis: If O units are ordered, an overstock results only if demand is $x < O$. We thus have the following:

$$\text{Expected overstock} = \int_{x=-\infty}^{O} (O - x)f(x)dx = \int_{x=-\infty}^{O} Of(x)dx - \int_{x=-\infty}^{O} xf(x)dx = OF_S\left(\frac{O-\mu}{\sigma}\right) - \int_{x=-\infty}^{O} xf(x)dx$$

Using Equation 9.8, we thus obtain the following:

$$\text{Expected overstock} = OF_S\left(\frac{O-\mu}{\sigma}\right) - \mu F_S\left(\frac{O-\mu}{\sigma}\right) + \sigma f_X\left(\frac{O-\mu}{\sigma}\right) = (O-\mu)F_S\left(\frac{O-\mu}{\sigma}\right) + \sigma f_S\left(\frac{O-\mu}{\sigma}\right)$$

APPENDIX 9E

Expected Understock from an Order

Objective: Assume demand to be normally distributed with a mean μ and standard deviation σ. Obtain an expression for the expected understock if O units are ordered.
Analysis: If O units are ordered, an understock results only if demand is $x > O$. We thus have the following:

$$\begin{aligned}\text{Expected understock} &= \int_{x=O}^{\infty} (x - O)f(x)dx = \int_{x=O}^{\infty} xf(x)dx - \int_{x=O}^{\infty} Of(x)dx \\ &= \int_{x=-\infty}^{\infty} xf(x)dx - \int_{x=-\infty}^{O} xf(x)dx - O\left[1 - F_S\left(\frac{O-\mu}{\sigma}\right)\right] \\ &= (\mu - O) + OF_S\left(\frac{O-\mu}{\sigma}\right) - \int_{x=-\infty}^{O} xf(x)dx\end{aligned}$$

Using Equation 9.8, we thus obtain the following:

$$\begin{aligned}\text{Expected understock} &= (\mu - O) + OF_S\left(\frac{O-\mu}{\sigma}\right) - \mu F_S\left(\frac{O-0\,\mu}{\sigma}\right) + \sigma f_S\left(\frac{O-\mu}{\sigma}\right) \\ &= (\mu - O)\left[1 - F_S\left(\frac{O-\mu}{\sigma}\right)\right] + \sigma f_S\left(\frac{O-\mu}{\sigma}\right)\end{aligned}$$

APPENDIX 9F

Simulation Using Spreadsheets

A **simulation** is a computer model that replicates a real-life situation, allowing the user to estimate what the potential outcome would be from each of a set of actions. Simulation is a very powerful tool that helps evaluate the impact of business decisions on performance in an uncertain environment. In some instances, future scenarios can be modeled mathematically without simulation and formulas obtained for the impact of different policies on performance. In other cases, formulas are difficult to obtain, and the manager can either "take a good guess" or use simulation. Simulations are powerful because they can accommodate any number of complications. Problems that are impossible to solve analytically can often be fairly easily solved with simulation. A good simulation is an inexpensive way to test different actions and identify the most effective decision given an uncertain future.

Consider Lands' End, a mail order firm selling apparel. Lands' End faces uncertain demand and has to make decisions regarding the number of catalogs to print and mail, the number of units of each product to order, and the contracts to enter into with its suppliers. The general manager at Lands' End would like to evaluate different policies before implementing them. A simulation requires the manager to create a computer model that mimics the orders placed, the inventory held, customer demand, and other processes that are part of the Lands' End supply chain.

An **instance** of demand refers to random demand obtained from a demand distribution. Each time demand is generated from a distribution, a new instance results. Based on estimates of the future demand distribution, instances of demand for different products are generated randomly. The impact of an ordering policy is evaluated for each instance of demand generated. Based on a large number of demand instances, the manager can evaluate the mean and variability of the performance of a policy. Different policies can then be compared.

GENERATING RANDOM NUMBERS USING EXCEL

A fundamental step in any simulation is the generation of random numbers that correspond to the distribution that has been estimated for future demand or some other parameter. For example, if Lands' End has estimated demand for cashmere sweaters from the winter catalog to be normally distributed with a mean of 3,000 and a standard deviation of 1,000, the manager needs to generate several instances of demand from this distribution. There are several functions available in Excel that generate random numbers.

The *RAND*( ) function generates a random number that is uniformly distributed between 0 and 1. There is thus a 10 percent probability that *RAND*( ) will generate a number between 0 and .1, a 50 percent probability that it will generate a random number between 0 and .5, and a 90 percent probability that it will generate a random number between 0 and .9. The *RAND*( ) function can be used to generate random numbers from a variety of distributions.

The Excel function *NORMINV*(*RAND*( ), μ, σ), generates a random number that is normally distributed with mean μ and standard deviation σ. The Excel function *NORMSINV*(*RAND*( )) generates a random number that is normally distributed with mean 0 and standard deviation 1. The fact that both *NORMINV* and *NORMSINV* can generate negative numbers often poses problems when they are used to generate demand. One option is to use the maximum of 0 and *NORMINV*(*RAND*( ), μ, σ) to generate demand. This is appropriate if the coefficient of variation *cv* is less than .4. For larger coefficients of variation, it is better to use the lognormal distribution (see Chapter 15) because it only generates non-negative numbers. The Excel function *LOGINV*(*RAND*( ), μ, σ) generates a random number X that follows the lognormal distribution where $ln(X)$ is normally distributed with mean μ and standard deviation σ. There are several other demand distributions that may be generated using other Excel functions.

SETTING UP A SIMULATION MODEL

Lands' End plans to sell cashmere sweaters in its winter catalog for $150 each. The manager expects demand to be normally distributed with a mean of $\mu = 3{,}000$ and a standard deviation $\sigma = 1{,}000$. Toward the end of the winter season, Lands' End sends out a sales catalog with discounted prices on unsold items. The discounted price determines the demand in response to the sales catalog. The manager anticipates that the sales catalog will generate demand for cashmere sweaters with a mean of $1{,}000 - 5p$ and a standard deviation of $(1{,}000 - 5p)/3$, where p is the discounted price charged. Any leftover sweaters after the sales catalog are donated to charity. Each sweater costs Lands' End $50. Thus, the donation to charity fetches $25 in tax benefits. Lands' End incurs a cost of $5 per unsold sweater to store and transport them to charity, resulting in a salvage value of $s =$ $20 per sweaters sent to charity. The manager has decided to charge a discount price of max($245, $150 − $n/20$), where n is the number of sweaters left over after the winter catalog. She would like to identify the number of sweaters that should be purchased at the start of the winter season.

The first step is to set up a simulation model that evaluates the net profit for an instance of demand during the winter season. The model constructed is shown in Figure 9F.1.

The relevant cell formulas are shown in Table 9F.1.

Figure 9F.1 contains the results for one instance of the simulation, in which the manager orders 3,000 sweaters. The random demand from the winter catalog is 2,637, leaving 363 sweaters to be discounted. Following the pricing rule, the manager discounts the sweaters to $131.9. The demand at the discounted price turns out to be 229, and 229 sweaters are sold. The remaining 134 sweaters are donated to charity. The net profit from this policy turns out to be $278,424 for this instance of demand.

USING DATA TABLES TO CREATE MANY INSTANCES

Having set up the simulation model, the next step is to create many instances of random demand and

FIGURE 9F.1 Excel Simulation Model for Lands' End

Microsoft Excel - landsend.xls

	A	B	C	D	E	F	G	H	I	J
1	*Ordering and Pricing at Lands' End*									
2										
3	Cost of sweaters =			$ 50						
4	Sale Price in winter catalog =			$ 150						
5	Mean demand from winter catalog =			3,000						
6	SD of demand from winter catalog =			1,000						
7	Mean discounted demand =			341						
8	SD of discounted demand =			113.58						
9										
10	Initial Quantity ordered =			3000		Cost of sweaters ordered =			$ 150,000	
11	Winter catalog demand =			2637		Revenue from winter sales =			$ 395,550	
12	Sweaters to be discounted =			363		Revenue from discounted sales			$ 30,194	
13	Discounted price, *p* =			$ 131.9		Net benefit from donation =			$ 2,680	
14	Demand at discounted price =			229		**Net profit =**			**$ 278,424**	
15	Number sold at discount =			229						
16	Number donated to charity =			134						
17										
18	Average profit =	$	264,910		Average number of sweaters discounted				392	
19	SD of profit =	$	61,778		Average number donated to charity =				191	
20										

TABLE 9F.1 Excel Cell Formulas for Figure 9F.1

Cell Number	*Cell Formula*	*Cell Number*	*Cell Formula*
D7	= 1000 − 5*D13	D16	= D12 − D15
D8	= D7/3	I10	= D3*D10
D11	= int(max(0, norminv(rand( ), D5, D6)))	I11	= min(D10, D11)*D4
D12	= max(0, D10 − D11)	I12	= D15*D13
D13	= max(25, 150 − D12/20)	I13	= D16*20
D14	= int(max(0, norminv(rand( ), D7, D8)))	I14	= sum(I11:I13) − I10
D15	= min(D12, D14)		

evaluate the average profits from ordering 3,000 units. In Excel, Data Tables can be used to achieve multiple replications of the simulation. The goal is to evaluate the mean and standard deviation of profits, average number of sweaters discounted, and average number of sweaters donated to charity over the multiple replications. A data table is constructed in the range A23:D522 to replicate the results of the simulation for 500 instances of demand as follows:

1. Enter formula = I14 in cell B23, = D12 in cell C23, and = D16 in cell D23. As a result, the profit is copied into cell B23, the quantity discounted copied into cell C23, and the quantity given to charity copied into cell D23.
2. Select the range A23:D522. From the toolbar select Data|Table. In the Table dialog box, point to cell A23 as the Column input cell. Click on OK.

The data table is created in the range A23:D522. Each row of the data table gives the profit, quantity discounted, and quantity given to charity for an instance of random demand. Excel recalculates the simulation using new random numbers for each row in the data table. We can now obtain the average profit, the average number of sweaters discounted, and the average number of sweaters donated to charity from the data table. These are calculated in cells C18, I18, and I19, respectively, in Figure 9F.1. From the data table the manager infers that ordering 3,000 sweaters results in an average profit (over 500 replications) of $264,910. On average, 392 sweaters are discounted and 191 donated to charity.

Each time the F9 key is pressed, new random numbers are generated and all entries recalculated. The manager at Lands' End can use the simulation to evaluate the impact of different initial ordering policies on performance.

PART FOUR

Transportation, Network Design, and Information Technology in a Supply Chain

CHAPTER 10

Transportation in a Supply Chain

CHAPTER 11

Facility Decisions: Network Design in a Supply Chain

CHAPTER 12

Information Technology in a Supply Chain

The goal of the chapters in this module is to discuss trade-offs when designing a supply chain network and describe how transportation, facilities, and information technology influence the performance of a supply chain. The design of a supply chain considers how facilities, transportation, inventory, and information should be used together to support the competitive strategy of a firm and maximize supply chain profits.

Chapter 10 describes the strengths and weaknesses of various modes of transportation and different options for designing transportation networks. Trade-offs among transportation cost, inventory cost, and responsiveness that must be considered when designing a supply chain are also discussed. Methodologies that firms can use to design delivery routes are described. Chapter 11 considers facility-related decisions that firms must make when designing their supply chain network. A framework for facility decisions in a supply chain is developed, and methodologies for locating facilities and allocating capacity and markets to each facility are described. Chapter 12 discusses the impact of information technology on the success of a supply chain. Different types of information systems and the role played by each system when designing, planning, and operating a supply chain are discussed.

CHAPTER 10

Transportation in a Supply Chain

Learning Objectives

After reading this chapter, you will be able to

1. understand the role of transportation in a supply chain;
2. evaluate the strengths and weaknesses of different modes of transportation;
3. identify various transportation network design options and their relative strengths and weaknesses;
4. identify trade-offs that shippers must consider when designing their transportation network; and
5. use methodologies for routing and scheduling deliveries in transportation networks.

In this chapter, we discuss the role of transportation within a supply chain and identify trade-offs that need to be considered when making transportation decisions. Our goal is to enable managers, responsible for transportation decisions within a supply chain, to make transportation strategy and design, planning, and operational decisions with an understanding of all the pros and cons of their choices.

10.1 THE ROLE OF TRANSPORTATION IN A SUPPLY CHAIN

Transportation refers to the movement of product from one location to another as it makes its way from the beginning of a supply chain to the customer's hands. Transportation plays a key role in every supply chain because products are rarely produced and consumed in the same location. Transportation is a significant component of the cost most supply chains incur. Freight transportation costs in the United States in 1996[1] were $455 billion, which amounted to about 6 percent of the gross domestic product. With the growth in e-commerce and the associated home delivery of products, transportation costs have become even more significant in retailing. From the book industry to the grocery industry, on-line firms are delivering products in small packages to the customer's home instead of in full trucks to a retail outlet. As a result, transportation cost is a larger fraction of the delivered cost of products sold on-line. For example, shipping a truck of books to a Borders retail store costs a few cents per book. In contrast, when Borders.com sends a package to a customer's home, the transportation cost is around a dollar per book.

Any supply chain's success is closely linked to the appropriate use of transportation. Wal-Mart has effectively used a responsive transportation system to lower its overall costs. To achieve a high level of product availability at a reasonable price, Wal-Mart carries a low level of inventory at its stores and replenishes frequently as product is sold. To lower the transportation cost of frequent replenishment, Wal-Mart aggregates products destined for different retail stores on trucks leaving a supplier. At distribution centers, Wal-Mart uses **crossdocking**, a process in which product is exchanged between trucks so that each truck going to a retail store has products from different suppliers. Wal-Mart also uses its transportation system to allow stores to exchange products based on where shortages and surpluses occur. The use of a responsive transportation system and crossdocking allows the company to lower inventories and costs, and increase profits. Transportation is thus a key to Wal-Mart's ability to improve the matching of supply and demand while keeping costs low.

7-Eleven Japan has a goal of carrying products in its stores to match the needs of customers as they vary by geographical location or time of day. To help achieve this goal, 7-Eleven uses a very responsive transportation system that replenishes its stores several times a day so that the products available match customers' needs. Products from different suppliers are aggregated on trucks according to the required temperature to help achieve very frequent deliveries at a reasonable cost. 7-Eleven uses a responsive transportation system along with aggregation to decrease its transportation and receiving costs while ensuring that product availability closely matches customer demand.

Supply chains also use responsive transportation to centralize and operate with fewer facilities. For example, Amazon.com relies on package carriers and the postal system to deliver customer orders from centralized warehouses. Dell manufactures out of one location in the United States and uses responsive transportation provided by package carriers like Airborne to provide customers with highly customized products at a reasonable price.

Effective transportation is a key to the success of any on-line business, because these businesses often attract customers from distant locations, and the product must be transported from the seller to the customer. With the growth in e-commerce over the Internet, on-line grocers like Webvan and Peapod are relying on effective trans-

[1]Distribution (1997).

portation to provide convenience to customers in the form of home delivery of groceries. As home deliveries of all products grow with e-commerce, transportation will play an even more significant role in the success of these supply chains.

Transportation is a significant link between different stages in a global supply chain. Dell currently has suppliers worldwide and sells to customers all over the world from plants in Texas, Ireland, Brazil, China, and Malaysia. Transportation allows products to move from suppliers to the assembly plants and from the assembly plants to customers. Similarly, global transportation allows Wal-Mart to sell products manufactured all over the world in the United States.

In the next section, we discuss factors that affect transportation decisions for different members of a supply chain.

10.2 FACTORS AFFECTING TRANSPORTATION DECISIONS

There are two key players in any transportation that takes place within a supply chain: The **shipper** is the party that requires the movement of the product between two points in the supply chain, and the **carrier** is the party that moves or transports the product. For example, when Dell uses UPS to ship its computers from the factory to the customer, Dell is the shipper and UPS is the carrier.

When making transportation-related decisions, factors to be considered vary, depending on whether one takes the perspective of a carrier or shipper. A carrier makes investment decisions regarding the transportation infrastructure (e.g., rails, locomotives, trucks, airplanes) and then operating decisions to try to maximize the return from these assets. A shipper, in contrast, uses transportation to minimize the total cost (transportation, inventory, information, and facility) while providing an appropriate level of responsiveness to the customer.

Factors Affecting Carrier Decisions

A carrier's goal is to make investment decisions and set operating policies that maximize the return on its assets. A carrier such as an airline, railroad, or trucking company must account for the following costs when investing in assets or setting pricing and operating policies:

1. **Vehicle-related cost**. This is the cost a carrier incurs for the purchase or lease of the vehicle used to transport goods. The vehicle-related cost is incurred whether the vehicle is used or not and is considered fixed for short-term operational decisions by the carrier. When making long-term strategic decisions or medium-term planning decisions, these costs are variable and the number of vehicles purchased or leased is one of the choices that a carrier makes. The vehicle-related cost is proportional to the number of vehicles leased or purchased.

2. **Fixed operating cost**. This includes any cost associated with terminals, airport gates, and labor that are incurred whether vehicles are used or not. Examples include the fixed cost of a trucking terminal facility or airport hub that is incurred independent of the number of trucks visiting the terminal or flights landing at the hub. If drivers were paid independent of their travel schedule, their salary would also be included in this category. For operational decisions, these costs are fixed. For planning and strategic decisions involving the location and size of facilities, these costs are variable. The fixed operating cost is generally proportional to the size of operating facilities.

3. **Trip-related cost**. This cost is incurred each time a vehicle leaves on a trip and includes the price of labor and fuel. The trip-related cost depends on the length and du-

ration of the trip but is independent of the quantity shipped. This cost is considered variable when making strategic or planning decisions. The cost is also considered variable when making operational decisions that affect the length and duration of a trip.

4. **Quantity related cost.** This category includes loading/unloading costs and a portion of the fuel cost that varies with the quantity being transported. These costs are generally variable in all transportation decisions unless labor used for loading and unloading is fixed.

5. **Overhead cost.** This category includes the cost of planning and scheduling a transportation network as well as any investment in information technology. When a trucking company invests in routing software that allows a manager to devise good delivery routes, the investment in the software and its operation is included in overhead. Airlines include the cost of groups that schedule and route planes and crew in overhead.

A large portion of a carrier's cost is independent of the quantity being carried on the truck, train, or ship. It does depend, however, on the utilization that is affected by the routing and scheduling of vehicles. For strategic and planning decisions, a carrier should consider all costs discussed previously to be variable. For operational decisions, most of these costs become fixed.

A carrier's decisions are also affected by the responsiveness it seeks to provide its target segment and the prices that the market will bear. For example, Federal Express (FedEx) designed a hub-and-spoke airline network for transporting packages to provide fast, reliable delivery times. UPS, in contrast, uses a combination of airlines and trucks to provide cheaper transportation with somewhat longer delivery times. The difference between the two transportation networks is reflected in the pricing schedule. FedEx charges for packages based primarily on the size. UPS, whereas, charges based on both size and destination. From a supply chain perspective, a hub-and-spoke air network is more appropriate when prices are independent of destination and rapid delivery is important, while a trucking network is more appropriate when prices vary with destination and somewhat slower delivery is acceptable.

Factors Affecting Shippers Decisions

Shipper's decisions include the design of the transportation network, choice of means of transport, and the assignment of each customer shipment to a particular means of transport. A shipper's goal is to minimize the total cost of fulfilling a customer order while achieving the responsiveness promised. A shipper must account for the following costs when making transportation decisions:

1. **Transportation cost.** This is the total amount paid to various carriers for transporting products to customers. It depends on the prices offered by different carriers and the extent to which the shipper uses inexpensive and slow or expensive and fast means of transportation. Transportation costs are considered variable for all shipper decisions as long as the shipper does not own the carrier.

2. **Inventory cost.** This is the cost of holding inventory incurred by the shipper's supply chain network. Inventory costs are considered fixed for short-term transportation decisions that assign each customer shipment to a carrier. Inventory costs are considered variable when a shipper is designing the transportation network or planning operating policies.

3. **Facility cost.** This is the cost of various facilities in the shipper's supply chain network. Facility costs are considered variable when supply chain managers make strategic design decisions but are considered fixed for all other transportation decisions.

4. **Processing cost.** This is the cost of loading/unloading orders as well as other processing costs associated with transportation. These are considered variable for all transportation decisions.

5. **Service level cost.** This is the cost of not being able to meet delivery commitments. In some cases it may clearly be specified as part of a contract, whereas in other cases it may be reflected as customer satisfaction. This cost should be considered in strategic, planning, and operational decisions.

A shipper must make a trade-off among all these costs when making transportation decisions. A shipper's decisions are also affected by the responsiveness it seeks to provide its customers and the margins generated from different products and customers. For example, Webvan, an on-line grocer, promises home delivery of groceries within a 30-minute time window selected by the customer. UPS, in contrast, does not deliver at a time selected by the customer but delivers packages at any time during working hours. The transportation networks designed by the two companies and the number of vehicles relative to demand reflect the difference in their strategies.

In the next section, we discuss different modes of transportation and their cost and performance characteristics.

10.3 MODES OF TRANSPORTATION AND THEIR PERFORMANCE CHARACTERISTICS

Supply chains use a combination of the following modes of transportation:

- Air
- Package carriers
- Truck
- Rail
- Water
- Pipeline
- Intermodal

We discuss the costs, pricing structure, and performance characteristics of the various modes summarized in Table 10.1.

TABLE 10.1 Transportation Facts

Mode	*Freight Expense ($ Billions)*	*Intercity Ton-Miles (Billions)*	*Intercity Tonnage (Millions)*	*Revenue/ Ton-Mile (Cents)*	*Average Length of Haul (Miles)*
Air	18.87	12.72	10.5	58.75	1,260
Truck (truckload)	348.11	921	3,373	9.13	289
Truck (less than truckload)				25.08	629
Rail	34.36	1,375	1,911	2.50	722
Water	22.24	258 (excludes coastwise)	1,000	0.73	Rivers/Canals 481 Great Lakes 509 Coastwise 1,653
Pipeline	8.29	599 (Oil)	1,118	1.40	Crude 761 Products 394

Adapted from *Transportation in America*, 1998.

Air

Major airlines in the United States that carry both passenger and cargo include American, Delta, US Airways, and United. Airlines have a high fixed cost in infrastructure and equipment. Labor and fuel costs are largely trip-related and independent of the number of passengers or amount of cargo carried on a flight. An airline's goal is to maximize the daily flying time of a plane and the revenue generated per trip. Given the large fixed costs and relatively low variable costs, revenue management, in which airlines vary seat prices and allocate seats to different price classes, is a significant factor in the success of passenger airlines. At present, airlines practice revenue management for passengers but not for cargo. As a result, two passengers traveling from Chicago to New York on the same plane may pay very different fares.

Air carriers offer a very fast and fairly expensive mode of transportation. Small, high-value items or time-sensitive emergency shipments that have to travel a long distance are best suited for air transport. Normally air carriers move shipments under 500 pounds, including high-value but lightweight high-tech products. For example, Dell uses airfreight to ship many of its components from Asia. Given the growth in high technology, the weight of freight carried by air has diminished over the last two decades of the 20th century even as the value of the freight has increased.

Key issues air carriers face include identifying the location and number of hubs, assigning planes to routes, setting up maintenance schedules for planes, scheduling crews, and managing prices and availability at different prices.

Package Carriers

Package carriers are transportation companies like FedEx, UPS, and the U.S. postal system that carry small packages ranging from letters to shipments weighing about 150 pounds. Package carriers use air, truck, and rail to transport time-critical smaller packages. Package carriers are expensive and cannot compete with less-than-truckload (LTL) carriers on price for large shipments. The major service they offer the shipper is rapid and reliable delivery. Therefore, shippers use package carriers for small and time-sensitive shipments. Package carriers also provide other value-added services that allow shippers to speed inventory flow and track order status. By tracking order status, shippers can proactively inform customers about their packages. Package carriers also pick up the package from the source and deliver it to the destination site. With an increase in just-in-time deliveries and focus on inventory reduction, demand for package carriers has grown.

Package carriers are the preferred mode of transport for e-businesses like Amazon and Dell as well as companies like Grainger and McMaster-Carr that send small packages to customers. With the growth in e-business, the use of package carriers has increased significantly over the last few years. Package carriers that primarily use airplanes, like FedEx, are similar to air cargo carriers except that they seek out smaller and more time-sensitive shipments for which tracking and other value-added services are more important. FedEx uses trucks to pick up packages at the source and deliver them to the final destination. Air cargo carriers do not provide this combined service. Companies use air cargo carriers for larger shipments and package carriers for smaller, more time-sensitive ones. For example, Dell uses air cargo to bring components from Asia but uses package carriers to deliver personal computers (PCs) to customers.

Given the small size of packages and several delivery points, consolidation of shipments is a key factor in increasing utilization and decreasing costs for package carriers. Package carriers have trucks that make local deliveries and pick up packages.

Packages are then taken to large sort centers from which they are sent by full truckload or air to the sort center closest to the delivery point. From the delivery point sort center, the package is sent to customers on small trucks making milk runs (discussed later in the chapter). Key issues in this industry include the location and capacity of transfer points as well as information capability to facilitate and track package flow. For the final delivery to a customer, an important consideration is the scheduling and routing of the delivery trucks.

Truck

Truck is the dominant mode of freight transportation in the United States and accounts for over 75 percent of the nation's freight bill.[2] The trucking industry consists of two major segments: full truckload (TL) and less than truckload (LTL). TL operations charge for the full truck independent of the quantity shipped. Rates vary with the distance traveled. LTL operations charge based on the quantity loaded and the distance traveled. The LTL rates exhibit economies of scale. Trucking is more expensive than rail but offers the advantage of door-to-door shipment and a shorter delivery time. It also has the advantage of requiring no transfer between pickup and delivery. Major truckload carriers include Schneider National, JB Hunt, Ryder Integrated, Werner, and Swift Transportation.

TL operations have relatively low fixed costs, and owning a few trucks is often sufficient to enter the business. As a result, there are many truckload carriers in the industry. Schneider National, the largest TL carrier, had only 17 percent of the market share among the top 40 firms in the United States in 1996. The idle time and travel distance between successive loads adds to cost in the TL industry. Carriers thus try to schedule shipments to meet service requirements while minimizing both their trucks' idle time and empty travel time.

TL pricing displays economies of scale with respect to the distance traveled. Given trailers of different size, pricing also displays economies of scale with respect to the size of the trailer used. TL shipping is suited for transportation between manufacturing facilities and warehouses or between suppliers and manufacturers. For example, Procter & Gamble offers TL shipping to customer warehouses.

LTL operations are priced to encourage shipments in small lots, usually less than half a truckload. TL tends to be cheaper for larger shipments. Prices display some economies of scale with the quantity shipped as well as the distance traveled. LTL shipments take longer than TL shipments because of other loads that need to be picked up and dropped off. LTL shipping is suited for shipments that are too large to be mailed as small packages but constitute less than half a truckload.

A key to reducing LTL costs is the degree of consolidation that carriers can achieve for the loads carried. LTL carriers use consolidation centers, where trucks bring in many small loads originating from a geographical area and leave with many small loads destined for the same geographical area. This allows LTL carriers to improve their truck use, although it increases delivery time somewhat. Larger firms enjoy an advantage in the LTL industry given the importance of consolidation and the fixed cost of setting up consolidation centers. Strong regional players have developed in the LTL industry because of the advantage offered by a high density of pickup and delivery points in a geographical area.

Key issues for the LTL industry include location of consolidation centers, assigning of loads to trucks, and scheduling and routing of pickup and delivery. The goal is to minimize costs through consolidation without hurting delivery time and reliability.

[2] *Transportation in America* (1998).

Rail

Major rail carriers in North America include Burlington Northern Santa Fe, Canadian National, CSX Transportation, and Norfolk Southern. Rail carriers incur a high fixed cost in terms of rails, locomotives, cars, and yards. There is also a significant trip-related labor and fuel cost that is independent of the number of cars (fuel costs do vary somewhat with the number of cars) but does vary with the distance traveled and the time taken. Any idle time, once a train is powered, is very expensive, because labor and fuel costs are incurred even though trains are not moving. Idle time occurs when trains exchange cars for different destinations. It also occurs because of track congestion. Labor and fuel together account for more than 60 percent of railroad expense. From an operational perspective, it is thus important for railroads to keep locomotives and crew well utilized.

Given the high fixed cost and low variable cost of operation, rail is priced to encourage large shipments over a long distance. Prices display economies of scale in the quantity shipped as well as the distance traveled. The price structure and the heavy load capability makes rail an ideal mode for carrying large, heavy, or high-density products over long distances. Transportation time by rail, however, can be long. Rail is thus ideal for very heavy, low-value shipments that are not very time-sensitive. The resulting transportation cost tends to be low. Coal, for example, is a major part of each railroad's shipment. Small, time-sensitive, short-distance or short-lead time shipments rarely use rail.

Railroad revenues have not grown significantly; they grew from $29 billion in 1980 to only $35 billion in 1996.[3] Most of the improvement in financial performance over that period has come from abandoning unprofitable lines and making better use of existing assets. The growth in the intermodal sector (discussed later in the chapter) has also helped railroad performance during this period.

A major goal in railroads is to keep locomotives and crew well utilized. Major operational issues at railroads include vehicle and staff scheduling, track and terminal delays, and on-time performance. Railroad performance is hurt by the large amount of time taken at each transition. The travel time is usually a small fraction of the total time for a rail shipment. Delays are exaggerated because trains today are typically not scheduled but "built"; in other words, a train leaves when there are enough cars to constitute the train. Cars wait for the train to build, adding to the uncertainty of the delivery time for a shipper. A railroad can improve on-time performance by scheduling some of the trains instead of building all of them. In such a setting, a more sophisticated pricing strategy that includes revenue management (as practiced by airlines) will need to be instituted for scheduled trains.

Water

Major ocean carriers include Sealand Service, Evergreen Line, Maersk, American President Line, and Hanjin Shipping Co. Water transport, by its nature, is limited to certain areas within the United States and the world. Within the United States, water transport takes place via the inland waterway system (Great Lakes and rivers) or coastal waters. Water transport is ideally suited for carrying very large loads at low cost. Within the United States water transport is used primarily for the movement of large bulk commodity shipments and is the cheapest mode for carrying such loads. It is, however, the slowest of all the modes, and significant delays occur at ports and ter-

[3] *Distribution* (1997).

minals. This makes water transport difficult to operate for short-haul trips, though it is used effectively in Japan and parts of Europe for daily short-haul trips of a few miles.

Within the United States, the passage of the Ocean Shipping Reform Act of 1998 was a significant event for water transport. This bill allows carriers and shippers to enter into confidential contracts, effectively deregulating the industry. The bill is similar to the deregulation that occurred in the trucking and airline industries in the 1970s and is likely to have a similar impact on the shipping industry.

In global trade, water transport is the dominant mode for shipping all kinds of products. Cars, grain, apparel, and other products are shipped to and from the United States by sea. For the quantities shipped and the distances involved, water transport is by far the cheapest mode of transport for global shipping. Delays at ports, customs, and the management of containers used are major issues in global shipping.

Pipeline

Pipeline is used primarily for the transport of crude petroleum, refined petroleum products, and natural gas. A significant initial fixed cost is incurred in setting up the pipeline and related infrastructure that does not vary significantly with the diameter of the pipeline. Pipeline operations are typically optimized at about 80 to 90 percent of pipeline capacity. Given the nature of the costs, pipelines are best suited when relatively stable and large flows are required. Pipeline may be an effective way of getting crude to a port or a refinery. Sending gasoline to a gas station does not justify investment in a pipeline and is done better with a truck. Pipeline pricing usually consists of two components: a fixed component related to the shipper's peak usage and a second charge relating to the actual quantity transported. This pricing structure encourages the shipper to use pipeline for the predictable component of demand and use other modes to cover fluctuations.

Intermodal

Intermodal transportation is the use of more than one mode of transport to move a shipment to its destination. A variety of intermodal combinations are possible, with the most common being truck/rail. Major intermodal providers with rail include CSX Intermodal, Pacer Stacktrain, and Triple Crown. Intermodal traffic has grown considerably with the increased use of containers for shipping and the rise of global trade. Containers are easy to transfer from one mode to another, and their use facilitates intermodal transportation. Containerized freight often uses truck/water/rail combinations, particularly for global freight. For global trade, intermodal is often the only option because factories and markets may not be next to ports. As the quantity shipped using containers has grown, the truck/water/rail intermodal combination has also grown. In 1996, intermodal activity contributed 16 percent of rail revenues.[4] On land, the rail/truck intermodal system offers the benefit of lower cost than truckload and delivery times that are better than rail. Intermodal brings together different modes of transport to create a price/service offering that cannot be matched by any single mode. It also creates convenience for shippers, which would deal with only one entity representing all carriers who together provide the intermodal service.

Key issues in the intermodal industry involve the exchange of information to facilitate shipment transfers between different modes because these transfers often involve considerable delays, hurting delivery time performance.

[4] *Distribution* (1997).

10.4 DESIGN OPTIONS FOR A TRANSPORTATION NETWORK

The design of a transportation network affects the performance of a supply chain by establishing the infrastructure within which operational transportation decisions regarding scheduling and routing are made. A well-designed transportation network allows a supply chain to achieve the desired degree of responsiveness at a low cost. We discuss a variety of design options for transportation networks and the strengths and weaknesses for each option in the context of a retail chain with many stores and several suppliers.

Direct Shipment Network

With the direct shipment network option, the retail chain structures its transportation network to have all shipments come directly from suppliers to retail stores, as shown in Figure 10.1. With a direct shipment network, the routing of each shipment is specified, and the supply chain manager only needs to decide on the quantity to ship and the mode of transportation to use. This decision involves a trade-off between transportation and inventory costs, as discussed later in the chapter.

The major advantage of a direct shipment transportation network is the elimination of intermediate warehouses and its simplicity of operation and coordination. The shipment decision is completely local, and the decision made for one shipment does not influence others. The transportation time from supplier to retail store will be short because each shipment is direct.

A direct shipment network is justified if retail stores are large enough such that optimal replenishment lot sizes are close to a truckload from each supplier to each retailer. With small retail stores, the direct shipment network, however, tends to have high costs. If a TL carrier is used for transportation, the high fixed cost of each truck results in large lots moving from suppliers to each retail store, resulting in high supply chain inventories. If an LTL carrier is used, the transportation cost and the delivery time increase, though inventories are lower. If package carriers are used, transportation cost will be very high. With direct deliveries from each supplier, receiving costs will be high because each supplier must make a separate delivery.

FIGURE 10.1 Direct Shipment Network

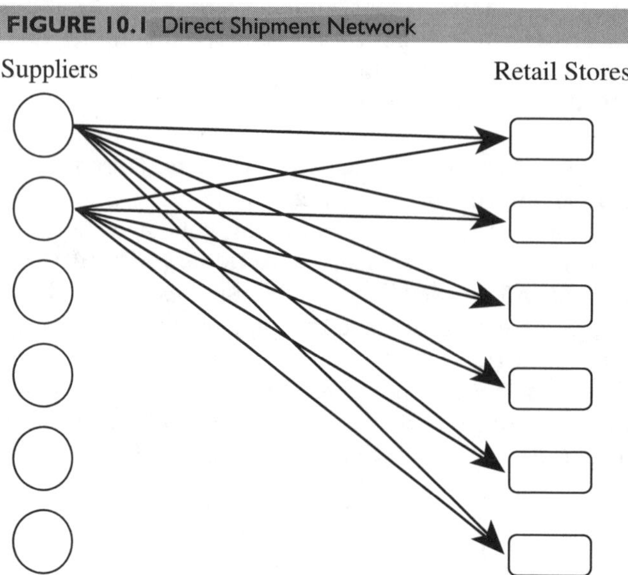

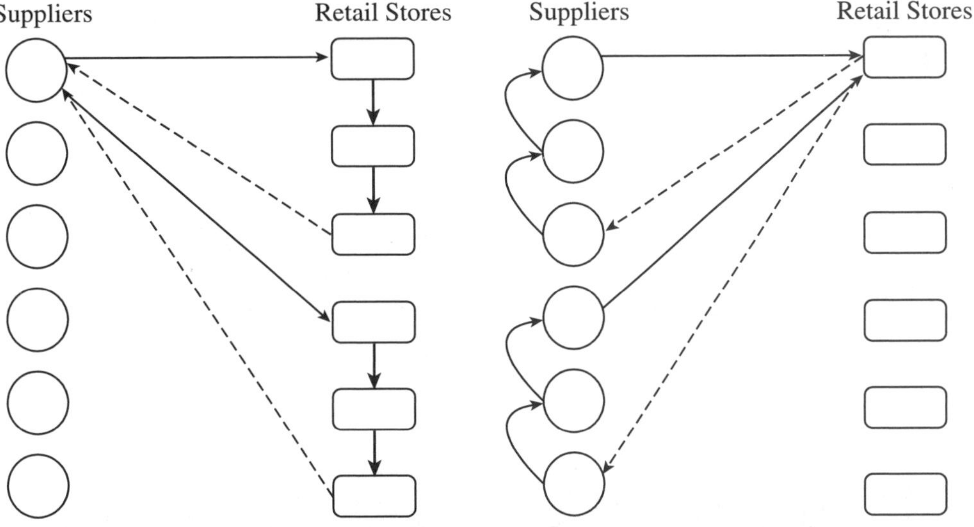

FIGURE 10.2 Milk Runs from Multiple Suppliers or to Multiple Retailers

Direct Shipping with Milk Runs

A **milk run** is a route in which a truck either delivers product from a single supplier to multiple retailers or goes from multiple suppliers to a single retailer, as shown in Figure 10.2. In direct shipping with milk runs, a supplier delivers directly to multiple retail stores on a truck or a truck picks up deliveries from many suppliers destined for the same retail store. When using this option, a supply chain manager has to decide on the routing of each milk run.

Direct shipping provides the benefit of eliminating intermediate warehouses, and milk runs lower transportation cost by consolidating shipments to multiple stores on a single truck. For example, the replenishment lot size for each retail store may be small and require LTL shipping if sent directly. The use of milk runs allows deliveries to multiple stores to be consolidated on a single truck, resulting in a better utilization of the truck and somewhat lower costs. Companies that make direct store deliveries, like Frito-Lay, use milk runs to lower their transportation cost. If very frequent, small deliveries are needed on a regular basis and either a set of suppliers or a set of retailers is in geographical proximity, using milk runs can significantly reduce transportation costs. For example, Toyota uses milk runs from suppliers to support its just-in-time (JIT) manufacturing system in both Japan and the United States. In Japan, Toyota has many assembly plants located close together and thus uses milk runs from a single supplier to many plants. In the United States, however, Toyota uses milk runs from many suppliers to its assembly plant in Kentucky.

All Shipments via Central Distribution Center

With the all shipments via central distribution center (DC) option, suppliers do not send shipments directly to retail stores. The retail chain divides stores by geographical region, and a DC is built for each region. Suppliers send their shipments to the DC, and the DC then forwards appropriate shipments to each retail store, as shown in Figure 10.3.

The DC is an extra layer between suppliers and retailers and can play two different roles. One is to store inventory and the other is to serve as a transfer location. In

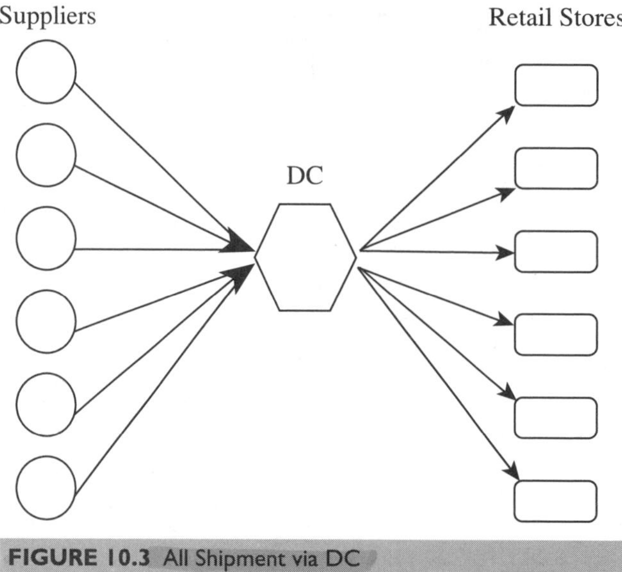

FIGURE 10.3 All Shipment via DC

either case, the presence of DCs can help reduce supply chain costs when suppliers are located far from the retail stores and transportation costs are high. The presence of a DC allows a supply chain to achieve economies of scale for inbound transportation to a point close to the final destination because each supplier sends a large shipment to the DC containing product for all stores the DC serves. Because DCs serve stores located nearby, the outbound transportation cost is not very large.

If transportation economies require very large shipments on the inbound side, DCs hold inventory and send product to retail stores in smaller replenishment lots. For example, when Wal-Mart sources from an overseas supplier, the product is held in inventory at the DC because the lot size on the inbound side is much larger than the sum of the lot sizes for the stores served by the DC. If replenishment lots for the stores served by the DC are large enough to achieve economies of scale on inbound transportation, the DC does not need to hold inventory. In this case the DC can crossdock product arriving from many suppliers on inbound trucks by breaking each inbound shipment into smaller shipments that are then loaded onto trucks going to each retail store. When a DC crossdocks product, each inbound truck contains product from a supplier for several retail stores, and each outbound truck contains product for a retail store from several suppliers. A major benefit of crossdocking is that little inventory needs to be held and product flows faster in the supply chain. Crossdocking also saves on handling cost because product does not have to be moved into and out of storage. Successful crossdocking, however, does require a significant degree of coordination and synchronization between the incoming and outgoing shipments.

Crossdocking is appropriate for products with large, predictable volumes and requires that DCs be set up such that economies of scale in transportation can be achieved on both the inbound and outbound sides. Wal-Mart has successfully used crossdocking to decrease inventories in the supply chain without incurring excessive transportation costs. Wal-Mart builds many large stores in a geographical area supported by a DC. As a result, the total lot size to all stores from each supplier fills trucks on the inbound side to achieve economies of scale. On the outbound side, the sum of the lot sizes from all suppliers to each retail store fills up the truck to achieve economies of scale.

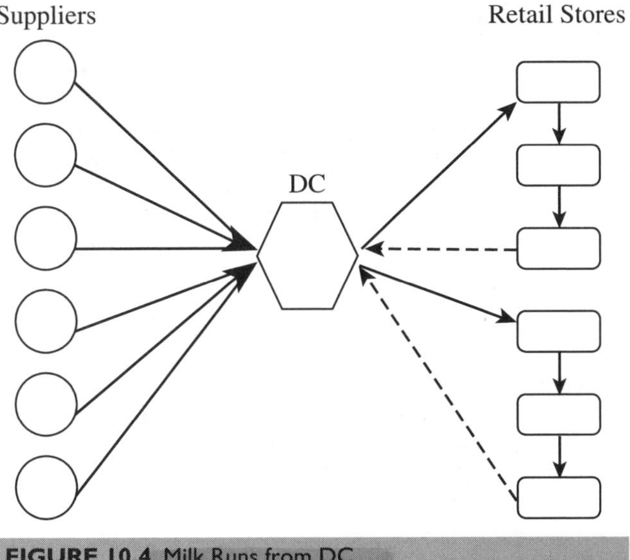

FIGURE 10.4 Milk Runs from DC

Shipping via Distribution Center Using Milk Runs

As shown in Figure 10.4, milk runs can be used from a DC if lot sizes to be delivered to each retail store are small. Milk runs reduce outbound transportation costs by consolidating small shipments. For example, 7-Eleven Japan crossdocks deliveries from its fresh food suppliers at its DCs and sends out milk runs to the retail outlets because the total shipment to a store from all suppliers does not fill a truck. Using crossdocking and milk runs allows 7-Eleven to lower its transportation cost while sending small replenishment lots to each store. Using crossdocking with milk runs requires a significant degree of coordination and suitable routing and scheduling of milk runs.

On-line grocers such as Webvan and Peapod use milk runs from DCs when making customer deliveries to help reduce transportation costs for small shipments to be delivered to homes. OshKosh B'Gosh, a manufacturer of children's wear, has used this idea to virtually eliminate LTL shipments from its distribution center in Tennessee to retail stores.

Tailored Network

The tailored network option is a suitable combination of previous options that reduces the cost and improves responsiveness of the supply chain. Here, transportation uses a combination of crossdocking, milk runs, TL and LTL carriers, along with package carriers in some cases. The goal is to use the appropriate option in each situation. High-volume products to high-volume retail outlets may be shipped directly, and low-volume products or shipments to low-volume retail outlets are consolidated to and from the DC. The complexity of managing this transportation network is high because different shipping procedures are used for each product and retail outlet. Operating a tailored network requires significant investment in information infrastructure to facilitate the coordination. Such a network, however, allows for the selective use of the shipment method to minimize the transportation as well as inventory costs.

Table 10.2 summarizes the pros and cons of the various transportation network options discussed.

In the next section we will discuss a variety of trade-offs that supply chain managers need to consider when designing and operating a transportation network.

TABLE 10.2 Pros and Cons of Different Transportation Networks

Network Structure	*Pros*	*Cons*
Direct Shipping	• No intermediate warehouse • Simple to coordinate	• High inventories (due to large lot size) • Significant receiving expense
Direct shipping with milk runs	• Lower transportation costs for small lots • Lower inventories	• Increased coordination complexity
All shipments via central DC with inventory storage	• Lower inbound transportation cost through consolidation	• Increased inventory cost • Increased handling at DC
All shipments via central DC with crossdock	• Very low inventory requirement • Lower transportation cost through consolidation	• Increased coordination complexity
Shipping via DC using milk runs	• Lower outbound transportation cost for small lots	• Further increase in coordination complexity
Tailored network	• Transportation choice best matches needs of individual product and store	• Highest coordination complexity

10.5 TRADE-OFFS IN TRANSPORTATION DESIGN

All transportation decisions in a supply chain network must be made taking into account their impact on inventory costs, facility and processing costs, cost of coordinating operations, as well as the level of responsiveness provided to customers. For example, Dell's use of package carriers for delivering PCs to customers increases transportation cost but allows Dell to centralize its facilities. If Dell wants to reduce its transportation costs, the company must either sacrifice responsiveness to customers or increase the number of facilities and resulting inventories to move closer to customers.

The cost of coordinating operations is generally hard to quantify. Companies should evaluate different transportation options in terms of various costs as well as revenues and then rank them according to coordination complexity. A manager can then make the appropriate transportation decision. Managers must consider the following trade-offs when making transportation decisions:

- Transportation and inventory cost trade-off
- Transportation cost and customer responsiveness trade-off

Transportation and Inventory Cost Trade-off

The trade-off between transportation and inventory costs is significant when designing a supply chain network. Two fundamental supply chain decisions involving this trade-off are as follows:

- Choice of transportation mode
- Inventory aggregation

Choice of Transportation Mode

Selecting a transportation mode is both a planning and an operational decision in a supply chain. The decision regarding carriers with which a company contracts is a planning decision, whereas the choice of transportation mode for a particular shipment is an operational decision. For both decisions, a shipper must balance transportation and inventory costs. The mode of transportation that results in the lowest transportation cost does not necessarily lower total costs for a supply chain. Cheaper modes of transport typically have longer lead times and larger minimum shipment

TABLE 10.3 Impact of Transportation Modes on Supply Chain Performance

	Rail	*TL*	*LTL*	*Package*	*Air*	*Water*
Lot size	5	4	3	1	2	6
Safety inventory	5	4	3	1	2	6
In-transit inventory	5	4	3	1	2	6
Transportation cost	2	3	4	6	5	1
Transportation time	5	3	4	1	2	6

quantities, both of which result in higher levels of inventory in the supply chain. Modes that allow for shipping in small quantities lower inventory levels but tend to be more expensive. Dell, for example, airfreights several of its components from Asia. This choice cannot be justified on the basis of transportation cost alone. It can only be justified because the use of a faster mode of transportation for shipping valuable components allows Dell to carry low levels of inventory.

The impact of using different modes of transportation on inventories, response time, and costs in the supply chain is shown in Table 10.3. Each transportation mode is ranked along various dimensions with 1 being the lowest and 6 being the highest.

Faster modes of transportation are preferred for products with a high value-to-weight ratio and for which reducing inventories is important, whereas slower modes are preferred for products with a low value-to-weight ratio and for which reducing transportation costs is important.

Ignoring inventory costs when making transportation decisions can result in choices that worsen the performance of a supply chain. To illustrate the importance of evaluating the trade-off between transportation and inventory costs, consider the example of Eastern Electric (EE), a major appliance manufacturer with a large plant in the Chicago area.[5] EE purchases all the motors for its appliances from Westview Motors, located near Dallas. EE currently purchases 120,000 motors each year from Westview at a price of $120 per motor. Demand has been relatively constant for several years and is expected to stay that way. Each motor averages about 10 pounds in weight, and EE has traditionally purchased in lots of 3,000 motors. Westview ships each EE order within a day of receiving it. At its assembly plant, EE carries a safety inventory equal to 50 percent of the average demand for motors during the delivery lead time.

The plant manager at EE has received several proposals for transportation and must decide on the one to accept. The details of various proposals are provided in Table 10.4, where one cwt is equal to 100 pounds.

TABLE 10.4 Transportation Proposals for Eastern Electric

Carrier	*Range of Quantity Shipped (cwt)*	*Shipping Cost ($/cwt)*
AM Railroad	200 +	6.50
Northeast Trucking	100 +	7.50
Golden Freightways	50–150	8.00
Golden Freightways	150–250	6.00
Golden Freightways	250–400	4.00

[5]This example is inspired by the *Honfleur Corporation* case in Shapiro and Heskett (1985).

Golden's pricing represents a marginal unit quantity discount (see Chapter 7). Golden's representative has proposed lowering the marginal rate for the quantity over 250 cwt in a shipment from \$4/cwt to \$3/cwt. Golden's new proposal will result in very low transportation costs for EE if the plant manager orders in lots of 4,000 motors.

The plant manager, however, decides to include inventory costs in the transportation decision. EE's annual cost of holding inventory is 25 percent, which implies an annual holding cost of $H = \$120 \times 0.25 = \$30$ per motor. Shipments by rail require a 5-day transit time, whereas shipments by truck have a transit time of 3 days. The transportation decision affects the cycle inventory, safety inventory, and in-transit inventory for EE. Therefore, the plant manager decides to evaluate the total transportation and inventory cost for each transportation option.

The AM Railroad proposal requires a minimum shipment of 20,000 pounds or 2,000 motors. The replenishment lead time in this case is $L = 5 + 1 = 6$ days. For a lot size of $Q = 2,000$ motors, the plant manager obtains the following (see Chapter 7):

$$\begin{aligned}
\text{Cycle inventory} &= Q/2 = 2{,}000/2 = 1{,}000 \text{ motors} \\
\text{Safety inventory} &= L/2 \text{ days of demand} = (6/2)(120{,}000/365) \\
&= 986 \text{ motors} \\
\text{In-transit inventory} &= 120{,}000(5/365) = 1{,}644 \text{ motors} \\
\text{Total average inventory} &= 1{,}000 + 986 + 1{,}644 = 3{,}630 \text{ motors} \\
\text{Annual holding cost using AM Rail} &= 3{,}630 \times 30 = \$108{,}900
\end{aligned}$$

AM Rail charges \$6.50 per cwt, resulting in a transportation cost of \$0.65 per motor because each motor weighs 10 pounds. Thus,

$$\text{Annual transportation cost using AM Rail} = 120{,}000 \times .65 = \$78{,}000$$

The total annual cost for inventory and transportation using AM Rail is thus \$186,900.

The plant manager then evaluates the cost associated with each transportation option, as shown in Table 10.5.

Based on the analysis in Table 10.5, the plant manager decides to sign a contract with Golden Freightways and order motors in lots of 500. This option has the highest transportation cost but the lowest overall cost. If the selection of the transportation option was made using only the transportation cost incurred, Golden's new proposal lowering the price for large shipments would look attractive. In reality, EE pays a

TABLE 10.5 Analysis of Transportation Options for EE

Alternative	*Lot Size (Motors)*	*Transportation Cost*	*Cycle Inventory*	*Safety Inventory*	*In-Transit Inventory*	*Inventory Cost*	*Total Cost*
AM Rail	2,000	\$78,000	1,000	986	1,644	\$108,900	\$186,900
Northeast Trucking	1,000	\$90,000	500	658	986	\$64,320	\$154,320
Golden	500	\$96,000	250	658	986	\$56,820	\$152,820
Golden	1,500	\$96,000	750	658	986	\$71,820	\$167,820
Golden	2,500	\$86,400	1,250	658	986	\$86,820	\$173,220
Golden	3,000	\$78,000	1,500	658	986	\$94,320	\$172,320
Golden (old proposal)	4,000	\$67,500	2,000	658	986	\$109,320	\$176,820
Golden (new proposal)	4,000	\$63,750	2,000	658	986	\$109,320	\$173,070

high overall cost for this proposal. Thus, considering the trade-off between inventory and transportation costs allows the plant manager to make a transportation decision that minimizes Eastern's total cost.

> ***Key Point*** When selecting a mode of transportation, managers must account for inventory costs. Modes with high transportation cost can be justified if they result in significantly lower inventories.

Inventory Aggregation

Firms can significantly reduce the safety inventory they require by physically aggregating inventories in one location (see Chapter 8). Most e-businesses have used this technique to gain advantage over firms with facilities in many locations. For example, Amazon.com has focused on decreasing its facility and inventory costs by holding inventory in a few warehouses, whereas booksellers like Borders and Barnes and Noble have to hold inventory in many retail stores.

Transportation cost, however, increases when inventory is aggregated. Consider a bookstore chain such as Borders. The inbound transportation cost to Borders derives from the replenishment of bookstores with new books. There is no outbound cost because customers transport their own books home. If Borders decides to close all its bookstores and only sell on-line, it will have to incur both inbound and outbound transportation costs. The inbound transportation cost to warehouses will be lower than to all bookstores. On the outbound side, however, transportation cost will increase significantly because the outbound shipment to each customer will be small and will require an expensive mode such as a package carrier. The total transportation cost will increase on aggregation because each book will travel the same distance as when it was sold through a bookstore, except that a large fraction of the distance will be on the outbound side using an expensive mode of transportation. As the degree of inventory aggregation increases, total transportation cost goes up. Thus, all firms planning inventory aggregation must consider the trade-off between transportation, inventory, and facility costs when making this decision.

Inventory aggregation is a good idea when inventory and facility costs form a large fraction of a supply chain's total costs. Inventory aggregation is useful for products with a large value-to-weight ratio and for products with high demand uncertainty. For example, inventory aggregation is very valuable in the PC industry for new products because PCs have a large value-to-weight ratio and demand is uncertain. Inventory aggregation is also a good idea if customer orders are large enough to ensure sufficient economies of scale on outbound transportation. When products have a low value-to-weight ratio and customer orders are small, however, inventory aggregation may hurt a supply chain's performance because of high transportation costs. Compared with PCs, the value of inventory aggregation is smaller for best-selling books that have a lower value-to-weight ratio and more predictable demand.

We illustrate the trade-off involved in making aggregation decisions in the context of HighMed Inc., a manufacturer of medical equipment used in heart procedures. HighMed is located in Wisconsin, and cardiologists all over North America use its equipment. The medical equipment is not sold through purchasing agents but directly to doctors. HighMed has currently divided the United States into 24 territories, each with its own sales force. All product inventories are maintained locally and replenished from Madison every four weeks using UPS, and the average replenishment lead time using UPS is one week. UPS charges at a rate of \$0.66 + 0.26x, where x is the quantity shipped in pounds. The products sold fall into two categories: Highval and Lowval. Highval products weigh 0.1 pounds and cost \$200 each. Lowval products weigh 0.04 pounds and cost \$30 each.

Weekly demand for Highval products in each territory is normally distributed with a mean of $\mu_H = 2$ and a standard deviation of $\sigma_H = 5$. Weekly demand for Lowval products in each territory is normally distributed with a mean of $\mu_L = 20$ and a standard deviation of $\sigma_L = 5$. HighMed maintains sufficient safety inventories in each territory to provide a cycle service level of 0.997 for each product. Holding cost at HighMed is 25 percent.

The management team at HighMed wants to evaluate the operating cost of the current operating procedure and compare it with two other options they have been considering:

1. **Option A**. Keep the current structure but start replenishing inventory once a week rather than once every four weeks.
2. **Option B**. Eliminate inventories in the territories, aggregate all inventories in a finished goods warehouse at Madison, and replenish the warehouse once a week.

If inventories are aggregated at Madison, orders will be shipped using FedEx, which charges \$5.53 + 0.53x per shipment, where x is the quantity shipped in pounds. The factory requires a one-week lead time to replenish finished goods inventories at the Madison warehouse. An average customer order is for 1 unit of HighVal and 10 units of LowVal.

HighMed can reduce transportation cost by aggregating the quantity shipped at a time because prices for both UPS and FedEx display economies of scale. When comparing Option A with the current system, the management team must trade off the savings in transportation cost through less frequent replenishment with the savings in inventory cost with more frequent replenishment. When considering Option B, the management team must trade off the increase in transportation cost upon aggregation of inventories and the use of a faster but more expensive carrier (FedEx) with the decrease in inventory cost.

The management team first analyzes the current situation. For each territory,

$$\begin{aligned}\text{Replenishment lead time } L &= 1 \text{ week}\\ \text{Reorder interval } T &= 4 \text{ weeks}\\ \text{Cycle service level } CSL &= 0.997\end{aligned}$$

HighMed Inventory Costs (Current Scenario) For HighVal in each territory, the management team obtains the following:

$$\begin{aligned}\text{Average lot size } Q_H &= \text{Expected demand during } T \text{ weeks} = T\mu_H = 4 \times 2 = 8 \text{ units}\\ \text{Safety inventory } ss_H &= F^{-1}(CSL) \times \sigma_{T+L} = F^{-1}(\text{CSL}) \times \sqrt{T+L} \times \sigma_H = F^{-1}\\ &\quad (0.997) \times \sqrt{4+1} \times 5 = 30.7 \text{ units (see Equation 8.16)}\\ \text{Total HighVal inventory} &= Q_H/2 + ss_H = (8/2) + 30.7 = 34.7 \text{ units}\end{aligned}$$

Across all 24 territories, HighMed thus carries HighVal inventory of 24 × 34.7 = 832.8 units. For LowVal in each territory, the management team obtains the following:

$$\begin{aligned}\text{Average lot size } Q_L &= \text{Expected demand during } T \text{ weeks} = T\mu_L = 4 \times 20 = 80 \text{ units}\\ \text{Safety inventory } ss_H &= F^{-1}(CSL) \times \sigma_{T+L} = F^{-1}(CSL) \times \sqrt{T+L} \times \sigma_L\\ &= F^{-1}(0.997) \times \sqrt{4+1} \times 5 = 30.7 \text{ units}\\ \text{Total LowVal inventory} &= Q_H/2 + ss_H = (80/2) + 30.7 = 70.7 \text{ units}\end{aligned}$$

Across all 24 territories HighMed thus carries LowVal inventory of 24 × 70.7 = 1696.8 units.

The management team thus obtains the following:

$$\text{Annual inventory holding cost for HighMed} = (\text{Average HighVal inventory} \times \$200 + \text{Average LowVal inventory} \times \$30) \times 0.25$$
$$= (832.8 \times \$200 + 1696.8 \times \$30) \times 0.25 = \$54{,}366$$

HighMed Transportation Cost (Current Scenario) The average replenishment order from each territory consists of Q_H units of HighVal and Q_L units of LowVal. Thus,

$$\text{Average weight of each replenishment order} = 0.1Q_H + 0.04Q_L = 0.1 \times 8 + 0.04 \times 80 = 4 \text{ lb}$$

$$\text{Shipping cost per replenishment order} = \$0.66 + 0.26 \times 4 = \$1.7$$

Each territory has 13 replenishment orders per year, and there are 24 territories. Thus,

$$\text{Annual transportation cost} = \$1.7 \times 13 \times 24 = \$530$$

HighMed Total Cost (Current Scenario) Annual inventory and transportation cost at HighMed = inventory cost + transportation cost = \$54,366 + \$530.4 = \$54,896. The HighMed management team evaluates the costs for Option A and Option B similarly, and the results are summarized in Table 10.6.

From Table 10.6 observe that increasing the replenishment frequency under Option A decreases total cost at HighMed. The increase in transportation costs is much smaller than the decrease in inventory costs resulting from smaller lots. HighMed is able to reduce total cost the most by aggregating all inventories and using FedEx for transportation because the decrease in inventories on aggregation is larger than the increase in transportation costs.

If customer order sizes are small, the increase in transportation cost on aggregation can be significant, and inventory aggregation may increase total costs. Consider what happens in the case of HighMed if each customer order averages 0.5 HighVal

TABLE 10.6 HighMed Costs under Different Network Options

	Current Scenario	*Option A*	*Option B*
Number of stocking locations	24	24	1
Reorder interval	4 weeks	1 week	1 week
HighVal cycle inventory	96 units	24 units	24 units
HighVal safety inventory	736.8 units	466 units	95.2 units
HighVal inventory	832.8 units	490 units	119.2 units
LowVal cycle inventory	960 units	240 units	240 units
LowVal safety inventory	736.8 units	466 units	95.2 units
LowVal inventory	1,696.8 units	706 units	335.2 units
Annual inventory cost	\$54,366	\$29,795	\$8,474
Shipment type	Replenishment	Replenishment	Customer order
Shipment size	8 HighVal + 80 LowVal	2 HighVal + 20 LowVal	1 HighVal + 10 LowVal
Shipment weight	4 lb	1 lb	0.5 lb
Annual transport cost	\$530	\$1,148	\$14,464
Total annual cost	\$54,896	\$30,943	\$22,938

and 5 LowVal (half the size considered earlier). The costs for the current option as well as Option A remain unchanged because HighMed does not pay for outbound transportation and only incurs the cost of transporting replenishment orders under both options. Option B, however, becomes more expensive because outbound transportation costs increase with a decrease in customer order size. The costs under Option B are as follows:

$$\text{Average weight of each customer order} = 0.1 \times 0.5 + 0.04 \times 5 = 0.25 \text{ lb}$$
$$\text{Shipping cost per customer order} = \$5.53 + 0.53 \times 0.25 = \$5.66$$
$$\text{Number of customer orders per territory per week} = 4$$
$$\text{Total customer orders per year} = 4 \times 24 \times 52 = 4{,}992$$
$$\text{Annual transportation cost} = 4{,}992 \times 5.66 = \$28{,}255$$
$$\text{Total annual cost} = \text{inventory cost} + \text{transportation cost} = \$8{,}474 + \$28{,}255 = \$36{,}729$$

Thus, with small customer orders, inventory aggregation is no longer the lowest-cost option for HighMed because of the large increase in transportation costs. The company is better off maintaining inventory in each territory and using Option A, which gives a lower total cost, as shown in Table 10.5.

Key Point Inventory aggregation decisions must account for inventory and transportation costs. Inventory aggregation decreases supply chain costs if the product has a high value-to-weight ratio and high demand uncertainty and if customer orders are large. If a product has a low value-to-weight ratio or low demand uncertainty or if customer orders are small, inventory aggregation may increase supply chain costs.

Trade-off Between Transportation Cost and Customer Responsiveness

The transportation cost a supply chain incurs is closely linked to the degree of responsiveness the supply chain aims to provide. If a firm has high responsiveness and ships all orders within a day of their receipt from the customer, it will have small outbound shipments, resulting in a high transportation cost. If it decreases its responsiveness and aggregates orders over a longer time horizon before shipping them out, it will be able to exploit economies of scale and incur a lower transportation cost because of larger shipments. **Temporal aggregation** is the process of combining orders across time. Temporal aggregation decreases a firm's responsiveness because of shipping delay but also decreases transportation costs because of economies of scale that result from larger shipments. Thus, a firm must consider the trade-off between responsiveness and transportation cost when designing its transportation network.

Consider Alloy Steel, a steel service center in the Cleveland area. Alloy ships all orders to customers using an LTL carrier that charges $\$100 + 0.01x$, where x is the number of pounds of steel shipped on the truck. The LTL carrier also charges \$10 for each customer delivery. Currently, Alloy Steel ships orders on the day they are received. Allowing for two days in transit, this policy allows Alloy to achieve a response time of two days. Daily demand at Alloy Steel over a two-week period is shown in Table 10.7.

TABLE 10.7 Daily Demand at Alloy Steel over Two-Week Period

Week 1	19,970	17,470	11,316	26,192	20,263	8,381	25,377
Week 2	39,171	2,158	20,633	23,370	24,100	19,603	18,442

The general manager at Alloy Steel feels that customers do not really value the two-day response time and would be satisfied with a four-day response. As the response time increases, Alloy Steel has the opportunity to aggregate demand over multiple days for shipping. For a response time of three days, Alloy Steel can aggregate demand over two successive days before shipping. For a response time of four days, Alloy Steel can aggregate demand over three days before shipping. The manager evaluates the quantity shipped and transportation costs for different response times over the two-week period, as shown in Table 10.8.

From Table 10.8 observe that the transportation cost for Alloy Steel decreases as the response time increases. The benefit of temporal consolidation, however, diminishes rapidly on increasing the response time. As the response time increases from two to three days, transportation cost over the two-week window decreases by $700. Increasing the response time from three to four days reduces the transportation cost by only $200. Thus, a limited amount of temporal aggregation can be very effective at reducing transportation cost in a supply chain. Firms, however, must trade off the decrease in transportation cost on temporal aggregation with the loss of revenue because of poorer responsiveness when choosing the appropriate response time.

Temporal consolidation also improves transportation performance because it results in more stable shipments. For example, in Table 10.7, when Alloy Steel sends daily shipments, the coefficient of variation is 0.44, whereas temporal aggregation across three days (achieved with a four-day response time) has a coefficient of variation of only .16. More stable shipments allow both Alloy Steel and the carrier to plan operations better and improve utilization of their assets.

TABLE 10.8 Quantity Shipped and Transportation Cost as a Function of Response Time

		Two-Day Response		*Three-Day Response*		*Four-Day Response*	
Day	***Demand***	***Quantity Shipped***	***Cost***	***Quantity Shipped***	***Cost***	***Quantity Shipped***	***Cost***
1	19,970	19,970	$ 299.7	0	$ —	0	$ —
2	17,470	17,470	$ 274.70	37,440	$ 474.40	0	$ —
3	11,316	11,316	$ 213.16	0	$ —	48,756	$ 587.56
4	26,192	26,192	$ 361.92	37,508	$ 475.08	0	$ —
5	20,263	20,263	$ 302.63	0	$ —	0	$ —
6	8,381	8,381	$ 183.81	28,644	$ 386.44	54,836	$ 648.36
7	25,377	25,377	$ 353.77	0	$ —	0	$ —
8	39,171	39,171	$ 491.71	64,548	$ 745.48	0	$ —
9	2,158	2,158	$ 121.58	0	$ —	66,706	$ 767.06
10	20,633	20,633	$ 306.33	22,791	$ 327.91	0	$ —
11	23,370	23,370	$ 333.70	0	$ —	0	$ —
12	24,100	24,100	$ 341.00	47,470	$ 574.70	68,103	$ 781.03
13	19,603	19,603	$ 296.03	0	$ —	0	$ —
14	18,442	18,442	$ 284.42	38,045	$ 480.45	38,045	$ 480.45
			$4,164.46		$3,464.46		$3,264.46

Key Point Temporal aggregation of demand results in a reduction of transportation costs because it entails larger shipments and also reduces the variation in shipment sizes from one shipment to the next. It does, however, hurt customer response time. The marginal benefit of temporal aggregation declines as the time window over which aggregation takes place increases.

In the next section we discuss how transportation networks can be appropriately structured to supply customers with differing needs.

10.6 TAILORED TRANSPORTATION

Tailored transportation is the use of different transportation networks and modes based on customer and product characteristics. Most firms sell a variety of products and serve many different customer segments. For example, W.W. Grainger sells more than 200,000 maintenance, repair, and operations supply products to both small contractors and very large firms. Products vary in size and value, and customers vary in the quantity purchased, responsiveness required, uncertainty of the orders, and distance from Grainger branches and DCs. Given these differences, a firm like Grainger should not design a common transportation network to meet all needs. A firm can meet customer needs at a lower cost by using tailored transportation to provide the appropriate transportation choice based on customer and product characteristics. In the following sections, we describe various forms of tailored transportation in supply chains.

Tailored Transportation by Customer Density and Distance

Firms must consider customer density and distance from warehouse when designing transportation networks. The ideal transportation options based on density and distance are shown in Table 10.9.

When a firm serves a very high density of customers close to the DC, it is often best for the firm to own a fleet of trucks that are used with milk runs to supply customers because this scenario makes very good use of the vehicles. If customer density is high but distance from the warehouse is large, it does not pay to send milk runs from the warehouse because trucks will travel a long distance empty on the return trip. In such a situation, it is better to use a public carrier with large trucks to haul the shipments to a crossdock center close to the customer area, where the shipments are loaded onto smaller trucks that deliver product to customers using milk runs. In this situation, it may not be ideal for a firm to own its own fleet. As customer density decreases, using an LTL carrier or a third-party doing milk runs is more economical because the third-party carrier can provide lower costs by aggregating shipments across many firms. If a firm wants to serve an area with a very low density of customers far

TABLE 10.9 Transportation Options Based on Customer Density and Distance

	Short Distance	*Medium Distance*	*Long Distance*
High density	Private fleet with milk runs	Crossdock with milk runs	Crossdock with milk runs
Medium density	Third-party milk runs	LTL carrier	LTL or package carrier
Low density	Third-party milk runs or LTL carrier	LTL or package carrier	Package carrier

from the warehouse, even LTL carriers may not be feasible, and the use of package carriers may be the best option. Boise Cascade Office Products, an industrial distributor of office supplies, has designed a transportation network consistent with the suggestion in Table 10.8.

Customer density and distance should also be considered when firms decide on the degree of temporal aggregation to use when supplying customers. Firms should serve areas with high customer density more frequently because these areas are likely to provide sufficient economies of scale in transportation, making temporal aggregation less valuable. To lower transportation costs, firms should use a higher degree of temporal aggregation when serving areas with a low customer density.

Tailored Transportation by Size of Customer

Firms must consider customer size and location when designing transportation networks. Very large customers can be supplied using a TL carrier, whereas smaller customers will require an LTL carrier or milk runs. When using milk runs, a shipper incurs two types of costs:

- Transportation cost based on distance from warehouse
- Delivery cost based on number of deliveries

The transportation cost is the same whether going to a large or small customer. If a delivery is to be made to a large customer, including other small customers on the same truck can save on transportation cost. For each small customer, however, the delivery cost per unit is higher than for large customers. Therefore, it is not optimal to deliver to small and large customers with the same frequency at the same price. One option firms have is to charge a higher delivery cost for small customers compared with large ones. Another option is to tailor milk runs so that they visit larger customers with a higher frequency than smaller customers. Firms can partition customers into large (L), medium (M), and small (S) based on the demand at each. The optimal frequency of visits can be evaluated based on the transportation and delivery costs (see Section 7.2). If large customers are to be visited every milk run, medium customers every other milk run, and low demand customers every three milk runs, suitable milk runs can be designed by combining large, medium, and small customers on each run. Medium customers would be partitioned into two subsets (M_1, M_2), and small customers partitioned into three subsets (S_1, S_2, S_3). The firm can sequence the following six milk runs to ensure that each customer is visited with the appropriate frequency: (L, M_1, S_1), (L, M_2, S_2), (L, M_1, S_3), (L, M_2, S_1), (L, M_1, S_2), (L, M_2, S_3). This tailored sequence has the advantages of each truck carrying about the same load and larger customers being provided with more frequent delivery than smaller customers consistent with their relative costs of delivery.

Tailored Transportation by Product Demand and Value

The degree of inventory aggregation and the modes of transportation used in a supply chain network should vary with the demand and value of a product as shown in Table 10.10.

The cycle inventory for high-value products with high demand is disaggregated to save on transportation costs because this allows replenishment orders to be transported less expensively. Safety inventory for such products can be aggregated to reduce inventories (see Chapter 8) and a fast mode of transportation used if the safety inventory is required to meet customer demand. For high-demand products with low value, all inventories should be disaggregated and held close to the customer to re-

TABLE 10.10 Impact of Value and Demand of Product on Aggregation

Product Type	*High Value*	*Low Value*
High demand	Disaggregate cycle inventory. Aggregate safety inventory. Inexpensive mode of transportation for replenishing cycle inventory and fast mode when using safety inventory.	Disaggregate all inventories and use inexpensive mode of transportation for replenishment inventory.
Low demand	Aggregate all inventories. If needed, use fast mode of transportation for filling customer orders.	Aggregate only safety inventory. Use inexpensive mode of transportation for replenishing cycle inventory.

duce transportation costs. For low-demand, high-value products, all inventories should be aggregated to save on inventory costs. For low-demand, low-value products, cycle inventories can be held close to the customer and safety inventories aggregated to reduce transportation costs while taking some advantage of aggregation. Cycle inventories are replenished using an inexpensive mode of transportation to save costs.

Key Point Tailoring transportation based on customer density and distance, customer size, or product demand and value allows a supply chain to achieve appropriate responsiveness and cost.

10.7 ROUTING AND SCHEDULING IN TRANSPORTATION

The most important operational decision related to transportation in a supply chain is the routing and scheduling of deliveries. Managers must decide on the customers to be visited by a particular vehicle and the sequence in which they will be visited. For example, on-line grocers like Webvan and Peapod and on-line delivery companies like Kozmo are built on delivering customer orders to their homes. The success of their operations turns on their ability to decrease transportation costs while providing the promised level of responsiveness to the customer. Kozmo promises one-hour delivery to customers, and Webvan promises home delivery within a half-hour time window. Given a set of customer orders, the goal at both companies is to route and schedule delivery vehicles such that the costs incurred to meet delivery promises are as low as possible. Typical objectives when routing and scheduling vehicles are a combination of minimizing cost by decreasing the number of vehicles needed, the total distance traveled by vehicles, and the total travel time of vehicles, as well as eliminating service failures such as a delay in shipments.

We discuss routing and scheduling problems in the context of the manager of a Webvan DC. After customers place orders for groceries on-line, staff at the DC must pick the items needed and load them on trucks for delivery. The manager must decide which trucks will deliver to which customers and the route that each truck will take when making deliveries. The manager must also ensure that no truck is overloaded and that promised delivery times are met.

One morning, the DC manager at Webvan has orders from 13 different customers that are to be delivered. The location of the DC, each customer on a grid, and the order size a_i from each customer i are shown in Table 10.11. The manager has four

TABLE 10.11 Customer Location and Demand for Webvan

	X Coordinate	*Y Coordinate*	*Order Size a_i*
Warehouse	0	0	
Customer 1	0	12	48
Customer 2	6	5	36
Customer 3	7	15	43
Customer 4	9	12	92
Customer 5	15	3	57
Customer 6	20	0	16
Customer 7	17	−2	56
Customer 8	7	−4	30
Customer 9	1	−6	57
Customer 10	15	−6	47
Customer 11	20	−7	91
Customer 12	7	−9	55
Customer 13	2	−15	38

trucks, each capable of carrying up to 200 units. The manager feels that the delivery costs are strongly linked to the total distance the trucks travel and that the distance between two points on the grid is correlated with the actual distance that a vehicle will travel between those two points. The manager thus decides to assign customers to trucks and identify a route for each truck with a goal of minimizing the total distance traveled.

The DC manager must first assign customers to be served by each vehicle and then decide on each vehicle's route. After the initial assignment, route sequencing and route improvement procedures are used to decide on the route for each vehicle. The DC manager decides to use the following computational procedures to support his decision:

- The savings matrix method
- The generalized assignment method

Next, we discuss how each method can be used to solve the routing and scheduling decision at Webvan.

Savings Matrix Method

The savings matrix method is simple to implement and can be used to assign customers to vehicles even when delivery time windows or other constraints exist. The major steps in the savings matrix method are as follows:

1. Identify the distance matrix
2. Identify the savings matrix
3. Assign customers to vehicles or routes
4. Sequence customers within routes

The first three steps are used to assign customers to vehicles, and the fourth step is used to route each vehicle to minimize the distance traveled.

Identify the Distance Matrix

The **distance matrix** identifies the distance between every pair of locations to be visited. The distance is used as a surrogate for the cost of traveling between the pair of locations. If the transportation costs between every pair of locations is known, the costs can be used in place of distances. The distance *Dist*(*A*, *B*) on a grid between a point *A* with coordinates (x_A, y_A) and a point *B* with coordinates (x_B, y_B) is evaluated as follows:

$$Dist(A, B) = \sqrt{(x_A - x_B)^2 + (y_A - y_B)^2} \quad \textbf{(10.1)}$$

The distance between the DC and every pair of customer locations for Webvan is shown in Table 10.12. The distances between every pair of locations are next used to evaluate the savings matrix.

Identify the Savings Matrix

The **savings matrix** represents the savings that accrue on consolidating two customers on a single truck. Savings may be evaluated in terms of distance, time, or money. The manager at Webvan constructs the savings matrix in terms of distance. A **trip** is identified as the sequence of locations a vehicle visits. The trip DC → Cust *x* → DC starts at the DC, visits customer *x*, and returns to the DC. The savings *S*(*x*, *y*) is the distance saved if the trips DC → Cust *x* → DC and DC → Cust *y* → DC are combined to a single trip DC → Cust *x* → Cust *y* → DC. This saving can be calculated by the following formula:

$$S(x, y) = Dist(\text{DC}, x) + Dist(\text{DC}, y) - Dist(x, y) \quad \textbf{(10.2)}$$

For example, using Table 10.12 the manager evaluates $S(1,2) = 12 + 8 - 9 = 11$. The savings matrix for the Webvan deliveries is shown in Table 10.13. The savings matrix is then used to assign customers to vehicles or routes.

TABLE 10.12 Distance Matrix for Webvan Deliveries

	DC	*Cust 1*	*Cust 2*	*Cust 3*	*Cust 4*	*Cust 5*	*Cust 6*	*Cust 7*	*Cust 8*	*Cust 9*	*Cust 10*	*Cust 11*	*Cust 12*	*Cust 13*
Cust 1	12	0												
Cust 2	8	9	0											
Cust 3	17	8	10	0										
Cust 4	15	9	8	4	0									
Cust 5	15	17	9	14	11	0								
Cust 6	20	23	15	20	16	6	0							
Cust 7	17	22	13	20	16	5	4	0						
Cust 8	8	17	9	19	16	11	14	10	0					
Cust 9	6	18	12	22	20	17	20	16	6	0				
Cust 10	16	23	14	22	19	9	8	4	8	14	0			
Cust 11	21	28	18	26	22	11	7	6	13	19	5	0		
Cust 12	11	22	14	24	21	14	16	12	5	7	9	13	0	
Cust 13	15	27	20	30	28	22	23	20	12	9	16	20	8	0

TABLE 10.13 Savings Matrix for Webvan Deliveries

	Cust 1	*Cust 2*	*Cust 3*	*Cust 4*	*Cust 5*	*Cust 6*	*Cust 7*	*Cust 8*	*Cust 9*	*Cust 10*	*Cust 11*	*Cust 12*	*Cust 13*
Cust 1	0												
Cust 2	11	0											
Cust 3	21	15	0										
Cust 4	18	15	28	0									
Cust 5	10	14	18	19	0								
Cust 6	9	13	17	19	29	0							
Cust 7	7	12	14	16	27	33	0						
Cust 8	3	7	6	7	12	14	15	0					
Cust 9	0	2	1	1	4	6	7	8	0				
Cust 10	5	10	11	12	22	28	29	16	8	0			
Cust 11	5	11	12	14	25	34	32	16	8	32	0		
Cust 12	1	5	4	5	12	15	16	14	10	18	19	0	
Cust 13	0	3	2	2	8	12	12	11	12	15	16	18	0

Assign Customers to Vehicles or Routes

When assigning customers to vehicles or routes, the manager attempts to maximize savings. An iterative procedure is used to make this assignment. Initially each customer is assigned to a separate route. Two routes can be combined into a **feasible** route if the total deliveries across both routes do not exceed the vehicle's capacity. At each iterative step, the Webvan manager attempts to combine routes with the highest savings into a new feasible route. The procedure is continued until no more combinations are feasible.

At the first step, the highest saving of 34 results on combining truck routes 6 and 11. The combined route is feasible because the total load is 16 + 91 = 107, which is below 200. The two customers are thus combined on a single route, as shown in Table 10.14, and the saving of 34 is eliminated from further consideration.

TABLE 10.14 Savings Matrix with Revised Routes for Webvan Deliveries

	Route	*Cust 1*	*Cust 2*	*Cust 3*	*Cust 4*	*Cust 5*	*Cust 6*	*Cust 7*	*Cust 8*	*Cust 9*	*Cust 10*	*Cust 11*	*Cust 12*	*Cust 13*
Cust 1	1	0												
Cust 2	2	11	0											
Cust 3	3	21	15	0										
Cust 4	4	18	15	28	0									
Cust 5	5	10	14	18	19	0								
Cust 6	6	9	13	17	19	29	0							
Cust 7	7	7	12	14	16	27	33	0						
Cust 8	8	3	7	6	7	12	14	15	0					
Cust 9	9	0	2	1	1	4	6	7	8	0				
Cust 10	10	5	10	11	12	22	28	29	16	8	0			
Cust 11	6	5	11	12	14	25	34	32	16	8	32	0		
Cust 12	12	1	5	4	5	12	15	16	14	10	18	19	0	
Cust 13	13	0	3	2	2	8	12	12	11	12	15	16	18	0

TABLE 10.15 Savings Matrix with Revised Routes for Webvan Deliveries after Second Iteration

	Route	*Cust 1*	*Cust 2*	*Cust 3*	*Cust 4*	*Cust 5*	*Cust 6*	*Cust 7*	*Cust 8*	*Cust 9*	*Cust 10*	*Cust 11*	*Cust 12*	*Cust 13*
Cust 1	1	0												
Cust 2	2	11	0											
Cust 3	3	21	15	0										
Cust 4	4	18	15	28	0									
Cust 5	5	10	14	18	19	0								
Cust 6	6	9	13	17	19	29	0							
Cust 7	6	7	12	14	16	27	33	0						
Cust 8	8	3	7	6	7	12	14	15	0					
Cust 9	9	0	2	1	1	4	6	7	8	0				
Cust 10	10	5	10	11	12	22	28	29	16	8	0			
Cust 11	6	5	11	12	14	25	34	32	16	8	32	0		
Cust 12	12	1	5	4	5	12	15	16	14	10	18	19	0	
Cust 13	13	0	3	2	2	8	12	12	11	12	15	16	18	0

The next highest saving is 33 on adding customer 7 to the route for customer 6. This is feasible because the resulting load is 107 + 56 = 163, which is under 200. Thus, customer 7 is also added to route 6, as shown in Table 10.15.

The next highest saving now is 32 on adding customer 10 to route 6 (we need not consider the saving of 32 on combining customer 7 with customer 11 because both are already in route 6). This, however, cannot be done because the addition of customer 10 results in a delivery of 47 units and adding this amount to the deliveries already on route 6 would exceed the vehicle capacity of 200. The next highest saving is 29 on adding either customer 5 or 10 to route 6. Each of these is also infeasible because of the capacity constraint. The next highest saving is 28 on combining routes 3 and 4, which is feasible. The two routes are combined into a single route, as shown in Table 10.16.

TABLE 10.16 Savings Matrix with Routes for Webvan Deliveries after Third Iteration

	Route	*Cust 1*	*Cust 2*	*Cust 3*	*Cust 4*	*Cust 5*	*Cust 6*	*Cust 7*	*Cust 8*	*Cust 9*	*Cust 10*	*Cust 11*	*Cust 12*	*Cust 13*
Cust 1	1	0												
Cust 2	2	11	0											
Cust 3	3	21	15	0										
Cust 4	3	18	15	28	0									
Cust 5	5	10	14	18	19	0								
Cust 6	6	9	13	17	19	29	0							
Cust 7	6	7	12	14	16	27	33	0						
Cust 8	8	3	7	6	7	12	14	15	0					
Cust 9	9	0	2	1	1	4	6	7	8	0				
Cust 10	10	5	10	11	12	22	28	29	16	8	0			
Cust 11	6	5	11	12	14	25	34	32	16	8	32	0		
Cust 12	12	1	5	4	5	12	15	16	14	10	18	19	0	
Cust 13	13	0	3	2	2	8	12	12	11	12	15	16	18	0

Continuing the iterative procedure, the manager partitions customers into four groups {1, 3, 4}, {2, 9}, {6, 7, 8, 11}, {5, 10, 12, 13} with each group assigned to a single vehicle. The next step is to identify the sequence in which each vehicle will visit customers.

Sequence Customers Within Routes

When sequencing customers within routes, the manager's goal is to minimize the distance each vehicle must travel. Changing the sequence in which deliveries are made can have a significant impact on the distance traveled by vehicles. Consider the truck that has been assigned deliveries to customers 5, 10, 12, and 13. If the deliveries are in the sequence 5, 10, 12, 13, the total distance traveled by the truck is 15 + 9 + 9 + 8 + 15 = 56 (distances are obtained from Table 10.12). However, if deliveries are in the sequence 5, 10, 13, 12, the truck covers a larger distance of 15 + 9 + 16 + 8 + 11 = 59. Delivery sequences are determined by obtaining an initial route sequence and then using route improvement procedures to obtain delivery sequences with a lower transportation distance or cost.

Route Sequencing Procedures The manager at Webvan can use route sequencing procedures to obtain an initial trip for each vehicle. The initial trip is then improved using the route improvement procedures, which are discussed later in the chapter. The following route sequencing procedures are illustrated for the vehicle assigned customers 5, 10, 12, 13.

1. **Farthest insert**. Given a vehicle trip (including a trip consisting of only the DC), for each remaining customer, evaluate the minimum increase in length if this customer is inserted at a suitable point in the trip and insert the customer with the largest minimum increase to obtain a new trip. This step is referred to as a **farthest insert** because the customer farthest from the current trip is inserted. The process is continued until all remaining customers to be visited by the vehicle are included in a trip.

For the Webvan example, the manager is seeking a trip starting at the DC and visiting customers 5, 10, 12, and 13. The initial trip consists of just the DC with a length of 0. Including customer 5 in the trip adds 30 to its length, including customer 10 adds 32, including customer 12 adds 22, and including customer 13 adds 30 (see Table 10.12). Using farthest insert, the manager adds customer 10 to obtain a new trip (DC, 10, DC) of length 32.

At the next step, inserting customer 5 raises the length of the trip to 40, inserting customer 12 raises it to 36, and inserting customer 13 raises it to 46. The manager thus inserts the farthest customer 13 to obtain the new trip (DC, 10, 13, DC) of length 46. This still leaves customers 5 and 12 to be inserted. The minimum cost insertion for customer 5 is (DC, 5, 10, 13, DC) for a length of 55, and the minimum cost insertion for customer 12 is (DC, 10, 12, 13, DC) for a length of 48. The manager thus inserts customer 5 to obtain the trip (DC, 5, 10, 13, DC) of length 55. Customer 12 is then inserted between customers 10 and 13 to obtain the trip (DC, 5, 10, 12, 13, DC) of length 56.

2. **Nearest insert**. Given a vehicle trip (including a trip consisting of only the DC), for each remaining customer, evaluate the minimum increase in length if this customer is inserted at a suitable point in the trip and insert the customer with the smallest minimum increase to obtain a new trip. This step is referred to as a **nearest insert** because the customer closest to the current trip is inserted. The process is continued until all remaining customers the vehicle will visit are included in a trip.

For the Webvan example, the manager applies nearest insert to the vehicle serving customers 5, 10, 12, and 13. Starting at the DC, the nearest customer is 12. Inserting customer 12 results in the trip (DC, 12, DC) of length 22. At the next step, inserting customer 5 results in a trip of length 40, inserting customer 10 in a trip of length 36, and inserting customer 13 in a trip of length 34. Customer 13 results in the smallest increase and is inserted to obtain the trip (DC, 12, 13, DC) of length 34. The next nearest insertion is customer 10, resulting in the trip (DC, 10, 12, 13, DC) of length 48, and the final insertion of customer 5 results in the trip (DC, 5, 10, 12, 13, DC) of length 56.

3. **Nearest neighbor**. Starting at the DC, this procedure adds the closest customer to extend the trip. At each step, the trip is built by adding the customer closest to the point last visited by the vehicle until all customers have been visited.

For the Webvan example, the customer closest to the DC is 12 (see Table 10.12). This results in the path (DC, 12). The customer closest to customer 12 is 10, extending the path to (DC, 12, 10). The nearest neighbor of customer 10 is 5, and the nearest neighbor of customer 5 is 13. The Webvan manager thus obtains the trip (DC, 12, 10, 5, 13, DC) of length 66.

4. **Sweep**. In the sweep procedure, any point on the grid is selected and a line swept either clockwise or counterclockwise from that point. The trip is constructed by sequencing customers in the order they are encountered during the sweep.

The Webvan manager uses the sweep procedure with the line centered at the DC. Customers are encountered in the sequence 5, 10, 12, 13 to obtain the trip (DC, 5, 10, 12, 13, DC) for a length of 56.

The initial trips resulting from each route sequencing procedure and their lengths are summarized in Table 10.17.

Route Improvement Procedures Route improvement procedures start with a trip obtained using a route sequencing procedure and improve the trip to shorten its length. The Webvan manager next applies route improvement procedures to alter the sequence of customers visited by a vehicle and shorten the distance a vehicle must travel. The following two route improvement procedures discussed are illustrated on the trip obtained as a result of the nearest neighbor procedure:

1. **2-OPT**. The 2-OPT procedure starts with a trip and breaks it at two places. This results in the trip breaking into two paths, which can be reconnected in two possible ways. The length for each reconnection is evaluated, and the smaller of the two used to define a new trip. The procedure is continued on the new trip until no further improvement results.

For example, the trip (DC, 12, 10, 5, 13, DC) resulting from the nearest neighbor procedure can be broken into two paths (13, DC) and (12, 10, 5) and reconnected into the trip (DC, 5, 10, 12, 13, DC), as shown in Figure 10.5. The new trip has length 56, which is an improvement over the existing trip.

2. **3-OPT**. The 3-OPT procedure breaks a trip at three points to obtain three paths that can be reconnected to form up to eight different trips. The length of each of the

TABLE 10.17 Initial Trips Using Different Route Sequencing Procedures at Webvan

Route Sequencing Procedure	*Resulting Trip*	*Trip Length*
Farthest insert	DC, 5, 10, 12, 13, DC	56
Nearest insert	DC, 5, 10, 12, 13, DC	56
Nearest neighbor	DC, 12, 10, 5, 13, DC	66
Sweep	DC, 5, 10, 12, 13, DC	56

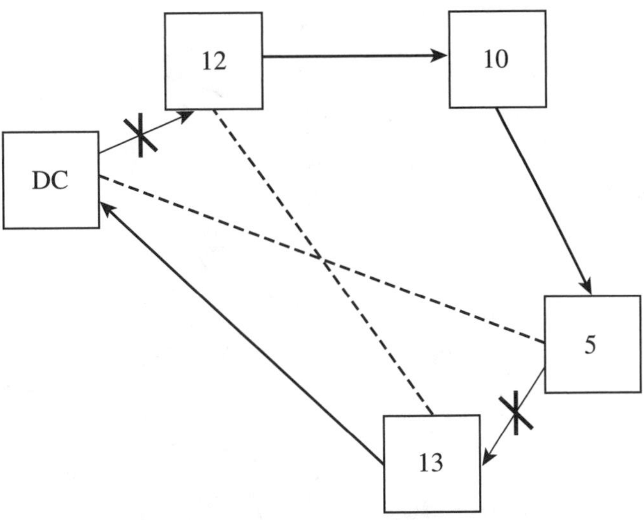

FIGURE 10.5 Improving Route Sequencing Using 2-OPT

eight possible trips is evaluated and the shortest trip retained. The procedure is continued on the new trip until no further improvement results.

The trip (DC, 5, 10, 12, 13, DC) resulting from the 2-OPT procedure is broken up into three paths (DC), (5, 10), (12, 13). The various resulting trips on reconnecting the three paths are (DC, 12, 13, 5, 10, DC), of length 65; (DC, 12, 13, 10, 5, DC), of length 81; and (DC, 13, 12, 5, 10, DC), of length 61. All other trips correspond to one of these four trips reversed. This application of the 3-OPT procedure does not improve the trip because the current trip is the shortest. At this stage, the Webvan manager can form three new paths from the trip and repeat the procedure.

The Webvan manager uses route sequencing and improvement procedures to obtain delivery trips for each of the four trucks, as shown in Table 10.18 and Figure 10.6. The total travel distance for the delivery schedule is 176.

Generalized Assignment Method

The generalized assignment method is more sophisticated than the savings matrix method and usually results in better solutions when there are few delivery constraints to be satisfied. The procedure for routing and sequencing of vehicles consists of the following steps:

1. Assign seed points for each route
2. Evaluate insertion cost for each customer
3. Assign customers to routes
4. Sequence customers within routes

TABLE 10.18 Webvan Delivery Schedule Using Saving Matrix Method

Truck	*Trip*	*Length of Trip*	*Load on Truck*
1	DC, 2, 9, DC	32	93
2	DC, 1, 3, 4, DC	39	183
3	DC, 8, 11, 6, 7, DC	49	193
4	DC, 5, 10, 12, 13, DC	56	197

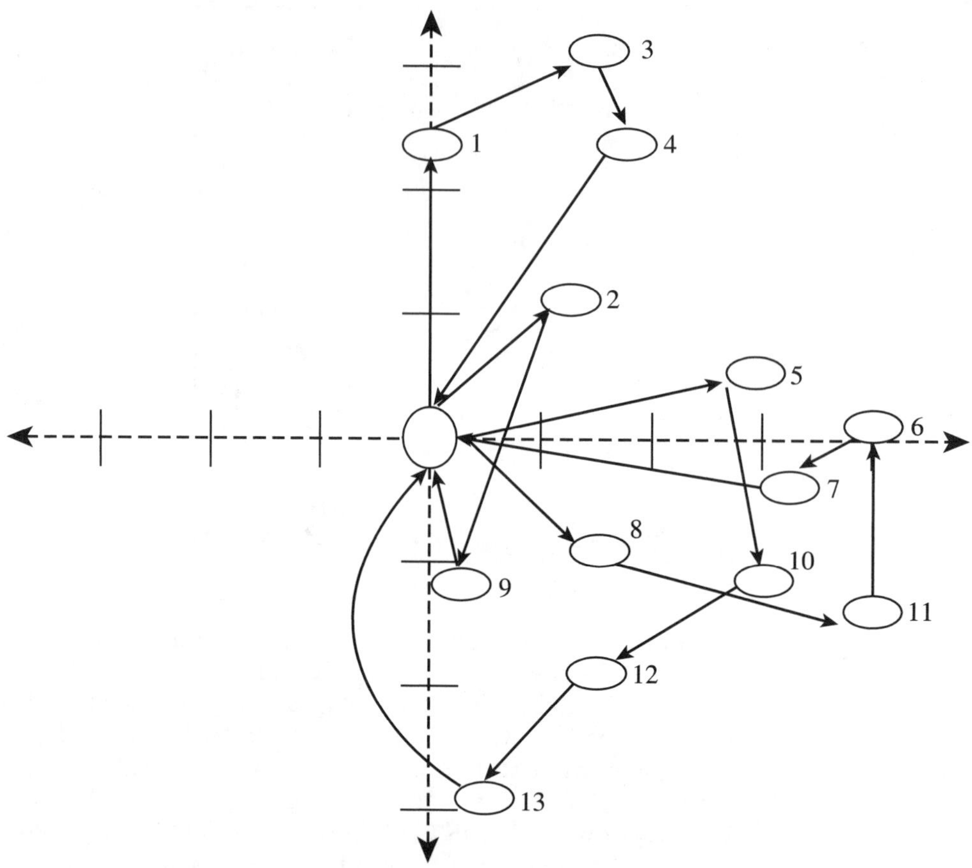

FIGURE 10.6 Delivery Routes at Webvan Using Savings Matrix Method

The first three steps assign customers to vehicles, and the fourth step identifies a route for each vehicle to minimize the distance traveled. We discuss each step in greater detail in the context of the delivery decision at Webvan.

Assign Seed Points for Each Route

When assigning seed points for each route, the goal is to determine a seed point corresponding to the center of the trip taken by each vehicle using the following procedure:

1. Divide the total load to be shipped to all customers by the number of trucks to obtain L_{seed}, the average load allocated to each seed point.
2. Starting at any customer, use a ray starting at the DC to sweep clockwise to obtain cones assigned to each seed point. Each cone is assigned a load of L_{seed}.
3. Within each cone, the seed point is located in the middle (in terms of angle) at a distance equal to that of the customer (with a partial or complete load allocated to the cone) farthest from the DC.

The manager at Webvan uses this procedure to obtain seed points for the deliveries described in Table 10.11. Given four vehicles and a total delivery load across all customers of 666 units, the manager obtains an average load per vehicle of $L_{seed} = 666/4 = 166.5$ units.

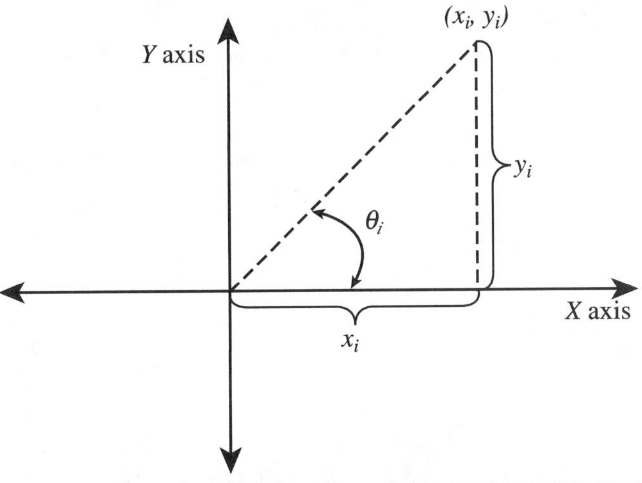

FIGURE 10.7 Angular Position of Customer *i*

The next step is to sweep clockwise with a ray emanating from the DC to obtain four cones, one for each vehicle, including all customers. The first step in defining the cones is to obtain the angular position of each customer. The angular position (θ_i) of customer i with coordinates (x_i, y_i), is the angle made relative to the X axis by the line joining the customer i to the origin (DC), as shown in Figure 10.7.

The angular position of each customer is obtained as the inverse tangent of the ratio of its y coordinate to the x coordinate:

$$\theta_i = \tan^{-1} (y_i/x_i) \quad \textbf{(10.3)}$$

The inverse tangent can be evaluated using the Excel function *ATAN()* as follows:

$$\theta_i = ATAN(y_i/x_i) \quad \textbf{(10.4)}$$

The angular position of each customer is obtained using Equation 10.4 as shown in Table 10.19. The next step is to sweep clockwise and order the customers as encountered. For Webvan, a clockwise sweep encounters customers in the order 1, 3, 4, 2, 5, 6, 7, 11, 10, 8, 12, 9, and 13. Starting with customer 1, four cones, each representing a load of L_{seed} = 166.5 units, are to be formed. Customers 1 and 3 combine to load 91 units on the truck. Customer 4 is encountered next in the sweep. Adding the entire load for customer 4 would result in a load of 183, which is larger than L_{seed} = 166.5. To get a load of 166.5, only 166.5 − 91 = 75.5 units of the load should be included. Thus, the first cone extends to a point that is 75.5/92 of the angle between customers 3 and 4. Customer 3 has an angular position of 1.13, and customer 4 has an angular position of 0.93, resulting in an angle between them of 1.13 − 0.93 = 0.20. The first cone thus extends to an angle (75.5/92) × 0.20 beyond customer 3 with a resulting angle of 1.13 − (75.5/92) × 0.20 = 0.97. The first cone thus has one end at customer 1 (angle of 1.57) and the other at an angle of 0.97, as shown in Figure 10.8.

TABLE 10.19 Angular Positions of Webvan Customers

	X Coordinate	*Y Coordinate*	*Angular Position (Radians)*	*Demand*
DC	0	0		
Customer 1	0	12	1.57	48
Customer 2	6	5	0.69	36
Customer 3	7	15	1.13	43
Customer 4	9	12	0.93	92
Customer 5	15	3	0.20	57
Customer 6	20	0	0.00	16
Customer 7	17	−2	−0.12	56
Customer 8	7	−4	−0.52	30
Customer 9	1	−6	−1.41	57
Customer 10	15	−6	−0.38	47
Customer 11	20	−7	−0.34	91
Customer 12	7	−9	−0.91	55
Customer 13	2	−15	−1.44	38

The seed point is then located at an angle $\alpha_1 = (0.97 + 1.57)/2 = 1.27$ in the middle of the cone at a distance equal to that of the farthest customer included. Customer 3, at a distance $d_1 = \sqrt{(7-0)^2 + (15-0)^2} = 17$ is the farthest customer in the first cone. Given the distance d_1, the coordinates (X_1, Y_1) of the seed point 1 are as follows:

$$X_1 = d_1\cos(\alpha) = 17\cos(1.27) = 5, \text{ and } Y_1 = d_1\sin(\alpha_1) = 17\sin(1.27) = 16$$

FIGURE 10.8 Sweep Method to Locate Seed I

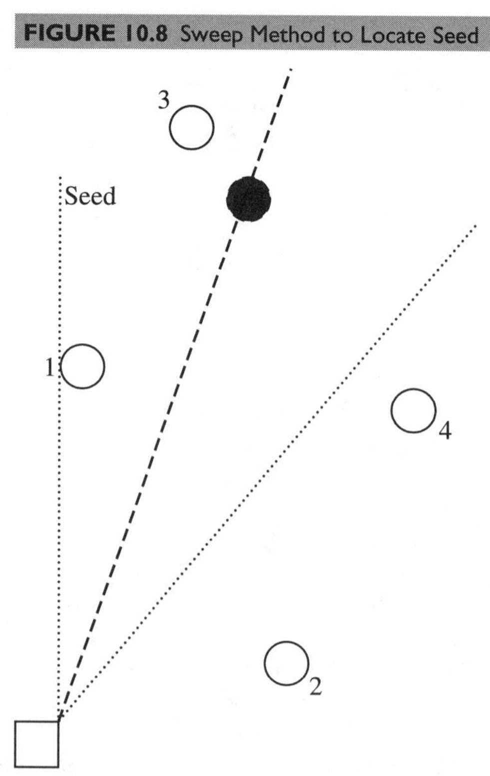

TABLE 10.20 Seed Point Coordinates for Webvan Deliveries

Seed Point	*X Coordinate*	*Y Coordinate*
S_1	5	16
S_2	18	9
S_3	19	−5
S_4	9	−12

The second cone starts at the angle 0.97 and includes 92 − 75.5 = 16.5 units of the customer 4 load. On sweeping clockwise, customers 2, 5, 6, and 7 are encountered before a load of 166.5 is exceeded. To get a load of exactly 166.5, only 41/56 of customer 7 load is needed. The angular position of the end of the cone is thus 41/56 between customers 6 and 7. Customer 6 is at an angle of 0.00, and customer 7 is at an angle of − 0.12. The second cone thus ends at an angle of 0.00 − 0.12 × (41/56) = − 0.09. The second cone has one end at an angle of 0.97 and the other at an angle of − 0.09. The seed point is thus located at an angle α_2 in the middle of the cone, that is, $\alpha_2 = (0.97 - 0.09)/2 = 0.44$. The distance d_2 of the seed point for the second cone is the same as customer 6, the farthest customer in the cone. This corresponds to a distance of $d_2 = 20$ (see Table 10.12). The coordinates (X_2, Y_2) of the seed point 2 are thus as follows:

$$X_2 = d_2 \cos(\alpha_2) = 20 \cos(0.44) = 18 \qquad \text{and} \qquad Y_2 = d_2 \sin(\alpha_2) = 20 \sin(0.44) = 9$$

Proceeding in the same manner, the manager at the Webvan DC forms four cones to determine the four seed points as shown in Table 10.20.

Evaluate Insertion Cost for Each Customer

For each seed point S_k and customer i, the **insertion cost** c_{ik} is the extra distance that would be traveled if the customer is inserted into a trip from the DC to the seed point and back and is given by the following:

$$c_{ik} = Dist(DC, i) + Dist(i, S_k) - Dist(DC, S_k),$$

where the *Dist()* function is evaluated as in Equation 10.1. For customer 1 and seed point 1, the insertion cost is given by the following:

$$c_{11} = Dist(DC, 1) + Dist(1, S_1) - Dist(DC, S_1) = 12 + 10 - 17 = 5$$

The manager at the Webvan DC evaluates all insertion costs c_{ik} as shown in Table 10.21.

Assign Customers to Routes

The manager next assigns customers to each of the four vehicles so as to minimize total insertion cost while respecting vehicle capacity constraints. The assignment problem is formulated as an integer program and requires the following input:

$$c_{ik} = \text{insertion cost of customer } i \text{ and seed point } k$$
$$a_i = \text{order size from customer } i$$
$$b_k = \text{capacity of vehicle } k$$

Define the following decision variables:

$$y_{ik} = 1 \text{ if customer } i \text{ is assigned to vehicle } k, 0 \text{ otherwise}$$

The integer program for assigning customers to vehicles is as follows:

$$Min \sum_{k=1}^{K} \sum_{i=1}^{n} c_{ik}\, y_{ik}$$

TABLE 10.21 Insertion Costs for Webvan Deliveries for Each Customer and Seed Point

Customer	*Seed Point 1*	*Seed Point 2*	*Seed Point 3*	*Seed Point 4*
1	2	10	18	23
2	2	0	5	10
3	2	9	20	29
4	4	4	15	24
5	15	2	5	16
6	25	9	5	21
7	22	8	1	15
8	11	5	0	1
9	12	9	4	1
10	24	11	1	10
11	32	17	4	18
12	20	12	4	0
13	30	24	15	8

subject to the following:

$$\sum_{k=1}^{K} y_{ik} = 1, i = 1, \ldots, n$$

$$\sum_{i=1}^{n} a_i y_{ik} \leq b_k, k = 1, \ldots, K$$

$$y_{ik} = 0 \text{ or } 1 \qquad \text{for all } i \text{ and } k$$

For Webvan, the order size for each customer is given in Table 10.11, the insertion cost c_{ik} is obtained from Table 10.21, and the capacity of each vehicle is 200 units. The manager at Webvan solves the integer program using the tool Solver in Excel to obtain the assignment of customers to vehicles as shown in Table 10.22 and Figure 10.9. The sequencing of customers within each trip is obtained using the route sequencing and route improvement procedures discussed earlier. The total distance traveled for the delivery schedule is 159.

Applicability of Routing and Scheduling Methods

The delivery schedule for Webvan resulting from the generalized assignment method in Table 10.21 is superior to the solution obtained from the savings matrix method in Table 10.17. The generalized assignment method is more sophisticated and generally gives a better solution than the savings matrix method when the delivery schedule has no constraints other than vehicle capacity. The main disadvantage of the generalized assignment method is that it has difficulty generating good delivery schedules as more constraints are included. For example, if Webvan has fixed time windows within which deliveries must be made to customers, it is difficult to use the generalized assignment

TABLE 10.22 Webvan Delivery Schedule Using Generalized Assignment Method

Truck	*Trip*	*Length of Trip*	*Load on Truck*
1	DC, 1, 3, 4, DC	39	183
2	DC, 2, 5, 6, DC	43	109
3	DC, 10, 7, 11, DC	47	194
4	DC, 8, 12, 13, 9, DC	36	180

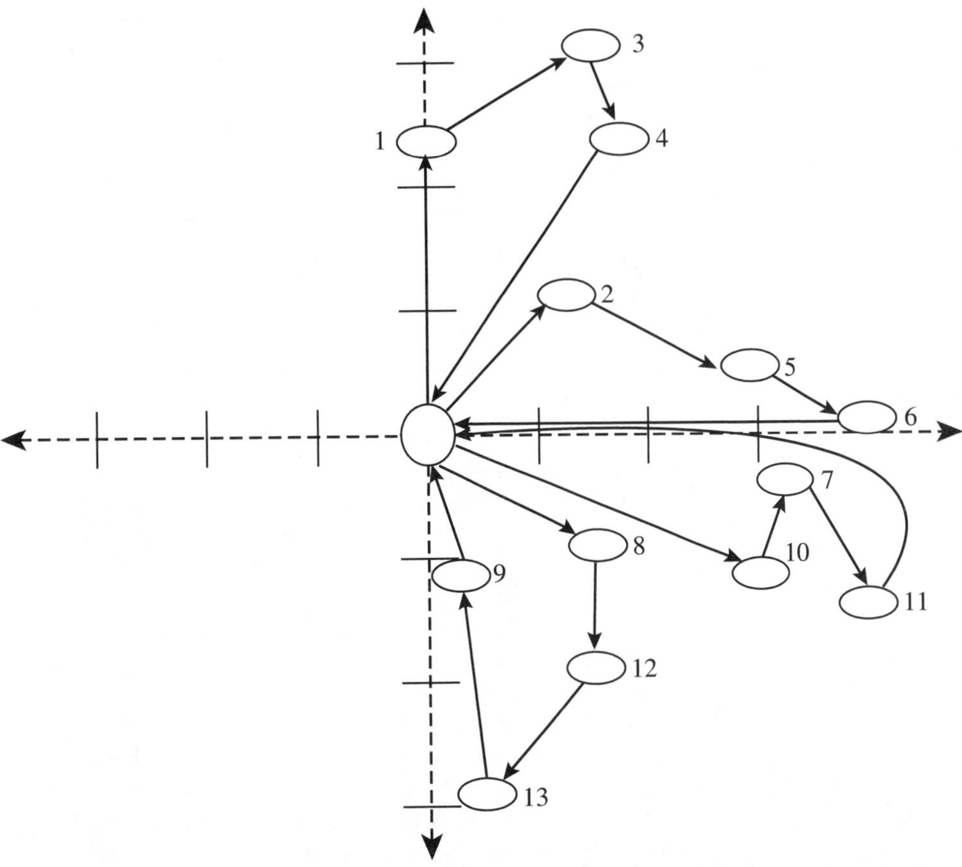

FIGURE 10.9 Delivery Routes at Webvan Using Generalized Assignment

method to generate a delivery schedule. The generalized assignment method is recommended if the constraints are limited to vehicle capacity or total travel time.

The main strength of the savings matrix method is its simplicity and robustness. The method is simple enough to be easily modified to include delivery time windows and other constraints, and robust enough to give a reasonably good solution that can be implemented in practice. Its main weakness is the quality of the solution. It is often possible to find better delivery schedules using more sophisticated methods. The savings matrix method is recommended when there are many constraints that need to be satisfied by the delivery schedule.

Software packages for transportation planning and routing and scheduling of deliveries are available from several companies including i2 Technologies, CAPS Logistics (a Baan company), and Logility.

10.8 MAKING TRANSPORTATION DECISIONS IN PRACTICE

Managers should keep the following issues in mind when making transportation decisions in a supply chain:

- **Align transportation strategy with competitive strategy**. Managers should ensure that a firm's transportation strategy supports its competitive strategy.

They should design functional incentives that help achieve this goal. Historically, the transportation function within firms has been evaluated based on the extent to which it can lower transportation costs. Such a focus leads to decisions that lower transportation costs but hurt the level of responsiveness provided to customers and may raise the firm's total cost. If the dispatcher at a DC is evaluated solely based on the extent to which trucks are loaded, she is likely to delay shipments and hurt customer responsiveness to achieve a larger load. Firms should evaluate the transportation function based on a combination of transportation cost, other costs such as inventory affected by transportation decisions, and the level of responsiveness achieved with customers.

- **Consider both in-house and outsourced transportation**. Managers should consider an appropriate combination of company-owned and outsourced transportation to meet their needs. This decision should be based on a firm's ability to handle transportation profitably as well as the strategic importance of transportation to the success of the firm. In general, outsourcing is a better option when shipment sizes are small, whereas owning the transportation fleet is better when shipment sizes are large and responsiveness is important. For example, Wal-Mart has used responsive transportation to reduce inventories in its supply chain. Given the importance of transportation to the success of its strategy, the company owns and manages its transportation fleet. This is made easier by the fact that it achieves good utilization from its transportation assets because most of its shipments are large. In contrast, firms like W.W. Grainger and McMaster-Carr send small shipments to customers; inventory management rather than transportation is the key to their success. A third-party carrier can lower costs for them by aggregating their shipments with those of other companies. As a result, both companies use third-party carriers for their transportation.
- **Design a transportation network that can handle e-commerce**. The growth in e-commerce for most business-to-consumer firms has resulted in a decrease in shipment sizes and a growth in home delivery. Transportation systems for the new economy need to be very responsive but must also be able to exploit every opportunity for aggregation, in some cases even with competitors, to help decrease the transportation cost of small shipments. Whereas replenishment orders are large and can use rail or truckload carriers, most e-commerce shipments require more expensive package carriers or LTL carriers given their smaller size. The growth in JIT manufacturing and the focus on reduced inventories and frequent replenishment has further increased the need to handle small shipments. If managers do not take these trends into account when designing their transportation networks, firms are likely to see a significant increase in transportation cost along with a drop in responsiveness to the customer.
- **Use technology to improve transportation performance**. Managers must use the information technology available to help decrease costs and improve responsiveness in their transportation networks. Systems available through several firms—including i2 Technologies, CAPS Logistics, and Logility—help managers do transportation planning and model selection, and build delivery routes and schedules. Available technology allows carriers to identify the precise location of each vehicle as well as the shipments the vehicle carries. Satellite-based communication systems allow carriers to communicate with each vehicle in their fleet. These technologies can help a carrier

become much more responsive and also help lower costs by better matching shipments from customers with vehicles that are best suited to carry them. These technologies also help a firm react better to unforeseen changes caused by the weather or other unpredictable factors.

- **Design flexibility into the transportation network**. When designing transportation networks, managers should take into account uncertainty in demand as well as availability of transportation. Ignoring uncertainty encourages a greater use of inexpensive and inflexible transportation modes that perform well when everything goes as planned. Such networks, however, perform very poorly when plans change. When managers account for uncertainty, they are more likely to include flexible, though more expensive, modes of transportation within their network. Although these modes may be more expensive for a particular shipment, including them in the transportation options allows a firm to reduce the overall cost of providing a high level of responsiveness.

10.9 SUMMARY OF LEARNING OBJECTIVES

1. Understand the role of transportation within a supply chain.

   Transportation refers to the movement of product from one location to another within a supply chain. The importance of transportation has grown with the increasing globalization in supply chains as well as the growth in e-commerce, because both trends increase the distance products travel. Transportation decisions affect supply chain profitability and influence both inventory and facility decisions within a supply chain.
2. Evaluate the strengths and weaknesses of different modes of transportation.

   The various modes of transportation include water, rail, intermodal, truck, air, pipeline, and package carriers. Water is typically the least expensive mode but is also the slowest, whereas air and package carriers are the most expensive and the fastest. Rail and water are best suited for low-value, large shipments that do not need to be moved in a hurry. Air and package carriers are best suited for small, high-value emergency shipments. Intermodal and full truckload carriers are faster than rail and water but somewhat more expensive. Less-than-truckload carriers are best suited for small shipments that are too large for package carriers but much less than a truckload.
3. Identify various transportation network design options and their relative strengths and weaknesses.

   Networks are designed to either ship directly from origin to destination or move the product through a consolidation point. Direct shipments are most effective when large quantities are to be moved. When shipments are small, using an intermediate warehouse or distribution center takes longer and is more complex but lowers transportation cost by aggregating the smaller shipments. Shipments may also be consolidated with a single vehicle either picking up from multiple locations or dropping off in multiple locations.
4. Identify trade-offs that shippers need to consider when designing their transportation network.

   When designing transportation networks, shippers must consider the trade-off between transportation cost, inventory cost, operating cost, and customer responsiveness. The supply chain goal is to minimize the total cost while providing the desired level of responsiveness to customers.

5. Use methodologies for routing and scheduling deliveries in transportation networks.

   The savings matrix and the generalized assignment methodology can be used to route vehicles and sequence deliveries. The methods can be used to minimize the transportation cost while meeting delivery commitments to customers. Several companies provide software that allows a manager to set delivery schedules.

Discussion Questions

1. What modes of transportation are best suited for large, low-value shipments? Why?
2. Wal-Mart designs its networks to have a DC support several large retail stores. Explain how the company can use such a network to reduce transportation costs while replenishing inventories frequently.
3. Compare the transportation costs for an e-business like Amazon.com and a retailer like Home Depot when selling home improvement materials.
4. What transportation challenges do on-line grocers like Webvan and Peapod face? Compare transportation costs at on-line grocers and supermarket chains.
5. Do you expect aggregation of inventory at one location to be more effective when a company like Dell sells computers or when a company like Amazon.com sells books? Explain by considering transportation and inventory costs.
6. Discuss key drivers that may be used to tailor transportation. How does tailoring help?
7. What are the strengths and weaknesses of using the savings matrix method and the generalized assignment method for routing and scheduling of vehicles?

Exercises

1. A power plant in California uses coal at the rate of 100,000 pounds each day. It also uses MRO material at the rate of 1,000 pounds each day. The coal comes from Wyoming, and the MRO material comes from Chicago. Coal costs $0.01 per pound, and MRO material costs $10 per pound, on average. Holding costs at the power plant are 25 percent. Transportation choices available are as follows:

   Train
   Lead time = 15 days
   Carload (100,000 lb) at $400 per carload
   Full train (70 cars) at $15,000 per train

   Truck
   Lead time = 4 days
   Minimum cost = $100
   Up to 10,000 lb at $0.08 per lb
   Between 10,000 and 20,000 lb at $0.07 per lb for entire load
   Between 25,000 and 40,000 lb at $0.06 per lb for entire load
   Full small truckload (40,000 lb) for $2,000
   Full large truckload (60,000 lb) for $2,600

   Safety inventory of coal and MRO materials is kept at twice the consumption during the lead time of supply. What mode of transport do you recommend for each of the two products? Why?
2. Books-On-Line, an on-line bookseller, charges its customers a shipping charge of $4 for the first book and $1 for each additional book. The average customer order contains 4 books. Books-On-Line currently has one warehouse in Seattle and ships all orders from there. For shipping purposes, Books-On-Line divides the United States into three zones: western, central, and eastern. Shipping cost incurred by Books-On-Line per customer order (average 4 books) is $2 within the same zone, $3 between adjacent zones, and $4 between nonadjacent zones.

Weekly demand from each zone is independent and normally distributed with a mean of 50,000 and a standard deviation of 25,000. Each book costs on average \$10, and the holding cost incurred by Books-On-Line is 25 percent. Books-On-Line replenishes inventory every week and aims for a 99.7 percent cycle service level. Assume a replenishment lead time of one week.

A warehouse is designed to carry 50 percent more than the replenishment order + safety stock. The fixed cost of a warehouse is \$200,000 + x, where x is its capacity in books. The weekly operating cost of a warehouse is \$0.01y, where y is the number of books shipped. Books-On-Line is planning its network strategy. Which zones should have warehouses? Detail all costs involved. Amortize fixed costs over ten years assuming a 10% cost of capital.

3. A European manufacturer of industrial furniture has a factory located in Munich and four warehouses in Western Europe. The warehouses collect customer orders, which are then shipped from the factory. Upon receipt, the warehouse distributes customer orders using small trucks. Daily demand at each of the four warehouses along with distance from Munich is as follows:

Warehouse	*Daily Demand (kg)*	*Distance (km)*
Milan	25,000	800
Paris	35,000	1,000
Copenhagen	20,000	600
Madrid	20,000	1,300

All shipments are by truck. There are three truck sizes available with the following capacities: 40,000 kg (small), 60,000 kg (medium), and 80,000 kg (large). Transportation costs for the three types of trucks are as follows:

Small: $100 + 0.1x$ Euro
Medium: $125 + 0.1x$ Euro
Large: $150 + 0.1x$ Euro

x is the distance to be traveled in kilometers. For replenishment frequency varying between 1 and 4 days for each warehouse, identify the optimal transportation option and the associated cost. What other factors should be considered before deciding on the replenishment frequency?

4. The manager at Albertson's, a grocery chain also selling on-line, has 12 orders that are to be delivered to customers. The location and order size for each customer are shown in Table 10.23.

TABLE 10.23 Customer Locations and Order Sizes for Albertson's

	X Coordinate	*Y Coordinate*	*Order Size*
DC	0	0	
Customer 1	−12	0	74
Customer 2	−5	6	55
Customer 3	−15	7	68
Customer 4	−12	9	109
Customer 5	−3	15	81
Customer 6	0	20	41
Customer 7	2	17	74
Customer 8	4	7	52
Customer 9	6	1	80
Customer 10	6	15	69
Customer 11	7	20	103
Customer 12	9	7	75

The Alberston's fulfillment store has five trucks, each capable of carrying up to 225 units. Use the savings matrix and generalized assignment methods to devise suitable delivery schedules. What is the total distance traveled under each schedule?

Bibliography

Ballou, Ronald H. *Business Logistics Management.* Upper Saddle River, N.J.: Prentice Hall, 1999.

Bowersox, D. J., D. J. Closs, and O. K. Helferich. *Logistical Management.* New York: Macmillan Publishing Company, 1986.

Coyle, John J., Edward J. Bardi, and Robert A. Novack. *Transportation.* Cincinnati: South-Western College Publishing, 2000.

Christofides, N., and S. Eilon. "An Algorithm for the Vehicle Dispatching Problem." *Operations Research Quarterly* 20, 3, (1969) 309–318.

Fisher, M. L., A. J. Greenfield, R. Jaikumar, and J. T. Lester III. "A Computerized Vehicle Routing Application." *Interfaces* (August 1982), 42–52.

Fisher, M. L., and R. Jaikumar. "A Generalized Assignment Heuristic for Vehicle Routing." *Networks* 11, 1981, pp. 109–124.

Hammond, J. H., and J. E. P. Morrison. "Note on the U.S. Transportation Industry." Harvard Business School note 688080.

Lin, S., and B. Kernighan. "An effective Heuristic Algorithm for the Traveling Salesman Problem." *Operations Research* 21 (1973), 498–516.

Robeson, J. F., and W. C. Copacino. *The Logistics Handbook.* New York: The Free Press, 1994.

Shapiro, R. D., and J. L. Heskett. *Logistics Strategy: Cases and Concepts.* St. Paul, Minnesota: West Publishing Co., 1985.

Tyworth, J. E., J. L. Cavinato, and C. J. Langley, Jr. *Traffic Management: Planning, Operations, and Control.* Prospect Heights, Ill.: Waveland Press, 1991.

CHAPTER 11

Facility Decisions: Network Design in a Supply Chain

Learning Objectives
After reading this chapter, you will be able to

1. understand the role of facility decisions in designing a supply chain network;
2. identify factors influencing supply chain network design decisions;
3. develop a framework for making network design decisions; and
4. use optimization for facility location and capacity allocation decisions.

In this chapter, we provide an understanding of the role of facilities within a supply chain. We focus on the fundamental questions of facility location and capacity allocation when designing a supply network. We identify and discuss the role of various factors that influence the facility location and capacity allocation decision. We then establish a framework and discuss various solution methodologies for facility location and capacity allocation decisions in a supply chain.

11.1 THE ROLE OF FACILITY DECISIONS IN A SUPPLY CHAIN

Supply chain **facility decisions** include the location of manufacturing, storage, or transportation-related facilities and the allocation of capacity and roles to each facility. Facility decisions are also referred to as **supply chain network design decisions** and are classified as follows:

1. **Facility role**. What role should each facility play? What processes are performed at each facility?
2. **Facility location**. Where should facilities be located?
3. **Capacity allocation**. How much capacity should be allocated to each facility?
4. **Market and supply allocation**. What markets should each facility serve? Which supply sources should feed each facility?

All network design decisions affect each other and must be made taking this fact into consideration. Decisions regarding the role of each facility are significant because they determine the amount of flexibility the supply chain has in changing the way it meets demand. For example, Toyota has plants located worldwide in each major market that it serves. Prior to 1997, each plant was capable of serving only its local market. This hurt Toyota when the Asian economy went into a recession. The local plants in Asia had a lot of idle capacity that could not be used to serve other markets that had excess demand. Toyota has now added flexibility to each plant to be able to serve markets other than the local one. This additional flexibility helps Toyota deal more effectively with changing global market conditions.

Facility location decisions have a long-term impact on a supply chain's performance. It is very expensive to shut down a facility or move it to a different location. As a result, companies must live with their location decisions for a long time—in many cases, decades. A good location decision can help a supply chain be responsive while keeping its costs low. Toyota, for example, built its assembly plant in the United States in Lexington, Kentucky, in 1988 and has used the plant since then. The Lexington plant proved very profitable for Toyota when the yen strengthened and cars produced in Japan were too expensive to be cost-competitive with cars produced in the United Sates. The plant allowed Toyota to be responsive to the American market while keeping costs low.

In contrast, a poorly located facility makes it very difficult for a supply chain to perform close to the efficient frontier. For example, Amazon.com found it very difficult to be responsive and cost-effective in supplying books throughout the United States when it had a single warehouse in Seattle. As a result, the company has added warehouses located in other parts of the country.

Capacity allocation decisions also have a significant impact on supply chain performance. Although capacity allocation can be altered more easily than location, capacity decisions do tend to stay in place for several years. Allocating too much capacity to a location results in poor utilization and as a result higher costs. Allocating too little capacity results in poor responsiveness if demand is not satisfied or high cost if demand is filled from a distant facility.

The allocation of supply sources and markets to facilities has a significant impact on performance because it affects total production, inventory, and transportation costs incurred by the supply chain to satisfy customer demand. This decision should be reconsidered on a regular basis so that the allocation can be changed as market conditions or plant capacities change. For example, as Amazon.com has grown its customer base, the company has built new warehouses and changed the markets supplied by each warehouse. As a result, it has lowered costs and improved responsiveness. Of course, the allocation of markets and supply sources can be changed only if the facilities are flexible enough to serve different markets and receive supply from different sources.

Network design decisions have a significant impact on performance because they determine the supply chain configuration and set constraints within which inventory, transportation, and information can be used to either decrease supply chain cost or increase responsiveness. A company has to focus on network design decisions as its demand grows and its current configuration becomes too expensive or provides poor responsiveness. For example, Dell has built a facility in Brazil to serve its South American market because the factories in Texas, Ireland, and Malaysia could not do so in the most profitable manner.

Network design decisions are also very important when two companies merge. Because the markets served by the combined firm are different from those served by either of the two separate firms, consolidating some facilities and changing the location and role of others can often help reduce cost and improve responsiveness.

We focus on developing a framework as well as methodologies that can be used for network design in a supply chain. In the next section, we identify various factors that influence network design decisions.

11.2 FACTORS INFLUENCING NETWORK DESIGN DECISIONS

Macroeconomic, political, strategic, technological, infrastructure, competitive, and logistical and operational factors influence network design decisions in supply chains. The following sections elaborate on these factors.

Strategic Factors

A firm's competitive strategy has a significant impact on network design decisions within the supply chain. Firms focusing on cost leadership will tend to find the lowest-cost location for their manufacturing facilities, even if that means locating very far from the markets they serve. For example, in the early 1980s, many apparel producers moved all their manufacturing out of the United States to countries with lower labor costs with the hope of lowering their costs.

Firms focusing on responsiveness will tend to locate facilities closer to the market and may select a high-cost location if this choice allows the firm to react quickly to changing market needs. Apparel manufacturers in Italy have developed very flexible production facilities that allow them to provide a high level of variety quickly. Companies that value this responsiveness use the Italian manufacturers in spite of their higher cost.

Convenience store chains aim to provide easy access to customers as part of their competitive strategy. Convenience store networks thus contain many stores that cover an area, though each store is not very large. In contrast, discount stores like Sam's Club have a competitive strategy that focuses on providing low prices. Thus, their networks have very large stores, and customers often have to travel some distance to get to one. An area covered by one Sam's Club store may contain many convenience stores.

Global supply chain networks can best support their strategic objectives with facilities in different countries playing different roles. For example, Nike has production facilities located in many countries in Asia. The facilities in China and Indonesia focus on cost and produce the mass-market, lower-priced shoes for Nike. In contrast, facilities in Korea and Taiwan focus on responsiveness and produce the higher-priced new designs. This differentiation allows Nike to satisfy a wide variety of demands in the most profitable manner.

It is important for a firm to identify the mission or strategic role of each facility when designing its global network. Ferdows suggests the following classification of possible strategic roles for various facilities in a global supply chain network:[1]

1. **Offshore facility—low-cost facility for export production**. An offshore facility serves the role of being a low-cost supply source for markets located outside the country where the facility is located. The location selected for an offshore facility should have low labor and other costs to facilitate low-cost production. Given that many Asian developing countries waive import tariffs if all the output from a factory is exported, they are preferred sites for offshore manufacturing facilities.

2. **Source facility—low-cost facility for global production**. A source facility also has low cost as its primary objective, but its strategic role is broader than that of an offshore facility. A source facility is often a primary source of product for the entire global network. Source facilities tend to be located in places where production costs are relatively low, infrastructure is well-developed, and a skilled workforce is available. Good offshore facilities evolve over time into source facilities. A good example is Nike's plants in Korea and Taiwan. Plants in both countries started out as offshore facilities because of low labor costs. Over time, however, these plants have become more involved with new product development and manufacture some products for sale all over the world.

3. **Server facility—regional production facility**. A server facility's objective is to supply the market where it is located. A server facility is built because of tax incentives, local content requirement, tariff barriers, or high logistics cost to supply the region from elsewhere. In the late 1970s, Suzuki partnered with the Indian government to set up Maruti Udyog. Initially, Maruti was set up as a server facility and only produced cars for the Indian market. The Maruti facility allowed Suzuki to overcome the high tariffs for imported cars in India.

4. **Contributor facility—regional production facility with development skills**. A contributor facility serves the market where it is located but also assumes responsibility for product customization, process improvements, product modifications, or product development. Most well-managed server facilities become contributor facilities over time. The Maruti facility in India today develops many new products for both the Indian and the overseas markets and has moved from being a server to a contributor facility in the Suzuki network.

5. **Outpost facility—regional production facility built to gain local skills**. An outpost facility is located primarily to obtain access to knowledge or skills that may exist within a certain region. Given its location, it also plays the role of a server facility. The primary objective remains one of being a source of knowledge and skills for the entire network. Many global firms have production facilities located in Japan in spite of the high operating costs. Most of these serve as outpost facilities.

6. **Lead facility—facility that leads in development and process technologies**. A lead facility creates new products, processes, and technologies for the entire network. Lead facilities are located in areas with good access to a skilled workforce and technological resources.

[1] Ferdows (1997).

Technological Factors

Characteristics of available production technologies have a significant impact on network design decisions. If production technology displays significant economies of scale, few high-capacity locations are the most effective. This is the case in the manufacture of computer chips, in which factories require a very large investment. As a result, most companies build few chip production facilities, and each one they build has a very large capacity.

In contrast, if facilities have lower fixed costs, many local facilities are preferred because this helps lower transportation costs. For example, bottling plants for Coca-Cola do not have a very high fixed cost. To reduce transportation costs, Coca-Cola sets up many bottling plants all over the world, each serving its local market.

Flexibility of the production technology affects the degree of consolidation that can be achieved in the network. If the production technology is very inflexible and product requirements vary from one country to another, a firm has to set up local facilities to serve the market in each country. Conversely, if the technology is flexible, it becomes easier to consolidate manufacturing in a few large facilities.

Macroeconomic Factors

Macroeconomic factors include taxes, tariffs, exchange rates, and other economic factors that are not internal to an individual firm. As trade has increased and markets have become more global, macroeconomic factors have had a significant influence on the success or failure of supply chain networks. Therefore, it is imperative that firms take these factors into account when making network design decisions.

Tariffs and Tax Incentives

Tariffs refer to any duties that must be paid when product or equipment are moved across international, state, or city boundaries. Tariffs have a strong influence on location decisions within a supply chain. If a country has very high tariffs, companies either do not serve the local market or set up manufacturing plants within the country to save on duties. High tariffs lead to more production locations within a supply chain network, with each location having a lower allocated capacity. As tariffs have come down with the World Trade Organization and regional agreements, like NAFTA (North America) and MERCOSUR (South America), firms can now supply the market within a country from a plant located outside that country without incurring high duties. As a result, firms have begun to consolidate their global production and distribution facilities. For global firms, a decrease in tariffs has led to a decrease in the number of manufacturing facilities and an increase in the capacity of each facility built.

Tax incentives are a reduction in tariffs or taxes that countries, states, and cities often provide to encourage firms to locate their facilities in specific areas. Many countries vary incentives from city to city to encourage investments in areas with lower economic development. Such incentives are often a key factor in the final location decision for many plants. General Motors built its Saturn facility in Tennessee primarily because of the tax incentives offered by the state. Similarly, BMW built its factory, which assembles the Z3, in Spartanburg, mainly because of the tax incentives offered by South Carolina.

Developing countries often create **free trade zones**, where duties and tariffs are relaxed as long as production is used primarily for export. This creates a strong incentive for global firms to set up a plant in these countries to be able to exploit their low labor costs. In China, for example, the establishment of a free trade zone near GuangZhou has led to several global firms locating facilities there.

Many developing countries also provide additional tax incentives based on training, meals, transportation, and other benefits offered to the workforce. Tariffs may also vary based on the product's level of technology. China, for example, waives tariffs entirely for high-tech products in an effort to encourage companies to locate there and bring in state-of-the-art technology. Motorola located a large chip manufacturing plant in China to take advantage of the reduced tariffs and other incentives available to high-tech products.

Many countries, including the United States and the European Union, also place minimum requirements on local content and limits on imports. Such policies lead companies to set up many facilities and source from local suppliers. For example, the United States has limits on the import of apparel from different countries. As a result, companies develop suppliers in many countries to avoid reaching the limit from any one country. Policies that restrict imports from countries lead to an increase in the number of production sites within the supply chain network.

Exchange Rate and Demand Risk

Fluctuation in exchange rates has a significant impact on the profits of any supply chain serving global markets. A firm that sells its product in the United States with production in Japan is exposed to the risk of appreciation of the yen. In this case, the cost of production is incurred in yen, while revenues are obtained in dollars. Thus, an increase in the value of the yen increases the production cost in dollars, decreasing the firm's profits. In the 1980s, many Japanese manufacturers faced this problem when the yen appreciated in value. At that time most of their production capacity was located in Japan, and they served large markets overseas. The appreciation of the yen decreased their revenues, and they saw their profits decline. Most Japanese manufacturers have responded by building production facilities all over the world.

Exchange rate risks may be handled using financial instruments that limit, or hedge against, the loss due to fluctuations. Suitably designed supply chain networks, however, offer the opportunity to take advantage of exchange rate fluctuations and increase profits. An effective way to do this is to build some overcapacity in the network and make the capacity flexible so that it can be used to supply different markets. This flexibility allows the firm to alter production flows within the supply chain to produce more in facilities that have a lower cost based on current exchange rates.

Companies must also take into account fluctuations in demand caused by fluctuations in the economies of different countries. For example, the Asian economies slowed down between 1996 and 1998. Firms that had plants with little flexibility saw a lot of unutilized capacity in their Asian plants. Firms with greater flexibility in their manufacturing facilities were able to use the extra capacity in their Asian plants to meet the needs of other countries where demand was high. As mentioned earlier in the chapter, in 1997 Toyota had assembly plants in Asia that were only capable of producing for the local market. The Asian crisis motivated Toyota to make the plants more flexible to be able to supply demand from other countries.

When designing supply chain networks, companies must build appropriate flexibility to help counter fluctuations in exchange rates and demand across different countries.

Political Factors

The political stability of the country under consideration plays a significant role in the location choice. Companies prefer to locate facilities in politically stable countries where the rules of commerce are well defined. Countries with independent and clear legal systems allow firms to feel that they have recourse in the courts should they need it. This makes it easier for companies to invest in facilities in these countries. Political stability is hard to quantify, so a firm makes an essentially subjective evaluation when designing its supply chain network.

Infrastructure Factors

The availability of good infrastructure is an important prerequisite to locating a facility in a given area. Poor infrastructure adds to the cost of doing business from a given location. Global companies have located their factories in China near Shanghai, Tianjin, or GuangZhuo, even though these locations do not have the lowest labor or land cost because of better infrastructure at these locations. Key infrastructure elements to be considered during network design include availability of sites, labor availability, proximity to transportation terminals, rail service, proximity to airports and seaports, highway access, congestion, and local utilities.

Competitive Factors

Companies must consider competitors' strategy, size, and location when designing their supply chain networks. A fundamental decision firms make is whether to locate their facilities close to competitors or far from them. How the firms compete and whether external factors such as raw material or labor availability force them to locate close to each other influence this decision.

Positive Externalities Between Firms

Positive externalities are instances in which the collocation of multiple firms benefits all of them. Positive externalities lead to competitors locating close to each other. For example, gas stations and retail stores tend to locate close to each other because doing so increases the overall demand, thus benefiting all parties. By locating together in a mall, competing retail stores make it more convenient for customers who need only drive to one location and find everything they are looking for. This increases the total number of customers who visit the mall, increasing demand for all stores located there.

Another example of positive externality occurs when the presence of a competitor leads to the development of appropriate infrastructure in a developing area. In India, for example, Suzuki was the first foreign auto manufacturer to set up a manufacturing facility. The company went to considerable effort and built a local supplier network. Given the well-established supplier base in India, Suzuki's competitors have also built assembly plants there, because they now find it more effective to build cars in India rather than import them to the country.

Locating to Split the Market

When there are no positive externalities, firms locate to be able to capture the largest possible share of the market. A simple model first proposed by Hotelling explains the issues behind this decision.[2]

When firms do not control price but compete on distance from the customer, they can maximize market share by locating close to each other and splitting the market. Consider a situation in which customers are uniformly located along the line segment between 0 and 1, and two firms compete based on their distance from the customer, as

[2]Tirole (1997).

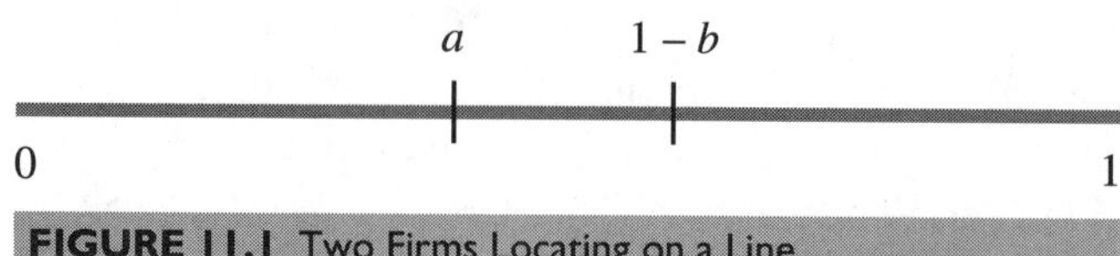

FIGURE 11.1 Two Firms Locating on a Line

shown in Figure 11.1. A customer goes to the closest firm, and customers that are equidistant from the two firms are evenly split between them.

If total demand is 1, firm 1 locates at point a, and firm 2 locates at point $1 - b$, the demand at the two firms, d_1 and d_2, is given by the following:

$$d_1 = \frac{1 - b + a}{2} \quad \text{and} \quad d_2 = \frac{1 + b - a}{2}$$

Clearly, both firms maximize their market share if they move closer to each other and locate at $a = b = 1/2$.

Observe that when both firms locate in the middle of the line segment, the average distance that customers have to travel is 1/4. If one firm locates at 1/4 and the other at 3/4, the average distance that customers travel drops to 1/8. This set of locations, however, gives both firms an incentive to try to increase market share by moving to the middle. The result of competition is for both firms to locate close together even though doing so increases the average distance to the customer.

If the firms compete on price and incur the transportation cost to the customer, it may be optimal for the two firms to locate as far apart as possible,[3] with firm 1 locating at 0 and firm 2 locating at 1. Locating far from each other minimizes price competition and helps the firms split the market and maximize profits.

Customer Response Time and Local Presence

Firms must consider the response time customers desire when designing their supply chain networks. Firms that target customers who can tolerate a large response time require few locations and can focus on increasing the capacity of each location. In contrast, firms that target customers who value short response times need to locate close to them. These firms must have many facilities, with each location having a low capacity. Thus, a decrease in the response time customers desire increases the number of facilities required in the network, as shown in Figure 11.2.

For example, customers are unlikely to come to a convenience store if they have to travel a long distance to get there. It is thus best for a convenience store chain to have many stores distributed in an area so that most people have a convenience store close to them. In contrast, customers shop for larger amounts at supermarkets and are willing to travel longer distances to get to one. Thus, supermarket chains tend to have stores that are much larger than convenience stores and not as densely distributed. Most towns have fewer supermarkets than convenience stores. Discounters like Sam's Club target customers who are even less time-sensitive. These stores are even larger than supermarkets, and there are fewer of them in an area. W.W. Grainger uses 350 facilities all over the United States to provide same-day delivery of maintenance, repair, and operation (MRO) supplies to many of its customers. McMaster-Carr, a competitor, targets customers who are willing to wait for next-day delivery. McMaster-

[3] Ibid.

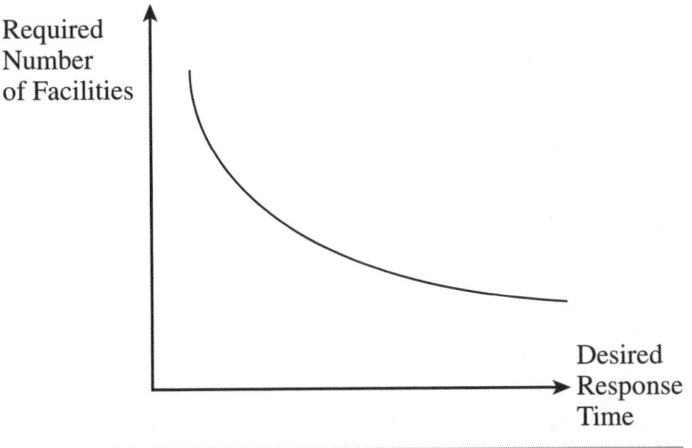

FIGURE 11.2 Relationship Between Desired Response Time and Number of Facilities

Carr has only five facilities throughout the United States and is able to provide next-day delivery to a large number of customers.

If a firm is delivering its product to customers, use of a rapid means of transportation allows it to build fewer facilities (see Chapter 10) and still provide a short response time. However, this option increases transportation cost. Moreover, there are many situations in which the presence of a facility close to a customer is important. For example, a coffee shop is likely to attract customers who live or work nearby. No faster mode of transport can serve as a substitute and be used to attract customers that are far away.

Logistics and Facility Costs

Logistics and facility costs incurred within a supply chain change as the number of facilities, their location, and capacity allocation is changed. Companies must consider inventory, transportation, and facility costs when designing their supply chain networks.

Inventory Costs

As the number of facilities in a supply chain increases, the inventory and resulting inventory costs also increase (see Chapter 8), as shown in Figure 11.3.

To decrease inventory costs, firms try to consolidate and limit the number of facilities in their supply chain network.

Transportation Costs

Inbound transportation costs are the costs incurred in bringing material into a facility. **Outbound transportation costs** are the costs incurred in sending material out of a facility. Outbound transportation costs per unit tend to be higher than inbound costs because inbound lot sizes are typically larger. For example, the Amazon.com warehouse receives full truckload shipments of books on the inbound side, but ships out small packages with a few books per customer on the outbound side. Increasing the number of warehouse locations decreases the average distance to a customer and thus the distance that a product has to travel on the outbound side. Thus, increasing the

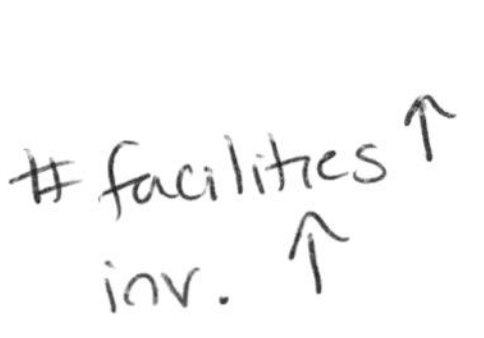

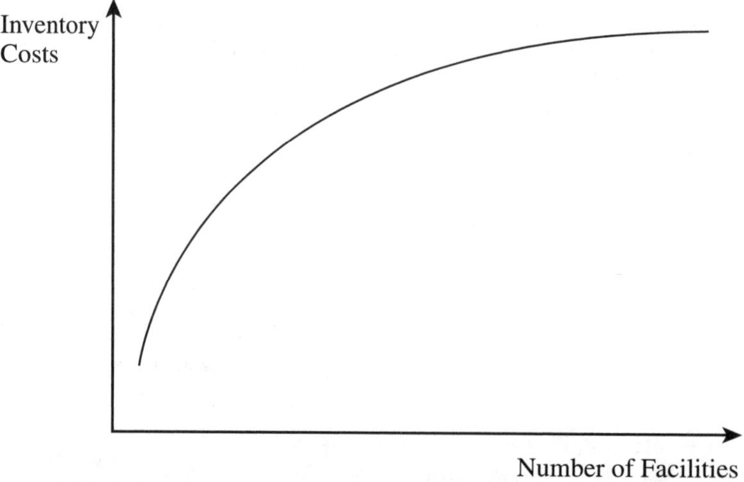

FIGURE 11.3 Relationship Between Number of Facilities and Inventory Costs

number of facilities decreases transportation cost, as shown in Figure 11.4. If the number of facilities is increased to a point where inbound lot sizes are also very small, increasing the number of facilities increases transportation cost, as shown in Figure 11.4. As it has grown, Amazon.com has increased the number of warehouses in its network in an effort to reduce transportation cost and improve response time.

When there is a significant reduction in material weight or volume as a result of processing, it may be better to locate facilities closer to the supply source rather than the customer. For example, when iron ore is processed to make steel, the amount of output is a small fraction of the amount of ore used. Locating the steel factory close to the supply source is preferred because it reduces the distance that the large quantity of ore has to travel.

FIGURE 11.4 Relationship Between Number of Facilities and Transportation Cost

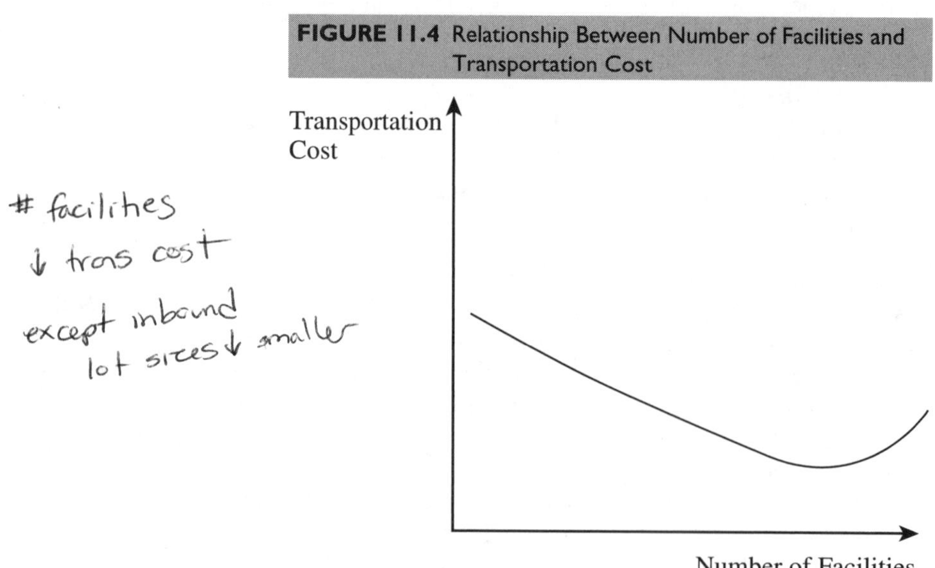

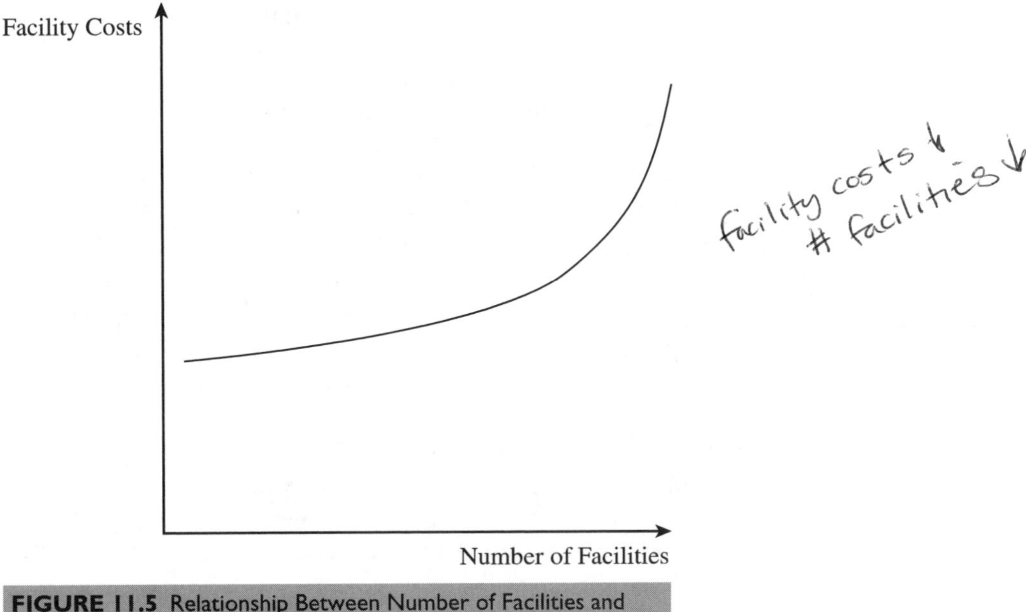

FIGURE 11.5 Relationship Between Number of Facilities and Facility Costs

Facility (Setup and Operating) Costs

Costs a firm incurs at any facility can be divided into two categories: fixed and variable. Costs such as leasing or construction costs are treated as fixed, because in the short term they do not vary with the quantity flowing through the facility. Costs associated with production or warehouse operation do vary with the quantity being handled and are thus considered variable. Facility costs decrease as the number of facilities is reduced, as shown in Figure 11.5, because a consolidation of facilities allows a firm to exploit some economies of scale in both fixed and variable costs.

Total logistics costs are the sum of inventory, transportation, and facility costs for a supply chain network. As the number of facilities is increased, total logistics costs first decrease and then increase, as shown in Figure 11.6. Each firm should have at

FIGURE 11.6 Variation in Logistics Cost and Response Time with Number of Facilities

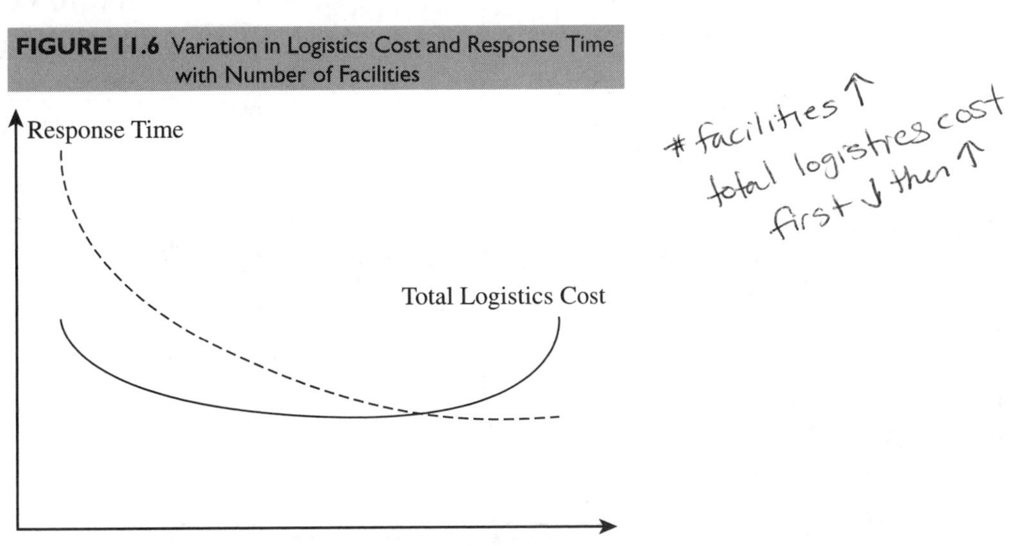

least the number of facilities that minimize total logistics costs. For example, Amazon.com has been adding to the number of warehouses it has primarily to reduce its logistics costs and improve response time. As a firm wants to further reduce the response time to its customers, it may have to increase the number of facilities beyond the point that minimizes logistics costs. A firm should add facilities beyond the cost-minimizing point only if managers are confident that the increase in revenues because of better responsiveness is greater than the increase in costs because of the additional facilities.

In the next section we discuss a framework for making network design decisions.

11.4 A FRAMEWORK FOR NETWORK DESIGN DECISIONS

Global network design decisions are made in four phases, as shown in Figure 11.7. In the following sections, we describe each phase in greater detail.

Phase I: Define a Supply Chain Strategy

The objective of the first phase of network design is to define a firm's supply chain strategy. The supply chain strategy specifies what capabilities the supply chain network must have to support a firm's competitive strategy (see Chapter 2).

FIGURE 11.7 A Framework for Network Design Decisions

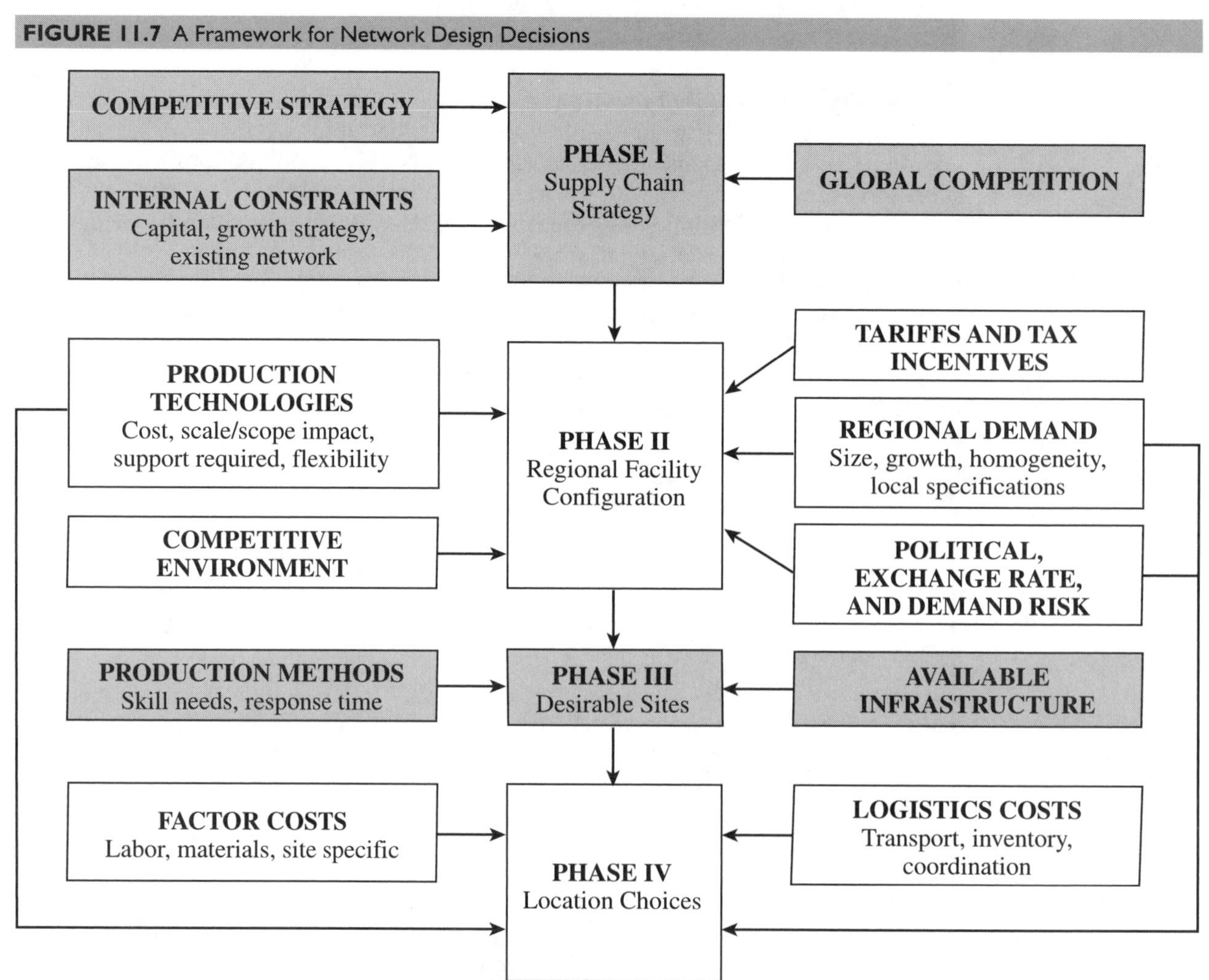

Phase I starts with a clear definition of the firm's competitive strategy as the set of customer needs that the supply chain aims to satisfy. Next, managers must forecast the likely evolution of global competition and whether competitors in each market will be local or global players. Managers must also identify constraints on available capital and whether growth will be accomplished by acquiring existing facilities, building new facilities, or partnering.

Based on the competitive strategy of the firm, an analysis of the competition, any economies of scale or scope, and any constraints, managers must determine the supply chain strategy for the firm.

Phase II: Define the Regional Facility Configuration

The objective of the second phase of network design is to identify regions where facilities will be located, their potential roles, and their approximate capacity.

An analysis of Phase II is started with a forecast of the demand by country. Such a forecast must include a measure of the size of the demand as well as a determination of whether the customer requirements are homogenous or variable across different countries. Homogenous requirements favor large consolidated facilities, whereas requirements that vary across countries favor smaller, localized facilities.

The next step is for managers to identify whether economies of scale or scope can play a significant role in reducing costs given available production technologies. If economies of scale or scope are significant, it may be better to have a few facilities serving many markets. If economies of scale or scope are not significant, it may be better for each market to have its own facility. For example, Coca-Cola has bottling plants in every market that it serves because the manufacturing technology does not include large economies of scale. Chip manufacturers like Motorola, in contrast, have very few plants for their global markets given the economies of scale in production.

Next, managers must identify demand risk, exchange rate risk, and political risk associated with different regional markets. They must also identify regional tariffs, any requirements for local production, tax incentives, and any export or import restrictions for each market.

Managers must identify competitors in each region and make a case for whether a facility needs to be located close to or far from a competitor's facility. The desired response time for each market must also be identified.

Based on all this information, managers will identify the regional facility configuration for the supply chain network. The regional configuration defines the approximate number of facilities in the network, regions where facilities will be set up, and whether a facility will make all products for a given market or a few products for all markets in the network.

Phase III: Select Desirable Sites

The objective of the third phase is to select a set of desirable sites within each region where facilities are to be located. The set of desirable sites should be larger than the desired number of facilities to be set up so that a precise selection may be made in Phase IV.

Sites should be selected based on an analysis of infrastructure availability to support the desired production methodologies. **Hard infrastructure requirements** include the availability of suppliers, transportation services, communication, utilities, and warehousing infrastructure. **Soft infrastructure requirements** include the availability of skilled workforce, workforce turnover, and the community receptivity to business and industry.

Phase IV: Choose Location

The objective of this phase is to select a precise location and capacity allocation for each facility. Attention is restricted to the desirable sites selected in Phase III. The network is designed to maximize total profits, taking into account the expected margin and demand in each market along with the various logistics and facility costs.

In the next section we discuss methodologies for making facility location and capacity allocation decisions during Phase IV.

11.4 MODELS FOR FACILITY LOCATION AND CAPACITY ALLOCATION

Managers' goal when locating facilities and allocating capacity should be to maximize the overall profitability of the resulting supply chain network. The following information must be available before the design decision can be made:

- Location of supply sources and markets
- Location of potential facility sites
- Demand forecast by market
- Facility, labor, and material costs by site
- Transportation costs between each pair of sites
- Inventory costs by site as well as a function of quantity

Given this information, either gravity or network optimization models may be used to design the network.

Gravity Location Models

Gravity models are used to find locations that minimize the cost of transporting raw materials from suppliers and finished goods to the markets served. Gravity models assume that both the markets and the supply sources can be located as grid points on a plane. All distances are calculated as the geometric distance between two points on the plane. These models also assume that the transportation cost grows linearly with the quantity shipped. We discuss a gravity model for locating a single facility that receives raw material from supply sources and ships finished product to markets. The basic inputs to the model are as follows:

x_n, y_n: Coordinate location of either a market or supply source n

F_n: Cost of shipping one unit for one mile between the facility and either market or supply source n

D_n: Quantity to be shipped between facility and market or supply source n

If (x, y) is the location selected for the facility, the distance d_n between the facility at location (x, y) and the supply source or market n is as follows:

$$d_n = \sqrt{(x - x_n)^2 + (y - y_n)^2} \qquad \textbf{(11.1)}$$

Then the total transportation cost TC is as follows:

$$TC = \sum_{n=1}^{k} d_n D_n F_n \qquad \textbf{(11.2)}$$

The location that minimizes the total cost TC is obtained by iterating through the following three steps where (x, y) is the location of the facility to begin each iteration:

1. For each supply source or market n, evaluate d_n as defined in Equation 11.1.
2. Obtain a new location (x', y') for the facility, where

$$x' = \frac{\sum_{n=1}^{k} \frac{D_n F_n x_n}{d_n}}{\sum_{n=1}^{k} \frac{D_n F_n}{d_n}} \quad \text{and} \quad y' = \frac{\sum_{n=1}^{k} \frac{D_n F_n y_n}{d_n}}{\sum_{n=1}^{k} \frac{D_n F_n}{d_n}}, \tag{11.3}$$

3. If the new location (x', y') is almost the same as (x, y) stop. Otherwise, set $(x, y) = (x', y')$ and go to step 1.

We illustrate the procedure for Steel Appliances, a manufacturer of high-quality refrigerators and cooking ranges. Steel Appliances has one assembly factory located near Denver from which it has supplied the entire United States. Demand has grown rapidly, and the chief executive officer of Steel Appliances has decided to set up another factory to serve its eastern markets. The supply chain manager is asked to find a suitable location for the new factory. Three parts plants located in Buffalo, New York; Memphis, Tennessee; and St. Louis, Missouri will supply parts to the new factory, which will serve markets in Atlanta, Boston, Jacksonville, Philadelphia, and New York. The coordinate location, the demand in each market, the required supply from each parts plant, and the shipping cost for each supply source or market are shown in Table 11.1.

The supply chain manager decides to obtain the location of the new facility using the iterative procedure described earlier. The manager selects the initial location of the factory to be coordinates $x = 0$ and $y = 0$. The analysis for the first iteration is provided in Table 11.2.

TABLE 11.1 Locations of Supply Sources and Markets for Steel Appliances

Sources/ Markets	*Transportation Cost \$/Ton Mile (F_n)*	*Quantity in Tons (D_n)*	*Coordinates*	
			x_n	y_n
Supply Sources				
Buffalo	0.90	500	700	1200
Memphis	0.95	300	250	600
St. Louis	0.85	700	225	825
Markets				
Atlanta	1.50	225	600	500
Boston	1.50	150	1050	1200
Jacksonville	1.50	250	800	300
Philadelphia	1.50	175	925	975
New York	1.50	300	1000	1080

TABLE 11.2 Analysis for First Iteration for Steel Appliances

Source Market	x_n	y_n	d_n	D_n	F_n	$D_nF_nx_n/d_n$	$D_nF_ny_n/d_n$	D_nF_n/d_n
Buffalo	700	1200	1389	500	0.90	226.7	388.7	0.32
Memphis	250	600	650	300	0.95	109.6	263.1	0.44
St. Louis	225	825	855	700	0.85	156.6	574.0	0.70
Atlanta	600	500	781	225	1.50	259.3	216.1	0.43
Boston	1050	1200	1595	150	1.50	148.2	169.3	0.14
Jacksonville	800	300	854	250	1.50	351.1	131.7	0.44
Philadelphia	925	975	1344	175	1.50	180.7	190.4	0.20
New York	1000	1080	1472	300	1.50	305.7	330.2	0.31

From Equation 11.3 and the analysis in Table 11.2, the manager obtains the following:

$$x' = \frac{\sum_{n=1}^{k} \frac{D_nF_nx_n}{d_n}}{\sum_{n=1}^{k} \frac{D_nF_n}{d_n}} = \frac{1737.9}{2.97} = 585 \qquad y' = \frac{\sum_{n=1}^{k} \frac{D_nF_ny_n}{d_n}}{\sum_{n=1}^{k} \frac{D_nF_n}{d_n}} = \frac{2263.5}{2.97} = 762$$

After the first iteration, $(x, y) = (0, 0) \neq (x', y') = (585, 762)$. Thus, the manager sets $(x, y) = (585, 799)$ and starts a new iteration, repeating steps 1 to 3. After 40 such iterations, the manager obtains $(x, y) = (681, 882)$. Repeating steps 1 to 3 again results in $(x', y') = (681, 882)$. The manager thus identifies the coordinates $(x, y) = (681, 882)$ as the location of the factory that minimizes total transportation cost. From a map, these coordinates are close to the border of North Carolina and Virginia. The precise coordinates provided by the gravity model may not correspond to a feasible location. However, by finding a desirable site close to the recommended coordinates, the supply chain manager can locate the factory at a site that results in low transportation cost for Steel Appliances.

Network Optimization Models

When designing a supply chain network, there are usually several stages, including suppliers, plants, warehouses, and markets. There may also be other intermediate facilities such as consolidation centers or transit points. A typical supply network may develop as shown in Figure 11.8.

FIGURE 11.8 Stages in a Supply Network

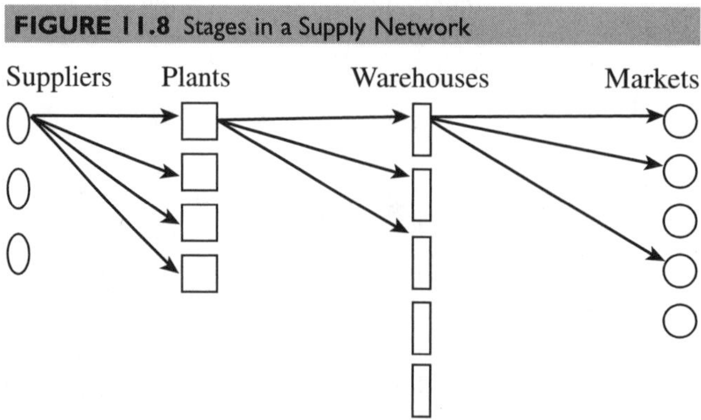

Besides locating the facilities, a manager must also decide how markets will be allocated to warehouses and how warehouses will be allocated to plants. The allocation decision can be altered on a regular basis as different costs change and markets evolve. When designing the network, both location and allocation decisions are made jointly.

There are fixed as well as variable costs associated with facilities, transportation, and inventories at each facility. Fixed costs are those that are incurred no matter how much is produced or shipped from a facility. Variable costs are those that are incurred in proportion to the quantity produced or shipped from a given facility. Variable facility, transportation, and inventory costs generally display economies of scale, and the marginal cost decreases as the quantity produced at a facility increases. However, in the models we consider, all variable costs grow linearly with the quantity produced or shipped.

We illustrate network optimization models using the example of two manufacturers of fiber optic telecommunication equipment. Both TelecomOne and HighOptic are manufacturers of the latest generation of telecommunication equipment. TelecomOne has focused on the eastern half of the United States. It has manufacturing plants located in Baltimore (B), Memphis (M), and Wichita, Kansas (W), and serves markets in Atlanta, Boston, and Chicago. HighOptic has targeted the western half of the United States and serves markets in Denver; Omaha, Nebraska; and Portland, Oregon. HighOptic has plants located in Cheyenne, Wyoming (C), and Salt Lake City (S).

Plant capacities, market demand, variable production and transportation cost per thousand units shipped, and fixed costs per month at each plant are shown in Table 11.3.

Allocating Demand to Production Facilities

From Table 11.3 observe that TelecomOne has a total production capacity of 71,000 units per month and a total demand of 30,000 units per month, and HighOptic has a production capacity of 51,000 units per month and a demand of 24,000 units per month. Managers in both companies must decide how to allocate the demand to their production facilities. This decision will be revisited every year as demand and costs change.

TABLE 11.3 Capacity, Demand, and Cost Data for TelecomOne and HighOptic

	Demand City *Production and Transportation Cost per Thousand Units (Thousand $)*							
Supply City	***Atlanta***	***Boston***	***Chicago***	***Denver***	***Omaha***	***Portland***	***Capacity (Thousand Units)*** K_i	***Monthly Fixed Cost (Thousand $)*** f_i
Baltimore (B)	1,675	400	685	1,630	1,160	2,800	18	7,650
Cheyenne (C)	1,460	1,940	970	100	495	1,200	24	3,500
Salt Lake City (S)	1,925	2,400	1,425	500	950	800	27	5,000
Memphis (M)	380	1,355	543	1,045	665	2,321	22	4,100
Wichita (W)	922	1,646	700	508	311	1,797	31	2,200
Monthly Demand (Thousand Units) D_j	10	8	14	6	7	11		

The demand allocation problem can be solved using a network optimization model. The model requires the following inputs:

n = Number of factory locations
m = Number of markets or demand points
D_j = Annual demand from market j
K_i = Annual capacity of factory i
c_{ij} = Cost of producing and shipping one unit from factory i to market j (cost includes production, inventory, and transportation)

The goal is to allocate the demand from different markets to the various plants to minimize the total cost of facilities, transportation, and inventory. Define the decision variables as follows:

$$x_{ij} = \text{Quantity shipped from factory } i \text{ to market } j \text{ each year}$$

The problem is formulated as the following linear program:

$$Min \sum_{i=1}^{n} \sum_{j=1}^{m} c_{ij}\, x_{ij}$$

Subject to the following constraints:

$$\sum_{i=1}^{n} x_{ij} = D_j \quad \text{for} \quad j = 1, \ldots, m \qquad \textbf{(11.4)}$$

$$\sum_{j=1}^{m} x_{ij} \leq K_i \quad \text{for} \quad i = 1, \ldots, n \qquad \textbf{(11.5)}$$

The constraints in Equation 11.4 ensure that all market demand is satisfied, and the constraints in Equation 11.5 ensure that no factory produces more than its capacity.

For both TelecomOne and HighOptic, the demand allocation problem can be solved using the Solver tool within Excel. The use of Solver is discussed later in the chapter, and only the optimal demand allocation is presented in Table 11.4.

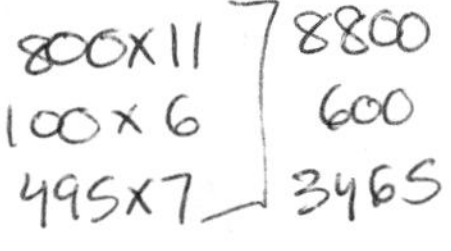

Observe that it is optimal for TelecomOne not to produce anything in the Wichita facility even though the facility is operational. With the demand allocation as shown in Table 11.4, TelecomOne incurs a monthly variable cost of $14,886,000 and a monthly fixed cost of $13,950,000, for a total monthly cost of $28,836,000. HighOptic incurs a monthly variable cost of $12,865,000 and a monthly fixed cost of $8,500,000, for a total monthly cost of $21,365,000.

TABLE 11.4 Optimal Demand Allocation for TelecomOne and HighOptic

		Atlanta	*Boston*	*Chicago*	*Denver*	*Omaha*	*Portland*
TelecomOne	Baltimore	0	8	2			
	Memphis	10	0	12			
	Wichita	0	0	0			
HighOptic	Salt Lake				0	0	11
	Cheyenne				6	7	0

Locating Plants: The Capacitated Plant Location Model

Managers at both TelecomOne and HighOptic have decided to merge the two companies into a single entity to be called TelecomOptic. They feel that significant benefits will result if the two networks are merged appropriately. TelecomOptic will have five factories from which to serve six markets. Management is debating whether all five factories are needed. They have assigned a supply chain team to study the network for the combined company and identify the plants that should be shut down.

The supply chain team decides to use a plant location network optimization model to solve the problem. The model requires the following inputs:

n = Number of potential factory locations
m = Number of markets or demand points
D_j = Annual demand from market j
K_i = Potential annual capacity of factory i
f_i = Annualized fixed cost of keeping factory i open
c_{ij} = Cost of producing and shipping one unit from factory i to market j (cost includes production, inventory, and transportation)

The team's goal is to decide on factory locations and then allocate demand to the open factories so as to minimize the total cost of facilities, transportation, and inventory. Define the following decision variables:

y_i = 1 if factory i is open, 0 otherwise
x_{ij} = Quantity shipped from factory i to market j each year

The problem is then formulated as the following integer program:

$$Min \sum_{i=1}^{n} f_i y_i + \sum_{i=1}^{n} \sum_{j=1}^{m} c_{ij} x_{ij}$$

Subject to the following constraints:

$$\sum_{i=1}^{n} x_{ij} = D_j \quad \text{for} \quad j = 1, \ldots, m \qquad \textbf{(11.6)}$$

$$\sum_{j=1}^{m} x_{ij} \leq K_i y_i \quad \text{for} \quad i = 1, \ldots, n \qquad \textbf{(11.7)}$$

$$y_i \in \{0, 1\} \quad \text{for} \quad i = 1, \ldots, n \qquad \textbf{(11.8)}$$

The objective function minimizes the total cost (fixed + variable) of setting up and operating the network. The constraint in Equation 11.6 requires that the demand at each market be satisfied. The constraint in Equation 11.7 states that no plant can supply more than its capacity. (Clearly the capacity is 0 if the plant is closed and K_i if it is open. The product of terms $K_i y_i$ captures this effect.) The constraint in Equation 11.8 enforces that each factory is either open ($y_i = 1$) or closed ($y_i = 0$). The solution will identify the factories that are to be kept open and the allocation of market demand to these plants.

The capacity and demand data, along with production, transportation, and inventory costs, at different factories for the merged firm TelecomOptic are given in Table 11.3. The supply chain team decides to solve the plant location model using the Solver tool in Excel.

The first step in setting up the Solver model is to enter the cost, demand, and capacity information. The fixed costs f_i for the five plants are entered in cells B3 to B7. The capacities K_i of the five plants are entered in cells I3 to I7. The variable costs c_{ij}

Microsoft Excel - table11.5to11.8.xls

	A	B	C	D	E	F	G	H	I
1	***Costs, Capacities, Demands***								
2		Fixed	Atlanta	Boston	Chicago	Denver	Omaha	Portland	Capacity
3	Baltimore	7650	1675	400	685	1630	1160	2800	18
4	Cheyenne	3500	1460	1940	970	100	495	1200	24
5	Salt Lake	5000	1925	2400	1425	500	950	800	27
6	Memphis	4100	380	1355	543	1045	665	2321	22
7	Wichita	2200	922	1646	700	508	311	1797	31
8			10	8	14	6	7	11	
9									
10	***Variables***	Open/Close	Atlanta	Boston	Chicago	Denver	Omaha	Portland	
11	Baltimore	0	0	0	0	0	0	0	
12	Cheyenne	0	0	0	0	0	0	0	
13	Salt Lake	0	0	0	0	0	0	0	
14	Memphis	0	0	0	0	0	0	0	
15	Wichita	0	0	0	0	0	0	0	

FIGURE 11.9 Spreadsheet Area for Decision Variables

are entered in cells C3 through H7. The demands D_j of the six markets are entered in cells C8 to H8. Next, corresponding to each decision variable x_{ij}, a cell is assigned as shown in Figure 11.9. Initially all variables are set to be 0. Cells B11 to B15 contain the decision variables y_i, and cells C11 through H15 contain the decision variables x_{ij}.

The next step is to construct cells for the constraints in Equations 11.6 and 11.7. The constraint cells are as shown in Figure 11.10. Cells B17 to B21 contain the capac-

FIGURE 11.10 Spreadsheet Area for Constraints

Microsoft Excel - table11.5to11.8.xls

	A	B	C	D	E	F	G	H	I
1	***Costs, Capacities, Demands***								
2		Fixed	Atlanta	Boston	Chicago	Denver	Omaha	Portland	Capacity
3	Baltimore	7650	1675	400	685	1630	1160	2800	18
4	Cheyenne	3500	1460	1940	970	100	495	1200	24
5	Salt Lake	5000	1925	2400	1425	500	950	800	27
6	Memphis	4100	380	1355	543	1045	665	2321	22
7	Wichita	2200	922	1646	700	508	311	1797	31
8			10	8	14	6	7	11	
9									
10	***Variables***	Open/Close	Atlanta	Boston	Chicago	Denver	Omaha	Portland	
11	Baltimore	0	0	0	0	0	0	0	
12	Cheyenne	0	0	0	0	0	0	0	
13	Salt Lake	0	0	0	0	0	0	0	
14	Memphis	0	0	0	0	0	0	0	
15	Wichita	0	0	0	0	0	0	0	
16	***Constraints***	***Capacity***	Atlanta	Boston	Chicago	Denver	Omaha	Portland	
17	Baltimore	0							
18	Cheyenne	0							
19	Salt Lake	0							
20	Memphis	0							
21	Wichita	0							
22	***Demand***		10	8	14	6	7	11	

TABLE 11.5 Cell Formulas in Constraint Area

Cell	*B17*	*C22*
Constraint	Capacity (Equation 11.7)	Demand (Equation 11.6)
Spreadsheet formula	=I3*B11 − sum(C11:H11)	=C8 − sum(C11:C15)
Actual formula	$K_1 y_1 - \sum_{j=1}^{6} x_{1j}$	$D_1 - \sum_{i=1}^{5} x_{i1}$

ity constraints in Equation 11.7, and cells C22 to H22 contain the demand constraints in Equation 11.6. The constraint in B17 corresponds to the capacity constraint for the factory in Baltimore. The cell C22 corresponds to the demand constraint for the market in Atlanta. The various formulas in the constraint cells are given in Table 11.5. The capacity constraints require that the cell value be greater than or equal to ($\geq$) 0, whereas the demand constraints require the cell value to equal 0.

The next step is to construct the objective function cell. The objective function measures the total fixed and variable cost of the supply chain network. In this case, the objective function is the fixed cost plus the variable cost of operating the network. It is located at cell B24 and contains the following formula:

= SUMPRODUCT(C3:H7, C11:H15) + SUMPRODUCT(B3:B7, B11:B15)

The next step is to use Tools/Solver to invoke Solver. Within the Solver parameters dialog box, the following information is entered to represent the plant location problem:

Set Target Cell: B24
Equal to: Select *Min*
By Changing Cells: B11:H15
Subject to the constraints:

B11:H15 ≥ 0 {All decision variables are non-negative}

B11:B15 *bin* {Location variables y_i are binary, that is, 0 or 1}

B17:B21 ≥ 0 $\{K_i y_i - \sum_{j=1}^{m} x_{ij} \geq 0$ for $i = 1, \ldots, 5\}$

C22:H22 = 0 $\{D_j - \sum_{i=1}^{n} x_{ij} = 0$ for $j = 1, \ldots, 6\}$

Within the Solver parameters dialog box, click on Options and then select Assume Linear Models. (This selection speeds up the solution time significantly.) Return to the Solver parameters dialog box; click on Solve. The optimal solution is returned in the variables area and is shown in Figure 11.11.

From Figure 11.11, the supply chain team concludes that it is optimal for TelecomOptic to close the plants in Salt Lake City and Wichita while keeping the plants in Baltimore, Cheyenne, and Memphis open. The total monthly cost of this network and operation is $47,401,000. This cost represents savings of about $3 million per month compared with the situation in which TelecomOne and HighOptic operate separate supply chain networks.

Locating Plants: The Capacitated Plant Location Model with Single Sourcing

In some cases, companies want to design supply chain networks, in which a market is supplied from only one factory, referred to as a **single source**. Companies may

Microsoft Excel - table11.5to11.8.xls

	A	B	C	D	E	F	G	H	I
1	***Costs, Capacities, Demands***								
2		Fixed	Atlanta	Boston	Chicago	Denver	Omaha	Portland	Capacity
3	Baltimore	7650	1675	400	685	1630	1160	2800	18
4	Cheyenne	3500	1460	1940	970	100	495	1200	24
5	Salt Lake	5000	1925	2400	1425	500	950	800	27
6	Memphis	4100	380	1355	543	1045	665	2321	22
7	Wichita	2200	922	1646	700	508	311	1797	31
8			10	8	14	6	7	11	
9									
10	***Variables***	Open/Close	Atlanta	Boston	Chicago	Denver	Omaha	Portland	
11	Baltimore	1	0	8	2	0	0	0	
12	Cheyenne	1	0	0	0	6	7	11	
13	Salt Lake	0	0	0	0	0	0	0	
14	Memphis	1	10	0	12	0	0	0	
15	Wichita	0	0	0	0	0	0	0	
16	***Constraints***	***Capacity***	Atlanta	Boston	Chicago	Denver	Omaha	Portland	
17	Baltimore	8							
18	Cheyenne	0							
19	Salt Lake	0							
20	Memphis	0							
21	Wichita	0							
22	***Demand***		0	0	0	0	0	0	
23									

FIGURE 11.11 Optimal Network Design for Telecom Optic

impose this constraint because it lowers the complexity of coordinating the network and requires less flexibility from each facility. The plant location model discussed earlier needs some modification to accommodate this constraint. The decision variables are redefined as follows:

y_i = 1 if factory is located at site i, 0 otherwise
x_{ij} = 1 if market j is supplied by factory i, 0 otherwise

The problem is formulated as the following integer program:

$$Min \sum_{i=1}^{n} f_i y_i + \sum_{i=1}^{n} \sum_{j=1}^{m} D_j c_{ij} x_{ij}$$

Subject to the following constraints:

$$\sum_{i=1}^{n} x_{ij} = 1 \qquad \text{for} \qquad j = 1, \ldots, m \tag{11.9}$$

$$\sum_{j=1}^{m} D_j x_{ij} \le K_i y_i \qquad \text{for} \qquad i = 1, \ldots, n \tag{11.10}$$

$$x_{ij}, y_i \in \{0, 1\} \tag{11.11}$$

The constraints in Equations 11.9 and 11.11 enforce that each market is supplied by exactly one factory.

TABLE 11.6 Optimal Network Configuration for TelecomOptic with Single Sourcing

	Open/ Closed	*Atlanta*	*Boston*	*Chicago*	*Denver*	*Omaha*	*Portland*
Baltimore	Closed	0	0	0	0	0	0
Cheyenne	Closed	0	0	0	0	0	0
Salt Lake	Open	0	0	0	6	0	11
Memphis	Open	10	8	0	0	0	0
Wichita	Open	0	0	14	0	7	0

Management at the merged company TelecomOptic described earlier would like to identify the optimal supply chain network if each market is to be supplied from a single factory. Using the data in Table 11.3, the plant location model with single sourcing is solved by the supply chain team to obtain the optimal network shown in Table 11.6.

If single sourcing is required, it is optimal for TelecomOptic to close the factories in Baltimore and Cheyenne. This is different from the result in Table 11.8, in which factories in Salt Lake City and Wichita were closed. The monthly cost of operating the network in Table 11.6 is $49,717,000. This cost is about $2.3 million higher than the cost of the network in Figure 11.11, in which single sourcing was not required. The supply chain team thus concludes that single sourcing, while making coordination easier and requiring less flexibility from the plants, will add about $2.3 million per month to the cost of the supply chain network.

Locating Plants and Warehouses Simultaneously

A much more general form of the plant location model needs to be considered if the entire supply chain network from the supplier to the customer must be designed. We consider a supply chain in which suppliers send material to factories that supply warehouses that supply markets. Location and capacity allocation decisions have to be made for both factories and warehouses. Multiple warehouses may be used to satisfy demand at a market, and multiple factories may be used to replenish warehouses. It is also assumed that units have been appropriately adjusted such that one unit of input from a supply source produces one unit of the finished product. The model requires the following inputs:

m = Number of markets or demand points
n = Number of potential factory locations
l = Number of suppliers
t = Number of potential warehouse locations
D_j = Annual demand from customer j
K_i = Potential annual capacity of factory at site i
S_h = Annual supply capacity at supplier h
W_e = Potential annual warehouse capacity at site e
F_i = Fixed annual cost of locating a plant at site i
f_e = Fixed annual cost of locating a warehouse at site e
c_{hi} = Cost of shipping one unit from supply source h to factory i
c_{ie} = Cost of producing and shipping one unit from factory i to warehouse e
c_{ej} = Cost of shipping one unit from warehouse e to customer j

The goal is to identify plant and warehouse locations as well as quantities shipped between various points that minimize the total fixed and variable costs. Define the following decision variables:

y_i = 1 if factory is located at site i, 0 otherwise
y_e = 1 if warehouse is located at site e, 0 otherwise
x_{ej} = Quantity shipped from warehouse e to market j per year
x_{ie} = Quantity shipped from factory at site i to warehouse e per year
x_{hi} = Quantity shipped from supplier h to factory at site i per year

The problem is formulated as the following integer program:

$$Min \sum_{i=1}^{n} f_i y_i + \sum_{e=1}^{t} f_e y_e + \sum_{h=1}^{l} \sum_{i=1}^{n} c_{hi} x_{hi} + \sum_{i=1}^{n} \sum_{e=1}^{t} c_{ie} x_{ie} + \sum_{e=1}^{t} \sum_{j=1}^{m} c_{ej} x_{ej}$$

Subject to the following constraints:

$$\sum_{i=1}^{n} x_{hi} \le S_h \quad \text{for} \quad h = 1, \ldots, 1 \qquad \textbf{(11.12)}$$

$$\sum_{h=1}^{l} x_{hi} - \sum_{e=1}^{t} x_{ie} \ge 0 \quad \text{for} \quad i = 1, \ldots, n \qquad \textbf{(11.13)}$$

$$\sum_{e=1}^{t} x_{ie} \le K_i y_i \quad \text{for} \quad i = 1, \ldots, n \qquad \textbf{(11.14)}$$

$$\sum_{i=1}^{n} x_{ie} - \sum_{j=1}^{m} x_{ej} \ge 0 \quad \text{for} \quad e = 1, \ldots, t \qquad \textbf{(11.15)}$$

$$\sum_{j=1}^{m} x_{ej} \le W_e y_e \quad \text{for} \quad e = 1, \ldots, t \qquad \textbf{(11.16)}$$

$$\sum_{e=1}^{t} x_{ej} = D_j \quad \text{for} \quad j = 1, \ldots, m \qquad \textbf{(11.17)}$$

$$y_i, y_e \in \{0, 1\} \qquad \textbf{(11.18)}$$

The objective function minimizes the total fixed and variable costs of the supply chain network. The constraint in Equation 11.12 specifies that the total amount shipped from a supplier cannot exceed the supplier's capacity. The constraint in Equation 11.13 states that the amount shipped out of a factory cannot exceed the quantity of raw material received. The constraint in Equation 11.14 enforces that the amount produced in the factory cannot exceed its capacity. The constraint in Equation 11.15 specifies that the amount shipped out of a warehouse cannot exceed the quantity received from the factories. The constraint in Equation 11.16 specifies that the amount shipped through a warehouse cannot exceed its capacity. The constraint in Equation 11.17 specifies that the amount shipped to a customer must cover the demand. The constraint in Equation 11.18 enforces that each factory or warehouse is either open or closed.

The model discussed here can be modified to allow direct shipments between factories and markets. All models discussed here can also be modified to accommodate economies of scale in production, transportation, and inventory costs. However, these requirements make the models more difficult to solve.

Accounting for Uncertainty in Network Design Decisions

Location and capacity allocation decisions in the design of a supply chain network are likely to stay in place for several years. Demand, price, cost, and other economic factors tend to fluctuate in the course of several years. It is thus important that companies account for the uncertainty in these factors when designing their networks. Network design decisions should not be evaluated based on the conditions at the time of the decision or on a specific vision of the future. Supply chain design decisions should be evaluated for a variety of future scenarios that reflect the underlying uncertainty. This is particularly important for firms setting up global networks, because other factors including tariffs and exchange rates may also fluctuate over time.

Future scenarios of demand, tariffs, costs, and exchange rates can be generated using simulation. For each network design, the resulting profits are evaluated for all generated scenarios to obtain a distribution of profits. The various designs should then be compared based on the mean and standard deviation of their profits.

Accounting for uncertainty will lead managers to build extra capacity into supply chain networks and make the available capacity more flexible in terms of the markets that can be served. If capacity is flexible, demand can be reallocated within the supply chain network to react best to changing demand, prices, costs, and exchange rates. If capacity is inflexible, production cannot be changed in response to changing conditions. The presence of flexibility thus increases potential profits. For example, Toyota has introduced greater flexibility in its factories worldwide, allowing the company to serve more than one market. The managers at Toyota expect this move to help them react better to fluctuations in global conditions. Just as safety inventory allows a supply chain to increase profits (see Chapter 9), safety capacity in a supply chain network also increases profits in the presence of uncertainty. Extra capacity is beneficial because it allows a firm to be responsive if market demand is higher than anticipated.

In general, all network design decisions in supply chains should be evaluated as options. We discuss a methodology for making this evaluation in Chapter 15.

11.5 MAKING NETWORK DESIGN DECISIONS IN PRACTICE

Managers should keep the following issues in mind when making network design decisions for a supply chain:

- **Do not underestimate the life span of facilities.** Facilities last a long time and have an enduring impact on a firm's performance. Therefore, it is very important that long-term consequences be thought through when making facility decisions. Managers must not only consider future demand and costs but also scenarios in which technology may change. Failure to do so may lead to facilities that are useless within a few years and become a financial burden to the firm. An insurance company moved its clerical labor from a metropolitan location to a suburban location to lower costs. With increasing automation, the need for clerical labor decreased significantly, and within a few years the facility was no longer needed. The company found it very difficult to sell the facility given its distance from residential areas and airports.[4]

  Within most supply chains, production facilities are harder to change than storage facilities. Supply chain network designers must consider that any factories that they put in place will stay in place for an extended period

[4]Harding (1988), p. 24.

of a decade or more. Warehouses or storage facilities, particularly those that are not owned by the company, can be changed within a year of making the decision. Managers must consider this difference in the lifetime of a facility when designing supply chain networks.

- **Do not gloss over the cultural implications**. Network design decisions regarding facility location and facility role have a significant impact on the culture of each facility and the firm. The culture at a facility will be influenced by other facilities in its vicinity. Network designers can use this fact to influence the role of the new facility and the focus of people working there. For example, when Ford Motor Company introduced the Lincoln Mark VIII model, management was faced with a dilemma. The Mark VIII shares a platform with the Mercury Cougar. However, the Mark VIII is part of Ford's luxury Lincoln division. Locating the Mark VIII line with the Cougar would have obvious operational advantages because of shared parts and processes. However, Ford decided to locate the Mark VIII line in the Wixom, Michigan, plant, where other Lincoln cars were produced. The primary reason for doing so was to ensure that the focus on quality for the Mark VIII would be consistent with other Ford luxury cars that were produced in Wixom. This decision has proved to be a good one for Ford; the Mark VIII has a reputation for quality.

  The location of a facility has a significant impact on the extent and form of communication that develops in the supply chain network. Locating a facility far from headquarters will likely give it more of a culture of autonomy. This may be beneficial if the firm is starting a new division that needs to function in a manner different from the rest of the company. In contrast, locating two facilities closer together is likely to encourage communication between them. Extensive communication can be very useful if decisions made at either facility have a strong impact on the performance of the other facility.
- **Do not ignore quality of life issues**. The quality of life at selected facility locations has a significant impact on performance because it influences the workforce available and their morale. In many instances, a firm may be better off selecting a higher-cost location if it provides a much better quality of life. Failure to do so can have dire consequences. For example, an aerospace supplier decided to relocate an entire division to an area with a lower standard of living to reduce costs. Most of the marketing team, however, refused to relocate. As a result, customer relations deteriorated, and the company had a very difficult transition. The effort to save costs hurt the company and effectively curtailed the firm's status as a major player in its market.[5]
- **Focus on tariffs and tax incentives when locating facilities**. Managers making facility location decisions should carefully consider tariffs and tax incentives. When considering international locations, it is astounding how often tax incentives drive the choice of location, often overcoming all of the other cost factors combined. For instance, Ireland has developed a large high-tech industry by using its low tax rates to entice companies to locate their European facilities there. Even within nations, local governments may offer generous packages of low to no taxes and free land when firms decide to locate facilities within their jurisdiction. Toyota, BMW, and Mercedes have all located their facilities in the United States primarily because of tax incentives offered by different states.

[5]Ibid.

11.6 SUMMARY OF LEARNING OBJECTIVES

1. Understand the role of facility decisions in designing a supply chain network.

   Facility decisions include identifying facility locations, roles, and capacities as well as allocating markets to be served by different facilities. These decisions are strategic in nature and define the physical constraints within which the network must be operated as market conditions change. Good network design decisions increase supply chain profits, and poor network design decisions hurt profits.
2. Identify factors influencing supply chain network design decisions.

   Network design decisions are influenced by macroeconomic, political, strategic, technological, infrastructure, competitive, and logistical and operational factors.
3. Develop a framework for making network design decisions.

   The goal of network design is to maximize the supply chain's long-term profitability. The process starts by defining the supply chain strategy, which must be aligned with the competitive strategy of the firm. The supply chain strategy, regional demand, political imperatives, and the competitive environment are used to define a regional facility configuration. For regions where facilities are to be located, potentially attractive sites are then selected based on available infrastructure. The optimal configuration is determined from the potential sites using demand, logistics cost, factor costs, and margins in different markets.
4. Use optimization for facility location and capacity allocation decisions.

   Gravity location models identify a location that minimizes inbound and outbound transportation costs. They are simple to implement but do not account for other important costs. Network optimization models can include contribution margins and production, transportation, and inventory costs and are used to maximize profitability. These models are useful when locating facilities, allocating capacity to facilities, and allocating markets to facilities.

Discussion Questions

1. How do the location and size of warehouses affect the performance of a firm like Amazon.com? What factors should Amazon take into account when making this decision?
2. How do import duties and exchange rates affect the location decision in a supply chain?
3. What are different roles played by production facilities within a global network?
4. Amazon.com has increased the number of warehouses as it has grown. How does this change various cost and response times in the Amazon supply chain?
5. McMaster-Carr sells MRO equipment from five warehouses in the United States. W.W. Grainger sells products from more than 300 retail locations, supported by several warehouses. In both cases, customers place orders using the Web or on the phone. Discuss the pros and cons of the two strategies.
6. Consider a firm like Dell with very few production facilities worldwide (at this writing only five). List the pros and cons of this approach and why it may or may not be suitable for the computer industry.
7. Consider a firm like Ford with more than 150 facilities worldwide. List the pros and cons of this approach and why it may or may not be suitable for the automobile industry.

Exercises

1. SC Consulting, a supply chain consulting firm, has to decide on the location of its home offices. Its clients are primarily in the 16 states in Table 11.7. There are four potential sites for home offices: Los Angeles, Tulsa, Denver, and Seattle. The annual fixed cost of locating an office at Los Angeles is $165,428, Tulsa is $131,230, Denver is $140,000, and Seattle is $145,000. The expected number of trips to each state and the travel costs from each potential site are shown in Table 11.7.
   Each consultant is expected to take at most 25 trips each year.
   a. If there are no restrictions on the number of consultants at a site, where should the home offices be located, and how many consultants should be assigned to each office? What is the annual cost in terms of the facility and travel?
   b. If at most 10 consultants are to be assigned to a home office, where should the offices be set up? How many consultants should be assigned to each office? What is the annual cost of this network?
   c. What do you think of a rule in which all consulting projects out of a given state are assigned to one home office? How much is this policy likely to add to cost compared with allowing multiple offices to handle a single state?
2. DryIce Inc. is a manufacturer of air conditioners that has seen its demand grow significantly. It anticipants nationwide demand for 2001 to be 180,000 units in the South, 120,000 units in the Midwest, 110,000 units in the East, and 100,000 units in the West. Managers at DryIce are designing the manufacturing network and have selected four potential sites: New York, Atlanta, Chicago, and San Diego. Plants could have a capacity of either 200,000 or 400,000 units. The annual fixed costs at the four locations are shown in Table 11.8 along with the cost of producing and shipping an air conditioner to each of the four markets. Where should DryIce build its factories, and how large should they be?

TABLE 11.7 Travel Costs and Number of Trips for SC Consulting

	Travel Costs ($)				
State	***Los Angeles***	***Tulsa***	***Denver***	***Seattle***	***Number of Trips***
Washington	150	250	200	25	40
Oregon	150	250	200	75	35
California	75	200	150	125	100
Idaho	150	200	125	125	25
Nevada	100	200	125	150	40
Montana	175	175	125	125	25
Wyoming	150	175	100	150	50
Utah	150	150	100	200	30
Arizona	75	200	100	250	50
Colorado	150	125	25	250	65
New Mexico	125	125	75	300	40
North Dakota	300	200	150	200	30
South Dakota	300	175	125	200	20
Nebraska	250	100	125	250	30
Kansas	250	75	75	300	40
Oklahoma	250	25	125	300	55

TABLE 11.8 Production and Transport Costs for DryIce Inc.

	New York	*Atlanta*	*Chicago*	*San Diego*
Annual fixed cost of 200,000-unit plant	$6 million	$5.5 million	$5.6 million	$6.1 million
Annual fixed cost of 400,000-unit plant	$10 million	$9.2 million	$9.3 million	$10.2 million
East	$211	$232	$238	$299
South	$232	$212	$230	$280
Midwest	$240	$230	$215	$270
West	$300	$280	$270	$225

3. Sunchem, a manufacturer of printing inks, has five manufacturing plants worldwide. Their locations and capacities are shown in Table 11.9 along with the cost of producing one ton of ink at each facility. The production costs are in the local currency of the country where the plant is located. The major markets for the inks are North America, South America, Europe, Japan, and the rest of Asia. Demand at each market is shown in Table 11.9. Transportation costs from each plant to each market in U.S. dollars are shown in Table 11.9. Management has to come up with a production plan for 2001.
   a. If exchange rates are expected as in Table 11.10, and no plant can run below 50 percent of capacity, how much should each plant produce, and which markets should each plant supply?
   b. If there are no limits on the amount produced in a plant, how much should each plant produce?
   c. Can adding 10 tons of capacity in any plant reduce costs?
   d. How should Sunchem account for the fact that exchange rates fluctuate over time?

TABLE 11.9 Capacity, Demand, Production and Transportation Costs for Sunchem

	North America	*South America*	*Europe*	*Japan*	*Asia*	*Capacity Tons/Year*	*Production Cost/Ton*
United States	600	1,200	1,300	2,000	1,700	185	$10,000
Germany	1,300	1,400	600	1,400	1,300	475	15,000 Marks
Japan	2,000	2,100	1,400	300	900	50	1,800,000 yen
Brazil	1,200	800	1,400	2,100	2,100	200	13,000 real
India	2,200	2,300	1,300	1,000	800	80	400,000 Rupees
Demand (tons/year)	270	190	200	120	100		

TABLE 11.10 Anticipated Exchange Rates for 2001

	US$	*Mark*	*Yen*	*Real*	*Rupee*
US$	1.000	1.993	107.7	1.78	43.55
Mark	0.502	1	54.07	0.89	21.83
Yen	0.0093	0.0185	1	0.016	0.405
Real	0.562	1.124	60.65	1	24.52
Rupee	0.023	0.046	2.47	0.041	1

Bibliography

Ballou, Ronald H. *Business Logistics Management.* Upper Saddle River, N.J.: Prentice Hall, 1999.

Ferdows, Kasra. "Making the Most of Foreign Factories." *Harvard Business Review* (March–April 1997), 73–88.

Harding, Charles F. "Quantifying Abstract Factors in Facility-Location Decisions." *Industrial Development* (May–June 1988), 24–24.

MacCormack, Alan D., Lawrence J. Newman III, and Donald B. Rosenfield. "The New Dynamics of Global Manufacturing Site Location." *Sloan Management Review* (Summer 1994), 69–79.

"Note on Facility Location." Harvard Business School note 9–689–059.

Robeson, James F., and William C. Copacino (eds.). *The Logistics Handbook.* New York: The Free Press, 1994.

Tayur, Sridhar, Ram Ganeshan, and Michael Magazine (eds.). *Quantitative Models for Supply Chain Management* Boston: Kluwer Academic Publishers, 1999.

Tirole, Jean. *The Theory of Industrial Organization.* Cambridge, Mass.: The MIT Press, 1997.

CASE STUDY

Managing Growth at SportStuff.com

In December 2000, Sanjay Gupta and his management team were busy evaluating the performance at SportStuff over the past year. Demand had grown by 80 percent over the year. This growth, however, was a mixed blessing. The venture capitalists supporting the company were very pleased with the growth in sales and the resulting increase in revenue. Sanjay and his team, however, could clearly see that costs would grow faster than revenues if demand continued to grow and the supply chain network was not redesigned. They decided to analyze the performance of the current network to see how it could be redesigned to cope best with the rapid growth anticipated over the next three years.

SPORTSTUFF.COM

Sanjay Gupta founded SportStuff in 1996 with a mission of supplying parents with more affordable sports equipment for their children. Parents complained about having to discard expensive skates, skis, jackets, and shoes because children outgrew them rapidly. Sanjay's initial plan was for the company to purchase used equipment and jackets from families and any surplus equipment from manufacturers and retailers and sell these over the Internet. The idea was very well received in the marketplace, demand grew rapidly, and by the end of 1996 the company had sales of $0.8 million. By this time a variety of new and used products were sold, and the company received significant venture capital support.

In June 1996, Sanjay leased part of a warehouse in the outskirts of St. Louis to manage the large amount of product being sold. Suppliers sent their product to the warehouse. Customer orders were packed and shipped by UPS from there. As demand grew, SportStuff leased more space within the warehouse. By 2000, SportStuff had leased the entire warehouse, and orders were shipped to customers all over the United States. Management divided the United States into six customer zones for planning purposes. Demand from each customer zone in 2000 was as shown in Table 11.11. Sanjay estimated that the next three years would see a growth rate of about 80 percent per year, after which demand would level off.

THE NETWORK OPTIONS

Sanjay and his management team could see that they needed more warehouse space to cope with the anticipated growth. One option was to lease more warehouse space in St. Louis itself. Other options included leasing warehouses all over the country. Leasing a warehouse involved fixed costs based on the size of the warehouse and variable costs that varied with the quantity shipped through the warehouse. Four potential locations for warehouses were identified in Denver, Seattle, Atlanta, and Philadelphia. Warehouses leased could be either small (about 100,000 square feet) or large (200,000 square feet). Small warehouses could handle a flow of up to 2 million units per year, whereas large warehouses could handle a flow of up to 4 million units per year. The current warehouse in St. Louis was small. The fixed and variable costs of small and large warehouses in different locations are shown in Table 11.12.

TABLE 11.11 Regional Demand at SportStuff for 2000

Zone	*Demand in 2000*	*Zone*	*Demand in 2000*
Northwest	320,000	Lower Midwest	220,000
Southwest	200,000	Northeast	350,000
Upper Midwest	160,000	Southeast	175,000

TABLE 11.12 Fixed and Variable Costs of Potential Warehouses

Location	*Small Warehouse*		*Large Warehouse*	
	Fixed Cost ($/year)	*Variable Cost ($/unit flow)*	*Fixed Cost ($/year)*	*Variable Cost ($/unit flow)*
Seattle	300,000	0.20	500,000	0.2
Denver	250,000	0.20	420,000	0.2
St. Louis	220,000	0.20	375,000	0.2
Atlanta	220,000	0.20	375,000	0.2
Philadelphia	240,000	0.20	400,000	0.2

TABLE 11.13 UPS Charges per Shipment (Four Units)

	Northwest	*Southwest*	*Upper Midwest*	*Lower Midwest*	*Northeast*	*Southeast*
Seattle	$2.00	$2.50	$3.50	$4.00	$5.00	$5.50
Denver	$2.50	$2.50	$2.50	$3.00	$4.00	$4.50
St. Louis	$3.00	$3.00	$2.50	$2.50	$3.00	$3.50
Atlanta	$4.00	$4.00	$3.00	$2.50	$3.00	$2.50
Philadelphia	$4.50	$5.00	$3.00	$3.50	$2.50	$4.00

Sanjay estimated that the inventory holding costs at a warehouse (excluding warehouse expense) was about $600 $\sqrt{F}$, where F is the number of units flowing through the warehouse per year. Thus, a warehouse handling 1 million units per year incurred an inventory holding cost of $600,000 in the course of the year.

SportStuff charged a flat fee of $3 per shipment sent to a customer. An average customer order contained four units. SportStuff in turn contracted with UPS to handle all its outbound shipments. UPS charges were based on both the origin and the destination of the shipment and are shown in Table 11.13. Management estimated that inbound transportation costs for shipments from suppliers were likely to remain unchanged, no matter what the warehouse configuration selected.

QUESTIONS

1. What is the cost SportStuff incurs if all warehouses leased are in St. Louis?
2. What supply chain network configuration do you recommend for SportStuff?

CHAPTER 12

Information Technology in a Supply Chain

Learning Objectives
After reading this chapter, you will be able to

1. understand the importance of information and information technology in a supply chain;
2. know at a high level how each supply chain driver uses information; and
3. understand the different information technologies that are used in a supply chain and how these have changed over time.

Information is crucial to the performance of a supply chain because it provides the basis upon which supply chain managers make decisions. Information technology consists of the tools used both to gain awareness of this information and to analyze the information to make the best decisions for the supply chain. In this chapter we explore the importance of information, its uses, and the technologies that enable supply chain managers to use information to make better decisions.

12.1 THE ROLE OF INFORMATION TECHNOLOGY IN A SUPPLY CHAIN

All of the supply chain drivers discussed to this point deal directly with some physical aspect of the supply chain. Chapters 7, 8, and 9 discuss how to manage product inventories, Chapter 10 discusses how to use transportation to move the product through the supply chain network, and Chapter 11 discusses issues regarding facility location and capacity that managers face when designing a supply chain network. This chapter, in contrast, focuses on information about both the product and the entire supply chain that makes the product. Information is the supply chain driver that serves as the glue allowing the other three drivers to work together to create an integrated, coordinated supply chain.

Information is crucial to supply chain performance because it provides the facts that supply chain managers use to make decisions. Without information, a manager will not know what customers want, how much inventory is in stock, and when more product should be produced and shipped. In short, without information, a manager can only make decisions blindly. Therefore, information makes the supply chain visible to a manager. Given this visibility, a manager can make decisions to improve the supply chain's performance. Without information, it is impossible for a supply chain to deliver products effectively to customers. With information, companies have the visibility they need to make decisions that improve company and overall supply chain performance. In this sense, information is the most important of the supply chain drivers because without it, none the other drivers can be used to deliver a high level of performance.

Managers must understand how information is gathered and analyzed because information is critical to a supply chain's success. This is where information technology comes into play. **Information technology** (IT) consists of the hardware and software used throughout a supply chain to gather and analyze information. IT serves as the eyes and ears of management in a supply chain, capturing and delivering the information necessary to make a good decision. For instance, an IT system at a personal computer (PC) manufacturer may tell a manager how many Pentium III chips are in stock to put into newly made PCs. IT is also used to analyze the information and recommend an action. In this role, a manager at a PC manufacturer could take the number of chips in inventory, look at demand forecasts, and determine whether to order more chips from Intel.

Using IT systems to capture and analyze information can have a significant impact on a firm's performance. For example, a major manufacturer of computer workstations and servers found that much of the information on customer demand was not being used to set production schedules and inventory levels. The manufacturing group lacked this demand information, and therefore demand visibility, which forced them to make inventory and production decisions blindly. By installing a supply chain IT system, the company was able to gather and analyze data to produce recommended stocking levels. Using the IT system enabled the company to cut its inventory in half because it could now make decisions based on information rather than educated guesses. Large impacts like this underscore the importance of IT as a driver of supply chain performance.

12.2 THE IMPORTANCE OF INFORMATION IN A SUPPLY CHAIN

Information is the key to the success of a supply chain because it enables management to make decisions over a broad scope that crosses both functions and companies. As discussed in Chapter 2, successful supply chain strategy results from viewing the supply chain as a whole rather than looking only at the individual stages. By taking a global scope across the entire supply chain, a manager is able to craft strategies that take into account all factors that affect the supply chain rather than just those factors affecting a particular stage or function within the supply chain. Taking the entire chain into account maximizes the profit of the total supply chain, which then leads to higher profits for each individual company within the supply chain.

How does a manager take this broad scope? The supply chain scope is made up entirely of information, and the breadth of this information determines whether the scope is global or local. To obtain a global scope of the supply chain, a manager needs accurate and timely information on all company functions and organizations in the supply chain. For example, it was not enough for the workstation manufacturer mentioned previously to know how much inventory was on hand within the company when trying to set the optimal inventory level. The company also needed to know the downstream demand and even the upstream supplier lead times and variability. With this broader scope, the company was able to set inventory levels that maximized profitability.

The information necessary to achieve a global scope may be divided into the following basic components, which correspond to different stages of the supply chain:

- **Supplier information**. What products can be purchased, at what price, with what lead time, and where they can be delivered. Supplier information also includes order status, modification, and payment arrangements.
- **Manufacturing information**. What products can be made, how many, by what facilities, with what lead time, with what trade-offs, at what cost, and in what batch size.
- **Distribution and retailing information**. What is to be transported where, in what quantity, by what mode, at what price, how much is stored at each site, and with what lead time.
- **Demand information**. Who is buying what, at what price, where, and in what quantity. Demand information includes forecasting and demand distribution information.

Supply chain managers use information to make many important decisions relating to each of the supply chain drivers. Setting inventory levels requires downstream information from customers on demand, upstream information from suppliers on availability, and information on current inventory levels, costs, and margins. Determining transportation policies requires information on customers, suppliers, routes, costs, times, and quantities to be shipped. Facility decisions require information on demand and suppliers, as well as information on capacities, revenues, and costs within the company.

Information must have the following characteristics to be useful when making supply chain decisions:

1. **Information must be accurate**. Without information that gives the true picture of the state of the supply chain, it is very difficult to make good decisions. That is not to say all information must be 100 percent correct, but rather that the data available paint a picture of reality that is at least directionally correct.

2. **Information must be accessible in a timely manner**. Often accurate information exists, but by the time is it available, either it is out of date or if it is current, it is not in an accessible form. To make good decisions, a manager needs to have up-to-date information that is easily accessible.

3. **Information must be of the right kind**. Decision makers need information that they can use. Often companies will have large amounts of data that are not helpful with decision making. Companies must think about what information should be recorded so that valuable resources are not wasted collecting meaningless data while important data go unrecorded.

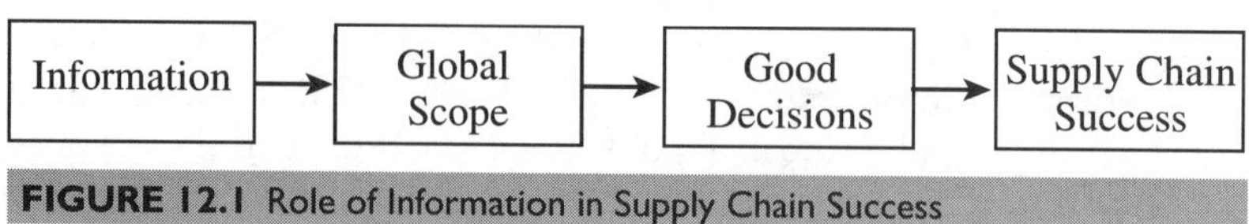

FIGURE 12.1 Role of Information in Supply Chain Success

In summary, when managers have good information, they have supply chain visibility, enabling them to take a global scope. With this global scope, they are able to make the best decisions for the supply chain. Therefore, information is a key to supply chain success, as captured in Figure 12.1.

12.3 USE OF INFORMATION IN A SUPPLY CHAIN

Information is a key ingredient not just at every stage of the supply chain, but also within each phase of supply chain decision making—from the strategic phase to the planning phase to the operational phase (see Chapter 1). For instance, information and analysis of that information plays a significant role during the formulation of supply chain strategy by providing the basis for decisions such as the location of the push/pull boundary in the supply chain. Information also plays a key role at the other end of the spectrum in operational decisions, such as what products will be produced during today's production run. Managers need to be able to understand how to analyze information to make good decisions. Much of this book deals with just that idea—how to identify a supply chain problem that needs to be solved, take information, analyze it, and then make a good decision to act on that information.

For example, Wal-Mart has been a pioneer not only in capturing information, but also in understanding how to analyze that information to make good supply chain decisions. Wal-Mart collects data in real time on what products are being purchased at each of its stores and sends these data back to the manufacturers. Wal-Mart analyzes this demand information to determine how much inventory to hold at each store and to decide when to ship new loads of product from the manufacturer. The manufacturer uses this information to set its production schedules so that it makes products in time to meet Wal-Mart's demand. Both Wal-Mart and its key suppliers do not just capture the information; they analyze it and base their actions on this analysis.

Information is used when making decisions about inventories, transportation, and facilities within a supply chain, as discussed here:

1. **Inventory**. Setting optimal inventory policies requires information that includes demand patterns, cost of carrying inventory, costs of stocking out, and costs of ordering (see Chapters 7, 8, and 9). For example, Wal-Mart collects detailed demand, cost, margin, and supplier information to make these inventory policy decisions.

2. **Transportation**. Deciding on transportation networks, routings, modes, shipments, and vendors all requires information including costs, customer locations, and shipment sizes to make good decisions (see Chapter 10). Wal-Mart uses information to integrate its operations tightly with those of its suppliers. This integration allows Wal-Mart to implement crossdocking in its transportation network, saving both inventory and transportation costs.

3. **Facility**. Determining the location, capacity, and schedules of a facility requires information on the trade-offs between efficiency and flexibility, demand, exchange rates, taxes, and so on (see Chapters 5 and 11). Wal-Mart's suppliers use the demand information from Wal-Mart's stores to set their production schedules. Wal-Mart uses

information on demand to determine where to place its new stores and crossdocking facilities.

The need for information to make good decisions regarding these drivers is clear. But as demonstrated in Chapter 13, information has the potential to add its highest value by improving supply chain coordination over all the supply chain drivers.

> ***Key Point*** Information is most important when it is used to create a global scope across all stages and drivers of a supply chain. This allows decisions to be made that maximize total supply chain profitability.

12.4 INFORMATION TECHNOLOGY: THE INFORMATION ENABLER

IT systems play a significant role in every stage of the supply chain by enabling companies to gather and analyze information. IT systems can be segmented according to the stages in the supply chain on which they focus and the phase of supply chain decisions for which they are used. These two segmentations can be used to create a matrix upon which any IT system used in the supply chain can be mapped. This matrix[1] is shown in Figure 12.2, where the horizontal axis corresponds to the stages in the supply chain and the vertical axis corresponds to the level of functionality that the systems perform.

The horizontal axis defines the scope of an IT system. There are IT systems throughout the entire supply chain, all the way from raw material suppliers to the customer. Some focus on only one stage or a function within a stage, whereas others cross multiple stages and give a broader scope. For instance, there are IT systems with a narrow scope that provide inventory levels for products in a particular warehouse or that provide manufacturing schedules for a particular plant. In contrast, there are IT systems that look at demand, inventory levels, and plant schedules across an entire network to determine what should be scheduled for production based on orders and inventories far downstream.

FIGURE 12.2 The Supply Chain IT Map

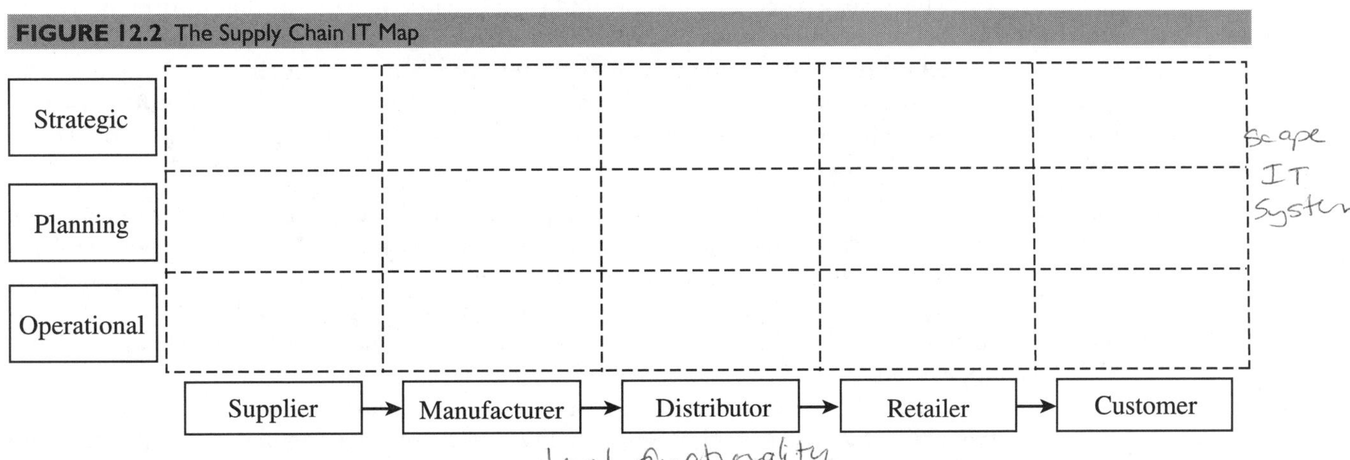

[1] A version of this matrix originated in Berquist, Kahl, and Kumar (1998).

The vertical axis defines the decision phase within a supply chain for which an IT system is used. IT systems have different levels of functionality that can capture and display information, analyze it to solve short-term problems, or analyze it to solve long-term problems. IT systems can be used to make strategic, planning, or operational decisions within a supply chain:

- **Strategic**. Strategic decisions involve time frames spanning several years in which managers must determine what products to make, how many plants to have, where they should be located, what types they should be, what type of distribution system to have, what functions to perform in house or outsource, and what type of demand to target. Strategic level information requirements tend to be very broad rather than detailed. IT systems used at this level are highly analytical because they focus on analyzing rather than gathering information. Strategic IT tools are targeted toward people at a higher level in the organization. Although this is an area that traditionally has not been served directly by IT solutions, new tools are being created for this purpose.
- **Planning**. Managers making planning decisions typically face time frames of several months to a year. The goal of planning decisions is to allocate available resources to best meet anticipated demand. Managers must decide approximate amounts of each type of product to be made and where it will be produced. Managers must also determine aggregate volumes through different distribution channels to different types of customers. Information requirements at this stage include costs, capacities, and demand at an aggregate level over the planning horizon. Planning decisions also focus on analyzing information rather than gathering it. Planning IT tools are targeted toward people at a middle to high level in the organization.
- **Operational**. At this level, IT systems aim to execute the plans and policies defined earlier. The operational level records transactions and deals with time frames all the way down to the second. Operational IT systems are involved with setting weekly production and delivery schedules. Often, this phase requires less analytical work, especially once schedules are set. Rather, operational IT systems focus on executing and recording transactions. For instance, operational IT systems may track whether a package has been delivered or what is to be manufactured by a line during the next shift. This level is very information-intensive because it requires that information be available for every transaction in the supply chain. Operational IT systems are used by people such as shop floor workers and delivery schedulers who are directly involved in executing supply chain transactions. Information gathered at this level is the foundation for all planning as well as strategic decisions.

All three decision-making phases and IT system levels are essential for each stage in a supply chain. Each stage needs to have a solid strategy: It needs to know where it wants to go. It needs a good plan: how to get there. And it needs good operations: It must execute the plan to get where it wants to go. The three levels of IT systems corresponding to the three phases of decision making and some of their characteristics appear in Figure 12.3.

These two dimensions—the scope of the supply chain that is covered by the IT system and the system's level of functionality—give a manager an understanding of where each type of IT system should be applied and what type of problems it can solve.

We next discuss the evolution of IT applications in the supply chain.

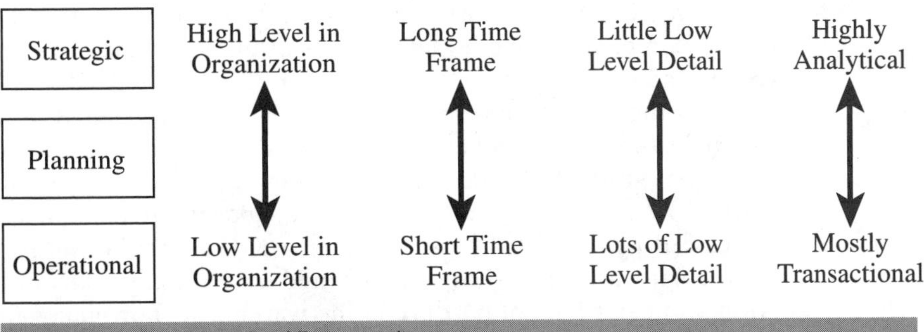

FIGURE 12.3 IT Levels of Functionality

The Past—Legacy Systems

Legacy systems are older IT systems based on mainframe technology that usually work at an operational level on only one stage or even one function within a stage of the supply chain. "Legacy system" is a very broad label and applies to a wide variety of systems with applications that can range from order entry to manufacturing scheduling to delivery. Although these functions are very different, they are all called legacy systems because of the older technology involved and because these systems continue to exist past their intended life span through numerous updates of the original code. Many legacy systems have lasted much longer than originally intended and are continually modified as requirements change. This continuous modification process can make them very cumbersome to work with, especially when considering that they were not very user-friendly in the first place. They can also become very complex after years of adding layer after layer of code.

Two important characteristics of legacy systems are the very narrow scope across which they have visibility and the operational nature of the tasks they perform. Legacy systems tend to focus solely on a particular function and are built as independent entities with little regard for other systems. Therefore, communication between systems is often minimal, and visibility across functions and supply chain stages is very limited. Legacy systems also have very limited analytical capabilities because they focus more on gathering information rather than on analyzing information to make decisions. Most were built to keep track of transactions rather than determine what transactions ought to be occurring.

Placing Legacy Systems on the Supply Chain Information Technology Map

Past legacy systems have focused on one specific function within one stage of the supply chain. For instance, a legacy system might deal only with inventory levels in a particular warehouse in a distributor's network. This system would monitor inventory levels in that warehouse but would likely have difficulty communicating with the legacy system that handled transportation for the same distributor. These limitations make it very difficult to coordinate transportation with the warehouse. Often there are different systems at different warehouses in the network that do not communicate. Therefore, even the warehouses are not coordinated because, with systems that do not communicate, they do not have visibility into each others' inventory. When looking across the various supply chain stages, the supply chain could literally have dozens or even hundreds of independent legacy systems that handle a product. Each stage would have little visibility into events at the other stages. With such limited visibility, companies using legacy systems often make decisions that have a very narrow scope and hurt the supply chain's total profits.

On the vertical axis measuring levels of functionality, legacy systems have little analytical capability and tend to look only at operational transactions that occur in the function on which they are focused. They rarely venture into the planning realm and virtually never attempt any sort of strategic supply chain decisions. For instance, as discussed previously, a legacy system could be monitoring inventory levels within a particular warehouse. The system would have the capability of telling users how many of a particular type of part are in the warehouse, how many are on order, how much the part costs, and possibly what the lead time is to order additional parts if they stock out. All of these data are at an operational level.

If we move up to a planning level, however, we find fewer legacy systems. For example, most legacy systems do not have the capability to analyze demand history to determine the proper level of safety inventory to hold to meet a certain service level. This sort of information would need to be manually entered by someone who, in most cases, would pick inventory levels based on a rule of thumb. Given this lack of planning capabilities, it is not surprising that legacy systems never ventured into the strategic realm.

Legacy systems exist at every horizontal stage in the supply chain. For our example, the warehouse inventory management system at the distributor is shown in Figure 12.4.

The following are the main advantages of legacy systems:

1. Legacy systems tend to *be able to get the operation done*. They may not be very efficient and they may be slow, but because legacy systems have often been up and running for more than a decade, they do work. Using legacy systems, therefore, is less risky in some respects than installing an untested new system whose operational abilities are unknown.

2. Legacy systems sometimes *take less incremental investment* to run than installing new applications because legacy systems already exist. The complex layers of code, however, often turn modifications into a quagmire that can be more difficult to complete than starting from scratch with a new system.

FIGURE 12.4 A Typical Legacy System's Mapping

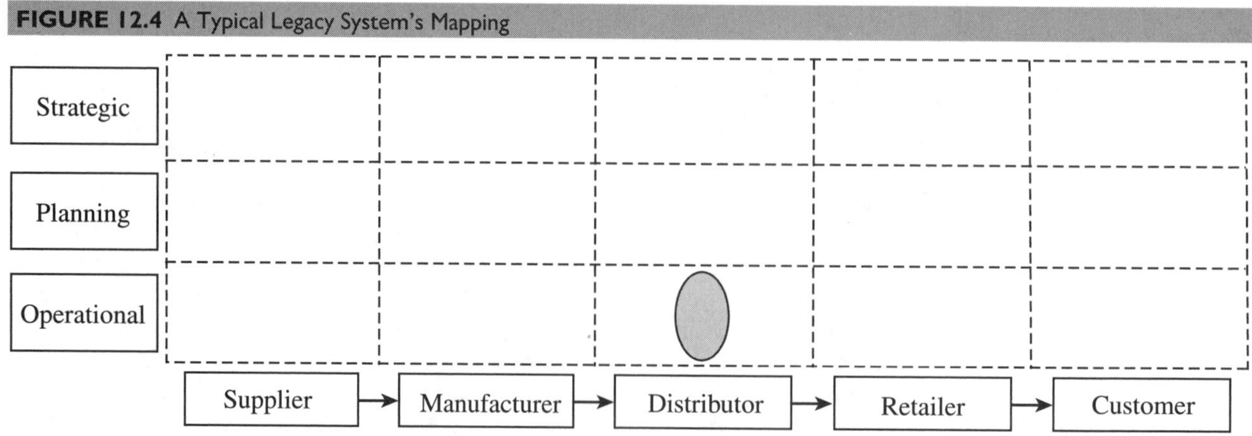

Legacy systems have a large number of disadvantages, which are summarized as follows:

1. Legacy systems *focus on only a small part* of a stage within the supply chain.
2. Legacy systems *usually have only transactional capabilities*, which relegates them to an operational rather than a planning or strategic role.
3. Legacy systems are usually based on mainframe technology that is *difficult to modify* and takes a long time to run when situations change.

The Present—Enterprise Resource Planning

Enterprise resource planning (ERP) systems are operational IT systems that gather information from across all of a company's functions, resulting in the entire enterprise having a broader scope. ERP systems monitor material, orders, schedules, finished goods inventory, and other information throughout the entire organization. ERP systems' main advantage over legacy systems is the clearly superior scope they provide to make better supply chain decisions.

ERP systems are good at monitoring transactions but generally lack the analytical capability to determine what transactions ought to happen. Therefore, they reside more in the operational area of the IT map than in the planning or strategic areas. This is beginning to change with ERP providers including some analytical modules in their systems. Although vertically limited, the ERP scope is obviously much broader than the typical legacy systems discussed previously. This breadth of scope is one of the features that make ERP systems as popular as they are. Their scope allows ERP systems to track orders through the entire company from procurement to delivery. The ability to keep track of orders and have broad visibility in general has become more important as supply chains become more global and more complex. Today's trend of using a product-based instead of a function-based organizational structure has also helped make ERP systems more attractive, because this structure increases the importance of the cross-functional scope that ERP systems provide.

ERP systems typically have many modules, each covering different functions within a company. These modules are linked together so that users in each function can see what is happening in other areas of the company. There are several key modules to an ERP system, each of which can be installed on its own or with a combination of other modules:

1. **Finance**. This module tracks financial information such as revenue and cost data through various areas within the company.
2. **Logistics**. This module is often broken into several sub modules covering different logistics functions such as transportation, inventory management, and warehouse management.
3. **Manufacturing**. This module tracks the flow of products through the manufacturing process, coordinating what is done to what part at what time.
4. **Order fulfillment**. This module monitors the entire order fulfillment cycle, keeping track of the progress the company has made in satisfying demand.
5. **Human resources**. This module handles all sorts of human resources tasks, such as the scheduling of workers.
6. **Supplier management**. This module monitors supplier performance and tracks the delivery of supplier's products.

All of these modules, and even other more specific ones not mentioned here, allow the ERP system to track the status of orders, products, supplies, people, and dollars.

ERP systems not only allow a company to track items throughout the system, they also allow a company to automate processes. By automating processes, companies are often able to increase efficiency and reduce errors. This combination can result in significant cost savings if executed properly. It is important to keep in mind, however, that automating poor processes only guarantees that they will be executed poorly each time. Thus, firms should review their processes before implementing ERP systems.

Beyond merely automating old processes, which can be akin to paving the cow paths, installing an ERP system often serves as a catalyst for a firm to redefine processes to make them more effective. ERP vendors build different versions of their software packages for different industries that are consistent with that industry's functional requirements. These different versions contain a variety of options for each function, process, or task that must be performed. One example is a scheduling module for a discrete manufacturing plant. By installing this module, the manufacturer can use the scheduling capabilities in the module to replace its existing scheduling system.

On the positive side, these functions, such as the scheduling module discussed previously, are often coded with best practice processes that can significantly improve the way a firm does business. Through the installation of an ERP system, a firm may be able to learn new best practices and increase its operational effectiveness.

There can be a downside to the prewritten processes in ERP software. These systems, although they can be modified, are usually difficult to change. Therefore, if there is a better way of performing a function that is not already coded into the ERP system, the superior process can be quite hard to implement. Often firms change their processes to fit the ERP way of doing things even though they realize that this is not the best way to operate for their particular situation. Thus, for the sake of visibility of information, firms may be forced to adopt less effective procedures.

Overall, where ERP systems excel is in the broad scope that they provide in real time. This is so attractive to customers that the ERP industry saw growth rates of between 30 percent and 40 percent in the mid- and late 1990s. However, growth has slowed as the market has become saturated, particularly within the world's largest companies. In summary, ERP systems are great at telling a company what *is* going on in the supply chain, because they are operationally focused, but fall short in helping a company determine what *ought* to be going on in the supply chain because they do not have sufficient analytic capability.

Placing Enterprise Resource Planning Systems on the Supply Chain Information Technology Map

ERP systems were developed to provide an integrated view of information across functions within a company and with the potential to go across companies. The enlarged scope of visibility along the horizontal axis is what chiefly differentiates ERP from legacy systems and is the main reason why the ERP industry was so successful during the mid- and late 1990s. Within a company, an ERP system will provide visibility of both incoming supplies and orders so that manufacturing managers can be sure when they schedule production that demand will be met and that appropriate materials will arrive on time. Salespeople can view production schedules and warehouse inventory levels in order to determine when a product might be delivered to a customer. ERP systems can also create the opportunity to share data across firms so that managers have visibility across the entire supply chain, although few companies have reached this stage of implementation. Nonetheless, the enlarged scope of visibility is the largest benefit that ERP systems offer because it allows company and supply chain managers to make much better decisions.

In terms of the vertical axis, ERP systems tend to focus on the operating level and do not have much analytical capability to help with decisions in the planning and strategic phases. They are great at telling managers what is going on but not good at telling them what should be going on. Similar to legacy systems, an ERP system can tell a manager what current inventory levels are for a product in a particular warehouse, for instance. But ERP systems are weak when it comes to determining how much inventory there should be to meet a certain service level. As an example, most ERP systems can develop a production schedule that attempts to find the best schedule possible. However, given the relatively unsophisticated optimization techniques used (such as material requirements planning [MRP]), they tend to arrive at a feasible rather than an optimal solution. ERP systems have problems trying to optimize over multiple types of constraints (such as capacity and material constraints) and multiple plants. Despite ERP's weakness in analytics, they still do have improved analytical capabilities compared with legacy systems.

The level of analytical power in ERP systems is changing as discussed. ERP companies have devoted large amounts of resources to developing analytical capabilities to add to their ERP packages. This analytical capability is delivered to customers in the form of add-on modules that bolt onto existing ERP systems. The focus on the analytics will improve ERP systems and move them into the planning and potentially even strategic levels of functionality.

On our IT map, ERP systems generally span all of the functions of a particular stage in the supply chain and have limited visibility into stages directly interacting with the ERP system. In addition, ERP systems have the potential to cross organizations and broaden scope even further, although this has not happened with much frequency. On the vertical axis, they solidly cover the operational area and have moved up into some of the planning arena, although they are not as well developed there. This is shown in Figure 12.5 for our distributor example.

The following are the main advantages of ERP systems:

1. ERP systems provide a *wider scope* to managers of supply chains. With an ERP system in place, managers have much broader information availability with which to make decisions that increase total supply chain profits.
2. ERP systems are fairly good at giving *real-time information* so there is little delay communicating information about changes in one part of the supply chain to other parts of the chain.
3. ERP systems are also better than legacy systems at using enabling technologies like the Internet to share information.

FIGURE 12.5 An ERP System's Mapping

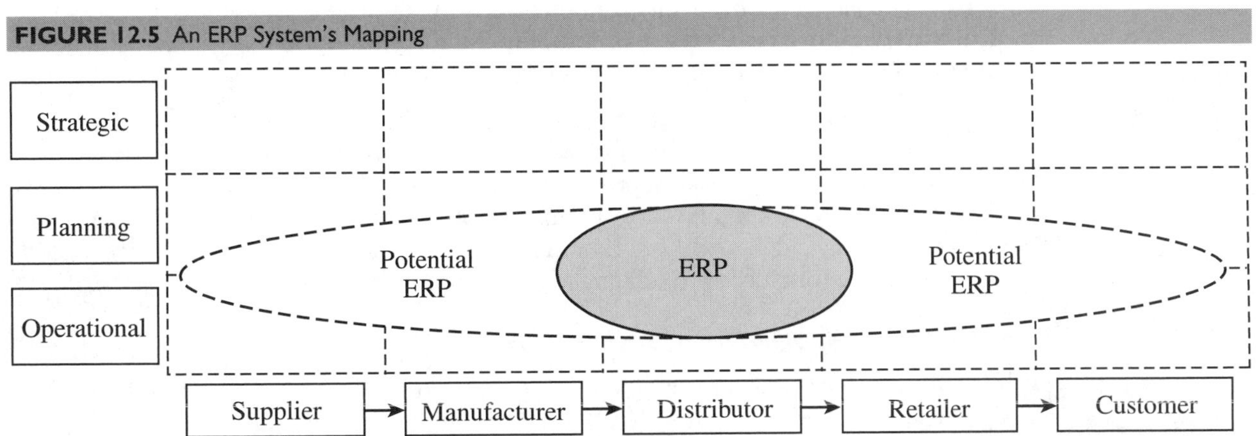

ERP systems have a number of disadvantages:

1. ERP systems still have relatively *weak analytical capabilities* because their focus is at an operational level. The ERP players are trying to move upward on the IT map, but it is a difficult move to make because software for the planning level requires quite a large amount of specific expertise to develop.

2. ERP systems have a reputation for being *very expensive and difficult to implement.* This can be especially true when the standard modules must be customized to accommodate different business processes. There are many stories of companies that have spent large amounts of time and money installing an ERP system only to have it fail and be forced to rip the entire system out and return to the old legacy systems. Of course, these are countered by great success stories. Nonetheless, installing an ERP system does have an element of risk to it.

The Enterprise Resource Planning Players

There are five major ERP players in the marketplace, which we describe here. In addition to these five, there are many smaller players that focus on small and midsize companies as their customers. The larger players have moved into these smaller markets, though, and these giants may become the major players there as well.

SAP The clear ERP market leader with around a 30 percent share of the market, SAP has its roots writing software for manufacturing environments. The firm has a strong tradition of building capabilities in-house, and they are expanding their product offerings vertically by developing more analytical functions to be used in supply chain planning.

Oracle The second largest player with about half the share of SAP, Oracle is the only one of the Big Five ERP players that is not solely an ERP firm. Oracle also writes database software, which led it to begin creating ERP systems. Oracle initially added financial applications to its database programs and eventually grew to be a full ERP provider. Oracle has had the most success with consumer packaged goods companies, although they have successfully expanded into other industries.

Peoplesoft Whereas SAP started with manufacturing applications and Oracle with finance, Peoplesoft started with human resources applications. It has acquired an analytical software firm in the supply chain realm (Red Pepper) in order to push its products up the vertical scale of the IT map.

J. D. Edwards This firm started out building cross-functional systems that were targeted toward midsize firms, generally those with around $1 billion in sales. J. D. Edwards has purchased Numetrix, a supply chain software company, in an effort to increase its offering in the analytical applications realm.

Baan Baan, like J. D. Edwards, began with the entire integrated view in mind rather than a specific function as is the case with the three leaders. Baan also focuses on midsize companies. Baan tends to perform better in manufacturing environments, although they have attempted to break out of this vertical industry. In order to improve its supply chain analytics, Baan has purchased CAPS Logistics. The years 1999 and 2000 were tough ones for Baan, and its future is uncertain.

The Present—Analytical Applications

Whereas an ERP system's greatest advantage is the broad scope it provides, an analytical application's advantage lies in the fact that it can be used for both planning and strategic decisions. Analytical systems are not focused at an operating level but rather on planning and strategic decisions. They analyze information supplied to them by legacy or ERP systems in order to help supply chain managers make good decisions. For example, ERP systems may provide demand history, inventory levels, and supplier lead times, and then an analytical application would determine what the inventory level should be to maximize profitability.

Analytical applications rely on sophisticated algorithms including linear programming, mixed integer programming, genetic algorithms, theory of constraints, and many types of heuristics. These algorithms are most often proprietary to the software company, and large amounts of R&D go into developing them. Due to the level of sophistication, this technology is relatively hard to develop if a firm has not had much experience in this area.

This segment of the IT industry has been growing rapidly in the last few years. Many segments of the analytical applications market are growing at 50 percent a year with little sign of a slow down.

Analytical applications are generally not as broad as ERP applications in their horizontal scope. In fact, many analytical applications focus only on a particular function within a supply chain stage, similar to the way legacy systems perform. However, they excel in their analytical capability, which gives them higher levels of functionality than either legacy or ERP systems. On the IT map, analytic applications therefore exist higher up on the vertical axis. There are many different types of analytical applications that focus on various stages and vertical niches in the supply chain. We have roughly categorized these systems into two groups according to their analytical capabilities: those systems focusing on planning capabilities and those focused more on an operational level. The following sections discuss the systems with some significant planning capabilities.

Procurement and Content Cataloging Applications

Procurement and cataloging applications focus on the relationship between a manufacturer and its suppliers and the procurement process that takes place between them. Though there are many such applications, the basic purposes of supplier-focused applications are to enable a streamlined procurement process, replace the supplier's catalog, and keep track of parts, specifications, prices, order processes, and the suppliers themselves. Supplier management systems allow analytical comparisons of supplier versus supplier and part versus part to help buyers make decisions on whom to buy from and what to buy. Ariba and Commerce One are leading suppliers of procurement software, and Aspect Development, a part of i2 Technologies, is a leading provider of content cataloging software.

Advanced Planning and Scheduling

Advanced planning and scheduling (APS) has been one of the fastest growing areas in analytical applications. APS systems produce schedules for what to make, where and when to make it, and how to make it while taking into account material availability, plant capacity, and other business objectives. APS can also encompass the functions of strategic supply chain planning, inventory planning, and available to promise (ATP). These systems are highly analytical and use sophisticated algorithms such as linear programming and genetic algorithms. APS systems can be used to develop detailed production schedules in plants, perform manufacturing planning, and perform supply chain planning to optimize the use of manufacturing, distribution, and transportation resources to meet demand. APS systems require inputs of transaction-level data that are collected by ERP or legacy systems. APS systems are an area that the ERP vendors have entered by building add-on modules with APS functionality. Supply chain software developer i2 Technologies is the leading developer of APS systems.

Transportation Planning and Content Systems

Transportation planning and content systems perform the analysis to determine how, when, where, and in what quantity materials ought to be transported. Comparisons of different carriers, modes, routes, and freight plans can be made using these systems. The planning vendors produce the engine that performs the analysis, and content vendors provide the data needed to perform the analysis, such as mileage and tariff requirements.

Demand Planning and Revenue Management

The demand planning and revenue management application helps companies forecast their demand using proprietary analytical tools. These systems take as inputs historical data and any information regarding future demand and come up with models to help explain past sales and forecast future demand. Good systems take into account demand trends as well as seasonality along with modifications for promotions to forecast future demand. The idea of revenue management is also often placed under the demand planning umbrella. Revenue management deals with using price discrimination to maximize the amount of consumer surplus one can get from product sales. This idea has been applied extensively in the airline industry and has now moved to both the hotel and car rental industries. Revenue management has a great deal of potential because it has not been applied in many other areas. i2 is a leading provider of demand planning solutions, and Talus is a leading provider of revenue management solutions.

Customer Relationship Management (CRM) and Sales Force Automation (SFA)

The customer relationship management (CRM) and sales force automation (SFA) applications automate relations between sellers and buyers by providing product and price information. They also allow for detailed customer and product information to be available in real time so that salespeople can direct their efforts or customers can configure orders themselves. Siebel Systems has been the clear leader in developing CRM applications.

Supply Chain Management

Supply chain management (SCM) systems are a combination of many of the preceding applications and are used to span the stages in the supply chain. They are delivered as a suite of different supply chain applications that are tightly integrated. SCM systems allow for a more global scope because they can span many supply chain stages with their different modules. For instance, an SCM system could come with APS, demand planning, transportation planning, and inventory planning. SCM systems have the analytical capabilities to produce planning solutions and strategic level decisions. Although they do not usually span all of the supply chain stages and they rely on legacy systems or ERP systems to provide the information necessary to perform the analysis, SCM systems currently provide the highest level of functionality with respect to the vertical axis of the IT map. SCM systems are the only systems to reach into the strategic level of functionality. i2 is the leader in developing SCM solutions. Manugistics is another major player in SCM.

The second group of applications is focused on operational issues such as executing tasks determined by the planning systems. Although not all systems fit neatly into either group, the systems described in the following sections tend to have more of an operational focus than a planning focus.

Inventory Management Systems

These systems observe demand patterns; take inputs on forecasting, costs, margins, and service levels; and then produce a recommended stocking policy. They are best used to achieve an optimal balance between inventory costs and stockout costs.

Manufacturing Execution System

A manufacturing execution system (MES) is less analytical than an APS system and is similar to the operationally focused ERP system, except that it concentrates only on executing production in a manufacturing facility. An MES generally produces short-term schedules and allocates resources with their analytical capabilities. The leading MES modules are from the ERP companies and a number of smaller players that develop only MESs.

Transportation Execution

Similar to an MES with respect to APS, transportation execution systems make transportation plans work. They are less analytical than their planning counterparts but serve as an operational link to the planning tools.

Warehouse Management System

Like transportation execution systems, warehouse management systems (WMSs) execute inventory planning commands and run the day-to-day operations of a warehouse. These systems also keep track of inventories in a warehouse.

Placing Analytical Applications on the Information Technology Map

On our IT map, analytical applications generally reside within various stages of the supply chain at the planning level, as we can see in Figure 12.6. Some planning applications have operational counterparts, which are also shown. SCM stretches across many supply chain stages. Note that some applications, such as the transportation applications, can exist between any two stages in the supply chain, and not simply where they are shown in Figure 12.6.

FIGURE 12.6 Analytical Applications Map

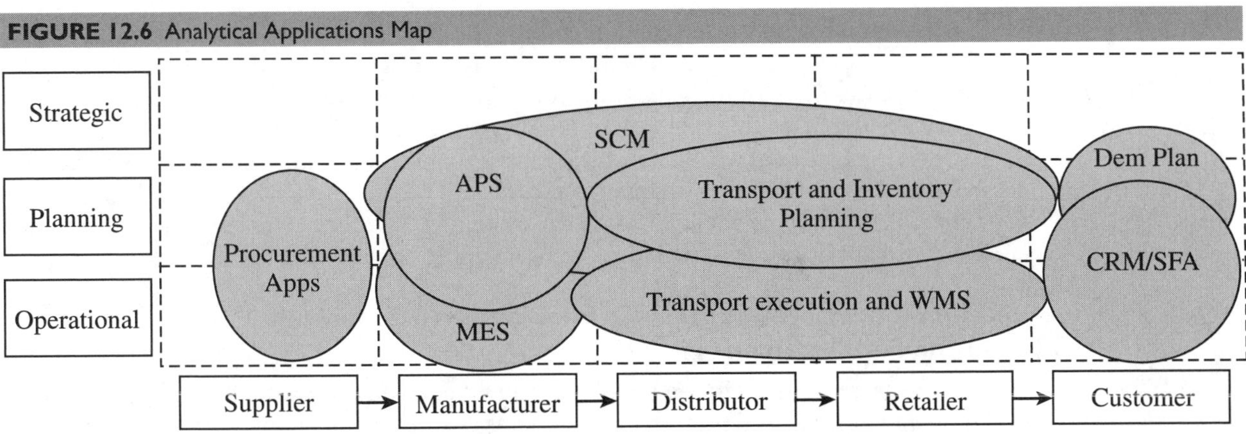

The IT map helps us see the major advantages of analytical applications, which are as follows:

1. Analytical applications have very sophisticated analytical capabilities and generate solutions that are far superior to what could be arrived at without them. Therefore, these applications can potentially greatly increase their users' profitability. This can be seen by analytic applications' penetration up the vertical scale of the IT map.
2. Analytical applications generally can respond in real time to problems and emergencies. For example, schedules can be instantly rerun if a machine goes down, thereby quickly shifting production.

Analytical applications do have one downfall in terms of the IT map: The biggest problem with analytical applications is that they do not have the broad scope of an ERP system. They must rely on data from either legacy or ERP systems, and when supply chain-wide data are not available, they must resort to estimates or default to local optimization. In any case, integrating the analytical application with a good data system is essential.

The Analytical Application Players

Within each of the analytical applications discussed, there are different leading providers, and we point this out where there is a clear leader. However, because this industry is relatively young, there is quite a bit of fragmentation. For the purposes of our discussion, we list only the two major SCM providers (along with the ERP players) because they provide the best combination of cross-stage scope and analytical capability:

1. **i2 Technologies**. i2 is the market leader in the SCM realm. i2's strength began with its powerful APS systems used for discrete manufacturers. i2 is particularly strong in the high-tech industry, although it now has a very broad base of customers.

2. **Manugistics**. The number-two player in SCM is Manugistics, although it is falling further behind i2. Manugistics' systems are best at demand planning and working with distribution-intensive products such as consumer goods.

3. **ERP players**. Some of the ERP players are also developing SCM capabilities using three different approaches. SAP is developing its capabilities in-house, Oracle has leaned toward partnering with existing SCM players (although it has developed an in-house supply chain solution as well), and Peoplesoft, J. D. Edwards, and Baan have acquired SCM companies and are incorporating their products into the ERP suites. At this writing, the ERP players have not made a significant dent in the analytical applications market, as their products are behind the leaders discussed.

In summarizing our discussion of the types of IT systems, it is important for supply chain managers to understand the interaction between ERP systems and analytical applications. Although they are sometimes viewed as competitors, they also rely on each other. The full value of an ERP system cannot be realized without the problem-solving ability of analytical solutions. Conversely, for analytic solutions to be productive, they need accurate data from a variety of functions. One of the best ways to obtain these data is through an ERP system. Therefore, managers often combine these two applications to produce the best supply chain.

The Future: Trends Shaping Information Technology in the Supply Chain

The importance of IT in the supply chain will continue to grow. As supply chains become more global and more complex and as customers and competition become more demanding, companies will need the supply chain capabilities that only sophisticated IT systems can give them. Therefore, the importance of IT to a supply chain can only increase. The future role of IT in the supply chain, however, is very difficult to predict. There are three main trends that will influence the supply chain software industry in the near future.

Best of Breed Versus Single Integrator

A battle is occurring, not just among the developers within a category of software, but also among developers of different types of software. The most vivid example is the conflict between the ERP and analytical applications developers. Developers of analytical applications strive to build a package that is the best at solving problems for that particular function within a stage in the supply chain. ERP providers build a system that allows a single, integrated view of many different functions in a supply chain stage. Analytical applications must integrate with some ERP or legacy system in order to get the data they analyze. The two types of systems thus naturally complement each other. However, there is conflict between the groups as the ERP players develop their analytical applications and begin to compete directly with the analytical developers.

Those who believe that the "best of breed" approach is the preferred solution pick the best application for each individual function or stage in the supply chain. These applications are the best of the breed of that function. Companies then wind up with several different types of systems that they must integrate to achieve global scope of the supply chain. This integration can be quite difficult because individual parts of the system come from different software firms and they may not be designed to work well together. The advantage is that a company does get the best solutions if it can overcome these problems.

Those who favor the "single integrator" approach look at the difficulties of integrating all of the different best of breed applications and opt instead for one single company's package to be used for all functions and potentially even all stages of the supply chain. The idea is that if all the modules come from a single firm, they will be designed to work well together, and therefore, getting them up and operational should be much easier than the best-of-breed approach. Of course, this ease of operation comes at the expense of being able to pick the best analytical tool for a particular problem a firm is facing. In addition, single sourcing of IT could cause the same problems that single sourcing from any supplier can create.

It is unclear which idea will win this battle or even if a clear winner will emerge. However, analytical applications have proven difficult to develop for those firms with little experience. And with regard to the acquisition strategy, it has not worked out well for the ERP players, either.

In the end, it is likely that both ideas will coexist, each serving those industries that are best suited to their particular attributes. For instance, in industries in which having the best inventory planning can be a competitive advantage, we might expect to see companies choose the best of breed solution so that they can take advantage of the absolute best inventory solutions. In industries in which one particular function does not offer a large advantage, we would expect to see companies choose single integrators because the ease of installation and operation would likely outweigh any gain from a more advanced analytical system.

Shifts in Platform Technology

As supply chain IT systems have moved from legacy to ERP and analytical systems, there has been a shift in technology from mainframes to client/server platforms.

Currently, two technologies are taking over the client/server technology that was the dominant platform for supply chain IT applications.

The first technology is the browser-based Internet application. Users of this application only need access to the Internet and a browser on their computers. These users utilize the browser to log into the IT system over the Internet. Any information or analysis they need is available over the browser. Calculations and storage take place on a central server. This technology is compelling, as it requires no costly software upgrades on the user's computer. Avoiding this expenditure and being able to easily use the latest application version make this option quite attractive. At this writing, just about every major software player discussed here is trying to take advantage of this technology by modifying products to make them Internet-accessible.

The second technology is the whole new business model of application service providers (ASPs). ASPs do not develop software themselves but rather host software developed by others and rent the use of the software to companies. The ASP is then responsible for running (generally remotely) the applications the customer rents. ASPs offer ERP systems and some analytical applications for rent. The ASP business model turns the traditional software model on its head in that customers pay a monthly subscription fee to use the software rather than a large up-front fee to acquire a license to the software. ASPs began by focusing on smaller businesses that lacked the capital to invest in expensive system installations. The benefits of ASPs, such as ease of upgrading and little up-front investment, may eventually win over some large companies, although penetration in larger companies is likely to be much lower than with small companies. ASPs exist not only as stand-alone companies but also within software developers (such as Oracle) that have begun offering their own ASP service. This trend toward a service-based model is very likely to continue and will significantly alter the way the software industry is structured. Leading ASPs include USInternetworking and Corio.

Convergence of Supply Chain Management and Business-to-Business Exchanges

Business-to-business (B2B) exchanges are electronic marketplaces on the Internet where suppliers and buyers interact to conduct transactions. Many B2B exchanges sprung up in 1999 and 2000, each generally focusing on an industry vertical, such as electronic components, plastics, or auto parts. Most of these B2B sites have focused their energy on developing a Web site and pulling in the potential buyers and sellers within their vertical industry. These exchanges provide the opportunity for huge value creation, through the reduction in transaction costs, improved supply chain visibility, and the more efficient allocation of supply and demand (for more, see Chapter 14).

These B2B exchanges have fostered many types of transactions. At their most basic level, exchanges create an efficient marketplace to make spot purchases or sales of goods. These can be done through a variety of transactional means such as auctions (one seller, multiple buyers), reverse auctions (one buyer, multiple sellers), fixed price transactions (one buyer and one seller), and bid/ask auctions (in which multiple buyers and sellers bid). Some of these transactions, such as auctions, are often best suited to short-term relationships. For a long-term relationship between a buyer and a seller, in which tight integration is beneficial, exchanges can provide even more value. Exchanges not only produce efficiencies in the transaction process and the creation of a market but they also enable tight collaboration between buyers and sellers. For example, exchanges can enable the sharing of demand forecasts between buyers and sellers so that sellers can more accurately manage their production. Exchanges can also allow the efficient combination of purchasing goods with the logistics services needed to fulfill an order.

As the exchanges have become operational, it has become increasingly clear that the key to exchanges creating value lies in this collaboration between buyers and sellers that an electronic market can enable. What the exchanges need to perform these functions are the supply chain IT applications discussed previously. As those involved in B2B exchanges realize they need this capability, they are seeking the services of the supply chain software developers discussed here.

At the same time, the supply chain software companies are realizing that they hold the key to successful B2B exchanges and, in addition to partnering with existing exchanges, are also starting their own exchanges. This is creating a convergence of the B2B exchanges and the supply chain companies, in which each offers a range of products that encompasses both B2B and SCM. This convergence creates a whole new set of opportunities for the supply chain software developers. It also brings a whole new set of competitors into the supply chain software world, which will alter the competitive landscape.

12.5 SUPPLY CHAIN INFORMATION TECHNOLOGY IN PRACTICE

Although there are different sets of practical suggestions for each component of the supply chain systems discussed here, there are several general ideas that managers need to keep in mind when making a decision regarding supply chain IT.

- **Select an IT system that addresses the company's key success factors**. Every industry and even companies within an industry can have very different key success factors. By key success factors, we mean the two or three elements that really determine whether a company is going to be successful. It is important to select supply chain IT systems that are able to give a company an advantage in the areas most crucial to the success of the business. For instance, the ability to set inventory levels optimally is crucial in the PC business, in which product life cycles are short and inventory becomes obsolete very quickly. In contrast, inventory levels are not nearly as crucial for an oil company, in which demand is fairly stable and the product has a very long life cycle. For the oil company, the key to success would depend more on utilization of the refinery. Given these success factors, a PC company might pick a package that is strong in setting inventory levels even if it is weak in maximizing utilization of production capacity, and the oil company should choose a different product, one that excels at maximizing utilization even if its inventory components are not especially strong.
- **Align the level of sophistication with the need for sophistication**. Management must consider the depth to which an IT system deals with the firm's key success factors. There can be a trade-off between the ease of implementing a system and that system's level of complexity. Therefore, it is important to consider just how much sophistication a company needs to achieve its goals and then ensure that the system a company chooses matches that level. This is important because erring on the less sophisticated side leaves the firm with a competitive weakness, whereas trying to be too sophisticated leads to a higher possibility of becoming bogged down in complexity. Managers need to think about how much sophistication they need.

If they do not need much, managers should keep it simple. If they need a lot, they should choose a system that provides it.

- **Use IT systems to support decision making, not to make decisions**. Although the analytical packages available today can make many optimal supply chain decisions for management, this does not mean that IT applications can make all of the decisions. A mistake companies can make is installing a supply chain system and then reducing the amount of managerial effort they spend on supply chain issues. Management must keep its focus on the supply chain because as the competitive and customer landscape changes, there needs to be a corresponding change in the supply chain. At the highest level, supply chain strategy needs to be determined by a firm's leaders. Therefore, management needs to stay focused on what is going on with its supply chain in order to make the best strategic supply chain decisions.
- **Think about the future**. Although it is more difficult to make a decision about an IT system with the future in mind than the present, it is very important that managers include the future state of the business in the decision process. If there are trends in a company's industry indicating that insignificant characteristics will become crucial in the future, then managers need to make sure their IT choices take these trends into account. One area that has affected every industry is the shift in technologies to Web-based applications. Managers need to select their IT systems with trends like this in mind. As IT systems often last for many more years than originally planned, managers need to spend time exploring how flexible the systems will be if, or rather when, changes are required in the future. This exploration can go so far as to include the viability of the supply chain software developer itself. If it is unclear whether a company will be able to get support from a software company in the future, management needs to be sure that the other advantages of the product outweigh this disadvantage. The key here is to ensure that the software not only fits a company's current needs but also, and even more importantly, that it will meet the company's future needs.

12.6 SUMMARY OF LEARNING OBJECTIVES

1. Understand the importance of information and information technology in a supply chain.

   Information is essential to making good supply chain decisions because it provides the global scope needed to make optimal decisions. Information technology provides the tools to gather this information and analyze it in order to make the best supply chain decisions.
2. Know at a high level how each supply chain driver uses information.

   Each of the supply chain drivers discussed in previous chapters (inventory, transportation, and facilities) require the fourth driver, information, in order to make decisions. Information is the factual component on which decisions about each of the other drivers are based. In essence, information is the glue that holds the entire supply chain together and allows it to function, making information the most important supply chain driver.
3. Understand the different information technologies that are used in a supply chain and how these have changed over time.

   As the importance of information grows, so does the importance of IT in gathering and analyzing those data to make decisions. IT systems can be categorized along a horizontal dimension that ranges across the stages of the supply chain. IT systems are also categorized along a vertical dimension that measures the system's level of functionality. This matrix allows us to see all of the roles of the various technologies that are used in the supply chain and provides an understanding of how different technologies interact with each other. The main categories of IT systems replacing older legacy systems are ERP systems, which focus on broadening the supply chain scope, and analytical applications, which focus on analyzing information to make strategic and planning decisions in supply chains.

Discussion Questions

1. Why might a well-funded startup make very different IT systems decisions than an established company faced with the same competitive situation?
2. What types of industries would be most likely to choose a best-of-breed approach to their IT systems? What types would be more likely to choose a single integrator approach?
3. Discuss how technology platform shifts have made supply chain IT systems more effective.
4. What types of companies will find the ASP model of delivering software more attractive than the traditional license model?
5. Discuss how the impact of ASPs and the various service-based rather than license-based software business models will change the software industry.
6. How will the emergence of B2B trading exchanges change the supply chain with respect to IT systems?
7. Will the analytical application industry be more fragmented, with different companies dominating different applications, or will one or two companies dominate the entire analytical applications industry? Explain the rationale behind your answer.
8. Discuss why the high-tech industry has been the leader in adopting supply chain IT systems.
9. Why have large automakers been leaders in promoting B2B exchanges?

Bibliography

Berquist, Thomas, Steven Kahl, Arun Kumar, "Supply and Demand Management." *Piper Jaffrey* (March 1998).

Fischer, Dave. "The Advantages of Planning Systems." *Supply Chain Management Review* (Global Supplement, Winter 2000), 8–11.

Sodhi, Mohan. "Getting the Most from Planning Technologies." *Supply Chain Management Review* (Global Supplement, Winter 2000), 19–23.

For More Information

For more information on IT, see the following publications:

Red Herring
InformationWeek
Manufacturing Systems
Upside
The Industry Standard
Business 2.0

PART FIVE

Coordinating a Supply Chain and the Role of E-Business

The goal of the chapters in this module is to highlight how concepts discussed earlier in the book may be used to help achieve coordination in a supply chain and identify the value of e-business for any firm.

Coordination helps ensure that each part of the supply chain takes actions that increase total supply chain profits and avoids actions that improve its local profits but hurt total profits. Chapter 13 discusses how the lack of coordination across different members of a supply chain can result in poor performance, even when each stage is doing the best it can given its own objectives. Ideas discussed in all previous chapters are brought together to identify managerial actions that can help a supply chain achieve coordination.

Chapter 14 uses the concepts developed in earlier chapters relating to the design, planning, and operation of a supply chain to analyze the development of e-business and discuss how firms can best integrate e-business when formulating strategy and designing their supply chains. Different industry examples are analyzed from a supply chain perspective to illustrate the value that e-business provides in each case.

CHAPTER 13

Coordination in a Supply Chain

Learning Objectives

After reading this chapter, you will be able to

1. describe supply chain coordination, the bullwhip effect, and their impact on performance;
2. identify causes of the bullwhip effect and obstacles to coordination in the supply chain;
3. discuss managerial levers that help achieve coordination in the supply chain; and
4. describe actions that facilitate the building of strategic partnerships and trust within the supply chain.

In this chapter, we discuss how lack of coordination leads to a degradation of service and an increase in cost within a supply chain. We describe various obstacles that lead to this lack of coordination and exacerbate variability through the supply chain. We then identify appropriate managerial levers that can help overcome the obstacles and achieve coordination. In this context, we also discuss actions that facilitate strategic partnerships and the building of trust within the supply chain.

13.1 LACK OF SUPPLY CHAIN COORDINATION AND THE BULLWHIP EFFECT

Supply chain coordination improves if all stages of the chain take actions that together increase total supply chain profits. Supply chain coordination requires each stage of the supply chain to take into account the impact its actions have on other stages.

A lack of coordination occurs either because different stages of the supply chain have objectives that conflict or because information moving between different stages becomes distorted. Different stages of a supply chain may have objectives that conflict if each stage has a different owner. As a result, each stage tries to maximize its own profits, resulting in actions that often diminish total supply chain profits (see Chapters 7 and 9). Today, supply chains often consist of stages with hundreds of different owners. For example, Ford Motor Company has thousands of suppliers, from Goodyear to Motorola, and each of these suppliers has several other suppliers in turn. Information is distorted as it moves within the supply chain because complete information is not shared between stages. This distortion is exaggerated by the fact that supply chains today produce a wide range of product variety. For example, Ford produces many different models with many options for each model. The increased variety makes it difficult for Ford to coordinate information exchange with thousands of suppliers and dealers. The fundamental challenge today is for supply chains to achieve coordination in spite of multiple ownership and increased product variety.

Many firms have observed the **bullwhip effect,** in which fluctuations in orders increase as they move up the supply chain from retailers to wholesalers to manufacturers to suppliers, as shown in Figure 13.1. The bullwhip effect distorts demand information within the supply chain, with different stages having a very different estimate of what demand looks like. The result is a loss of supply chain coordination.

Procter & Gamble (P&G) has observed the bullwhip effect in the supply chain for Pampers diapers.[1] The company found that raw material orders from P&G to its suppliers fluctuated significantly over time. Further down the chain, when sales at retail stores were studied, it was found that the fluctuations, though present, were small. It is reasonable to assume that the consumers of diapers (babies) at the last stage of the supply chain used them at a steady rate. Although consumption of the end product was stable, orders for raw material were highly variable, increasing costs and making it difficult for supply to match demand.

Hewlett Packard (HP) also found that the fluctuation in orders increased significantly as it moved from the resellers up the supply chain to the printer division to the integrated circuit division.[2] Once again, although product demand showed some variability, orders placed with the integrated circuit division were much more variable. This made it difficult for HP to fill orders on time and increased the cost of doing so.

Studies of the apparel and grocery industry have shown a similar phenomenon; the fluctuation in orders increases as we move upstream in the supply chain from retail to manufacturing. Barilla, an Italian manufacturer of pasta, observed that weekly orders placed by a local distribution center fluctuated by up to a factor of 70 in the course of the year, but weekly sales at the distribution center (representing orders placed by supermarkets) fluctuated by a factor of less than 3.[3] Barilla was thus facing demand that was much more variable than customer demand. This led to increased inventories, poorer product availability, and a drop in profits.

A similar phenomenon, over a longer time frame, has been observed in several industries that are prone to "boom and bust" cycles. A good example is the production of memory chips for computers. Between 1985 and 1998, there were at least two cycles in which prices of memory chips fluctuated by a factor of more than 3. These large

[1]Lee, Padmanabhan and Whang (1997).
[2]Ibid.
[3]Hammond (1994).

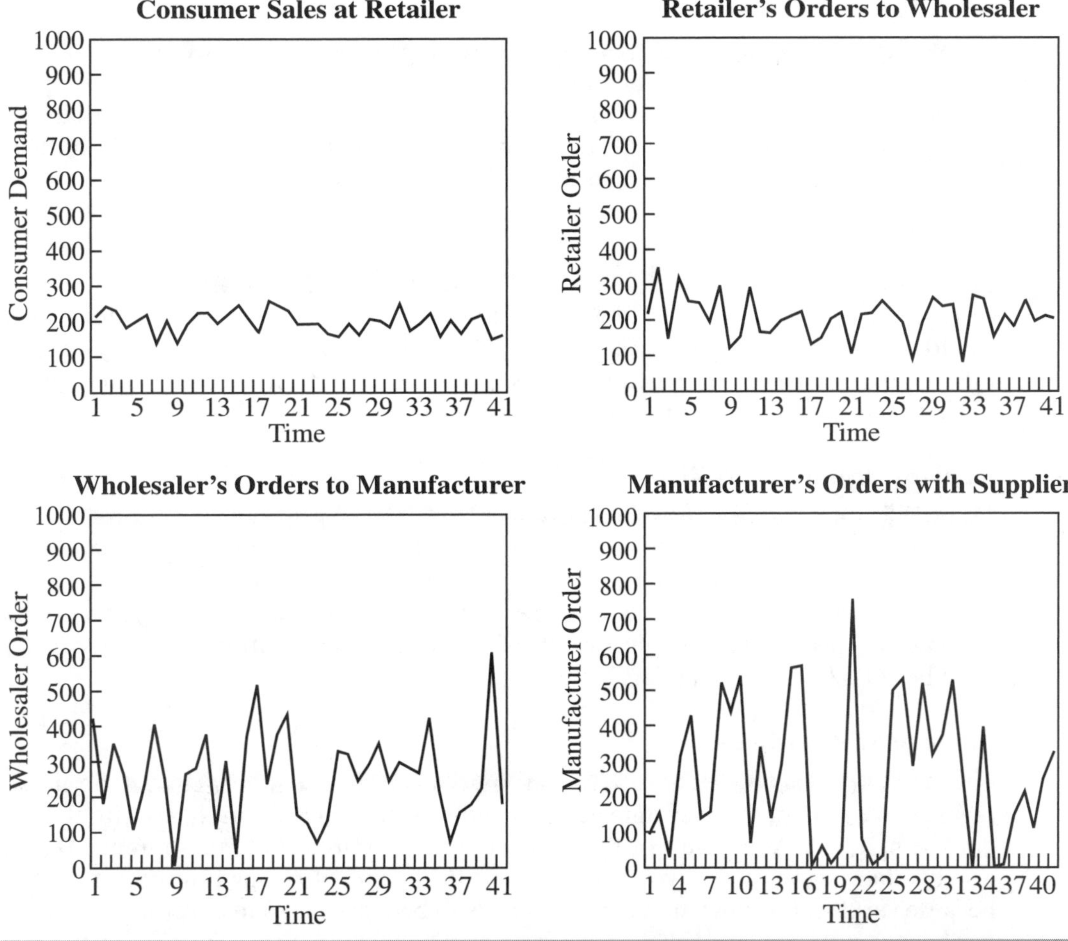

FIGURE 13.1 Demand Fluctuations at Different Stages of a Supply Chain

fluctuations in price were driven by either large shortages or surpluses in capacity. The shortages were exacerbated by panic buying and overordering followed by a sudden drop in demand.

In the next section we consider how the lack of coordination affects supply chain performance.

13.2 EFFECT OF LACK OF COORDINATION ON PERFORMANCE

Lack of coordination results if each stage of the supply chain only optimizes its local objective without considering the impact on the complete chain. Total supply chain profits are thus less than what could be achieved through coordination (see Chapters 7 and 9). Each stage of the supply chain, in trying to optimize its local objective, takes actions that end up hurting the performance of the entire supply chain.

Lack of coordination also results if information distortion occurs within the supply chain. As an example, consider the bullwhip effect P&G observed within the diaper supply chain. As a result of the bullwhip effect, orders P&G receives from its distributors are much more variable than demand for diapers at retailers. We discuss the impact of this increase in variability on various measures of performance in the diaper supply chain.

Manufacturing Cost

The bullwhip effect increases manufacturing cost in the supply chain. As a result of the bullwhip effect, P&G and its suppliers try to satisfy a stream of orders that is much more variable than customer demand. P&G can respond to the increased variability by either building excess capacity or holding excess inventory (see Chapter 5), both of which increase the manufacturing cost per unit produced.

Inventory Cost

The bullwhip effect increases inventory cost in the supply chain. To handle the increased variability in demand, P&G has to carry a higher level of inventory than would be required in the absence of the bullwhip effect. As a result, inventory costs in the supply chain increase. The high levels of inventory also increase the warehousing space required and thus the warehousing cost incurred.

Replenishment Lead Time

The bullwhip effect increases replenishment lead times in the supply chain. The increased variability as a result of the bullwhip effect makes scheduling at P&G and supplier plants much more difficult compared with a situation with level demand. There are times when the available capacity and inventory cannot supply the orders coming in. This results in higher replenishment lead times within the supply chain from both P&G and its suppliers.

Transportation Cost

The bullwhip effect increases transportation cost within the supply chain. The transportation requirements over time at P&G and its suppliers are correlated with the orders being filled. As a result of the bullwhip effect, transportation requirements will also fluctuate significantly over time. This has the impact of raising transportation cost because surplus transportation capacity needs to be maintained to cover high demand periods.

Labor Cost for Shipping and Receiving

The bullwhip effect increases labor costs associated with shipping and receiving in the supply chain. Labor requirements for shipping at P&G and its suppliers will fluctuate with orders. A similar fluctuation will occur for the labor requirements for receiving at distributors and retailers. The various stages have the option of carrying excess labor capacity or varying labor capacity in response to the fluctuation in orders. Either option increases total labor cost.

Level of Product Availability

The bullwhip effect hurts the level of product availability and results in more stockouts within the supply chain. The large fluctuations in orders make it less likely that P&G will be able to supply all distributor and retailer orders on time. This increases the likelihood that retailers will run out of stock, resulting in lost sales for the supply chain.

Relationships Across the Supply Chain

The bullwhip effect negatively affects performance at every stage and thus hurts the relationships between different stages of the supply chain. There is a tendency to assign blame to other stages of the supply chain because people involved at each stage

TABLE 13.1 Impact of Bullwhip Effect on Supply Chain Performance

Performance Measure	*Impact of Bullwhip Effect*
Manufacturing cost	Increases
Inventory cost	Increases
Replenishment lead time	Increases
Transportation cost	Increases
Shipping and receiving cost	Increases
Level of product availability	Decreases
Profitability	Decreases

feel they are doing the best they can. The bullwhip effect thus leads to a loss of trust between different stages of the supply chain and makes any potential coordination efforts more difficult.

From the preceding discussion, it follows that the bullwhip effect and the resulting lack of coordination have a significant negative impact on the supply chain's performance. The bullwhip effect moves a supply chain away from the efficient frontier by increasing cost and decreasing responsiveness. The impact of the bullwhip effect on different performance measures is summarized in Table 13.1.

> ***Key Point*** The bullwhip effect reduces the profitability of a supply chain by making it more expensive to provide a given level of product availability.

In the next section we discuss various obstacles to achieving coordination in the supply chain.

13.3 OBSTACLES TO COORDINATION IN A SUPPLY CHAIN

Any factor that leads to either local optimization by different stages of the supply chain or an increase in information distortion and variability within the supply chain is an obstacle to coordination. If managers in a supply chain are able to identify the key obstacles, they can then take suitable actions that help achieve coordination. We divide the major obstacles into five categories:

- Incentive obstacles
- Information processing obstacles
- Operational obstacles
- Pricing obstacles
- Behavioral obstacles

Incentive Obstacles

Incentive obstacles refer to situations in which incentives offered to different stages or participants in a supply chain lead to actions that increase variability and reduce total supply chain profits.

Local Optimization Within Functions or Stages of a Supply Chain

Incentives that focus only on the local impact of an action result in decisions that do not maximize total supply chain profits. For example, if a transportation manager's compensation is linked to the average transportation cost per unit, she is likely to take actions that lower transportation costs even if they increase inventory costs or hurt customer service. It is natural for any participant in the supply chain to take actions that optimize performance measures along which he or she is evaluated. For example, managers at a retailer such as K-Mart make all their purchasing and inventory decisions to maximize K-Mart profits, not total supply chain profits. Buying decisions based on maximizing profits at a single stage of the supply chain lead to ordering policies that do not maximize supply chain profits (see Chapters 7 and 9).

Evaluating a function in the supply chain based only on that function's costs also leads to actions that reduce supply chain profits. For example, transportation policies that minimize transportation costs rarely minimize total cost in the supply chain, or even in the company (see Chapter 10). Thus, objectives within the supply chain that are not aligned form a significant obstacle to coordination in the supply chain.

Sales Force Incentives

Improperly structured sales force incentives are a significant obstacle to coordination in the supply chain. In many firms, sales force incentives are based on the amount the sales force sells during an evaluation period of a month or quarter. The sales typically measured by a manufacturer are the quantity sold to distributors or retailers (sell-in), not the quantity sold to final customers (sell-through). Measuring performance based on sell-in is often justified on the grounds that the manufacturer's sales force does not control sell-through. For example, Barilla offered its sales force incentives based on the quantity sold to distributors during a four- to six-week promotion period. To maximize their bonuses, the Barilla sales force urged distributors to buy more pasta toward the end of the evaluation period, even if distributors were not selling as much to retailers. The sales force offered discounts they controlled to spur end-of-period sales. This increased variability in the order pattern, with a jump in orders toward the end of the evaluation period followed by very few orders at the beginning of the next evaluation period. Order sizes from distributors to Barilla fluctuated by a factor of up to 70 from one week to the next. A sales force incentive based on sell-in thus results in order variability being larger than customer demand variability.

Information Processing Obstacles

Information processing obstacles refer to situations in which demand information is distorted as it moves between different stages of the supply chain, leading to increased variability in orders within the supply chain.

Forecasting Based on Orders, not Customer Demand

When forecasts are based on orders received, any variability in customer demand is magnified as orders move up the supply chain to manufacturers and suppliers. In supply chains that exhibit the bullwhip effect, the fundamental means of communication between different stages are the orders that are placed. Each stage views its primary role within the supply chain as one of filling orders placed by its downstream partner. Thus, each stage views its demand to be the stream of orders received and produces a forecast based on this information.

In such a scenario, a small change in customer demand becomes magnified as it moves up the supply chain in the form of customer orders. Consider the impact of a random increase in customer demand at the retailer. The retailer may interpret part of this random increase to be a growth trend. This interpretation will lead the retailer to order more than the observed increase in demand because the retailer expects growth to continue into the future and thus orders to cover for future anticipated growth. The increase in the order placed with the wholesaler is thus larger than the observed increase in demand at the retailer. Part of the increase is a one-time increase. The wholesaler, however, has no way to interpret the order increase correctly. The wholesaler simply observes a jump in the order size and infers a growth trend. The growth trend inferred by the wholesaler will be larger than that inferred by the retailer. (Recall that the retailer had increased the order size to account for future growth.) The wholesaler will thus place an even larger order with the manufacturer. As we go further up the supply chain, the order size will be magnified.

Now assume that periods of random increase are followed by periods of random decrease in demand. Using the same forecasting logic just described, the retailer will now anticipate a declining trend and reduce order size. This reduction will also become magnified as we move up the supply chain.

> ***Key Point*** The fact that each stage in a supply chain forecasts demand based on the stream of orders received from the downstream stage results in a magnification of fluctuations in demand as we move up the supply chain from the retailer to the manufacturer.

Lack of Information Sharing

The lack of information sharing between stages of the supply chain magnifies the bullwhip effect. For example, a retailer such as Wal-Mart may increase the size of a particular order because of a planned promotion. If the manufacturer is not aware of the planned promotion, it may interpret the larger order as a permanent increase in demand and place orders with suppliers accordingly. The manufacturer and suppliers thus have a lot of inventory right after Wal-Mart has finished its promotion. Given the excess inventory, as future Wal-Mart orders return to normal, manufacturer orders will be smaller than before. The lack of information sharing between the retailer and manufacturer thus leads to a large fluctuation in orders placed by the manufacturer.

Operational Obstacles

Operational obstacles refer to actions taken in the course of placing and filling orders that lead to an increase in variability.

Ordering in Large Lots

When a firm places orders in lot sizes that are much larger than the lot sizes in which demand arises, variability of orders is magnified up the supply chain. Firms may order in large lots because there is a significant fixed cost associated with placing, receiving, or transporting an order (see Chapter 7) or because the supplier offers quantity discounts based on lot size (see Chapter 7). Ordering in large lots results in an order stream that is far more erratic than the demand stream. Figure 13.2 shows both the demand and the order stream for a firm placing an order every five weeks.

Because orders are batched and placed every five weeks, the order stream has four weeks without orders followed by a large order that equals five weeks of demand. A manufacturer supplying several retailers who batch their orders will face an order stream that is much more variable than the demand the retailers experience. If the manufacturer further batches their orders to suppliers, the effect is further magnified. In many instances there are certain focal point periods like the first or last week of a

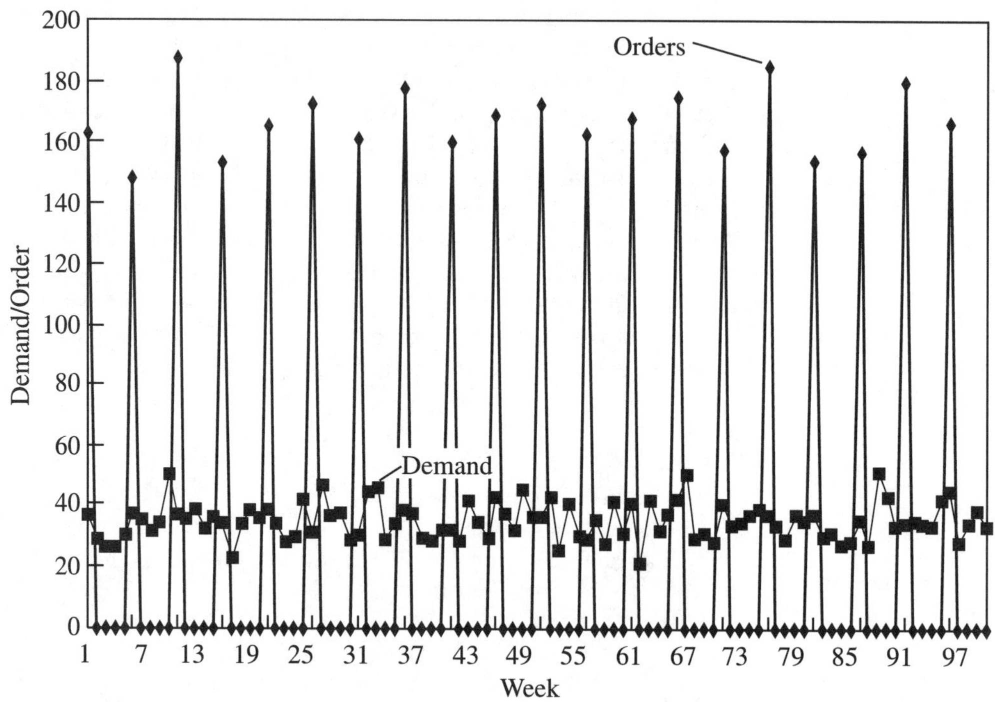

FIGURE 13.2 Demand and Order Stream with Orders Every Five Weeks

month when a majority of the orders arrive. This concentration of orders further exacerbates the impact of batching.

Large Replenishment Lead Times

The bullwhip effect is magnified if replenishment lead times between stages are long. Consider a situation in which a retailer has misinterpreted a random increase in demand as a growth trend. If the retailer faces a lead time of two weeks, it will incorporate the anticipated growth over two weeks when placing the order. If, in contrast, the retailer faces a lead time of two months, it will incorporate into its order the anticipated growth over two months (which will be much larger). The same applies when a random decrease in demand is interpreted as a declining trend.

Rationing and Shortage Gaming

Rationing schemes that allocate limited production in proportion to the orders placed by retailers lead to a magnification of the bullwhip effect. A situation in which a high-demand product is in short supply often arises within the supply chain. HP, for example, has faced several situations in which its newest product has demand that far exceeds supply. In such a situation, manufacturers come up with a variety of mechanisms to ration the scarce supply of product among various distributors or retailers. One commonly used rationing scheme is to allocate the available supply of product based on orders placed. Under this rationing scheme, if the supply available is 75 percent of the total orders received, each retailer receives 75 percent of its order.

This rationing scheme results in a game in which retailers try to increase the size of their orders to increase the amount supplied to them. A retailer needing 75 units will order 100 units in the hope that 75 will then be made available. The net impact of this rationing scheme is to inflate orders for the product artificially. What is worse, a retailer ordering based on what it expects to sell will get less and, as a result, lose sales, whereas a retailer inflating its order is rewarded.

If the manufacturer is using orders to forecast future demand, it will interpret the increase in orders as an increase in demand, even though customer demand is unchanged. The manufacturer may respond by building enough capacity to be able to fill all orders received. Once sufficient capacity becomes available, orders return to their normal level because they were inflated in response to the rationing scheme. The manufacturer is now left with a surplus of product and capacity. These boom and bust cycles then tend to alternate.

This phenomenon is fairly common in the computer industry, in which alternating periods of component shortages followed by a component surplus are often observed. In particular, memory chip manufacturing has experienced several such cycles during the 1990s.

Pricing Obstacles

Pricing obstacles refer to situations in which the pricing policies for a product lead to an increase in variability of orders placed.

Lot Size–Based Quantity Discounts

Lot size–based quantity discounts increase the lot size of orders placed within the supply chain (see Chapter 7). As discussed earlier, the resulting large lots magnify the bullwhip effect within the supply chain.

Price Fluctuations

Trade promotions and other short-term discounts offered by a manufacturer result in forward buying, in which a wholesaler or retailer purchases large lots during the discounting period to cover demand during future periods. Forward buying results in large orders during the promotion period followed by very small orders after that (see Chapter 7), as shown in Figure 13.3 for chicken noodle soup.

FIGURE 13.3 Retailer Sales and Manufacturer Shipments of Soup

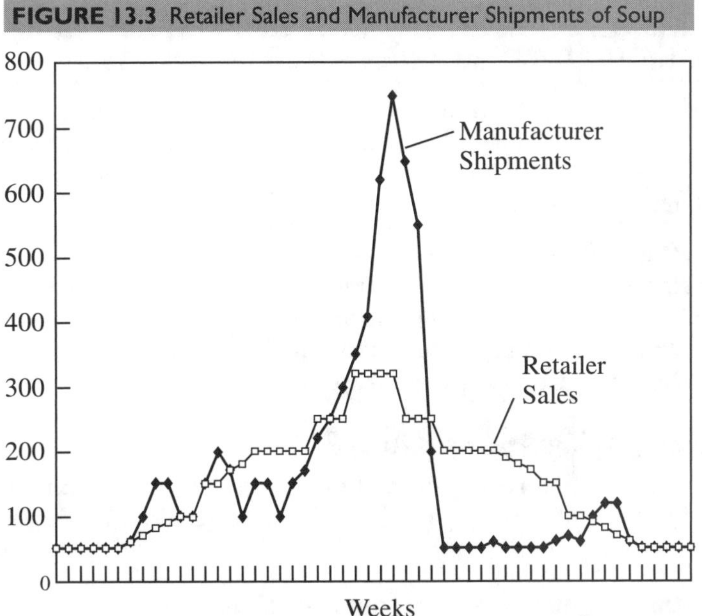

Source: Adapted from Marshall Fisher, "What Is the Right Supply Chain for Your Product?" *Harvard Business Review* (March–April 1997), 83–93.

Observe that the shipments during the peak period are higher than the sales during the peak period because of a promotion offered during this period. The peak shipment period is followed by a period of very low shipments from the manufacturer, indicating significant forward buying by distributors. The promotion thus results in a variability in manufacturer shipments that is significantly higher than the variability in retailer sales.

Behavioral Obstacles

Behavioral obstacles refer to problems in learning within organizations that contribute to the bullwhip effect. These problems are often related to the way the supply chain is structured and the communication between different stages. Some of the behavioral obstacles follow:

1. Each stage of the supply chain views its actions locally and is unable to see the impact of its actions on other stages.
2. Different stages of the supply chain react to the current local situation rather than identify the root causes.
3. Based on local analysis, different stages of the supply chain blame each other for the fluctuations, with successive stages in the supply chain becoming enemies rather than partners.
4. No stage of the supply chain learns from its actions over time because the most significant consequences of the actions any one stage takes occur elsewhere. The result is a vicious circle in which actions taken by a stage create the very problems that stage blames on others.
5. A lack of trust between supply chain partners causes them to be opportunistic at the expense of overall supply chain performance. The lack of trust also results in significant duplication of effort. More importantly, information available at different stages is either not shared or is ignored because it is not trusted.

13.4 MANAGERIAL LEVERS TO ACHIEVE COORDINATION

Having identified obstacles to coordination, we now focus on actions a manager may take to help overcome the obstacles and achieve coordination in the supply chain. The following managerial actions in the supply chain increase total supply chain profits and moderate the bullwhip effect:

- Aligning goals and incentives
- Improving information accuracy
- Improving operational performance
- Designing pricing strategies to stabilize orders
- Building partnerships and trust

Aligning Goals and Incentives

Managers can improve coordination within the supply chain by aligning goals and incentives such that every participant in supply chain activities works to maximize total supply chain profits.

Aligning Incentives Across Functions

One key to coordinated decisions within a firm is to ensure that the objective any function uses to evaluate a decision is aligned with the firm's overall objective. All facility, transportation, information, and inventory decisions should be evaluated based on their impact on profitability, not total costs, or even worse, just local costs. This helps avoid situations such as a transportation manager making decisions that lower transportation cost but increase overall supply chain costs (see Chapter 10).

Pricing for Coordination

A manager can use lot size–based quantity discounts to achieve coordination for commodity products if both the retailer and the manager have large fixed costs associated with each lot (see Chapter 7). For products for which a firm has market power, a manager can use two-part tariffs and volume discounts to help achieve coordination (see Chapter 7). Given demand uncertainty, manufacturers can use buyback contracts and quantity flexibility contracts to spur retailers to provide levels of product availability that maximize supply chain profits (see Chapter 9). Buyback contracts have been used in the publishing industry to increase total supply chain profits. Quantity flexibility contracts have helped Benetton increase supply chain profits.

Altering Sales Force Incentives from Sell-In to Sell-Through

Any change that reduces the incentive for a salesperson to push product to the retailer will reduce the bullwhip effect. If sales force incentives are based on sales over a rolling horizon, the incentive to push product is reduced. This helps reduce forward buying and the resulting fluctuation in orders. Another action that managers can take is to link incentives for the sales staff to sell-through by the retailer rather than sell-in to the retailer. This action eliminates any motivation that sales staff may have to encourage forward buying. The elimination of forward buying helps reduce fluctuations in the order stream.

Improving Information Accuracy

Managers can achieve coordination by improving the accuracy of information available to different stages in the supply chain.

Sharing Point-of-Sale Data

Sharing point-of-sale (POS) data across the supply chain can help reduce the bullwhip effect. A primary cause for the bullwhip effect is the fact that each stage of the supply chain uses orders to forecast future demand. Given that orders received by different stages vary, forecasts at different stages also vary. In reality, the only demand that the supply chain needs to satisfy is from the final customer. If retailers share POS data with other supply chain stages, all supply chain stages can forecast future demand based on customer demand. Sharing POS data helps reduce the bullwhip effect because all stages now respond to the same change in customer demand. Use of appropriate information systems facilitates the sharing of such data (see Chapter 12). Companies have also used the Internet to share data with suppliers. For direct sales companies like Dell, and companies involved in e-business, POS data are available in a form that can easily be shared. Dell shares demand data as well as current inventory positions of components with many of its suppliers on the Internet, thereby helping to avoid unnecessary fluctuations in supply and orders placed. P&G has convinced many retailers to share demand data. P&G in turn shares the data with its suppliers, improving coordination in the supply chain. Wal-Mart shares POS data with its suppliers to improve coodination.

Implementing Collaborative Forecasting and Planning

Once POS data are shared, different stages of the supply chain must forecast and plan jointly if complete coordination is to be achieved. Without collaborative planning, sharing POS data does not guarantee coordination. A retailer may have observed large demand in the month of January because it ran a promotion. If no promotion is planned in the following January, the retailer's forecast will differ from the manufacturer's forecast even if both have past POS data. The manufacturer must be aware of the retailer's promotion plans to achieve coordination. The key is to ensure that the entire supply chain is operating to a common forecast.

Wal-Mart has observed that a lack of collaborative planning has a significant impact on its supply chain performance. Wal-Mart has a joint initiative with P&G, called collaborative forecasting and replenishment, (CFAR) that has had significant success in this regard. Teams consisting of managers from both Wal-Mart and P&G jointly forecast sales of P&G products at Wal-Mart stores and then jointly plan replenishment strategies. This ensures that there is no gap between what Wal-Mart plans to sell and what P&G plans to produce. To facilitate this type of coordination in the supply chain environment, the Voluntary Interindustry Commerce Standards Association has set up a collaborative planning, forecasting, and replenishment (CPFR) committee to identify best practices and design guidelines for collaborative forecasting and planning. The use of both enterprise resource planning (ERP) and demand planning systems helps facilitate collaborative forecasting and planning within the supply chain (see Chapter 12).

Designing Single Stage Control of Replenishment

Designing a supply chain in which a single stage controls replenishment decisions for the entire supply chain can help diminish the bullwhip effect. As mentioned earlier, a key cause for the bullwhip effect is the fact that each stage of the supply chain uses orders from the previous stage as its historical demand. As a result, each stage views its role as one of replenishing orders placed by the next stage. In reality, the key replenishment is at the retailer, because that is where the final customer purchases. When a single stage controls replenishment decisions for the entire chain, the problem of multiple forecasts is eliminated and coordination within the supply chain follows.

For a manufacturer that sells directly to customers, like Dell, single control of replenishment is automatic because there is no intermediary between the manufacturer and the customer. The manufacturer automatically becomes the single point control of replenishment decisions.

When sales occur through retailers, there are several industry practices that result in single point control of replenishment. In **continuous replenishment programs** (CRP), the wholesaler or manufacturer replenishes a retailer regularly based on POS data. The CRP could be supplier, distributor, or third-party managed. In most instances, CRP systems are driven by actual withdrawals of inventory from retailer warehouses rather than POS data at the retailer level. Tying CRP systems to warehouse withdrawals is easier to implement, and retailers are often more comfortable sharing data at this level. ERP systems that are linked across the supply chain provide a good information infrastructure on which a continuous replenishment program may be based.

In **vendor-managed inventories** (VMI), the distributor or manufacturer monitors and manages inventories at the wholesaler or retailer. This centralizes the replenishment decision for all retailers at the upstream distributor or manufacturer. This practice existed in retailing before the growth of enabling technologies. Frito-Lay truck drivers restock retailer shelves without first going through the store owner. The existence of suitable information systems facilitates the implementation of VMI. VMI has been implemented with significant success by, among others, K-Mart (with about 50 suppliers) and Fred Meyer. K-Mart has seen inventory turns on seasonal items increase from 3 to between 9 and 11, and for nonseasonal items from 12–15 to 17–20. Fred Meyer has seen inventories reduce by 30 percent to 40 percent and fill rates increase to 98 percent.

In each of the instances cited here, the single forecast and control of replenishment by a single stage are what help eliminate the increased fluctuations because of the bullwhip effect.

Improving Operational Performance

Managers can help dampen the bullwhip effect by improving operational performance and designing appropriate product rationing schemes in case of shortages.

Reducing Replenishment Lead Time

By reducing the replenishment lead time, managers can decrease the uncertainty of demand during the lead time (see Chapter 8). A reduction in lead time is especially beneficial for seasonal items, because it allows for multiple orders to be placed in the season with a significant increase in the accuracy of the forecast (see Chapter 9). Thus, a reduction in replenishment lead time helps dampen the bullwhip effect by reducing the underlying uncertainty of demand.

Managers can take a variety of actions at different stages of the supply chain to help reduce replenishment lead times. Electronic data interchange (EDI) and other electronic forms of communication can be used to significantly cut the lead time associated with order placement and information transfer. At manufacturing plants, increased flexibility and cellular manufacturing can be used to achieve a significant reduction in lead times. A dampening of the bullwhip effect further reduces lead times because of stabilized demand and, as a result, improved scheduling. This is particularly true when manufacturing is producing a large variety of products. Advance shipment notices (ASN) can be used to reduce the lead time as well as effort associated with receiving. Crossdocking can be used to reduce the lead time associated with moving the product between stages in the supply chain. Wal-Mart has successfully used many of these approaches to significantly reduce lead time within its supply chain.

Reducing Lot Sizes

Managers can dampen the bullwhip effect by implementing operational improvements that reduce lot sizes. Reducing lot sizes decreases the amount of fluctuation that can accumulate between any pair of stages of a supply chain, thus decreasing the bullwhip effect. To reduce lot sizes, managers must take actions that help reduce the fixed costs associated with ordering, transporting, and receiving each lot (see Chapter 7). Wal-Mart and 7-Eleven Japan have been very successful at reducing replenishment lot sizes by aggregating deliveries across many products and suppliers.

Computer-assisted ordering (CAO) refers to using a computer instead of a retail order clerk in preparing an order. The computers integrate information about product sales, market factors affecting demand, inventory levels, product receipts, and desired service levels. CAO and EDI help reduce the fixed costs associated with placing each order. Today, the growing use of Web-based ordering by companies such as W. W. Grainger and McMaster-Carr has facilitated ordering in small lots because of reduced ordering costs for customers and reduced fulfillment costs for companies themselves. The growth of business-to-business (B2B) Internet exchanges is also reducing ordering costs. For example, General Motors and Ford will require all their suppliers to be equipped to receive orders on the Web to make ordering more efficient.

In some cases, managers can simplify ordering by eliminating the use of purchase orders. In the auto industry, some suppliers are paid based on the number of cars produced, eliminating the need for individual purchase orders. This reduces the order processing cost associated with each replenishment order. Information systems also facilitate the settlement of financial transactions, eliminating the cost associated with individual purchase orders.

On the transportation side, the large gap in the prices of truckload (TL) and less than-truckload (LTL) shipping encourages shipment in TL quantities. In fact, with the efforts to reduce order processing costs, transportation costs are now the major barrier to smaller lots in most supply chains. Managers can reduce lot sizes without increasing transportation costs by filling a truck using smaller lots from a variety of products (see Chapter 7). P&G, for example, requires all orders from retailers to be a full truckload. The truckload, however, may be built from any combination of products. A retailer can thus order small lots of each product as long as a sufficiently large variety of products is included on each truck. 7-Eleven Japan has effectively used this strategy with combined trucks, in which the separation is by the temperature at which the truck is maintained. All products to be shipped at a particular temperature are on the same truck. This has allowed 7-Eleven to reduce the number of trucks sent to retail outlets while keeping product variety large. Some firms in the grocery industry use trucks with different compartments, each at a different temperature and carrying a variety of products, to help reduce lot sizes.

Managers can also reduce lot sizes by having milk runs that combine shipments for several retailers on a single truck (see Chapter 10). In many cases, third-party transporters combine shipments to competing retail outlets on a single truck. This reduces the fixed transportation cost per retailer and allows each retailer to order in smaller lots. In Japan, Toyota uses a single truck from a supplier to supply multiple assembly plants, which enables managers to reduce the lot size received by any one plant. Managers can also reduce lot sizes by combining shipments from multiple suppliers on a single truck. In the United States, Toyota uses this approach to reduce the lot size it receives from any one supplier.

As smaller lots are ordered and delivered, both the pressure on and the cost of receiving can grow significantly. Therefore, managers must implement technologies that simplify the receiving process and reduce the cost associated with receiving. For example, ASN electronically identify shipment content, count, and time of delivery and help reduce unloading time and increase crossdock efficiency. ASNs can be used to update inventory records electronically, thus reducing the cost of receiving. Bar coding of pallets also facilitates receiving and delivery. DEX and NEX are two receiving technologies that allow the direct updating of inventory records once the item count has been verified.

Each of these technologies works to simplify the task of shipping, transporting, and receiving complex orders with small lots of many products. This facilitates the reduction of lot size, counteracting the bullwhip effect.

Another simple way to minimize the impact of batching is to encourage different customers to order in a way that demand is evenly distributed over time. Frequently, customers that order once a week tend to do so on either a Monday or Friday. Customers ordering once a month tend to do so either at the beginning or end of the month. In such situations, it is better to evenly distribute customers ordering once a week across all days of the week, and customers ordering once a month across all days of the month. In fact, regular ordering days may be scheduled in advance for each customer. This generally does not affect retailers but it does level out the order stream arriving at the manufacturer, thus dampening the bullwhip effect.

Rationing Based on Past Sales and Sharing Information to Limit Gaming

To diminish the bullwhip effect, managers can design rationing schemes that discourage retailers from artificially inflating their orders in case of a shortage. One approach, referred to as **turn and earn**, is to allocate the available supply based on past retailer sales rather than current retailer orders. Tying allocation to past sales removes any incentive a retailer may have to inflate orders, as a result dampening the bullwhip effect. In fact, during low demand periods, the turn-and-earn approach pushes retailers to try to sell more to increase the allocation they receive during periods of shortage. Several firms, including General Motors, have historically used the turn-and-earn mechanism to ration available product in case of a shortage. Others, like HP have historically allocated based on retailer orders but are now switching to past sales.

Other firms have tried to share information across the supply chain to minimize shortage situations. Firms like Sport Obermeyer offer incentives to their large customers to preorder at least a part of their annual order. This information allows Sport Obermeyer to improve the accuracy of its own forecast and allocate production capacity accordingly. Once capacity has been allocated appropriately across different products, it is less likely that shortage situations will arise, thus dampening the bullwhip effect. The availability of flexible capacity can also help in this regard, because flexible capacity can easily be shifted from a product whose demand is lower than expected to one whose demand is higher than expected.

Designing Pricing Strategies to Stabilize Orders

Managers can diminish the bullwhip effect by devising pricing strategies that encourage retailers to order in smaller lots and reduce forward buying.

Moving from Lot Size–Based to Volume-Based Quantity Discounts

As a result of lot size–based quantity discounts, retailers increase their lot size to take full advantage of the discount. Offering volume-based quantity discounts eliminates the incentive to increase the size of a single lot because volume-based discounts consider the total purchases during a specified period (say a year) rather than purchases in a single lot (see Chapter 7). Volume-based quantity discounts result in smaller lot sizes, thus reducing order variability in the supply chain. Volume-based discounts with a fixed end date at which discounts will be evaluated may lead to large lots close to the end date. Offering the discounts over a rolling time horizon helps dampen this effect. HP is experimenting with a move away from lot size–based discounts to volume-based discounts.

Stabilizing Pricing

Managers can dampen the bullwhip effect by eliminating promotions and charging an **every day low pricing** (*EDLP*). The elimination of promotions removes forward buying by retailers and results in orders that match customer demand. P&G, Campbell Soup, and several other manufacturers have implemented EDLP to dampen the bullwhip effect.

Managers can place limits on the quantity that may be purchased during a promotion to decrease forward buying. This limit should be retailer specific and linked to historical sales by the retailer. Another approach is to tie the promotion dollars paid to the retailer to the amount of sell-through rather than the amount purchased by the retailer. As a result, retailers obtain no benefit from forward buying and purchase more only if they can sell more. Promotions based on sell-through significantly dampen the bullwhip effect. The presence of specific information systems facilitates the tying of promotions directly to customer sales.

Building Strategic Partnerships and Trust

Managers find it easier to use the levers discussed in the previous section to diminish the bullwhip effect and achieve coordination if trust and strategic partnerships are built within the supply chain. Sharing of accurate information that is trusted by every stage results in a better matching of supply and demand throughout the supply chain and a lower cost. A better relationship also tends to lower the transaction cost between supply chain stages. For example, a supplier can eliminate its forecasting effort if it trusts orders and forecast information received from the retailer. Similarly, the retailer can lessen the receiving effort by decreasing counting and inspections if it trusts the supplier's quality and delivery. In general, stages in a supply chain can eliminate duplicated effort on the basis of improved trust and a better relationship. This lowering of transaction costs along with accurate shared information helps mitigate the bullwhip effect. Wal-Mart and P&G have been trying to build a strategic partnership that will be mutually beneficial and help reduce the bullwhip effect.

Managerial levers that help a supply chain achieve better coordination fall into two broad categories: **Action-oriented levers** include information sharing, changing of incentives, operational improvements, and stabilization of pricing, and **relationship-oriented levers** involve the building of cooperation and trust within the supply chain. In the next section we discuss relationship-oriented levers in greater detail.

13.5 BUILDING STRATEGIC PARTNERSHIPS AND TRUST WITHIN A SUPPLY CHAIN

A **trust-based relationship** between two stages of a supply chain includes **dependability** of the two stages and the ability of each stage to make a **leap of faith**.[4] Trust involves a belief that each stage is interested in the other's welfare and would not take actions without considering their impact on the other stage. Cooperation and trust within the supply chain help improve performance for the following reasons:

1. A more natural aligning of incentives and objectives is achieved. When stages trust each other, they are more likely to take the other party's objective into consideration when making decisions.
2. Action-oriented managerial levers to achieve coordination become easier to implement. Sharing of information is natural between parties that trust each other. Similarly, operational improvements are easier to implement and appropriate pricing schemes easier to design if both parties are aiming for the common good.
3. An increase in supply chain productivity results, either by elimination of duplicated effort or by allocating effort to the appropriate stage. For example, a manufacturer receives material from a supplier without inspecting it as long as the supplier shares process control charts. Another example is the situation in which a distributor aids the postponement strategy of a manufacturer by performing customization just before the "point of sale."
4. A greater sharing of detailed sales and production information results. This sharing allows the supply chain to coordinate production and distribution decisions. As a result, the supply chain is better able to match supply and demand, resulting in better coordination.

[4]Kumar (1996).

The benefits of trust are highlighted in Table 13.2, in the context of a replacement automotive parts supply chain. The table contains average ratings of more than 400 retailers classified into low or high categories based on their trust in the manufacturer.

Table 13.2 illustrates that retailers with a high trust in the manufacturer were more committed to the manufacturer, sold more of the manufacturer's products, and were rated higher by the manufacturer. It also highlights that the retailers themselves were happier when they had greater trust in the manufacturer because they were less likely to search for alternative supply sources. Thus, trust creates a win-win situation in which both stages of the supply chain benefit.

Historically, supply chain relationships have been based either on power or trust. In a power-based relationship, the stronger party dictates its view. Although exploiting power may be advantageous in the short term, its negative consequences are felt in the long term for three main reasons:

1. Exploiting power often results in one stage of the supply chain maximizing its profits, often at the expense of other stages. This decreases total supply chain profits.
2. Exploiting power to extract unfair concessions can hurt a company once the balance of power changes. This reversal of power has occurred from the 1980s to the present, as retailers have become more powerful than manufacturers in many supply chains.
3. When a stage of a supply chain systematically exploits its power advantage, other stages seek ways to resist. In many instances in which retailers have tried to exploit their power, manufacturers have sought ways to directly access the consumer. These include selling over the Internet and setting up company stores. The result can be a decrease in supply chain profits because different stages are competing rather than cooperating.

Although everybody agrees that cooperation and trust in a supply chain is valuable, these qualities are very hard to initiate and sustain. There are two views regarding how cooperation and trust can be built into any supply chain relationship:

- **Deterrence-based view**. In this view, the parties involved use a variety of formal contracts to ensure cooperation. With the contracts in place, parties are assumed to behave in a trusting manner purely for reasons of self-interest.
- **Process-based view**. With this view, trust and cooperation are built over time as a result of a series of interactions between the parties involved. Positive interactions strengthen the belief in the cooperation of the other party.

In most practical situations, neither view holds exclusively. It is impossible to design a contract that will take into account every contingency that may arise in the fu-

TABLE 13.2 Comparison of Retailers by Level of Trust

Measure of Comparison	*Low Trust*	*High Trust*
Retailers' development of alternative supply sources	100	78
Retailers' commitment to the manufacturer	100	112
Retailers' sales of manufacturer product line	100	178
Retailers' performance as rated by manufacturer	100	111

Adapted from N. Kumar "The Power of Trust in Manufacturer–Retailer Relationships," *Harvard Business Review* (November–December 1996), 92–106.

ture. Therefore, parties that may not yet trust each other have to rely on the building of trust to resolve issues that are not included in the contract. Conversely, parties that trust each other and have a long relationship still rely on contracts. In most effective partnerships, a combination of the two approaches is used. An example is the situation in which American suppliers sign an initial contract containing contingencies with Japanese manufacturers and then the manufacturers never refer to the contract again. Their hope is that all contingencies can be resolved through negotiation in a way that is best for the supply chain.

In most strong supply chain relationships, the initial period often relies more on the deterrence-based view. Over time, the relationship evolves toward a greater reliance on the process-based view. From the supply chain perspective, the ideal goal is **co-identification,** in which each party considers the other party's objective as its own. Co-identification ensures that each stage accounts for total supply chain profits when making decisions.

There are two phases to any long-term supply chain relationship. In the **design phase**, ground rules are established and the relationship is initiated. In the **management phase**, interactions based on the ground rules occur, and the relationship as well as the ground rules evolve. A manager seeking to build a supply chain relationship must consider how cooperation and trust can be encouraged during both phases of the relationship. Careful consideration is very important because in most supply chains, power tends to be concentrated in relatively few hands. The concentration of power often leads managers to ignore the effort required to build trust and cooperation, hurting supply chain performance in the long term.

Next we discuss how a manager can design a supply chain relationship to encourage cooperation and trust.

Designing a Relationship with Cooperation and Trust

The key steps in designing effective supply chain partnerships are as follows:

1. Assessing the value of the relationship
2. Identifying operational roles and decision rights for each party
3. Creating effective contracts
4. Designing effective conflict resolution mechanisms

Assessing the Value of the Relationship

The first step in designing a supply chain relationship is to identify clearly the mutual benefit that the relationship provides. In most supply chains, each member of the partnership brings distinct skills, all of which are needed to supply a customer order. For example, a manufacturer produces the product, a carrier transports it between stages, and a retailer makes the product available to the final customer. The next step is to identify the criteria used for evaluating the relationship as well as the contribution of each party. A common criterion is the increase in total profits as a result of the relationship. **Equity**, defined as fair dealing, should be another important criterion when evaluating and designing a relationship.[5] Equity, in this discussion, measures the fairness of the division of the total profits between the parties involved.

Stages of the supply chain are unlikely to work at utilizing the various managerial levers that achieve coordination unless they are confident that the resulting increase in profits will be shared equitably. For example, when suppliers work hard to reduce replenishment lead times, the supply chain benefits because of reduced safety invento-

[5] Ring and Van de Ven (1994).

ries at manufacturers and retailers. Suppliers are unlikely to put in the effort if the manufacturers and retailers are not willing to share the increase in profits with them. Thus, a supply chain relationship is likely to be sustainable only if it increases total profits, and this increase is shared equitably between the parties involved.

The next step is to clarify the contribution of each party as well as the benefits that will accrue to each. For example, if a manufacturer and distributor are to implement postponement together, it is important to clarify the role of each party in implementing postponement, the value of this strategy to the supply chain, and how the increased profits are to be shared between the parties. Flexible mechanisms should be designed that allow the partners to monitor the relationship periodically and adjust both contributions and the allocation of resulting benefits. For example, Chrysler negotiates a certain level of improvement per year with each supplier. It does not, however, specify areas within which the improvement must be achieved. This flexibility allows suppliers to identify areas where the largest improvement can result with the minimum effort and creates a win-win situation for both sides.

Identifying Operational Roles and Decision Rights for Each Party

When identifying operational roles and decision rights for different parties in a supply chain relationship, managers must consider the resulting interdependence between the parties. A source of conflict may arise if the tasks are divided in a way that makes one party more dependent on the other. In many partnerships, an inefficient allocation of tasks results simply because neither party is willing to give the other a perceived upper hand based on the tasks assigned.

The allocation of tasks results in a **sequential interdependence** if the activities of one partner precede the other. Traditionally, supply chain relationships have been sequential, with one stage completing all its tasks and then handing off to the next stage. In **reciprocal interdependence**, parties come together and exchange information and inputs in both directions. P&G and Wal-Mart are attempting to create reciprocal interdependence through collaborative forecasting and replenishment teams. The teams contain people from both Wal-Mart and P&G. Wal-Mart brings in demand information and P&G brings in information on available capacity. The teams then decide on the production and replenishment policy that is best for the supply chain.

Reciprocal interdependence requires a significant effort to manage and can increase the transaction costs if not managed properly. However, reciprocal interdependence is more likely to result in decisions that maximize supply chain profitability because all decisions must take the objectives of both parties into account. Reciprocal interdependence increases the interactions between the two parties, increasing the chances of trust and cooperation if positive interactions occur. Reciprocal interdependence also makes it harder for one party to be opportunistic and take self-serving actions that hurt the other party. Thus, greater reciprocal interdependence in the allocation of operational roles and decision rights increases the chances of an effective relationship, as shown in Figure 13.4.

Managers must ensure that tasks that are required from each party for a successful handoff of the product from one to the other be well defined. Consider the relationship among Dell, Sony, and Airborne. Dell takes orders for computers it assembles and monitors that Sony manufactures. Airborne picks up the computer from the Dell warehouse in Texas and the monitor from the Sony warehouse in Mexico. It then merges the two and sends a combined order to the customer. For an order to be filled on time, all three parties must coordinate and complete their tasks. To achieve cooperation, managers must also put in place some mechanism, such as appropriate information systems, that helps accurately track all failures to their source.

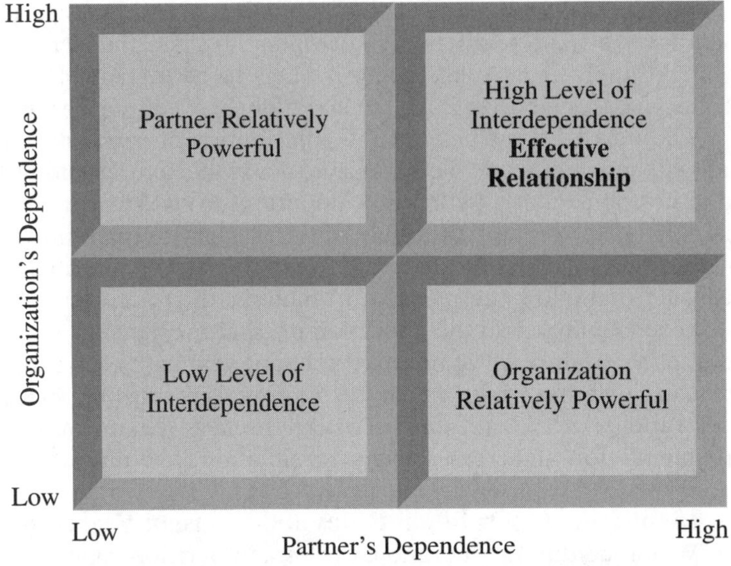

FIGURE 13.4 Effect of Interdependence on Supply Chain Relationships

Source: Adapted from N. Kumar, "The Power of Trust in Manufacturer-Retailer Relationships," *Harvard Business Review* (November–December 1996), 92–106.

Creating Effective Contracts

Managers can help promote trust by creating contracts that encourage negotiation as unplanned contingencies arise. Contracts are most effective for governance when complete information is available and all future contingencies can be accounted for. In practice, uncertainty with respect to the future value of the relationship and the future business environment makes it impossible to design a contract with all contingencies included. For example, when considering vendor-managed inventories or continuous replenishment programs, it is very difficult to design a contract for all possible future scenarios. Thus, it is essential that the supplier and the retailer develop a relationship that allows trust to compensate for gaps in the contract. The relationship often develops between appropriate individuals that have been assigned from each side. Over time, the informal understandings and commitments between the individuals tend to be formalized when new contracts are drawn up. When designing the partnership and initial contract, it should be understood that informal understandings will operate side by side, and these will contribute to the development of the formal contract over time. Thus, contracts that evolve over time are likely to be much more effective than contracts that are completely defined at the beginning of the partnership.

Over the long term, contracts can play only a partial role in maintaining effective partnerships in a supply chain. A good example is the relationship between Caterpillar and their dealerships, in which either the dealer or Caterpillar can terminate agreements without cause with 90 days' notice. Clearly it is not the contract alone that keeps the relationship effective. A combination of a contract, the mutual benefit of the relationship, along with trust that compensates for gaps in the contract, results in effective supply chain partnerships.

Designing Effective Conflict Resolution Mechanisms

Effective conflict resolution mechanisms can significantly strengthen any supply chain relationship. Conflicts are bound to arise in any relationship. Unsatisfactory resolutions cause the partnership to worsen, whereas satisfactory resolutions strengthen the partnership. A good conflict resolution mechanism should give the parties an opportunity to communicate and work through their differences, in the process building greater trust.

An initial formal specification of rules and guidelines for financial procedures and technological transactions can help build trust between partners. The specification of rules and guidelines facilitates the sharing of information among the partners in the supply chain. The sharing of information over time helps move the relationship from deterrence-based trust to process-based trust. When process-based trust is built between the parties, it facilitates conflict resolution.

To facilitate communication, regular and frequent meetings should be held between managers and staff assigned to the partnership. These meetings allow issues to be raised and discussed before they turn into major conflicts. They also provide a basis for resolution at a higher level, should resolution at a lower level not take place. An important goal of meetings and other formal conflict resolution mechanisms is to ensure that disputes about financial or technological issues do not turn into interpersonal squabbles.

When designing conflict resolution mechanisms, it is important to be sensitive to the context of the partnership. In the United States, parties are often comfortable returning to the detailed contract to resolve a dispute. The help of a court or an intermediary can also be sought to interpret the contract. Therefore, detailed contracts can be quite effective in the United States. In Asia, in contrast, conflict resolution mechanisms involving courts are unlikely to be very effective. Parties are much more comfortable directly negotiating resolutions to every conflict. Flexible contracts that allow for such negotiation are effective in building trust in that context.

Managing Supply Chain Relationships for Cooperation and Trust

Effectively managed supply chain relationships foster cooperation and trust, thus increasing supply chain coordination. In contrast, poorly managed relationships lead to each party's being opportunistic, resulting in a loss of total supply chain profits. The management of a relationship is often seen as a tedious and routine task. Top management, in particular, is often very involved in the design of a new partnership but rarely involved in its management. This has led to a mixed record in running successful supply chain alliances and partnerships.

Figure 13.5 shows the basic process by which any supply chain partnership or alliance evolves. Once the partnership has been designed and established, both partners learn about the environment in which the partnership will operate, the tasks and processes to be performed by each partner, the skills required and available on each side, and the emerging goals of each side. The performance of each side is evaluated based on the improvement in profitability and on equity or fairness. At this stage, a better evaluation of the value of the partnership becomes available, which provides both parties in the supply chain partnership an opportunity to revise the conditions of the partnership to improve profitability and fairness. It is important that the initial contracts be designed with sufficient flexibility to facilitate such alterations. Formal contracts may be restructured to reflect the changes. As the business environment and company goals change, the cycle repeats itself and the relationship evolves. Any successful supply chain partnership will go through many such cycles.

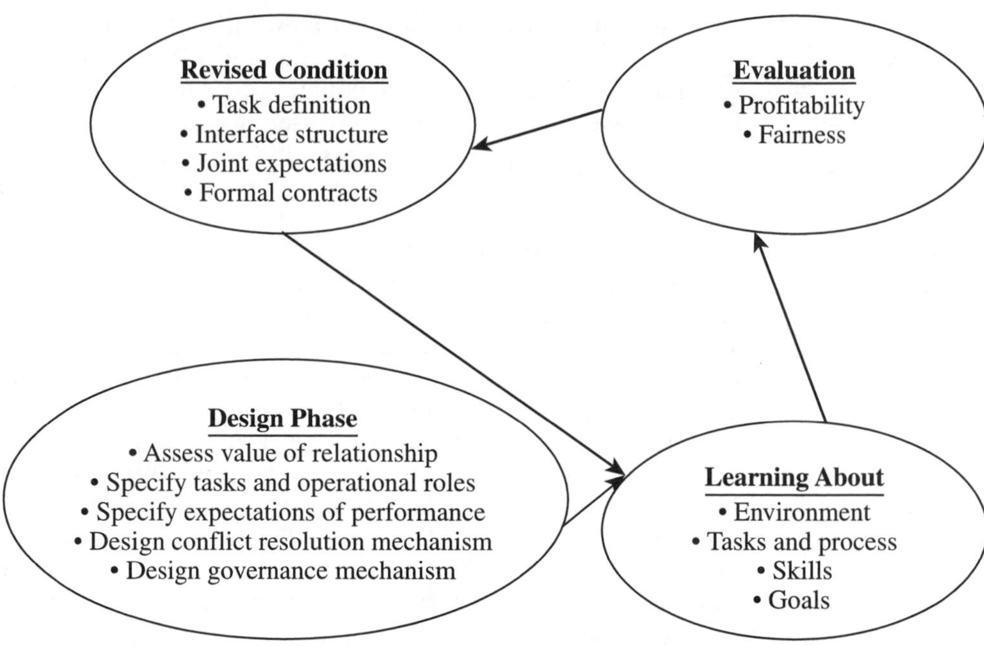

FIGURE 13.5 Process of Alliance and Partnership Evolution

Adapted from *Alliance Advantage* by Y.L. Doz and G. Hamel

A supply chain partnership falters if the perceived benefit from the relationship diminishes or one party is seen as being opportunistic. Problems arise when communication between the two parties is weak and the mutual benefit of the relationship is not reiterated regularly. When managing a supply chain relationship, managers should focus on the following factors to improve the chances of success of a supply chain partnership:

1. The presence of flexibility, trust, and commitment in both parties helps a supply chain relationship succeed. In particular, commitment of top management on both sides is crucial for success. The manager directly responsible for the partnership can also facilitate the development of the relationship by clearly identifying the value of the partnership for each party in terms of his own expectations.
2. Good organizational arrangements, especially for information sharing and conflict resolution, improve chances of success. Lack of information sharing and the inability to resolve conflicts are the two major factors that lead to the breakdown of supply chain partnerships.
3. Mechanisms that make the actions of each party and resulting outcomes visible help avoid conflicts and resolve disputes. Such mechanisms make it harder for either party to be opportunistic and help identify defective processes, increasing the value of the relationship for both parties.
4. The more fairly the stronger partner treats the weaker, vulnerable partner, the stronger the supply chain relationship tends to be.

The issue of fairness is extremely important in the supply chain context because most relationships will involve parties with unequal power. Unanticipated situations that hurt one party more than the other often arise. The more powerful party often has greater control over how the resolution occurs. The fairness of the resolution influences the strength of the relationship in the future.

Fairness requires that the benefits and costs of the relationship be shared between the two parties in a way that makes both winners. A relationship based on power would maximize all benefits on one side. A long-term supply chain relationship cannot be maintained if this is the case. For a strong supply chain relationship to develop, the stronger party must realize its responsibility for its partner's profitability. The relationship between the retailer Marks & Spencer and a manufacturer of a kitchen product provides an excellent example of a fair sharing of benefits.[6] A few months after the product's introduction, the manufacturer realized that costs had been miscalculated and exceeded the price at which the product was being sold to Marks & Spencer. Meanwhile, given its low retail price, customers found the product an outstanding value and made it a big hit. When the manufacturer brought the problem to the attention of Marks & Spencer, the retailer's managers helped the manufacturer reengineer both the product and the process to lower cost. Marks & Spencer also lowered its margin to provide a sufficient profit for the manufacturer. The outcome is one in which the relationship is strengthened between the two partners because Marks & Spencer's fairness allowed a resolution that recognized the manufacturer's needs. In the long run, both partners benefit and a higher level of trust develops.

Procedures and policies govern the interaction between parties in a supply chain relationship. It is thus important that the weaker party perceive the fairness of the stronger party's procedures and policies for dealing with its partners. The stronger party is in control of its policies and procedures and should not bias the policies in a way that is opportunistic and does not benefit the entire supply chain. Fair procedures should encourage two-way communication between the partners. The procedures should be impartial and allow the weaker party an opportunity to appeal the stronger party's decisions. Finally, the stronger party should be willing to explain all its decisions.

As discussed previously, managers can build trust and cooperation in a supply chain relationship by designing and managing the relationship in a way that is mutually beneficial and fair. The presence of trust and cooperation facilitates coordination in the supply chain, increasing profits for all stages involved.

13.6 ACHIEVING COORDINATION IN PRACTICE

Managers should consider the following ideas to focus attention on coordination and facilitate the use of the managerial levers discussed to help achieve coordination:

- **Quantify the bullwhip effect**. Companies often have no idea that the bullwhip effect plays a significant role in their supply chain. Managers should start by comparing the variability in the orders they receive from their customers with the variability in orders they place with their suppliers. This helps a firm quantify its own contribution to the bullwhip effect. When its contribution is visible, it becomes easier for a firm to accept the fact that all stages in the supply chain contribute to the bullwhip effect, leading to a significant loss in profits. In the absence of this concrete information, companies try to react better to the variability rather than eliminate the variability

[6]Kumar (1996).

itself. This leads companies to invest significant amounts in inventory management and scheduling systems, only to see little improvement in performance or profits. Evidence of the size of the bullwhip effect is very effective in getting different stages of the supply chain to focus on efforts to achieve coordination and eliminate the variability created within the supply chain.

- **Get top management commitment for coordination**. More than any other aspect of supply chain management, coordination can succeed only with top management's commitment. Coordination requires managers at all stages of the supply chain to subordinate their local interests to the greater interest of the firm or the supply chain. Coordination often requires the resolution of trade-offs in a way that requires many functions in the supply chain to change their traditional practices. These changes often run counter to approaches that were put in place when each function focused only on its local objective. Such changes within a supply chain cannot be implemented without strong top management commitment. Top management commitment was a key factor in helping Wal-Mart and P&G set up collaborative forecasting and replenishment teams.
- **Devote resources to coordination**. Coordination cannot be achieved without all parties involved devoting significant managerial resources to this effort. Companies often do not devote resources to coordination because they either assume that lack of coordination is something they have to live with or hope that coordination will occur on its own. The problem with this approach is that it leaves all managers involved with only the separate areas that they control, while no one is responsible for highlighting the impact one manager's actions have on other parts of the supply chain. One of the best ways to solve coordination problems is through teams made up of members from different companies throughout the supply chain. These teams should be made responsible for coordination and given the power to implement the changes required. Setting up a coordination team is fruitless unless the team has the power to act because the team will run into conflict with functional managers who are currently maximizing local objectives. Coordination teams can be effective only when a sufficient level of trust builds between members from different firms. If used properly, coordination teams can provide significant benefit, as is the case with the collaborative forecasting and replenishment teams set up by Wal-Mart and P&G.
- **Focus on communication with other stages**. Good communication with other stages of a supply chain often creates situations that highlight the value of coordination for both sides. Companies often do not communicate with other stages of the supply chain and are unwilling to share information. However, often all companies in the supply chain are frustrated with the lack of coordination and would be happy to share information if it helped the supply chain operate in a more effective manner. Regular communication between the parties involved facilitates change in such a setting. For instance, a major personal computer (PC) company had been ordering its microprocessors in batches of several weeks of production. It was trying to move to a build-to-order environment in which it would place microprocessor orders on a daily basis. Its managers assumed that the microprocessor supplier would be reluctant to go along with this approach. However, when communication was opened up with the supplier, the opposite turned out to be true. The supplier also wanted to reduce lot sizes and increase the frequency of orders. Its managers had just assumed that the PC manufacturer

wanted large lots and thus never requested a change. Regular communication helps different stages of the supply chain share their goals and identify common goals and mutually beneficial actions that improve coordination.

- **Try to achieve coordination in the entire supply chain network**. The complete benefit of coordination is achieved only when the entire supply chain network is coordinated. It is not enough for two stages in a supply chain to coordinate. The most powerful party in a supply chain should make an effort to achieve coordination in the entire network. Toyota has been very effective in achieving knowledge sharing and coordination in its entire network.
- **Use technology to improve connectivity in the supply chain**. The Internet, ERP systems, and other information systems can be used to increase the visibility of information throughout the supply chain. Until now, most ERP implementations have achieved visibility of information only within a firm. Visibility across the supply chain still requires additional effort in most cases. From the discussion in this chapter, it should be clear that the major benefits of ERP systems can be realized only if the systems help increase visibility across the supply chain and facilitate coordination. If firms are to realize the full benefit of the huge investments they make in ERP systems, it is crucial that they make the extra effort required to use these systems to facilitate collaborative forecasting and planning across the supply chain. The Internet should be used to share information and increase connectivity in the supply chain. The growth of Internet exchanges can be very effective in this regard.
- **Share the benefits of coordination equitably**. The greatest hurdle to coordination in the supply chain is the feeling on the part of any stage that the benefits of coordination are not being shared equitably. Managers from the stronger party in the supply chain relationship must be sensitive to this fact and ensure that all parties perceive that the way benefits are shared is fair.

13.7 SUMMARY OF LEARNING OBJECTIVES

1. Describe supply chain coordination, the bullwhip effect, and their impact on supply chain performance.

   Supply chain coordination requires all stages to take actions that maximize total supply chain profits. A lack of coordination results if different stages focus on optimizing their local objectives or if information is distorted as it moves across the supply chain. The phenomenon in which the fluctuation in orders increases as one moves up the supply chain from retailers to wholesalers to manufacturers to suppliers is referred to as the bullwhip effect. The bullwhip effect results in an increase in all costs in the supply chain and a decrease in customer service levels. The bullwhip effect moves all parties in the supply chain away from the efficient frontier and results in a decrease of both customer satisfaction and profitability within the supply chain.
2. Identify causes of the bullwhip effect and obstacles to coordination in the supply chain.

   A key obstacle to coordination in the supply chain is misaligned incentives that result in different stages optimizing local objectives instead of total supply chain profits. Other obstacles include lack of information sharing, operational inefficiencies leading to large replenishment lead times and large lots, sales force incentives that encourage forward buying, rationing schemes that encourage inflation of orders, promotions that encourage forward buying, and a lack of trust that makes any effort toward coordination difficult.

3. Discuss managerial levers that help achieve coordination in the supply chain.

Managers can help achieve coordination in the supply chain by aligning goals and incentives across different functions and stages of the supply chain. Other actions that managers can take to achieve coordination include sharing of sales information and collaborative forecasting and planning, implementation of single point control of replenishment, improving operations to reduce lead times and lot sizes, every day low pricing and other strategies that limit forward buying, and the building of trust and strategic partnerships within the supply chain.

4. Describe actions that facilitate the building of strategic partnerships and trust within the supply chain.

A manager can help build trust and strategic partnerships by designing a relationship in which the mutual benefit to both sides is clear, both parties are mutually interdependent, contracts are allowed to evolve over time, and conflicts are effectively resolved. When managing the relationship, flexibility, information sharing, visibility of effort and performance of each party, and fairness on the part of the stronger party when distributing costs and benefits help foster trust and facilitate coordination in the supply chain.

Discussion Questions

1. What is the bullwhip effect, and how does it relate to lack of coordination in the supply chain?
2. What is the impact of lack of coordination on the performance of the supply chain?
3. In what way can improper incentives lead to a lack of coordination in the supply chain? What countermeasures can be used to offset this effect?
4. What problems result if each stage of the supply chain views its demand as the orders placed by the downstream stage? How should firms within the supply chain communicate to facilitate coordination?
5. What factors lead to a batching of orders within a supply chain? How does this affect coordination? What actions can minimize large batches and improve coordination?
6. How do trade promotions and price fluctuations affect coordination in the supply chain? What pricing and promotion policies can facilitate coordination?
7. How is the building of strategic partnerships and trust valuable within a supply chain?
8. What issues must be considered when designing a supply chain relationship to improve the chances of developing cooperation and trust?
9. What issues must be considered when managing a supply chain relationship to improve the chances of developing cooperation and trust?

Bibliography

Bowersox, Donald J., David J. Closs, and Theodore P. Stank. "21st Century Logistics: Making Supply Chain Integration a Reality." *Supply Chain Management Review* (Fall 1999), 44–49.

Brunell, Tom. "Managing a Multicompany Supply Chain." *Supply Chain Management Review* (Spring 1999), 45–52.

Child, John, and David Faulkner. *Strategies of Cooperation*. Oxford: Oxford University Press, 1998.

Doz, Yves L. "The Evolution of Cooperation in Strategic Alliances: Initial Conditions or Learning Process?" *Strategic Management Journal*, 17 (1996), 55–83.

Doz, Yves L., and Gary Hamel. *Alliance Advantage*. Boston: Harvard Business School Press, 1998.

Dyer, J. H., and K. Nobeoka. "Creating and Managing a High-Performance Knowledge-Sharing Network: The Toyota Case." *Strategic Management Journal*, 21 (March 2000), 345–367.

Gulati, R., and Harbir Singh. "The Architecture of Cooperation: Managing Coordination Costs and Appropriation Concerns in Strategic Alliances." *Administrative Science Quarterly* 43 (1998), 781–814.

Hammond, J. H. "Barilla Spa (A-D)." *Harvard Business School* case 9–694–046, 1994.

Joint Industry Project on Efficient Consumer Response. *Continuous Replenishment: An ECR Best Practices Report.* Kurt Salmon and Associates, 1994.

Joint Industry Project on Efficient Consumer Response. *Computer Assisted Ordering: An ECR Best Practices Report.* Kurt Salmon and Associates, 1994.

Kumar, N. "The Power of Trust in Manufacturer-Retailer Relationships." *Harvard Business Review* (November–December 1996), 92–106.

Lee, Hau L., V. Padmanabhan, and S. Whang. "The Bullwhip Effect in Supply Chains," *Sloan Management Review* (Spring 1997), 93–102.

Mariotti, John L. "The Trust Factor in Supply Chain Management." *Supply Chain Management Review* (Spring 1999), 70–77.

Ring, P. S., and A. H. Van de Ven. "Developmental Processes of Cooperative Interorganizational Relationships." *Academy of Management Review*, 19 (1994), 90–118.

Senge, Peter M. *The Fifth Discipline.* New York: Currency and Doubleday, 1990.

APPENDIX 13A

The Beer Game

The Beer Game originated at MIT and has been used to simulate the performance of a simple supply chain with one player at each stage. The game is often used to illustrate the bullwhip effect in a simple supply chain. The supply chain consists of a manufacturer, a distributor, a wholesaler, and a retailer as shown in Figure 13A.1

Customers come to the retailer to purchase beer. The retailer tries to fill customer orders from beer in inventory. Any unfilled demand is carried over to the future as backlogged demand. The retailer places replenishment orders with the wholesaler, who tries to fill the orders from beer in inventory. The wholesaler in turn orders from the distributor and the distributor from the manufacturer. The manufacturer receives raw materials from a supplier. It takes two periods for orders and product to move between stages. In the game, the delay is accomplished by introducing an in-transit stage between every pair of stages in the supply chain, as shown in Figure 13A.1. The game is played by assigning two people to each of the four stages (retailer to manufacturer) of the supply chain. Several supply chains can operate simultaneously.

Each supply chain requires a customer board, a supplier board, four identical boards corresponding to each of the four stages, and three identical in-transit boards. The four different types of boards are shown in Figure 13A.2.

The boards are ordered as in Figure 13A.1 with the retailer, wholesaler, distributor, and manufacturer getting a stage board each. An in-transit board is placed between every pair of stages, resulting in three in-transit boards. The customer board is placed before the retailer, and the supplier board after the manufacturer. Each of the four stages gets a recording sheet, as shown in Table 13A.1.

"Current Period Demand" is the size of the order received in this period. "Gross Demand" during a period is the sum of the "Current Period Demand" and "Backlog" from the previous period. "Gross Demand" represents the amount that a stage has to try to supply this period. "Amount Shipped" is the quantity shipped during the period. Amount shipped should equal gross demand if there is sufficient inventory available. If gross demand exceeds inventory available, then the entire inventory will be shipped and the unfilled demand

FIGURE 13A.1 Beer Game Supply Chain

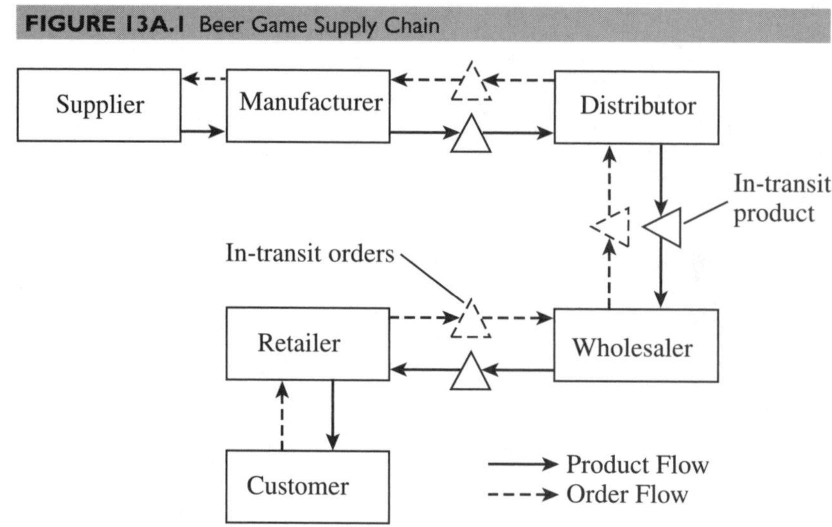

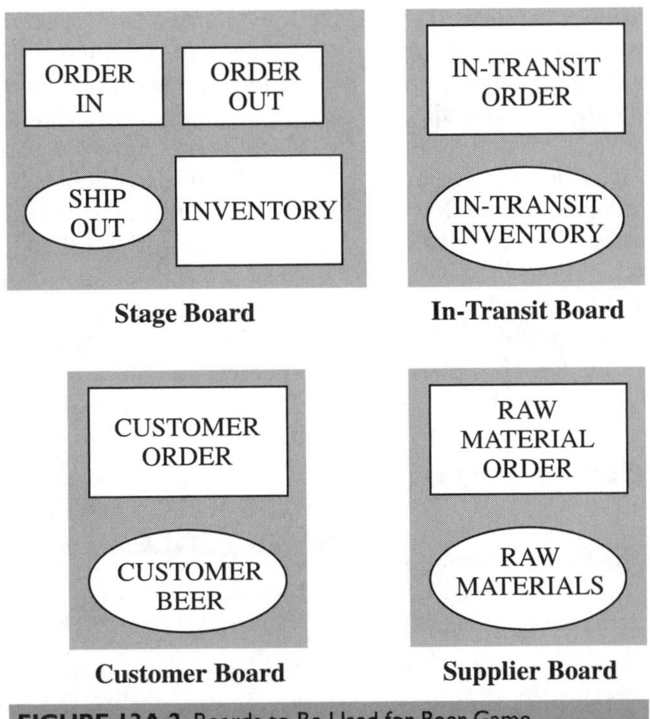

FIGURE 13A.2 Boards to Be Used for Beer Game

added to the backlog. "Ending Inventory" measures the cases of beer in inventory right after a shipment has been sent. "Backlog" is the amount of demand that has not yet been supplied. For any period,

Backlog = previous period backlog + max {0, gross demand − amount shipped}

"Order Placed" is the amount ordered by a stage with its supplier.

A cost of $1 is incurred for each case of beer in "Ending Inventory" per period. A cost of $2 is incurred for each case of demand in "Backlog" per period. The goal of each stage is to minimize the total cost incurred over the period when the game is played. The performance of a stage will be compared with the performance of the same stage in other supply chains.

During the game, orders are written on pieces of paper and pennies are used to represent cases of beer. The game starts with a sequence of orders placed in the customer order box. The game is played through multiple periods. At the start of each period, the following layout exists:

1. The ORDER-IN box at each of the four stages contains an order.
2. Each IN-TRANSIT ORDER box contains an order and each IN-TRANSIT INVENTORY box contains some pennies representing beer in transit.
3. The RAW-MATERIAL ORDER box contains an order.

TABLE 13A.1 Recording Sheet for Beer Game

Period	*Current Period Demand*	*Gross Demand*	*Amount Shipped*	*Ending Inventory*	*Backlog*	*Order Placed*
1						
2						

During each period, the activities performed by each stage are divided into two phases. The game works best if one person at each stage takes responsibility for the first phase and the other person takes responsibility for the second phase. The completion of both phases completes all activities to be performed during a period. All four stages must have finished phase I before any of them can start phase II in a period. At the end of each period, the layout looks the way it did at the start of the period. The supply chain then moves on to the next period. We now describe the activities performed in each phase of a period at all four stages.

PHASE I ACTIVITIES (COMMON TO ALL FOUR STAGES)

The goal during this phase is to fill the incoming order and place a replenishment order. Phase I activities are identical for all four stages of the supply chain:

1. Pick order from ORDER-IN box and record on recording sheet as Current Period Demand.
2. Compute Gross Demand by adding Current Period Demand (from this period) and Backlog (from previous period).
3. Transfer the minimum of the amount in the INVENTORY box and Gross Demand from the INVENTORY box to the SHIP OUT box. Record the amount transferred as the Amount Shipped.
4. Record Ending Inventory as the amount remaining in the INVENTORY box.
5. Compute Backlog = max {Gross Demand − Amount Shipped, 0} and record on recording sheet.
6. Place a replenishment order with the supplier on an order slip and place the order slip in the ORDER-OUT box. Record Order Placed on the recording sheet.

PHASE II ACTIVITIES FOR RETAILER

In this phase the retailer receives orders from the customer, beer from the wholesaler, and moves beer to the customer and orders to the wholesaler:

1. Move order from IN-TRANSIT ORDER box between retailer and wholesaler to the ORDER-IN box of the wholesaler.
2. Move order from ORDER-OUT box of retailer to IN-TRANSIT ORDER box between retailer and wholesaler.
3. Move beer from IN-TRANSIT INVENTORY box between retailer and wholesaler to INVENTORY box at retailer.
4. Move beer from SHIP-OUT box of wholesaler to IN-TRANSIT INVENTORY box between retailer and wholesaler.
5. Move order at top of pile in CUSTOMER ORDER box to ORDER-IN box of retailer.
6. Move beer from SHIP-OUT box of retailer to CUSTOMER BEER box.

PHASE II ACTIVITIES FOR WHOLESALER

In this phase, the wholesaler moves orders to the distributor and receives beer from the distributor:

1. Move order from IN-TRANSIT ORDER box between wholesaler and distributor to ORDER-IN box at distributor.
2. Move order from ORDER-OUT box at wholesaler to IN-TRANSIT ORDER box between wholesaler and distributor.
3. Move beer from IN-TRANSIT ORDER box between wholesaler and distributor to INVENTORY box at wholesaler.
4. Move beer from SHIP-OUT box at wholesaler to IN-TRANSIT ORDER box between retailer and wholesaler.

PHASE II ACTIVITIES FOR DISTRIBUTOR

In this phase, the distributor moves orders to the manufacturer and receives beer from the manufacturer:

1. Move order from IN-TRANSIT ORDER box between distributor and manufacturer to ORDER-IN box at manufacturer.
2. Move order from ORDER-OUT box at distributor to IN-TRANSIT ORDER box between distributor and manufacturer.
3. Move beer from IN-TRANSIT ORDER box between distributor and manufacturer to INVENTORY box at distributor.
4. Move beer from SHIP-OUT box at distributor to IN-TRANSIT ORDER box between distributor and manufacturer.

PHASE II ACTIVITIES FOR MANUFACTURER

In this phase, the manufacturer receives raw materials from the supplier and moves the next order to the supplier:

1. Take order from RAW-MATERIAL ORDER box at SUPPLIER and move equivalent amount of beer from RAW MATERIALS box at supplier to INVENTORY box at manufacturer.
2. Move order from ORDER-OUT box at manufacturer to RAW-MATERIAL ORDER box at supplier.

The game is stopped after a suitable number of periods have expired. Each stage then evaluates the total cost it has incurred and plots the orders it received. With this information, each stage should come up with a guess at what the customer demand pattern looked like for the periods that the game is played.

CHAPTER 14

E-Business and the Supply Chain

Learning Objectives
After reading this chapter, you will be able to

1. identify the role of e-business in a supply chain;
2. evaluate the impact of setting up an e-business on revenues for a supply chain;
3. evaluate the impact of setting up an e-business on costs for a supply chain; and
4. identify factors that influence the value of e-business in a supply chain.

In this chapter we discuss how e-business can be used to improve supply chain performance. We discuss why the value of e-business varies based on product and industry characteristics. Our goal is to enable managers to analyze their supply chains and identify how they can use e-business most beneficially.

14.1 THE ROLE OF E-BUSINESS IN A SUPPLY CHAIN

E-business is the execution of business transactions over the Internet. Supply chain transactions that involve e-business include the flow of information, product, and funds. Companies conducting e-business can perform some or all of the following supply chain transactions over the Internet.

- Providing information across the supply chain
- Negotiating prices and contracts with customers and suppliers
- Allowing customers to place orders
- Allowing customers to track orders
- Filling and delivering orders to customers
- Receiving payment from customers

All these transactions have been conducted in the past using other "channels," such as retail stores, salespeople, and catalogs. For example, mail order companies like Lands' End have used catalogs to convey product information to customers. Supermarkets convey product information by displaying the physical product. Other companies have used sales forces to convey product information. Some companies have used electronic means of communication such as electronic data interchange (EDI). The Internet, however, is the first channel that makes it possible for information located at a central source (the seller's Web server) to be available to anybody. Using a catalog, a company only provides information to people who receive the catalog. Similarly, EDI information is only available to those customers that have a dedicated EDI link to the seller. The Internet does not require a dedicated connection between a company and its customer; it simply requires that both be linked to the Internet, which is a public channel.

Today, the Internet plays a significant role in many supply chains; companies are using the Internet to conduct a wide variety of supply chain transactions. For example, Dell displays all its product information over the Internet. Customers are able to identify all options available for a personal computer (PC) they want to purchase along with the price of the configuration they select. Dell also shares demand and inventory information on-line with its suppliers. Using Web-based systems, Solectron, a contract manufacturer, collaborates with PC companies on product design. Companies use the Internet for negotiations and auctions to set prices of products and services. Companies like eBay allow people to auction products over the Internet. Exchanges like Freemarkets.com allow companies to auction their products and services over the Internet and seek bids from potential suppliers.

Companies with an e-business allow customers to place orders over the Internet. A customer can order PCs at Dell.com and books at Amazon.com or Borders.com. UPS and Federal Express (FedEx) allow customers to track their packages over the Internet. Companies like Netscape and shockwave.com fill and deliver orders over the Internet through downloads of electronic products. Most companies involved in e-business allow customers to pay over the Internet using their credit cards if they are consumers or to electronically pay their invoices if they are businesses.

A **business-to-consumer** (B2C) e-business involves transactions between a company and a consumer. Examples include Amazon, Dell, and Wal-Mart selling products to customers over the Internet. A **business-to-business** (B2B) e-business involves transactions between two companies. Examples include Dell, as well as W. W. Grainger and McMaster-Carr selling maintenance, repair, and operations (MRO) supplies to other companies over the Internet. General Motors and Ford are attempting to conduct all future transactions with suppliers over the Internet. Other companies involved in B2B e-business include software makers like i2, Ariba, Commerce One, and Freemarkets.com; these companies set up Internet exchanges and auction sites for manufacturers dealing with suppliers.

The initial growth of e-business was in B2C supply chains. The most famous examples include Amazon.com, which started by selling books over the Internet and has now expanded to include music, toys, electronics, software, and home improvement materials. Amazon has transformed the retail supply chains in several of the product categories it has entered. Today, no large retailer of books or music can think of operating without an e-business. The Boston Consulting Group estimated that on-line retailer transactions exceeded $36 billion in 1999.[1] This represents a

[1] *The State of Online Retailing 2.0*, Boston Consulting Group.

growth of almost 150 percent compared with 1998. However, on-line transactions in 1999 were only around 2 percent of total retail sales across all channels. Considerable growth of e-business is still expected in the B2C area because most experts feel that online retail sales could reach high single-digit percentages of total retail sales.

E-business also grew significantly in 1999 in B2B supply chains. B2B supply chains have used the Internet in a variety of ways to improve performance. Companies like W. W. Grainger, Cisco Systems Inc., and Intel Corporation were the first to move many supply chain processes on-line. At Intel, automated on-line ordering systems have replaced several hundred order clerks. Cisco handles more than 75 percent of its sales on-line. Companies like General Motors are setting up e-businesses to handle procurement of everything from staples to steering wheels. At General Electric, employees order office supplies from prequalified vendors over the Internet. Ford Motor Co. is using the Internet to bring together engineers from its operations all over the world to collaborate on projects with a goal of designing basic components that can be used everywhere. Companies like i2, Ariba, and Commerce One provide software and services that connect buyers and suppliers and automate purchasing processes in supply chains. Given the variety of ways that companies are setting up B2B e-businesses, tremendous growth is anticipated in the area. Goldman, Sachs & Co. projects that B2B sales on the Internet will reach $1.5 trillion by 2004 compared with $114 billion in 1999.[2] The growing interest in B2B e-business is also reflected by the fact that in 1999, venture capitalists poured $17 billion into B2B endeavors, compared with $11 billion in B2C ventures.[3]

E-business is expected to provide significant payoff in most B2B supply chains. Speculation abounds that e-business will lead to reduced prices, higher productivity, and lower labor costs. A Goldman Sachs study concluded that business costs overall could fall by as much as 12.5 percent, with the decrease being as high as 20 percent in industries such as electronics and freight transport.[4] Based on this optimism, virtually every large firm has either set up or is in the process of setting up e-businesses in its supply chain.

In the next section we consider how e-business is different from using traditional channels for the flow of information, products, and funds in a supply chain. Based on these differences, we identify the potential opportunities that e-business offers to a firm.

14.2 THE IMPACT OF E-BUSINESS ON SUPPLY CHAIN PERFORMANCE

If a firm is to exploit the advantages of setting up an e-business fully, it must understand the key differences between using the Internet and other channels for the flow of information, products, and funds. A company must identify the value created by using the Internet before replacing other channels.

[2] "To B2B or not to B2B," *U.S. News & World Report* (Feb. 7, 2000), p. 36.
[3] Ibid.
[4] "B2B: The Hottest Net Bet Yet?" *Business Week,* (Jan. 17, 2000), p. 36.

Revenue Impact of E-business

An e-business allows a firm or supply chain to exploit the following revenue enhancing opportunities:

- Offering direct sales to customers
- Providing 24-hour access from any location
- Aggregating information from various sources
- Providing personalization and customization of information
- Speeding up time to market
- Implementing flexible pricing
- Allowing price and service discrimination
- Facilitating efficient funds transfer

Offering Direct Sales to Customers

An e-business allows manufacturers and other members of the supply chain that do not have direct contact with customers in traditional channels to enhance revenues by bypassing intermediaries and selling directly to customers. The elimination of intermediary margins may also be viewed as a decrease in costs. For example, Dell Computers sells PCs on-line directly to customers. As a result, Dell is able to enhance margins because it shares no part of the margin with a distributor or retailer. In contrast, a PC manufacturer that sells through retailers, like Compaq, must share some of the product margin with the distributor and retailer, resulting in lower margins for Compaq. Moreover, Compaq has to deal with conflict with retailers when they decide to use the Internet for direct sales to customers.

Providing 24-Hour Access from Any Location

Unlike most retail stores, an e-business can attract customers who may not be able to place orders during regular business hours because it is always open for placing orders. At a retail store, customers place an order and receive the product at the same time. At an e-business, however, a customer can place an order even if the fulfillment process is shut down. For example, a customer can place an order at Grainger.com even though the Grainger store where he will pick up his order is closed. Grainger has observed a surge in on-line orders after its brick-and-mortar stores close.

E-business also allows a firm to access customers who may be geographically distant. For example, a small specialty retail store located near Chicago can reach customers all over the United States, or even the world, by setting up an e-business. Without an e-business, only the customers located near the store are likely to shop there. Access to an e-business is limited only by the customers' access to the Internet. If a person changes location, this does not alter Internet accessibility. For example, a customer can use Internet banking to access her bank account no matter where she is in the world as long as she has access to the Internet.

Aggregating Information from Various Sources

An e-business allows a firm to increase sales by offering information regarding a very large selection of products. For example, Dell offers customers a very large selection of computers and peripherals. Offering the same selection at a retail store would require a huge site with a correspondingly huge amount of inventory. Another example is Yahoo! Shopping, which provides product information from a large number of retailers that are allied with the site. A customer can go to Yahoo! Shopping and can purchase products from all retailers that are part of the site. Customers are attracted to Yahoo! Shopping because, given the large number of retailers on the site, they are very likely to find the product they are seeking. Retailers see increased sales by attracting customers from all over the United States. Without e-business, these retailers would only attract local customers.

Making a large variety available does not necessarily mean that a customer will be able to access all the variety offered. Firms have often gone overboard by offering seemingly limitless variety without giving customers the tools to navigate the site and quickly identify what they want. The ability to offer a large selection is effective only if appropriate search tools are provided. Without good search tools and intelligent product recommendations, a large inaccessible selection of products is of little value.

Providing Personalization and Customization of Information

The Internet offers an e-business the ability to use personal information to intelligently guide each customer's buying experience and increase sales. Some e-businesses use information on birthdays and other events provided by customers to send reminders and purchase recommendations. In a B2B environment, firms can set up customer-specific sites to display information on products that the customer buys most frequently. Available technologies allow an e-business to use existing preferences and a customer's historical purchases to rank currently available choices in terms of each individual customer's preference. The Internet thus offers the potential of creating an individualized buying experience for each customer, which can increase the look-to-buy ratios significantly compared with a physical store.

Firms that focus on mass customization can use the Internet to help customers select products that suit their needs. For example, Dell allows customers to customize their computers by using the options available on the Dell Web site. Lands' End allows shoppers to use a body measurement system to virtually try on clothing before they buy it.

Speeding Up Time to Market

A firm with an e-business can increase revenues by introducing new products much faster than a firm that uses physical channels. A firm selling PCs through physical channels must produce enough units to stock the shelves at each distributor or retailer and arrange for these units to reach these stores. This requires considerable time and effort. An e-business, in contrast, introduces a new product by making it available on the Web site. The distribution lag to fill the physical channels is not present. A new product can be made available as soon as the first unit is produced. This is evident in the computer industry where Dell often introduces new products earlier than its competitors using traditional channels. The advantage is also evident for firms like W. W. Grainger. Using traditional marketing, Grainger has to print new catalogs and send them to customers to give them information regarding new products. On the other hand, information regarding a new product can be added to the Grainger Web site as soon as it becomes available.

Implementing Flexible Pricing

An e-business can easily alter prices over time by changing one entry in the database linked to its Web site. This ability allows an e-business to maximize revenues by setting prices based on current inventories and demand. The airlines provide a good example of this ability; they make last-minute low-cost fares available on the Web on routes with unsold seats. Dell also changes prices for different PC configurations regularly based on demand and component availability. Firms can change prices at an e-business much more easily than via most traditional channels. If Dell and L.L. Bean were to use catalogs to convey a discount in prices, they would have to print new catalogs and mail them to potential customers. With an e-business, however, they update only the price on their Web site.

Allowing Price and Service Discrimination

Potentially, an e-business can price-discriminate and alter prices based on the buying power of individual customers to enhance revenues. The ability to ask different customer segments to pay different prices based on services offered allows a firm to increase revenues compared with a situation in which a firm charges a single price to all customers. Airlines increase revenues by charging different customers different fares for the same flight based on the duration of stay and advance booking. Airlines also use the Internet to increase revenues by offering last-minute low fares for flights with many unsold seats. Auction sites like eBay and exchanges built by companies like i2, Commerce One, and Ariba allow people to bid for goods and services, with the potential for different people to pay different amounts. Other e-businesses offer customers a menu of services at different prices, allowing them to select the desired service and the corresponding price. For example, Amazon.com provides a customer ordering multiple books with shipping times for each book. Some titles may be available for next-day shipping, whereas others involve a five-day lead time. Amazon offers customers the flexibility of receiving one order after five days (at a lower price) or two separate shipments (at a higher price) with the currently available book arriving first.

Facilitating Efficient Funds Transfer

An e-business can enhance revenues by speeding up collection. An excellent example comes from John McCain's 2000 presidential campaign. Within 48 hours of his primary victory in New Hampshire, Senator McCain's campaign collected $1 million over his Web site. In contrast, it would have taken a campaign receiving checks worth $1 million much more time and effort to process all the payments.

Potential Revenue Disadvantage of E-Business

For the sale of physical products that cannot be downloaded, an e-business has one potential disadvantage relative to physical channels. Whereas a retail store selling jeans can provide a customer the desired clothes immediately, an e-business without a physical retail outlet will take longer because of the shipping time. Therefore, customers that require a short response time may not use the Internet to order a product.

There is no such delay, however, for products that can be downloaded. Going online may offer a time advantage in many cases. For example, the prospectus for a mutual fund or even music can be downloaded from the Web. A physical mailing of these products or even making a trip to a music store takes much longer.

Cost Impact of E-Business

An e-business allows a firm or supply chain to take advantage of the following cost-reduction opportunities:

- Reducing product handling with a shorter supply chain
- Postponing product differentiation until after an order is placed
- Decreasing delivery cost and time with downloadable product
- Reducing facility and processing costs
- Decreasing inventory costs through centralization
- Improving supply chain coordination through information sharing

Reducing Product Handling with a Shorter Supply Chain

A manufacturer using e-business to sell directly to customers is able to reduce handling costs because fewer supply chain stages touch the product as it makes its way to a customer.

Postponing Product Differentiation Until After an Order Is Placed

An e-business can significantly lower its inventories if it can postpone the introduction of variety until after the customer order is received. The time lag between when a customer places the order and when he or she expects delivery offers an e-business a window of opportunity to implement postponement. For example, Dell keeps its inventory as components and assembles its PCs after receiving the customer order. The amount of component inventory required is much lower than it would be if Dell kept its inventories in the form of assembled PCs (see Chapter 8). E-business thus allows Dell to decrease its inventory holding costs as well as any depreciation of products in inventory.

Decreasing Delivery Cost and Time With Downloadable Product

If a firm can put its product in a form that can be downloaded, the Internet will save on the cost and time for delivery. For example, the MP3 format for music on the Internet offers an opportunity to eliminate all costs associated with transporting CDs. Similarly, the ability to download software eliminates the cost and time associated with producing CDs, packaging them, and transporting them to retail stores.

Reducing Facility and Processing Costs

An e-business can reduce facility costs by centralizing all inventories and decreasing the number of facilities required. For example, Amazon.com is able to supply demand from a few warehouses, whereas Borders and Barnes and Noble must incur facility costs for all the retail outlets they operate. A bookstore also costs more per square foot than a warehouse.

In many cases, customer participation in selection and order placement allows an e-business to lower its resource costs. For example, when a customer goes to the Lands' End Web site, she makes the effort to check on product availability and then place the order. When the same customer phones in an order, the firm incurs the additional cost of its employees checking product availability.

An e-business can lower its order fulfillment costs because it does not have to fill an order as soon as it arrives. A retail store or supermarket must staff its sales counters so that more cashiers are available when more customers are shopping. As a result, the store requires more staffing during weekends and at times when people are not at work. At an e-business, if a reasonable buffer of unfilled orders is maintained, the rate of order fulfillment can be made significantly smoother than the rate at which orders arrive, which reduces the peak load for order fulfillment and thus reduces resource requirements and cost (see Chapter 5).

Decreasing Inventory Costs through Aggregation

An e-business can aggregate inventories because it does not have to carry inventory close to the customer. Due to geographical aggregation, an e-business requires less inventory (see Chapter 8). Because customers are willing to wait for delivery, Amazon is able to aggregate all its inventory of books and music at a few warehouses. In contrast, Borders and Barnes and Noble need more inventory because they must carry a significant fraction of their inventory at retail stores. A key point here is that the relative benefit of aggregation is small for high-demand items with a small coefficient of variation but large for low-demand items with a high coefficient of variation (see Chapter 8).

Improving Supply Chain Coordination through Information Sharing

An e-business can easily share demand information throughout the supply chain to dampen the bullwhip effect and improve coordination. The Internet may also be used to share planning and forecasting information within the supply chain, further improving coordination. This helps reduce overall supply chain costs and better match supply and demand (see Chapter 13). Information processing costs also tend to be lower for an e-business if it has successfully integrated systems across the supply chain.

Potential Cost Disadvantages of E-Business

An e-business tends to have higher costs in the following situations:

- Increased transportation costs due to inventory aggregation
- Increased handling costs if customer participation is reduced
- Large initial investment in information infrastructure

Increased Transportation Cost Due to Inventory Aggregation For any business, two components of transportation cost must be considered: inbound and outbound. A firm incurs inbound transportation costs to bring the replenishment order in from the supplier. A firm incurs outbound transportation cost to take the product to the customer. Typically, replenishment orders tend to be larger than customer orders, and thus the unit transportation cost is lower for inbound transportation than for outbound transportation (see Chapter 10). Aggregating inventories increases the distance a customer order travels while decreasing the distance a replenishment order travels. Thus, compared with a business with several physical outlets, an e-business with aggregated inventories will tend to have higher transportation costs (across the entire supply chain) per unit.

Increased Handling Cost If Customer Participation Is Reduced For some products, like groceries, an e-business has to perform some tasks currently performed by the customer at retail stores. In such situations, an e-business will incur higher handling and delivery cost than a retail store. For example, whereas a customer picks out the required items at a grocery store, an e-business like Webvan incurs higher handling costs because it must pick a customer's order from the warehouse shelves and deliver it to the customer's home.

Large Initial Investment in Information Infrastructure Setting up an e-business requires a large initial investment in the information technology that will support it. A firm will have to invest in both Web servers and programming expertise to help set up the e-business. Today, the software to set up an e-business is evolving rapidly, and there are several application service providers (ASPs) that help set up the e-business infrastructure.

The effect of e-business on the costs of the drivers of supply chain performance is summarized in Table 14.1.

In the next section we discuss the impact that e-business has on the performance of firms in different industries.

TABLE 14.1 Impact of E-Business on Cost of Supply Chain Drivers

Supply Chain Driver	*Impact of E-Business on Cost*
Inventory	Decline
Transportation	Increase
Facility	Decline
Information	• Improve coordination and reduce costs through information sharing • Large initial investment with lower processing costs

14.3 VALUE OF E-BUSINESS IN DIFFERENT INDUSTRIES

The value of setting up an e-business is not the same in every industry. Whereas Dell has seen its profits increase after going on-line, Amazon.com has yet to show a profit after several years in existence, and Peapod, an on-line grocery business, is finding it difficult to remain in business. The value of e-business for an industry depends on the extent to which firms are able to exploit opportunities offered by the Internet to increase revenues and decrease costs.

Using E-Business to Sell PCs: Dell

The PC industry is well-suited to exploit the opportunities the Internet offers to increase profits. Firms like Dell have already used e-business extensively, and all PC manufacturers are working to expand their sales over the Internet.

As shown in Figure 14.1, Dell sells PCs directly to customers and starts assembly after receiving a customer order. Traditional PC manufacturers, in contrast, must have an assembled PC available for purchase at a retail store.

Revenue Impact of E-Business on the PC Industry

The main revenue disadvantage for Dell of selling PCs over the Internet is that customers who are unwilling to wait 5 to 10 days to receive their PC cannot be attracted. However, the PC is usually a planned purchase, and most people are willing to wait for its delivery. Dell also does not attract customers who need a lot of help when selecting a PC. However, the segment of people who are comfortable selecting their own PC and are willing to wait for its delivery is quite large and growing. Dell and other PC manufacturers selling over the Internet target this group of customers.

FIGURE 14.1 Supply Chains for Dell and a Traditional PC Manufacturer

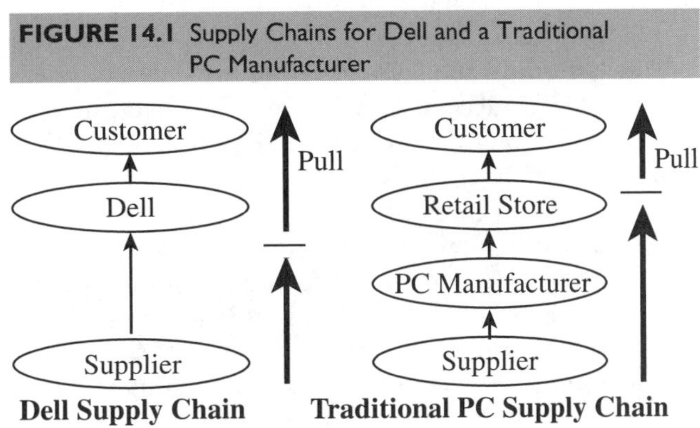

Dell is able to exploit most of the revenue-enhancing opportunities offered by an e-business. The company uses the Internet to increase revenues by offering a virtually unlimited number of different PC configurations. Customers are allowed to select recommended PC configurations or customize them to have the desired processor, memory, hard drive, and other components. Customization allows Dell to satisfy customers by giving them a product that is close to their specific requirements. The customization options are very easy to display over the Internet and allow Dell to attract customers that value this choice. Dell also uses customized Web pages to enable large business customers to place orders. The company constructs special Web pages for suppliers so that they can view orders for components they produce as well as current levels of inventory at Dell. This allows suppliers to plan based on customer demand and as a result dampens the bullwhip effect.

Dell has fully exploited the Internet to increase revenues by bringing new products to market faster, allowing the company to attract customers who are willing to pay higher prices to get the latest technology. Products in the PC industry have short life cycles of a few months. In addition, PCs across different manufacturers are substitutable because they often have the same components. Thus, a firm like Dell that brings products to market faster than the competition enjoys huge revenue advantages until competing products come to market. Competing firms that sell through distributors and retailers have to fill shelves at all retailers before a product reaches the customer. Dell, in contrast, introduces a new product to customers on the Internet as soon as the first PC of that model is ready to be assembled. As a result, Dell can offer new components in its products as soon as they are available. It takes PC manufacturers selling through distributors and retailers much longer to bring new components to market.

Although the company cannot compete with a retailer in terms of response time for a PC the retailer has in stock, Dell is one of the fastest at providing customers with customized PCs. Decreasing the response time by a few days allows Dell to attract more time-sensitive customers. The company has designed products and the assembly process to assemble the customized components after a customer order arrives. Without the direct interaction between the consumer and Dell that e-business affords, Dell's reaction would be slower and it could not be as responsive for customized products.

Dell also uses the price flexibility the Internet offers to increase revenues. The salespeople at Dell change prices daily based on demand and supply of components to maximize the revenue that can be extracted from available resources. The company lowers prices on configurations that contain components with excess inventory to spur sales.

By using the Internet to sell PCs directly to customers, Dell is able to eliminate distributor and retailer margins and increase its own margin. The Internet allows Dell customers to place orders at any time of the day. Dell also uses call centers to provide 24-hour access. The Internet, however, makes it much cheaper to provide access by decreasing the workforce required; computer stores would find it very expensive to stay open all day.

E-business allows Dell to collect payment for its PCs in a matter of days after they are sold. However, Dell pays its suppliers according to the more traditional schedules, in which payment is due in a given time period (30 days, for instance). Given its low levels of inventory, Dell is able to operate the business with negative working capital because it receives payment for its PCs about five days before it pays its suppliers for their components. A PC supply chain including distributors and retailers would find it nearly impossible to achieve these results.

Cost Impact of E-Business on the PC Industry

Dell is also able to exploit many of the cost reduction opportunities offered by selling PCs over the Internet. The only cost disadvantage of selling PCs on-line is the additional transportation cost.

Inventory Costs E-business offers Dell the opportunity to reduce its inventories by geographically aggregating them in a few locations (see Chapter 8). Whereas a chain of retail stores selling computers must carry inventory in each store, Dell aggregates all inventories in few locations. However, the benefit of geographical aggregation for a product like a PC will be marginal because a model that is selling well on the East Coast is also likely to sell well on the West Coast. Therefore, PC demand across different geographical regions is likely to be strongly correlated. As a result, the benefits of geographical aggregation for an e-business like Dell are relatively small.

The real benefit comes because e-business enables Dell to reduce inventories by exploiting the fact that time elapses from the point at which an online order arrives to the point at which it must be shipped. Dell products and assembly lines are designed such that all components on which customers are offered customization can be assembled in a very short period of time. This allows Dell to postpone assembly until after the customer order has been placed. As a result, Dell holds all inventory in the form of components that are common across multiple finished products. Postponement, coupled with component commonality, allows Dell to reduce inventories significantly (see Chapter 8). Dell maximizes the benefit of postponement by focusing on new PC models for which demand is hard to forecast (see Chapters 8 and 9).

A PC manufacturer that sells through distributors and retailers finds it difficult to implement postponement. As a result, traditional PC manufacturers often find that they are stuck with PC configurations that are not selling while being out of the configurations that are selling. Dell, in contrast, is better able to match supply and demand.

E-business also allows Dell to reduce inventories by enabling the company to share information across the supply chain, thereby dampening the bullwhip effect. This fact reduces costs and improves performance in the Dell supply chain by a significant amount (see Chapter 13).

Facility Costs E-business allows the Dell supply chain to lower facility costs because the company has no physical distribution or retail outlets. Dell only incurs the cost of the manufacturing facility and warehousing space for components. A PC supply chain selling through retail stores must pay for the distribution warehouses and retail stores as well.

E-business also allows Dell to take advantage of customer participation in order placement and decrease processing costs at its facility. Dell saves on the cost of call center representatives because customers do all the work when placing an order online. Given the time lag between when an on-line order is placed and when it must be filled, Dell is able to produce PCs at a more stable rate than the rate at which orders come in. This allows Dell to reduce production costs at its plants.

Transportation Costs As a result of e-business, total transportation costs in the Dell supply chain are higher than in a supply chain selling PCs through distributors and retailers. Dell sends individual PCs to customers from its factories, whereas a manufacturer selling through distributors and retailers sends large shipments on trucks to warehouses and to the retailer. The Dell supply chain thus has higher outbound transportation costs. Relative to the price of a PC, however, the outbound transportation cost is low (typically 2 to 3 percent), and thus it does not have a major impact on the overall cost.

E-Business Impact on Performance at Dell

As summarized in Table 14.2, e-business allows Dell to significantly improve its performance. Dell, to the delight of its shareholders, has exploited every advantage that the Internet offers to improve performance. Among all factors listed, the abilities to postpone assembly until after the customer has placed the order (build-to-order), delay product differentiation, and use component commonality are key if any PC manufacturer is to take full advantage of e-business.

Value of E-Business for a Traditional PC Manufacturer

Although it may seem at first glance that Dell, with its build-to-order business model, is best equipped to exploit the benefits of e-business, a careful study indicates that a traditional PC manufacturer, selling through distributors and retailers, has a lot to gain as well. The PC manufacturer should use e-business to sell new products or customized PC configurations whose demand is hard to forecast, and let the regular channel sell standard configurations whose demand is easier to forecast. Manufacturers should introduce new models on the Internet, and as demand for some of them grows, these models should be moved to the retail channel. The manufacturer is thus able to lower inventories by aggregating all high variability production and satisfying that demand on line. These models should be built to order using as many common components as is feasible. The standard models can be produced using a longer lead time but low-cost approach. Selling standardized models through distributors and retail stores allows the supply chain to save on transportation costs, which are likely to be more significant for these low-cost configurations. Retailers can be allowed to participate in the e-business by having kiosks where customers can configure models of their choice or order standardized models that are out of stock. It is important that traditional PC manufacturers give retailers a chance to participate in any e-business to avoid damaging existing channel relationships.

A traditional PC manufacturer can use the two-pronged approach outlined here to utilize both the strengths of e-business and those of traditional retail and distribution channels to the characteristics of the products sold by each.

TABLE 14.2 Impact of E-Business on Dell Performance

Factor	*Impact*	*Primary Causes*
Revenue	Increase	• Direct Sales to customer • Flexible pricing • Large variety and customization • Faster new product introduction • Fast delivery of customer order
Inventory costs	Decrease	• Aggregation using postponement and component commonality • Geographical aggregation • Information sharing
Facility costs	Decrease	• No retail outlets • Customer participation in order placement
Transportation costs	Increase	• Higher outbound transportation cost

Using E-business to Sell Books: Amazon.com

The book industry was one of the first to feel the impact of e-business with the launching of Amazon.com in July 1995. Since 1995, Amazon has added music, toys, electronics and software, and home improvement equipment to its list of product offerings. Unlike the PC industry and Dell, however, Amazon has been losing money in spite of dramatic growth in sales. For all of 1999, Amazon had total losses of nearly $600 million from revenues of about $1.6 billion.

Amazon purchases some of its books directly from the publisher and buys the remaining titles from distributors, as shown in Figure 14.2. A traditional bookstore chain, in contrast, purchases all books directly from publishers.

Revenue Impact of E-Business on the Book Industry

There are several reasons why e-business has hurt revenues in the book industry. As shown in Figure 14.2, the Amazon supply chain is longer than that of a bookstore chain such as Borders or Barnes and Noble because of the presence of an additional intermediary—the distributor. Unlike the PC industry, where e-business facilitates direct sales by manufacturers, e-business has resulted in longer supply chains in the book industry. Given distributor margins, this leaves lower margins for Amazon. The distributor margins can also be viewed as an increase in cost because of e-business in the book industry.

A factor hurting revenues for Amazon has been the steady downward pressure on book prices on the Internet. Amazon was the leader in offering deeper discounts on best-sellers and other books sold on-line. Traditional bookstores discounted best-sellers by about 30 percent, until Amazon started to offer discounts of 50 percent. The deeper discounts have contradicted the argument that people buy books on-line because of the convenience. If convenience drives on-line book sales, e-businesses selling books should charge for the convenience rather than offering deeper discounts. Price cuts have hurt the PC industry, too, but it has been more rampant for Internet booksellers than for Internet PC manufacturers.

As is the case with Dell, customers wanting a book quickly cannot shop at Amazon. Therefore, Amazon can only attract customers that are willing to wait a few days to get the book. Amazon also cannot attract customers who value the ability to leaf through books. The company tries to counter this problem by providing reviews and other information on books to allow customers to get a feel for the book on-line.

Amazon has exploited several opportunities on the Internet to attract customers and increase revenues. Amazon uses the Internet to attract customers by offering mil-

FIGURE 14.2 Supply Chains for Amazon.com and a Traditional Bookstore

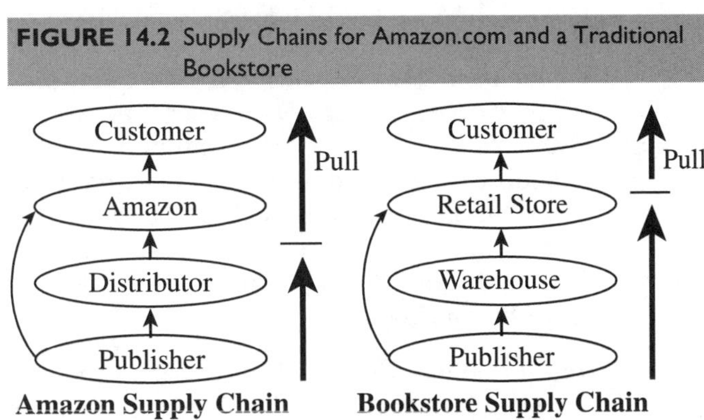

lions of books. Customers can search for hard-to-find books or those of special interest. A large physical bookstore, in contrast, can carry fewer than 100,000 titles. Amazon also uses the Internet to recommend books to customers based on their purchase history. E-mails are sent out to customers informing them of new titles that match their interests. Amazon also provides reviews and comments from other customers on the titles available. New titles are quickly introduced and made available on-line, whereas in a brick-and-mortar bookstore chain, all retail stores have to be stocked.

Amazon uses the Internet to allow customers to order a book any time of the day from the comfort of their own homes. If customers know the books they want, they can place the order on-line within a few minutes, and the books are delivered to their door. There is no need to leave the house and spend time that going to a physical bookstore would take. This fact allows Amazon to attract customers who value this convenience and are willing to wait for delivery.

Cost Impact of E-Business on the Book Industry

Amazon also uses e-business to lower its inventory and some of its facility costs. However, processing costs at facilities and transportation costs increase as a result of selling books on-line.

Inventory Costs Amazon is able to decrease inventories by geographically aggregating the inventories in a few locations (see Chapter 8). A bookstore chain, in contrast, has higher inventories because titles are carried at every store. The reduction of inventories on aggregation is most significant for low-volume books with high demand uncertainty (see Chapters 8 and 9). The benefit is less significant for best-sellers that sell in large volumes with demands that are more predictable. Amazon carries high-volume titles in inventory, and it purchases very low volume titles from the distributor in response to a customer order. This allows the Amazon supply chain to further reduce inventories of very low volume titles, because distributors are able to aggregate across other booksellers in addition to Amazon.

Facility Costs E-business allows Amazon to lower facility costs because it does not need the retail infrastructure that a bookstore chain like Borders or Barnes and Noble must have. Initially, Amazon did not have a warehouse and purchased all books from distributors. When demand volumes were low, the distributor was a better location to carry inventories because it could aggregate demand across other booksellers besides Amazon. However, as demand has grown, Amazon has opened its own warehouses, where it stocks high-volume books. Amazon now purchases the high-volume books directly from publishers and only goes to distributors for the lower-volume books. Thus, facility costs at Amazon are growing. However, they are still much lower than the facility costs for a bookstore chain because Amazon has no retail sites.

Amazon, however, incurs higher order processing costs than a bookstore chain. At a bookstore, the customer selects the books and only cashiers are needed to receive payment. At Amazon, no cashiers are needed, but every order is picked off the warehouse shelves and packed for delivery. For books that are received from distributors, additional handling at Amazon adds to the cost of processing the order. For some on-line bookstores, distributors directly ship the customer order to save on handling costs. However, this adds to the distributor margin, further squeezing the margin for the on-line bookseller.

Transportation Costs The Amazon supply chain incurs higher transportation costs than a book store chain selling through retail stores. Local bookstores do not have the cost of individually shipping books to customers. Amazon, in contrast, incurs the cost of shipping books to its customers from warehouses. The shipping cost from an Amazon warehouse represents a significant fraction of the cost of a book. (It could be as high as 100 percent for an inexpensive book.) As demand has grown, Amazon has opened a total of seven warehouses with more than 3 million square feet, in an effort to get closer to customers, decrease its transportation costs, and improve response time.

E-Business Impact on Performance at Amazon

Some of the opportunities and disadvantages of selling books over the Internet are summarized in Table 14.3. A comparison of Tables 14.2 and 14.3 shows that e-business offers far greater advantages when selling PCs than when selling books. The major difference between the two products is that whereas product differentiation in PCs can be postponed until after the customer has placed an order, books are currently published well in advance of a sale. The benefits of e-business when selling books would be significantly larger if the form of books changed and they could be downloaded on-line. If books become downloadable, Amazon will be able to exploit all the advantages that Dell currently exploits, along with being able to ship the product over the Internet. As a result, many of Amazon's current disadvantages would disappear.

Other potentially downloadable products that Amazon currently sells include software and music. In both instances, Amazon could increase the benefit of e-business if it either creates CDs in response to a customer order or allows customers to download these products. For other products like toys and hand tools, limited possibilities exist for postponement. The advantages of e-business for Amazon in those product categories will continue to be smaller compared with physical retail outlets.

Value of E-Business for a Traditional Bookstore Chain

Traditional bookstore chains have a lot to gain by setting up an e-business to complement their retail stores. Going on-line allows a bookstore chain to offer the same convenience and variety as a brick-and-mortar store and exploit all the other revenue advantages that e-business provides Amazon.

Bookstore chains can also use the fact that the benefits of aggregation are most significant for low-volume books whose demand is hard to forecast. The chains should structure themselves such that retail outlets carry many copies of best-sellers for customer purchase and few copies of low-volume books to encourage customers to browse and make impulse purchases. Terminals or Internet kiosks should be provided

TABLE 14.3 Impact of E-Business on Amazon.com Performance

Factor	*Impact*	*Primary Causes*
Revenue	Increase	• Convenience • Large variety of books • Customer specific recommendations
	Decrease	• Distributor margins • Downward price pressure • Inability to browse
Inventory cost	Decrease	• Geographical aggregation (major benefit is for low-volume books)
Facility costs	Decrease	• No retail outlets, only warehouses • No cashiers required
	Increase	• Each customer order is picked and packed
Transportation cost	Increase	• Higher outbound transportation costs

so that customers wanting to order any low-volume books can place their orders on-line. The presence of kiosks also increases the variety of books that the bookstore can offer. This approach would allow bookstore chains to reduce inventories by aggregating low-volume books sold on-line. The chains would also be able to incur low transportation costs for best sellers sold at retail stores.

Bookstore chains can also reduce inventory costs by using technology that allows a book to be printed in a few minutes on demand. With suitable printers available in bookstores, low-volume books can be printed on demand rather than carried in inventory.

Traditional bookstores also have the option of providing some service discrimination by using both the mail and retail stores to deliver orders. Customers can have books shipped directly to their homes at higher prices or pick up books at the bookstore at lower prices. The second option would allow the chain to include the order as part of a replenishment shipment to the bookstore, thus lowering transportation cost.

A traditional bookstore chain can integrate e-business into its retail stores to take advantage of the strengths of each and provide an effective ordering and delivery network that a pure e-business like Amazon cannot. Amazon has tried to gain some of the advantages available to bookstore chains by building more warehouses such that no customer is very far from a warehouse.

Using E-Business to Sell Groceries: Peapod

The grocery industry saw a spurt in new e-businesses in 1998 and 1999, although none has proved profitable so far. Peapod, one of the oldest on-line grocers, saw its financial performance and stock price suffer in 1999. For the first three quarters of 1999, Peapod revenues fell compared with 1998, and losses grew by more than 40 percent. Over that period, Peapod suffered losses of more than $19 million on sales of $51.6 million. The higher losses were attributed to higher grocery fulfillment costs. An investment of over $70 million by Dutch supermarket company Royal Ahold NV rescued Peapod from bankruptcy.

Peapod started by supplying orders using people at grocery stores to pick and deliver orders. The company has now moved to supplying orders from centralized fulfillment centers in areas that it serves. Each fulfillment center is much larger than a supermarket and is comparable to a warehouse. As shown in Figure 14.3, the Peapod and supermarket supply chains are comparable except that with a supermarket, some products come from a warehouse and the rest come directly from suppliers.

Revenue Impact of E-Business on the Grocery Industry

Peapod and other on-line groceries have tried to sell convenience and the time savings they offer customers. For most people, grocery shopping is a chore that is

FIGURE 14.3 Supply Chains for Peapod and a Traditional Supermarket

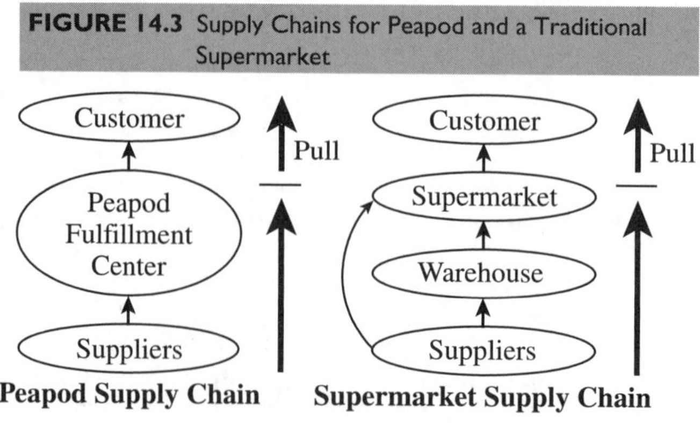

time-consuming and rarely enjoyable. Peapod allows customers to place orders at any time and have them delivered at home, eliminating a trip to the supermarket. This can be a significant convenience in urban areas where customers have to walk to a supermarket and carry all their groceries home. In a suburban area, the benefit is smaller because people can easily drive to supermarkets that are open until late at night. Supermarkets in suburban areas are easily accessible, and Peapod does not enjoy as significant an advantage as in urban areas by providing 24-hour access on-line.

The convenience factor and access are more significant if a specialty food provider goes on-line. For example, ethnic food stores are not as accessible as supermarkets, and people often drive long distances to reach them. Offering ethnic foods on the Internet provides easy access to customers and saves a long drive. Ethnicgrocer.com is an e-business that specializes in ethnic groceries and products.

Peapod is able to increase revenues by creating a personalized shopping experience for customers and delivering customized, one-to-one advertising and promotions. This is done using extensive member profiles that Peapod creates based on on-line shopping behavior, purchase histories, and surveys. Unlike a supermarket, where the store does not know what customers have selected until they check out, Peapod can guide on-line customers based on what they purchase. For example, if a customer buys some pasta, Peapod can suggest a type of pasta sauce or some Parmesan cheese. Over longer periods, Peapod can collect shopping patterns and suggest products that match a customer's preferences. Such suggestions enhance revenues by increasing customers' impulse purchases.

Peapod also adds to its revenues by giving consumer goods companies a forum for targeted interactive advertising and electronic coupons. Peapod increases revenues by selling data on consumer choices to product manufacturers. Consumer choice data available to an on-line grocer are more valuable than scanner data from a supermarket because scanner data reveal only the customer's final purchases. An on-line grocer, in contrast, can record the customer's decision process. For example, an on-line grocer can record a customer's substitution patterns for items that are out of stock. With scanner data, a supermarket cannot record substitutions because it has no way of finding out if the customer looked for something that is out of stock.

The revenue generated based on information gathered by on-line grocers contributes significantly to their earnings. At this stage, most on-line grocers have lost money on the actual sale of groceries but made money selling the information they gather.

Cost Impact of E-Business on the Grocery Industry

Peapod and other on-line grocers use e-business to lower facility costs and, to some extent, inventory costs. Processing costs at facilities and transportation costs, however, are much higher than for traditional supermarkets.

Inventory Costs Compared with a supermarket chain, an on-line grocer like Peapod can lower inventories by aggregating the inventory in a few large replenishment centers. The degree of aggregation, however, is less than that achieved by Amazon or Dell because Peapod needs fulfillment centers in every urban area it serves to get food to the customer in an acceptable condition. The benefits of aggregation for Peapod are not very significant relative to a supermarket because supermarkets tend to be fairly large and achieve sufficient forecast accuracy because of aggregation. For supermarkets, further aggregating to the level of a fulfillment center would result in only a marginal reduction in inventories.

The benefits of aggregation are further diminished by the fact that the majority of products sold at a supermarket are staple items with steady demand. For these products, demand is predictable with a low coefficient of variation. Thus, aggregation provides a marginal benefit in terms of improved forecast accuracy and reduced inventories (see Chapter 8). The benefits of aggregation are higher for specialty, low-demand items with high demand uncertainty. These products constitute a small fraction of overall sales at a supermarket. Thus, aggregation allows e-grocers to lower their inventory costs only marginally compared with a typical supermarket. If on-line grocers focused primarily on specialty items like ethnic foods, the inventory benefits of aggregation would be larger.

Facility Costs E-business allows Peapod to lower facility costs because it only needs warehouse facilities and can save on the cost of retail outlets such as supermarkets. Processing costs at Peapod to fulfill an order, however, are higher than those for a supermarket. Peapod saves on checkout clerks compared with a supermarket. An on-line grocer, however, must pick the customer order, a task the customer performs at a supermarket. Thus, e-business results in a loss of customer participation compared with a supermarket and raises processing costs.

Transportation An on-line grocer like Peapod has significantly higher transportation costs than a supermarket. Supermarkets have the advantage of having to bear only inbound transportation cost for products, with customers providing transportation from the supermarket to their homes. Inbound transportation costs tend to be low because supermarkets have large deliveries that enable them to exploit economies of scale in transportation. Peapod, in contrast, has to bear inbound transportation cost to its fulfillment centers and then outbound delivery costs from the fulfillment centers to customer homes. Outbound delivery costs are high because customer orders do not fill a truck, resulting in low utilization for delivery trucks and personnel. The task becomes all the more problematic given the different temperature requirements for different types of food.

Compared with computers and books, groceries have a low value-to-weight/volume ratio. For example, paper towels and bathroom tissues have very low value but occupy a lot of space in the truck. Thus, transportation costs are a significant fraction of the cost incurred by on-line grocers. This makes it very difficult for an on-line grocer to compete with a supermarket on prices.

Peapod charges customers extra for delivery to offset the additional transportation and delivery expense. Nonetheless, Peapod's losses grew in 1999 primarily because of high fulfillment costs. Webvan, another on-line grocer, at this writing does not charge for delivery of its on-line orders. This practice has resulted in situations in which customers order a pack of chewing gum for home delivery. The delivery cost of gum is many times the cost of the gum itself! Such scenarios have resulted in Webvan's incurring large losses in its first few months of existence.

E-Business Impact on Performance at Peapod

E-business offers some revenue enhancement opportunities in the grocery industry. Costs, however, are likely to be significantly higher for an on-line grocer than a supermarket. The impact of e-business on performance of the grocery industry is summarized in Table 14.4.

A comparison of Tables 14.2, 14.3, and 14.4 shows that e-business offers a lower cost advantage when selling groceries compared with books and PCs. Supermarkets are large enough to enjoy most of the inventory benefits that aggregation has to offer without having to incur the additional delivery cost that an on-line grocer incurs. On-line grocers cannot compete with supermarkets on price, and on-line profits from the sale of groceries are likely to be small. On-line grocers will succeed only if there are enough people willing to pay the additional price for the convenience of home deliv-

TABLE 14.4 Impact of E-Business on Peapod Performance

Factor	*Impact*	*Primary Causes*
Revenue	Increase	• Convenience (benefit larger in urban areas and for specialty foods) • Customization and personalization • Sale and use of customer information
Inventory cost	Marginal decrease	• Geographical aggregation (primarily for low-volume items)
Facility costs	Decrease	• No retail outlets, only warehouses • No checkout clerks needed
	Increase	• Each customer order is picked
Transportation cost	Large increase	• Outbound transportation cost increases

ery. In the short term, the growth of on-line groceries is adding to capacity in the grocery industry in the form of warehousing space and delivery capacity. Although delivery capacity will be useful in the future to satisfy the needs of home delivery, the excess warehousing capacity will drive margins lower within the industry.

Value of E-Business to a Traditional Grocery Chain

Traditional supermarket chains can benefit by using an e-business to complement the strengths of their existing network. The e-business can be used to offer convenience to customers who value it and are willing to pay for it. Supermarkets can be used to target the customers who value the lower prices offered.

A supermarket chain with an e-business has the opportunity to offer an entire array of services at differing prices based on the amount of work the customer does. The cheapest service involves customers walking into the supermarket and shopping for the products they want. In this case, the customer picks the order from the shelves and provides outbound transportation for it. For an additional charge, a supermarket could allow customers to place orders on-line to be picked up at a later time. In this case, the supermarket personnel pick the order from the shelf but the customer provides outbound transportation. The most expensive service is when the customer places orders on-line for home delivery. In this case, the supermarket chain is responsible for both picking the order from the shelf, and delivering it to the customer's home. The varying services and prices would allow supermarket chains to satisfy the needs of a variety of customers efficiently.

Among the supermarket chains, Albertson's has taken the lead in combining e-business with physical supermarkets. It has renamed some of its stores Albertsons.com. Half the store remains a traditional supermarket, and the other half is used to fulfill on-line grocery orders. This allows the firm to exploit economies of scale on inbound transportation while keeping delivery distances to customers short on the outbound side. Currently, customers are allowed to pick up their orders at the store for no fee or have the order delivered to their home. The company charges $5.95 for orders under $60; larger orders are delivered free.[5] The company plans to convert more of its supermarkets to have fulfillment capability for on-line orders as demand grows. Based on our analysis, Albertson's model is likely to be the most effective method for combining e-business with existing supermarkets in the grocery industry and pure online grocers are likely to be less effective.

[5] "Grocer Feeds Growing On-line Appetite," *The Seattle Times* (November 11, 1999), D1.

Using E-Business to Sell Maintenance, Repair, and Operations Supplies: Grainger.com

W. W. Grainger is a (B2B) distributor of maintenance, repairs, and operations (MRO) supplies. Grainger sells more than 200,000 different products ranging from consumables like machine lubricants to hardware items like nuts and bolts needed to make repairs. Grainger has traditionally sold its products using a catalog. Customers place orders on the phone or walk up to one of 380 branches (similar to a large retail store) in the United States. Orders placed over the phone are either picked up at a branch or shipped to the customer using a package carrier.

In 1995, Grainger established an e-business when it set up Grainger.com, allowing customers to place orders on-line. Sales at Grainger.com are currently around $160 million per year.[6] Grainger has also set up FindMRO, which lists 5-million low-demand, hard-to-find items, and OrderZone, where customers can order products from Grainger as well as several companies that serve noncompeting segments of the business market. E-business has grown rapidly in the MRO supplies industry, with competitors like McMaster-Carr going on-line and e-businesses like ProcureNet developing MRO buying sites where many different companies place their products.

Revenue Impact of E-Business for Grainger

Grainger is likely to see margins drop as a result of the growth of e-business in the MRO supply industry. With customers able to compare prices easily over the Internet, the growth in e-business will put pressure on MRO supply companies to reduce prices. The Aberdeen Group has forecast that e-business is likely to result in MRO's supply prices dropping by 5 to 10 percent.[7]

Grainger is in a position to exploit several of the revenue enhancing opportunities offered by the Internet. Grainger.com allows a customer access to all the 220,000 products that Grainger sells, whereas the catalog only offers about 80,000 products. Compared with a catalog, searching for a product is simpler on the Internet using search engines that Grainger has developed. With OrderZone and FindMRO, Grainger has used the Internet to significantly increase the range of products that it makes available to its customers. Such a large range would be impossible to provide using just a catalog. The increased variety allows Grainger to attract more customers and satisfy more needs of existing customers. The Internet allows Grainger to enhance revenues by introducing a new product as soon as it becomes available. With direct mail marketing, Grainger had to wait for a new catalog to be shipped before customers were informed about new products. An e-business also allows Grainger to offer promotions and change prices easily without having to send out new catalogs.

Grainger.com allows customers to place orders and check their status at any time of the day. This is a significant benefit to customers who can use this ability to improve their MRO purchase process. For example, a customer's night shift personnel can use the Internet to place and check on orders for supplies they need. They no longer have to wait for people from the day shift to place their orders. This improves the accuracy of orders from customers and reduces the time needed to process them. A study by the Aberdeen Group indicates that on-line purchases decrease the duration of the order and fulfillment cycle from an average of 7.3 days to an average of 2 days.[8] The decreased order fulfillment times allow Grainger to attract more orders through its

[6]"A Super Middleman," *Internet World* (January 15, 2000).
[7]"E-procurement: The Next Frontier," *Industrial Distribution* (January 31, 2000), 65.
[8]Ibid.

e-business. A study by Grainger Consulting estimates that MRO distributors could see incremental sales gains of 10 to 20 percent by selling online.[9]

E-business, however, cannibalizes demand from traditional sales channels at Grainger, reducing the revenue benefits to some extent. Strategically, Grainger is better off cannibalizing itself rather than allowing a competitor to steal customers.

Cost Impact of E-Business at Grainger

Grainger uses e-business to lower its order processing costs and to some extent its facility costs. Grainger customers will also see a significant reduction in order processing costs and a smaller reduction in the price of products as a result of e-business.

Inventory Costs As Internet orders that are shipped by package carrier grow, Grainger will be able to aggregate more of it inventories, resulting in some reduction. Grainger will achieve further inventory reduction if on-line sales grow large enough to enable the company to close some of its branches. The inventory benefits, however, are likely to be small because Grainger's existing supply chain network is also well suited to on-line sales. Customers also save on inventory costs as a result of e-business because replenishment lead times over the Internet are lower than with traditional procurement methods.

Facility Costs Grainger's facility costs will come down to some extent if more Internet sales are shipped using package carriers and some branches are closed. Grainger will see a bigger reduction in processing costs from on-line sales. Customers placing orders over the Internet perform all order placement activities. This allows Grainger to decrease the number of customer service representatives in its call centers.

Customers also save on order processing costs as a result of e-business. E-business is a convenient way for corporations to place content-rich catalogs in the hands of end users of MRO supplies. As a result, companies no longer require staff to process MRO purchase orders. E-business offers many companies a quick and convenient chance to get away from inefficient manual methods of procurement. The Aberdeen Group estimates that on-line purchase of MRO supplies saves about $30 per order in administrative costs.[10]

Transportation Costs Transportation costs in the Grainger supply chain are unlikely to change significantly as a result of e-business. Transportation costs may increase somewhat if more Internet orders are shipped using package carriers rather than being picked up at branches.

E-Business Impact on Performance at Grainger

MRO distributors like Grainger are likely to see a marginal improvement in revenue as a result of e-business. Both distributors and customers will also see a decrease in their order processing costs, as summarized in Table 14.5.

As Table 14.5 indicates, the benefit of e-business in MRO supply chains is likely to be greater for customers, though distributors like Grainger will also benefit by saving on processing costs. This is an industry in which customers will drive the conversion to e-business because of the convenience it offers them. Companies like Grainger can benefit by taking the lead in setting up effective e-businesses ahead of their competitors.

Manufacturers and buyers in other industries have also used e-business to reduce the transaction cost of fulfilling orders. For example, Whirlpool Corporation has set

[9]Ibid.
[10]Ibid.

TABLE 14.5 Impact of E-Business on Grainger Performance

Factor	*Impact*	*Primary Causes*
Revenue	Increase Decrease	• Larger product selection • Some drop in prices • Intermediary margin in on-line marketplaces
Facility costs	Decrease	• Save on call center costs at Grainger • Potential branch closings • Save on administrative costs at customer
Inventory cost	Unchanged	• Degree of aggregation similar to fulfillment of phone orders • Marginal decrease if branches close
Transportation cost	Unchanged	• Network similar to fulfillment of phone order • Some increase if more shipments by package carriers

up a business portal WhirlpoolWebWorld.com to allow retailers to place orders.[11] Placing orders from the portal allows buyers to reduce their order placement costs and enables Whirlpool to reduce their order fulfillment costs. The resulting decrease in transaction costs allows the supply chain to reduce batch sizes and replenishment lead times and achieve a better matching of supply and demand. Whirlpool's e-business has been quite successful with retailers that account for 60 percent of Whirlpool's sales placing orders from the portal. Whirlpool estimates that this figure will rise to more than 90 percent by the middle of 2001.

Using E-Business to Create Markets: Internet Exchanges

Internet exchanges, **Internet marketplaces**, or portals are electronic marketplaces and communities of interest on the Internet where companies can obtain information and buy and sell products. These exchanges are typically sponsored and hosted by independent third parties. An example is mySAP.com, which includes a collection of electronic marketplaces under the banner of mySAP.com Marketplace. MySAP contains communities in several industries—including banking, aerospace and retail—as well as functional areas such as human resources and information technology. Each community supports on-line catalogs, auctions, news reports, and online price quotes. Another example is TradeMatrix from i2 Technologies. TradeMatrix also provides functionality to exchanges in a variety of industries, including the high-tech, aerospace, retail, and apparel industries. Other examples of these exchanges include PlasticsNet.com for the plastics industry, iShip.com for the shipping industry, ChemConnect.com for the chemicals industry, and Truckstop.com and National Transportation Exchange for the trucking industry.

Each exchange provides industry specific information to attract visitors. Exchanges also provide on-line catalogs from a variety of product suppliers in the industry. The primary benefit of these exchanges is that they bring together many buyers and many sellers from an industry. A key functionality that many of these exchanges provides is the facilitation of on-line buying transactions and auctions for B2B commerce. Ariba, Commerce One, i2, and Freemarkets.com provide platforms to set up on-line marketplaces and also operate some of these markets themselves.

[11]"Putting the 'E' Back in E-business," *Information Week* (January 31, 2000).

There are two potential ways in which buyers can use Internet exchanges. One is to use private or third-party exchanges on the Internet to facilitate transactions and cement long-standing relationships between partners. The other is to use the exchange as an on-line marketplace for conducting auctions connecting many buyers and suppliers. Companies must understand the difference between the two approaches and use them appropriately.

Impact of Internet Exchanges and Auction Marketplaces on Buyers

Internet exchanges can help reduce transaction costs and improve performance from collaborative planning within the supply chain, as discussed earlier for MRO supplies. Companies can use exchanges to conduct transactions, exchange information, and analyze this information so that both parties benefit. Without a common exchange that companies are both hooked into, it is difficult for them to collaborate, aggregate, analyze, and share information. All the benefits of going on-line discussed in the Grainger example are available to a firm using an Internet exchange. The important point here is that the exchange is used to make existing relationships more efficient and beneficial to both parties, not to drive prices down by having sellers bid against each other. Even though auction marketplaces have received a lot of press, it is the use of Internet exchanges to foster long-term collaborative relationships that is likely to provide the greatest benefit to supply chains.

In addition, Internet exchanges and auction marketplaces offer a buyer the ability to search across multiple suppliers when looking for a product. Buyers can make comparisons and select the products that best suit their needs. If *best* is interpreted by companies to mean the least expensive, growth in exchanges and auction marketplaces is likely to push prices for commodity products lower because of increased competition.

It has been suggested that all buyers of commodity products should shop through auction marketplaces because of the price reduction that will result. There are, however, potential downsides to this approach if it is not implemented properly. From a supply chain perspective, it is important for a buyer to consider not just the purchase price but the total cost of buying a product from a supplier. If a buyer makes a decision based only on the purchase price, it is likely to increase other supply chain costs. Consider an auto manufacturer that needs a few tons of sheet steel daily for cars produced at its assembly plant. One option for the manufacturer is to buy the lowest-cost steel on a daily basis. Although this may reduce the purchase price somewhat, it will raise overall costs by disrupting any just-in-time manufacturing system that the car manufacturer may use. Making all purchases using auctions will have a negative impact on relations between suppliers and manufacturers. An auction facilitates a one time transaction, not a long-term relationship. In the auto industry, the last two decades of the 20th century focused on improving supply chain relationships so that suppliers and auto manufacturers could work closely to improve the way products were designed, manufactured, and delivered. Chrysler significantly improved its performance by getting suppliers involved in the design phase of a new product. This level of supplier involvement is only possible given a long-term relationship between suppliers and manufacturers. Thus, core products that a buyer requires in significant and steady quantities should not be handled through an auction process with the goal of reducing purchase price. E-business between the buyer and seller should be used in this setting to reduce transaction costs of order placement and fulfillment and improved information exchange during both order fulfillment and product design.

A good example of this approach is Dell and its use of e-business when dealing with its suppliers. Dell does not use the Internet to create a marketplace in which suppliers compete against each other for orders. Dell uses the Internet to exchange demand and inventory information with its suppliers. This allows suppliers to set appropriate production levels and help the Dell supply chain to match supply and demand better. Dell uses e-business primarily to improve information flows and decrease transaction costs, allowing the supply chain to better match supply and demand and decrease overall costs considerably.

Auction marketplaces, however, do offer a considerable advantage to buyers who are suddenly short of a product they need. An example is a manufacturer seeking to transport product and finding that its regular trucking company has no trucks available. In such a situation, an auction marketplace for trucking allows the manufacturer to place its emergency shipment out to bid. All truckers with surplus capacity can now bid on the job, allowing the manufacturer to find the required capacity at a good price. Clearly, the ability of an on-line marketplace to match surplus capacity and unfilled demand is of considerable value to each company as well as the industry overall. An online marketplace allows the industry (and each company) to match supply and demand better while operating with lower overall capacity by aggregating the uncertain component of demand as well as surplus capacity.

Thus, buyers should focus on using Internet exchanges to reduce transaction costs and improve supply chain coordination for their steady, stable demand and using on-line auction markets to match shortages and surpluses for which the value of aggregation is the greatest.

Impact of Internet Exchanges and Auction Marketplaces on Sellers

The impact of Internet exchanges on sellers will depend on how they are used. If exchanges are used to reduce transaction costs and improve collaborations in supply chains, sellers will benefit, as discussed earlier for Grainger in the MRO supply business. With Internet exchanges, sellers will find it easier to introduce new products and offer all the available variety. Sellers should also be able to reduce replenishment lead times and achieve a better match between supply and demand through improved coordination.

However, the growth of Internet exchanges and auction marketplaces and the resulting competition will put considerable downward pressure on prices that sellers will be able to charge for their products. If all products move to auction marketplaces, supplier margins will shrink considerably for core products that have a steady and significant demand. While seller margins shrink as a result of selling through auctions, supply chain costs will not necessarily decrease. The cost of coordinating different suppliers for each order and the lack of long-term relationships can overwhelm any benefits that the reduced seller margins will provide the supply chain. Therefore, for products with steady and significant demand, sellers are better off establishing long-term relationships and e-business transactions that do not involve auctions. The e-business should focus on decreasing the transaction cost of receiving and fulfilling orders and improving information exchange so that the supply chain can better match supply and demand.

Sellers will find auction marketplaces run by intermediaries very useful when selling surplus inventory or capacity. Using auction marketplaces, sellers are able to access a large market in which to offer their surplus. The ability of an on-line marketplace to aggregate surplus supply and unmet demand makes it a highly effective channel in which sellers can offer their surplus. Effective auction marketplaces will allow both buyers and sellers to account for the total cost of product exchange when setting up auctions. For example, if a seller is offering a stamping press in Detroit, an offer for $1 million from the Detroit area is better than an equivalent offer from Asia, because the seller incurs a lower transportation cost. An auction marketplace that allows both the buyer and seller to be aware of total cost will result in a final sale that is the most effective from a supply chain perspective.

Impact of Internet Exchanges and Auction Marketplaces on Industry Performance

Internet exchanges can be very effective at decreasing transaction costs between different supply chain stages. They can also help improve the coordination and collaboration between stages in the supply chain. To achieve these benefits, however, Internet exchanges should be used primarily to improve buyer-seller communication as opposed to creating on-line auction marketplaces where firms search for the best price.

Auction marketplaces will be most effective at matching surplus inventory and capacity with unmet demand because of their ability to aggregate demand as well as supply. The use of third party–owned auction marketplaces for this purpose should grow in all industries. Auction marketplaces, however, are not particularly effective for the selling and buying of products with a steady and significant demand. The use of auctions for buying and selling such products is likely to shrink seller margins without necessarily decreasing the total cost to the buyer. For products with steady and significant demand, the most effective use of e-business is a long-term relationship between buyer and seller, coupled with the use of the Internet to decrease transaction costs and share demand and supply information.

14.4 SETTING UP E-BUSINESS IN PRACTICE

A firm can be successful with e-business only if it can integrate the Internet with existing channels of distribution in a way that uses the strengths of each appropriately. The Internet's capability to provide access to many customers must be coupled with a suitable supply chain network to fulfill those orders. Managers should consider the following ideas when setting up an e-business in practice:

- **Integrate the Internet with the existing physical network**. To extract maximum benefit from e-business, firms should integrate it with their existing supply chain networks. This coupling of the e-business with the existing physical network has been referred to as **clicks and mortar**. The success of an e-business is closely linked to the distribution capabilities of the existing supply chain network. Separating them will add to inefficiencies within the supply chain.

  An example of a company that has not yet integrated the two units effectively is W. W. Grainger. Grainger currently separates its e-business from its branch sales units, and the e-business unit is stealing orders from the branches. The success of the Grainger e-business unit will come from the use of an appropriate mix of package carriers and branches to ship orders. A key to success for Grainger is to exploit economies in the fulfillment network for both the branches and e-business. Keeping branches and the e-business separate makes this integration harder.

  Alberston's use of its physical assets to satisfy both on-line orders and people who want to shop in a supermarket is an effective integration of e-business within a supply chain network. Another example of an effective clicks-and-mortar strategy is The Gap, which allows customers to place on-line orders through computers placed in the stores and also return items purchased on-line at retail stores. The Internet is used to expand the variety available to customers at a Gap store. Gap stores stock popular items, and customers can order on-line the colors or sizes that may not be available in the store. This allows The Gap to centralize low-volume items while increasing the variety available to customers and extract the maximum benefit from integrating its e-business with its physical network.

- **Devise shipment pricing strategies that reflect costs**. Incomplete consideration of shipping costs has played a significant role in the losses incurred by e-businesses to date. Forrester reports that less than half the companies it surveyed make a profit on each shipped package.[12] Companies must be aware of the average cost to fulfill an order and reflect this cost in the prices they charge. Charging standard fees regardless of size or weight adds to losses that firms incur. As long as carriers charge based on weight, size, and destination, e-businesses must account for these factors when charging customers for shipping. Firms may want to forgo shipping costs in the beginning to attract customers. Over time, however, they must have a plan to recover these costs. An example of the potential problems is Ethnicgrocer.com based in the Chicago area. By offering free shipping, Ethnicgrocer has attracted customers who live in suburban or rural areas that are far from ethnic grocery stores. Ethnicgrocer cannot make money by shipping 10-pound bags of rice for free. Without a plan for charging customers for shipping or getting out of the business of selling 10-pound bags of rice, Ethnicgrocer will have difficulty becoming profitable.
- **Optimize e-business logistics to handle packages, not pallets**. The growth of e-business increases the amount shipped in small packages to customers. For example, whereas Borders and Barnes and Noble send all their merchandise using large shipments to replenish their stores, on-line booksellers must send packages containing a few books to each customer. With smaller packages, it becomes critical for companies to exploit every possible opportunity to consolidate shipments to lower costs. This may involve partnering with other firms to consolidate shipments. To increase consolidation and reduce transportation costs, e-businesses must try to bundle an entire customer order into a single package.
- **Design the e-business supply chain to handle returns efficiently**. Customers purchasing product on-line are likely to have a higher rate of returns than customers purchasing from a physical store. Regardless of how good a Web site is, it cannot match the customer experience of touching and seeing the product at a retail store. As a result, the product purchased on-line is often different from the customer's expectation. E-businesses have had a lot of difficulty handling returns, and this has contributed to customers' having a bad experience. E-businesses like Gap.com that are integrated with retail stores have handled returns by allowing customers to return unwanted merchandise at a store. Pure e-businesses, however, have no other choice at this stage but to allow customers to mail back the unwanted merchandise. This adds to supply chain costs and tarnishes the customer's experience. The problem is magnified when an e-business allows a customer to place a single

[12]"Mastering Commerce Logistics" (1999).

order across several suppliers. Ideally, the returns should be sent to a single location as well. Most e-businesses, however, are not structured to allow a customer to do this. In many instances, customers must return the product to the supplier that it came from. The problem is magnified when different suppliers have different return policies.

- **Keep customers informed throughout the order fulfillment cycle.** E-businesses must keep customers involved as their orders proceed through fulfillment. Customers must be allowed to check the status of their order on-line or be informed proactively by e-mail about the order's status. On-line customers are more likely to check on the status of their order than customers ordering through other channels. An e-business loses its cost advantage in order placement if a customer has to call back to check on the status of the order. E-businesses should inform customers about the total fulfillment cycle time rather than just the shipping time. This will set customer expectations in line with reality and reduce the number of customers calling back to ask why their order did not arrive when it was promised.

14.5 SUMMARY OF LEARNING OBJECTIVES

1. Identify the role of e-business in a supply chain.

   E-business is the execution of business transactions over the Internet. Firms have used e-business to provide information across the supply chain, negotiate prices and contracts, allow customers to place and track orders, allow customers to download orders, and receive payment from customers.
2. Evaluate the impact of setting up an e-business on revenues for a supply chain.

   Supply chains have used e-business to enhance revenues by selling directly to customers, providing 24-hour access, aggregating product information from many suppliers, providing customers with a personalized and customized shopping experience, speeding up the delivery of customized products, reducing the time taken to bring new products to market, changing prices based on product availability and services provided, and using the Internet for efficient funds transfer. The revenue enhancement achieved has varied with the extent to which an e-business has been able to exploit these opportunities.
3. Evaluate the impact of setting up an e-business on costs for a supply chain.

   Supply chains have used e-business to reduce costs by decreasing product handling with a shorter supply chain, postponing product differentiation until after the order is placed, decreasing delivery cost and time with a downloadable product, reducing facility and processing costs, decreasing inventory costs through centralization, and improving supply chain coordination through information sharing. The cost reduction achieved has varied with the extent to which an e-business has exploited these opportunities.
4. Identify factors that influence the value of e-business in a supply chain.

   Supply chains that have used e-business successfully are able to move several supply chain activities from the push to the pull phase and postpone product differentiation until after a customer has placed his or her order. Successful e-businesses are also able to gain considerable reduction in facility and inventory costs as a result of centralization. Achieving this cost reduction also requires that transportation be a small fraction of the total product cost. Successful B2B supply chains have used e-business to lower their transaction costs for processing an order and exchange information to better match supply and demand. For unpredictable demand, Internet exchanges offer a significant opportunity because of their ability to aggregate both unmet demand and excess supply, and more efficiently match the two.

Discussion Questions

1. Discuss how a catalog retailer like L.L. Bean can use e-business to its advantage.
2. Consider the sale of home improvement products at Amazon, Home Depot, or a chain of hardware stores like True-Value. Who can extract the greatest benefit from going on-line? Why?
3. Amazon.com sells books, music, electronics, software, toys, and home improvement products on-line. In which product category does e-business offer the greatest advantage compared with a retail store chain? In which product category does e-business offer the smallest advantage (or a potential cost disadvantage) compared with a retail store chain? Why?
4. Why should an e-business like Amazon build more warehouses as its sales volume grows?
5. The Gap has completely integrated its e-business with its retail stores. What potential advantages does this strategy offer compared with having a separate e-business?
6. Why is the benefit from e-business larger in the PC industry than in the book or grocery industry?
7. Why is it difficult for an e-business in the grocery industry to compete against supermarkets on the basis of price?

Bibliography

Business Trade & Technology Strategies, The Forrester Report (August 1998.)

Evans, Philip, and Thomas S. Wurster. "Getting Real About Virtual Commerce." *Harvard Business Review* (November–December 1999), 84–94.

Hanson, Ward. *Principles of Internet Marketing*. Cincinnati: South-West College Publishing, 2000.

Mastering Commerce Logistics, The Forrester Report (August 1999.)

Poirier, Charles C. "The Convergence of Business & Technology." *Supply Chain Management Review* (Fall 1999), 52–58.

Retail's Growth Spiral, The Forrester Report (November 1998.)

Ricker, Fred R., and Ravi Kalakota. "Order Fulfillment: The Hidden Key to E-Commerce Success." *Supply Chain Management Review* (Fall 1999), 60–70.

Salcedo, Simon, and Ann Grackin. "The e-Value Chain." *Supply Chain Management Review* (Winter 2000), 63–70.

Shapiro, Carl, and Hal R. Varian. *Information Rules: A Strategic Guide to the Network Economy*. Boston: Harvard Business School Press, 1999.

"The e-Enabled Supply Chain." Global Supplement, *Supply Chain Management Review* (Fall 1999.)

Turban, Efraim, Jae Lee, David King, and H. Michael Chung. *Electronic Commerce: A Managerial Perspective*. Upper Saddle River, N.J.: Prentice Hall, 2000.

PART SIX

Financial Factors Influencing Supply Chain Decisions

CHAPTER 15

Financial Evaluation of Supply Chain Decisions

The goal of this module is to highlight how uncertainties in financial factors such as prices, exchange rates, and inflation should be accounted for in supply chain decisions. Various financial factors that influence supply chain decisions are identified and methodologies for financial evaluation of supply chain decisions are discussed. These methodologies are then used to evaluate several supply chain decisions.

CHAPTER 15

Financial Evaluation of Supply Chain Decisions

Learning Objectives

After reading this chapter, you will be able to

1. identify financial factors that influence supply chain performance;
2. understand the financial tools used to evaluate supply chain decisions; and
3. perform financial analysis on supply chain decisions.

In previous chapters, we focus on how supply and demand uncertainty influences supply chain strategy, planning, and operation. In this chapter we focus on how financial uncertainties influence the performance of supply chains. We discuss the methodologies used to evaluate supply chain decisions given this uncertainty and show how they can be used to make better supply chain decisions.

15.1 THE IMPACT OF FINANCIAL FACTORS ON SUPPLY CHAIN DECISIONS

During the supply chain design phase, decisions are made regarding significant investments in the supply chain. Firms make such supply chain decisions as how many plants to build and how large they should be, how many trucks to purchase or lease, and whether to build warehouses or lease warehouse space. These decisions, once made, often cannot be altered in the short term. They can remain in place for several years and define the boundaries within which the supply chain must compete. Therefore, it is important that these decisions be evaluated correctly. Besides such factors as supply and demand uncertainty, several financial factors also affect these decisions. Managers must consider financial uncertainties when making supply chain decisions, particularly when designing global supply chains. Toyota, for example, has made its global assembly plants more flexible so that each plant can supply multiple markets. One of the main benefits of this flexibility is that it allows Toyota to react to both fluctuations in exchange rates and local prices by altering production to maximize profits. A firm may choose to build a flexible global supply chain even in the presence of little demand or supply uncertainty if uncertainty exists in exchange rates or prices. Thus, both supply and demand uncertainty and financial uncertainty must be considered when making supply chain decisions.

This sort of financial analysis can also be used to tie supply chain performance to the performance of shareholders' investments in the company. Financial analysis is used to compare different supply chain decisions in terms of their financial performance. Therefore, financial analysis is an important tool that must be well understood by supply chain managers when they make decisions about the supply chain.

15.2 DISCOUNTED CASH FLOW ANALYSIS

Since supply chain design decisions remain in place for an extended period of time, they should be evaluated as a sequence of cash flows over that period. The **present value** of a stream of cash flows is what that stream is worth in today's dollars. **Discounted cash flow** (DCF) analysis evaluates the present value of any stream of future cash flows and allows management to compare two streams of cash flows in terms of their financial value. Discounted cash flow analysis is based on the fundamental premise that "a dollar today is worth more than a dollar tomorrow" because a dollar today may be invested and earn a return in addition to the dollar invested. This premise provides the basic tool for comparing the relative value of future cash flows that will arrive during different time periods.

The present value of future cash flow is found by using a discount factor. If a dollar today can be invested and earn a rate of return k over the next period, an investment of \$1 today will result in $1 + k$ dollars in the next period. An investor would therefore be indifferent between obtaining \$1 in the next period or $\$1/(1 + k)$ in the current period. Thus, \$1 in the next period is discounted as follows to obtain its present value:

$$\text{Discount factor} = \frac{1}{1+k} \tag{15.1}$$

The rate of return k is also referred to as the discount rate, hurdle rate, or opportunity cost of capital. Given a stream of cash flows $C_0, C_1, \ldots, C_T$ over the next T periods, and a rate of return k, the net present value (NPV) of this cash flow stream is given by the following:

$$NPV = C_0 + \sum_{t=1}^{T}\left(\frac{1}{1+k}\right)^t C_t \tag{15.2}$$

The NPV of different options should be compared when making supply chain decisions. A negative NPV for an option indicates that the option will lose money for the supply chain. The decision with the highest NPV will provide a supply chain with the highest financial return.

Consider Trips Logistics, a third-party logistics firm that provides warehousing and other logistics services. The general manager at Trips Logistics is facing a decision regarding the amount of space to lease for the upcoming three-year period. He has forecast that Trips Logistics will need to handle a demand of 100,000 units for each of the three years. Historically, Trips Logistics has required 1,000 square feet of warehouse space for every 1,000 units of demand. For the purposes of this discussion, the only cost Trips Logistics faces is the cost for the warehouse.

Trips Logistics receives revenue of $1.22 for each unit of demand. The general manager must decide whether to sign a three-year lease or obtain warehousing space on the spot market each year. The three-year lease will cost $1 per square foot per year, and the spot market rate is expected to be $1.20 per square foot per year for each of the three years. Trips Logistics has a discount rate of $k = 0.1$.

The general manager decides to compare the NPV of signing a three-year lease for 100,000 square foot of warehouse space with obtaining the space from the spot market each year.

If the general manager obtains warehousing space from the spot market each year, Trips Logistics will earn $1.22 for each unit and pay $1.20 for one square foot of warehouse space required. The expected annual profit for Trips Logistics in this case is given by the following:

$$\text{Expected annual profit if warehousing space is obtained from spot market} = 100{,}000 \times \$1.22 - 100{,}000 \times \$1.20 = \$2{,}000$$

Obtaining warehouse space from the spot market provides Trips Logistics with an expected positive cash flow of $2,000 in each of the three years. The NPV may be evaluated as follows:

$$NPV(\text{No lease}) = C_0 + \frac{C_1}{1+k} + \frac{C_2}{(1+k)^2} = 2{,}000 + \frac{2{,}000}{1.1} + \frac{2{,}000}{1.1^2} = \$5{,}471$$

If the general manager leases 100,000 square feet of warehouse space for the next three years, Trips Logistics pays $1 per square foot of space leased each year. The expected annual profit for Trips Logistics in this case is given by the following:

$$\text{Expected annual profit with three-year lease} = 100{,}000 \times \$1.22 - 100{,}000 \times \$1.00 = \$22{,}000$$

Signing a lease for three years provides Trips Logistics with a positive cash flow of $22,000 in each of the three years. The NPV may be evaluated as follows:

$$NPV(\text{Lease}) = C_0 + \frac{C_1}{1+k} + \frac{C_2}{(1+k)^2} = 22{,}000 + \frac{22{,}000}{1.1} + \frac{22{,}000}{1.1^2} = \$60{,}182$$

The NPV of signing the lease is $60,182 − $5,471 = $54,711 higher than obtaining warehousing space on the spot market. The general manager at Trips Logistics thus decides to sign the three-year lease. However, as we discuss in the next section, including additional factors in the decision may cause the manager to rethink the decision.

15.3 REPRESENTATIONS OF UNCERTAINTY

The manager at Trips Logistics considered both future demand and spot market prices to be predictable. In reality, demand and prices are highly uncertain and are likely to fluctuate during the life of any supply chain decision. For a global supply chain, exchange rates and inflation are also likely to vary over time in different locations. Supply chain managers must incorporate these uncertainties when making decisions. We next discuss some models that can be used to represent uncertainty in financial factors such as price and exchange rate.

Binomial Representation of Uncertainty

The binomial representation of uncertainty is based on the assumption that when moving from one period to the next, the value of the underlying factor (such as price) has only two possible outcomes: up or down. In the commonly used multiplicative binomial, it is assumed that the underlying factor either moves up by a factor $u > 1$ with probability p, or down by a factor $d < 1$ with probability $1-p$. Given a price P in period 0, the possible outcomes in future periods are as follows:

Period 1: Pu, Pd
Period 2: Pu^2, Pud, Pd^2
Period 3: Pu^3, Pu^2d, Pud^2, Pd^3
Period 4: Pu^4, Pu^3d, Pu^2d^2, Pud^3, Pd^4

In general, period T has all possible outcomes $Pu^td^{(T-t)}$, for $t = 0, 1, \ldots, T$. From a state $Pu^ad^{(T-a)}$ in period t, the price may move to either $Pu^{a+1}d^{(T-a)}$ with probability p or $Pu^ad^{(T-a)+1}$ with probability $(1 - p)$ in period $t + 1$. This is represented as the binomial tree shown in Figure 15.1.

FIGURE 15.1 The Multiplicative Binomial Tree

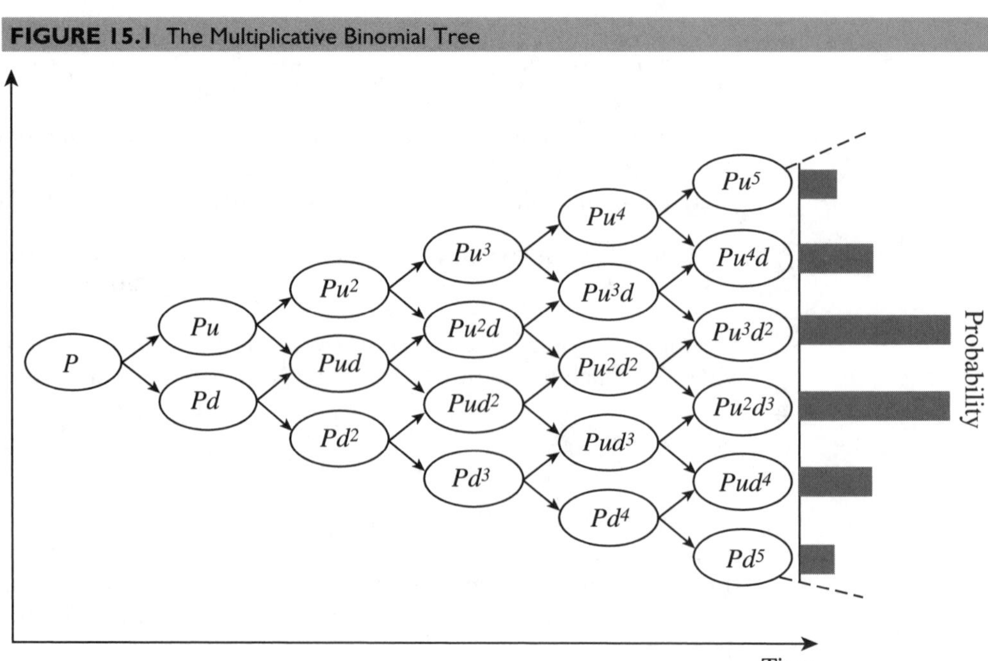

In the additive binomial, it is assumed that the underlying factor increases by u in a given period with probability p and decreases by d with probability $1 - p$. The additive binomial has the following states in a given period:

Period 1: $P + u, P - d$
Period 2: $P + 2u, P + u - d, P - 2d$
Period 3: $P + 3u, P + 2u - d, P + u - 2d, P - 3d$
Period 4: $P + 4u, P + 3u - d, P + 2u - 2d, P + u - 3d, P - 4d$

In general, period T has all possible outcomes $P + tu - (T - t)d$, for $t = 0, 1, \ldots, T$.

The multiplicative binomial cannot take on negative values and can be used for factors like price and exchange rates that cannot become negative. It also has the advantage of the growth or decline in the given factor being proportional to the current value of the factor and not fixed independent of size. For example, a product with a unit price of \$10 is much less likely to see a fluctuation in price of \$5 than a product with a unit price of \$100. This fact is better captured by the multiplicative binomial.

A logical objection to both the multiplicative and additive binomial is the fact that the underlying factor takes on only one of two possible values at the end of each period. Certainly, a price can change to more than just two values. But by making the period short enough, this assumption may be justified. The time period selected depends on the factor under consideration. Whereas a period of a week or a month may be appropriate for product prices, a shorter time horizon may be more appropriate for exchange rates.

As the number of periods increases, the probability distribution among the end states of the multiplicative binomial becomes smoother and begins to resemble the normal distribution. Observe that as we go further into the future, the range of possibilities of the underlying factor increases. This is a common property of all binomial distributions and is a reasonable assumption for most financial factors such as price or exchange rates.

Log-Transformed Binomial Representation of Uncertainty

The form of the log-transformed binomial distribution is similar to the standard additive binomial discussed in the preceding section, except that the probability p and the increase u or decrease d in value are different. The log-transformed binomial representation of uncertainty is computationally attractive and is evaluated as follows.[1]

It is assumed that changes in the underlying factor will be evaluated after discrete intervals Δt, and $\sigma^2 \Delta t$ is the observed variance of the factor value over this period. For example, if the factor being considered is price and the duration of a period is 4 weeks, then σ^2 represents the variance of price over a week and $\Delta t = 4$. Ideally, we want the period over which σ^2 is evaluated to be as small as possible. If r represents the risk-free return, the transition probability p and the increase u and decrease d from one period to the next are given by the following:

$$p = (1 + \mu k/H)/2, H = u = -d = \sqrt{k + (\mu K)^2} \qquad \textbf{(15.3)}$$

where

$$k = \sigma^2 \Delta t \text{ and } \mu = r/\sigma^2 - 1/2$$

The distribution is then represented as an additive binomial.

[1] Trigeorgis (1996).

Other Representations of Uncertainty

In the valuation of options, the underlying asset price is often allowed to vary continuously over time. A commonly used process to describe the evolution of the asset price is the log-normal diffusion process.[2] A key feature of this process is that the price never drops below zero. Another feature of the log-normal diffusion process that is similar to the binomial is that the variance of the asset price grows with time. The variance in fact grows proportionally to the length of the time horizon.

Another common representation of the evolution of a financial factor is as a mean reverting process. The idea here is that the factor fluctuates about a mean and experiences shocks. When it deviates from the mean, it is pulled back toward the mean over time. The further from the mean that the factor deviates, the stronger it is pulled back toward the mean.

15.4 EVALUATING SUPPLY CHAIN DECISIONS USING DECISION TREES

A **decision tree** is a graphic device used to evaluate decisions under uncertainty. Decision trees with discounted cash flows can be used to evaluate supply chain decisions given uncertainty in prices, demand, exchange rates, and inflation.

The first step in setting up a decision tree is to identify the number of time periods into the future that will be considered when making the decision. The decision maker should also identify the duration of a period, which could be a day, a month, a quarter, or any other time period. The duration of a period should be the minimum period of time over which factors affecting supply chain decisions may change by a *significant* amount. *Significant* is hard to define, but in most cases it is appropriate to use the duration over which an aggregate plan holds as a period. If planning is done monthly, we set the duration of a period at a month. In the following discussion, T represents the number of time periods over which the supply chain decision is to be evaluated.

The next step is to identify factors that will affect the value of the decision and are likely to fluctuate over the next T periods. These factors include demand, price, exchange rate, and inflation. Having identified the key factors, the next step is to identify probability distributions that define the fluctuation of each factor from one period to the next. If, for instance, demand and price are identified as the two key factors that affect the decision, the probability of moving from a given value of demand and price in one period to any other value of demand and price in the next period must be defined.

The next step is to identify a periodic discount rate k to be applied to future cash flows. It is not essential that the same discount rate apply to each period. The discount rate should take into account the inherent risk associated with the investment. In general, a higher discount rate should apply to investments with higher risk.

The decision is now evaluated using a decision tree, which contains the present and T future periods. Within each period a node must be defined for every possible combination of factor values (say demand and price) that can be achieved. Arrows are drawn from origin nodes in period i to end nodes in period $i+1$. The probability on an arrow is referred to as the **transition probability** and is the probability of transitioning from the origin node in period i to the end node in period $i+1$.

The decision tree is evaluated starting from nodes in period T and working back to period 0. For each node, the decision is optimized taking into account current as

[2]Ibid.

well as future values of various factors. The analysis is based on **Bellman's principle**, which states that for any choice of strategy in a given state, the optimal strategy in the next period is the one that is selected if the entire analysis is assumed to begin in the next period. This principle allows the optimal strategy to be solved in a backward fashion starting at the last period. Expected future cash flows are discounted back and included in the decision currently under consideration. The value of the node in period 0 gives the value of the investment as well as the decisions taken during each time period. Tools like Treeplan are available that help solve decision trees on spreadsheets.

The decision tree analysis methodology is summarized as follows:

1. Identify the duration of each period (e.g., week, month) and the number of periods T over which the decision is to be evaluated.
2. Identify factors whose fluctuation will be considered over the next T periods such as demand, price, and exchange rate.
3. Identify representations of uncertainty for each factor, that is, determine what distribution to use to model the uncertainty.
4. Identify the periodic discount rate k for each period.
5. Represent the decision tree with defined states in each period as well as the transition probabilities between states in successive periods.
6. Starting at period T, work back to period 0, identifying the optimal decision and the expected cash flows at each step. Expected cash flows at each state in a given period should be discounted back when included in the previous period.

We illustrate the decision tree analysis methodology by using the lease decision facing the general manager at Trips Logistics. The manager must decide whether to lease warehouse space for the coming three years and the quantity to lease. Recall that 1,000 square feet of warehouse space is required for every 1,000 units of demand and the current demand at Trips Logistics is for 100,000 units per year. The manager anticipates uncertainty in demand and spot prices for warehouse space over the coming three years. He decides to use a multiplicative binomial representation of uncertainty for both demand and price. From one year to the next, demand may go up by 20 percent with a probability of .5 or go down by 20 percent with a probability of .5. The probabilities of the two outcomes are unchanged from one year to the next.

The general manager can sign a three-year lease at a price of \$1 per square foot. per year. Warehouse space is currently available on the spot market for \$1.20 per square foot per year. From one year to the next, spot prices for warehouse space may go up by 10 percent with probability .5 or go down by 10 percent with probability .5 according to a binomial process. The probabilities of the two outcomes are unchanged from one year to the next.

The general manager feels that prices of warehouse space and demand for the product fluctuate independently. Each unit Trips Logistics handles results in revenue of \$1.22, and the company is committed to handling all demand that arises. Trips Logistics uses a discount rate of $k = 0.1$ for each of the three years.

The general manager assumes that all costs are incurred at the beginning of each year and thus constructs a decision tree with $T = 2$. The decision tree is shown in Figure 15.2, with each node representing demand (D) in thousands of units and price (p) in dollars. The probability of each transition is .25, because price and demand fluctuate independently.

The manager first analyzes the option of not signing a lease and obtaining all warehouse space from the spot market. He starts with period 2 and evaluates the

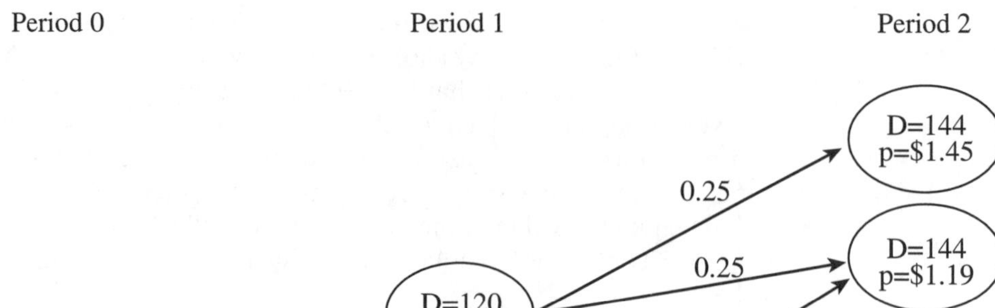

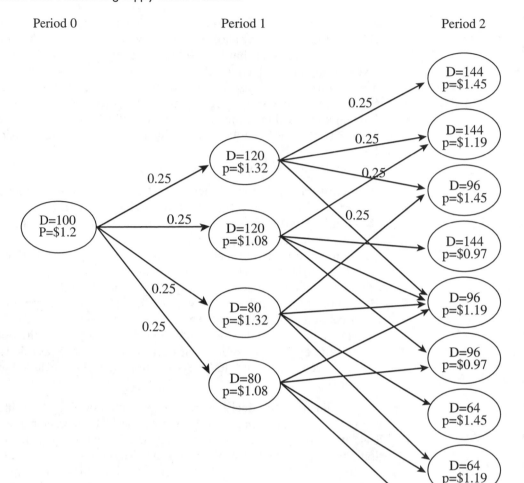

FIGURE 15.2 Decision Tree for TL Considering Demand and Price Fluctuation

profit for Trips Logistics at each node. At the node $D = 144$, $p = \$1.45$, Trips Logistics must satisfy a demand of 144,000 and faces a spot price of \$1.45 per square foot for warehouse space in period 2. The cost incurred by Trips Logistics in period 2 at the node $D = 144$, $p = \$1.45$ is represented by $C(D = 144,p = 1.45,2)$ and is given by the following:

$$C(D = 144,p = 1.45,2) = 144{,}000 \times 1.45 = \$208{,}800$$

The profit at Trips Logistics in period 2 at the node $D = 144$, $p = \$1.45$ is represented by $P(D = 144,p = 1.45,2)$ and is given by the following:

$$\begin{aligned} P(D = 144,p = 1.45,2) &= 144{,}000 \times 1.22 - C(D = 144,p = 1.45,2) \\ &= 175{,}680 - 208{,}800 = -\$33{,}120 \end{aligned}$$

The profit for TL at each of the other nodes in period 2 is evaluated similarly as follows:

$P(D = 144,p = 1.19,2) = 144{,}000 \times 1.22 - 144{,}000 \times 1.19 = \$4{,}320$
$P(D = 144,p = 0.97,2) = 144{,}000 \times 1.22 - 144{,}000 \times 0.97 = \$36{,}000$
$P(D = 96,p = 1.45,2) = 96{,}000 \times 1.22 - 96{,}000 \times 1.45 = -\$22{,}080$
$P(D = 96,p = 1.19,2) = 96{,}000 \times 1.22 - 96{,}000 \times 1.19 = \$2{,}880$
$P(D = 96,p = 0.97,2) = 96{,}000 \times 1.22 - 96{,}000 \times 0.97 = \$24{,}000$
$P(D = 64,p = 1.45,2) = 64{,}000 \times 1.22 - 64{,}000 \times 1.45 = -\$14{,}720$
$P(D = 64,p = 1.19,2) = 64{,}000 \times 1.22 - 64{,}000 \times 1.19 = \$1{,}920$
$P(D = 64,p = 0.97,2) = 64{,}000 \times 1.22 - 64{,}000 \times 0.97 = \$16{,}000$

The manager next evaluates the expected profit at each node in period 1 to be the profit during period 1 plus the present value (at the time of period 1) of the expected profit in period 2. The expected profit $EP(D= \ , p = \ , 1)$ at a node is the expected profit over all four nodes in period 2 that may result from this node. $PVEP(D= \ , p = \ , 1)$ represents the present value of this expected profit, and $P(D= \ , p= \ , 1)$, the total expected profit, is the sum of the profit in period 1 and the present value of the expected profit in period 2. From the node $D = 120$, $p = \$1.32$ in period 1, there are four possible states in period 2. The manager thus evaluates the expected profit in period 2 over all four states possible from the node $D = 120$, $p = \$1.32$ in period 1 to be $EP(D = 120,p = 1.32,1)$, where

$EP(D = 120,p = 1.32,1) = 0.25 \times P(D = 144,p = 1.45,2) + 0.25 \times P(D = 144,p = 1.19,2) + 0.25 \times P(D = 96,p = 1.45,2) + 0.25 \times P(D = 96,p = 1.19,2) = -0.25 \times 33{,}120 + 0.25 \times 4{,}320 - 0.25 \times 22{,}080 + 0.25 \times 2{,}880 = -\$12{,}000$

The present value of this expected value in period 1 is given by the following:

$PVEP(D = 120,p = 1.32, 1) = EP(D = 120,p = 1.32,1)/(1+k) = -12{,}000/1.1 = -\$10{,}909$

The manager obtains the total expected profit $P(D = 120,p = 1.32,1)$ at node $D = 120$, $p = 1.32$ in period 1 to be the sum of the profit in period 1 at this node, as well as the present value of future expected profits:

$P(D = 120,p = 1.32,1) = 120{,}000 \times 1.22 - 120{,}000 \times 1.32 + PVEP(D = 120,p = 1.32,1) = -\$12{,}000 - \$10{,}909 = -\$22{,}909$

The total expected profit for all other nodes in period 1 is evaluated as follows:

$EP(D = 120,p = 1.08,1) = 0.25 \times P(D = 144,p = 1.19,2) + 0.25 \times P(D = 144,p = 0.97,2) + 0.25 \times P(D = 96,p = 1.19,2) + 0.25 \times P(D = 96,p = 0.97,2) = 0.25 \times 4{,}320 + 0.25 \times 36{,}000 + 0.25 \times 2{,}880 + 0.25 \times 24{,}000 = \$16{,}800$

$PVEP(D = 120,p = 1.08, 1) = EP(D = 120,p = 1.08, 1)/(1+k) = 16{,}800/1.1 = \$15{,}273$

$P(D = 120,p = 1.08,1) = 120{,}000 \times 1.22 - 120{,}000 \times 1.08 + PVEP(D = 120,p = 1.08, 1) = \$16{,}800 + \$15{,}273 = \$32{,}073$

$EP(D = 80,p = 1.32,1) = 0.25 \times P(D = 96,p = 1.45,2) + 0.25 \times P(D = 96,p = 1.19,2) + 0.25 \times P(D = 64,p = 1.45,2) + 0.25 \times P(D = 64,p = 1.19,2) = -0.25 \times 22{,}080 + 0.25 \times 2{,}880 - 0.25 \times 14{,}720 + 0.25 \times 1{,}920 = -\$8{,}000$

$PVEP(D = 80,p = 1.32, 1) = EP(D = 80,p = 1.32, 1)/(1+k) = -8{,}000/1.1 = -\$7{,}273$

$P(D = 80,p = 1.32,1) = 80{,}000 \times 1.22 - 80{,}000 \times 1.32 + PVEP(D = 80,p = 1.32, 1) = -\$8{,}000 - \$7{,}273 = -\$15{,}273$

$EP(D = 80,p = 1.08,1) = 0.25 \times P(D = 96,p = 1.19,2) + 0.25 \times P(D = 96,p = 0.97,2) + 0.25 \times P(D = 64,p = 1.19,2) + 0.25 \times P(D = 64,p = 0.97,2) = 0.25 \times 2{,}880 + 0.25 \times 24{,}000 + 0.25 \times 1{,}920 + 0.25 \times 16{,}000 = \$11{,}200$

$PVEP(D = 80,p = 1.08, 1) = EP(D = 80,p = 1.08, 1)/(1+k) = 11{,}200/1.1 = \$10{,}182$

$P(D = 80,p = 1.08,1) = 80{,}000 \times 1.22 - 80{,}000 \times 1.08 + PVEP(D = 80,p = 1.08, 1) = \$11{,}200 + \$10{,}182 = \$21{,}382$

For period 0, the total profit $P(D = 100,p = 1.20,0)$ is obtained as the sum of the profit at period 0 and the present value of the expected profit over the four nodes in period 1:

$EP(D = 100,p = 1.20,0) = 0.25 \times P(D = 120,p = 1.32,1) + 0.25 \times P(D = 120,p = 1.08,1) + 0.25 \times P(D = 80,p = 1.32,1) + 0.25 \times P(D = 80,p = 1.08,1) = -0.25 \times 22{,}909 + 0.25 \times 32{,}073 - 0.25 \times 15{,}273 + 0.25 \times 21{,}382 = \$3{,}818$

$PVEP(D = 100,p = 1.20, 1) = EP(D = 100,p = 1.20, 0)/(1+k) = 3{,}818/1.1 = \$3{,}471$

$P(D = 100,p = 1.20,0) = 100{,}000 \times 1.22 - 100{,}000 \times 1.20 + PVEP(D = 100,p = 1.20, 0) = \$2{,}000 + \$3{,}471 = \$5{,}471$

Thus, the expected net present value of not signing the lease and obtaining all warehousing space from the spot market is given by the following:

$$NPV(\text{No lease}) = \$5{,}471$$

The manager next evaluates the alternative in which the lease for 100,000 square feet of warehouse space is signed. The evaluation procedure is very similar to the previous case, but the outcome in terms of profit changes. For example, at the node $D = 144,p = 1.45$, the manager will have to obtain 44,000 square feet of warehouse space from the spot market at $1.45 per square foot because only 100,000 square feet of space has been leased at $1 per square foot. If demand happens to be less than 100,000 units, Trips Logistics still has to pay for the entire 100,000 square feet of leased space. For period 2, the manager obtains the profit at each of the nine nodes as shown in Table 15.1.

The manager next evaluates the total expected profit for each node in period 1. Again, the expected profit $EP(D = ,p = , 1)$ at a node is the expected profit over all

TABLE 15.1 Period 2 Profit Calculations at Trips Logistics

Node	*Leased Space*	*Warehouse Space at Spot Price*	*Profit P(D=,p=, 2)*
$D = 144,p = 1.45$	100,000 sq. ft.	44,000 sq. ft.	$144{,}000 \times 1.22 - (100{,}000 \times 1 + 44{,}000 \times 1.45) = \$11{,}880$
$D = 144,p = 1.19$	100,000 sq. ft.	44,000 sq. ft.	$144{,}000 \times 1.22 - (100{,}000 \times 1 + 44{,}000 \times 1.19) = \$23{,}320$
$D = 144,p = 0.97$	100,000 sq. ft.	44,000 sq. ft.	$144{,}000 \times 1.22 - (100{,}000 \times 1 + 44{,}000 \times 0.97) = \$33{,}000$
$D = 96,p = 1.45$	100,000 sq. ft.	0 sq. ft.	$96{,}000 \times 1.22 - 100{,}000 \times 1 = \$17{,}120$
$D = 96,p = 1.19$	100,000 sq. ft.	0 sq. ft.	$96{,}000 \times 1.22 - 100{,}000 \times 1 = \$17{,}120$
$D = 96,p = 0.97$	100,000 sq. ft.	0 sq. ft.	$96{,}000 \times 1.22 - 100{,}000 \times 1 = \$17{,}120$
$D = 64,p = 1.45$	100,000 sq. ft.	0 sq. ft.	$64{,}000 \times 1.22 - 100{,}000 \times 1 = -\$21{,}920$
$D = 64,p = 1.19$	100,000 sq. ft.	0 sq. ft.	$64{,}000 \times 1.22 - 100{,}000 \times 1 = -\$21{,}920$
$D = 64,p = 0.97$	100,000 sq. ft.	0 sq. ft.	$64{,}000 \times 1.22 - 100{,}000 \times 1 = -\$21{,}920$

four nodes in period 2 that may result from this node, $PVEP(D = ,p = , 1)$ is the present value of this expected profit, and $P(D = ,p = , 1)$ is the total expected profit from both period 1 and 2. The manager thus obtains the results in Table 15.2.

For period 0, the expected profit $EP(D = 100,p = 1.20,0)$ over the four nodes in period 1 is given by the following:

$$EP(D = 100,p = 1.20,0) = 0.25 \times P(D = 120,p = 1.32,1) + 0.25 \times P(D = 120,p = 1.08,1) + 0.25 \times P(D = 80,p = 1.32,1) + 0.25 \times P(D = 80,p = 1.08,1) = 0.25 \times 35{,}782 + 0.25 \times 45{,}382 - 0.25 \times 4{,}582 - 0.25 \times 4{,}582 = \$18{,}000$$

The present value of the expected profit in period 0 is given by the following:

$$PVEP(D = 100,p = 1.20, 0) = EP(D = 100,p = 1.20, 0)/(1+k) = 18{,}000/1.1 = \$16{,}364$$

The total expected profit is obtained as the sum of the profit in period 0 and the present value of the expected profit over all four nodes in period 1. It is as follows:

$$P(D = 100,p = 1.20,0) = 100{,}000 \times 1.22 - 100{,}000 \times 1 + PVEP(D = 100, p = 1.20, 0) = \$22{,}000 + \$16{,}364 = \$38{,}364$$

The NPV of signing a three-year lease for 100,000 square feet of warehouse space is thus the following:

$$NPV(\text{Lease}) = \$38{,}364$$

Observe that the NPV of the lease option is considerably lower than when uncertainty is ignored ($60,182). This is because the lease is a fixed decision and Trips Logistics is unable to react to market conditions by leasing less space if demand is lower. Rigid contracts are less attractive in the presence of uncertainty.

The presence of uncertainty in demand and price reduces the value of the lease and increases the value of the spot market option. However, the manager still prefers to sign the three-year lease for 100,000 square feet because this option has a higher expected profit.

TABLE 15.2 Period 1 Profit Calculations at Trips Logistics

Node	*EP(D = ,p = ,1)*	*PVEP(D = ,p = ,1)*	*P(D = ,p = ,1)*
$(D = 120, p = 1.32,1)$	$0.25 \times P(D = 144,p = 1.45,2) + 0.25 \times P(D = 144,p = 1.19,2) + 0.25 \times P(D = 96,p = 1.45,2) + 0.25 \times P(D = 96,p = 1.19,2) = 0.25 \times 11{,}880 + 0.25 \times 23{,}320 + 0.25 \times 17{,}120 + 0.25 \times 17{,}120 = \$17{,}360$	$EP(D = 120,p = 1.32,1)/(1+ k) = 17{,}360/1.1 = \$15{,}782$	$= 120{,}000 \times 1.22 - (100{,}000 \times 1 + 20{,}000 \times 1.32 + PVEP(D = 120,p = 1.32\ 1) = \$20{,}000 + \$15{,}782 = \$35{,}782$
$(D = 120,p = 1.08,1)$	$0.25 \times 23{,}320 + 0.25 \times 33{,}000 + 0.25 \times 17{,}120 + 0.25 \times 17{,}120 = 22{,}640$	$22{,}640/1.1 = \$20{,}582$	$120{,}000 \times 1.22 - (100{,}000 \times 1 + 20{,}000 \times 1.08) + PVEP(D = 120,p = 1.08, 1) = \$24{,}800 + \$20{,}582 = \$45{,}382$
$(D = 80,p = 1.32,1)$	$0.25 \times 17{,}120 + 0.25 \times 17{,}120 - 0.25 \times 21{,}920 - 0.25 \times 21{,}920 = -\$2{,}400$	$-2{,}400/1.1 = -\$2{,}182$	$80{,}000 \times 1.22 - 100{,}000 \times 1 + PVEP(D = 80,p = 1.32, 1) = -\$2{,}400 - \$2{,}182 = -\$4{,}582$
$(D = 80,p = 1.08,1)$	$0.25 \times 17{,}120 + 0.25 \times 17{,}120 - 0.25 \times 21{,}920 - 0.25 \times 21{,}920 = -\$2{,}400$	$-2{,}400/1.1 = -\$2{,}182$	$= 80{,}000 \times 1.22 - 100{,}000 \times 1 + PVEP(D = 80,p = 1.09, 1) = -\$2{,}400 - \$2{,}182 = -\$4{,}582$

> ***Key Point*** Uncertainty in economic factors should be included in the financial evaluation of supply chain decisions. The inclusion of uncertainty may have a significant impact on this evaluation.

Evaluating Flexibility Using Decision Trees

The decision tree analysis methodology is very useful when evaluating flexibility within a supply chain. We consider the evaluation of flexibility with decision trees in the context of warehousing choices for Trips Logistics.

The general manager at Trips Logistics has been offered a contract in which, for an up-front payment of $10,000, Trips Logistics will have the flexibility of using between 60,000 square feet and 100,000 square feet of warehouse space at $1 per square foot. Trips Logistics must pay $60,000 per year for the first 60,000 square feet and can then use up to another 40,000 square feet on demand at $1 per square foot. The general manager decides to use decision trees to evaluate whether this flexible contract with an up-front payment of $10,000 is preferable to a fixed contract for 100,000 square feet of warehouse space.

The underlying decision tree for evaluating the flexible contract is exactly as in Figure 15.2. The profit at each node, however, will change because of the flexibility. If demand is larger than 100,000 units, Trips Logistics uses all 100,000 square feet of warehouse space even under the flexible contract. If demand is between 60,000 and 100,000 units, however, Trips Logistics only need pay for the exact amount of warehouse space used rather than the entire 100,000 square feet under the contract without flexibility. The profit at each node for period 2 is evaluated as follows:

$$P(D = 144, p = 1.45, 2) = 144{,}000 \times 1.22 - (100{,}000 \times 1 + 44{,}000 \times 1.45) = \$11{,}880$$

$$P(D = 144, p = 1.19, 2) = 144{,}000 \times 1.22 - (100{,}000 \times 1 + 44{,}000 \times 1.19) = \$23{,}320$$

These first two nodes have the same profit regardless of whether the flexible lease is offered. However, in the next node, Trips Logistics is able to take advantage of the flexibility when spot prices drop below the lease price for the optional space and only use the first 60,000 square feet of lease space, getting the rest from the spot market at a lower price. The resulting profit for $D = 144, p = 0.97$ is as follows:

$$P(D = 144, p = 0.97, 2) = 144{,}000 \times 1.22 - (60{,}000 \times 1 + 84{,}000 \times 0.97) = \$34{,}200$$

If demand drops below 100, Trips Logistics is also able to take advantage of the flexible lease by not using, and therefore not paying for, all 100,000 square feet. The resulting profits for the remaining nodes are as follows:

$$P(D = 96, p = 1.45, 2) = 96{,}000 \times 1.22 - 96{,}000 \times 1 = \$21{,}120$$
$$P(D = 96, p = 1.19, 2) = 96{,}000 \times 1.22 - 96{,}000 \times 1 = \$21{,}120$$
$$P(D = 96, p = 0.97, 2) = 96{,}000 \times 1.22 - (60{,}000 \times 1 + 36{,}000 \times 0.97) = \$22{,}200$$
$$P(D = 64, p = 1.45, 2) = 64{,}000 \times 1.22 - 64{,}000 \times 1 = \$14{,}080$$
$$P(D = 64, p = 1.19, 2) = 64{,}000 \times 1.22 - 64{,}000 \times 1 = \$14{,}080$$
$$P(D = 64, p = 0.97, 2) = 64{,}000 \times 1.22 - (60{,}000 \times 1 + 4{,}000 \times 0.97) = \$14{,}200$$

The general manager evaluates the expected profit $EP(D = , p = , 1)$ from period 2, the present value in period 1 of the profit in period 2, and the total expected profit for each node in period 1 as discussed earlier. The results are shown in Table 15.3.

TABLE 15.3 Period 1 Profit Calculations at Trips Logistics With Flexible Contract

Node	*EP(D = ,p = ,1)*	*PVEP(D = ,p = ,1)*	*P(D = ,p = ,1)*
$(D = 120,p = 1.32,1)$	$0.25 \times 11{,}880 + 0.25 \times 23{,}320 + 0.25 \times 21{,}120 + 0.25 \times 21{,}120 = 19{,}360$	$19{,}360/1.1 = \$17{,}600$	$120{,}000 \times 1.22 - (100{,}000 \times 1 + 20{,}000 \times 1.32) + PVEP(D = 120,p = 1.32\ 1) = \$20{,}000 + \$17{,}600 = \$37{,}600$
$(D = 120,p = 1.08,1)$	$0.25 \times 23{,}320 + 0.25 \times 34{,}200 + 0.25 \times 21{,}120 + 0.25 \times 22{,}200 = \$25{,}210$	$25{,}210/1.1 = \$22{,}918$	$120{,}000 \times 1.22 - (100{,}000 \times 1 + 20{,}000 \times 1.08) + PVEP(D = 120,p = 1.08,1) = \$24{,}800 + \$22{,}918 = \$47{,}718$
$(D = 80,p = 1.32,1)$	$0.25 \times 21{,}120 + 0.25 \times 21{,}120 + 0.25 \times 14{,}080 + 0.25 \times 14{,}080 = \$17{,}600$	$17{,}600/1.1 = \$16{,}000$	$80{,}000 \times 1.22 - 80{,}000 \times 1 + PVEP(D = 80,p = 1.32,1) = \$17{,}600 + \$16{,}000 = \$33{,}600$
$(D = 80,p = 1.08,1)$	$0.25 \times 21{,}120 + 0.25 \times 22{,}200 + 0.25 \times 14{,}080 + 0.25 \times 14{,}200 = \$17{,}900$	$17{,}900/1.1 = \$16{,}273$	$80{,}000 \times 1.22 - 80{,}000 \times 1 + PVEP(D = 80,p = 1.08,1) = \$17{,}600 + \$16{,}273 = \$33{,}873$

The total expected profit in period 0 is the sum of the profit in period 0 and the present value of the expected profit in period 1. The manager thus obtains the following:

$EP(D = 100,p = 1.20,0) = 0.25 \times P(D = 120,p = 1.32,1) + 0.25 \times P(D = 120,p = 1.08,1) + 0.25 \times P(D = 80,p = 1.32,1) + 0.25 \times P(D = 80,p = 1.08,1) = 0.25 \times 37{,}600 + 0.25 \times 47{,}718 + 0.25 \times 33{,}600 + 0.25 \times 33{,}873 = \$38{,}198$

$PVEP(D = 100,p = 1.20, 1) = EP(D = 100,p = 1.20, 0)/(1+k) = 38{,}198/1.1 = \$34{,}725$

$P(D = 100,p = 1.20,0) = 100{,}000 \times 1.22 - 100{,}000 \times 1 + PVEP(D = 100,p = 1.20, 0) = \$22{,}000 + \$34{,}725 = \$56{,}725$

The value of flexibility may now be obtained as the difference between the expected present values of the two contracts:

Expected present value of flexible contract = \$56,725
Expected present value of rigid contract (100,000 square feet) = \$38,364
Net present value of flexibility = \$56,725 − \$38,364 = \$18,361

The flexible contract is thus beneficial for Trips Logistics because it only requires an up-front payment of \$10,000. An up-front payment of \$10,000 would still result in the flexible contract being \$8,361 more valuable than the rigid contract.

Key Point Flexibility should be valued by taking into account uncertainty in economic factors. In general, flexibility will tend to increase in value with an increase in uncertainty.

15.5 AM TIRES: FINANCIAL EVALUATION OF SUPPLY CHAIN DESIGN DECISIONS

In this section we discuss a supply chain design decision at AM Tires, a tire manufacturer, to illustrate the power of the decision tree analysis methodology. AM tires is faced with a plant location decision in a global network with fluctuating exchange rates and demand uncertainty.

AM Tires sells its products in both Mexico and the United States. Demand in the United States is currently 100,000 tires per year, and that in Mexico is 50,000 tires per year. From one year to the next, demand in either country may go up by 20 percent with probability .5 or go down by 20 percent with probability .5. Demand fluctuations in the two countries are independent.

Tires sell for $30 each in the United States and 240 pesos each in Mexico. The current exchange rate is $1US = 9 pesos. Exchange rates are expected to fluctuate as per the binomial distribution. From one year to the next, the peso may rise 25 percent or drop 25 percent, each with a probability of .5. Exchange rate fluctuations are independent of demand fluctuations.

AM Tires is designing its manufacturing network, which will be in place over the next two years. The company is planning to build a 100,000-unit plant in the United States and a 50,000-unit plant in Mexico. The plants may be dedicated, in which case they can only supply the local market, or flexible, in which case they can supply either market. The fixed and variable costs for each option are shown in Table 15.4. Observe that the fixed costs have been given per year rather than up front with a future salvage value. Transportation costs between the United States and Mexico are $1 per tire either way. The plant decision has to stay in place over the next two years, and the discount rate used by AM Tires is $k = 0.1$. The vice president of operations at AM Tires is working with the CEO to decide on the type of facility to build in each location. The company is bound by agreements with each local government to build a plant in each country.

The vice president constructs a decision tree, as shown in Figure 15.3. Each node in a given period leads to eight possible nodes in the next period because demand in each country and the exchange rate may go up or down. The detailed links in period 2 for one node in period 1 are shown in Figure 15.3. The transition probability between each pair of linked nodes is $.5 \times .5 \times .5 = .125$ because demand in the United States as well as Mexico and exchange rate fluctuations are independent and take place with .5 probability each. Demand is represented by *RU* for the United States, and *RM* for Mexico, and is expressed in thousands. The exchange rate is represented by *E*, where *E* is the number of pesos to one U.S. dollar.

There are four possible capacity and flexibility combinations between plants in Mexico and the United States. The vice president at AM Tires first evaluates the case in which a dedicated capacity of 100,000 is installed in the United States and a dedicated capacity of 50,000 is installed in Mexico.

Dedicated Capacity of 100,000 in United States and 50,000 in Mexico

The vice president starts by evaluating profits at each node in period 2. Each node is represented by the corresponding value of *RU*, *RM*, and *E*.

TABLE 15.4 Fixed and Variable Production Costs

	Dedicated Plant		*Flexible Plant*	
Plant	***Fixed Cost***	***Variable Cost***	***Fixed Cost***	***Variable Cost***
U.S. 100,000	$1 million/year	$15/tire	$1.1 million/year	$15/tire
Mexico 50,000	4 million pesos/year	110 pesos/tire	4.4 million pesos/year	110 pesos/tire

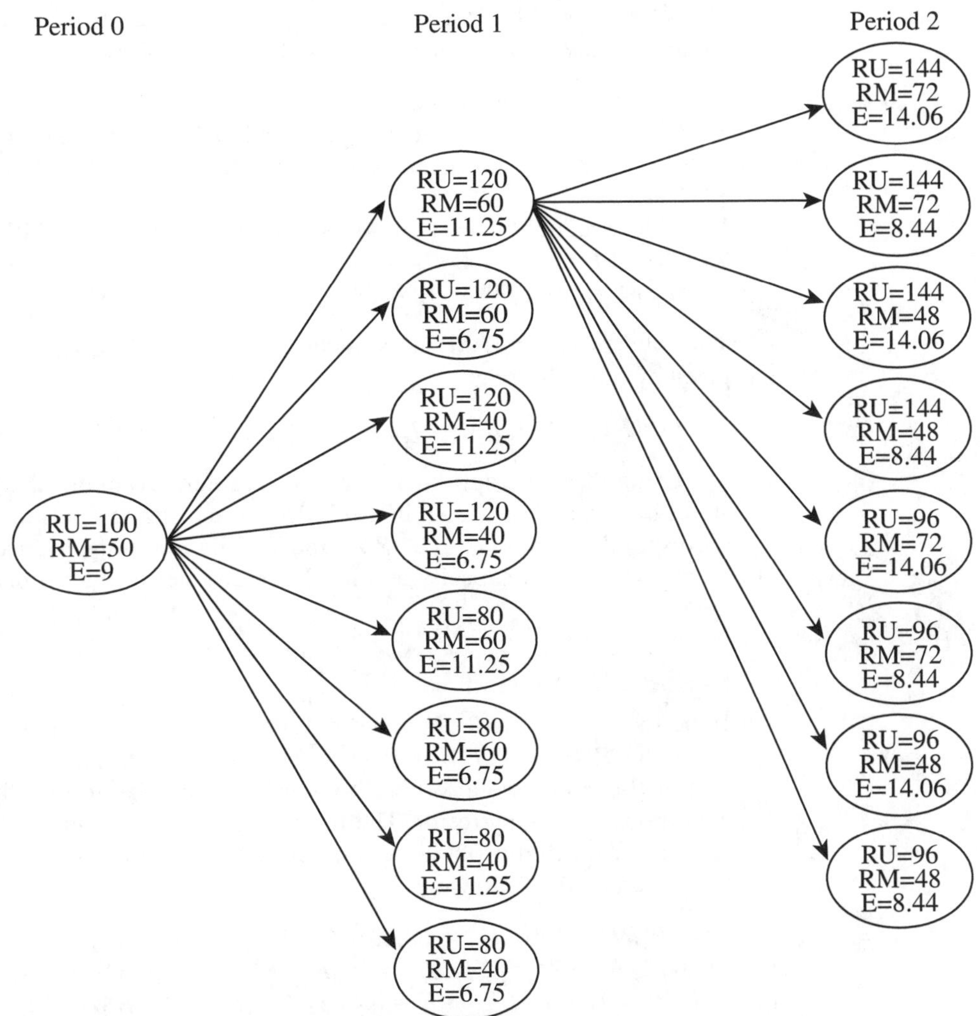

FIGURE 15.3 Partial Decision Tree for AM Tires

Period 2 Evaluation

The detailed analysis for the node RU = 144, RM = 72, E = 14.06 is as follows. All 100,000 of the United States capacity and all 50,000 of the Mexican capacity is used for the local markets because capacity is dedicated, and demand exceeds capacity in both markets. Revenues and costs are evaluated as follows.

Revenues for RU = 144, RM = 72, E = 14.06 The revenues in the United States and Mexico are evaluated as follows:

U.S. revenue from manufacture and sale of 100,000 tires = 100,000 × \$30 = \$3,000,000
Mexico revenue from manufacture and sale of 50,000 tires = 50,000 × 240 = 12,000,000 pesos = \$12,000,000/E = 12,000,000/14.06 = \$853,485
Total revenue = \$3,853,485

Costs for $RU = 144$, $RM = 72$, $E = 14.06$ The costs in the United States and Mexico are evaluated from the data in Table 15.4 as follows:

Fixed cost of U.S. plant = \$1,000,000
Variable production cost at U.S. plant = 100,000 × 15 = \$1,500,000
Fixed cost of Mexico plant = 4,400,000 pesos = \$4,400,000/E = 4,400,000/14.06 = \$312,944
Variable production cost at Mexico plant = 50,000 × 110 = 5,500,000 pesos = \$5,500,000/E = 5,500,000/14.06 = \$391,181
Total cost = 1,000,000 + 1,500,000 + 312,944 + 391,181 = \$3,204,125

The total profit for AM Tires at the node $RU = 144$, $RM = 72$, $E = 14.06$, is thus given by the following:

$$P(RU = 144, RM = 72, E = 14.06, 2) = 3{,}853{,}485 - 3{,}204{,}125 = \$649{,}360$$

Using the same approach, the vice president evaluates the profit in each of the 27 states in period 2 as shown in Table 15.5. Each state in period 2 is represented by the corresponding value of RU, RM, and E. The amount produced in each plant is the minimum of plant capacity and local demand because both plants are assumed to be dedicated.

Period 1 Evaluation

In period 1 there are 8 outcome nodes to be analyzed. A detailed analysis for one of the nodes $RU = 120$, $RM = 60$, $E = 11.25$ is presented here. Besides the revenue and cost at this node, we also need to consider the expected profit in period 2 from the eight nodes that may result. The transition probability into each of the eight nodes is .125. The expected profit in period 2 from the node $RU = 120$, $RM = 60$, $E = 11.25$ is thus given by the following:

$$EP(RU = 120, RM = 60, E = 11.25, 1) = 0.125 \times [P(RU = 144, RM = 72, E = 14.06, 2) + P(RU = 144, RM = 72, E = 8.44, 2) + P(RU = 144, RM = 48, E = 14.06, 2) + P(RU = 144, RM = 48, E = 8.44, 2) + P(RU = 96, RM = 72, E = 14.06, 2) + P(RU = 96, RM = 72, E = 8.44, 2) + P(RU = 96, RM = 48, E = 14.06, 2) + P(RU = 96, RM = 48, E = 8.44, 2)]$$

From Table 15.3 we thus obtain the following:

$$EP(RU = 120, RM = 60, E = 11.25, 1) = 0.125 \times [649{,}360 + 748{,}815 + 630{,}868 + 718{,}009 + 589{,}360 + 688{,}815 + 570{,}868 + 658{,}009] = \$656{,}763$$

The present value of the expected profit in period 2 discounted to period 1 is given by

$$PVEP(RU = 120, RM = 60, E = 11.25, 1) = EP(RU = 120, RM = 60, E = 11.25, 1) / (1+k) = 656{,}763/1.1 = \$597{,}057$$

Revenues for $RU = 120$, $RM = 60$, $E = 11.25$ The revenues in the United States and Mexico are evaluated as follows:

U.S. revenue from manufacture and sale of 100,000 tires = 100,000 × \$30 = \$3,000,000
Mexico revenue from manufacture and sale of 50,000 tires = 50,000 × 240 = 12,000,000 pesos = \$12,000,000/E = 12,000,000/11.25 = \$1,066,667
Total revenue = \$4,066,667

TABLE 15.5 Period 2 Profits for Dedicated Capacity in Both United States and Mexico

			United States			*Mexico*			
RU	***RM***	***E***	***Production***	***Revenue ($)***	***Variable cost ($)***	***Production***	***Revenue (Pesos)***	***Variable cost (Pesos)***	***Profit ($)***
144	72	14.06	100,000	3,000,000	1,500,000	50,000	12,000,000	5,500,000	649,360
144	72	8.44	100,000	3,000,000	1,500,000	50,000	12,000,000	5,500,000	748,815
144	72	5.06	100,000	3,000,000	1,500,000	50,000	12,000,000	5,500,000	915,020
144	48	14.06	100,000	3,000,000	1,500,000	48,000	11,520,000	5,280,000	630,868
144	48	8.44	100,000	3,000,000	1,500,000	48,000	11,520,000	5,280,000	718,009
144	48	5.06	100,000	3,000,000	1,500,000	48,000	11,520,000	5,280,000	863,636
144	32	14.06	100,000	3,000,000	1,500,000	32,000	7,680,000	3,520,000	482,930
144	32	8.44	100,000	3,000,000	1,500,000	32,000	7,680,000	3,520,000	471,564
144	32	5.06	100,000	3,000,000	1,500,000	32,000	7,680,000	3,520,000	452,569
96	72	14.06	96,000	2,880,000	1,440,000	50,000	12,000,000	5,500,000	589,360
96	72	8.44	96,000	2,880,000	1,440,000	50,000	12,000,000	5,500,000	688,815
96	72	5.06	96,000	2,880,000	1,440,000	50,000	12,000,000	5,500,000	855,020
96	48	14.06	96,000	2,880,000	1,440,000	48,000	11,520,000	5,280,000	570,868
96	48	8.44	96,000	2,880,000	1,440,000	48,000	11,520,000	5,280,000	658,009
96	48	5.06	96,000	2,880,000	1,440,000	48,000	11,520,000	5,280,000	803,636
96	32	14.06	96,000	2,880,000	1,440,000	32,000	7,680,000	3,520,000	422,930
96	32	8.44	96,000	2,880,000	1,440,000	32,000	7,680,000	3,520,000	411,564
96	32	5.06	96,000	2,880,000	1,440,000	32,000	7,680,000	3,520,000	392,569
64	72	14.06	64,000	1,920,000	960,000	50,000	12,000,000	5,500,000	109,360
64	72	8.44	64,000	1,920,000	960,000	50,000	12,000,000	5,500,000	208,815
64	72	5.06	64,000	1,920,000	960,000	50,000	12,000,000	5,500,000	375,020
64	48	14.06	64,000	1,920,000	960,000	48,000	11,520,000	5,280,000	90,868
64	48	8.44	64,000	1,920,000	960,000	48,000	11,520,000	5,280,000	178,009
64	48	5.06	64,000	1,920,000	960,000	48,000	11,520,000	5,280,000	323,636
64	32	14.06	64,000	1,920,000	960,000	32,000	7,680,000	3,520,000	(57,070)
64	32	8.44	64,000	1,920,000	960,000	32,000	7,680,000	3,520,000	(68,436)
64	32	5.06	64,000	1,920,000	960,000	32,000	7,680,000	3,520,000	(87,431)

Costs for $RU = 120$, $RM = 60$, $E = 11.25$ The costs in the United States and Mexico are evaluated from the data in Table 15.4 as follows:

Fixed cost of US plant = \$1,000,000
Variable production cost at U.S. plant = $100{,}000 \times 15$ = \$1,500,000
Fixed cost of Mexico plant = 4,400,000 pesos = \$4,400,000/E = 4,400,000/11.25 = \$391,111
Variable production cost at Mexico plant = $50{,}000 \times 110$ = 5,500,000 pesos = \$5,500,000/E = 5,500,000/11.25 = \$488,889
Total cost = 1,000,000 + 1,500,000 + 391,111 + 488,889 = \$3,380,000

The expected profit for AM Tires at the node $RU = 120$, $RM = 60$, $E = 11.25$ is given by the following:

$$P(RU = 120, RM = 60, E = 11.25, 1) = 4{,}066{,}667 - 3{,}380{,}000 + PVEP(RU = 120, RM = 60, E = 11.25, 1) = 686{,}667 + 597{,}057 = \$1{,}283{,}724$$

The expected profit for all nodes in period 1 is given in Table 15.6.

TABLE 15.6 Period 1 Profits for Dedicated Capacity in Both United States and Mexico

				United States			Mexico			
RU	*RM*	*E*	*Expected Profit in Period 2 EP($)*	*Production*	*Revenue ($)*	*Variable Cost ($)*	*Production*	*Revenue (Pesos)*	*Variable Cost (Pesos)*	*Profit ($)*
120	60	11.25	656,763	100,000	3,000,000	1,500,000	50,000	12,000,000	5,500,000	1,283,724
120	60	6.75	781,370	100,000	3,000,000	1,500,000	50,000	12,000,000	5,500,000	1,521,447
120	40	11.25	545,843	100,000	3,000,000	1,500,000	40,000	9,600,000	4,400,000	1,067,332
120	40	6.75	596,445	100,000	3,000,000	1,500,000	40,000	9,600,000	4,400,000	1,160,741
80	60	11.25	386,763	80,000	2,400,000	1,200,000	50,000	12,000,000	5,500,000	738,269
80	60	6.75	511,370	80,000	2,400,000	1,200,000	50,000	12,000,000	5,500,000	975,993
80	40	11.25	275,843	80,000	2,400,000	1,200,000	40,000	9,600,000	4,400,000	521,877
80	40	6.75	326,445	80,000	2,400,000	1,200,000	40,000	9,600,000	4,400,000	615,287

Period 0 Evaluation

In period 0 the demand and exchange rate are given by $RU = 100$, $RM = 50$, $E = 9$. Besides the revenue and cost at this node, we also need to consider the expected profit from the eight nodes in period 1. The expected profit is given by the following:

$EP(RU = 100, RM = 50, E = 9, 0) = 0.125 \times [P(RU = 120, RM = 60, E = 11.25, 1) + P(RU = 120, RM = 60, E = 6.75, 1) + P(RU = 120, RM = 40, E = 11.25, 1) + P(RU = 120, RM = 40, E = 6.75, 1) + P(RU = 80, RM = 60, E = 11.25, 1) + P(RU = 80, RM = 60, E = 6.75, 1) + P(RU = 80, RM = 40, E = 11.25, 1) + P(RU = 80, RM = 40, E = 6.75, 1)]$

From Table 15.6 we thus obtain the following:

$EP(RU = 100, RM = 50, E = 9, 0) = 0.125 \times (1{,}283{,}724 + 1{,}521{,}447 + 1{,}067{,}332 + 1{,}160{,}741 + 738{,}269 + 975{,}993 + 521{,}877 + 615{,}287) = \$985{,}584$

The present value of the period 1 profit discounted to period 0 is given by the following:

$PVEP(RU = 100, RM = 50, E = 9, 0) = EP(RU = 100, RM = 50, E = 9, 0) / (1+k) = 985{,}584/1.1 = \$895{,}985$

Revenues for $RU = 100, RM = 50, E = 9$ The revenues in period 0 are as follows:

U.S. revenue from manufacture and sale of 100,000 tires = 100,000 × \$30 = \$3,000,000
Mexico revenue from manufacture and sale of 50,000 tires = 50,000 × 240 = 12,000,000 pesos = \$12,000,000/E = 12,000,000/9 = \$1,333,333
Total revenue = \$4,333,333

Costs for $RU = 100, RM = 50, E = 9$. The costs in period 0 are given by

Fixed cost of U.S. plant = \$1,000,000
Variable production cost at U.S. plant = 100,000 × 15 = \$1,500,000
Fixed cost of Mexico plant = 4,400,000 pesos = \$4,400,000/E = 4,400,000/9 = \$488,889
Variable production cost at Mexico plant = 50,000 × 110 = 5,500,000 pesos = \$5,500,000/E = 5,500,000/9 = \$611,111
Total cost = 1,000,000 + 1,500,000 + 488,889 + 611,111 = \$3,600,000

The expected profit for AM Tires from installing 100,000 units of dedicated capacity in the United States and 50,000 units of dedicated capacity in Mexico is as follows:

$$P(RU = 100, RM = 50, E = 9, 0) = 4{,}333{,}333 - 3{,}600{,}000 + 895{,}985 = \$1{,}629{,}318$$

The vice president of AM Tires thus obtains the following:

NPV(dedicated 100,000 unit capacity in U. S. and 50,000 in Mexico) = $1,629,318

Flexible Capacity of 100,000 in United States and 50,000 in Mexico

The vice president next evaluates the NPV of installing flexible capacity in both the United States and Mexico. Flexible capacity may be used to produce tires for either country, depending on the profit from doing so. The decision tree in this case is as shown in Figure 15.3 but the profit at each node changes. The vice president first evaluates the profit at each node in period 2.

Period 2 Evaluation

The detailed analysis for the node $RU = 144$, $RM = 72$, $E = 14.06$ for period 2 is as follows. The vice president first evaluates the margin contribution of producing a tire in one place and selling in each of the two markets as shown in Table 15.7.

From Table 15.7 it is clear that under the given conditions, both U.S. and Mexican production should first be used to satisfy U.S. demand. Only the surplus should be used to satisfy Mexican demand, because this action maximizes profits for AM Tires. The example considered here is simple enough for the optimal solution to be obtained by observation. In general, network design methodologies to allocate market demand to plants must be used (see Chapter 11).

U.S. production contribution for $RU = 144$, $RM = 72$, $E = 14.06$ Given a demand in the United States of 144,000 units, all 100,000 units of U.S. production are sent to the local market. Given a margin of $15 per unit the vice president obtains the following:

Contribution margin from U.S. production = 100,000 × $15 = $1,500,000
Fixed cost of U.S. plant = $1,100,000
Profit from U.S. production = $400,000

Mexican production contribution for $RU = 144$, $RM = 72$, $E = 14.06$ Given that there is a higher margin of $21.2 per tire from selling Mexican tires in the United States, 44,000 tires from Mexico are sent to the United States. The remaining 6,000 tires are sold in Mexico with each tire contributing $9.2. Thus,

Contribution margin from Mexican production = 44,000 × $21.2 + 6,000 × $9.2 = $988,000
Fixed cost of Mexican plant = 4,400,000 pesos = $312,945
Profit from Mexican production = $675,055

TABLE 15.7 Source/Destination Margins for $RU = 144$, $RM = 72$, $E = 14.06$

Source	*Destination*	*Variable Cost*	*Shipping Cost*	*E*	*Sale Price*	*Margin ($)*
U.S.	U.S.	$15	0	14.06	$30	$15
U.S.	Mexico	$15	$1	14.06	240 pesos	$1.1
Mexico	U.S.	110 pesos	$1	14.06	$30	$21.2
Mexico	Mexico	110 pesos	0	14.06	240 pesos	$9.2

The total profit for AM Tires is the sum of the profit from U.S. and Mexican production and is as follows:

$$P(RU = 144, RM = 72, E = 14.06, 2) = \$400{,}000 + \$675{,}055 = \$1{,}075{,}055$$

Compare the profit at this node with and without flexibility. Flexibility results in a profit of $1,075,055, whereas dedicated capacity results in a profit of $649,360. The production flexibility allows AM Tires to exploit exchange rate fluctuations and increase profit by adjusting the markets being served by each plant.

The vice president of operations repeats this analysis for each of the 27 nodes in period 2. The results are shown in Table 15.8.

Period 1 Evaluation

In period 1 there are eight outcome nodes to be analyzed. The detailed analysis for the node $RU = 120$, $RM = 60$, $E = 11.25$ is provided. Besides the revenue and cost at this node, we also need to consider the present value of the expected profit from the

TABLE 15.8 Period 2 Profits With Flexible Capacity in Both U.S. and Mexico

			Contribution Margin ($/unit)				*U.S. Production*			*Mexico Production*			
RU	***RM***	***E***	***U.S./ U.S.***	***U.S./ Mex***	***Mex/ U.S.***	***Mex/ Mex***	***For U.S.***	***For Mexico***	***Profit in U.S. ($)***	***For U.S.***	***For Mexico***	***Mexico Profit ($)***	***Total Profit ($)***
144	72	14.06	15	1.1	21.2	9.2	100,000	—	400,000	44,000	6,000	675,055	1,075,055
144	72	8.44	15	12.4	16.0	15.4	100,000	—	400,000	44,000	6,000	273,630	673,630
144	72	5.06	15	31.4	7.3	25.7	78,000	22,000	761,478	—	50,000	415,020	1,176,498
144	48	14.06	15	1.1	21.2	9.2	100,000	—	400,000	—	48,000	130,868	530,868
144	48	8.44	15	12.4	216.0	14.5	100,000	—	400,000	—	48,000	218,009	618,009
144	48	5.06	15	31.4	7.3	25.7	100,000	—	400,000	2,000	48,000	378,158	778,158
144	32	14.06	15	1.1	21.2	9.2	100,000	—	400,000	44,000	6,000	674,293	1,074,293
144	32	8.44	15	12.4	16.0	15.4	100,000	—	400,000	44,000	6,000	273,630	673,630
144	32	5.06	15	31.4	7.3	25.7	100,000	—	400,000	18,000	32,000	83,265	48,265
96	72	14.06	15	1.1	21.2	9.2	96,000	4,000	344,279	—	50,000	149,60	493,639
96	72	8.44	15	12.4	16.0	15.4	96,000	4,000	389,744	—	50,000	248,815	638,559
96	72	5.06	15	31.4	7.3	25.7	96,000	4,000	465,723	—	50,000	415,020	880,743
96	48	14.06	15	1.1	21.2	9.2	96,000	—	340,000	—	48,000	130,868	470,868
96	48	8.44	15	12.4	16.0	15.4	96,000	—	340,000	—	48,000	218,009	558,009
96	48	5.06	15	31.4	7.3	25.7	96,000	—	340,000	—	48,000	363,636	703,636
96	32	14.06	15	1.1	21.2	9.2	96,000	—	340,000	—	32,000	(17,070)	322,930
96	32	8.44	15	12.4	16.0	15.4	96,000	—	340,000	—	32,000	(28,436)	311,564
96	32	5.06	15	31.4	7.3	25.7	96,000	—	340,000	—	32,000	(47,41)	292,569
64	72	14.06	15	1.1	21.2	9.2	64,000	22,000	(116,467)	—	50,000	149,360	32,893
64	72	8.44	15	121.4	16.0	15.4	64,000	22,000	133,592	—	50,000	248,815	382,408
64	72	5.06	15	31.4	7.3	25.7	64,000	36,000	991,510	—	36,000	55,336	1,046,846
64	48	14.06	15	1.1	21.2	9.2	64,000	—	(140,000)	—	48,000	130,868	(9,132)
64	48	8.44	15	12.4	16.0	15.4	64,000	—	(140,000)	—	48,000	218,009	78,009
64	48	5.06	15	31.4	7.3	25.7	64,000	36,000	991,510	—	12,000	(561,265)	430,245
64	32	14.06	15	1.1	21.2	9.2	64,000	—	(140,000)	—	32,000	(17,070)	(157,070)
64	32	8.44	15	12.4	16.0	15.4	64,000	—	(140,000)	—	32,000	(28,436)	(168,436)
64	32	5.06	15	31.4	7.3	25.7	64,000	32,000	865,787	—	—	(869,565)	(3,779)

TABLE 15.9 Source/Destination Margins for $RU = 120$, $RM = 60$, $E = 11.25$

Source	*Destination*	*Variable cost*	*Shipping cost*	*E*	*Sale price*	*Margin ($)*
U.S.	U.S.	$15	0	11.25	$30	$15
U.S.	Mexico	$15	$1	11.25	240 pesos	$5.3
Mexico	U.S.	110 pesos	$1	11.25	$30	$19.2
Mexico	Mexico	110 pesos	0	11.25	240 pesos	$11.6

eight nodes in period 2 that may result from this node. The transition probability to each of the eight nodes is 0.125. The expected profit is thus as follows:

$EP(RU = 120, RM = 60, E = 11.25, 1) = 0.125 \times [P(RU = 144, RM = 72, E = 14.06, 2) + P(RU = 144, RM = 72, E = 8.44, 2) + P(RU = 144, RM = 48, E = 14.06, 2) + P(RU = 144, RM = 48, E = 8.44, 2) + P(RU = 96, RM = 72, E = 14.06, 2) + P(RU = 96, RM = 72, E = 8.44, 2) + P(RU = 96, RM = 48, E = 14.06, 2) + P(RU = 96, RM = 48, E = 8.44, 2)]$

From Table 15.8, the vice president thus obtains the following:

$EP(RU = 120, RM = 60, E = 11.25, 1) = 0.125 \times [1{,}075{,}055 + 673{,}630 + 530{,}868 + 618{,}009 + 493{,}639 + 638{,}559 + 470{,}868 + 558{,}009] = \$632{,}330$

The present value of the expected profit discounted to period 1 is given by the following:

$PVEP(RU = 120, RM = 60, E = 11.25, 1) = EP(RU = 120, RM = 60, E = 11.25, 1) / (1+k) = 632{,}330/1.1 = \$574{,}845$

The next step is to evaluate the margin contribution of producing a tire in one place and selling in each of the two markets with an exchange rate of $E = 11.25$. The details are contained in Table 15.9. The next step is to evaluate the profit contribution from each plant. Given the simple example, the evaluation is done directly in this case.

U.S. production contribution for $RU = 120$, $RM = 60$, $E = 11.25$ Given that there is a higher margin from selling U.S. production in the United States, all 100,000 U.S. tires are sent to the local market. Thus,

Contribution margin from U.S. production = 100,000 × $15 = $1,500,000
Fixed cost of U.S. plant = $1,100,000
Profit from U.S. production = $400,000

Mexican production contribution for $RU = 120$, $RM = 60$, $E = 11.25$ Given that there is a higher margin from selling Mexican production in the United States, 20,000 tires from Mexico are sent to the United States and 30,000 tires are sold in Mexico. Given the margins in Table 15.9, the vice president thus obtains the following:

Contribution margin from Mexican plant = 20,000 × $19.2 + 30,000 × $11.6 = $732,000
Fixed cost of Mexican plant = 4,400,000 pesos = $391,111
Profit from Mexican plant = $340,889.

The total expected profit for AM Tires for $RU = 120$, $RM = 60$, $E = 11.25$ in period 1 is thus given by the following:

$P(RU = 120, RM = 60, E = 11.25, 1) = \$400{,}000 + \$391{,}111 + PVEP(RU = 120, RM = 60, E = 11.25, 1) = \$400{,}000 + \$340{,}889 + \$574{,}845 = \$1{,}315{,}734$

The expected profit for all other nodes in period 1 is calculated the same way and is shown in Table 15.10.

TABLE 15.10 Period 1 Profits With Flexible Capacity in Both United States and Mexico

				Contribution Margin (unit)				*U.S. Production*			*Mexico Production*			
RU	*RM*	*E*	*Expected Profit in Period 1 EP ($)*	*U.S./ U.S.*	*U.S./ Mex*	*Mex/ U.S.*	*Mex/ Mex*	*For U.S.*	*For Mexico*	*Profit in U.S. ($)*	*For U.S.*	*For Mexico*	*Profit in Mexico ($)*	*Total Profit ($)*
120	60	11.25	632,330	15	5.3	19.2	11.6	100,000	—	400,000	20,00	30,000	340,889	1,315,734
120	60	6.75	753,405	15	19.6	12.7	19.3	90,000	10,000	446,000	—	50,000	313,148	1,444,062
120	40	11.25	570,022	15	5.3	19.2	11.6	90,000	—	250,000	30,000	20,000	416,889	1,185,091
120	40	6.75	552,355	15	19.6	12.7	19.3	100,000	—	400,000	10,000	40,000	247,148	1,149,289
80	60	11.25	330,657	15	5.3	19.2	11.6	80,000	—	100,000	20,000	30,000	340,889	741,486
80	60	6.75	589,807	15	19.6	12.7	19.3	90,000	10,000	446,000	—	50,000	313,148	1,295,336
80	40	11.25	175,843	15	5.3	19.2	11.6	60,000	—	(200,000)	20,000	30,000	340,889	300,746
80	40	6.75	275,227	15	19.6	12.7	19.3	80,000	20,000	492,000	—	20,000	(265,852)	476,355

Period 0 Evaluation

In period 0 the demand and exchange rate are given by $RU = 100$, $RM = 50$, $E = 9$. Besides the revenue and cost at this node, we also need to consider the present value of the expected profit from all nodes in period 1. Given a transition probability of .125 to each node, the expected profit from period 1 is as follows:

$EP(RU = 100, RM = 50, E = 9, 0) = 0.125 \times [P(RU = 120, RM = 60, E = 11.25, 1) + P(RU = 120, RM = 60, E = 6.75, 1) + P(RU = 120, RM = 40, E = 11.25, 1) + P(RU = 120, RM = 40, E = 6.75, 1) + P(RU = 80, RM = 60, E = 11.25, 1) + P(RU = 80, RM = 60, E = 6.75, 1) + P(RU = 80, RM = 40, E = 11.25, 1) + P(RU = 80, RM = 40, E = 6.75, 1)]$

From Table 15.8, the vice president thus obtains the following:

$EP(RU = 100, RM = 50, E = 9, 0) = .125 \times (1{,}315{,}734 + 1{,}444{,}062 + 1{,}185{,}091 + 1{,}149{,}289 + 741{,}486 + 1{,}295{,}336 + 300{,}746 + 476{,}355) = \$988{,}512$

The present value of the expected profit in period 1 discounted to period 0 is as follows:

$PVEP(RU = 100, RM = 50, E = 9, 0) = EP(RU = 100, RM = 50, E = 9, 0) / (1+k) = 988{,}512/1.1 = \$898{,}647$

The next step is to evaluate the margin contribution of producing a tire in one place and selling in each of the two markets in period 0. The details are listed in Table 15.11.

The vice president next evaluates the profit contribution from each plant.

TABLE 15.11 Source/Destination Margins for $RU = 100$, $RM = 50$, $E = 9$

Source	*Destination*	*Variable Cost*	*Shipping Cost*	*E*	*Sale price*	*Margin ($)*
U.S.	U.S.	$15	0	9	$30	$15
U.S.	Mexico	$15	$1	9	240 pesos	$10.7
Mexico	U.S.	110 pesos	$1	9	$30	$16.8
Mexico	Mexico	110 pesos	0	9	240 pesos	$14.4

U.S. production contribution for $RU = 100$, $RM = 50$, $E = 9$ All 100,000 units produced in the United States are sold locally because the U.S. market provides a higher margin. Thus,

Contribution margin from U.S. production = 100,000 × \$15 = \$1,500,000
Fixed cost of U.S. plant = \$1,100,000
Profit from U.S. production = \$400,000

Mexican production contribution for $RU = 100$, $RM = 50$, $E = 9$ All of the Mexican capacity is used to satisfy Mexican demand because there is no unmet demand in the United States. Thus, 50,000 tires are sold in Mexico.

Contribution margin from Mexican production = 50,000 × \$14.4 = \$720,000
Fixed cost of Mexican plant = 4,400,000 pesos = \$488,889
Profit from Mexican production = \$231,111

The total expected profit for AM Tires in period 0 is thus given by the following:

$P(RU = 100, RM = 50, E = 9, 0) = \$400{,}000 + \$231{,}111 + PVEP(RU = 100, RM = 50, E = 9, 0) = \$400{,}000 + \$231{,}111 + \$898{,}647 = \$1{,}529{,}758$

The vice president thus obtains the following:

NPV(Flexible 100,000-unit capacity in United States and 50,000 in Mexico) = \$1,529,758

The option of having both plants be flexible yields a lower expected NPV compared with both plants being dedicated. A similar analysis can be used to evaluate the cases in which one of the two plants is flexible. The results for the four options are shown in Table 15.12.

Based on the results in Table 15.12, the CEO of AM Tires decides to build a dedicated plant in the United States and a flexible plant in Mexico.

In summary, the decision tree methodology is quite powerful. As mentioned earlier, a major factor is in the choice of discount rate. The appropriate discount rate should be risk-adjusted, and risk may vary by period. It is not appropriate to use either the risk-free discount rate or a constant risk-adjusted discount in each period. One option is to find the risk-adjusted rate for each period and each state and apply that in our decision tree analysis. This would allow for a fair comparison between different investment options.

Other approaches available include contingent claims analysis (CCA) for discrete time analysis and real options for the continuous time case.[3,4] In both cases, transition

TABLE 15.12 *NPV of Various Plant Configurations for AM Tires*

Plant Configuration		
United States	***Mexico***	***NPV***
Dedicated	Dedicated	\$1,629,319
Flexible	Dedicated	\$1,514,322
Dedicated	Flexible	\$1,722,447
Flexible	Flexible	\$1,529,758

[3]Ibid.
[4]Amram and Kulatilaka (1999).

probabilities are adjusted so that the risk-free discount rate may be applied in each period. This allows for the proper valuation of risk. The solution methodology at that point is exactly the same as with decision tree analysis.

When underlying decision trees are very complex and explicit solutions for the underlying decision tree are difficult to obtain, firms should use simulation for evaluating decisions (see Chapter 9). In a complex decision tree, there are thousands of possible paths that may result from the first period to the last. Transition probabilities are used to generate probability weighted random paths within the decision tree. For each path, the stage-by-stage decision as well as the payoff is evaluated. The paths are generated in such a way that the probability of a path being generated during the simulation is the same as the probability of the path in the decision tree. After generating many paths and evaluating the payoffs in each case, the payoffs obtained during the simulation are used as a representation of the payoffs that would result from the decision tree. The present value is then found by averaging the payoffs obtained in the simulation and discounting them back to the present.

Simulation methods are very good at evaluating a decision for which the path itself is not decision-dependent. In other words, transition probabilities from one period to the next are not dependent on the decision taken during a period. They can also take into account real world constraints as well as complex decision rules. In addition, they can easily handle different forms of uncertainty, even in instances in which uncertainty between different factors is correlated.

Simulation models require a higher setup cost to start and operate compared with decision tree tools. However, their main advantage is that they can provide high-quality evaluations of complex situations.

15.6 FINANCIAL ANALYSIS OF SUPPLY CHAIN DECISIONS IN PRACTICE

Here are some ideas to help managers apply financial analysis to supply chains in practice:

- **Use multiple financial methodologies and metrics**. This chapter presents many different ways to use financial analysis to make supply chain decisions. They each add a lot of value when making a decision. However, each methodology presents only a subset of the possible perspectives a manager can take on the decision. As one methodology can give only part of the picture, it is beneficial to examine decisions using multiple methodologies and metrics. Often, different methodologies will recommend different decisions, and by using multiple methodologies, the differences between the strategic choices will become clearer. This can be especially true for financial metrics. There is no single metric that can be used for making decisions. The best decisions can be made when a multitude of metrics are available, because many metrics provide the best overall view of the alternatives being considered. Therefore, when making decisions, managers should use a variety of metrics instead of relying on just one.
- **Use financial analysis as an input to decision making, not as the decision-making process**. Financial analysis is a great tool in the decision-making process, as it often produces an answer and an abundance of quantitative data to back up that answer. However appealing this may be, management should not rely solely on financial analysis to make decisions. Use of this analysis as a large part of the decision-making process is fine, but other inputs into the decision process that

are difficult to quantify should be included in the analysis as well. Financial methodologies alone do not provide a complete picture of the alternatives. For instance, there may be strategic benefits to locating a plant in a certain country that are hard to quantify. These impacts should be considered in addition to the raw financial analysis. In the final analysis, management must use other inputs beyond financial analysis in the decision-making process in order to get the most complete view of the alternatives possible.

- **Use estimates along with sensitivity analysis.** Many of the inputs into financial analysis can be difficult, if not impossible, to nail down in a very accurate fashion. This can cause financial analysis to be a long and drawn-out process. One of the best ways to speed the process along and arrive at a good decision is to use estimates of inputs when it appears that finding a very accurate input would take an inordinate amount of time. As discussed in some of the other practice-oriented sections, using estimates is fine when the estimates are backed up by sensitivity analysis. It is almost always easier to come up with a range for an input than it is to come up with a single point. By performing sensitivity analysis on the input's range, managers can often show that no matter where the true input lies within the range, the outcome remains the same. When this is not the case, they can highlight a key variable to making the decision that likely deserves more attention to arrive at a more accurate answer. In summary, in order to use financial analysis effectively to make supply chain decisions, managers need to make estimates of inputs and then back up those estimates with sensitivity analysis.

15.7 SUMMARY OF LEARNING OBJECTIVES

1. Identify financial factors that influence supply chain performance.

   The main financial measurement in terms of evaluating supply chain alternatives is present value of the stream of cash flows generated by each alternative. These streams are affected by uncertainty and flexibility, which must be taken into account when valuing the cash flows.

2. Understand the financial tools used to evaluate supply chain decisions.

   When valuing the streams of cash flows, decision trees are a basic approach to valuing alternatives. Incorporating a binomial representation of uncertainty allows the decision tree to value alternatives given uncertainty. When decision trees become too complex to reasonably solve, simulation can be used to perform financial evaluations on the decision alternatives.

3. Perform financial analysis on supply chain decisions.

   The basic steps in performing financial analysis involve gathering financial data on the alternatives, determining what the uncertainties affecting the decision are, quantifying the cash flows for each alternative in each time period, quantifying the uncertainties' impact on the cash flows, and using one of the methodologies to calculate a financial valuation for the different alternatives.

Discussion Questions

1. Why is it important to consider financial factors when evaluating supply chain decisions?
2. What are the major financial factors that can affect the value of supply chain decisions?

3. Describe the basic principle of discounted cash flows and how it can be used to compare different streams of cash flows.
4. How does the binomial representation of uncertainty relate to the normal distribution?
5. Summarize the basic steps in the decision tree analysis methodology.
6. What are the major financial uncertainties faced by an electronic components manufacturer deciding whether to build a plant in Thailand or the United States?
7. What are some major nonfinancial factors that a company should consider when making decisions on where to source product?

Exercises

1. Moon Micro is a small manufacturer of servers that currently builds all of its product in Santa Clara, California. As the market for servers has grown dramatically, the Santa Clara plant has reached capacity of 10,000 servers per year. Moon is considering two options to increase its capacity. The first option is to add 10,000 units of capacity to the Santa Clara plant at an annualized fixed cost of $10 million plus $500 labor per server. The second option is to have Molectron, an independent assembler, manufacture servers for Moon at a cost of $2,000 for each server (excluding raw materials cost). Moon sells each server for $15,000 and raw materials cost $8,000 per server.

   Moon must make this decision for a two-year time horizon. During each year, demand for Moon servers has an 80 percent chance of increasing 50 percent from the year before and a 20 percent chance of remaining the same as the year before. Molectron's prices may change as well. They are fixed for the first year but have a 50 percent chance of increasing 20 percent in year 2 and a 50 percent chance of remaining where they are.

   Use a decision tree to determine whether Moon should add capacity to its Santa Clara plant or if it should outsource to Molectron. What are some other factors that would affect this decision that have not been mentioned?
2. Unipart, a manufacturer of auto parts, is considering two different B2B marketplaces to purchase their maintenance, repair, and operations (MRO) supplies. Both marketplaces offer a full line of supplies at very similar prices for products and shipping. Both provide very similar service levels and lead times.

   However, their fee structures are quite different. The first marketplace, Parts4u.com, sells all of its products with a 5 percent commission tacked on top of the price of the product (not including shipping). AllMRO.com's pricing is based on a subscription fee of $10 million which must be paid up-front for a two-year period, and a commission of 1 percent on each transaction's product price.

   Unipart spends about $150 million on MRO supplies each year, although this varies with their utilization. Next year will likely be a strong year, in which high utilization will keep MRO spending at $150 million. However, there is a 25 percent chance that spending will drop by 10 percent. The second year, there is a 50 percent chance the spending level will stay where it was in year 1 and a 50 percent chance it will drop by another 10 percent. Unipart uses a discount rate of 20 percent. Assume all costs are incurred at the end of each year (so year 1's costs are incurred at the end of year 1 and year 2 costs are incurred at the end of year 2).

   Which B2B marketplace should Unipart buy its parts from?
3. Alphacap, a manufacturer of electronic components, is trying to select a single supplier for the raw materials that go into its main product, the doublecap, a new capacitor that is used by cellular phone manufacturers to protect microprocessors from power spikes. Two companies can provide the necessary materials: MultiChem and Mixemat.

MultiChem has a very solid reputation for its products and charges a higher price due to their reliability of supply and delivery. MultiChem dedicates plant capacity to each customer, and therefore, supply is assured. This allows MultiChem to charge $1.20 for the raw materials used in each doublecap.

Mixemat is a small raw materials supplier that has limited capacity. It charges only $0.90 for a unit's worth of raw materials, but its reliability of supply is in question. It does not have enough capacity to supply all its customers all the time. This means that orders to Mixemat are not guaranteed. In a year of high demand for raw materials, Mixemat will have 90,000 units available for Alphacap. In low-demand years, all product will be delivered.

If Alphacap does not get raw materials from its suppliers, it needs to buy them on the spot market to supply its customers. Alphacap relies on one major cellular phone manufacturer for the majority of its business, and failing to deliver could cause it to lose this contract, essentially putting the firm at risk. Therefore, Alphacap will buy raw material on the spot market to make up for any shortfall. Spot prices for single lot purchases (such as Alphacap would need) are $2.00 when raw materials demand is low and $4.00 when demand is high.

Alphacap sold 100,000 doublecaps the previous year and there is a 75 percent chance that it will sell 110,000 this year. However, there is a 25 percent chance it will only sell 100,000. Next year, the demand has a 75 percent chance of rising 20 percent over this year and a 25 percent chance of falling 10 percent. Alphacap uses a discount rate of 20 percent. Assume that costs are incurred at the end of each year (year 1's costs are incurred in a year and year 2 costs are incurred at the end of year 2) and that Alphacap must make a decision with a two-year horizon. Only one supplier can be chosen, as these two suppliers refuse to supply someone who works with their competitor.

Which supplier should Alphacap choose? What other information would you like to have to make this decision?

4. Bell Computer is reaching a crossroads. This PC manufacturer has been growing at a rapid rate. This has been causing problems for its operations as it tries to keep up with the surging demand. Bell executives can plainly see that within the next half year, the systems used to coordinate their supply chain are going to fall apart since they will not be able to handle the volume Bell projects it will have.

To solve this problem, Bell has brought in two supply chain software companies that have made proposals on systems that could handle the volume and the complexity of tasks Bell needs to have occur. These two software companies are offering very different types of products, however.

The first company, SCSoftware, proposes a system that Bell will purchase a license for. This would allow Bell to use the software as long as it wants. However, Bell would be responsible for maintaining this software, which would require significant resources.

The second company, SC-ASP, proposes that Bell pay a subscription fee on a monthly basis for SC-ASP to host Bell's supply chain applications on SC-ASP's machines. Bell employees would access information and analysis via a Web browser. Information would automatically be fed from the ASP servers to the Bell servers whenever necessary. Bell would continue to pay this monthly fee for the software, but all maintenance would be performed by SC-ASP.

How should Bell go about making a decision on which software company to go with? What are the specific pieces of information that Bell needs to know (both about the software and about the future conditions Bell will experience) in order to make a decision? What are some of the qualitative issues Bell must think about in addition to the costs?

Bibliography

Amram, Martha, and Nalin Kulatilaka, *Real Options*. Boston: Harvard Business School Press, 1999.

Brealey, Richard A., and Stewart C. Myers. *Principles of Corporate Finance*, New York: McGraw-Hill, 1996.

Horngren, Charles T., George Foster, and Srikant M. Datar. *Cost Accounting*, Upper Saddle River, N.J.: Prentice Hall, 1997.

Johnson, Norman L., Samuel Kotz, and N. Balakrishnan. *Continuous Univariate Distributions*, New York: John Wiley & Sons 1994.

Luehrman, Timothy A. "Investment Opportunities as Real Options: Getting Started on the Numbers." *Harvard Business Review* (July–August 1998), 51–67.

Ross, Sheldon M. *Introduction to Stochastic Dynamic Programming*. New York: Academic Press,1983.

Stokey, Nancy L., Robert E. Lucas Jr., and Edward C. Prescott. *Recursive Methods in Economic Dynamics*. Cambridge, Mass: Harvard University Press, 1989.

Trigeorgis, Lenos. *Real Options*. Cambridge Mass:, The MIT Press, 1996.

Name Index

P

Q

S

T

U

W

Y

Subject Index

D

E

F

V

W